MARRIAGES

of

RUTHERFORD COUNTY, TENNESSEE

1804-1872

$\mathcal{M}$ARRIAGES

of

$\mathcal{R}$UTHERFORD $\mathcal{C}$OUNTY, $\mathcal{T}$ENNESSEE

1804-1872

Compiled by
EDYTHE RUCKER WHITLEY

With an Index by Gary Parks

CLEARFIELD

Reprinted for
Clearfield Company, Inc. by
Genealogical Publishing Co., Inc.
Baltimore, Maryland
1999

Introduction

UTHERFORD COUNTY, Tennessee was erected on October 25, 1803 from Davidson County, and was named in honor of General Griffith Rutherford of North Carolina. With the exception of a few deed books which were destroyed during the Civil War, most of the old records of Rutherford County are extant, and most—like the marriage records—can be found at the courthouse in Murfreesboro.

The first group of marriage records published herein was copied by me during the years 1920 to 1925 when I was compiling my own family history. In the late 1930s I had reason to bring the marriages down a few more years. In 1964 I added more, including some I missed earlier. In 1971 I added the balance given in this compilation.

The reader should note that marriage bonds were frequently issued the same day as licenses, but the marriage itself was usually—though not always—solemnized at a later date. If no date of marriage, or solemnization (abbreviated *Sol.*), is given, then the single date provided refers to the date of issue of either the bond or the license.

Edythe Rucker Whitley
Nashville, Tennessee
July 1980

Section 1: 1804-1837

Acklen, Christopher to Martha Kirby, Aug. 27, 1810.
Surety, Henry Kirby.
Acree, Dandridge to Susan Bowman, May 13, 1817. Surety,
Thomas Yardley.
Acuff, Benjamine to Eleanor Butler, Aug. 22, 1835. Sol.
Aug. 23, 1835 by Nancy Overall, M.G. Surety, Kellar
Mathis.
Adams, Absolom to Mary C. Richardson, Sept. 1834.
Sureties, Henry Ewing, Joseph W. Clay and John
McGregor.
Adams, Edward to Nancy Gilliam, May 8, 1827. Surety,
William McKinney.
Adams, Luke P. to Sarah Uselton, Dec. 22, 1830. Sol.
Dec. 23, 1830 by William Keele, M.G.
Adams, William to Elizabeth Goodloe, April 24, 1819.
Sol. April 26, 1819 by Jacob Wright, J.P.
Adams, William to Jane Hall, Dec. 27, 1836. Surety,
Charles D. Morse.
Adcock, Barney to Martha Higgins, Dec. 24, 1814.
Surety, Adam Struder.
Adcock, Harman to Priscilla White, Feb. 29, 1820. Sol.
March 2, 1820 by Wm. Vinson, J.P.
Adcock, Henderson to Mary Foster, June 17, 1834. Sol.
June 17, 1834 by J. F. Shaperd, J.P. Surety, Wm.
Adcock.
Adcock, John to Miss Bersheba Green, Nov. 9, 1822.
Sol. Nov. 9, 1822 by G. W. Oliver, J.P.
Adcock, Stephen to Polly Fox, June 12, 1824. Sol. June
12, 1834 by Wm. Vinson, J.P. Surety, Lewis Dyal.
Akers, Wm. R. to Mary E. McKnight, Jan. 2, 1836. Sol.
Jan. 7, 1836 by Jesse Alexander, V.D.M. Surety,
George McElroy.
Akin, William to Mary Wright, Aug. 7, 1822.
Akin, Christian to Mary Brady, May 26, 1810. Surety,
Henry Kirby.
Alderson, Richard D. to Mary Millins, Feb. 2, 1831.
Sol. Feb. 3, 1831 by Henry Ridley, J.P.
Alexander, Adlia (Adlai) to Sarah W. Sims, Oct. 3, 1833.
Sol. --------. Surety, Elisha Cox.
Alexander, Doran L. to Nancy Powell, June 21, 1824.
Alexander, James to Elizabeth Doss, May 27, 1829. Sol.
May 27, 1829 by Sam'l Jones, J.P. Surety, James
Pybass.
Alexander, John to Kissey Carter, June 25, 1811.
Alexander, John D. to Mary R. Baird, Nov. 11, 1837.
Sol. Nov. 16, 1837 by William Eagleton, V.D.M.

Alexander, Jonathan to Tressy Williams, April 27, 1838.
Surety, J. W. Hunt.
Alexander, Levi to Elizabeth Alford, Feb. 20, 1830.
Surety, John D. Fletcher.
Alexander, Pritchard to Nancy Norman, July 2, 1840.
Surety, Furney G. Norman.
Alexander, William to Matilda Allen, Aug. 26, 1834.
Surety, Lafayette Epps.
Alexander, Wm. H. to Nancy Laughlin issued Nov. 5, 1834.
Surety, James H. Alexander.
Allen, Benjamine to Jane Johnson, Aug. 8, 1834. Sol.
Aug. 9, 1834 by Wm. Vinson, J.P. Surety, Edmund C.
Lovern.
Allen, David L. to Julia Read, Sept. 1, 1830. Sol. Sept.
7, 1830 by Peyton Smith. Surety, William Barksdale.
Allen, John to Nancy C. Morton, Aug. 18, 1823. Surety,
John Still.
Allen, Reuben to Darky Cobb, Nov. 18, 1834. Sol. Nov.
25, 1834 by J. P. Shepard. Surety, William Under-
wood.
Allen, R. B. to Malinda Vawter, July 27, 1833. Surety,
H. Tennison.
Allen, William to Sarah Read, April 7,1828. Sol. April
22, 1828 by Peyton Smith.
Alley, Ezekiel T. to Rebecca Webb, Aug. 28, 1824. Sol.
Sept. 9, 1824 by J. Higgins, J. P. Surety, Phineas
Parker.
Allison, Mathias H. to Mary Ann Howland, Aug. 31, 1829.
Surety, John F. Howland.
Allman, Richard to Florida Lowry, June 19, 1836. Sol.
June 19, 1836 by Geo. A. Sublett, J.P. Surety,
Isaac Miller.
Alsop, William to Elizabeth Eades, April 10, 1823. Sol.
April 10, 1823 by H. Robinson, J.P.
Anderson, Charles to Mary Gilliland, June 4, 1817.
Anderson, Charles to Polly Jetton, June 4, 1817. Sol.
June 5, 1817 by Jas. S. Jetton, J.P.
Anderson, Charles M. to Mary C. King, June 27, 1832.
Sol. June 28, 1832 by V. D. Cowan, J.P.
Anderson, Edmund R. to Martha T. Henderson, Nov. 20,
1820. Sol. Nov. 20, 1820 by R. Henderson, V.D.M.
Anderson, Gabriel to Martha Walker, Aug. 9, 1833.
Surety, John Burnett.
Anderson, George W. to Martha Carter, Nov. 30, 1820.
Sol. Nov. 30, 1820 by Cary James, D.M.E.C.
Anderson, Jackson to Patsey Pace, Dec. 19, 1825. Sol.
Dec. 22, 1825 by Wm. Stanfield.
Anderson, James M. to Sarah A. Kirby, Oct. 6, 1832.
Sol. Oct. 11, 1832 by V. D. Cowan, J.P.
Anderson, John to Nancy Pollard, March 26, 1835.
Surety, James M. Blanton.
Anderson, Levi C. to Mariah Earp, Sept. 12, 1833. Sol.
Sept. 12, 1833 by A. S. Edwards, J. P. Surety,
Woodfin Nailor.

Anderson, Robert to Mary Smith, Nov. 30, 1830. Sol. Dec. 2, 1830 by Peyton Smith. Surety, William Pate.

Anderson, Samuel to Elizabeth Burrus, Jan. 21, 1819. Sol. Jan. 21, 1819 by Robert Henderson. Surety, Henry D. Jamison.

Anglin, Peyton to Malinda Couch, March 26, 1836. Surety, Anderson Anglin.

Anglin, Thomas to Edith Culver, Dec. 21, 1824. Sol. Dec. 21, 1824 by James Sandford. Surety, David W. Anglin.

Arbuckle, Joseph to Lewhanna Clarke, Sept. 21, 1822. Sol. Sept. 22, 1822 by David Gordon.

Arbuckle, Ralston to Elizabeth Johns, June 17, 1837. Sol. June 18, 1837 by Jordan Williford, J.P.

Armstrong, Ezekiel to Sally Hall, July 4, 1818. Surety, George McCrackin.

Armstrong, Knox to Pernissa S. Witherspoon, Dec. 22, 1834. Sol. Dec. 24, 1834 by Jesse Alexander, V.D.M.

Armstrong, Martin W. to Mary M. Armstrong, Sep. 24, 1834. Sol. Sep. 24, 1834 by Jesse Alexander. Surety, John Alexander.

Armstrong, Zenas to Magdalen Knox, Dec. 23, 1825. Sol. Dec. 27, 1825 by Jesse Alexander, V.D.M.

Arnold, Asa to Tenacy Rucker, Jan. 30, 1832 by O. W. Crockett, J.P.

Arnold, Becker to Sophia Smith, Sept. 18, 1830. Surety, James W. Glass.

Arnold, Enoch to Sally Sullings, Dec. 23, 1809. Surety, Presley Edwards.

Arnold, Ezekiel to Mary Gilliland, Jan. 2, 1816. Sol. Jan. 4, 1816 by L. Davis, J.P.

Arnold, Hubert to Temperance Weaver, March 26, 1834. Sol. Oct. 28, 1834 by A. S. Edwards, J.P. Surety, Daniel Weaver.

Arnold, James to Milly Gilliland, Dec. 2, 1815. Surety, Winifred Pope.

Arnold, James G. to Mary S. Lannon, Feb. 7, 1835. Surety, Tilman W. Lannom.

Arnold, John to Cara Warren, Jan. 15, 1821. Sol. Jan. 17, 1821 by Cary James.

Arnold, Peter to Nancy Harp, May 16, 1835. Sol. May 17, 1825 by A. S. Edwards, J.P. Surety, Andrew S. Edwards.

Arnold, William to Cassendra Acklin, Nov. 12, 1833. Surety, Robert B. Warren.

Arnold, William to Eleanor Robinson, Oct. 2, 1829. Sol. Oct. 2, 1829 by Henry Ridley, J.P. Surety, John Drennon.

Ashford, Michael to Harriett Lockhard, Oct. 26, 1827. Sol. Oct. 30, 1827 by Wm. H. Davis, J.P. Surety, Hugh Tomlinson.

Ashley, James to Lucy McCrary, Sept. 3, 1823. Sol. Sept. 4, 1823 by B.L. McFerrin, J.P. Surety, George McCrary.

Atkinson, James H. to Susan Ellis, Feb. 20, 1832. Sol.
  March 1, 1832 by Peyton Smith.
Austin, Owen E. to Tabitha Jane Covington, Nov. 23,
  1829. Surety, Jerry W. Kirby.
Aveant, Benjamine W. to Nancy Lytle, Sept. 9, 1835.
  Sol. Sept. 9, 1835 by G. Baker. Surety, Wm. H. Sneed.
Avaritt, Littleton to Sarah Head, April 19, 1821. Sol.
  April 19, 1821.
Aymette, William to Louisa J. Hamilton, Jan. 24, 1820
  by Edm'nd Jones, D.M.E.C.
Bacchus, John to Sary James, Aug. 22, 1818. Surety,
  David Hayes.
Bailey, Campion (Campain) to Jane Hall, Feb. 18, 1833.
  Surety, Edward Johnson.
Bailey, Jamison to Mary Smothers, Aug. 18, 1835.
  Surety, Archibald Stinson.
Baird, James P. to Eleanor W. Kirk, Aug 8, 1833.
Baird, James W. to Sara Jane McLean, Sept. 23, 1835.
  Surety, J. M. Baird.
Baird, Lemuel M. to Violet L. Henderson, July 25, 1827.
  Surety, Thomas C. Nelson.
Baird, Martin to Elizabeth A. Henderson, Oct. 29, 1835.
  Surety, C. R. Johns.
Baker, Hampton A. to Menerci E. Harris, Oct. 21, 1837,
  by Wm. H. Murray, J.P.
Baker, Jacob to Elizabeth Finger, March 7, 1818.
  Surety, Vincent Taylor.
Baker, William to Jane Miller, Dec. 20, 1814. Surety,
  James Henderson.
Baker, William D. to Marilla Martin, Nov. 4, 1823.
  Surety, Joseph D. Baker.
Baldridge, David C. to Sarah Howell, Feb. 21, 1834.
  Surety, John L. Dickey.
Baldridge, Francis to Frances Dickey, Nov. 18, 1811.
Baldridge, Matthew to Elizabeth Howell, Jan. 16, 1836.
Ballard, Avery to Anne Wallis, Aug. 4, 1825.
Ballard, Lewis to Ruth Pace, July 19, 1824. Surety,
  Willie Ballard.
Ballard, William to Lucy B. Graham, Nov. 18, 1835.
  Surety, Robert Anderson.
Ballentine, Jesse to Lydia Ballentine, Dec. 26, 1827.
  Surety, James C. Fathera.
Ballew, Aaron to Martha Nichols, Aug. 26, 1823. Surety,
  Daniel Nichols.
Banks, David to Elizabeth Lawrence, Nov. 28, 1823.
Banks, George F. to Maria W. Sims, Dec. 29, 1832.
Banning, Alexander to Elizabeth Smith, Nov. 5, 1822.
Barber, James to Nancy Lovin, Feb. 17, 1827. Surety,
  William Barber.
Barber, Joel to Elizabeth Tucker, June 3, 1827.
  Surety, John Sanders.
Barber, Thomas to Margaret Barber, April 10, 1834.
  Surety, Wade Jarrett.
Barber, William to Sarah Williams, March 4, 1833.
  Surety, Nelson P. Modrell.

Barbour, John A. to Jonah L. Barbour, Jan. 2, 1830.
Surety, Overton B. Morris.
Barksdale, Randolph to Susan Williams, Nov. 16, 1824.
Surety, Thomas H. Read.
Barksdale, William to Ann Eliza Calhoun, May 14, 1829.
Surety, Ransford McGrigor.
Barlow, Alfred to Elizabeth Gibson, June 23, 1834.
Barlow, Benjamine D. to Fanny Molloy, Oct. 15, 1832.
Barlow, Benjamine D. to Mary Jane Kirby, Dec. 22, 1834.
Surety, Wm. Spence.
Barlow, William to Elizabeth C. Hall, Dec. 5, 1837.
Barnes, Daniel T. to Susan E. Sims, Oct. 31, 1816.
Barnett, Ambrose to Sarah Sanders, Feb. 15, 1832.
Barnett, Levi to Elizabeth Williams, Oct. 9, 1835.
Surety, William Holt.
Barnhill, James M. to Delilah Stephens, Feb. 4, 1818.
Surety, Bachel Barnhill.
Barr, Delemore to Jane Jetton, Aug. 29, 1833. Surety,
H. Graham.
Barrett, Levi to Minerva Hainey, Nov. 12, 1829. Surety,
William Stokes.
Harrington, Washington to Susan Easters, Dec. 13, 1821.
Barton, Hale to Lucinda E. Rucker, Jan. 12, 1829.
Surety, Wm. T. Christy.
Barton, Joshua to Elizabeth A. Barton, March 1, 1834.
Surety, John Smith.
Barton, Robert to Polly Bankhead, Jan. 7, 1817.
Barton, Robert D. to Ruthey Barton, Aug. 15, 1836.
Surety, Wm. H. Ivie.
Bass, Benjamine F. to Mrs. Rebecca Thompson, Nov. 15,
1834. Surety, J. M. Barry.
Bass. James Jr. to Eliza House, Sept. 22, 1819.
Bass, William to Lucinda Farnbrough, Oct. 10, 1838.
Surety, Isaac L. Howse.
Batey, Benjamine to Evaline A. Morton-, Dec. 6, 1824.
Batey, Christopher to Mahaley Puckett, Jan. 18, 1822.
Batey, Eleazer to Winney Roberts, Aug. 16, 1835. Surety,
John Cooper.
Batey, George Washington to Mary Jane Crockett, Dec. 20,
1836. Surety, George W. House.
Batey, Isaac to Susan Gwin, Aug. 3, 1824. Surety, John
Calvert.
Batey, Joseph to Anne B. Webber, Sept. 27, 1827. Surety,
Moses G. Reeves.
Batey, William to America S. Crockett, Dec. 5, 1836.
Surety, Geo. W. Batey.
Batey, William D. to Matilda McKee, March 1, 1827.
Surety, John Sullivan.
Batey, William F. to Elizabeth Sills, Nov. 16, 1815.
Surety, Thomas G. Watkins.
Batte, William to Amanda Pryor, Feb. 28, 1827. Surety,
Overton W. Crockett.
Battle, Joel Allen to Sarah M. Searcy, Dec. 12, 1831.
Battle, William M. to Sarah Jane Smith, July 24, 1828.

Batton, Money to Nancy Featherstone, Oct. 14, 1817.
Surety, Henry M. Hutson.
Batts, Thomas to Viola A. Bowman, Nov. 17, 1825.
Baugh, John A. to Mary Anne Marable, Aug. 13, 1829.
Surety, Harrison Patillo.
Baumgarner, Peter to Nancy Gregory, Sept. 29, 1817.
Baxter, David to Cynthia H. Dickson, Nov. 28, 1822.
Baxter, Samuel to Sarah M. Dickson, March 24, 1825.
Bendles, John to Mary Sublett, Aug. 2, 1821.
Bean, Jesse to Polly Kirkendol, Dec. 21, 1805. Surety,
Robert Bean.
Bean, John to Matilda Strain, Dec. 13, 1825.
Beard, Thomas C. to Nancy Hall, March 21, 1816.
Bearfoot, Noah to Elizabeth Cook, Jan. 7, 1819.
Beaty, James to Judith Scott, Sept. 7, 1815. Surety,
Alexander Pool.
Beaty, Nathaniel to Margaret Smith, May 2, 1829. Surety,
Nicholas Harris.
Beavers, Abraham to Dilly Crutchfield, Nov. 21, 1823.
Surety, Gilbert B. Clark.
Becton, Frederick, E. to Eliza P. Yandell, Jan. 13, 1824.
Becton, Frederick E. to Catherine Harris, Aug. 9, 1823.
Becton, George W. to Martha L. Henderson, April 30,
1833. Surety, B. W. Avent.
Becton, John M. to Eleanor E. Sharpe, Jan. 16, 1827.
Surety, Pleasant H. Mitchell.
Bedford, John R. to Matilda Smith, Dec. 6, 1809. Surety,
Joseph Herndon.
Bedford, Robert to Mary Coleman Bedford, Feb. 10, 1804.
Surety, Peter LeGrand.
Bedford, Thomas to Nancy Wade, Feb. 12, 1828.
Becton, William J. to Mary Y. Robb, May 26, 1827.
Surety, William S. Butler.
Beesley, Christopher to Susan J. Ridout, Dec. 16, 1835.
Surety, Isaac L. House.
Beesley, Durant to Harriet Blackman, Dec. 6, 1823.
Surety, Jesse Covington.
Beesley, John P. to Eveline T. Avent, Sept. 16, 1834.
Surety, John P. Graham.
Beesley, Major P. to Emeline Simmons, April 5, 1834.
Surety, Benjamine Marable.
Bell, John to Sally Dickinson, Dec. 10, 1815. Surety,
Jonathan Currin.
Bell, John to Mary Sullivant, Aug. 29, 1818. Surety,
Zachariah P. Bell.
Bell, Joseph W. to Nancy Mosley, Dec. 28, 1835. Surety,
Benjamine H. Bell.
Bell, Samuel to Rebecca M. Peay, March 19, 1827.
Surety, Joseph Hollis.
Bell, Samuel P. to Mary A. Sanford, Aug. 28, 1837.
Bell, Zadock to Katherine Lowrance, July 26, 1821.
Bellah, John to Sarah Davidson, April 30, 1816.
Bellen, Reuben to Catherine Vaughan, Jan. 1825.

RUTHERFORD COUNTY MARRIAGES

Belt, Arthur to Peggy Todd, Aug. 26, 1835. Surety, Arthur H. Belt.
Belt, Benjamine to Louisa Todd, Aug. 1, 1834.
Belt, Hyram to Aberilla Medford, June 26, 1818. Surety, Thomas Keels.
Benoit, Ernest to Fanny Gains, Oct. 30, 1817. Surety, Walter Keeble.
Bennett, William to Susannah Tucker, Jan. 10, 1816.
Benson, John to Mary Anne Higginbotham, Nov. 7, 1829. Surety, Allen Gowen.
Benson, Washington to Margaret Dunn, Sept. 16, 1833. Surety, Hardy Traviɔ.
Benson, William to Catherine Higenbotham, Dec. 25, 1830.
Benthall, Laben to Levina Lannum, April 1, 1824. Surety, Alexander Carter.
Bernard, William to Catherine Barksdale, Nov. 15, 1823. Surety, William Dickinson.
Berry, John C. to Nancy B. Ramsey, Dec. 20, 1833. Surety, Sam'l G. Thompson.
Berry, Thomas S. to Eliza Ann Puckett, Jan. 16, 1833. Surety, James C. Taylor.
Berryman, Talliaferro to Margaret E. Whitsett, March 1, 1837.
Best, George to Sarah A. Blankenship, July 1, 1829. Surety, Allen Blankenship.
Bethshares, Thomas to Ersula Burlison, April 6, 1821.
Bethshears, Wm. S. to Martha L. Johnson, Nov. 15, 1825.
Bickerton, James to Mary Thomas, Sept. 3, 1822.
Bingham, Elihu H. to Mary Lisenby, April 18, 1823. Surety, Robert Bingham (Bigham).
Biles, Herbert to Martha Anne Rutledge, March 22, 1825.
Bingham, William to Mary Hoover, Oct. 15, 1829. Surety, Christopher Hoover.
Binkley, John H. to Mary Walker, Dec. 23, 1829. Surety, Henry McCullough.
Bishop, Neal to Annie Davis, May 6, 1823.
Bishop, Drury to Margaret Watt, March 1, 1821.
Bishop, Joseph to Elizabeth Childress, Jan. 31, 1829. Surety. Sol. Reed.
Bishop, Sterling to Judith Davis, July 27, 1823. Surety, John M. Davis.
Bishop, Sterling to Mary Cochran, May 19, 1815. Surety, Abner Howell.
Bishop, Sterling to Mary Tucker, July 20, 1816.
Bishop, William to Mary Davis, March 2, 1829. Surety, Pleasant Childress.
Bivins, David to Elizabeth Hunt, Feb. 24, 1834. Surety, Benjamine Lillard.
Bivins, James to Leodocia Brasher, June 26, 1826.
Bivins, Richard W. to Rebecca Barnes (Banes), July 2, 1833. Surety, Joshua Barton.
Black, Robert to Rebecca Miller, April 6, 1833. Surety, Samuel H. Laughlin.

7

RUTHERFORD COUNTY MARRIAGES

Black, Spotwood H. to Anne Acklin, Oct. 6, 1829. Surety, Elijah Staton.
Black, Thomas C. to Catherine W. Morton, May 5, 1835. Surety, Geo. D. Crosthwait.
Blackburn, Ferninand to Mary Anne Marable, Jan. 16, 1827. Surety, William C. Edwards.
Blackman, Ollie M. to Johanna F. Mayfield, Dec. 15, 1834. Surety, E. A. C. Norman.
Blackwood, James to Anna Thomas, May 11, 1819.
Blair, Alexander M. to Matilda W. Henderson, Sept. 14, 1829. Surety, Levi Reeves.
Blair, Benjamine T. to Jane G. Nevins, March 12, 1827. Surety, William Nevins.
Blair, Ira L. to Mary A. Sodler, July 28, 1832.
Blair, James to Marilla May, 1825.
Blair, William to Sally Staggs, Dec. 13, 1814. Surety, Hugh Blair.
Blair, Wm. L. J. to Margaret Williams, Feb. 23, 1825. Surety, James P. Thompson.
Blakely, William to Elizabeth Sanders, Aug. 1, 1818. Surety, Thomas Sanders.
Blakemore, James B. to Margaret W. Russell, Sept. 25, 1828.
Blakemore, William to Jane Davis, Jan. 30, 1822.
Blalock, Giles to Martha Beverly, Aug. 3, 1837.
Blalock, Jesse to Nancy Averitt, Dec. 27, 1833. Surety, Asa Coulter.
Bland, Charles to Nancy Cates, July 25, 1825.
Blankenship, Benjamine to Mary G. Butts, Dec. 19, 1827. Surety, John Blankenship.
Blankenship, John M. to Lucy Via, Aug. 12, 1836. Surety, Robert W. Searcy.
Blankenship, Matthew to Naomi Owen, Oct. 1, 1825.
Blankenship, Sylvester to Hannah Witherspoon, Oct. 13, 1830. Surety, David Witherspoon.
Blankenship, Thomas to Mary McKelvey, Oct. 10, 1824. Surety, Gilbert B. Clark.
Blessing, Jacob to Lucretia Gallathan, March 9, 1817. Surety, Nicholas Null.
Bloodworth, David to P. Harris, July 18, 1835. Surety, Delon Devaden.
Blount, Willie Augustus to Delia Blakemore, Dec. 22, 1823.
Boles, Robert to Patsey Barker, Dec. 4, 1817. Surety, Amos Reynolds.
Bolles, Reuben to Catherine Vaughan, Jan. 6, 1825.
Bone, Elihu to Nancy B. Warnick, March 1, 1815.
Bone, James to Thelia Shaperd, Oct. 29, 1829. Surety, Hugh S. Locke.
Bone, John M. to Sarah Anne Rebecca Coleman, April 15, 1836. Surety, Benjamin C. James.
Booker, William B. to Anne Smith, Nov. 9, 1824. Surety, William Ledbetter.
Boone, James to Sophia Smith, Aug. 31, 1825.

Booth, Samuel to Mary P. Tilman, March 10, 1823. Surety, Geo. C. Booth.

Boren, Elijah F. to Sarah Nance, April 17, 1825.

Boring, Amos to Nancy Etter, Jan. 11, 1817. Surety, Eli Smith.

Borpo, Alexander to Mary McCormack, July 26, 1817.

Bowen, Abner to Elizabeth Renshaw, Aug. 22, 1824. Surety, Arnet Jones.

Bowen, Charles to Salley Vasser, June 29, 1827. Surety, Caswell Vasser.

Bowen, James to Catherine Maclin, Jan. 5, 1816.

Bowen, Thomas to Rebecca Walkup, Oct. 15, 1821.

Bowling, John to Ruan Flemming, Jan. 1, 1836. Surety, James Pybass.

Bowman, James to Dovery Hamilton, Feb. 20, 1819.

Bowman, James P. to Mary Brown, July 11, 1830.

Bowman, John to Caroline Smith, Oct. 4, 1837.

Bowman, Samuel P. to Mary A. Trigg, April 19, 1837.

Boyd, James H. to Rosannah E. Boyd, Jan. 12, 1836. Surety, David M. Henderson.

Boyd, James H. to Fanny Weatherspoon, Dec. 30, 1822. Surety, William D. Jordan.

Boyd, John to Elizabeth E. Boyd, Jan. 17, 1836. Surety, Wm. Boyd.

Boyd, Mack to Derinda Summers, Nov. 30, 1830.

Boyd, Paul W. to Isabella Boyd, May 11, 1833. Surety, Robert Boyd.

Boyd, Robert to Margaret T. Witherspoon, Aug. 24, 1829. Surety, James H. Boyd.

Boyd, William M. to Isabella M. McKnight, March 24, 1834.

Boyles, Obadiah to Sally Espey, May 21, 1816.

Braddy, Benjamine to Charlotte Farriss, Sept. 30, 1822.

Bradley, Edmond S. to Mary B. Denoho, Dec. 4, 1833. Surety, Burson Harris.

Brady, Frederick to Betsey Hooker, March 10, 1818.

Brady, William to Harrietta Keeble, Nov. 20, 1818.

Bragg, Thomas to Catherine Cherry, Feb. 10, 1818.

Brandon, Cornelius to _____ , Jan. 25, 1805. Surety, Joseph Tennison.

Brandon, George to Jane Tilford, Sept. 16, 1823. Surety, Thomas Smott.

Brandon, James to Rebecca Craft, Jan. 3, 1825.

Brashears, Isaac W. to Sally Trott, Feb. 12, 1833. Surety, Z. W. Bivins.

Brashears, Nathan to Lucinda Pearson, Jan. 21, 1833. Surety, Robert Sanders.

Brawley, Hugh to Jemima Todd, Aug. 17, 1821.

Brawley, Levi to Polly Glasscocke, Nov. 19, 1818. Surety, David Patton.

Britton, William T. to Susan Thompson, Jan. 22, 1832. Surety, John L. Dillard.

Brittenham, John to Mary Miller, Jan. 25, 1819.

Britton, John to Martha Smith, June 27, 1818.

RUTHERFORD COUNTY MARRIAGES

Brockman, John to Nancy Hardin, July 3, 1827. Surety,
  Nathan L. Douglas.
Brookshire, Benjamine to Elizabeth Bateman, Nov. 17,
  1817.
Brookshire, Mannering to Sally Shelton, Nov. 25, 1816.
Brothers, James to Elizabeth Page, Nov. 5, 1835. Surety,
  Wm. D. Page.
Brothers, Thomas to Polley Kelton, March 12, 1827.
  Surety, John L. Lynch.
Broughton, Thomas to Lucy E. Weever, July 23, 1822.
Brown, Alexander to Polly Jonican (Jamison), March 7,
  1833.
Brown, David C. to Amy Smith, Sept. 26, 1817.
Brown, Elisha to July Peak, Jan. 10, 1833. Surety, Wm.
  Mitchell.
Brown, George to Patsey Head, Dec. 28, 1824.
Brown, George H. to Nancy Hamilton, April 4, 1836.
Brown, Isaac C. to Jane Wade, Nov. 4, 1824. Surety,
  Nathaniel Douglas.
Brown, James to Sarah Jonakin, Dec. 30, 1829. Surety,
  Wm. Brown.
Brown, James A. to Lucy A. Rowland, Dec. 20, 1836.
  Surety, Travis Windrow.
Brown, James M. to Esther Fleming, Jan. 5, 1829. Surety,
  Wm. T. Christy.
Brown, John to Betsy Wheeler, May 5, 1819.
Brown, John to Nancy A. Jetton, Sept. 10, 1834. Surety,
  Edmund Pendleton.
Brown, Richard to Mariah Lowry, Dec. 12, 1827. Surety,
  F. P. Crockett.
Brown, Robert to Mary Stewart, Aug. 4, 1827. Surety,
  High Smith.
Brown, Thomas to Rebecca Cooper, July 8, 1822.
Brown, Thomas to Rebecca Smothers, Nov. 27, 1823.
  Surety, Archibald Stinson.
Brown, Willie to Kessiah Gambrel, Oct. 12, 1829. Surety,
  Jesse Brown.
Brown, William to Jane Hamilton, Jan. 18, 1834. Surety,
  Arthur McCrary.
Brown, William to Rebecca Wigger, Oct. 5, 1819.
Brown, William S. to Elizabeth Wills, Nov. 10, 1829.
  Surety, John Taber.
Brown, William S. to Patsy Bruce, Dec. 7, 1829.
Brown, William T. to Louisa Burns, Oct. 30, 1817.
Broyles, Alfred to Susan Mankins, Nov. 17, 1822.
Broyles, Joel to Mary Fox, July 24, 1835. Surety,
  Joseph Fox.
Brubker, Garrett to Elizabeth Madison, Dec. 21, 1830.
  Surety, John Crow.
Bruce, John to Mary R. Henderson, May 8, 1821.
Bruce, James H. to Zady Smith, May 16, 1835. Surety,
  James Castleman.
Bryant, Samuel H. to Mary Manley, June 22, 1836. Surety,
  Robert S. Morris.
Bryant, William to Lucy Kirby, Aug. 2, 1816.

Bryant, William L. J. to Elizabeth A. Thomas. Surety, Alfred Shitfield.
Bryant, William T. to Jane Kerr, Dec. 16, 1829. Surety, Robert S. Morris.
Buchanan, James to Mariah T. Ott, Nov. 17, 1836. Surety, Richard Lyons.
Buford, John to Sarah Elliott, April 3, 1824. Surety, George W. Lee.
Bugs, Willeby to Polly Wills, Aug. 7, 1816.
Bulla, James to Sally Carlisle, Jan. 21, 1805. Surety, James Carlisle.
Bullard, John to Rebecca Bumgarner, Dec. 26, 1817. Surety, Hezekiah Rhodes.
Bullard, Peter H. to Louisa Jane Herod, Sept. 14, 1834. Surety, James R. Smith.
Bullock, Thomas to Francis Williams, June 13, 1829. Surety, John F. McQuischeon.
Bumgarner, Peter to Nancy Gregory, Sept. 29, 1817.
Bumpass, Robert H. to Martha Wade, July 30, 1821.
Bunny, Samuel to Jane Davis, Dec. 22, 1824.
Burchett, Anderson to Sally Vernon, June 21, 1823. Surety, Thos. Burchett.
Burchett, Bradley to Elizabeth Burgess, Dec. 23, 1834. Surety, John Johnston.
Burge, Henry to Elizabeth Knox, Nov. 4, 1824. Surety, William Faulkenbury.
Burge, Jeremiah to Zibeath Clemmons, Feb. 20, 1816.
Burge, Richard to Nancy Massey, April 30, 1818.
Burgess, Edward to Mary Blanton, Dec. 10, 1829. Surety, John Burgess.
Burgess, John to Nancy Johnson, June 10, 1825.
Burgess, Thomas to Sally Blanton, Jan. 2, 1821.
Burkes, Willis to Charlotte Miller, Oct. 29, 1827. Surety, John F. Howland.
Burks, Leroy to Rebecca Harbern, April 17, 1816.
Burks, Willis to Lucinda Blakely, Feb. 1, 1834. Surety, William Ledbetter.
Burleson, Hilkey to Penelope Pope, Sept. 22, 1810. Surety, Ezekiel Pope.
Burleson, Joseph to Patience Ward, Jan. 7, 1817.
Burleson, David to Ruthy Hobson, March 6, 1819.
Burlison, Isaac to Fanny Morton, March 17, 1818. Surety, Thos. G. Watkins.
Burnett, Joseph to Anna Beesley, March 22, 1819.
Burnett, Lewis G. to Temperance A. Perry, March 5, 1835. Surety, Andrew Finney.
Burnett, Samuel to Cinthia McCall, July 20, 1813.
Burns, Jesse to Petty Freeman, June 9, 1816.
Barpo, Joseph to Delila Baker, April 24, 1820.
Burrus, Phillip J. to Martha W. Yandell. Surety, John W. Childress.
Burt, William to Christian Thomas, April 16, 1823. Surety, Jesse Hudson.

Burton, Richard to Mahulda Sanders, Sept. 6, 1824.
Surety, John Hudson.
Bush, John H. to Martha Williams, ____ 1830. Surety,
Micjaha Whitley.
Bush, Zachariah to Lucinda Gilly, Nov. 1, 1821.
Butler, Benjamine to Elizabeth Shoemaker, Aug. 24, 1824.
Surety, Thomas Butler.
Butler, James to Nancy Smith, July 21, 1813.
Butler, James to Anne West, Oct. 22, 1823. Surety,
Andrew Higdon.
Butler, Thomas to Polly Huff, Oct. 22, 1816.
Butler, William to Martha Hughes, Dec. 16, 1822.
Surety, Jonathan Higgins.
Butler, William S. to Julia G. Marshall, Dec. 9, 1823.
Byford, Aaron to Jane Franklin, May 6, 1829. Surety,
Richard Holt.
Byford, David to Lear McGoigal. (No date).
Byford, George to Jane Smith, Aug. 3, 1817.
Byford, Hardy to Mary Cooke, Feb. 24, 1824. Surety,
James Sissum.
Byford, John to Sarah Elliott, April 3, 1824. Surety,
George W. Lee.
Byford, William to Lear McGoigal, April 17, 1819.
Byford, William to Sarah Lennex, July 26, 1837. Surety,
William Leigh.
Bynum, William to Martha McCullouch, Dec. 16, 1834.
Surety, J. W. McCullouch.
Caffey, Alexander H. to Nancy E. Weatherly, Aug. 2, 1828.
Caffey, Medford to Rutha Ann Yardley, May 27, 1820.
Cain, George to Elizabeth Nevils, Dec. 18, 1829. Surety,
Henry R. Kirby.
Calan, Thomas to Nancy Woods, May 29, 1828.
Caldwell, William to Emily Hutchison, Nov. 17, 1834.
Surety, Millington Harrell.
Campbell, Archibald to Susan F. Neilly, Dec. 20, 1821.
Campbell, James to Betsey Pace, Nov. 18, 1817.
Campbell, John to Levicy Williams, June 30, 1827.
Surety, John McClain.
Campbell, Lowellen to Lindsey Vaught, Oct. 22, 1833.
Surety, Richard Alman.
Campbell, Matthew to Jane Valentine, Sept. 15, 1829.
Surety, Berryman G. Hankins.
Campbell, Thomas to Frances Culver, Dec. 25, 1827.
Surety, Thomas Williams.
Cannon, Abraham W. to Mary Y. Sharpe, May 24, 1820.
Cannon, Clement to Susan Locke. Aug. 1810. Surety,
William White.
Cannon, John T. to Sarah A. Harrison, July 15, 1829.
Surety, James D. Glinn.
Cantrell, Ota to Nelton Cummins, July 27, 1818. Surety,
James Thompson.
Cardwell, Thomas G. to Martha Acklin, March 15, 1835.
Surety, Sam'l B. Tinsley.
Carithers, John G. to Charlotte Dyer, May 14, 1816.

Carlton, William to Emily Rucker, May 23, 1832.
Carmen, Elisha to Alley Carmen, Dec. 13, 1822. Surety,
Stephen Parsley.
Carnahan, Abraham to Cynthia Price, Feb. 3, 1829.
Surety, Archibald Tenison.
Cranahan, Hugh to Elizabeth Thompson, June 21, 1806.
Surety, Abraham Thompson.
Carns, Alexander B. to Cynthia M. Gowan. May 9, 1832.
Carpenter, Asa to Elizabeth Mason, Sept. 23, 1815.
Carrick, Thomas to Sarah Smith, Jan. 5, 1825.
Carroll, Michum to Oney Bryant, May 24, 1817.
Carroll, Stephen to Anne Locke, March 31, 1810. Surety,
Henry Botyer.
Carter, Burwell to Nancy Burgess, Oct. 13, 1830. Surety,
Henry D. Ransom.
Carter, Cullin to Emily C. Bloodworth, Aug. 5, 1834.
Carter, Henry to Mary E. Hardeman, Nov. 16, 1833.
Surety, Walker Peak.
Carter, Hiram C. to Elizabeth McDowell, Sept. 26, 1837.
Carter, Nathan W. to Mary Thompson, Dec. 20, 1836.
Surety, Joseph Flowers.
Carter, Robert to Elizabeth Todd, Dec. 28, 1830. Surety,
Alexander A. Nesbett.
Carter, William to Elizabeth Stanley, Sept. 7, 1830.
Surety, Robert Carter.
Carter, William to Mary Moore, Apr. 21, 1835. Surety,
Alexander Nesbett.
Cartwright, Benajah to Delila Davis, June 26, 1823.
Surety, William Taylor.
Cartwright, Isaac to Sally Morris, March 15, 1806.
Surety, Frederick White.
Castleman, Joseph to Susanna Smith, April 13, 1816.
Castleman, Lewis to Lucinda Starkey, March 12, 1836.
Surety, Josiah H. Castleman.
Castleman, William S. to Susannah Sanders, July 13, 1836.
Surety, Joseph Flowers.
Catheym, Alexander to Mary Locke, Aug. 1, 1805. Surety,
Alex McKnight.
Cathey, James to Sally Oliver, May 8, 1817. Surety,
John Darrah.
Cawthon, James to Nancy McDowell, March 17, 1834.
Surety, Joseph E. Basham.
Cawthen, Martin B. to Nancy Elliott, April 16, 1823.
Cawthon, Pleasant to Jane Robinson, Dec. 14, 1823.
Chappell, John to Mary F. Smith, Aug. 2, 1834. Surety,
Jas. F. Fletcher.
Cheatham, John A. to Anne McLin, Oct. 11, 1836. Surety,
Thomas ___.
Cherry, John to Elizabeth Boyer, Jan. 26, 1818. Surety,
Thomas Bragg.
Childers, William to Betsey Jordan, Nov. 24, 1821.
Childress, David to Susan Smith, Jan. 24, 1826.
Childress, Henry to Nancy Harris, April 20, 1830.
Surety, Travis Watts.

Childress, James to Rebecca Kinkade, May 28, 1818.
Childress, John to Levina Wray, Aug. 7, 1838.
Childress, Joseph to Sara Craford, Aug. 11, 1827. Surety,
Joseph Sursa.
Childress, Logan to Elizabeth Seymore, Sept. 23, 1829.
Surety, Walter Lowe.
Childress, William to Betsy Jordan, Nov. 24, 1821.
Childress, William to Elizabeth Bryant, May 4, 1835.
Surety, Samuel Jones.
Chizenhall, John to Ehoda Pinson, Aug. 17, 1821.
Chrisp, William to Mary Elder, April 4, 1821.
Christian, Peyton to Peggy Pace, Feb. 4, 1833. Surety,
James Pace.
Christopher, John to Elizabeth Jones, Dec. 30, 1824.
Christopher, John to Jincy Carter, June 23, 1818.
Surety, James Baldridge.
Christopher, Joshua to Rosemond Rutledge, April 22, 1822.
Church, John A. to Margaret L. Ramsey, Dec. 16, 1819.
Church, Robert to Amanda Bryant, March 3, 1835. Surety,
James Ramsey.
Clack, John to Sarah May, Nov. 24, 1825.
Clark, Anderson A. to Nancy C. Robb, June 7, 1836.
Surety, Thos. P. Clark.
Clark, Elisha B. to Ann Dickinson, Jan. 21, 1817.
Surety, Thos. Washington.
Clark, James to Nelly Burks, Aug. 13, 1836. Surety,
Leroy Burks.
Clark, James M. to Asenath Jetton, Aug. 27, 1835.
Surety, William B. Holloway.
Clark, John N. to Caroline McFadden, Jan. 11, 1837.
Surety, William R. McFadden.
Clark, Jourdin to Elizabeth Brewer, Aug. 7, 1837.
Surety, Ezekiel Morrison.
Clark, William to Emily Kelton, Sept. 17, 1835. Surety,
Reuben Curry.
Clarke, George to Susan Burchett, March 1, 1823. Surety,
John Hall.
Clay, Samuel T. to Martha Ann Edwards, Nov. 2, 1822.
Clay, Sydney to Clara Barnett, Sept. 6, 1833. Surety,
John Barnett.
Clayton, William to Rosannah Norman, Jan. 26, 1808.
Surety, Pritchard Alexander.
Clayton, William C. to Elizabeth Norman, Feb. 13, 1833.
Surety, J. B. Jones.
Clements, John G. to Charity Sharpe, Oct. 23, 1827.
Surety, Alfred Bell.
Clendenan, John to Elizabeth Herndon, April 6, 1825.
Clendennon, John to Mary Meadors, Sept. 4, 1837.
Clopton, Walter Jr. to Martha Ann Duffer, Aug. 12, 1825.
Coats, Armstead to Nancy Brown, Oct. 20, 1825.
Coats, Peyton H. to Elizabeth Richardson, Aug. 31, 1825.
Cobb, Thomas to Eliza G. Pearson, Jan. 8, 1820.
Cochran, Edward A. to Elizabeth Wade, July 16, 1825.

Cocke, James W. to Caroline E. Howell, Jan. 15, 1835.
Surety, William T. Roberts.
Coleman, Chastain A. to Lucy Smith, Dec. 11, 1829.
Surety, Jesse Roberts.
Coleman, Grief to Rebecca Coleman, July 30, 1824.
Surety, Ephraim Meadors.
Coleman, Jesse to Elizabeth Bivins, Oct. 26, 1836.
Surety, Wiley Harman.
Coleman, John to Temperance W. Harris, April 5, 1827.
Surety, Joel Neal.
Coleman, John to Milley Coleman, Sept. 25, 1833. Surety,
Charles A. Frensley.
Coleman, Jordan to Nancy Anderson, Dec. 18, 1809.
Surety, James H. Gambill.
Coleman, Joseph to Temperance Rogers, June 7, 1824.
Coleman, Mordecai to Elizabeth Coleman, Dec. 6, 1834.
Surety, D. Caldwell.
Coleman, William to Elizabeth Hodge, 1834. Surety, Wm.
A. Coleman.
Coleman, William to Susan Lewis, Nov. 20, 1833. Surety,
Lewelling Williams.
Collier, Ingram B. to Martha Covington, Dec. 13, 1817.
Collier, P. P. to Susan D. Bryan, July 21, 1830.
Collingsworth, Benjamine F. to Elizabeth Mason, Sept. 19,
1825.
Collins, Jas. S. to Harkles P. Thompson, Jan. 11, 1827.
Surety, John Smothers.
Colwell, William to Polly Curry, May 19, 1806. Surety,
John Curry.
Con, James N. to Elizabeth McMurray, Jan. 25, 1834.
Conatser, Nicholas to Sally L. Wherry, Sept. 4, 1823.
Surety, Eli Nicholas.
Conn, George A. to Martha A. Dillard, July 24, 1822.
Conn, Josephus H. to Jane C. McFerrin, Aug. 4, 1822.
Connelly, George W. to Rebecca Young, Dec. 5, 1821.
Connelly, Hardy S. to Elizabeth B. Read, July 8, 1824.
Surety, Robert C. Owen.
Connelly, James B. to Elizabeth W. Tweedy, March 12,
1818.
Connelly, John W. to Sally Nichols, Nov. 24, 1824.
Surety, Caleb Ballew.
Connelly, Thomas J. to Stacy Hewitt, Jan. 21, 1834.
Surety, R. Blair.
Cook, George W. to Mary Mathenia, June 24, 1819.
Cook, James to Mary Smith, Jan. 30, 1837.
Cook, John to Anna Teel, Nov. 20, 1830. Surety, Hardy
Byford.
Cook, Joseph to Mary Ferguson, May 7, 1818.
Cook, Thomas to Karon Smith, Jan. 16, 1835. Surety,
William Forbs.
Cook, Wiett W. to Mariah Clark, Feb. 3, 1830. Surety,
George Jones.
Cooke, Green to Lurainy Nixon, July 20, 1822.
Cooke, John D. to Christian Mullins, Nov. 17, 1825.

Cooper, Bedford C. to Elizabeth Turner, Aug. 25, 1836.
Surety, William K. Wilson.
Cooper, John B. to Jane McGuffin, June 22, 1835. Surety,
Charles D. Cooper.
Cooper, Charles D. to Elizabeth V. Lindsay, Oct. 31,
1835. Surety, Richard Ledbetter.
Cooper, Edward to Celia Wheeler, March 24, 1825. Surety,
Richard Lennox.
Cooper, John to Levicy Goodin, Nov. 6, 1824. Surety,
Jacob Davis.
Cooper, John L. to Frances C. Lindsey, April 21, 1834.
Surety, Thomas Edwards.
Cooper, Micajah T. to Sarah A. Vinson, March 31, 1829.
Surety, Joseph Hollis.
Cooper, Nelson to Eliza Jacobs, Dec. 24, 1833. Surety,
Jonathan Owen.
Cooper, Noah to Eliza M. Farr, Oct. 20, 1835. Surety,
E. L. Farr.
Cooper, Richard to Elizabeth Miller, April 23, 1804.
Surety, William Nash.
Coplin, James to Nancy Lowry, March 23, 1820.
Cosbey, Alfred G. to Sarah McKinley, July 28, 1836.
Surety, Robert S. Morris.
Cosbey, Williamson to Mary Ann Cook, Dec. 2, 1836.
Surety, A. D. Marshall.
Cosby, Wallace to Sarah Rankin, Jan. 16, 1823. Surety,
Richard Neill.
Cotten, Abner to Polly Crosslin, April 23, 1805.
Surety, Wm. Crass.
Couch, William to Susan Anglin, May 30, 1834. Surety,
Anderson Anglin.
Coulter, Asa to Barbara Everett, Aug. 30, 1821.
Counts, George to Sally Rich, July 23, 1806. Surety,
Thomas Rich.
Counts, George S. to Nancy A. Hays, May 20, 1834.
Surety, James Pybass.
Counts, Jesse to Margaret Holloway, April 3, 1834.
Surety, William Davis.
Counts, William to Sara Freeman, Dec. 13, 1804. Surety,
Geo. Counts.
Coursey, William to Catherine Gregory, Jan. 26, 1835.
Surety, Anglen Anglen.
Covington, David to Judith Kindrick, Jan. 29, 1817.
Covington, Edmund to Emelia D. Underwood, Dec. 20, 1830.
Surety, Ellis W. Hankins.
Covington, Jackson to Mary Corder, Feb. 3, 1835. Surety,
N. C. Goodloe.
Covington, Jesse to Levica Beesley, Oct. 22, 1816.
Covington, John to Jane Marlin, Feb. 19, 1824. Surety,
Bedford Crawford.
Covington, Larkin to Ann Minifee, March 12, 1817.
Surety, Andrew Griffin.
Cowan, Varner D. to Susan B. Johns, June 28, 1827.
Surety, Wm. T. Christy.

RUTHERFORD COUNTY MARRIAGES

Cowan, Varner D. to Margaret Jetton, June 7, 1824.
Surety, William Ladbetter.
Cowan, William to Mary E. Johns, April 23, 1833. Surety,
D. B. Molloy.
Cowan, William B. to Nancy Sublett, July 2, 1823.
Cowan, William M. to Mary M. Briant, March 10, 1832.
Cox, Elisha to Frances W. Vis, Dec. 17, 1835. Surety,
Isaac Ledbetter.
Cox Ephraim to Anne Bell, April 6, 1825.
Cox, Ezekial to Mary L. Watson, July 14, 1835. Surety,
Richard Ledbetter.
Cox, Hiram to Elizabeth Chisenhall, Nov. 15, 1823.
Surety, William Warren.
Cox, Hiram to Elizabeth Ridgeway, March 21, 1814.
Surety, John Ridgeway.
Cox, James I. to Rebecca W. Chisenhall, Nov. 17, 1834.
Surety, Alexr. S. Dickson.
Cox, James L. to Susan Porterfield, Jan. 31, 1835.
Surety, James H. Alexander.
Cox, Thomas W. to Millanda D. Bradford, Aug. 22, 1823.
Surety, Ralph McFadden.
Craddock, Elicum to Anne Sutherland, Nov. 2, 1829.
Surety, Oliver M. Crutchfield.
Craddock, John N. to Anne Edmondson, Aug. 10, 1829.
Surety, John G. Keeble.
Crawford, Charles B. to Mary I. Clayton, Nov. 24, 1835.
Surety, James W. Leiper.
Crawford, David to Elizabeth Casey, Jan. 21, 1805.
Surety, James Carlisle.
Craig, John to Nancy Cowan, Jan. 22, 1823. Surety,
Absolom Stout.
Crawford, William to Nancy Bell, Jan. 5, 1837.
Crawford, William C. to Mary Anne Killiam, Dec. 17,
1824. Surety, John Crawford.
Creek, John to Frances Calton, July 23, 1836. Surety,
James Hill.
Crews, Squire to Piety Prewitt, Aug. 21, 1819. Surety,
Wm. Rawlins.
Crocker, John T. to Eliza Winston, June 19, 1834.
Crocker, Lambert to Lucy Williams, Oct. 4, 1830. Surety,
Moses B. Wadley.
Crockett, Fountain O. to Julia G. Smith, Dec. 5, 1820.
Crockett, Granville S. to Sarah Sims, May 16, 1821.
Cross, John to Mary D. Joy, Dec. 1, 1835. Surety,
Thomas Boyd.
Crosshwait, George D. to Frances E. Burton, Oct. 11,
1836. Surety, Wm. H. Sneed and John W. Jetton.
Crouse, Matthias to Mary Hunt, Oct. 27, 1827. Surety,
James Pybass.
Crouse, Spencer to Derindia Hunt, Dec. 20, 1830.
Surety, P. G. Noland.
Crowder, Jesse to Elizabeth Lee, Sept. 22, 1823. Surety,
Hezekiah Watkins.

Crowder, Nathaniel to Nancy Neisbet, Feb. 5, 1827.
Surety, Allen Gowen.
Crutchfield, Gideon to Marcia Walker, March 7, 1818.
Surety, Zachariah P. Bell.
Cuff, John W. to Susanna Baker, July 3, 1820.
Culan, Thomas to Nancy Wood, May 29, 1828.
Cummins, Benjamine to Parmely Gray, May 2, 1833. Surety,
Micajah Thompson.
Cummins, Robert to Elizabeth A. McFarlin, Nov. 20, 1830.
Cummins, Robert G. to Isabela McKnight, Oct. 9, 1823.
Surety, James Wilson.
Cummins, Uriah to Margaret Smith, July 27, 1816.
Cunningham, James to Rachel Thorn, Jan. 12, 1820.
Cunningham, Joseph to Anny Knox, Nov. 29, 1817.
Curle, Portland J. to Milly Marshall, June 15, 1819.
Curry, James to Rebecca Hoshone, June 15, 1814.
Dalton, Thomas to Martha McCay, Oct. 22, 1832.
Dalton, John to Eliza J. Parrish, Sept. 28, 1837.
Surety, Edwin Rowton.
Dalwood, John to Marthy Mynight, June 7, 1806. Surety,
William Laughlin and Peter Devault.
Daniel, Elisha to Sally Alsup, Jan. 22, 1821.
Daniel, James to Elizabeth Alsup, Aug. 29, 1827. Surety,
Edward Daniel.
Daniel, Joseph R. to Mary E. Randolph, May 30, 1836.
Surety, William C. J. Burrus.
Daniel, Stephen to Abigail Allsup, Aug. 29, 1827. Surety,
Edward Daniel.
Daniel, Walter W. to Jane A. Berry, Aug. 25, 1835.
Surety, John C. Berry.
Darnul, William to Condice Freeman, Dec. 12, 1820.
Daughtry, Jeremiah to Martha Mankin, March 1, 1837.
Surety, Jesse Mankin.
Davenport, Reuben to Ruth M. Sauls, March 28, 1825.
Surety, John Sauls.
David, Benjamine to Franky Vessor, Aug. 22, 1817.
Davidson, John to Mary Hare, July 30, 1829. Surety,
Benjamine H. Billings.
Davidson, Jonah to Mary Finch, Jan. 26, 1825.
Davidson, Richard to Elizabeth Toombs, Feb. 26, 1821.
Davis, Abel Jr. to Tabitha Daniel, Jan. 4, 1836.
Surety, W. G. Parrish.
Davis, Acquilla to Mary F. Morton, July 14, 1835.
Surety, Benj. W. Avent.
Davis, Andrew F. to Elizabeth R. Nuckles, Aug. 10, 1815.
Surety, Joshua Nuckles.
Davis, Benjamine to Elizabeth Spraggins, Aug. 23, 1820.
Davis, David to Mary Martin, Sept. 28, 1825.
Davis, Eaton to Deborah Moore, July 2, 1825.
Davis, Edward to Nancy Battle, Feb. 26, 1829. Surety,
Charles Guyger.
Davis, George W. to Sarah Rucker, April 1, 1837.
Davis, Goodman to Henrietta Pryor, Sept. 14, 1834.
Surety, Thomas Smith.

RUTHERFORD COUNTY MARRIAGES

Davis, Henry to Ann Sullivan, April 7, 1818. Surety,
Thomas Price.
Davis, Isaac to Lucy Via, Jan. 28, 1826.
Davis, James to Rachel Read, Sept. 27, 1827. Surety,
John Hicks.
Davis, James B. to Martha D. Shearman, Nov. 23, 1830.
Surety, Malcomb R. Nelson.
Davis, John P. to Anny Sullivan, April 13, 1816.
Surety, James Sullivan.
Davis, Duckett to Eliza J. M. Jones, Dec. 29, 1835.
Surety, James W. Morton.
Davis, Thomas to Martha Hogins, Feb. 28, 1829. Surety,
William Potts.
Davis, Thomas D. to Arey Johnson, June 7, 1827. Surety,
Moses Lynch.
Davis, Thomas P. to Lucinda Beesley, June 25, 1830.
Surety, James McDowell.
Davis, Thomas P. to Lucinda Wright, March 7, 1834.
Surety, A. J. Hoover.
Davis, Thomas P. to Nancy Popp, Aug. 19, 1836. Surety,
Richard D. Allison.
Davis, Timothy to Frances Ross, Nov. 30, 1805. Surety,
Norton Gum.
David, William to Martha Trimble, Feb. 10, 1821.
Deason, John to Sally Arnold, Dec. 16, 1815.
Debs, Samuel C. to Mary C. Cannon, Oct. 24, 1836.
Surety, James R. Cannon.
Deloath, Boykin to Sally Bell, Feb. 6, 1816.
Dement, Abraham to Mary Nance, March 28, 1821.
Dement, Allen to Catherine Robertson, Feb. 18, 1824.
Surety, William Dickson.
Dement, Cader to Mary M. Andrews, Oct. 27, 1821.
Dement, Charles to Sarah H. Tarpley, March 1, 1820.
Dement, James to Rosannah Posey, June 5, 1835. Surety,
Josephus Moore.
Dement, John to Cecelia W. Lowe, Sept. 27, 1820.
Demumber, William to Mary Patton, Jan. 9, 1819.
Denen, Hiram A. to Martha Hill, Sept. 5, 1829.
Denny, Robert A. to Clementine C. Bobitt, Nov. 13, 1837.
Denny, Samuel to Jane Davis, Dec. 22, 1824. Surety,
Evan Taylor.
Denny, Robert to Lucy Farmer, Aug. 12, 1830. Surety,
Jas. R. Cox.
Denton, Charles to Mary Anne Parsley, June 23, 1827.
Surety, Jesse Garner.
Depriest, Charles C. to Polly T. Edwards, Nov. 7, 1817.
Surety, Charles B. Turley.
Davenport, George to Jane Kilpatrick, May 23, 1836.
Surety, Joseph Bogle.
Dial, John C. to Mary Johnson, Aug. 23, 1832.
Dickey, James to Mary Wells, Oct. 23, 1810.
Dickey, Matthew to Marah Jourdan, May 18, 1814.
Dickey, John L. to Martha B. Taylor. Surety, Amon
Boring.

Dickins, Baxter to Nancy Holton, Feb. 14, 1820.
Dickins, William to Elizabeth Adams, Sept. 1, 1818.
Dickinson, Alfred to Elizabeth Hall, Oct. 3, 1836.
Dickinson, Gallant D. to Isabella McCrary, Nov. 3, 1828.
Dickinson, Isham S. to Sarah Warren, Dec. 23, 1825.
Dickinson, Samuel to Agnes Pallet, March 30, 1820.
Dickinson, William to Elizabeth Adams, Sept. 1, 1818.
Surety, George Adams.
Dickson, Amos to Elizabeth Monday, May 23, 1814.
Surety, Francis Monday.
Dickson, David to Anny Owen, Dec. 31, 1833. Surety,
A. M. Hamilton.
Dickson, Enos H. to Cynthia Howell, April 20, 1824.
Surety, Samuel Nelson.
Dickson, Ezekiel to Rebecca L. Davis, Oct. 21, 1820.
Dickson, Joseph to Mary Hare, May 30, 1821.
Dickson, William to Perminty Reeves, May 23, 1825.
Dickson, William R. to Rody F. Johns, March 19, 1827.
Surety, Varner D. Cowan.
Dickson, Alfred to Elizabeth Hall, Oct. 3, 1836. Surety,
Levi Jones.
Dill, Joseph to Nancy K. Wilson, May 20, 1835. Surety,
Wilson H. Kerr.
Dill, Marvell M. to Mary Ann Sanders, May 3, 1831.
Dill, Newton C. to Narcissa Kerr, Feb. 8, 1827. Surety,
Simeon Hogue.
Dill, Noah W. to Martha A. Harwell, Dec. 13, 1837.
Dillion, Allen to Lucy Loftin, June 15, 1836. Surety,
Samuel Winston.
Dirikson, Davis S. to May L. Wilson, Jan. 16, 1836.
Surety, Robert H. Cate.
Dismukes, Thomas U. to Mary Jane Hager, Oct. 5, 1836.
Doak, Joseph to Maria T. Stovall, May 9, 1822.
Doak, Robert to Jane Wilson, May 23, 1822.
Dobson, Benjamine to Nancy Lannum, March 22, 1834.
Surety, John H. Flowers.
Dobson, Joseph C. to Mary N. Tweedy, Sept. 10, 1822.
Dobyns, Dennis R. D. to Matilda Wadley, Dec. 8, 1836.
Surety, William G. Parrish.
Donelson, Andrew J. to Catherine Nelson, Oct. 10, 1835.
Surety, Burton Yandell.
Donelson, Calvin to Martha Weatherspoon, Sept. 7, 1836.
Surety, Levi Donnell.
Donnell, Levi to Elizabeth Sherrill, Oct. 26, 1836.
Surety, James M. Weatherly.
Donnell, Samuel to Jane Andres, Feb. 1, 1804. Surety,
James Andres.
Donnell, William to Mary Todd, Aug. 20, 1827. Surety,
Archibald Tennison.
Donoho, William to Jane C. Ready, July 14, 1835.
Surety, R. D. Donoho.
Doran, Alexander to Nancy Powell, June 21, 1824.
Surety, Thomas Powell.

Doran, James G. to Elizabeth Knox, Dec. 24, 1818.
Surety, James McKnight.
Dorsey, Charles to Eleanor Broyles, Oct. 13, 1823.
Surety, John Howland.
Dosher, John to Rachel Pain, Nov. 26, 1823. Surety,
Daniel Dosher.
Douglas, Rodham to Elizabeth Gillespie, Jan. 6, 1819.
Douglas, Rodham to Sally Pearson, June 23, 1827.
Surety, William Webb.
Drennon, John to Mary Robinson, Oct. 2, 1829. Surety,
William Arnold.
Drennon, Joseph A. to Menerva C. Sander, Feb. 11, 1833.
Surety, Joseph Robertson.
Drew, Jonathan to Jane Martin, Sept. 1, 1821.
Driskill, George to Elizabeth Campbell, Dec. 24, 1818.
Surety, Jacob Campbell.
Drumwright, George M. to Harriet Mustain, Dec. 21, 1829.
Surety, Richard R. Rainey.
Drury, Daniel to Bridgett Epps, Sept. 22, 1827. Surety,
Curry McGrier.
Duboise, James to Margaret Duboise, Feb. 19, 1816.
Dunaway, Elijah to Ann Todd, Dec. 27, 1836.
Dunlap, John C. to Elizabeth R. Jarrett. Surety,
Jesse Adcock.
Dunn, Henry to Ann Moore, June 9, 1835. Surety, Marcus
Smotherman.
Dunn, John P. to Nancy Brown, Dec. 4, 1823. Surety,
Jacob Spear.
Dunn, John R. to Jerana Catherine Bevins, June 29, 1833.
Surety, John G. Holloway.
Durham, Thomas to Elizabeth Johnson, April 20, 1816.
Dyer, Isaiah to Frances P. Gambill, July 6, 1829.
Surety, Dugald G. Ferguson.
Dyer, William H. to Martha Ann Marshall, May 21, 1816.
Eades, Isaac to Cynthia George, Oct. 14, 1823. Surety,
John Sweet.
Eades, William to Sally Wells, Jan. 21, 1822.
Early, Henry to Olive Reed, Sept. 1, 1823. Surety,
William Cobb.
Earwood, William to Eleanor Rankin, Oct. 30, 1822.
East, Anderson to Sarah Johns, Aug. 1, 1834. Surety,
John Lamar.
Eastland, Thomas B. to Josephine M. Green, April 2,
1829. Surety, William T. Christy.
Eastus, Henderson to Nancy Bond, Jan. 8, 1835. Surety,
William Mullins.
Edens, Ezekiel to Mary Gammil, Feb. 2, 1814. Surety,
John McCain.
Edmondson, John to Amanda K. Randolph, Oct. 11, 1830.
Surety, William H. Mitchell.
Edwards, Arthur M. to Nancy Harrell, Aug. 19, 1829.
Surety, Hubbard S. Wilkinson.
Edwards, Augustus to Mary Robertson, Feb. 21, 1824.
Surety, Elisha Sanders.

Edwards, Charles A. to Tabitha V. Ivie, Dec. 1, 1834. Surety, Robert B. Warren.
Edwards, Edward to Catherine Countryman, Oct. 14, 1816.
Edwards, John to Sarah Cummins, July 21, 1804. Surety, O. M. Benge.
Edwards, John J. to Nancy Ward, Sept. 23, 1829. Surety, John W. Richardson.
Edwards, Levi to Delilah Smith, March 5, 1818.
Edwards, Richard A. to Frances A. Mathis, Sept. 16, 1833. Surety, R. H. White.
Edwards, Roderick to Anne D. Brumfield, Sept. 24, 1823. Surety, William Wilson.
Edwards, Thomas J. to Jane Dunlap, Feb. 11, 1834. Surety, Thomas Edwards.
Edwards, Welden to Rachel West, July 20, 1835. Surety, William G. Cook.
Edwards, Wm. C. to Eliza A. Nelson, April 1, 1830. Surety, Wm. T. Christy.
Eggleston, John W. to Ann W. West, Oct. 22, 1836. Surety, Richmond Wood.
Ehart, Christian to Mary Brady, May 26, 1810. Surety, Matthew McClahahan.
Elam, Edward to Rebecca Wade, April 18, 1821.
Elam, Joel to Mary Aiken, June 11, 1824. Surety, Reuben Wright.
Elam, William to Jemima Strange, Feb. 2, 1830. Surety, Samuel Winston.
Elder, Benjamine to Eliza A. Wade, Feb. 7, 1827. Surety, Charles Guyger.
Elder, James to Polly Wood, July 2, 1816.
Elder, James to Jane Watson, March 26, 1829. Surety, David Myers.
Elder, Joshua to Lydia Etter, Jan. 29, 1824. Surety, Hezekiah House.
Elder, William to Tabitha Nance, Dec. 18, 1828.
Elgin, Samuel to Lucinda Jones, March 25, 1829. Surety, S. H. Laughlin.
Elliott, Barney to Rebecca Freeman, Sept. 22, 1818. Surety, Charles Lock.
Elliott, Knacy H. to Martha W. Slack, May 6, 1834. Surety, Martin Clark.
Elliott, Richard S. to Margaret Eselton, Dec. 12, 1832.
Elliott, Robert to Ann Thorn, Jan. 1, 1827. Surety, William Brady.
Elliott, Simon to Candas Dean, May 28, 1820.
Elliott, Thomas to Margaret Miller, Oct. 8, 1824. Surety, William Johnston (Johnson).
Elliott, Thomas to Jane Rushing, Jan. 16, 1837. Surety, Peter N. Elliott.
Ellis, Josiah to Ann Loyd, July 31, 1824. Surety, Hick Ellis.
Ellis, Thomas B. to Susan M. Robinson, Dec. 8, 1832.
Ellis, William W. to Rhoda Curtis, June 27, 1829. Surety, Joseph P. Holt.

Ellis, Wyatt H. to May Dixon, Nov. 9, 1836. Surety,
    L. D. Baker.
Ellis, Wyley to Sarah H. James, Aug. 29, 1836. Surety,
    C. G. Mitchell.
Ellison, Hugh H. to Nancy Becton, March 9, 1820.
Elrod, Adam A. to Margaret Work, Jan. 20, 1836. Surety,
    James Brown.
Elrod, George to Thussey Peas, Oct. 11, 1823. Surety,
    John R. Rogers.
Elrod, Harmond to Jincy McKee, July 15, 1818. Surety,
    Ambrose McKee.
Elrod, John to Mary Bishop, Dec. 9, 1836. Surety,
    Joseph Trimble.
Elrod, Montgomery to Mary E. Batey, Dec. 19, 1833.
    Surety, Thos. W. Batey.
Epps, Ely to Rebecca Miller, Dec. 16, 1822. Surety,
    Isaac Johnston (Johnson).
Epps, Lafayette to Rebecca Allen, Dec. 12, 1834.
    Surety, James McR. Fresley.
Erwin, Charles to Sarah Corder, Jan. 22, 1820.
Espey, Alexander to Mirna Todd, April 6, 1837. Surety,
    Miles Herrald.
Espey, Charles to Elizabeth White, May 10, 1825.
Espey, George to Mary Gillespie, Sept. 22, 1820.
Espey, John to Catherine Wright, Dec. 22, 1828.
Espey, John to Mariah Cook, Sept. 25, 1837. Surety,
    Jefferson Earp.
Espey, Robert to Lucinda Biles, July 31, 1823. Surety,
    Willie Biles.
Espey, Robert to Amelia George, Sept. 4, 1827. Surety,
    Alexander Espey.
Edualy, David to Lucy E. Blankenship, Dec. 19, 1816.
Evans, John to Martha Williams, Aug. 20, 1836. Surety,
    Thomas Williams.
Evans, John to Dokey McDowell, Feb. 7, 1832.
Evans, Joseph to Susannah Vann, Oct. 2, 1829. Surety,
    William B. Evans.
Evins, Daniel to Elizabeth Williams, Nov. 19, 1834.
    Surety, Hays B. Snell.
Ewell, Dabney to Dovey Davidson, June 7, 1821.
Ewell, Jesse to Cynthia H. Robertson, Jan. 27, 1834.
    Surety, Isaac Robinson.
Eyson, Richard to Pietta Gasaway, July 18, 1816.
Ezell, Uberto D. to Isabella Marshall, Feb. 10, 1829.
    Surety, Benjamine Fisher.
Fagan, Henry W. to Martha V. Barton, Dec. 17, 1834.
    Surety, Wm. A. McCombs.
Fagan, Robert to Patsey Gibson, Jan. 2, 1816.
Falkenberry, Thomas J. to Martha S. Wright. Surety,
    William Barton.
Farbus, Robert to Martha Childress, June 3, 1830.
    Surety, Henry Haley.
Farmer, Bailey W. to Catherine Hartwell, March 3, 1835.
    Surety, Isaac L. Howse.

RUTHERFORD COUNTY MARRIAGES

Farmer, Thomas to Nancy Ward, June 8, 1830. Surety,
E. C. Wilkinson.
Farr, William L. to Sarah Wilson, Sept. 29, 1835.
Surety, E. L. Farr.
Farris, John to Mary Seawell, Aug. 15, 1822.
Farris, William D. to Mary Ward, Jan. 8, 1833.
Faulkenbury, Jacob to Jane M. Flaming, Sept. 26, 1827.
Surety, Hiram Tennison.
Favour, James to Anna Meban, Nov. 2, 1804. Surety,
William Howell.
Fears, Eben E. to Elizabeth Spence, June 17, 1833.
Surety, Samuel Spence.
Featherstone, Presley to Elizabeth Harris, Dec. 30,
1834. Surety, Robert Jarrett.
Fentress, David to Matilda C. McIver, Jan. 17, 1833.
Ferguson, Toliver to Catherine Minters, Oct. 5, 1821.
Ferrell, James to Zina Jones, Feb. 18, 1824.
Ferriss, John C. to Christiana H. Clay, Feb. 22, 1834.
Surety, Sam Clark.
Ferriss, Wm. D. to Mary Ward, Jan. 8, 1833. Surety,
E. W. Staton.
Fields, Riley to Susan Wood, Jan. 26, 1835. Surety,
Presly Stewart.
Finch, George to Polina Arbuckle, Sept. 12, 1833.
Surety, Thos. Cook.
Finch, Jarrott to Elizabeth Hill, Nov. 17, 1818.
Surety, Thomas Broughton.
Finch, John to Sarah Cook, Aug. 24, 1833. Surety,
Jarrott Finch.
Finley, Isaac to Elinder Fowler, Aug. 26, 1820.
Finney, Andrew to Mary Ann Goley, Sept. 20, 1834.
Surety, R. Blair.
Finney, William to Ruth Penn, July 22, 1823. Surety,
Amos S. Wallis.
Fisher, Edward to Martha Ann Hartwell, Dec. 8, 1823.
Surety, Joseph H. Wortham.
Fisher, John to Elizabeth Killingworth, July 2, 1818.
Fleming, John to Eleanor Fleming, Dec. 27, 1825.
Fleming, John to America Parrish, Jan. 22, 1835. Surety,
James Blanton.
Fleming, Richard L. to Eleanor Rankin, May 16, 1814.
Flemming, Thomas F. to Charlotte Parrish, Sept. 20, 1831.
Fletcher, Granderson to Sarah A. J. Pritchett, Oct. 12,
1837. Surety, William C. Duffy.
Fletcher, James F. to Jane M. Sims, Oct. 26, 1824.
Surety, M. H. Fletcher.
Fletcher, John to Mary D. Gleaves, March 28, 1834.
Surety, Richard Ledbetter.
Fletcher, John to Elizabeth Yandell, Sept. 17, 1829.
Surety, Fredk E. Becton, Jr.
Fletcher, John D. to Catherine Featheton, Dec. 19, 1823.
Surety, Montfort H. Fletcher.
Fletcher, John W. to Tabitha Jinkins, Aug. 20, 1822.

24

Fletcher, Montford H. to Susan C. Smith, Dec. 18, 1824.
Surety, F. E. Becton.
Fletcher, William C. to Nancy G. MacGowen, Jan. 22,
1835. Surety, Stephen D. Watkins.
Flowers, Josiah to Cinthia Lannom, Oct. 20, 1832.
Flowers, Larry to Mazana Green, March 27, 1833.
Surety, William Flowers.
Fly, William D. to Augusta Edwards, Feb. 26, 1835.
Surety, John Heriford.
Forbs, William to Judith McDowell, Feb. 22, 1836.
Surety, James Cooke.
Ford, Edward to Sarah Whittle, Oct. 16, 1826. Surety,
Robert Barton.
Ford, John to Love Northcutt, Oct. 10, 1821.
Ford, Simeon to Margaret Sanders, Jan. 10, 1824.
Ford, Solomon to Ann Moody, June 22, 1830. Surety,
James Gilliam.
Forrest, Elisha to Sally Vincent, Jan. 2, 1821.
Fortenberry, James to Cinthia Prawley, Sept. 5, 1821.
Foster, George to Phoebe Todd, Oct. 30, 1834. Surety,
Wm. Johnson.
Foster, Guinn to Sarah Reeves, Dec. 21, 1830. Surety,
Michael Comer.
Foster, James J. to Mildred Johnson, Oct. 25, 1823.
Surety, John D. Fletcher.
Foster, John to Mary Wright, Jan. 2, 1836. Surety,
Henry Childress.
Foster, John to Elizabeth Allen, Feb. 27, 1836.
Surety, Reuben Allen.
Foster, John to Patsy Fuller, Dec. 31, 1823.
Foster, William to Rebecca W. Rains, Jan. 3, 1825.
Foster, William to Sally Staggs, July 4, 1822.
Foutch, Thomas to Caroline Reed, July 18, 1835. Surety,
Kellar Mathis.
Fowler, Rezin to Hester Craft, Nov. 17, 1829. Surety,
Nathan Findly.
Fowler, Thomas C. A. to Frances Norris, Nov. 27, 1823.
Surety, William Loftin.
Fox, John to Margaret Carter, June 20, 1827. Surety,
Bartlett Anderson.
Fox, Joseph to Tabitha Pointed, Feb. 11, 1835. Surety,
Henry Pruett.
Fox, Matthias to Jemimah Broyles, Oct. 9, 1827. Surety,
Green Holland.
Frederick, Hezekiah to Ezelly Hobson, May 17, 1809.
Surety, John Spence.
Freeman, Asberry to Elizabeth Candike, Jan. 23, 1822.
Freeman, Cader to Patsey Parker, Jan. 24, 1821.
Freeman, Daniel to Margaret Hayley, July 28, 1836.
Surety, John W. Yardley.
Freeman, Green to Priscilla Bowman, Jan. 1, 1817.
Freeman, John to Elizabeth Gable, Aug. 23, 1819.
Surety, John Stroud.
Freeman, Mathew to Anne King, July 18, 1831.

Freeman, Squire to Clarissa Chism, July 21, 1824.
Surety, William Freeman.
Frensley, James M. R. to Jane Nance, Feb. 16, 1835.
Surety, Charles A. Frensley.
Frensley, Matthew P. to Mary Baldridge, Jan. 30, 1836.
Surety, Allen Nance.
Frizelle, Isaac to Susan Arnold, Jan. 5, 1816.
Frizzelle, Brice to Jane Alexander, Sept. 10, 1833.
Surety, Allen Frizzell.
Frizzell, Hugh to Frances Harris, Dec. 12, 1835.
Surety, John Fletcher.
Frizzell, William J. to Mary Deer, Feb. 27, 1836.
Surety, Reuben Curry.
Fryor, Isaac to Nancy Goodner, July 3, 1818. Surety,
Garrett Fryor.
Fudge, John B. to Pamelia Barnes, April 5, 1824.
Surety, Washington Barrington.
Fulks, John D. to Mary Rawlings, Sept. 8, 1824. Surety,
Joel Fulks.
Fuller, Benjamine to Hannah Gum, Dec. 9, 1815. Surety,
Marable Travis.
Fuller, James to Elizabeth Dement, Oct. 30, 1833.
Surety, Isaac Parker.
Fuquay, William B. to Judith Ford, Aug. 24, 1831.
Furgason, Joel J. to Ruth Stovall, March 1, 1824.
Surety, Obadiah Furgason.
Gage, Jeremiah to Elizabeth Welsh, Feb. 26, 1805.
Surety, Adam Cronister.
Gale, William H. to Sarah A. Harris, Dec. 11, 1823.
Gambill, Hiram H. to Elizabeth Julia Andrews, May 6,
1821.
Gambill, John to Hannah Raney, April 2, 1834. Surety,
Martin Clark.
Gannaway, Burwell to Sally H. Batey, March 12, 1817.
Surety, Henry D. Jamison.
Gannon, Geo. to Susan Stacey, Aug. 7, 1834. Surety,
James Ready.
Garner, Jesse to Elizabeth Caulk, Jan. 31, 1826.
Surety, William Garner.
Garner, John to Paggy Guess, Feb. 7, 1816.
Garner, John N. to Rebecca H. Walpoole, Jan. 3, 1833.
Surety, Benjamine C. James.
Garner, Lewis to Louisa A. Ridley, April 1, 1835.
Surety, S. B. Christy.
Garner, Thomas to Sarah Warren, Nov. 12, 1829. Surety,
John Warren.
Garner, William to Obedience Haley, Feb. 12, 1823.
Garrett, Jacob to Mary Morris, Jan. 16, 1827. Surety,
John J. Choate.
Garrison, James to Mourning Basham, Aug. 6, 1823.
Surety, David S. Philips.
Garrison, Samuel to Nancy Fortenberry, Aug. 17, 1821.
Gassaway, William to Nancy Pope, July 29, 1812.
Gasaway, Samuel to Louisa Mitchell, Oct. 27, 1824.
Surety, Joel D. Mitchell.

Gasaway, Thomas to Nancy Boatright, June 11, 1810.
Surety, John A. Shelby.
Geaslin, Ezekil to Anne Rankin, May 29, 1827. Surety,
Henry Johnson.
Geno, Lewis to Mary Winters, June 29, 1827. Surety,
Daniel Sailors.
Gentry, Samuel L. to Mary Robinson, March 28, 1825.
Surety, Wm. L. Featherson.
Gentry, Thomas G. to Elizabeth Campbell, Jan. 5, 1819.
Surety, Russell Dance.
Gentry, William W. to Virginia B. Campbell, Feb. 27,
1823. Surety, William Ellison.
George, Leonard to Martha Ivy, June 2, 1917. Sureties,
Isaac Erwin and Daniel P. Perkins.
George, William F. to Elizabeth Clifton, May 1, 1834.
Surety, Henry Clifton.
Gibbons, James to Hannah Gasaway, Sept. 20, 1815.
Surety, Benjamine Ward.
Gibbons, John to Sarah Mitchell, Nov. 21, 1836. Surety,
Kellar Matthews.
Gibbons, Stephen to Nancy Rutherford, Nov. 1, 1815.
Surety, Thomas Rutherford.
Gibonay, John W. to Sarah Ann Wilman, March 9, 1832.
Gibson, Hezekiah to Mary Ridgeway, Oct. 25, 1817.
Surety, Wm. Ridgeway.
Gibson, James to Nancy Keele, July 23, 1824. Surety,
Washington Gibson.
Gibson, Moses to Nancy A. McKee, Dec. 5, 1837. Surety,
Kendrick Barlow.
Gilbert, James to Elizabeth Stephens, April 6, 1836.
Surety, George Stephens.
Gilchrist, Daniel to Nancy Phillips, Dec. 29, 1819.
Giles, Wilson B. to Elizabeth A. Banton, Nov. 15, 1836.
Surety, J. M. Barry.
Gillespie, John to Polly Goforth, June 27, 1817.
Surety, Berryman Norman.
Gilley, Caleb to Ibby Bynum, Feb. 27, 1827. Surety,
Benjamine Whitfield.
Gilley, Jesse H. to Sarah Carnahan, Nov. 6, 1835.
Surety, Thomas Y. Whitfield.
Gilley, Peterson to Elizabeth Carhahan, March 13, 1833.
Surety, Thomas Y. Whitfield.
Gilley, Simeon to Sarah Bynum, May 6, 1835. Surety,
Jesse H. Gilley.
Gilliam, James to Margaret C. Lowrence, Sept. 29, 1831.
Gilliam, John to Malissa Bone, Oct. 13, 1831.
Gilliam, Thomas to Elizabeth Travis, May 27, 1830.
Surety, John Travis.
Gilliam, William to Martha Molloy, May 8, 1823. Surety,
Edward Fisher.
Gilliland, Joseph to Nelly Hill, May 2, 1812.
Gilliland, Joseph to Susan Taylor, May 28, 1816.
Gillmore, John to Nancy Arnold, Jan. 22, 1825.
Gilmore, Arthur M. to Elizabeth Sloss, Feb. 4, 1823.

Gingery, Jacob to Elizabeth Fisher, Sept. 28, 1826.
Surety, Henry C. Bradford.
Glaze, William to Mary Stone, Jan. 18, 1825.
Glouchland, Joseph W. to Elizabeth Erwin, April 9,
1811.
Godsey, Lacy to Julia Angel, Dec. 17, 1823.
Godwin, Samuel to Bedy Sanders, Feb. 7, 1824.
Godwin, Samuel to Jasina Jackson, May 30, 1836.
Surety, Micha Robinson.
Godwin, William P. to Mary M. Burton, June 20, 1836.
Surety, Richard Ledbetter.
Goforth, John M. to Jane Johnson, Oct. 14, 1817.
Surety, Andrew Johnson.
Gooch, Allen T. to Elizabeth V. Morton, Aug. 31, 1826.
Gooch, John C. to Eliza A. Sanders, Dec. 5, 1831.
Gooch, Thomas T. to Nancy White, July 27, 1827.
Surety, William T. Bryant.
Good, Hugh to Betsy Brandon, Aug. 2, 1816.
Goode, Edward to Nancy Dosheta, Nov. 17, 1805. Surety,
Robt. Hancock.
Gooden, Cornelius to Margaret Long, Feb. 22, 1825.
Gooding, Nicholas to Margaret Cooper, Sept. 1, 1830.
Surety, Isaac Cooper.
Goodloe, Aquilla to Joannah Hall, Jan. 12, 1836.
Surety, R. Peek.
Goodloe, George to Rachel Espey, March 22, 1810.
Surety, Jesse Brasher.
Goodloe, Henry, Jr. to Miriam H. Barton, Dec. 23, 1834.
Surety, John King.
Goodloe, John, Jr. to Catherine Totty, Dec. 27, 1828.
Goodman, Edmund to Elizabeth Neal, Nov. 1, 1827.
Surety, William Vaughter.
Goodman, William to Mary F. Hill, Nov. 30, 1836.
Surety, Edmund Goodman.
Goodman, William B. to Sarah W. Carter, March 22, 1824.
Goodrich, John to Rebecca McKinney, May 20, 1833.
Surety, Jas. B. Buchanan.
Goodrich, Washington to Mary James, May 17, 1833.
Surety, Henry M. Jones.
Goodwin, James to Sarah Donald, Nov. 19, 1828.
Goodwin, James to Sally Bland, Dec. 21, 1809. Surety,
Wm. Davidson.
Gordon, Issac to Polly Landers, March 30, 1821.
Gordon, John to Margaret White, Aug. 20, 1832.
Gott, Joseph to Caroline McKee, Sept. 11, 1833. Surety,
Harmon Elrod.
Gowan, A. P. to Elizabeth S. Lowe, Jan. 14, 1829.
Sureties, Levi Reeves and Richard Allman.
Graham, Daniel to Maria McIver, May 8, 1823. Surety,
John D. Martin.
Gray, Henry L. to Mary Henrietta Dyer, April 4, 1820.
Surety, Harmon Elrod.
Green, John to Delila Ford, June 4, 1815.

Gregory, Alexander to Barbara Mooney, May 26, 1810.
Surety, Sterling Stokes.
Gregory, Edwin to Ann E. Hoover, April 7, 1834.
Gregory, John D. to Melvina Jacobs, June 28, 1837.
Surety, Thomas Lee.
Gregory, Jonathan to Alizira Featherston, Oct. 3, 1833.
Surety, William Keith.
Gregory, Joseph L. to Francis B. Nixon, April 14, 1823.
Surety, Wright Gregory.
Gregory, Madison to Julia E. Mason, March 2, 1836.
Surety, James R. Cannon.
Gregory, Robert to Nancy Broils, Nov. 14, 1816.
Gregory, Thomas to Francis E. Rowton, March 8, 1830.
Surety, Jeremiah Brown.
Grubb, Alfred B. to Sally Castleman, Jan. 14, 1830.
Surety, William Chrisp.
Grubbs, Thomas W. to Lena Underwood, April 27, 1825.
Gum, Robert E. to Mary Ann Fulks, April 19, 1821.
Gum, William to Melindah Nugent, March 22, 1819.
Guthrey, Henry to Henley Nevins, Feb. 8, 1832.
Guthrey, Wm. H. to Mary Jones, June 25, 1835.
Surety, James Dement.
Guthrey, William H. to Francis Read, Nov. 10, 1831.
Surety, Travis C. Guthrey.
Hail, William H. to Didema Hankins, Dec. 15, 1829.
Surety, John Pogue.
Haile, Leeman to Marillis Edwards, Jan. 11, 1832.
Hailey, Elijah W. to Elizabeth A. Coleman, March 28,
1837. Surety, Armstead Neel.
Hainey, Jesse to Betsy T. Blakemore, Aug. 24, 1816.
Hale, Ellis to Mary Miller, Dec. 15, 1827. Surety,
Isaac Miller.
Hale, Stephen to Priscilla Goodloe, Oct. 19, 1819.
Hale, Thomas to Celia Dabney, Feb. 3, 1810. Surety,
Oswell Neilson.
Haley, Henry to Susan Haley, March 5, 1825.
Haley, Henry to Ann Mullins, Aug. 25, 1831.
Haley, John C. to Catherine Mullins, Aug. 19, 1823.
Surety, Spencer Haley.
Haley, Thomas to Sarah Estes, Jan. 27, 1828. Surety,
John Howell.
Hall, Andrew to Elizabeth Countryman, Dec. 26, 1809.
Surety, Hugh Kirk.
Hall, Irvin to Susannah Stewart, Nov. 16, 1827.
Surety, Samuel T. Stewart.
Hall, James to Nancy Hamilton, April 15, 1806. Surety,
Jeptha Stanley.
Hall, John to Charlotte Gambrill, Oct. 27, 1818.
Surety, Joseph Kindrick.
Hall, John to Susannah Stewart, Nov. 16, 1824.
Hall, John to Temperance Perry, Oct. 30, 1815. Surety,
John Walden.
Hall, John A. to Louisa Wallace, July 16, 1836.
Surety, John H. Benson.

Hall, John C. to Eliza Marshall, Oct. 1, 1810. Surety, John Flemming.
Hall, John W. to Martha Edmonds, May 3, 1836.
Hall, Randolph B. to Charlott Anderson, April 5, 1817.
Hall, Thomas to Sarah Paty, Sept. 12, 1836. Surety, Nathaniel Haynes.
Hall, William to Sarah Curry, March 1, 1814.
Hall, William to Ann Eliza Lyle, April 22, 1837. Surety, Nathaniel Haynes.
Hall, William M. to Jane Maben, Aug. 23, 1808.
Hall, Zacharaih to Sarah Dement, Feb. 17, 1825.
Hallyburton, John E. to Mary Ann Ivie, Dec. 26, 1837. Surety, William B. Buckner.
Ham, James to Polly Broils, Oct. 27, 1818. Surety, Alexander Patterson.
Hamilton, Andrew M. to Mary Bryan, Aug. 28, 1824. Surety, William Aymett.
Hamilton, Eleazer to Emily Perry, Nov. 15, 1823. Surety, Jonathan Huggins.
Hamilton, Francis T. to Jane Travis, Dec. 27, 1832.
Hamilton, George to Jane Stovall, Aug. 12, 1829. Surety, Joseph Youree.
Hamilton, Hance to Charlotte Spence, Dec. 5, 1837. Surety, Richmond S. Fletcher.
Hamilton, James D. to Sarah McFarlin, Aug. 22, 1826.
Hamilton, John to Elizabeth Smith, Jan. 20, 1816.
Hamilton, William to Elizabeth H. Walker, May 2, 1836.
Hammon, Hiram to Jane Harris, Nov. 7, 1814. Surety, Benj. Walker.
Hamon, John to Sally Langston, Feb. 23, 1815.
Hampton, James to Ollie _____, March 15, 1806. Surety, John Davis.
Hampton, John to Nancy McCoy, June 10, 1815. Surety, Thomas Wheeler.
Hampton, Thomas to Sally Davis, Feb. 1, 1816.
Hancock, Benjamine to Caroline Ready, Sept. 25, 1817. Surety, John Darrah.
Hancock, Benj. C. to Fredonia Bennett, Dec. 17, 1833. Surety, O. Arnold.
Hancock, Francis to Catherine Blakemore, March 27, 1821.
Hancock, James to Sarah Fergason, Jan. 3, 1833. Surety, Isham S. Green.
Hancock, Samuel to Mary Barker, Dec. 9, 1837. Surety, Benjamine Hampton.
Hand, Samuel to Eliza Wallace, Sept. 7, 1818. Surety, Gideon Rucker.
Haney, Isaac to Lethey Bruce, April 2, 1836.
Haney, William to Eliza Sagely, Feb. 16, 1818.
Hankins, John to Susan Moore, Feb. 27, 1818.
Hanna, Andrew to Peggy Patton, May 12, 1805. Surety, James Cochran.
Hannis, David P. to Berintha M. Featherston, Dec. 16, 1819.

Harbin, Alfred S. to Henrietta Lowe, Dec. 18, 1827.
Surety, Alfred P. Gowen.
Harbour, Elisha to Nancy Cooper, March 21, 1825.
Harmon, John T. to Nancy Wilson, Oct. 30, 1817.
Harmon, Willie to Tabitha Nance, Nov. 30, 1826.
Surety, Peyton Smith.
Harper, Joel to Kitty Lassiter, Feb. 22, 1816.
Harper, Samuel to Polly Gambill, Dec. 1, 1804. Surety,
Aaron Gambill.
Harpole, John to Mary Anne McMinamy, Sept. 20, 1824.
Surety, James McMinamy.
Harrell, David to Polly Ann Carter, Dec. 8, 1837.
Surety, Legrand H. Carney.
Harrell, Thomas to Margaret Espey, Aug. 26, 1835.
Surety, Henry Harrell.
Harris, Alsea to Jane Modrell, April 24, 1837. Surety,
John D. Fletcher.
Harris, Benjamine to Lucinda W. Harris, July 14, 1824.
Surety, Robert D. Harris.
Harris, Claiborne to Mary Summers, Aug. 18, 1835.
Harris, David to Nancy D. Stovall, Feb. 17, 1834.
Surety, John M. Barry.
Harris, Evan to Margaret Henry, June 14, 1833.
Surety, Wm. Wells.
Harris, George E. to Julia Marshall, Aug. 21, 1819.
Harris, John P. to Margaret Bowman, June 21, 1832.
Harris, Oliver B. to Jemima Patterson.
Harris, Robert D. to Lucy N. Legrand, July 19, 1827.
Surety, Charles R. Abbott.
Harris, Thomas E. to Sarah E. Thompson, May 23, 1836.
Surety, Joseph Bogle.
Harris, Thomas S. to Polly Sloan, June 1, 1824.
Surety, John Stevenson.
Harris, Virgil H. to Rachel Thomas, July 28, 1835.
Surety, Nathan Harris.
Harris, William to Rhoda Benson, May 3, 1836.
Harris, William to Eliza Mitchell, May 13, 1819.
Harris, William G. to Esther McFarland, Sept. 30, 1815.
Surety, A. B. Morris.
Harrison, Eli to Rebecca Gibson, Feb. 1, 1823.
Harrison, Gideon to Rody Harrison, Sept. 20, 1827.
Surety, Samuel McDowell.
Harrison, James to Mary Sikes, April 15, 1823. Surety,
Bradley Acuff.
Harrison, John to Polly Smith, Dec. 25, 1804. Surety,
George Caperton.
Harrison, Lewis to Peggy Love, July 14, 1825.
Harrison, Washington to Nancy Harrison, Jan. 16, 1836.
Surety, Joseph Tatum.
Harrison, Wm. H. to Mary W. Puckett, Sept. 28, 1827.
Surety, William Smith.
Hart, Hiram to Sarah Hall, Dec. 30, 1823.
Hartman, John to Burchett Neal, Oct. 18, 1823. Surety,
John Neal.

Hatfield, James to Martha Williams, Aug. 31, 1837.
Surety, Charles A. Fransley.
Hawkins, Berryman G. to Nancy J. Fuller, March 30, 1829.
Surety, Moses G. Reaves.
Hawkins, James S. to Susannah Hoover, Jan. 7, 1837.
Surety, William L. Watkins.
Hayes, John to Rebecca Matthews, Feb. 8, 1835. Surety,
Surety, Donaldson Saunders.
Haynes, Everett to Jane Hayes, Feb. 15, 1834. Surety,
A. J. Hoover.
Haynes, Everett to Sarah Nance, Jan. 18, 1831. Surety,
Wm. H. Posey.
Haynes, John M. to Sarah Span, Jan. 18, 1831. Surety,
James Vannata.
Haynes, Thomas K. to Sarah Tutor, Sept. 17, 1833.
Surety, Boling King.
Haynes, William A. to Julia A. Covington, July 30, 1836.
Surety, Peter Campbell.
Hays, James to Margaret McCarrill, May 31, 1810.
Surety, Timothy Trigg.
Hays, William J. to Seluda Nash, Nov. 30, 1833. Surety,
William Spann.
Hazelett, Melzer W. to Nancy DePriest, March 25, 1833.
Surety, C. W. Heist.
Head, John F. to Elizabeth Ann Snell, Dec. 19, 1820.
Head, John R. to Eliza Thompson, Aug. 2, 1837. Surety,
Geo. A. Sublett.
Heath, James to Delaney Pate, Aug. 5, 1826. Surety,
L. Christopher Beesley.
Heath, Levi to Sarah Underwood, Dec. 18, 1825.
Heath, Levy to Sally Brashears, July 31, 1818. Surety,
Benajah Carlton.
Heath, Solomon to Betsey Vault, Nov. 25, 1817.
Helfin, Jesse to Susan Rhodes, June 2, 1819.
Heflin, Jonathan to Delilah Harris, April 11, 1810.
Surety, James Heflin.
Helton, James to Permela Stewart, Oct. 20, 1832.
Helton, John to Nancy Lyons, June 1, 1833. Surety,
John Thompson.
Helton, John to Elizabeth Wilson, Jan. 21, 1820.
Helton, William to Nancy Shipp, Oct. 26, 1836. Surety,
Augustus Iron.
Henderson, Albert G. to Evalina S. Morris, Sept. 12,
1827. Surety, Robert Binford.
Henderson, Greenville to Matilda Keyser, March 23, 1833.
Surety, Richard Ledbetter.
Henderson, John to Sarah McEwen, Sept. 18, 1810. Surety,
James McEwen.
Hendrick, Daniel to Elizabeth Jarratt, April 22, 1823.
Surety, George Morris.
Henley, Turner B. to Rebecca Ledbetter, Oct. 11, 1823.
Surety, John R. Laughlin.
Henry, James B. to Sophia McNeely, May 25, 1821.
Henry, James P. to Sarah L. McEwen, March 24, 1827.
Surety, James Bone.

Henry, John to Jane Gibson, June 1, 1813.
Henson, John to Susan Thurman, July 28, 1824. Surety,
    William Thurman.
Herndon, Reuben to Martha Cross, March 14, 1825.
Herrin, William D. to Sarah Garner, Dec. 3, 1831.
Herring, Charles to Sarah Owens, July 30, 1828.
Harrol, William to Jerusha Jarnagan, Dec. 24, 1827.
    Surety, Jesse Thompson.
Hess, Joseph D. to Sally D. Stovall, Sept. 23, 1816.
Hess, William R. to Sophia W. Dyer, June 4, 1817.
Hewett, John to Any Young, Jan. 4, 1820.
Hibbett, Joseph F. to Martha S. Cannon, April 26, 1833.
    Surety, James R. Cannon.
Hickman, John to Jane Beesley, Aug. 9, 1837. Surety,
    S. N. Tuder.
Hickman, Nathaniel to Judith Wills, Aug. 22, 1817.
    Surety, John Rutledge.
Hickman, Nathaniel to Nancy Vaughan, Sept. 24, 1818.
    Surety, Ollie Blakemore.
Hicks, Isaac M. to Sarah Ann Patillo, Dec. 12, 1837.
    Surety, George W. Marable.
Hicks, John to Sarah Butler, July 23, 1823. Surety,
    Adam Simmons.
Hicks, William D. to Sarah Tucker, Jan. 13, 1835.
    Surety, Bailey W. Farmer.
Higdon, Andrew to Mary Baum, March 18, 1826.
Higdon, Elijah to Sarah Bishop, June 13, 1836. Surety,
    J. D. Baum.
Hight, Stephen to Elizabeth Dubois, May 17, 1821.
Hight, William to Naomi Patterson, Feb. 6, 1837.
    Surety, W. F. Short.
Higinbotham, Andrew to Catherine Tucker, Oct. 8, 1823.
    Surety, William Wren.
Hill, Abram to Edatha Hunter, Dec. 11, 1827. Surety,
    William Patrick.
Hill, Alfred to Elizabeth Fuller, Jan. 26, 1830.
    Surety, William M. Marable.
Hill, Cary G. to Eliza J. Doodman, Sept. 21, 1832.
Hill, Daniel H. to Lacy (Lucy) Smalley, March 20, 1804.
    Surety, Teenan Moore.
Hill, Green to Rachel Wilson, Jan. 4, 1825.
Hill, Israel M. C. to Christian Gray, Oct. 4, 1821.
Hill, James H. to Eve Garner, Oct. 15, 1827. Surety,
    Jesse Garner.
Hill, John to Margaret P. Roulhac, Oct. 23, 1823.
    Surety, Jas. P. Roulhac.
Hill, John W. to Catherine Morgan, Jan. 5, 1827.
    Surety, John D. Stovall.
Hill, Joshua D. to Elizabeth McCutchen, Feb. 4, 1829.
    Surety, Levi Reeves.
Hill, Moses G. to Mildred E. Vaughan, Oct. 5, 1835.
    Surety, E. G. Grinage.
Hill, Thomas to Sally Basye, Jan. 15, 1817. Surety,
    Thomas H. Cannon.

Hill, William to Elizabeth Brown, Aug. 7, 1833.
Surety, Pleasant Cauthron.
Hill, William to Susannah Pitts, Dec. 22, 1836. Surety,
Benjamine Lillard.
Hill, William A. to Elizabeth G. Cooke (Cocke), Dec. 10,
1836. Surety, James M. Blanton.
Hilliard, Isaac H. to Levinia A. Leinan, May 26, 1836.
Surety, William H. Bowman.
Hobson, Nathaniel to Martha James, Oct. 27, 1812.
Hodge, James, Jr. to Rebecca A. Neel, Dec. 13, 1828.
Hodge, Samuel to Sarah Mitchell, March 22, 1823.
Hodges, Thomas to Malinda Curlee, Sept. 14, 1835.
Surety, B. L. McFerrin.
Hogan, Jesse to Phoebe Taylor, Dec. 18, 1818.
Hogwood, Dennison to Priscilla Burkly, Dec. 26, 1836.
Surety, Levi Bowling.
Hogwood, Ransom to Elizabeth Nance, July 8, 1824.
Surety, George Brown.
Holden, Charles to Matilda Crocker, April 21, 1830.
Surety, John Sneed.
Holden, Charles to Sarah Webb, April 5, 1833. Surety,
Madison H. Alexander.
Holden, Dennis to Sarah Nash, Feb. 14, 1820.
Holden, Jordan to Tabitha Patterson, Aug. 15, 1836.
Surety, James Wadley.
Holden, Joseph to Fanny Douglas, April 14, 1814.
Surety, George Holden.
Holden, Rolly to Martha H. Leathers, Feb. 27, 1837.
Surety, Adam Comer.
Holley, Crawford to Sally Valentine, Dec. 23, 1822.
Surety, Thomas Mitchell.
Hollis, David to Delina Walker, Nov. 26, 1833. Surety,
Simeon Hollis.
Hollis, James to Martha Saffle, April 18, 1829.
Surety, David Hollis.
Hollis, John to Esther Bell, Sept. 4, 1823. Surety,
James Bell.
Hollis, John to Sarah Smith, April 1, 1816.
Hollis, Joseph to Elizabeth Dolly, Oct. 15, 1827.
Surety, James Manahan.
Hollis, Simeon to Mary Jones, Aug. 23, 1834. Surety,
James B. Hollis.
Holloway, John B. to Mildred V. Tucker, June 29, 1833.
Surety, Geo. A. Sublett.
Hollowell, Edwin C. to Ann M. Crockett, Oct. 18, 1836.
Surety, William K. Ransom.
Hollowell, Joseph to Louiza Beesley, Feb. 15, 1832.
Hollowell, William B. to Sarah Wade, Feb. 8, 1837.
Surety, William F. Leiper.
Holmes, James to Mary Ready, May 16, 1829. Surety,
Robert Locke.
Holt, James to Manerva Mitchell, Oct. 11, 1830.
Holt, Harold to Lucinda Thompson, May 6, 1829. Surety,
Baswell C. Glascock.

RUTHERFORD COUNTY MARRIAGES

Holt, Richard to Sarah Byford, June 28, 1823.
Holton, William B. to Sally P. Tilman, June 11, 1823.
Hood, Chesley to Eleanor Brady, April 27, 1830. Surety,
  Drury Dance.
Hood, Chesley to Martha G. Collier, Jan. 15, 1833.
  Surety, George Cain.
Hooker, James to Margaret Collins, Dec. 5, 1825.
Hooker, Joshua to Fanny Wynne, Oct. 14, 1816.
Hooper, George to Jane Higgenbotham, Nov. 8, 1834.
  Surety, Abraham Cook.
Hoosby, John H. to Jane Trimble, Feb. 6, 1821.
Hoover, Abraham to Mary McKee, Oct. 31, 1837. Surety,
  Robert D. Rankin.
Hoover, Daniel to Eliza Hamm, Jan. 28, 1837. Surety,
  Dollison Parker.
Hoover, Ephraim to Margaret Smith, Aug. 25, 1827.
  Surety, John L. Hoover.
Hoover, Frederick to Mary Ann Yardly, Jan. 28, 1837.
  Surety, John Johnson.
Hope, David B. to Elizabeth Puckett, Sept. 3, 1832.
Hope, William P. to Tabitha Fletcher, Sept. 22, 1834.
  Surety, Isham Cox.
Hopkins, Elisha to Polly Franklin, April 3, 1830.
  Surety, Isham Franklin.
Hopkins, Hampton to Frances Saterwhite, July 29, 1824.
  Surety, Joseph R. Taylor.
Hopkins, Willie to Feraby Simpson, Dec. 21, 1829.
  Surety, Peter Simpson.
Hord, Thomas to Mary E. McCullough, April 3, 1834.
  Surety, Drury Dance.
Horton, Elijah to Rachel Wadley, Aug. 3, 1833.
  Surety, Michael Comer.
Horton, Jefferson to Elizabeth Norvell, Dec. 19, 1829.
  Surety, John D. Fletcher.
Hoskins, John to Nancy North, Jan. 31, 1825.
House, Claiborne to Susan Hutton, March 4, 1823.
House, Hezekiah to Julia A. Blackman, Nov. 13, 1828.
Howell, Benjamine W. to Mary Pope, May 2, 1829.
  Surety, John Denny.
Howell, David to Lucinda Fuller, May 23, 1827. Surety,
  Willie Jernigan.
Howell, James D. to Martha Pope, July 27, 1833. Surety,
  Benjamine Warren.
Howell, John to Sarah Vardell, Sept. 28, 1827. Surety,
  Richard Blair.
Howland, Lewis to Elizabeth Jacobs, March 2, 1827.
  Surety, Allen Gowen.
Howse, Robert C. to Nancy Beaty, Oct. 16, 1828.
Hubbard, John to Elizabeth Briant, April 12, 1830.
  Surety, William Gilliam.
Hubbard, William to Mark Peek, March 31, 1825.
Hudson, Enoch M. to Mary C. Clark, Feb. 20, 1832.
Hudson, John to Nancy Pitts, Sept. 25, 1824. Surety,
  John Harrel.

Hudson, Lodewick to Mary C. Mayfield, Dec. 15, 1835.
Surety, Robert M. Loftin.
Hughs, David H. to Elizabeth Smith, July 15, 1820.
Hughs, Richardson to Nancy Flemming, Dec. 6, 1825.
Huist, Christian to Rebecca Owens, Oct. 22, 1829.
Surety, Fredk. B. Becton.
Hunt, Francis A. to Mary Ann Creech, Feb. 26, 1834.
Surety, John Pace.
Hunt, Henry to July Ann Wood, Nov. 23, 1835. Surety,
James Blankenship.
Hunt, Hickman to Nancy Sutton, Sept. 12, 1837. Surety,
Felix G. Kelly.
Hunt, Jeremiah to Sarah Taylor, Jan. 9, 1829. Surety,
John Taylor.
Hunt, Samuel to Nancy Rowton, March 27, 1821.
Hunt, William to Nancy Davis, Dec. 8, 1827. Surety,
Shadrack Coon.
Hunter, Joab to Margaret Sherwood, Dec. 20, 1825.
Hutchison, David C. to Martha A. McGowen, Oct. 12, 1830.
Hutchison, William to Jane Lorance, March 28, 1823.
Surety, Aaron Yearwood.
Hutton, John W. to Frances F. Moore, July 19, 1833.
Surety, Thos. S. Watkins.
Hynds, Benjamine D. to Sarah E. Hardeman, Sept. 25,
1837. Surety, James M. Blanton.
Ingles, George W. to Mary M. W. Thompson, Sept. 29,
1835. Surety, William D. Page.
Irby, Willis to Elizabeth S. Reed, Sept. 6, 1824.
Surety, William Edding.
Iron, Augustus to Mary Helton, May 25, 1836. Surety,
William J. Walkup.
Ivey, Benjamine to Adeline Mabery, Jan. 28, 1833.
Surety, Burrel Ivey.
Ivey, Benjamine W. to Elizabeth E. McClroy, May 1,
1837. Surety, John Forbs.
Ivery, Charles to Judith Wood, Sept. 11, 1834. Surety,
Isaac Howse.
Ivins, John to Phebe Spencer, June 11, 1836. Surety,
James Williams.
Jackson, Aaron to Hannah Keel, Oct. 18, 1835. Surety,
James Gibson.
Jackson, Hosea to Mary Kimbrough, Sept. 30, 1833.
Surety, Samuel Jackson.
Jackson, Matthew to Percilla A. Finney, Aug. 16, 1836.
Surety, James A. Charlton.
Jackson, Nathan to Indiana Windrow, Nov. 15, 1827.
Surety, Richard Jackson.
Jackson, Willis to Nancy Carlton, Sept. 21, 1835.
Surety, John Crick.
Jacobs, Alfred to Polly Conner, Jan. 12, 1819.
Jacobs, Alfred to Martha Brookshire, Sept. 4, 1827.
Surety, William Glaze.
Jacobs, John to Mary Summers, Oct. 12, 1824. Surety,
Jerry Jacobs.

Jacobs, Matthias to Ellen Cola, Dec. 26, 1834. Surety, Richard D. Gaither.
Jacobs, Pleasant to Nancy Rawlins, Aug. 19, 1829. Surety, Richard Gaither.
James, Benjamine C. to Jane E. Bone, May 3, 1836. Surety, Thomas E. Goodrich.
James, John P. to Eddy Powell, June 9, 1827. Surety, Moses G. Reaves.
James, Robert L. to Johannah Robertson, Feb. 13, 1817. Surety, Nathaniel Hobson.
James, Thomas to Dorothy Sanders, June 2, 1833. Surety, Wm. Ledbetter.
James, William N. to Clementine L. Nance, Oct. 23, 1824. Surety, Josiah S. Kelly.
Jameson, Samuel to Elizabeth Brothers, Dec. 9, 1837. Surety, John Brothers.
Jamison, Allen to Caroline Fulks, April 22, 1835. Surety, Thomas Brandon.
Jamison, Henry D. to Elizabeth Batey, Jan. 20, 1819. Surety, Parker Alexander.
Jamison, Hugh B. to Susan White, Aug. 25, 1817.
Jarratt, Benjamine to Anne Murphey, Feb. 11, 1825.
Jarratt, David M. to Rebecca Brasher, May 4, 1821.
Jarratt, Higdon R. to Eliza R. Rucker, June 24, 1825.
Jarratt, John J. to Martha Manor, Nov. 15, 1823. Surety, William E. North.
Jarrett, Jonichan to Matilda Reed, Feb. 9, 1829. Surety, James Yearwood.
Jarrett, Thompson to Elmira L. Dodd, June 5, 1822.
Jarratt, Wade to Judith M. Jarrett, June 19, 1821.
Jenkins, Hiram to Nancy J. C. Puckett, Sept. 7, 1837. Surety, H. B. Snell.
Jennings, Gordon to Elizabeth Jones, Aug. 2, 1813. Surety, James Pearce.
Jetton, Isaac to Henrietta Elam, Nov. 12, 1817. Surety, Edward Elam.
Jetton, John to Rachel Winsett, Oct. 26, 1827. Surety, Jeremiah W. Fletcher.
Jetton, John L. to Elizabeth Jetton, March 18, 1805. Surety, Robert Marley.
Jetton, John L. to Mariah Trott, March 3, 1829. Surety, Henry Trott.
Jetton, John W. to Miss C. H. Morton, July 3, 1837. Surety, James R. Burrus.
Jetton, Lewis to Rebecca Goodloe, Jan. 31, 1829. Surety, J. W. McElroy.
Jetton, Robert to _____ Wilson, Jan. 9, 1805. Surety, John Thompson.
Jetton, Rufus B. to Mary M. Fletcher, Nov. 5, 1829. Surety, James Elder.
Jinkins, William to Peggy Rodgers, Feb. 17, 1817.
Job, Elihu C. to Mary Smith, Jan. 12, 1833. Surety, Davis Caldwell.
Jobe, Berry P. to Minerva M. Newman, Dec. 30, 1836. Surety, Thomas Elliott.

RUTHERFORD COUNTY MARRIAGES

Johns, Frederick to Margaret Thompson, Oct. 4, 1825.
Johns, Isaac to Hannah Long, Nov. 19, 1827. Surety,
Thomas Powell.
Johns, Joseph G. to Zane Lassiter, Dec. 15, 1835.
Surety, Randolph V. Johns.
Johns, Paul V. to Sophonia E. Nelson, Oct. 26, 1836.
Surety, William B. Robertson.
Johns, Randolph V. to Lucinda Wade, Jan. 8, 1832.
Surety, Jas. W. Hamilton.
Johns, Stephen B. to Martha Harrison, Dec. 21, 1836.
Surety, James C. Christy.
Johns, Thomas to Unity C. Smith, Oct. 9, 1832.
Johnson, Archibald to Harriet B. Smith, Nov. 30, 1819.
Johnson, James H. to Arena Alley, Aug. 4, 1831.
Johnson, James M. to Nancy Adcock, Feb. 10, 1835.
Surety, Columbus M. Johnson.
Johnson, John to Sarah Beesley, Dec. 2, 1828.
Johnson, John to Lucretia Burgess, May 12, 1835.
Surety, A. Mitchell.
Johnson, John to Mariah Rollin, Dec. 22, 1829. Surety,
Donelson Parker.
Johnson, Joshua to Clementine Wright, Oct. 29, 1835.
Surety, Henry H. Treadway.
Johnson, Larkin to Nancy Arnold, Aug. 10, 1804. Surety,
Levi Arnold.
Johnson, Larkin to Jane McMurry, Dec. 15, 1831.
Johnson, Oliver C. to Melison E. Clay, Oct. 2, 1827.
Surety, Rensford McGregor.
Johnson, Oliver C. to Elizabeth W. Clay, Dec. 18, 1829.
Johnson, Camuel C. to Elizabeth McClure, Jan. 2, 1817.
Surety, Joseph Gammell.
Johnson, Thomas to Mary N. Smith, Jan. 24, 1820.
Johnson, William to Patsey Bailey, June 1, 1815.
Johnson, William to Matilda Ballard, Aug. 17, 1837.
Surety, John Johnson.
Johnston, Benjamine to Caroline M. Smith, Feb. 3, 1820.
Johnston, Isaac to Elizabeth Elliott, Aug. 9, 1823.
Surety, Simon Elliott.
Johnston, John to Elizabeth Gray, Sept. 3, 1823.
Surety, Edward Johnston.
Johnston, Robert to Martha Whitmore, Sept. 5, 1836.
Surety, Henry T. Killen.
Johnston, Thomas to Ellen McFarland, Sept. 23, 1810.
Surety, John McKain.
Johnston, William to Catherine Finney, Jan. 2, 1822.
Johnston, Zachariah to Elizabeth Nevins, Feb. 12, 1823.
Surety, Peyton Rowton.
Jones, Allen to Elizabeth Sutherland, April 21, 1821.
Jones, Amzi to Ann Bradford, Dec. 14, 1837. Surety,
Levi White.
Jones, Anderson to Anna Thompson, Feb. 26, 1834.
Surety, John R. Laughlin.
Jones, Arnett to Esther Nichols, Dec. 10, 1827. Surety,
Eli Nichols.

Jones, Daniel to Elizabeth Massey, Dec. 21, 1824.
Surety, David Jones.
Jones, David, Jr. to Lucy Duffer, Aug. 15, 1825.
Jones, Elijah to Riney Pace, June 18, 1827. Surety,
David Jones.
Jones, Enoch to Eunice McLin, March 23, 1825.
Jones, Giles to Zilphia Phelps, Mar. 20, 1835.
Surety, Benjamine Bugg.
Jones, H. H. to Eliza Marable, July 12, 1834. Surety,
Wm. Nelson.
Jones, John to Elizabeth Molloy, Oct. 16, 1821.
Jones, John to Margaret Evans, May 10, 1834. Surety,
James Killough.
Jones, John to Rachel Barber, Feb. 11, 1835. Surety,
A. East.
Jones, John B. to Elizabeth Clayton, Nov. 3, 1837.
Surety, Edward Featherstone.
Jones, Joseph B. to Martha Ann Heath, Jan. 13, 1835.
Surety, Wilson H. Kerr.
Jones, Littleberry to Phillips Counts, March 11, 1818.
Surety, Felix Jones.
Jones, Matthew to Elizabeth Lewis, Aug. 24, 1835.
Surety, Ephraim Nesbett.
Jones, Nathan to Elizabeth Hall, Dec. 18, 1829. Surety,
Alexander Rankin.
Jones, Peter B. to Mary R. Parrish, Jan. 2, 1836.
Surety, James Rankin.
Jones, Pinkey to Elizabeth Aldridge, Dec. 25, 1833.
Jones, Samuel to Julia Goodloe, Jan. 9, 1821.
Jones, Spotwood to Sally Thurman, Dec. 16, 1822.
Surety, Berry Thurman.
Jones, Spottwood to Elizabeth Davis, Jan. 16, 1827.
Surety, Wm. L. Davis.
Jones, Thomas to Sarah Jones, Dec. 24, 1827. Surety,
Moses G. Reeves.
Jones, William to Patsey Thornton, March 24, 1821.
Jones, William L. to Mary Phelps, April 7, 1834.
Jones, Willie to Patsey McKafee, April 10, 1809.
Surety, Geo. R. Nash.
Jordan, Alexander to Jane Wilson, June 4, 1829. Surety,
David Jordan.
Jordan, David to Elizabeth Jones, April 18, 1827.
Surety, Adam Cluch.
Jordan, Mark to Barbara McGonagil, Feb. 12, 1823.
Joslin, Lewis to Delia M. Crawford, Aug. 30, 1817.
Julian, Charles to Peggy Seymour, Jan. 12, 1822.
Keeble, Edwin A. to Mary W. Maney, Nov. 30, 1836.
Surety, W. S. Puckett.
Keeble, Humphrey W. to Anne Hill, July 25, 1825.
Keeble, Robert R. to Martha M. Marable, June 9, 1828.
Keeble, Walter to Jane C. Smith, Sept. 28, 1829.
Surety, Robert L. Weakley.
Keith, Lee to Martha Jane Wood, Dec. 11, 1830.
Keith, Washington to Rebecca Belt, Aug. 11, 1830.

Keesee, Charles to Sarah McGrew, Oct. 25, 1825.
Kelly, Albert to Pamela Miller, Nov. 5, 1833. Surety,
   Isaac L. Miller.
Kelley, Samuel to Elizabeth Thompson, Dec. 17, 1822.
Kelley, Stephen to Susan Clark, Sept. 11, 1837. Surety,
   George A. Sublett.
Kelton, George to Sarah Clarke, Aug. 23, 1827. Surety,
   Jesse Gilliam.
Kelton, John to Lucinda Page, Feb. 28, 1827. Surety,
   Thomas Brothers.
Kelton, Samuel to Elizabeth Manly, Oct. 1, 1817.
   Surety, James Wilson.
Kelton, William to Lucinda White, Aug. 17, 1820.
Kendal, Ephraim to Elizabeth Painter, Feb. 22, 1837.
   Surety, Robert Stephenson.
Kennedy, John to Frances Barbery, April 19, 1817.
   Surety, James Patton.
Kennedy, Edmond to Susannah Davis, Dec. 11, 1815.
   Surety, Charles Davis.
Kennedy, Sam'l to Eliza Barber, June 8, 1836. Surety,
   Robert Jarrett.
Kerr, G. W. to Sarah Barnes, Dec. 27, 1837. Surety,
   Philip Thompson.
Kerr, Wilson to Rachel Wilson, May 29, 1809. Surety,
   William Hall.
Kerr, Wilson Hugh to Mary Ann Edwards, July 5, 1836.
   Surety, John P. Smith.
Keys, Samuel to Frankie Getly (Gentry), April 12, 1816.
Killingsworth, William B. G. to Rebecca Jones, Sept. 3,
   1821.
Killough, Isaac to Mary D. McKeen, Feb. 21, 1827.
   Surety, James W. Stewart.
Killough, John to Elinder Kirk, Jan. 6, 1816.
Kimbro, John to Martha Walden, Sept. 15, 1815. Surety,
   Robert Smith.
Kimbro, Joseph to Lucinda T. Gooch, Dec. 24, 1821.
Kincannon, Landon A. to Cyrena Robertson, Aug. 31, 1834.
   Surety, Josephus Moore.
Kindrick, William R. to Nancy Finch, Nov. 22, 1824.
   Surety, Thos. Hardeman.
King, Adam C. to Jane C. Bone, Aug. 15, 1837. Surety,
   James W. Hamilton.
King, Daniel to Patsey Nipper, Nov. 18, 1825.
King, Edwin J. to Julia Ledbetter, Jan. 11, 1837.
   Surety, Philip M. Howse.
King, Enes to Mary Stapleton, March 13, 1809. Surety,
   John Stapleton.
King, James H. to Margaret Houston, Dec. 5, 1818.
   Surety, Hugh H. Elliston.
King, James M. to Martha Batey, Nov. 24, 1821.
King, Patterson W. to Rebecca Health, May 23, 1832.
King, Samuel to Mary Fears, Aug. 9, 1827. Surety,
   James Gibson.

King, Wm. P. to Sarah M. Edwards, Jan. 20, 1824.
Surety, Isham G. Searcy.
Kirby, Henry to Mary Hudson, Dec. 21, 1811.
Kirby, Jeremiah W. to Miss Eliza Covington, Nov. 18,
1822.
Kirk, Hugh to Jane Jetton, Feb. 13, 1816.
Kirk, John, Jr. to Mary Davidson, Oct. 28, 1815.
Surety, John Killough.
Kirk, Thomas to Peggy Lipsey, Dec. 13, 1815. Surety,
Joseph Dillard.
Kirkendall, Bean to Sally Bean, Jan. 11, 1823. Surety,
Jacob Kirkendall.
Kirkendall, Jacob to Cynthis Bean, March 5, 1823.
Surety, Wm. Bean.
Kneeland, Ira C. to Margaret R. Cannon, Dec. 14, 1833.
Surety, W. W. Masterson.
Knight, John to Sally Anderson, Feb. 7, 1819.
Knight, Ralph to Isabella Byford, Aug. 5, 1827.
Surety, Daniel Bowen.
Knight, Wm. S. to Elizabeth King, Sept. 29, 1827.
Surety, Ezekiel Knight.
Knox, Benjamine to Margaret McKnight, July 29, 1816.
Knox, John to Sarah Ann Howland, April 20, 1835.
Surety, John Jakes.
Knox, Joseph to Cinthia A. Smith, May 23, 1822.
Knox, Robert to Martha Brawley, May 20, 1809. Surety,
Thomas Brawley.
Lain, Longshore to Patsey Towle, Oct. 7, 1815. Surety,
Manuel Tombs.
Lamb, Barrum to Lucinda Sage, March 9, 1822.
Lamb, Enoch to Polly Ann Pool, July 9, 1821.
Lamb, William to Joicy Lamb, Feb. 7, 1819.
Lamb, William F. to Emeline Phillips, Nov. 28, 1836.
Surety, Travis Windrow.
Lambert, Jarvis to Mourning Mason, Dec. 26, 1835.
Surety, John Cheshier.
Lambert, Thomas to Elizabeth Fulton, Aug. 5, 1822.
Landers, Thomas to Elizabeth Thomas, Dec. 2, 1834.
Surety, William Hobbs.
Lane, George W. to Mary Mason, Dec. 14, 1829. Surety,
Samuel Patterson.
Lane, Micajah to Anne Norsworthy, Nov. 29, 1823.
Surety, Thomas A. Harris.
Lane, Malcijah to Martha Thompson, March 5, 1831.
Lannon, Green to Mary G. Dickson, April 21, 1823.
Surety, John Lannon.
Lannum, William to Mary P. Cloddy, July 11, 1832.
Lassiter, Alexander to Isabella Higgenbotham, Aug. 3,
1829. Surety, William Douglas.
Lassiter, William to Margaret Culp, March 11, 1837.
Surety, Richard Allman.
Lester, Brinkley to Mary Rowen, May 15, 1830. Surety,
John Sparrow.
Laughlin, John R. to Nancy Ladbetter, Oct. 1, 1823.
Surety, Benjamine P. Seawell.

Laughlin, Samuel H. to Mary C. Bass, Oct. 21, 1816.
Laughlin, Young to Christian Thompson, July 25, 1816.
Lawing, Robert to Mary Ann Sublett, Oct. 2, 1816.
Lawrence, Edmund to Rebecca Callahan, Sept. 1, 1829.
    Surety, Bartlett Yeargan.
Lawrence, Jeremiah to Rebecca Fleming, Sept. 9, 1822.
Lawrence, Jesse to Delilah Hawkins, Sept. 13, 1817.
Lawrence, Samuel to Lucinda May, Aug. 10, 1836. Surety,
    Isaac N. Oliphant.
Lawrence, Samuel W. to Evaline M. Brittain, Sept. 26,
    1833. Surety, Alfred Miller.
Lawrence, William H. to Judith W. Edwards, Jan. 4, 1825.
Leatherman, Charles to Eliza Alexander, June 30, 1834.
    Surety, Thomas Johnson.
Leatherman, Jefferson to Malinda Fletcher, Dec. 21,
    1837. Surety, Jas. C. Carter.
Lee, George W. to Mary Wallace, Aug. 30, 1823.
Lee, Washington to Martha Byford, March 15, 1827.
    Surety, Aaron Byford.
Lee, William to Polly Byford, Sept. 8, 1823. Surety,
    Henry Byford.
LeGrand, William T. to Frances O. Gayle. Surety,
    Benjamine F. Currey.
Leiper, John to Elizabeth A. Rucker, July 14, 1835.
    Surety, William P. Leiper.
Lenoir, John P. H. to Nancy Vaughan, 1808. Surety,
    William Neale.
Leonard, Frederick to Evelina Finney, July 19, 1836.
    Surety, James H. Charlton.
Level, John to Patsy Claybrook, Nov. 16, 1805. Surety,
    Benjamine Saunders.
Lewis, Andrew to Margaret Jones, Jan. 5, 1832.
Lewis, Archibald to Prudence Laciter, Jan. 18, 1834.
    Surety, Peter J. Thomas.
Lewis, Gabriel to Tabitha Ivy, March 8, 1822.
Lewis, James to Sally Barfield, Sept. 18, 1815.
Lillard, Alexander to Martha M. Ivey, Sept. 9, 1835.
    Surety, John Wallace.
Lillard, William B. to Mary Smith, Sept. 7, 1831.
Linch, Aden to Susan Linch, Nov. 25, 1834. Surety,
    Gilbert Dyer.
Linch, Erasmus C. to Sarah Swan, Dec. 4, 1833. Surety,
    Moses Swan.
Linch, Hugh to Harriett West, Jan. 21, 1828.
Lindsey, Dudley H. to Charlotte T. Puckett, Oct. 12,
    1829. Surety, James B. Woods.
Lion, Elijah to May Carnahan, Nov. 27, 1833. Surety,
    C. D. Neil.
Lipsey, Morgan to Deborah Parker, Nov. 21, 1823.
    Surety, Hardy Parker.
Lipsey, Morgan to Polly Pearson, June 21, 1824. Surety,
    Joshua Morgan.
Locke, Joseph to Gilla Moore, Nov. 18, 1819.

Lockhart, Elias to Rachel McPeak, Nov. 23, 1827.
Surety, John Drennon.
Loftin, Thomas to Catherine Howell, Nov. 30, 1815.
Surety, James Edwards.
Long, John to Vaney Long, Aug. 22, 1824. Surety, Squire
Long.
Long, Squire to Malinda Byford, May 4, 1829. Surety,
Alexander F. McFerrin.
Long, Solomon to Betsy Byford, Dec. 20, 1820.
Lorance, Ephraim M. to Nancy Bell, Nov. 4, 1818.
Lorance, George W. to Sarah Jones, Dec. 18, 1829.
Surety, Moses G. Reeves.
Lorance, William to Mary Renshaw, Sept. 10, 1829.
Surety, Daniel Bradfield.
Lord, William to Elizabeth Baumgarner, May 21, 1829.
Surety, John Todd.
Love, Allen R. to Nancy A. Clark, Dec. 20, 1837.
Surety, William H. Bowman.
Love, Charles to Minerva Oliphant, Aug. 7, 1837.
Surety, James M. Tompkins.
Lovell, Markham to Nancy Coleman, Oct. 28, 1834. Surety,
Wm. Ross.
Lowell, William to Elizabeth Gambill (Gambrell), June
10, 1825.
Lowe, Gabriel to Lavinia Still, Sept. 8, 1827. Surety,
John Elliott.
Lowe, James to Malinda Summers, May 5, 1833. Surety,
Sam Clark.
Lowe, John S. to Susan R. Thomas, Oct. 14, 1823.
Surety, Joel M. Lloyd.
Lowe, Walter, Jr. to Mary L. White, Feb. 13, 1825.
Lowe, William to Rhoda Plummer, March 4, 1818. Surety,
Joel Howell.
Lowery, William to Mary Brown, Jan. 2, 1827. Surety,
Mills A. Britt.
Lowrance, George W. to Polexany Northcutt, March 6,
1834.
Lowrie, John W. to Elizabeth Drennon, Dec. 11, 1824.
Surety, James Tucker.
Lowry, Albin to Jane Simmons, Sept. 18, 1823. Surety,
Nathaniel Perry.
Lumly, Green to Rachel Roden, Dec. 20, 1815.
Lusk, Burton to Tabitha Summers, Dec. 28, 1833.
Lusk, Samuel to Polly Todd, Nov. 11, 1818.
Lynch, John L. to Elizabeth Maner, Aug. 9, 1827.
Surety, Thomas Newson.
Lyon, Richard to Isabel Jones, Nov. 4, 1823. Surety,
Swinfield Everett.
Lyons, Elijah to Mary Carnahan, Nov. 27, 1833.
Lytle, John to Mary Turner, Oct. 24, 1820.
Lytle, William J. to Mary J. Smith, March 26, 1834.
Surety, Richard Ledbetter.
McAdoo, Brantley H. to Elizabeth Osborne, July 11, 1829.
Surety, Robert S. Donnell.

RUTHERFORD COUNTY MARRIAGES

McBride, Charles to Nancy Toom, April 9, 1816.
McBroom, J. D. to Rutha Moore, Feb. 23, 1834.
McCain, James to Judith Wills, Nov. 6, 1817. Surety,
James Dickey.
McCain, James to Jane Edmonson, May 12, 1805, Surety,
John McCain.
McCaslin, Matthew to Hannah Robinson, Jan. 1, 1822.
Surety, Sol. Beesly.
McClain, John to Emelia Williams, March 28, 1826.
McClaren, William L. to Frances B. Anthony, Aug. 29,
1834. Surety, James C. Christy.
McClary, Garland to Sara Ann Read, Dec. 9, 1835.
Surety, Jas. S. Morris.
McClendon, Green to Cynthia J. Phelps, Jan. 2, 1835.
McCombs, Robert to Jane Hall, Oct. 25, 1820.
McCombs, William to Catherine Overall, Jan. 16, 1835.
Surety, H. W. Fagan.
McCord, Rich'd E. to Catherine W. Hazlett, Feb. 26,
1833. Surety, Noel Sanders.
McCorkle, Jehiel M. to Elizabeth Smith, Jan. 17, 1824.
Surety, John McCorkle.
McCormack, Joseph to Levina Bradshaw, May 11, 1816.
McCormick, Eli to Anny Stevens, Jan. 8, 1816.
McCoy, Hardy to Louise Thornton, Sept. 23, 1822.
McCoy, William to Polly Welch, Dec. 20, 1824. Surety,
Jas. Higgins.
McCrackin, George to Mary Baxter, Nov. 5, 1827.
Surety, William Wallis.
McCrary, Arthur to Iby Hamilton, Nov. 17, 1824. Surety,
David Youree.
McCrary, George M. to Jane L. Porter, Jan. 6, 1827.
Surety, Samuel Porter.
McCrie, Edward to Polly Moody, April 30, 1818.
McCulley, Joseph to Rachel Robertson, May 15, 1824.
Surety, Robert McCulley.
McCulley, William to Kessian Kilian, May 23, 1829.
Surety, Henry McCulley.
McCullouch, David to Mariah Johnson, July 4, 1836.
Surety, Samuel Patton.
McCullough, Robert L. to Mary Smith, Oct. 4, 1830.
Surety, Green B. Lannun.
McCullough, Richard P. to Nancy Posey, Dec. 4, 1824.
Surety, John Arnett.
McCutchen, David C. to Priscilla Hair, Sept. 30, 1824.
Surety, William Vandike.
McCutchen, John F. to Priscilla P. McLean, Nov. 1, 1827.
Surety, George W. Mabry.
McCutchen, Thomas to Crecy Tyler, Oct. 7, 1836.
McDaman, James to Mary Fouch, March 13, 1837. Surety,
William D. Rowton.
McDaniel, George to Ezabella Neely, May 1, 1816.
McDaniel, Staunton, M. to Martha Heard, Dec. 6, 1833.
Surety, Andrew Finney.
McDaniel, Wilson to Jane Finney, Oct. 28, 1824. Surety,
Armstrong Herd.

44

McDeanman, Richard to Susan Hood, May 9, 1829. Surety, Joseph McDeannan.
McDowell, Gideon to Elizabeth Norris, Jan. 24, 1833. Surety, John H. Smith.
McDowell, Harrison to Cassandra Webb, Oct. 9, 1834. Surety, John Williams.
McDowell, Jesse to Mariah Freeman, Dec. 5, 1829. Surety, Nathan Thurman.
McDowell, Jesse to Sally Cooke, Oct. 27, 1829. Surety, Daniel Smith.
McElroy, Adam to Martha McDaniel, Oct. 25, 1834. Surety, William M. Knox.
McElroy, Andrew M. to May Swan, April 29, 1835. Surety, T. G. Wooten.
McElroy, Matthew L. to Jane M. Witherspoon, March 21, 1835. Surety, William ____?.
McFarland, Thomas to Nancy Rawlins, June 12, 1817. Surety, Benjamine McFarland.
McFarlin, Benjamine to Elizabeth Berry, July 24, 1818. Surety, Stith M. Laughlin.
McFerrin, Alexander F. to Eliza H. Mason, June 1, 1835. Surety, U. S. Cummins.
McGowan, Harpeth H. to Nancy Locke, Nov. 25, 1828.
McGough, Matthew to Nancy Clarke, June 2, 1824. Surety, Martin Lamb.
McGowan, John to Sara T. Williams, Dec. 13, 1834. Surety, Jas. D. Currin.
MacGowan, Thomas to Martha J. Locke, Nov. 24, 1824. Surety, Thomas Batte.
McGowen, William B. to Martha J. Batey, Aug. 15, 1837. Surety, Alfred Elliott.
McGraw, Caleb to Mary Cocke, Feb. 18, 1818. Surety, Charles Niles.
McGregor, Albert to Mary E.O. Hamblin, April 30, 1834. Surety, Geo. D. Crosthwait.
McGregor, Ransford to Isabella S. Handerson, Aug. 20, 1834. Surety, J. W. Jetton.
McHenry, John to Rachel Brown, Dec. 12, 1815. Surety, William Hall.
McIver, Evander to Matilda C. Wendel, Oct. 18, 1827. Surety, James P. Lowery.
McKay, William to Rebecca Lambert, June 1, 1826.
McKean, Eli to Polly M. McGahey, Nov. 5, 1804. Surety, Wm. Howell.
McKee, Andrew M. to Eliza Hoskins, Jan. 11, 1827. Surety, Spill C. Hoskins.
McKee, John to Sarah Elrod, July 28, 1831.
McKee, John B. to Ann L. Ramsey, May 2, 1827. Surety, Robert Sullivan.
McKee, William to Sophia Blankenship, Dec. 20, 1824.
McKelvey, Hugh to Nancy Williamson, July 22, 1829. Surety, Calvin T. Clark.
McKelvey, Willis W. to Nancy Barnes, Jan. 6, 1823. Surety, John McKelvey.

McKelvey, Willis W. to Saluda M. Barnes, Dec. 21, 1833.
Surety, James McKelvey.
McKerley, John to Johannah Farr, Feb. 4, 1823.
McKinley, John to Rebecca Powell, May 19, 1819.
McKissick, Daniel to Margaret B. Henderson, March 5,
1822.
McKnight, Calvin H. to Polly Z. Keys, Sept. 7, 1831.
McKnight, James to Susannah Knox, Sept. 10, 1818.
McKnight, James to Nancy Alexander, Nov. 20, 1820.
McKnight, Robert to Mrs. Elizabeth Gardner, March 14,
1832.
McKnight, Samuel F. to Elizabeth Youree, March 15, 1833.
Surety, George W. Knox.
McKnight, Thomas to Nancy Robertson, May 22, 1813.
McKnight, William to Neoma S. Doran, July 2, 1823.
McLaughlin, Isaac to Susan Herrod, Dec. 23, 1829.
Surety, Alfred S. Harbin.
McLaughlin, Levi to Ruthy McCree, March 14, 1816.
McLean, Charles G. to Sarah S. Blackman, Dec. 14, 1835.
Surety, O. M. Blackman.
McLean, James to Susanna Gooding, Oct. 9, 1834. Surety,
Allen Beaty.
McLean, John to Ruth Elkins, Oct. 5, 1829. Surety,
Edmund Tennison.
McLendon, Geo. T. to Susan O. Worrell, May 22, 1834.
Surety, Thomas J. McLendon.
McMahan, James A. to Mary Coleman, Aug. 10, 1822.
McMenamy, James to Sarah Robertson, June 19, 1830.
Surety, William Sanders.
McMillan, Malcolm to Nancy Richards, July 23, 1830.
Surety, Philemon W. Oliphant.
McMillan, Jackson to Nancy Thornton, Sept. 6, 1824.
Surety, James Wright.
McMurry, John to Brinthey M. Hannis, Oct. 5, 1833.
Surety, Alexander Neisbet.
McMurry, William to Celia Belieu, Feb. 9, 1819.
McMurry, William H. to Rheny Johnson, Jan. 22, 1833.
Surety, Alexander Neisbet.
McNary, John N. to Matilda B. Henderson, Jan. 8, 1833.
Surety, Hugh Kukuiam.
McNees, Samuel C. to Elizabeth Cummins, May 16, 1806.
Surety, John Spence.
McNight, James to Ellis Sanders, Oct. 30, 1817.
McPeak, Henry to Milly Arnold, Feb. 21, 1805. Surety,
John McPeak.
McPeak, John to Nancy Hedgeth, Oct. 17, 1822.
McRay, Curtis to Elizabeth Ivey, Dec. 27, 1833. Surety,
John J. Warren.
McRae, William A. to Sarah E. Vaughan, Feb. 11, 1837.
Surety, Richard Spann.
McRea, William to Mary Lovel, Oct. 4, 1827. Surety,
William Gilliam.
McSpadden, Robert D. to Margaret Porter, Aug. 7, 1832.
Maban, Stephen to Jean Thompson, June 21, 1805. Surety,
Andrew Hall.

Maberry, Benjamin to Sally Thornton, Jan. 24, 1822.
Maberry, James to Mary Peek, Aug. 15, 1835. Surety,
    James Blanton.
Mackey, Charles to Elizabeth Hedgpath, Feb. 11, 1823.
Maddox, Natty to Sarah B. Moore, Feb. 5, 1835. Surety,
    Natty W. Maddox.
Major, William to Glover H. Gentry, Nov. 19, 1824.
    Surety, John Matthews.
Majors, Alexander W. to Malinda Crook, Sept. 26, 1827.
    Surety, Joseph L. Majors.
Majors, Robert H. to Sarah Fugitt, Aug. 28, 1824.
    Surety, John W. Ragsdale.
Mallard, Alfred to Sarah Gregory, Dec. 3, 1832.
Mallard, George W. to Anny Foster, April 9, 1812.
Mallard, Joseph to Sally Holden, Nov. 17, 1818. Surety,
    William Holden.
Malone, William N. to Mariah J. Hoover, June 29, 1824.
    Surety, Wm. E. North.
Maney, William to Martha A. Murfree, March 10, 1819.
Mankin, Charles to Martha Burke, Aug. 8, 1836. Surety,
    James Howland.
Mankin, James to Lydia Hodge, Nov. 26, 1823. Surety,
    John Mankin.
Mankin, Jesse to Cynthia Oaks, June 26, 1827. Surety,
    John Ott.
Mankin, Stephen B. to Sarah Robertson, --- 8, 1835.
    Surety, Joseph Smith.
Manely, Jesse to Tabitha Cooper, Jan. 23, 1823. Surety,
    Samuel McMurry.
Manley, Turner B. to Susan House, Dec. 21, 1820.
Manning, Francis S. to Rebecca Montgomery, Nov. 11, 1828.
Manning, Willie D. to Sally Thurman, April 1, 1821.
Mannon, John to Nancy Key, Jan. 11, 1820.
Manor, James to Phebe Foster, June 26, 1824. Surety,
    Montfort H. Fletcher.
Manor, Levi to Levina Jarret, May 29, 1824. Surety,
    David M. Jarrett.
Marable, Isaac M. to Elizabeth Williams, May 13, 1815.
Marable, John to Catherine Hazlett, Feb. 28, 1833.
    Surety, Berry Ryan.
Marable, William M. to Nancy Harris, Aug. 26, 1828.
Marchbanks, James to Elizabeth Gilley, Oct. 8, 1835.
    Surety, Wm. Mankin.
Marlin, James to Nancy Taylor, Jan. 26, 1816.
Marlin, John to Mary C. Dean, April 2, 1817.
Marlin, Lemuel L. to Elizabeth Pinkard, Nov. 22, 1837.
    Surety, James G. Wooten.
Marlin, Thomas to Evelina Alexander, Oct. 17, 1825.
Marlin, William to Lucinda Miller, July 4, 1832.
Marrs, Alfred to Ann McElroy, Feb. 13, 1837. Surety,
    Thomas Vaughan.
Marsh, Sion to Margaret Baker, Oct. 20, 1816.
Marshall, Robert to Nancy Hoskins, Sept. 12, 1820.
Marshall, William to Mrs. Martha Brown, Nov. 21, 1835.
    Surety, M. G. Reeves.

Martin, Caleb to Susan Batey, Dec. 5, 1836. Surety,
John Elrod.
Martin, John to Martha Ann Vaughan, Dec. 20, 1834.
Surety, Wm. Johns.
Martin, Lewis G. to Belinda Rucker, Sept. 12, 1816.
Martin, Thomas to Martha Mason, April 29, 1821.
Mason, Henry to Rebecca Thacker, Sept. 9, 1836. Surety,
John J. Lawing.
Mason, Isaac H. to Rebecca A. Ferguson. Surety, Geo.
W. Lane.
Mason, John F. to Leah Hensley, Aug. 5, 1835. Surety,
Abner W. Blair.
Mason, Reynsor H. to Harriet Burnett, Dec. 19, 1834.
Surety, Moses G. Reeves.
Massey, Drury to Sally Woods, Oct. 23, 1818. Surety,
Owen Wood.
Massey, Osburn to Elizabeth Fortenberry, Sept. 5, 1821.
Massey, William G. to Caroline M. Blakemore. Surety,
William Hunter.
Masterson, Thomas to Sally Washington, Dec. 2, 1807.
Surety, Henchy Pettway.
Matheny, Job to Nancy Cooke, Sept. 7, 1822.
Matthews, Chappel to Sarah Dunn, Aug. 21, 1833. Surety,
John Jones.
Matthew Chappel to Catherine Holden, July 23, 1835.
Surety, Wm. A. Dun.
Matthews, Drury to Pauline Rucker, June 7, 1830.
Surety, Drury Robertson.
Matthews, Jacob to Prudence Esther, Dec. 18, 1825.
Matthews, James H. to Harriet Allen, Aug. 5, 1834.
Surety, Kelley Matthews.
Matthews, James R. T. to Stacy Elliott, Nov. 29, 1831.
Matthews, Robt. to Louisa Tucker, May 29, 1827. Surety,
Thos. W. Marshall.
Matthews, Tennessee to Priscilla W. Morton, Nov. 20,
1835. Surety, John Curd.
Matthews, William R. to Tabitha M. E. Knox, April 26,
1833. Surety, Andrew J. Hoover.
Maxey, Joel to Jane Goodson, July 6, 1827. Surety,
Elam McCracken.
Maxwell, Jno. to Elizabeth Covington, Jan. 13, 1818.
May, Edmund to Jane Neal, Nov. 16, 1836. Surety,
Nelson W. Baldridge.
May, Thomas to Sarah R. King, Nov. 18, 1837. Surety,
Joshua King.
Mayfield, Christopher to Margaret Hughes, Aug. 17,
1825
Mayfield, Hance W. to Malinda Prater, Sept. 16, 1835.
Surety, Lodden Hudson.
Mayfield, Tolbert to Elizabeth Johnston, Sept. 29, 1824.
Surety, Alfred P. Gowan.
Mayfield, William to Ann Jones, Dec. 18, 1834. Surety,
Ephraim Norman.
Mayhew, David to Margaret Boggs, Dec. 2, 1816.

Mayho, Benjamin to Caroline Bangston, July 31, 1833.
Surety, Joel Parker.
Maze, Sherrod to Parthenia Grimes, Nov. 20, 1834.
Surety, Henry Hayes.
Mences, James to Elizabeth M. Anthony, June 29, 1816.
Meller, Lewis to Elizabeth Haney, May 24, 1817.
Meridy, William to Lucinda Guthrie, July 17, 1837.
Surety, Isham Traylor.
Merritt, James P. to Elizabeth A. Mathews, Feb. 2, 1824.
Michael, Lemuel C. to Mary Burchett, Aug. 11, 1835.
Surety, A. J. Jetton.
Michael, Thomas to Milley Taylor, Jan. 3, 1824.
Miller, Charles to Patsy Lowry, Aug. 18, 1815. Surety,
John Lowry.
Miller, Felix G. to Elizabeth Mayfield, Dec. 21, 1827.
Surety, William W. Miller.
Miller, James R. to Rebecca Johnston, July 6, 1815.
Miller, Nathaniel to Martha Ann E. Read, May 4, 1835.
Surety, James Elder.
Miller, William to Margaret Acree, Oct. 6, 1817.
Surety, Dandridge Acree.
Miller, William to Margaret Norman, March 12, 1834.
Surety, Moses G. Reeves.
Minor, William to Mary Booker, Sept. 17, 1819.
Minter, Jeptha to Levina Manor, Dec. 15, 1834. Surety,
James W. Baird.
Mitchell, Charles C. to Ann Bevirt, July 11, 1833.
Mitchell, David to Margaret V. Peebles, Jan. 1, 1829.
Surety, William H. Bowman.
Mitchell, Ebenezer to Nancy Currin, Dec. 16, 1833.
Surety, John H. Burke.
Mitchell, James to Mary Maxey, Jan. 30, 1833. Surety,
Philip Maxey.
Mitchell, James C. to Fanny A. Bedford, Jan. 3, 1821.
Mitchell, John to Ann Burnett, Dec. 12, 1835. Surety,
John H. Smith.
Mitchell, Stephen to Nancy Finley, Oct. 28, 1829.
Surety, John N. Mitchell.
Mitchell, Thomas C. to Susanna Robinson, Nov. 13, 1823
Mitchell, Thomas R. to Nancy Pullum, Oct. 7, 1837.
Surety, Joab B. Freeman.
Mitchell, William to Miss ----- Burnett, Jan. 22, 1824.
Surety, Robert B. Warren.
Mobb, Andrew J. to Nancy Merritt, Aug. 20, 1837.
Surety, John H. Bush.
Modrell, Nelson P. to Nancy Sharp, May 12, 1835.
Surety, Thomas Warren.
Molloy, David B. to Eleanor P. Harrison, March 13, 1834.
Surety, Jno. W. Jetton.
Molloy, John to Nancy Elam, March 8, 1827. Surety,
Robert D. Harris.
Monahan, James to Eppy Newton, Oct. 24, 1809. Surety,
John L. Jetton.
Montford, Tenpenny to Mary Gannon, Aug. 11, 1832.
Montgomery, Joseph A. to Mary M. Rankin, Sept. 10, 1831.

Montgomery, Milton to Nancy Gordon, March 18, 1822.
Mooney, Joseph to Anny Holden, Dec. 25, 1837. Surety,
T. Holden.
Moore, David to Elizabeth Bradley, Oct. 9, 1815.
Moore, James to Elizabeth Montgomery, Aug. 13, 1810.
Surety, Wm. McMurry.
Moore, James to Rebecca Wade, May 3, 1824. Surety,
James Foster.
Moore, James R. to Elizabeth Heard, Oct. 30, 1815.
Surety, John Vaden.
Moore, John to Matilda Brooks, Aug. 19, 1826. Surety,
James Higgins.
Moore, John D. to Phebe Edwards, Aug. 23, 1820.
Moore, John E. to Mary Mankins, Dec. 30, 1819.
Moore, Joseph P. to Matilda C. Abbott, Oct. 18, 1832.
Moore, Leroy to Martha Ann Gordon, Dec. 30, 1833.
Surety, Reuben M. Gordon.
Moore, Peter to Sarah McNight, Oct. 23, 1804. Surety,
John McKnight.
Moore, Robert R. to Isabella W. Moore, June 15, 1835.
Surety, T. H. Stokes.
Moore, Samuel T. to Elizabeth Nevins, Sept. 13, 1823.
Surety, Baker Wrather.
Moore, Walter to Mary Smotherman, Aug. 26, 1839. Surety,
William Mallard.
Moore, William M. to Mildred L. Vaughan, Sept. 21, 1829.
Surety, Drury Vaughan.
Moppin, Burrell to Rosanna Parsley, July 27, 1835.
Surety, Moses M. Parsley.
Moran, John to Elizabeth Edwards, Sept. 12, 1830.
Morgan, Carey to Nancy Winston, Oct. 23, 1817. Surety,
Jonathan Currin.
Morgan, Gardner to Margaret Rouse, Dec. 30, 1835.
Surety, Berry Rouse.
Morgan, John to Betsy Summers, Nov. 11, 1817.
Morgan, Samuel to Harriett Harris, July 16, 1817.
Surety, Rolly Morgan.
Morris, James to Susan Wade, Aug. 10, 1836. Surety,
Nathaniel Haynes.
Morton, James to Amanda Smith, Aug. 21, 1830. Surety,
Alexander Smith.
Morton, John Z. to Jane K. Whitsett, Sept. 30, 1830.
Surety, John Guthrie.
Morton, Joseph to Martha A. Sneed, Oct. 29, 1834.
Surety, Clement W. Horn.
Mosley, Guilliam to Rebecca Hogans, Sept. 15, 1817.
Surety, Jeremiah Underwood.
Mosby, John to Nancy Smith, Jan. 4, 1816.
Moss, George H. to Nancy Walker, Jan. 7, 1824.
Moss, Gilbert to Sarah Adams, May 22, 1829. Surety,
James H. Wilson.
Motheral, Joseph to Anney L. Williams, Sept. 29, 1820.
Mullins, David to Nancy Taylor, Dec. 24, 1833. Surety,
Nelson Mullins.

Mullins, Edward to Dorothy Read, May 6, 1837. Surety, Nathaniel Miller.
Mullins, Jesse to Sarah Read, April 26, 1837. Surety, Edwin A. Keeble.
Mullins, Jesse to Mary Ann Marable, Sept. 6, 1837. Surety, Daniel N. Tune.
Mullins, John to Silvy Read, March 7, 1827. Surety, Silas Read.
Mullins, John to Frances E. Ferguson, March 13, 1827. Surety, L. F. R. Henderson.
Mullins, John to Harriet Smothers, March 22, 1831.
Mullins, John to Rebecca Taylor, Sept. 12, 1836. Surety, Joshua Elder.
Mullins, John R. to Mary Johns, May 19, 1834. Surety, Randolph V. Johns.
Mullins, Nelson to Martha Mullins, Dec. 25, 1837. Surety, James Taylor.
Mullins, William to Armedia Lassiter, Oct. 7, 1837. Surety, Asop Bond.
Murfree, Miles P. to Elizabeth Maxwell, Nov. 6, 1829. Surety, John Brockman.
Murphy, Ezekiel to Louisa Jones, Dec. 24, 1835. Surety, Levi Reeves.
Murphy, John to Louisa W. Edwards, Nov. 13, 1831.
Murphy, Nathaniel G. to Eliza V. Morris, Nov. 26, 1833. Surety, W. J. Lytle.
Murphy, Wayne, W. to Ann M. Mindrow, Jan. 10, 1835. Surety, William A. Haney.
Murray, Robert to Catherine Koonce, Aug. 3, 1822.
Murry, James to Elizabeth Dement, May 25, 1830. Surety, Isaac T. Wright.
Murry, Samuel to Sereany Dement, Dec. 18, 1829. Surety, John W. Hunt.
Myers, Benjamine to Melberry Williams, Feb. 9, 1824.
Myrick, Walter to Sally Tarpley, Aug. 31, 1815.
Myrick, Walter to Jane McKnight, Sept. 21, 1818.
Nairy, Francis E. to Elizabeth Lisenby, Aug. 31, 1833. Surety, Green L. Poplin (name was probably McNairy-E.R.W.).
Nance, Clement W. to Ann Avent, Feb. 11, 1836. Surety, Tennessee Mathews.
Nance, Henry to Lucy Lovel, Dec. 2, 1817. Surety, Dougald Ferguson.
Nance, John to Ann Gambrill, March 18, 1818.
Nance, Martin to Elizabeth Chissenhall, Aug. 12, 1828.
Nance, Richard to Elizabeth Hill, Oct. 30, 1833. Surety, A. A. Vincents.
Nance, William to Mary Coleman, Aug. 15, 1837. Surety, Samuel Jones.
Nash, George to Eliza Carbell, Oct. 31, 1837. Surety, Abram C. Penn.
Nash, George R. to Martha Griffin, May 31, 1810. Surety, Thomas Johnson.

Nash, Travis C. to Johanna Miller, Oct. 3, 1808.
Surety, John Miller.
Nash, William W. to Nancy Roberts, Nov. 25, 1830.
Neal, Seth to Frances Kimbro, Dec. 29, 1823.
Neal, William to Grace Atkinson, Oct. 10, 1823. Surety,
Hicks E. Ellis.
Neel, Alexander to Anny Shedy, June 13, 1817.
Neelly, Joshua to Polly Crownover, Sept. 27, 1818.
Neilly, Benjamine F. to Elizabeth A. McCoy, Dec. 10,
1822.
Neilly, John to Mary Bowles, Dec. 27, 1817. Surety,
William Youree.
Neilly, William to Elizabeth Reid, Jan. 13, 1818.
Surety, Constant Hardeman.
Nelson, Beverly to Elizabeth Robertson, Dec. 12, 1815.
Surety, Samuel C. Rucker.
Nelson, Daniel to Mary Matthews, March 3, 1836. Surety,
Wm. Ledbetter.
Nelson, James C. to Louisa Norman, Nov. 4, 1834.
Surety, William M. McClure.
Nelson, Joseph to Susan Gowen, June 19, 1829. Surety,
David Wendel.
Nelson, Pleasant H. to Henrietta S. Barnett, Dec. 10,
1827. Surety, Absolom Fowler.
Nelson, Samuel to Eunice R. Williams, Dec. 18, 1824.
Surety, Thomas Hardeman.
Nelson, Thomas to Mrs. Judith Edwards, April 16, 1832.
Nelson, William D. to Martha L. Marable, Dec. 21, 1831.
Newman, James to Mary Parker, Aug. 1, 1835. Surety,
Thos. Bailey.
Newman, John to Martha Gowen, --- -- ----.
Newman, Joseph to Nancy Mankins, Dec. 16, 1816.
Newsom, Francis C. to Susan Ridley. Surety, Sam'l C.
Muse.
Newsom, John B. to Sarah B. Ridley. Surety, Jonathin
Currin.
Newsom, Thomas to Elizabeth Coleman, Dec. 6, 1834.
Surety, D. Caldwell.
Nichol, William to Julia Lytle, Oct. 6, 1825.
Nichols, Daniel B. to Martha W. Morris, Nov. 25, 1833.
Nichols, James L. to Mildred Miller, July 27, 1835.
Surety, Wm. D. Clark.
Nichols, Joshua to Mary A. Youree, March 11, 1835.
Surety, Richard Ledbetter.
Nisbet, Joseph to Rosanna Newman, Jan. 20, 1818.
Surety, Samuel McMurray.
Nixon, John to Edney Simpson, Sept. 12, 1815. Surety,
Reuben Rion.
Noe, James to Sarah House, July 2, 1833. Surety, John
Noe.
Norfleet, Thomas M. to Virginia A. Bernard, Dec. 23,
1834. Surety, Francis B. Mabry.
Norman, Berryman to Tempy Oden, July 23, 1818. Surety,
Owen Wood.

Norman, Furney G. to Elizabeth Clater, April 29, 1809.
Surety, Joe Herndon.
Norman, Furney G. to Elizabeth Norris, Feb. 20, 1824.
Surety, Pritchett Alexander.
Norman, John to Nancy Neal, Sept. 13, 1827. Surety,
Richard Neal.
Norman, Thomas H. to Martha Waller, May 14, 1821.
Norman, William J. G. to Catherine McCoy, Dec. 20, 1834.
Surety, Jas. G. Wooten.
Norman, William M. to Lucretta McKay, Dec. 19, 1834.
Surety, Samuel Morgan.
Norris, James D. to Adaline Morris, July 7, 1821.
Norris, Joseph to Eve Winston, Nov. 22, 1817. Surety,
David P. Hannis.
North, Anthony to Sarah P. Lawrence, Nov. 5, 1832.
North, William E. to Purliner D. Jarrett, Dec. 9, 1825.
Northcutt, Hosey to Phebe Potty, Jan. 21, 1831.
Northcutt, William to Caty Soap, Aug. 17, 1805. Surety,
George Soap.
Norton, William to Mary Keele, Sept. 13, 1834. Surety,
Winston Taylor.
Norvill, Nathaniel to Lucy Loftin, Nov. 2, 1815.
Surety, J. C. Caldwell.
Oaks, Isaac to Elizabeth Broyles, Oct. 15, 1823.
Surety, Alfred Broyles.
Oaks, Isable (Isble) to Elizabeth Mankin, May 18, 1827.
Surety, James Mankin.
Odell, Jeremiah to Patsey Freeman, Dec. 31, 1822.
Surety, Archibald Cooper.
Olds, Daniel S. to Elizabeth Vernon, April 14, 1827.
Surety, Samuel Lewis.
Oliver, William to Winifred Summers, Dec. 27, 1817.
Surety, Matthew Simmons.
Olliphant, Philemon W. to Catherine Stanley, Jan. 29,
1827. Surety, James Stanley.
Olliphant, Sam. H. to Nancy Shackleford, Jan. 15, 1820.
Orr, Alexander to Jane McKnight, March 26, 1805.
Surety, Henry McCoy.
Orr, James to Frances M. Barker, Nov. 30, 1836.
Surety, Dollarson Barker.
Orr, James B. to Cinthy Goodloe, April 1, 1833. Surety,
David McKnight.
Orrand, Thomas to Sarah Hays, April 15, 1817. Surety,
James Haley.
Osburn, Jesse to Dorotha James, July 31, 1805. Surety,
Joseph James.
Ott, Anderson D. to Mary Ann Kelton, April 19, 1836.
Surety, Alfred G. Cosby.
Ott, John to Rebecca Cosby, Aug. 7, 1827. Surety,
Robert Walker.
Overall, Andrew J. to Narcissia Overall, July 22, 1836.
Surety, Nathaniel S. Overall.
Overall, James to Lucinda Butler, Oct. 1, 1825.
Overall, John to Jean McLin, Dec. 17, 1817.

Owen, Jonathan to Margey J. Ivey, Sept. 2, 1829.
Surety, F. P. Crockett.
Owens, John to Rebecca Thompson, Feb. 10, 1826.
Owens, Richard to Mary May, Nov. 12, 1826. Surety,
John Owens.
Owens, Thomas to Patsey Anderson, March 19, 1821.
Pace, James to Elizabeth George, Feb. 9, 1837. Surety,
William H. Ivie.
Pace, John to Sarah McCracken, Sept. 24, 1834. Surety,
Hardin Allmon.
Page, John B. to Nancy M. Brothers, Dec. 4, 1827.
Surety, Burton D. Brothers.
Page, William to Eliza Patton, Aug. 24, 1829. Surety,
Levi Wade.
Pallett, Thomas A. to Sarah Moore, March 4, 1828.
Palmer, William to Patsey Booth, Sept. 3, 1823. Surety,
Andrew Higgenbotham.
Palmer, William H. to Mildred Johns, June 15, 1822.
Parham, Joshua N. to Elizabeth Broomfield, Sept. 20,
1827. Surety, Sanford G. Allen.
Parham, Peter to Sarah Broomfield, Jan. 4, 1826.
Parker, Dollison to Elizabeth Yardley, June 24, 1833.
Parker, Francis to Penelope Edwards, July 12, 1837.
Surety, Moses G. Reeves.
Parker, Garrison to Polly Johnson, April 27, 1824.
Surety, Peter Hilton.
Parker, Hardy to Delila Morse, June 26, 1827. Surety,
Adam S. Butler.
Parker, Isaac to May Fuller, March 13, 1834. Surety,
B. C. Powell.
Parish, William G. to Elizabeth C. Fleming, Sept. 5,
1820.
Parrish, William to Amy Noakes, March 12, 1816.
Parsley, Jesse S. to Sarah W. Coleman, Nov. 18, 1831.
Parsley, Jesse S. to Susannah Coleman, June 26, 1837.
Surety, John L. Parsley.
Partee, Charles M. to Narcissa L. A. Smith, July 2,
1822.
Pate, William to Sarah Forbs, Dec. 20, 1830. Surety,
Edward Seward.
Pate, William to Elizabeth J. Moore, Feb. 7, 1837.
Surety, James H. Heath.
Patillo, Samuel to Sarah Ann Newgent, Dec. 12, 1832.
Patrick, Levi to Mary Wallace, Jan. 24, 1826.
Patterson, Bailey to Nancy Neal, July 24, 1818. Surety,
John Patterson.
Patterson, Edward to Sarah Burks, Sept. 4, 1818.
Surety, Leroy Burks.
Patterson, Fenton M. to Mary Johns, Feb. 6, 1826.
Patterson, Gideon to Susanna Gambill, March 16, 1822.
Patterson, John to Mary McCoy, Dec. 3, 1817.
Patterson, Thomas to Elizabeth Ward, Nov. 5, 1827.
Surety, Ezekiel (Azekiel) Ward.
Patterson, Turner to Martha Weatherford, Oct. 27, 1835.
Surety, Jackson Wallace.

Patton, Matthew to Isabella Whitmore, July 16, 1817.
Surety, Jacob Rice.
Patton, Samuel to Jane Robinson, Nov. 2, 1815. Surety,
Thos. Woods.
Payne, Edward to Polly Link, Feb. 3, 1835. Surety,
Cornelius Sanders.
Payne, S. Payne to Minerva Sanders, July 16, 1830.
Pace, John L. to Frances Keele, April 17, 1830.
Pea, William to Jemima Keel, Dec. 20, 1830 (1828).
Surety, James Gibson.
Peake, William to Elizabeth Read, March 1, 1827.
Surety, Thomas Powell, Jr.
Pearce, Jesse to Elizabeth Lyon, Aug. 12, 1837. Surety,
John P. Dunn.
Pearce, McKinnie to Mary Walker, June 25, 1825.
Pearcy, William to Sarah Traylor, Oct. 18, 1834.
Surety, Francis W. Pearcy.
Peay, Thomas T. to Margaret L. Kelton, June 9, 1836.
Surety, Joseph Edwards.
Peebles, Herbert I. to Monen Jones, March 17, 1832.
Peek, Thomas to Elizabeth Wright, July 2, 1836.
Surety, John A. McLin.
Penn, George D. to Telitha P. Clay, Oct. 15, 1831.
Penn, Josiah to Ruth W. Broughton, June 11, 1825.
Peoples, George to Jane Black, Nov. 6, 1817.
Perkins, Jesse to Mariah Williams, Feb. 1824.
Perry, Henry to Jane Young, May 9, 1831.
Perry, Strother to Elizabeth Lowry, May 28, 1829.
Surety, James C. Standley.
Perryman, Stephen to Elizabeth Ewes, Sept. 27, 1832.
Pettypool, Thomas to Mary Nixon, April 29, 1817.
Peyton, Benjamine to Mary Cherry, Aug. 9, 1824. Surety,
Samuel Burke.
Peyton, Harrison to Winney Vaper, March 22, 1836.
Surety, Jas. W. Hamilton.
Phelps, Elisha to Jane Steel, June 3, 1809. Surety,
Amos Phelps.
Phelps, Ephraim to Mary Davis, Nov. 11, 1817.
Phelps, Silas to Jane Ridgeway, Nov. 17, 1818.
Phelps, Zadoc to Demaris Sander, July 15, 1835. Surety,
Leonard Burchett.
Philips, Alfred to Ann Pace, Jan. 28, 1834.
Philips, Cornelius to Mary J. Murphy, Dec. 12, 1837.
Surety, Francis Owens.
Philips, Cornelius to Mary Robertson, April 11, 1835.
Surety, John D. Murphey.
Phillips, David S. to Peggy Knox, Feb. 16, 1825.
Phillips, William B. to Mary Davis, Oct. 20, 1825.
Pearcy (Piearcy), Thomas to Sarah L. Johns, Nov. 12,
1829. Surety, Benjamine Davis.
Pierce, Granville S. to Elizabeth V. Abbott, Oct. 21,
1830. Surety, Uriah S. Cummings.
Pierson, John to Polly Booth, Feb. 8, 1820.

Pinkard, Bailey to Elizabeth Newman, May 27, 1834.
Surety, U. S. Clemmons.
Pinkston, James T. to Mary G. Johns, Feb. 20, 1834.
Surety, Robert D. Donoho.
Pinson, Joel to Nancy Collier, Dec. 2, 1829. Surety,
William Nevil.
Pitts, Kinchen to Betsy Elder, Jan. 21, 1824. Surety,
Matthew Pitts.
Pogue, James E. to Nancy McGill, April 10, 1820.
Pogue, John to Matilda Haynes, Dec. 17, 1822.
Poindexter, James K. to Susan C. McCall, April 20, 1833.
Surety, Wm. Poindexter.
Polk, Charles to Ruth Gibson, Sept. 22, 1824. Surety,
James McBride.
Polk, James K. to Susan Childress, Jan. 1, 1824.
Polk, William to Susanna Gamble, April 14, 1808.
Pope, Benjamine to Sarah Read, Nov. 9, 1824. Surety,
Benjamine Howell.
Pope, Charles to Eliza Smith, Dec. 28, 1815.
Pope, Hardy to Evaline J. Gambrell, Sept. 26, 1833.
Surety, Sam'l Clark.
Pope, John to Dorothy Etter, July 17, 1834. Surety,
Sam Clark.
Pope, Solomon to Peggy Hobson, Dec. 21, 1808.
Pope, William to Peachy Thurman, March 21, 1833.
Surety, Geo. A. Sublett.
Porter, John N. to Katherine Rucker, June 20, 1816.
Porter, Samuel to Jane Laughlin, May 16, 1806. Surety,
James Laughlin.
Porter, Thomas B. to Mary Covington, Dec. 3, 1827.
Surety, William B. Stewart.
Porterfield, Samuel S. to Edney A. Monahan, July 29,
1835. Surety, J. G. Cox.
Porterfield, William S. to Sarah Pearson, June 24, 1829.
Surety, William J. Todd.
Posey, Dennis to Susan Read, March 21, 1822.
Posey, John to Mary Hoggett, Jan. 1, 1816.
Posey, William to Barbary Haynes, Dec. 16, 1819.
Posey, William S. to Anna Nance, Nov. 22, 1817. Surety,
Benjamine Lane.
Potter, Benjamine H. to Martha Pryor, Nov. 2, 1835.
Surety, W. G. Crockett.
Potts, George B. to Ann Nevina, April 1, 1836. Surety,
William A. Haynes.
Potts, William to Martha Estes, Nov. 16, 1824. Surety,
Alfred Ransom.
Powell, Osburn to Elizabeth Boatright, March 18, 1819.
Powell, Tenison to Angelina Carter, Dec. 22, 1818.
Powell, Thomas to Sarah S. Puckett, Sept. 11, 1827.
Surety, William Ledbetter.
Powell, William to Rachel Kerr, Nov. 16, 1815. Surety,
Geo. A. Sublett.
Powell, William E. to Martha L. Rideout, Oct. 6, 1827.
Surety, William Wills.

RUTHERFORD COUNTY MARRIAGES

Powers, George to Mary Anne McGrew, Feb. 6, 1825.
Prater, Elijah to Cynthia Hail, March 4, 1837. Surety,
Aaron Prater.
Prater, Jennier to Margaret Miller, Nov. 17, 1827.
Surety, Herod Burks.
Prater, Thomas to Sarah Jacobs, Aug. 22, 1837. Surety,
William Summers.
Prewett, Henry to Sarah Fox, Jan. 17, 1833. Surety,
M. H. Prewitt.
Price, John to Johanna Rucker, Dec. 29, 1814. Surety,
Samuel C. Rucker.
Price, John M. to Zilpha Claiton (Clayton), June 3,
1824. Surety, William B. Claiton (Clayton).
Price, John W. to Matilda Pace, Dec. 7, 1829. Surety,
George W. Williamson.
Priestly, James to Susan M. Nelson, Nov. 9, 1835.
Surety, Joseph W. Nelson.
Prior, John to Rebecca Cooke, Aug. 28, 1823. Surety,
Job Metheny.
Pruett, Matthias H. to Eliza Fox, Oct. 26, 1829.
Surety, John L. Hoover.
Pucket, Elam to Elizabeth Adams, Jan. 30, 1818. Surety,
George Thompson.
Puckett, Isham to Mary Ann Page, Feb. 26, 1829. Surety,
John Bond.
Puckett, Leonard to Nancy Smith, June 24, 1820.
Puckett, Leonard to Theresa Whitlock, Aug. 21, 1830.
Surety, William H. Harrison.
Puckett, Lodwick to Nancy Still, Sept. 16, 1820.
Puckett, Luke to Lucy Ann Michael, Feb. 13, 1818.
Surety, William Mederith.
Puckett, William to Martha Owens, Dec. 24, 1818.
Surety, Andrew Griffin.
Puckett, William to Malisa Ledbetter, Dec. 11, 1827.
Surety, Francis Hancock.
Puckett, William A. to Nancy Warren, Oct. 18, 1836.
Surety, George A. Sublett.
Puckett, William S. to Milley Manor, Jan. 6, 1833.
Surety, D. V. McLean.
Puckett, Woodson to Margaret Farr, April 2, 1825.
Pugh, Joseph to Anne Chisa, Sept. 9, 1822.
Pugh, William to Margaret Castleman, Dec. 17, 1823.
Pulley, Robert to Sarah Dancey, Aug. 2, 1834. Surety,
Price Curd.
Pursell, Samuel M. to Mary Barchlay (Barkley), Aug. 22,
1834. Surety, Thos. R. Peek.
Purtle, Samuel to Sally Hust, Feb. 20, 1821.
Quarles, Milton W. to Martha Smith, Aug. 10, 1829.
Surety, Swinfield Smith.
Quinby, John R. to Eliza Gowen, Oct. 12, 1837. Surety,
Wm. Matthews.
Quin, Michael to Eliza Ballentine, Jan. 5, 1835.
Surety, John Ballentine.
Rabey, James to Isabella Phillips, Nov. 28, 1836.
Surety, Travis Windrow.

Ragsdale, Baxter to Martha Bradfield, Dec. 26, 1827.
Surety, Moses G. Reeves.
Ragdsale, Baxter H. to Mary Anne Rucker, Jan. 17, 1827.
Surety, Charles R. Abbott.
Rainey, Anderson to Lucinda McPeake, Nov. 25, 1835.
Surety, Samuel Patton.
Ramsey, Hardy B. to Nancy Barber, Jan. 5, 1837. Surety,
R. S. Ricketts.
Ramsey, James to Catherine Thomas, Oct. 19, 1837.
Surety, Lemuel B. Herrold.
Ramsey, John to Elizabeth Trimble, Nov. 1, 1815.
Surety, Joseph Trimble.
Ramsey, William to Elizabeth Barber, Dec. 25, 1827.
Surety, Richard W. Ramsey.
Ramsey, William F. to Nancy Knox, Jan. 17, 1832.
Ramsey, William, Jr. to Polly Overall, July 3, 1804.
Surety, Jas. McKee.
Randolph, Beverly to Lucy W. Searcy, Nov. 25, 1818.
Surety, S. R. Rucker.
Randolph, Grief to Nancy E. Anderson, Oct. 31, 1829.
Surety, William W. Anderson.
Randolph, Peyton to Miss A. S. Keeble, Sept. 18, 1822.
Rankin, Joseph to Mary Ivy, Feb. 6, 1837. Surety,
William H. Ivie.
Rankin, Samuel to Nancy Vaughan, Aug. 28, 1827. Surety,
Henry J. Johnston.
Rankin, Thomas C. to Louisa Warren, Feb. 24, 1825.
Rankin, William C. to Mary Ann Powell, Dec. 5, 1833.
Surety, S. D. Watkins.
Ransom, Alfred to Sarah Snell, Dec. 6, 1825.
Ransom, Athelston to Eliza Clark, Dec. 8, 1823.
Ransom, Benjamine to Sally Jarrett, June 9, 1810.
Surety, Thomas Smith.
Ransom, Henry D. to Priscilla Manor, March 29, 1831.
Ransom, John to Elizabeth Bowman, Sept. 2, 1817.
Surety, Thompson Jarrett.
Ransom, Lemuel to Jane Commer, Oct. 18, 1836. Surety,
Moses G. Reeves.
Rawls, John to Frances Anderson, May 22, 1823. Surety,
Horace Oliver.
Rawlings, John W. to Elizabeth Brooks, March 29, 1837.
Surety, Matthias Rawlings.
Rawlings, Mathias to Louisa Blair, June 3, 1834.
Surety, John Rawlings.
Rawlins, John to Sally Hoover, July 21, 1817.
Ray, John to Milley Webb, June 11, 1814.
Ray, John G. to Rebecca Williams, Feb. 6, 1836. Surety,
James Jackson.
Ray, Thomas to Elicia Hains, July 2, 1824. Surety,
William Vandike.
Read, James A. to Zabieth F. Lanom, Jan. 8, 1827.
Durety, Hiram Drennon.
Read, John to Patsy Wade, Feb. 27, 1823. Surety, John
Bradley.

Read, John A. to Nancy McKee, Sept. 9, 1834. Surety, William McCombs.
Read, John H. to Anne Beavers, Jan. 2, 1816.
Read, John N. to Mary Barksdale, May 16, 1810. Surety, Blackman Coleman.
Read, Silast L. to Letty J. Pollard, June 7, 1824.
Read, Sion L. to Hardencia Spencer, Aug. 2, 1819.
Read, Solomon to Nancy Barlow, Jan. 21, 1833. Surety, William A. Guthrey.
Ready, James to Crecy Carithers, Feb. 27, 1826.
Reames, James to Sarah May, Feb. 15, 1835. Surety, John S. Hardy.
Reece, Isham to Lucy Mitchell, Dec. 25, 1826.
Reed, Clack to Jane E. Shoemaker, Feb. 19, 1829. Surety, Grief Carroll.
Reed, Isaac to Elizabeth Potts, Aug. 7, 1829. Surety, Terry Vaughan.
Reed, James to Eleanor Rankin, April 23, 1817.
Reed, Jesse to Matilda Montgomery, March 25, 1823. Surety, Reuben Wright.
Reed, Levi to Mary Young, Feb. 10, 1827. Surety, James S. Leech.
Reed, Martin to Sarah Gibson, Jan. 25, 1827. Surety, Jesse Wood.
Reed, Mordecai to Sarah Stacy, Oct. 6, 1824. Surety, Aaron Stacy.
Reed, Nathan to Mary Clouse, Aug. 10, 1821.
Reese, John to Eliza Traylor, Nov. 28, 1835. Surety, Wm. H. Marable.
Reese, John to Martha Traylor, Dec. 16, 1834. Surety, Wm. L. Jones.
Reese, John to Polly E. Brandon, March 8, 1823. Surety, Nathan Kenashaw.
Reid, Peter to Delana Lassiter, Feb. 23, 1835. Surety, Lester Lassiter.
Renshaw, Elijah to Nancy Moore, Dec. 21, 1824. Surety, George Moore.
Renshaw, John to Martha Walker, Aug. 9, 1827.
Renshaw, Richard to Eliza Walkup, Oct. 8, 1830. Surety, Abner Bowen.
Replogle, Henry to Mary Coleman, March 27, 1833. Surety, F. P. Crockett.
Revel, Kinchin to Sally Burlison, Dec. 13, 1820.
Revel, Theophilus to Polly Ward, Dec. 21, 1820.
Rey, Solomon to Margaret Blackburn, Feb. 25, 1816.
Reynolds, Calvin to Caroline Smith, Jan. 13, 1836. Surety, Charles Leatherman.
Reynolds, Peter to Jane Cawthorn, Aug. 16, 1816.
Reynolds, Peter to Matilda Strother, Jan. 19, 1825.
Reynolds, Squire to Crecy Lewis, Dec. 10, 1825.
Rhoddin, David to Polly Lumly, May 8, 1816.
Rhodes, Claiborne H. to Lucisaiana Wood, Jan. 13, 1823. Surety, John D. Newgent.

Rice, John to Sarah Hill, Nov. 9, 1824. Surety, Brooking Burnett.
Richards, James to Martha Wooten, May 4, 1833. Surety, Noland Anberry (Asberry).
Richards, John to Jane Patterson, July 26, 1810. Surety, William Stockird.
Richards, John to Nancy Ann Freeman, Sept. 10, 1835. Surety, William C. Stanley.
Richardson, Christopher to Rebecca Daniel, Feb. 10, 1835. Surety, William M. McCan.
Richardson, James to Angelina Alexander, Dec. 22, 1823. Surety, James Jones.
Richardson, James T. to Mary Lorance, March 15, 1834. Surety, S. D. Watkins.
Richardson, John W. to _____ Starns, June 18, 1833. Surety, George D. Crosthwait.
Richard T. to Elizabeth Moore, Oct. 16, 1831.
Richardson, Thomas to Rebecca Miller, April 4, 1821.
Richardson, William M. to Mary C. Crosthwait, Aug. 18, 1824. Surety, Wm. H. Gayle.
Richie, John to Elizabeth Simpson, Oct. 10, 1815. Surety, Hugh Wallace.
Richmond, Anderson to Jane C. Dodd, Jan. 29, 1833. Surety, Griffin Dodd.
Ricks, Exum to Esther Watson, Nov. 9, 1820.
Ridley, Bromfield L. to Rebecca Crosthwait, Oct. 10, 1829. Surety, Geo. A. Sublett.
Ridley, George V. to Emma Cannon, July 12, 1836. Surety, Lewis Garner.
Ridley, James to Hannah H. Williams, June 30, 1836. Surety, Hance A. Ridley.
Ridley, John C. to Caroline E. Morton, June 16, 1831.
Riding, Thomas to Frances Vaughan, Jan. 9, 1816.
Ring, Thomas to Nancy G. McCabe, Aug. 6, 1836. Surety, Alexander L. McCabe.
Rippetoe, Burrus W. to Elizabeth Bland, July 16, 1825.
Ritter, Preston H. to Mary Massey, April 17, 1817. Surety, Alexander M. Bainbridge.
Roberts, Thomas to Polly Langston, July 15, 1816.
Robertson, Christopher to Partheny Smith, Jan. 30, 1828.
Robertson, Edward to Betsy Miller, Aug. 31, 1816.
Robertson, Edward H. to Nancy H. Dodd, Oct. 28, 1824. Surety, Joseph Spence.
Robertson, Elisha to Anne Miller, March 8, 1825.
Robertson, Kinchen to Julia Ann Wade, July 27, 1824. Surety, James Bigham.
Robertson, Luke S. to Emeline Dickson, April 19, 1834. Surety, Thomas Sanders.
Robertson, Pleasant to Rena McKay, Jan. 12, 1836. Surety, Samuel Crowder.
Robertson, Richard to Elizabeth Eaton, March 8, 1837. Surety, William Robertson.
Robertson, Richard to Sarah Dycus, Sept. 9, 1810.
Robertson, Thomas to Tabitha Bishop, Aug. 19, 1816.

Robertson, William to Rebecca Manor, June 24, 1825.
Robertson, William to Jane Crowder, March 2, 1836.
  Surety, Pleasant Robertson.
Robbins, Thomas to Mary Cunningham, July 8, 1830.
  Surety, Lemuel Wright.
Robins, Lemuel to Martin Cunningham, Sept. 23, 1826.
Robinson, Christopher to Jane Patterson, Sept. 14, 1836.
  Surety, Benton Woods.
Robinson, Edward H. to Nancy H. Dodd, Oct. 28, 1824.
Robinson, Isaiah to Nancy Esatrop, Feb. 2, 1829. Surety,
  Moses G. Reeves.
Robinson, John to Nancy Bowman, Oct. 31, 1822.
Robinson, John H. to Mary A. House, May 17, 1830.
Robinson, Micajah to Nelly Sanders, March 6, 1834.
  Surety, Luke S. Robinson.
Robinson, Samuel B. to Mary North, Jan. 7, 1837.
  Surety, John Randsom (Ransom).
Robinson, David to Nancy Robinson, July 5, 1831.
Robinson, Fulton to Jane Blair, June 19, 1819.
Robinson, William to Mary Culbertson, April 29, 1805.
  Surety, Thomas Marlin.
Rodgers, Andrew to Frances North, Aug. 23, 1820.
Rogers, Ervin to Celia Reeves, Dec. 21, 1824.
Rogers, John to Sally Crowder, Jan. 1, 1829. Surety,
  John J. Cooke.
Rogers, John to Sally Mosley, Oct. 3, 1831.
Rogers, John D. to Mary Gambill, Aug. 27, 1832.
Roland, John to Polly Robertson, July 7, 1812.
Roulhac, George to Agatha Hardeman, Dec. 27, 1828.
Roulhac, William G. to Elizabeth L. Hill, March 29, 1832.
Rooker, Jennings to Mary Miller, July 1, 1835. Surety,
  Martin Clark.
Rooney, Michael C. to Mary Rankin, April 10, 1823.
Ross, John to Nancy Taylor, Feb. 19, 1824. Surety,
  Josiah Taylor.
Rosewell, Buford A. to Margaret C. Burnett, June 19,
  1833. Surety, Martin Clark.
Rouse, Edmund to Sally Hill, Aug. 1, 1827. Surety,
  John Rouse.
Rouse, William to Eliza Anne Smith, Aug. 26, 1825.
Rowland, Benjamine to Sarah Johnson, Aug. 16, 1819.
Rowlett, Leonard to Susan Beesley, Jan. 2, 1822.
Rowton, Richmond, to Jane P. Barkley, July 26, 1826.
  Surety, John Prewett.
Rozella, Ashley B. to Henrietta S. Nelson, Oct. 8, 1832.
Rucker, Benjamine to Temperance W. Smith (alias Temper-
  ance W. Bass), Oct. 6, 1825.
Rucker, Edmund M. to Susan Overall, July 7, 1835.
  Surety, James M. Tompkins.
Rucker, Gideon L. to Rebecca Wright, Oct. 27, 1824.
  Surety, William Ledbetter.
Rucker, James H. to Elizabeth G. Ferriss, Jan. 16, 1826.
Rucker, John W. to Mariah M. Keeble, March 23, 1829.
  Surety, John W. Childress.

Rucker, Joseph B. to Susan Edmondson, Aug. 16, 1830.
Surety, John W. Childress.
Rucker, Joseph B. to Susan Seward, July 29, 1835.
Surety, John H. King.
Rucker, Martin to Catherine Hill, Feb. 23, 1836.
Surety, Ring W. Batteryn.
Rucker, Ransom to Charlotte Manning, Sept. 23, 1817.
Surety, William Ridgeway.
Rucker, Samuel C. to Lucinda A. Alexander, July 13, 1819.
Rucker, Terry to Elizabeth Ridgeway, Dec. 28, 1815.
Rucker, Thomas O. G. to Mirah Mitchell, Jan. 9, 1818.
Surety, Elisha B. Clarke.
Rucker, Thomas S. to Joice R. Rucker, March 19, 1823.
Surety, John R. Laughlin.
Rucker, William R. to Susan Childress, Nov. 10, 1819.
Rushing, Abel to Elizabeth Vencent, Dec. 7, 1835.
Surety, Alexander A. Vincent.
Rutledge, Joseph M. to Mary Watkins, March 2, 1835.
Surety, Thomas C. Black.
Rushing, Patrick to Sheriba Burks, Sept. 2, 1834.
Surety, Nelson E. Rushing.
Rushing, William to Decca Lisenby, Feb. 5, 1820.
Russell, Alexander to Elizabeth Hannah, Sept. 11, 1815.
Surety, John Wallace.
Russell, William to Sarah Youngblood, June 5, 1816.
Rust, Isaac to Margaret S. McElroy, Jan. 9, 1837.
Surety, John L. Henderson.
Rutledge, David to Angelina Williamson, July 3, 1816.
Rutledge, Joseph M. to Mary Watkins, March 2, 1835.
Surety, Thomas C. Black.
Rutledge, Pleasant to Harriet Barlow, March 28, 1821.
Ryan, George to Amanda M. F. Owen, Aug. 6, 1836.
Surety, Benjamine Forbs.
Ryan, Michael T. to Elizabeth Thornton, Jan. 11, 1833.
Surety, Pulaski Nixon.
Sage, Jesse to Eleanor Wright, June 4, 1827. Surety,
John F. McCutcheon.
Sagely, Joseph to Jane Gilliland, Sept. 29, 1814.
Surety, John Gilliland.
Salmons, Watson to Lucy Dunn, Oct. 21, 1830. Surety,
Abner Salmons.
Sanders, Cornelius to Susan Barnett, April 15, 1822.
Sanders, Elisha to Mary A. Jarret, Dec. 19, 1837.
Surety, John W. Hall.
Sanders, Elisha to Zilly Dickinson, March 25, 1818.
Sanders, Frederick to Frances Spain, June 7, 1837.
Surety, Wm. W. Ross.
Sanders, Garrett to Elizabeth Old, Sept. 7, 1829.
Surety, James McMennemy.
Sanders, George to Elizabeth Hayse, Oct. 21, 1830.
Surety, Charles Locke.
Sanders, Hiram to Catherine Barnes, March 21, 1836.
Sanders, Isaac to Sarah Mitchell, April 11, 1836.

Sanders, James to Mary Wilson, Feb. 24, 1823. Surety, Thomas McKnight.
Sanders, James to Martha Jackson, May 18, 1833. Surety, Joshua Underwood.
Sanders, James M. to Jane F. Hart, Feb. 17, 1834. Surety, Thomas Sanders.
Sanders, John H. to Mary Brown, July 4, 1837. Surety, William H. Wright.
Sanders, Pinkney G. to Eliza Ivins, Nov. 8, 1836. Surety, Noah W. Dill.
Sanders, Richard to Mary C. Travis, Jan. 7, 1831.
Sanders, Thomas to Edney Burton, April 22, 1818. Surety, Isaac Sanders.
Sanders, Wiley to Martha B. Hart, Feb. 20, 1832.
Sanders, William to Cherry Sanders, Feb. 9, 1822.
Sanford, George W. to Elizabeth B. Payne, July 19, 1824. Surety, James Sanford.
Sandford, John to Lucy Newsom, Sept. 7, 1810. Surety, Isaac Nance.
Saulter, John to Elizabeth Dunkin, Feb. 4, 1836. Surety, James M. Roberts.
Saunders, Robert W. to Kesiah Johnson, March 11, 1834. Surety, Jesse A. House.
Saunders, Thomas to Polly Lannum, April 19, 1821.
Savage, James to Mary Read, Sept. 24, 1836. Surety, John Bishop.
Sawyers, James to Susan Tippet, Sept. 30, 1817. Surety, James Alexander.
Scales, Peter P. to Caroline M. Hancock, Oct. 14, 1826.
Scoggins, John to Cynthia Davis, Oct. 4, 1830. Surety, Abraham Overall.
Scott, John W. to Alzira Johnson, May 4, 1833. Surety, Wm. H. McMurry.
Scott, Moses to Jane Webb, Oct. 28, 1808. Surety, Joseph Thompson.
Screws, Littleton to Malinda Ivy, May 8, 1824. Surety, Nathaniel Perry.
Scruggs, William to Sarah W. Good, Jan. 9, 1833. Surety, D. R. Gooch.
Searcy, Anderson to Elizabeth White, Oct. 8, 1833. Surety, Burton Yandell.
Searcy, Isaac to Elizabeth Marable, Dec. 14, 1820.
Searcy, John W. to Ann Sneed, May 11, 1836. Surety, Anderson East.
Seem, Abraham B. to Mahala Northcutt, March 10, 1823. Surety, John Ford.
Self, Nathan to Usley Burleson, Oct. 1, 1816.
Sellars, Alfred to Hannah P. Miller, Aug. 18, 1823.
Sessom, Jesse to Catharine Parker, April 7, 1855. Surety, Wm. Byford.
Seward, David to Ledy Holly, Nov. 7, 1836. Surety, A. S. Harris.
Sexton, William to Julian Wimberly, March 6, 1835. Surety, Isaac Whitworth.
Shackleford, Reuben to Milberry Darnell, Jan. 17, 1823.

Shapard, Robert P. to Parthenia Mitchell, Nov. 12, 1829.
Surety, Henry H. Treadway.
Sharpe, Alfred to Narcissa Davis, Jan. 20, 1815.
Surety, William H. Davis.
Sharpe, Cyrus to Charity Perry, Sept. 29, 1817. Surety,
James Sharpe.
Sharpe, James to Isabella McKnight, May 28, 1806.
Surety, Theophilus A. Cannon.
Sharpe, Theophilus A. to Lavenia S. Penn, Dec. 30, 1829.
Surety, Edwin R. Dickson.
Sharpe, William to Mary Wilson, Nov. 27, 1815. Surety,
Samuel Wilson.
Shaw, Milo to Elizabeth Ferris, Dec. 31, 1825.
Shaw, Robert P. to Sarah A. Morris, Oct. 18, 1834.
Surety, A. B. Robertson.
Shelton, John to Sarah Bennett, March 25, 1834. Surety,
John McKinley.
Shelton, Stephen to Nancy Hoover, April 10, 1837.
Surety, Martin Hoover.
Shelton, Thomas to Elizabeth Nance, April 18, 1820.
Shepard, B. to B. J. Cl____, Nov. 10, 1825.
Shepard, Peyton to Mary Davis, Dec. 18, 1834. Surety,
Thos. Peake.
Shepard (Shepherd) Robert to Serena Bishop, Feb. 26,
1833. Surety, Samuel Pursel.
Shepman, Abraham to Letitia Magby, June 14, 1805.
Surety, Isaac Shepman.
Sherard, Thomas to Pertandy Wallden, Feb. 22, 1836.
Surety, Henry Barkley.
Sherrod (Sherrold), Austin W. to Sarah L. Henry, Sept.
11, 1834. Surety, John W. McElroy.
Sherwood, Benjamine to Sally Brown, Jan. 13, 1818.
Surety, Hugh Sherwood.
Sherwood, John H. to Mary Skidmore, July 22, 1834.
Surety, Robert Todd.
Sherwood, Jonathan to Margaret Dicus, Sept. 30, 1817.
Surety, Daniel Sherwood.
Shoemaker, William C. to Elizabeth Stallin, Sept. 24,
1829. Surety, Daniel Williams.
Short, Anderson to Winney Leath, Dec. 21, 1824. Surety,
William H. Robinson.
Short, Moses to Hannah Baley, March 4, 1814.
Sikes, Jesse to Martha L. Howse, March 14, 1827.
Surety, Rolly Morgan.
Simmons, Eleanor (Eleazer) to Elizabeth Edwards, Oct.
17, 1827. Surety, Thomas C. Nelson.
Simmons, James F. to Eliza E. Henderson, Nov. 11, 1829.
Surety, Ransford McGrigor.
Simmons, John to Louisa McKay, July 23, 1834. Surety,
William McKay.
Simmons, Wyatt to Malinda Clark, Oct. 21, 1837.
Surety, Tilford Butler.
Simms, John W. to Jane C. Duffer, Nov. 10, 1835.
Surety, William A. Mitchell.

Simpson, Harris to Mary H. Thomas, March 27, 1827.
Surety, Robert Walker.
Simpson, James M. to Martha Clark, Dec. 10, 1832.
Simpson, John W. to Ann C. Vinson, Sept. 18, 1834.
Surety, Jesse Adcock.
Simpson, Kennedy to Catherine Saylors, Oct. 26, 1819.
Simpson, Peter to Jane Brandon, Jan. 31, 1829. Surety,
Richard Cunningham.
Simpson, Thomas F. to Cinthia Jacobs, Sept. 22, 1820.
Surety, Alexander Downing.
Simpson, William to Nancy Roberts, August 24, 1819.
Simpson, William to Sarah Higgins, August 28, 1820.
Sims, Robert L. to Catherine C. Hawkins, May 19, 1831.
Singletary, John L. to Margaret Eudaley, Oct. 30, 1832.
Sloan, James D. to Harriet A. Vaughan, Nov. 18, 1833.
Surety, Joseph Edwards.
Slocum, David to Patsy Nash, May 13, 1806. Surety,
Francis Nash.
Sloss, Joseph to Sarah Harrison, Jan. 12, 1825.
Smelledge, Edward E. to Amelia E. Oliphant, Aug. 23,
1823. Surety, Wm. L. J. Blair.
Smith, Absolom to Caty Dummery, Aug. 19, 1818. Surety,
John Jones.
Smith, Andrew M. to Rebecca P. Smith, Jan. 26, 1836.
Surety, Robert S. Jones.
Smith, Bird to Susan Garner, Sept. 10, 1819.
Smith, Charles to Oney Smith, July 31, 1834. Surety,
Wm. D. Rowton.
Smith, Charles G. O. to Susan T. May, Jan. 9, 1837.
Smith, Cunningham to Sarah Jones, Jan. 8, 1834.
Smith, Daniel to Mary Summers, Oct. 7, 1829. Surety,
Jesse McDowel.
Smith, Daniel to Locky McAdoo, Dec. 3, 1836. Surety,
Nelson Doak.
Smith, Eli to Elizabeth Etter, Dec. 13, 1818.
Smith, George W. to Martha M. Morton, Dec. 16, 1835.
Surety, Levi B. White.
Smith, Griffith to Nancy Myers, July 27, 1818. Surety,
John Jones.
Smith, Isham to Jane Stevenson, Oct. 21, 1815. Surety,
John Stevenson.
Smith, James to Anne Curlee, Aug. 29, 1821.
Smith, James to Patsey Vickery, Aug. 3, 1838. Surety,
John Moore.
Smith, James to Patsey Summer, March 7, 1835. Surety,
Jacob Tyler.
Smith, James to Delaney Tyler, March 9, 1822.
Smith, James H. to Talitha Jacobs, Jan. 16, 1836.
Smith, James S. to Susan C. Tucker, Aug. 10, 1830.
Surety, William Bennett.
Smith, John to Patience Perry, Sept. 4, 1822.
Smith, John to Francis Brown, Dec. 27, 1828.
Smith, John to Elizabeth Sims, April 26, 1830. Surety,
Alexander W. Smith.

Smith, John to Sarah McCulloch, June 6, 1833. Surety, Anderson Ott.
Smith, John P. to Frances L. Sims, Jan. 5, 1815. Surety, William A. Liddon.
Smith, John, Jr. to Sarah S. Puckett, Dec. 10, 1828.
Smith, Josiah to Nancy Coburn, Jan. 13, 1814.
Smith, Joseph to Elizabeth Thweate, May 15, 1809. Surety, John Smith.
Smith, Larkin to Nancy Mooney, Feb. 20, 1823. Surety, Wm. Hubbard.
Smith, Matthew to Amelia Floyd, May 31, 1827. Surety, Edmund Penn.
Smith, Meredith to Elizabeth Tucker, March 14, 1817.
Smith, Millington to Mary G. Gardner, Jan. 1, 1834. Surety, Chastain Coleman.
Smith, Nimrod to Margaret Moody, Oct. 17, 1820.
Smith, Noah to Rebecca Watson, April 25, 1835. Surety, Benjamine C. James.
Smith, Richard W. F. to Esther Sherwood, Oct. 7, 1823. Surety, Samuel Baxter.
Smith, Robert D. to Eliza English, March 25, 1834. Surety, Littleberry.
Smith, Samuel to Isabel Bradley, Oct. 23, 1822.
Smith, Thomas to Margaret D. Graves, July 18, 1810. Surety, Thomas C. Vaughan.
Smith, Thomas to Martha Ann Howerton, March 18, 1834. Surety, Richard Fields.
Smith, Thomas B. to Temperance W. Bass, March 26, 1810. Surety, Jno. B. Hogg.
Smith, Thos. Washington to Sarah M. Ivy, March 25, 1835. Surety, David Philips.
Smith, William to Cicily M. Morton, July 21, 1825.
Smith, William to Lucinda Nivins, Jan. 20, 1825.
Smith, William to Mary Elliott, Dec. 22, 1830. Surety, John W. Arnold.
Smith, William H. to United America Smith, April 24, 1816.
Smith, Wilson R. to Temperance J. Smith, May 7, 1829. Surety, Samuel Clark.
Smott, Thomas to Margaret Bogue, Sept. 16, 1823. Surety, George Brandon.
Smotherman, Abraham to Mary Williams, Sept. 18, 1827. Surety, George Comer.
Smotherman, Lewis to Mary Williams, Sept. 6, 1815. Surety, John Wood.
Smotherman, Marcus to Mary D. Moore, Oct. 19, 1835. Surety, Jas. S. Dunn.
Smotherman, Samuel to Levina Oldridge, Sept. 14, 1824. Surety, William Smotherman.
Smothers, James to Clarissa Spencer, Jan. 15, 1829.
Smothers, John to Mima Ridley, March 18, 1836. Surety, Moses G. Reeves.
Smothers, Thomas F. to Sarah White, Nov. 13, 1830. Surety, Lawrence C. Thompson.

Sneed, Constantine P. to Susannah P. Hardeman, Feb. 12, 1825.

Sneed, William H. to Sarah A. Rucker, Nov. 1, 1837. Surety, Geo. D. Corsthwait.

Snell, Hardy I. to Jane Woods, Nov. 15, 1827. Surety, Richard Ransom.

Snell, Roger to Martha Lawrence, Nov. 30, 1829. Surety, Richard Ransom.

Snell, William to Eliza Wade, Nov. 1, 1836. Surety, William F. Leiper.

Snell, Willis to Rebecca C. Smith, Sept. 18, 1834. Surety, Richard Ledbetter.

Soap, Isaac to Nancy Cooper, March 4, 1824. Surety, William Fortenbury.

Soap, James to Elizabeth Fowler, August 30, 1822.

Soape, Roswell to Jemima Fowler, July 21, 1835. Surety, A. E. McFerrin.

Somers, Abner to Sarah Simmons, May 14, 1827. Surety, Charles F. Lowe.

Sotherland, Claton to Polly T. Edwards, March 27, 1826.

Sowell, Wilson to Catherine Smith, Feb. 11, 1825.

Spain, Littleberry to Elizabeth Cook, July 26, 1817.

Spain, William to Transiquilla Flowers, June 28, 1836. Surety, William Flowers.

Spann, Bird to Sarah McCrary, Oct. 4, 1837. Surety, Richard Spann.

Spann, William to Mary P. Delbridge, July 30, 1836. Surety, Thomas G. Vaughan.

Sparrow, John to Catherine Lassater, Sept. 1, 1821.

Spence, John to Elizabeth Spence, Sept. 16, 1834. Surety, Wm. F. Leiper.

Spence, Joseph to Mary Ann Fears, Dec. 3, 1833. Surety, Oben Fears.

Spence, Samuel to Martha Anglin, Nov. 19, 1833. Surety, O. B. Fears.

Spencer, Thos. H. to Martha Barksdale, March 9, 1824. Surety, John B. Morris.

Sperry, Lewis to Sarah C. Wade, Dec. 12, 1827. Surety, Peter Campbell.

Springer, John to Sarah West, Feb. 26, 1829. Surety, Thos. A. Sikes.

Stacy, Aaron to Mary Person, Sept. 29, 1824. Surety, Daniel Peerson.

Stacy, Benedict to Elizabeth Gray, July 1, 1835.

Stafford, John to Jemima Hoover, Dec. 15, 1835. Surety, Leruer B. Blair.

Stanley, John to Mary Ann Sailors, July 7, 1818. Surety, John Saylors.

Stanley, John to Elizabeth Posey, March 17, 1829. Surety, Wm. H. Blanton.

Stansil, Harvey to Wealthy Smith, Feb. 15, 1813.

State, James A. to Catherine Smith, Oct. 6, 1818.

Statham, John G. to Mary Jane Stovall, May 16, 1822.

Statham, William P. to Sarah Tatum, Sept. 22, 1829. Surety, William H. Statham.

RUTHERFORD COUNTY MARRIAGES

Stattler, Samuel to Nancy R. Lillard, Sept. 20, 1837.
   Surety, Wm. H. Hallyburton.
Stegall, Elijah to Jane Cunningham, Nov. 3, 1818.
   Surety, Joshua Elder.
Stegall, Obediah G. to Mary Hodge, Oct. 8, 1830.
   Surety, Henry Potts.
Stegar, Francis to Nancy Thomas, March 12, 1834.
Steger, Charles C. to Mary Smith, July 13, 1833.
   Surety, William Goodman.
Steger, William to Mary Neel, March 8, 1834. Surety,
   William Goodman.
Stephens, Aminadah to Catharine Adams, Sept. 28, 1829.
   Surety, James H. Wilson.
Stephens, Joseph D. to Isabella B. Wright, Nov. 17,
   1829. Surety, James L. Porter.
Stevens, Sampson to Maduci E. Dickson, Dec. 28, 1821.
Stevens, William to Betsy Holt, Sept. 26, 1820.
Stevenson, John to Christiana Roberts, Oct. 21, 1815.
   Surety, Isham Smith.
Steward, Wesley B. to Cintha A. Steward, Feb. 7, 1836.
   Surety, Edward Rowse.
Stewart, Daniel M. to Martha Montgomery, Dec. 1, 1818.
   Surety, Jonathan M. Wallace.
Stewart, James B. to Rhoda Ann Williams, Nov. 28, 1833.
   Surety, William Prim.
Stewart, John E. to Hariet N. Hancock, April 29, 1835.
   Surety, I. L. Taylor.
Stewart, Peyton to Lila Mitchell, Jan. 18, 1837.
   Surety, John Tilar.
Stewart, Presley to Jinsey Rouse, Dec. 24, 1834.
   Surety, John Rouse.
Stewart, William to Rachel Scott, May 18, 1819.
Stewart, William to Elizabeth Cook, Sept. 1, 1836.
   Surety, Austin Cook.
Still, Littleberry to Elizabeth Babbett, Nov. 12, 1819.
Stinson, Green to Malinda Jane Perry, June 29, 1833.
   Surety, William Owen.
Stockird, Absolom to Nancy Ward, Jan. 1, 1834.
Stockird, James to Charlotte Billingsley, March 28,
   1804. Surety, John Norman.
Stokes, Sterling to Jane Johnson, June 24, 1809.
   Surety, Burwell Featherstone.
Stokes, Thomas H. to Peggy B. Porterfield, Jan. 21,
   1824.
Stokes, William to Margaret Wheeler, July 14, 1827.
   Surety, Moses G. Reeves.
Stovall, Jesse C. to Sarah Oaks, Nov. 10, 1835. Surety,
   Francis A. Youree.
Stovall, John A. to Susan Ferguson, May 24, 1822.
Stovall, Patten A. to Sarah Ann Bynum, April 6, 1825.
   Surety, William M. Knox.
Stovall, Samuel to Catherine Pendleton, Aug. 23, 1823.
Stovall, William P. to Mary P. McFerrin, Feb. 19, 1822.

Strong, Francis to Elizabeth Hearn, July 27, 1833.
Surety, William T. Brothers.
Strong, Nelson to Winifred Fan., Aug. 13, 1827.
Surety, Edmund Arnold.
Strong, William S. to Jerusha M. Clark, Nov. 22, 1827.
Surety, Samuel Vest.
Stroop, John to Mary E. Fathara, Sept. 17, 1821.
Strother, John to Elizabeth Matthews, Dec. 4, 1816.
Strother, Robert to Hannah Alrid, Sept. 22, 1811.
Surety, John Neely.
Stroud, John W. to Mary Ann Good, Sept. 13, 1836.
Surety, William A. Dunn.
Stroud, Thomas to Mary Gum, May 17, 1818. Surety,
Henry D. McBroom.
Stuart, Samuel T. to Lucretia Holleck, Jan. 26, 1824.
Sturdivant, John to Melinda Forgy, Jan. 28, 1804.
Surety, Thomas Bedford.
Sublett, George A. to Elizabeth M. Ledbetter, May 29,
1821.
Sublett, William to Ann Robertson, Dec. 7, 1821.
Sublett, William to Esther Smith, Nov. 14, 1835.
Surety, Martin Edwards.
Sugg, Aquilla to Mary Gentry, Dec. 20, 1834. Surety,
Samuel Gentry.
Sugg, John H. to Elizabeth Brothers, Sept. 11, 1815.
Surety, Peter Arnold.
Sugg, Thomas to Jane Ramsey, Aug. 13, 1816.
Sullivan, James to Jane Warren, Feb. 15, 1831.
Sullivan, Jesse to Susannah Howell, July 25, 1829.
Surety, Oliver W. Crutchfield.
Sullivan, Robert to Phebe Elrod, Aug. 16, 1822.
Sullivant, John to Rachel Rushing, Jan. 27, 1820.
Summerall, Henry to Manerva Day, Sept. 9, 1820.
Summers, Alfred to Lucinda Summers, March 29, 1826.
Summers, David to Martha Jones, Sept. 25, 1833.
Summers, George to Sally Jacobs, Nov. 16, 1815.
Surety, Reubin Todd.
Summers, James Ira to Sarah Todd, Aug. 21, 1834.
Surety, Benjamine Todd.
Summers, John to Jane Hayes, Nov. 1, 1837. Surety,
Epenitus Carlock.
Summers, Lewis to Ruthy Hogshead, Dec. 2, 1817.
Sutherland, James to Jincy Erwin, June 15, 1818.
Sutherland, Jesse to Cuzi Huring, June 29, 1831.
Suttle, Ellis to Martha Jane Overall, April 11, 1836.
Surety, Madison H. Alexander.
Sutton, Elisha to Mary Barr, Dec. 29, 1829. Surety,
Dan'l Coggins.
Sutton, Lemuel to Anne W. Thomas, July 14, 1823.
Swan, George D. to Sarah Gillespie, Nov. 18, 1819.
Sweet, David to Elizabeth Beshield, Dec. 14, 1831.
Swink, Michael to Rebecca Bivins, July 13, 1818.
Surety, Jesse Thompson.

Swope, Roseow (Roscow) to Zineby Fowler, Sept. 30, 1829.
Surety, Thomas Faulkenbury.
Tabour, John to Unice Bullard, July 29, 1824. Surety,
William Wells.
Tailor, John to Martha Richardson, Dec. 3, 1827. Surety,
Paiton H. Coats.
Tally, Newman to Zena Carter, Oct. 11, 1809.
Tally, Pleasant to Amelia Bishop, Oct. 20, 1823.
Surety, John Noland.
Tarpley, Edward to Peggy Davis, Nov. 9, 1816.
Tarpley, James A. to Charlotte Dement, Dec. 7, 1821.
Tarver, Nelson to Parthena A. Mason, Dec. 17, 1827.
Surety, Abner B. Currey.
Tatum, Jesse M. to Martha J. W. Austin, Dec. 23, 1834.
Surety, Jacob T. Taylor.
Tatum, John B. to Sarah B. Morris, Feb. 2, 1836.
Surety, Absolom Tatum.
Tatum, Luke to Elizabeth Walker, Jan. 27, 1820.
Tatum, Marcus to Mary Tatum, April 15, 1823. Surety,
David Tatum.
Tatum, William to Mary Statham, Jan. 10, 1824.
Taylor, Aaron to Martha Daniel, Sept. 17, 1816.
Taylor, David to Rachael Witherspoon, March 11, 1833.
Surety, Robert Shepard.
Taylor, James to Mary Mullins, Sept. 22, 1835. Surety,
William Hooker.
Taylor, James J. to Eliza L. Vinson, Jan. 27, 1837.
Surety, William K. Ransom.
Taylor, James R. to Elizabeth Barton, Jan. 2, 1827.
Surety, Benjamine Rucks.
Taylor, Jesse to Caty Holt, July 30, 1816.
Taylor, Jesse to Lydia Williams, July 20, 1819.
Taylor, John to Jane Wrather, June 19, 1837. Surety,
Alfred Elliott.
Taylor, John D. to Mary Pybas, Nov. 17, 1829. Surety,
Adin Taylor.
Taylor, Josiah to Sophia Zachy (Zachry), May 31, 1827.
Surety, James H. Blakely.
Taylor, Josiah R. to Elizabeth Blakeley, Sept. 24, 1822.
Taylor, Lewis to Tabitha Beesley, March 3, 1823.
Surety, Charles Niles.
Taylor, Michael to Jane Smith, May 2, 1810. Surety,
Thomas Carlton.
Taylor, Nehemiah to Rebecca Freeman, June 14, 1827.
Surety, William Hearn.
Taylor, Powell to Ann Post, Aug. 18, 1826. Surety,
Wyat H. Ellis.
Taylor, Robert to Permelia Ann Buckner, Sept. 17, 1827.
Surety, John Frazier.
Taylor, Robert to Catherine Vernon, Nov. 29, 1824.
Surety, Thomas Michael.
Taylor, Vincent to Mary R. Puckett, Dec. 11, 1820.
Taylor, William to Ann Parker, Jan. 21, 1824. Surety,
Henry Crouse.

Teague, John to Sarah Sutton, Sept. 20, 1835. Surety, Elijah Stevens.
Teal, James to Elizabeth Barber, Jan. 30, 1827. Surety, William Barber.
Tear, Richard V. to Susan Vaughan, April 4, 1817.
Tear, Richard V. to Elizabeth Dunnagin, Aug. 5, 1833. Surety, A. J. Hoover.
Tedder, William to Mary K. Church, Sept. 29, 1834. Surety, David Travis.
Teeter, Stout to Minerva Edwards, Oct. 31, 1829. Surety, Samuel Statler.
Tenison, Rutherford to Rody Whitfield, Dec. 17, 1822. Surety, George Brandon.
Tenning, William A. to Ann Wade, Nov. 18, 1817. Surety, William Mitchell.
Tennison, Abraham to Mildred Caraghan, March 17, 1824. Surety, Archibald Tennison.
Tennison, Martin to Peggy Bell, May 11, 1824. Surety, Archibald Tennison.
Tharp, James to Sarah Hutcherson, Dec. 9, 1824. Surety, Ebenezer MacGowan.
Thomas, Edward to Frances Atkinson, April 16, 1827. Surety, Moses G. Reeves.
Thomas, Henry to Sarah McKee, Aug. 11, 1827. Surety, Daniel McKee.
Thomas, Jacob to Mary M. Donald, Sept. 3, 1813.
Thomas, John F. to Cintha Orr, Sept. 15, 1829. Surety, Robert Orr.
Thomas, Peter to Esther Jane Lester, Feb. 13, 1830. Surety, James L. Young.
Thomas, Thomas to Sally Eads, Oct. 20, 1821.
Thomas, William to Harriet Keys, March 15, 1817.
Thomas, William to Mary Dill, June 9, 1834. Surety, John McKinley.
Thomas, Wilson to Solina A. Oliver, May 8, 1834. Surety, Peter Campbell.
Thomas, Wilson B. to Sarah Vance, April 24, 1819.
Thompson, Henry D. to Susan Smith, Jan. 31, 1816.
Thompson, Jacob to Temperance B. Crawford, March 1, 1817. Surety, Alfred Blackman.
Thompson, James to Avey Ward, Feb. 23, 1824. Surety, Samuel Nelson.
Thompson, James A. to Eleanor C. Manus, Oct. 8, 1834. Surety, W. W. Masterson.
Thompson, Jesse to Patience Carr, Aug. 9, 1821.
Thompson, John to Polly Snell, Aug. 11, 1804. Surety, Joseph Thompson.
Thompson, John to Rebecca Thompson, Oct. 6, 1834. Surety, Wm. M. Yearwood.
Thompson, Joseph to Mary Thompson, Dec. 17, 1804. Surety, Joseph Williams.
Thompson, Joseph to Letha Pulley, Jan. 26, 1810.
Thompson, Lawrence C. to Elizabeth Ransom, Jan. 11, 1830. Surety, Richard Ransom.

Thompson, Mansfield to Charity Banks, Dec. 6, 1824.
Thompson, Orville to Tabitha Powell, Nov. 26, 1823.
Surety, John McKinley.
Thompson, Robert to Anne Banks, Nov. 11, 1824. Surety,
William Thompson.
Thompson, Robert C. to Elizabeth G. Henderson, May 16,
1820.
Thompson, Sam'l C. to Louisa Henderson, Aug. 28, 1834.
Surety, Matthew Gray.
Thompson, Wilie B. to Elizabeth Collier, Jan. 9, 1837.
Surety, John Sanford.
Thompson, William L. to Martha Johns, April 4, 1828.
Threet, Henry to Elizabeth Wright, Dec. 26, 1827.
Surety, Robert S. Morris.
Thresher, George to Nancy Felker, Sept. 15, 1824.
Thorn, William to Eliza Jones, Nov. 11, 1830. Surety,
John Robertson.
Thornton, John to Patience Pinson, Nov. 19, 1822.
Thurman, Benjamine to Malinda Perry, Sept. 14, 1829.
Surety, Willie D. Manning.
Thurman, Benjamine to Nancy Ann Brothers, Jan. 22, 1834.
Surety, Wm. G. Parrish.
Thurman, Berry to Willy Ann Davis, Oct. 4, 1817.
Surety, Lewis Davis.
Thurman, Hollis to Elizabeth Carter, Sept. 14, 1835.
Surety, James G. Wooten.
Thurman, Wiley to Elizabeth Lee, Dec. 31, 1829. Surety,
Albian Lowry.
Tilford, James M. to Margaret H. Dickson, Jan. 7, 1819.
Tilman, Benjamine to Julia Scott, March 23, 1810.
Surety, Patton Anderson.
Tippet, John to Nelly Sawyers, Feb. 12, 1818. Surety,
James Sawyers.
Tippett, Richard to Rebecca Thomas, March 25, 1825.
Surety, William Holden.
Todd, Benjamine to Elvira Summers, Nov. 11, 1834.
Surety, Hiram Todd.
Todd, Hiram to Rachel Lusk, Feb. 4, 1835. Surety, Asa
Todd.
Todd, James to Mary Russell, Sept. 7, 1835. Surety,
James A. Good.
Todd, Jefferson to Mary Simmons, Sept. 11, 1835.
Surety, Abner Simmons.
Todd, Pinkney to Synthia Todd, Oct. 3, 1835. Surety,
James L. Berry.
Todd, Reuben to Jemima Todd, April 11, 1827. Surety,
Samuel Lusk.
Todd, William to Eda A. Todd, March 8, 1836. Surety,
Ephraim Nesbitt.
Tompkins, Silas to Cinthy Parks, Oct. 10, 1818. Surety,
John Allen.
Toombs, Hardin to Elizabeth Coleman, May 5, 1833.
Surety, Francis Coleman.
Tooms, Manuel to Sarah Pettypool, April 30, 1816.

Tooms, William to Elizabeth Foster, Dec. 14, 1836.
Surety, Harden Tooms.
Trail, Young to Katherine Rhodes, June 19, 1819.
Travers, Daniel, Junr. to Rhody Gibson, March 20, 1804.
Surety, Daniel Travers, Sr.
Travis, Amos to Gaither Milley, Sept. 19, 1829. Surety,
Barton S. Travis.
Travis, Arthur to Elizabeth Higgenbotham, Nov. 3, 1823.
Surety, James Montgomery.
Travis, Milus to Synthia Wharry, Sept. 20, 1820.
Travis, Solomon to Jane Hoyle, Oct. 12, 1818.
Traylor, Isham to Mary Crosthwait, Feb. 29, 1836.
Surety, Robert S. Morris.
Traylor, Peter to Lucy Jones, Dec. 30, 1834. Surety,
A. Rankin.
Trollinger, Joseph to Susanna Plummer, May 22, 1816.
Trott, Henry, Jr. to Laura E. Laughlin, Aug. 3, 1830.
True, David H. to Nelly Glass Cock, March 27, 1817.
Surety, John Hewitt.
Tucker, Beverly to Dicy Tooms, Jan. 4, 1836. Surety,
Harden Tooms.
Tucker, Silas to Elmira F. C. Bowman, June 7, 1836.
Surety, Sam'l H. Hodge.
Tucker, Silas to Malissa A. Bowman, Oct. 14, 1829.
Surety, John R. Wilson.
Tucker, Thomas to Nancy Nance, Nov. 26, 1833. Surety,
Spencer Hazlett.
Tumline, Humphrey to Euphraima Nichols, April 8, 1805.
Surety, Wm. Orman.
Tune, Daniel N. to Jane Mullins, Oct. 16, 1837. Surety,
John Mullins.
Turentine, James to S. Thompson, Sept. 12, 1822.
Turner, William W. to Frances Anne Vaughan, Feb. 21,
1829. Surety, William Vaughan.
Turpin, John H. to Charlotte C. Ward, July 23, 1821.
Tyler, Elias to Anne Yearwood, May 25, 1824. Surety,
James Yearwood.
Tyrone, Adam to Elizabeth Smith, Dec. 24, 1814. Surety,
R. W. Cunningham.
Underwood, Anthony to Elizabeth Wright, Nov. 26, 1824.
Surety, William Hill.
Underwood, Claiborn to Nancy Dunn, Aug. 11, 1835.
Surety, Admiral Blackman.
Underwood, Elisha to Jane Thorne, May 10, 1831.
Underwood, James to Martha Ann Rowland, Sept. 5, 1834.
Surety, Martin Clark.
Underwood, John to Mary Anne Matthews, April 11, 1830.
Surety, Abel Underwood.
Underwood, Matthew to Jane Rowland, Oct. 17, 1836.
Surety, William Smotherman.
Underwood, William to Mary Dunn, April 19, 1817. Surety,
Throneberry Holt.
Urby, Harrison to Sisan Mason, Sept. 28, 1818. Surety,
William Reurs.
Usselton, George to Catherine Hoover, Aug. 5, 1822.

Vaden, Lemuel to Delaney Ward, Sept. 22, 1827. Surety,
Allen Blankenship.
Vance, Peter to Lucy Simmons, April 1, 1818. Surety,
John Painter.
VanCleave, Isaac J. to Jane Thomas, Nov. 20, 1837.
Surety, Frederick Renshaw.
Vancleave, Stephen to Nancy Philips, Nov. 10, 1821.
Vancleif, Stephen to Elenor Phillips, Feb. 1, 1819.
Surety, Bennett Phillips.
Vardell, John T. to Rebecca Cook, Jan. 25, 1817.
Surety, Uriah Nixon.
Vardell, Thomas to Sarah Finch, Feb. 11, 1820.
Vaughn, Anderson to Louisa P. Miles, Sept. 12, 1835.
Surety, Thomas W. Miles.
Vaughan, Coleman H. to Lucinda Mullins, May 28, 1828.
Vaughan, Elisha B. to Mahala Wade, March 27, 1823.
Surety, Edward A. Cochran.
Vaughan, James to Mary Kennedy, June 19, 1824. Surety,
Jacob Payne.
Vaughan, James W. to Jemima McNeely, Dec. 1, 1825.
Vaught, John to Margaret Smith, July 14, 1834. Surety,
Joseph Dill.
Vaught, William to Mary Knox, Sept. 21, 1835. Surety,
George Vaught.
Venerable, Richard to Jane Gammill, Feb. 6, 1816.
Vickery, John M. to Louisa Heartless, Feb. 26, 1834.
Surety, Reuben Carney.
Vickery, Winright to Martha Reobertson, Jan. 9, 1821.
Vincent, John N. to Mary Roberts, May 3, 1836. Surety,
Wm. W. Nash.
Vinson, George to Caroline Trail, Dec. 22, 1829.
Surety, Greenberry Smith.
Vinson, George to Naomy Pearson, Oct. 17, 1833. Surety,
Greenberry Smith.
Vinson, Henry, Sr. to Rachel Caits, Feb. 3, 1837.
Vivrett, John B. to Mary McClain, Sept. 5, 1832.
Waddey, Geo. W. to Margaret Hill, Aug. 7, 1834. Surety,
A. M. Hamilton.
Wade, George to Frances Basey, Dec. 13, 1825.
Wade, James to Elizabeth Miller, June 10, 1806. Surety,
William Drennon.
Wade, James to Abigail Ann Wade, April 2, 1834. Surety,
Simeon Seward.
Wade, John C. to Lucinda Kimbro, Dec. 20, 1831.
Wade, John M. to Harriet Calhoun, Dec. 31, 1829.
Surety, Willis Snell.
Wade, John M. to Susanna A. Pruett, Oct. 4, 1827.
Surety, Levi Wade.
Wade, Levi to Mary A. P. Bedford, Jan. 17, 1822.
Wade, Levi to Mary Henderson, Jan. 8, 1828.
Wade, Lewis to Frances Ferriss, Oct. 3, 1827. Surety,
Patrick H. Bowman.
Wade, Mordecai B. to Martha Ann Campbell, Nov. 24, 1835.
Surety, Jas. W. Nelson.

Wade, Noah to Rachael Wade, Oct. 17, 1820.
Walker, Bird B. to Louisa Taylor, Nov. 17, 1834.
  Surety, Leonard Taylor.
Walker, Ephraim to Martha McDowell, Dec. 11, 1820.
Walker, George to Sarah T. Kellough, Nov. 11, 1837.
Walker, Pleasant H. to Susan Lane, May 25, 1824.
  Surety, James Sharpe.
Walkup, James to Levivey Tennison, Jan. 2, 1824.
Walkup, Robert to Nancy Neely, Aug. 20, 1827. Surety,
  John Renshaw.
Wall, Henry M. to Susannah Higdon, July 22, 1823.
  Surety, Andrew Higdon.
Wallace, Jackson to Mary Bradley, Sept. 2, 1829.
  Surety, James W. Stewart.
Wallace, John to Jane Davis, Feb. 26, 1822.
Wallace, Jonathan to Louise Hickinbottom, May 13, 1816.
Wallace, Jonathan M. to Sarah Thorn, Aug. 28, 1820.
Wallace, Joseph to Charlotte Martin, Dec. 30, 1825.
Wallace, Joseph to Mary Wallace, Nov. 16, 1835. Surety,
  Jackson Wallace.
Wallace, Samuel to Kesiah Hardcastle, Aug. 1, 1816.
Waller, Edward to Matilda C. Calton, Feb. 17, 1824.
Wallis, Amos S. to Martha Penn, June 11, 1825.
Wallis, William P. to Nancy Stone, Dec. 5, 1827.
  Surety, Spencer Thomason.
Walls, Simeon D. to Eliza J. Carr, Dec. 27, 1836.
  Surety, John P. Smith.
Walpool, William E. to Rebecca S. James, Dec. 2, 1823.
  Surety, Wm. J. Phillips.
Walters, William to Sally Saunders, Oct. 29, 1821.
Walton, Charles H. to Elizabeth R. Phillips, Dec. 15,
  1826.
Ward, Austin to Eliza Walpole, July 25, 1829. Surety,
  Thomas Gregory.
Ward, Best to Casandra McClanahan, Aug. 6, 1833.
  Surety, Simeon Taylor.
Ward, Burwell to Mary McClanahan, Jan. 21, 1822.
Ward, Ezekiel to Louisa Furgerson, May 15, 1837.
  Surety, George Nash.
Ward, Henry to Polly Pitt, Oct. 24, 1818. Surety,
  Matthew Pitt.
Ward, Jesse to Rebecca Dobson, Dec. 18, 1823.
Ward, John to Polly Read, Sept. 2, 1826.
Ward, Thomas C. to Sarah A. Stone, July 11, 1836.
  Surety, Thomas E. Spain.
Ward, Thomas S. to Harriet Reed, Aug. 30, 1825.
Ward, William to Polly Roberson, Oct. 24, 1812.
Warnick, John to Abigail Montgomery, Sept. 24, 1827.
  Surety, John Blankenship.
Warren, Benjamine to Elizabeth Mosby, April 23, 1837.
  Surety, Geo. W. Lillard.
Warren, Burrell to Elizabeth Nance, Aug. 24, 1816.
Warren, Enoch to Susan Broiles, Oct. 24, 1836. Surety,
  John Mankin.

Warren, George E. to Eddy Thompson, Oct. 2, 1823.
Surety, John Thompson.
Warren, Jeremiah to Elizabeth Williams, Nov. 28, 1817.
Surety, John Williams.
Warren, John to Susan Hill, April 13, 1827. Surety,
Jesse Garner.
Warren, Nathaniel to Nancy Newman, Sept. 4, 1810.
Surety, Enoch Arnold.
Warren, Peterson G. to Elizabeth Pybas, Dec. 7, 1832.
Warren, Robert to Sarah Osborne, Nov. 14, 1835. Surety,
R. Peak.
Warren, Thomas to Mary O. Clark, Oct. 12, 1835. Surety,
William D. Clark.
Warren, William to Elizabeth Nance, July 22, 1819.
Warren, William M. to Elizabeth Hooker, Nov. 28, 1829.
Surety, Joshua T. Hill.
Wasson, John to Nicey Posey, Dec. 7, 1833. Surety,
Alexander Nisbett.
Wasson, Richard P. to Elizabeth Bellah, May 21, 1836.
Watkins, Isaiah to Mary Jane Gilliman, Feb. 7, 1817.
Surety, Henry Reed.
Watkins, Joseph to Nancy Robertson, Sept. 2, 1829.
Surety, William H. Bowman.
Watkins, Joseph M. to Lavinia Sharpe, Jan. 22, 1833.
Surety, Andrew J. Hoover.
Watkins, Thos. G. to Mary Nelson, March 10, 1818.
Surety, John R. Laughlin.
Watkins, Wilson L. to Caroline Wade, Dec. 24, 1833.
Surety, Benj. Marable.
Watson, David H. to Nancy D. James, Jan. 25, 1833.
Surety, William R. James.
Watson, Merida to Amelia Asby, Sept. 22, 1834. Surety,
J. R. Robinson.
Watson, Wilkins W. to Elizabeth M. Kite, May 25, 1837.
Surety, N. B. Hamilton.
Weakley, William to Peggy Stoe, June 22, 1820.
Weatherly, James M. to Mary A. E. M. Batey, Aug. 3, 1837.
Surety, Stephen D. Watkins.
Weaver, Adam to Jane Robertson, Nov. 24, 1836. Surety,
Robert S. Morris.
Weaver, David to Mary Taylor, Dec. 16, 1834. Surety,
John D. Gilmore.
Weaver, William to Lucinda Austin, Sept. 9, 1835.
Surety, Peter Arnold.
Webb, Aaron to Mary Owen, Jan. 27, 1823. Surety, Hugh
Webb.
Webb, Greenberry to Pamelia Heflin, Jan. 15, 1830.
Surety, William McKay.
Webb, Isaiah to Franky May, Nov. 16, 1818. Surety,
Aden Webb.
Webb, Wesley to Sarah Lloyd, Dec. 17, 1834. Surety,
Willie Snell.
Webber, Benjamine to Jane G. Mosely, Dec. 31, 1823.

Welborn, John C. to Lucy Donnelly, Jan. 16, 1836.
Surety, Moses G. Reeves.
Welch, John to Mildred Ann Barksdale, Oct. 23, 1830.
Surety, Ambrose B. Niper.
Welch, Nicholas to Martha Johnson, Nov. 29, 1824.
Welch, William M. to Mary C. Smith, Jan. 16, 1836.
Surety, Alvin Smith.
Welcher, Charles to Caroline Mitchell, Sept. 2, 1836.
Surety, H. Yoakum.
Wendel, David D. to Sarah Keeble, Dec. 19, 1837.
Surety, Thomas E. Taylor.
Wendel, Thomas N. to Mary Ann Hancock, Oct. 4, 1836.
Surety, George D. Crosthwait.
West, Amos to Nancy Nash, Jan. 2, 1837. Surety, William
W. Nash.
West, Andy N. to Polly Harris, Nov. 30, 1818. Surety,
Allsea Harris.
West, George to Penelope D. Estes, Feb. 18, 1835.
Surety, David M. Estes.
West, John to Eliza Maryweathers, July 26, 1830.
Surety, Obid Ramsey.
Wharey, John to Elizabeth Spear, June 3, 1809. Surety,
John Spence.
Wharry, Jonathan to Jane Walkup, March 24, 1820.
Wharton, Nelson to Perlina Stovall, May 23, 1837.
Surety, Allsea Harris.
Wheeler, Henry to Peggy Barnett, Nov. 16, 1815. Surety,
Samuel Gray.
Wheeler, James to Martha Cruse, Jan. 25, 1818. Surety,
William Rucker.
Wheeler, James to Peggy (Margaret) Mayberry, June 24,
1818. Surety, Samuel Smith.
White, B. F. to Rebecca Johnston, Aug. 5, 1823.
Surety, A. H. White.
White, Burrell G. to Elizabeth Miller, April 6, 1833.
Surety, J. C. Wilburn.
White, Henry to Lucy Searcy, Dec. 1, 1832.
White, Richard H. to Mildred F. Nelson, Oct. 23, 1834.
Surety, Henry White.
White, Robert to Malinda Lowe, Feb. 8, 1825.
White, Robert M. to Nancy Benton, April 11, 1805.
Surety, Henry White.
White, Stephen F. to Hannah H. Dickson, June 23, 1814.
Whitehead, Charles to Malinda Erwin, Jan. 15, 1820.
Whitfield, Benjamine to Elizabeth Herrod, July 5, 1827.
Surety, John Espey.
Whitfield, Matthew to Fanny R. Manahan, July 30, 1834.
Surety, Eli. Whitfield.
Whitfield, Thomas G. to Melinda Guiley, Dec. 31, 1825.
Whitfield, Willis to Alementer Rhodes, July 25, 1825.
Whithorne, Thomas to Polly Hampton, Sept. 21, 1818.
Surety, James Hampton.
Whitmore, William to Mary Gilly, Oct. 14, 1818. Surety,
Matthew Patton.

RUTHERFORD COUNTY MARRIAGES

Whitsett, Thomas to Jane Collins, Sept. 9, 1812.
Wiggs, Henry to Anne Epps, Jan. 7, 1830. Surety,
Norman Norton.
Wilcox, Hezekiah to Susannah Chism, Sept. 10, 1821.
Wildy, James A. to Jane W. Daughtry, Nov. 29, 1827.
Surety, Moses G. Reeves.
Wiley, Henry to Sally P. Trott, Feb. 26, 1829. Surety,
V. M. Sublett.
Wilkinson, Edward C. to Diana Mayfield, Jan. 8, 1833.
Surety, Edward A. Keeble.
Wilkinson, Hubbard S. to Adaline W. Howse, Dec. 10, 1832.
Williams, David to Julia Ann Anderson, March 19, 1827.
Surety, Joseph C. Dobson.
Williams, Gabriel to Mary Lewis, Aug. 16, 1829. Surety,
Isaac Alley.
Williams, Henry C. to Elizabeth L. James, Feb. 9, 1829.
Surety, James Crichlow.
Williams, Isaac to Wiggy Walkup, July 15, 1816.
Williams, James to Lavinea Evans, Sept. 6, 1834. Surety,
Martin Crocker.
Williams, James to Phebe Spence, June 11, 1836.
Williams, James to Tempy Whitfield, Aug. 18, 1818.
Surety, Robert Fagan.
Williams, Jason to Mary Parker, Sept. 5, 1817. Surety,
Bryant Hare.
Williams, Jesse to Rachel Tucker, Jan. 6, 1806. Surety,
Wm. Smith.
Williams, John to Susannah Teal, Dec. 12, 1829. Surety,
Squire Long.
Williams, John to Mary Bishop, Dec. 26, 1827. Surety,
Samuel Williford.
Williams John H. to Martha Green, Dec. 9, 1831.
Williams, Lewellen to Martha Beesley, July 21, 1834.
Surety, John J. Polk.
Williams, Loderick to Shady Lockhart, July 30, 1834.
Surety, Jesse Perkins.
Williams, Richard to Sarah Owen, Oct. 11, 1830. Surety,
Alenbert Crocker.
Williams, Robert to Elizabeth Beesley, Aug. 26, 1825.
Williams, Samuel M. to Lucretia Lockhard, Feb. 17, 1835.
Surety, Lorenzo D. Young.
Williams, Thomas to Martha J. Gambill, May 17, 1829.
Surety, James S. Smith.
Williams, William to Milly Brookshire, March 30, 1816.
Williams, William to Vesty Holden, Feb. 27, 1836.
Surety, John Evans.
Williams, William to Zelphy Lester, Jan. 13, 1836.
Surety, Jesse Williams.
Williams, William L. to Polly Alsup, Feb. 10, 1820.
Williamson, Bowling to Sally Nichols, Nov. 14, 1815.
Surety, Samuel Hill.
Williamson, Geo. W. to Edna Dejernett, Dec. 30, 1829.
Surety, Alexander McCullough.
Williamson, Henry C. to Elizabeth L. James, Feb. 9, 1829.
Surety, James Crichlow.

Williamson, Richard to Elizabeth Posey, April 16, 1827.
Surety, Lewis Noland.
Williamson, Robert to Elizabeth Uselton, April 19, 1836.
Surety, David Lyon.
Williford, Samuel to Mary Northcutt, June 1, 1821.
Willis, Willis to Temperance Whitfield, Nov. 29, 1821.
Wilson, Aron to Hannah Martin, March 13, 1812.
Wilson, Benjamine F. to Elizabeth A. Hooper, April 13,
  1837. Surety, John McKinley.
Wilson, David S. to Louisa Elliott, May 17, 1829.
Surety, Simon Elliott.
Wilson, Henry to Martha J. Brumfield, Jan. 8, 1824.
Wilson, James to Elizabeth Kelton, Oct. 31, 1821.
Wilson, John R. to Eliza P. Black, Oct. 20, 1825.
Wilson, Josiah L. to Rachel G. Cox, Feb. 8, 1827.
Surety, William Cox.
Wilson, Samuel to Ann Heart, Dec. 26, 1805. Surety,
  Wm. Tucker.
Wilson, Samuel to Martha Sharpe, Nov. 27, 1815. Surety,
  William Sharpe.
Wilson, Samuel S. to Eliza C. Keys, Jan. 19, 1822.
Wilson, William to Jane McHenry, Nov. 10, 1816.
Wills, George to Sarah Shackleford, March 19, 1825.
Willis, James B. to Anny W. Shackleford, Jan. 3, 1810.
Surety, Benjamine W. Lane.
Windrow, Byars to Jane W. Traylor, Jan. 8, 1836. Surety,
  Matthew McDowell.
Winfrey, George to Nelly Beverly, Oct. 19, 1813.
Winfrey, Henry to Susan Mayo, Sept. 11, 1837. Surety,
  John A. Felker.
Winfrey, James to Milkey Smothers, July 29, 1830.
Surety, William Thrasher.
Winsett, Harley to Matilda Brown, Dec. 3, 1833.
Surety, Amos Winsett.
Winston, Anthony to Priscilla Harris, Aug. 7, 1823.
Surety, Andrew Cummins.
Witherspoon, Thos. A. to Rachel E. Youree, Feb. 25,
  1833. Surety, Samuel McKnight.
Witherspoon, William to Margaret Davis, Nov. 30, 1821.
Witherspoon, Winphrey to Mary Orr, Jan. 26, 1827.
Surety, Samuel H. Andrews.
Witherspoon, Wimphrey to Susan Thompson, Dec. 9, 1837.
Surety, N. G. Murphey.
Womack, Michael to Judah T. Rutledge, Oct. 19, 1825.
Wood, David S. to Cynthia Ann Webb, Sept. 19, 1829.
Surety, Hugh S. Webb.
Wood, Drury to Matilda Vanphat, Oct. 9, 1827. Surety,
  Jackson Wallace.
Wood, James to Mary Nevins, Oct. 7, 1824. Surety,
  Thomas Tarpley.
Wood, John to Elizabeth Brasher (Brashear), May 9, 1823.
Surety, John L. Jetton.
Wood, John H. (of Warren) to Roxannah P. Sutton, June
  15, 1827. Surety, Edward Fisher.

Wood, John J. to Dorothy Hoskins, Aug. 26, 1833.
Surety, Charles A. Edwards.
Wood, William to Eliza Vaughan, Jan. 4, 1827. Surety,
Jesse Watt.
Woodfin, Samuel to Mariah Barnwell, Feb. 12, 1816.
Woodruff, Allen N. to Sarah Williams, Nov. 17, 1829.
Surety, John R. Nelson.
Woodruff, James to Sarah Perkins, Sept. 26, 1829.
Surety, Sam'l P. Braynt.
Woodrum, Stephen to Jane Smith, Dec. 8, 1823.
Woods, James B. to Margaret Finger, Oct. 12, 1829.
Surety, Dudley H. Lindsey.
Woods, John to Mary F. Jarratt, Oct. 29, 1833. Surety,
Robert S. Morris.
Wooten, William N. to Elenor Welch, Nov. 12, 1836.
Surety, James G. Wooten.
Work, John to Peggy Louisa Jetton, Aug. 11, 1825.
Wrather, Alexander B. to Jane Tarpley, Nov. 30, 1831.
Wrather, Alexander B. to Louisiana Wade, Aug. 18, 1836.
Surety, Baker Wrather.
Wrather, Baker to Sally G. Masterson, Aug. 29, 1815.
Wrather, Baker to Roxy Rowden, Dec. 2, 1816.
Wrather, Daniel to Ann Wrather, May 26, 1835. Surety,
A. B. Wrather.
Wrather, John to Martha Fletcher, May 11, 1837. Surety,
Joseph Clough.
Wrather, William to Nancy Dejearnett, Oct. 3, 1836.
Surety, John Wrather.
Wren, William to Susan Higenbotham, March 28, 1824.
Wright, Ezekiel to Sarah Dunn, Oct. 15, 1827. Surety,
William Thorn.
Wright, George to Catherine Featherston, Feb. 11, 1835.
Surety, Henry Threat.
Wright, John to Lear Dicas, Nov. 6, 1810.
Wright, Kinchin to Martha Read, April 24, 1816.
Wright, Richard to Luvicey Plummer, Jan. 26, 1822.
Wright, Thomas C. to Kesiah Hart, July 24, 1837.
Surety, William A. Ridley.
Wright, Thomas M. to Elizabeth T. Finch, Sept. 23, 1834.
Surety, Francis A. Youree.
Wright, William H. to Mary Smith, March 6, 1837. Surety,
Stephen D. Abbott.
Wynn, Washington to Jane Gillespie, Feb. 7, 1821.
Wynne, William to Elizabeth Jane Brooks, June 8, 1822.
Yager, Paschel to Margaret Cox, June 22, 1829. Surety,
Martin Clark.
Yancy, Sanford to Jane Harris, March 25, 1816.
Yandell, William M. to Catherine W. Searcy, June 28,
1827. Surety, Hugh D. Neilson.
Yardley, Thomas to Mary Cox, Nov. 10, 1829. Surety,
Jonathan W. McClary.
Yardly, Thomas to Margarett Warren, Oct. 21, 1817.
Yearwood, Aaron to Sally Webber, Dec. 29, 1821.
Yearwood, James J. to Elizabeth Pybas, Sept. 5, 1818.
Surety, Lewis B. Shipp.

Yearwood, John to Anney Pace, Aug. 25, 1824. Surety, William Pace.
Yearwood, William M. to Hannah P. Wallis, Sept. 19, 1837. Surety, Charles Ready, Jr.
Young, Alphia to Olivia D. Martin, Nov. 9, 1836. Surety, James S. Davis.
Young, Hiram to Judith L. Molloy, Nov. 25, 1835. Surety, Jos. W. Nelson.
Young, James to Nancy Sullivan, March 20, 1810. Surety, James McKey.
Young, Jesse to Dolly Williams, March 6, 1835.
Young, John to Elizabeth Han, Dec. 14, 1809. Surety, Jas. Blackledge.
Young, Lorence D. to Mary Ann Goldin, Dec. 27, 1831.
Young, Samuel to Sarah Goulding, Jan. 5, 1829.
Young, Sam'l to Nancy Lee, Aug. 10, 1823. Surety, John Simpson.
Youngblood, William to Edy Reid, Dec. 18, 1817. Surety, John Reid.
Yount (Young), Abram to Susan Rowe, Sept. 4, 1818.
Youree, Andrew H. to Anne Porter, Aug. 6, 1828.
Zachary, Caleb to Mary Zachary, May 23, 1809. Surety, Joshua Zachary.
Zachary, Godlpho (Godolpho) to Margaret Nichols, April 22, 1837. Surety, J. S. Zachary.
Zachary, Spencer to Elizabeth Zachary, March 6, 1818. Surety, James Harrison.
Zachary, Hartwell S. to Nancy C. Yandell, March 6, 1835.
Zachary, Josiah W. to Josie Zachary, March 29, 1818.

RUTHERFORD COUNTY MARRIAGES

Section 2: 1838-1840

William D. Clark and Eliza R. Kelton, Feb. 9, 1838.
William Read and Piety Adcock, Feb. 15, 1838.
James McCullough and Mary Davis, Feb. 12, 1838.
John B. Brown and Nancy Tucker, Feb. 22, 1838.
John McFarland and Jane Thomas, Feb. 18, 1838.
Richard V. Teer and Nancy Elder, Feb. 19, 1838.
William Craddock and Eliza Holmes, April 2, 1838.
John Neal and Mary May, Feb. 19, 1838.
William D. Rowton and Eliza McClure, Feb. 20, 1838.
Green Patterson and Frances Copeland, Feb. 20, 1838.
Samuel Knox and Eliza Dill, Feb. 20, 1838.
Bartlett Coulter and Marial L. Biles, Feb. 20, 1838.
William R. Philips and Edy Thompson, Feb. 22, 1838.
William Burnett and Uriah Busley, Feb. 22, 1838.
John O. Twigg and Elizabeth Newsom, Feb. 27, 1838.
James M. Roberts and Louisa Jane Conly, Feb. 28, 1838.
Admiral Blackman and Margaret Underwood, Feb. 28, 1838.
Archibald Y. Sloan and Margarett W. Jetton, Feb. 28, 1838.
Thomas Dobbins and Amanda Oden, Feb. 28, 1838.
Ezra Keyser and Sophia S. Pryor, Mar. 5, 1838.
James Wallace and Jane Todd, Mar. 7, 1838.
Archibald Hays and May Marshall, Mar. 7, 1838.
Alfred Ross and Ann C. Ridout, Mar. 7, 1838.
Robert M. White and Ann G. Braksdale, Mar. 10, 1838.
Richmond S. Fletcher and Nancy Goodloe, Mar. 15, 1838.
John N. Taylor and Nancy Thomas, Mar. 15, 1838.
Simeon Hoover and Elizabeth Elliott, Mar. 24, 1838.
Robert Daulton and Sarah A. Davenport, Mar. 26, 1838.
William Holden and Jane Marlin, Mar. 26, 1838.
George Holden and Martha Davidson, Mar. 26, 1838.
Robert S. Morris and Catherine U. Keyser, Mar. 29, 1838.
David Travis and Mary Earthman, April 4, 1838.
James G. Wooten and Serenia Pinkard, April 4, 1838.
John H. Quesenberry and Menervia Hazelett, April 7, 1838.
Thomas Marshall and Rody Ellis, April 9, 1838.
Berry Reed and Mary Wallace, April 10, 1838.
William H. Posey and Rebecca Underwood, April 11, 1838.
Ephraim A. C. Norman and Frances M. Hudson, April 12, 1838.
Elijah Goss and Sophia Smith, April 12, 1838.
Milton Lannom and Mary Griffin, April 16, 1838.
William H. Grady and Betsy A. Whitehead, April 19, 1838.
Isaac N. Oliphant and Martha A. Lane, April 26, 1838.
Bryant Hare and Giney Dennes, April 20, 1838.
John Yearwood and Elizabeth Jamison, April 20, 1838.

Thomas F. Wetherford and Jane Wallace, April 21, 1838.
Washington McPeak and Margaret Jones, April 21, 1838.
Jonathan H. Alexander and Tressy William, April 27,
1838.
William Herrill and Jane Yardly, May 4, 1838.
Joel B. Northcutt and Mary Ralph, May 10, 1838.
Patton McPeak and Mary Weatherly, May 16, 1838.
James Mitchell and Elizabeth Weatherford, May 23, 1838.
John Burnett and Ann Gregory, May 25, 1838.
Henry Mabry and Mary J. Thompson, May 29, 1838.
Samuel Fulks and Sarah Bell, June 4, 1838.
Joseph T. B. Turner and Sarah W. Jetton, June 6, 1838.
William Neal and Frances Estes, June 16, 1838.
John McGill and Margaret W. Anderson, July 2, 1838.
John W. Bobbett and Margaret J. Rose, July 7, 1838.
Thomas S. Word and Lamora Farris, July 9, 1838.
Jacob Batson and Frances Wrather, July 10, 1838.
Alfred Pierce and Harriett Alfred (Alford), July 12,
1838.
Abram M. Coleman and Sarah Yearwood, July 17, 1838.
Samuel Fulks and Sarah Bell, July 23, 1838.
William W. Moseley and Mary E. Frost, July 25, 1838.
Thomas E. Woodfin and Harriett Pattrick, Aug. 4, 1838.
John Seward and Martha J. Underwood, Aug. 7, 1838.
George Youes and Sioty Adcock, Aug. 9, 1838.
Edward F. Sanders and L. Smith, Aug. 20, 1838.
William H. Newgent and Catherine Peak, Aug. 18, 1838.
John S. Farr and Anna C. Pinkston, Aug. 24, 1838.
John W. Overall and Mary J. Woods, Aug. 24, 1838.
Alexander Landers and Nancy Vinson, Aug. 6, 1838.
Joseph McCrcken and Adaline Lorance, Aug. 25, 1838.
Isaac Mayfield and Eliza Robertson, Aug. 30, 1838.
Andrew W. Johnson and Susan F. Ellis, Sept. 4, 1838.
Isaac H. Ledbetter and Julia A. Jamison, ------, 1838.
Lewis Rawlings and Elizabeth Hoover, Sept. 5, 1838.
John McKay and Martha Auberry, Sept. 5, 1838.
Benjamine B. Pattillo and Nancy Ward, Sept. 18, 1838.
Silas M. Phelps and Mary Crutchfield, Sept. 19, 1838.
Edward Williamson and Lucretia Wade, Sept. 20, 1838.
Nathan Petty and Rebecca Coosa, Sept. 20, 1838.
John Sudberry and Sarah Wood, Sept. 24, 1838.
James Priestly and Eliza Ragsdalle, Sept. 24, 1838.
Best Ward and Sarah Ann Nevils, Sept. 25, 1838.
Jesse Brashear and Sarah Ann Brown, Sept. 25, 1838.
Fanning Coulter and Mary Mullins, Sept. 26, 1838.
James Hayes and Nancy Jarratt, Sept. 26, 1838.
William G. Woodfin and Nancy E. Davis, Oct. 1, 1838.
Larkin J. Johnson and Nancy Johnson, Oct. 2, 1838.
William Walker and Sarah W. Stephens, Oct. 5, 1838.
Franklin Knox or Knox Franklin and Eliza Brown, Oct. 6,
1838.
John Low and Christian Dunn, Oct. 8, 1838.
William J. McGregor and Eliza Evans, Oct. 11, 1838.
James McGill and Margaret C. Laurence, Oct. 15, 1838.

William H. McCabe and Margaret Ricks, Oct. 16, 1838.
William H. Lyon and Martha Sims, Oct. 17, 1838.
Benjamin Brothers and Sarah Moore, Oct. 18, 1838.
Garland Anderson and Sarah A. McFarland, Oct. 20, 1838.
James Patterson and Frances Forbes, Oct. 20, 1838.
James N. Champion and Elenor Harrison, Oct. 25, 1838.
James S. Dunn and Martha Acuff, Oct. 30, 1838.
Wiley B. Gordon and Virginia Russworm, Oct. 30, 1838.
Wright Herrild and Annis Jeregin, Nov. 2, 1838.
Thomas Thorn and Margaret A. Jones, Nov. 5, 1838.
William Summers and Isabella Youree, Nov. 8, 1838.
William Reed and Nancy Burchett, Nov. 15, 1838.
Henry F. Box and Amelia Brinkley, Nov. 16, 1838.
Nathaniel Haynes and Menervia Beesley, Nov. 18, 1838.
Thomas M. Arnold and Nancy A. Johnson, Nov. 18, 1838(?).
Abner Marlin and Nancy Blakly, Nov. 18, 1838.
James Merritt and Martha M. Sanders, Nov. 21, 1838.
Nathan W. Cochran and Alamento May, Nov. 19, 1838.
Thomas McDaniel and Martha J. McElroy, Nov. 20, 1838.
John Meredith and Mary A. Huggins, Nov. 24, 1838.
Nathaniel Newgent and Mary Shepherd, Nov. 24, 1838.
Abram D. Endsley and Mary A. Tennon, Nov. 26, 1838.
James W. McDaniel and Matilda Monday,Nov. 27, 1838.
Edward Haggard and Eliza Cooper, Nov. 27, 1838.
Elias E. Pinkard and Sarah Jones, Nov. 28, 1838.
Kendrick G. Pearson and Mary E. Flemming, Nov. 29, 1838.
Joel Farriss and Rebecca Maberry, Dec. 4, 1838.
Jesse Carter and Sarah Todd, Dec. 6, 1838.
John Johnson and Sarah Adcock, Dec. 8, 1838.
John A. Thomas and Eveline Cox, Dec. 11, 1838.
John Brothers and Nancy Pendleton, Dec. 11, 1838.
William L. Vaughan and Melissa Brock, Dec. 11, 1838.
James Odell and Syotha Watts, Dec. 12, 1838.
Alexander C. Rutledge and Louisa Carlton, Dec. 12, 1838.
Hiram H. Wood and Ann Hall, Dec. 12, 1838.
Adam Taylor and ----- Taylor, Dec. 13, 1838.
Ramsey Weatherford and Elizabeth Wallace, Dec. 15, 1838.
Alexander Orr and Jane White, Dec. 17, 1838.
William C. Claitor and Eveline R. Daniel, Dec. 19, 1838.
William Summer (free man of color) and Betsy Smith (free
  of color), Dec. 19, 1838.
Ambrose McKee and Catherine Thomas, Dec. 19, 1838.
John F. Bruce and Milly Smith, Dec. 20, 1838.
Joel T. Lee and Sarah Newsom, Dec. 22, 1838.
John W. Hoover and Julia A. McCabe, Dec. 24, 1838.
James M. Newman and Henrietta Low, Dec. 24, 1838.
Joseph Walker and Barbery Hoover, Dec. 26, 1838.
Jordan Holden and Phebe West, Dec. 27, 1838.
Clement R. Davis and Elizabeth Jones, Dec. 29, 1838.
Joseph W. Rodgers and Elizabeth W. Rodgers, Dec. 29,
  1838.
Preston Lochard and Mary Underwood, Dec. 30, 1838.
Frederick W. Nance and Margaret Shacklett, Jan. 2, 1839.
Charles C. Abanathy and Narcissa A. L. Wright, Jan. 3,
  1839.

John G. Murphey and Sarah A. Lehue, Jan. 4, 1839.
Jacob Hoobury and Mary A. Conly, Jan. 7, 1839.
William C. Lewis and Elizabeth Thompson, Jan. 7, 1839.
James Wilkinson and Rebecca Hester, Jan. 9, 1839.
Thomas Lannon and Susan Tucker, Jan. 12, 1839.
John Ross and Eliza Barker, Jan. 15, 1839.
Joseph W. Nelson and Mary E. Greaves, Jan. 16, 1839.
Jacob Whitworth and Ledy Bowes, -------- ?
George Batey and Frances B. Traylor, Jan. 21, 1839.
William Walker and Sarah Hicks, Jan. 21, 1839.
Iverson G. Smith and Elizabeth Burton, Jan. 24, 1839.
Obed Woodson and Susan Moss, Jan. 24, 1839.
Lytle Adcock and Nancy Gaines, Jan. 26, 1839.
Levi Reeves and Mary Jane Baswell, Jan. 27, 1839.
William Marlin and Rebecca Jacobs, Jan. 29, 1839.
Richard Brown and Elizabeth Thompson, Jan. 30, 1839.
Eli Tribble and Rebecca Fox, Feb. 4, 1839.
John Koonce and Emeline Parkson, Feb. 4, 1839.
John T. Neil and Carolina Coleman, Feb. 4, 1839.
Peyton Keel and Margaret E. Mayfield, Feb. 6, 1839.
Hardy Miller and Sarah Mayfield, Feb. 11, 1839.
John Wilson and Rhody Manor, Feb. 12, 1839.
William G. Barndon and Tilmesia M. Goodloe, Feb. 12, 1839.
Tudor N. Smith and Elizabeth James Tite, Feb. 13, 1839.
Edmund Rouse and Delila Watkins, Feb. 13, 1839.
Thomas A. Buford and Mary L. James, Feb. 14, 1839.
Samuel Kelton and Margaret Shapard, Feb. 19, 1839.
Geo. W. Knox and Rebecca L. Doran, Feb. 20, 1839.
E. D. Mathews and M. L. Stewart, Mar. 4, 1839.
Monroe Rutledge and Rebecca L. Crowder, Mar. 4, 1839.
Thomas Batte and Ann O. Hunter, Mar. 4, 1839.
Radford W. Read and Frances E. A. Hart, Mar. 6, 1839.
Henry Crowse and Mary Taylor, Mar. 9, 1839.
John N. Raines and Sarah Batton, Mar. 16, 1839.
Thomas C. Hayes and Mary A. Smith, Mar. 19, 1839.
Jacob S. Howberry and Mary Ann Conley, Mar. 20, 1839.
Lewis Jarrell and Cynthia Lowry, Mar. 23, 1839.
William Reynolds and Isabella E. Witherspoon, Mar. 25, 1839.
Ivy J. C. Haynes and Elvira A. Fletcher, April 4, 1839.
Joseph Robinson and Elizabeth Campbell, April 20, 1839.
Robert W. Martin and Mary J. McAdo, April 23, 1839.
Adam S. Butler and Nancy Foster, April 24, 1839.
Obediah Smith and Mary Rodgers, April 27, 1839.
William Coleman and Nancy Taylor, April 30, 1839.
Felix H. Patterson and Nancy Dillon, May 4, 1839.
John Gollerher and Tabitha Adams, May 6, 1839.
Thomas Arnold and Amanda Daulton, May 9, 1839.
Lawrence G. Hays and Frances Johns, May 9, 1839.
Henry Hunt and Smithie Manor, May 11, 1839.
Andrew J. Ivie and Jane Hunt, May 18, 1839.
William Gegg and Rebecca Walker, May 22, 1839.
Jeffers, J. Hoobery and Nancy Conley, May 24, 1839.

Francis Winston and Harriet M. Winston, May 28, 1839.
Thomas H. Vaughan and Sarah R. Thompson, May 30, 1839.
William S. Whitman and Catherine Reed, June 10, 1839.
Franklin Binkley and Rebecca J. Worrell, June 4, 1839.
Fountain C. Mosby and Amanda T. Dill, June 4, 1839.
Mathew H. Brady and Sarah N. Cox, June 6, 1839.
Jethro Goodman and Mary Good, June 8, 1839.
Robert M. Brown and Mary A. Soap, June 12, 1839.
Edmond P. Grant and Elizabeth Brockman, June 17, 1839.
John Gilley and Lucinda Young, June 24, 1839.
James O. Good and Eliza Kelton, June 25, 1839.
Thomas Drake and Catherine Cosby, June 26, 1839.
Robert B. Warren and Nancy Davis, June 28, 1839.
Thomas W. Beasley and Martha A. Haynes, July 3, 1839.
Geo. Parnack (Parnck) and Melvina Todd, July 6, 1839.
Geo. E. Kennedy and Elizabeth Wood, July 8, 1839.
Lewis Creason and Jane K. Barkley, July 10, 1839.
Jacob Seek and Louisia Robinson, July 13, 1839.
Isaac Young and Mary Sanford, July 14, 1839.
Joshua King and Judah M. May, July 15, 1839.
Christopher Acklin and Eliza A. Ward,   1839.
Robert Good and Margaret A. McElroy, July 23, 1839.
Wm. C. Duffer and Frances Fletcher, July 25, 1839.
James Bell and Susan Farmer, Aug. 2, 1839.
Malery Parker and Sarah Evans, Aug. 3, 1839.
Theophilus H. Leathers and Malitie A. Holden, Aug. 5,
  1839.
Enoch N. Dickson and Martha L. Davis, Aug. 7, 1839.
John E. Dromgoole and Rebecca Blanch, Aug. 12, 1839.
Alfred Miller and Narcissa Bradford, Aug. 12, 1839.
Stephen T. Davidson and Ester Mitchell, Aug. 14, 1839.
G. C. Keel or Maston and Rachel Hoover, Aug. 20, 1839.
Daniel Robertson and Margarett D. Haynes, Aug. 21, 1839.
Walter Moore and Mary Smotherman, Aug. 26, 1839.
Pleasant Underwood and Rebecca Smotherman, Aug. 27,
  1839.
John B. Feltcher and Catherine E. Bell, Aug. 31, 1839.
John A. Crockett and Margaret K. Ransom, Sept. 2, 1839.
William A. Donels and Catherine Finney, Sept. 2, 1839.
Mathew J. Duke and Martha E. Phillips, Sept. 7, 1839.
Thomson Pugh and Mary A. Parkman, Sept. 14, 1839.
Amos L. Pearson and Druzilla Holt, Sept. 16, 1839.
Taylor Beasley and Hollow N. Jones, Sept. 17, 1839.
Henry Barnes and Elizabeth A. Barton, Sept. 19, 1839.
Jesse F. Todd and Nancy Russell, Sept. 24, 1839.
Daniel Evans and Lewana Martin, Sept. 28, 1839.
Charles B. Ferris and Mary J. Ransom, Sept. 28, 1839.
Amos Hays and Delila Taylor, Oct. 3, 1839.
Thomas M. Golden and Susan Ryan, Oct. 5, 1839.
Harry Osburn and Ann Read, Oct. 10, 1839.
John Wallace and Lucy Martin, Oct. 12, 1839.
George W. Cantrell and Mary E. Phillips, Oct. 12, 1839.
Thomas Hogwood and Rebecca J. Church, Oct. 19, 1839.
William Hudson and Martha Beasley, Oct. 22, 1839.

RUTHERFORD COUNTY MARRIAGES

Abner Jones and Mildred Holloway, Oct. 23, 1839.
Geo. W. McMahan and Menervi Holden, Oct. 23, 1839.
James A. Russell and Nancy T. Keys, Oct. 24, 1839.
Alfred Mallard and Sarah Comer, Oct. 26, 1839.
Andrew Palmer and Ann M. Sullivan, Oct. 26, 1839.
James Tedo and Martha Ramsey, Oct. 27, 1839.
Charles P. Morton and Eliza Hancock, Oct. 30, 1839.
John Q. Parsley and Jane Bennett, Nov. 2, 1839.
Levi Wade and Virginia A. Braksdale, Nov. 4, 1839.
Nathaniel Burnett and Elizabeth Crutchfield, Nov. 6,
  1839.
Benjamine Harrison and Sarah Lannon, Nov. 6, 1839.
Caswell A. Lee and Mary A. Tucker, Nov. 7, 1839.
Nathaniel Batey and Nancy Smith, Nov. 11, 1839.
Morgan Ailor and Sarah Smith, Nov. 15, 1839.
William J. Pope and Sophia Griffin, Nov. 15, 1839.
James Jenkins and Mary A. Beesley, Nov. 16, 1839.
Nathaniel Greer and Mary Greer, Nov. 16, 1839.
Isaac Hall and Margaret Munday, Nov. 20, 1839.
John S. Haynes and Ann Sneed, Nov. 20, 1839.
Alfred T. Howell and Cyntha Neal, Nov. 20, 1839.
Williamson Smith and Jane McCullough, Nov. 22, 1839.
Elijah T. Dunn and Mary Smotherman, Nov. 23, 1839.
Charles Parks and Martha Price, Nov. 27, 1839.
James A. Alexander and Elizabeth McHenry, Nov. 27, 1839.
Berry Wright and Sarah Denney, Dec. 2, 1839.
John J. Lawing and Nancy Critchlow, Dec. 4, 1839.
S. H. Underwood and Levinia Jarratt, Dec. 7, 1839.
Alexander Nesbit and Susan C. Fletcher, Dec. 7, 1839.
John A. Miller and Mary Marlin, Dec. 7, 1839.
Abel Rushing and Amanda Kimbro, Dec. 9, 1839.
Sanpherd H. Little and Agness Nance, Dec. 9, 1839.
John F. Cox and Margaret J. Eathman, Dec. 12, 1839.
Blackman L. Rozell and Martha E. Sharpe, Dec. 13, 1839.
Aaron Botts and Martha D. Rozell, Dec. 13, 1839.
John H. Thompson and Margarett Sharpe, Dec. 14, 1839.
Edmund G. Cook and Emily H. Collier, Dec. 16, 1839.
Michaell Ashford and Mary Robbins, Dec. 16, 1839.
George N. Taylor and Jane McClanahan, Dec. 18, 1839.
John L. Donnelson and Sarah J. Anglin, Dec. 19, 1839.
Andrew Jackson Jetton and Tabitha Searcy, Dec. 19, 1839.
Lewis Smith and Elizabeth Buttler, Dec. 24, 1839.
Evritt B. Haynes and Lucinda Dickson, Dec. 24, 1839.
John Reed and Mary Spain, Dec. 25, 1839.
Edward J. Hall and Hannah Bailey, Dec. 26, 1839.
John Murphey and Elizabeth R. Parish, Dec. 29, 1839.
Milton J. Garrett and Syote E. Holden, Jan. 2, 1840.
William W. Nance and Agness Cook, Jan. 1, 1840.
George Roromines and Rebecca M. Trail, Jan. 4, 1840.
Green Phelps and Drucilla Staky, Jan. 6, 1840.
Robert B. Jetton and Mary S. Childress, Jan. 7, 1840.
John Mullins and Eliza J. Griffin, Jan. 8, 1840.
Adam McElroy and Margaret J. J. Youree, Jan. 8, 1840.
Isham R. Peebles and Sarah A. Puckett, Jan. 9, 1840.

James H. Biles and Fissonia Watson, Jan. 16, 1840.
Johnson Wilborn and Elalia P. Knight, Jan. 23, 1840.
Adam Weaver and Mary Hunt, Jan. 23, 1840.
Robert McKay and Jane P. Hillrose, Jan. 25, 1840.
Paul Patton and Mihaley Newman, Jan. 27, 1840.
James Lawrence and Elizabeth McGill, Jan. 28, 1840.
William Lawrence and Dorcas Ann Richardson, Jan. 28, 1840.
James Norwell and Nancy B. Vaughan, Feb. 3, 1840.
Jackson C. Brothers and Elizabeth L. Ross, Feb. 4,1840.
Epps L. Matthews and Eliza J. Wade, Feb. 11, 1840.
James W. Clark and Sarah B. Jetton, Feb. 10, 1840.
Robert Thompson and Martha Allman, Feb. 11, 1840.
Nathan S. Overall and Elizabeth Wood, Feb. 12, 1840.
Peterson G. Leath and Selina H. Lannom, Feb. 12, 1840.
William S. Holman and Sophia A. Robb, Feb. 14, 1840.
James H. Taylor and Sarah A. E. Coleman, Feb. 20, 1840.
Anderson Heath and Mary McDowell, Feb. 20, 1840.
William B. Fuquay and Nancy E. Sims, Feb. 18, 1840.
James A. Grider and Elizabeth A. McDowell, Feb. 19, 1840.
John W. Hall and Clementine Johnson, Feb. 19, 1840.
William Hollingsworth and Eliza Taylor, Feb. 21, 1840.
Martin L. Crocker and Margaret Read, Feb. 26, 1840.
James McInlise and Elizabeth Ward, Feb. 29, 1840.
James R. McClanahan and C. M. Wallace, Feb. 22, 1840.
William Perryman and Mary Heath, Mar. 4, 1840.
William Burnett and Elizabeth Burnett, Mar. 9, 1840.
Eliza Cates and Mary A. Harrison, March 11, 1840.
John N. Porter and Eliza Whittaker, March 12, 1840.
Lewis D. Jetton and Jane Petty, March 12, 1840.
Alexander Robinson and Elizabeth Tudor, March 17, 1840.
William Summers and Susan Lowe, March 17, 1840.
Zedock C. Bell and Barbara Shepherd, March 18, 1840.
Roderick Edwards and Elizabeth Harwell, March 19, 1840.
Jackson Fleming and Elizabeth Jamison, March 23, 1840.
William Warren and Martha J. Lasswell, March 25, 1840.
Thomas G. Vaughan and Francis J. Lillard, March 26, 1840.
James H. Short and Harriet Pitts, March 27, 1840.
Michael Swink and Martha Parkes, April 16, 1840.
John D. Wilson and Lucy Hayes, April 1, 1840.
Thomas Rogers and Oliver Rogers, April 10, 1840.
John D. Summers and Mary Green, April 6, 1840.
John D. Stockard and Mary A. Berryman, April 8, 1840.
James Thomas and Harriet Oakley, April 8, 1840.
Zachariah T. Summers and Phebe Sanders, April 9, 1840.
John McDermott and Eveline M. Boring, April 16, 1840.
Joseph Fuller and Emnline Corder, April 27, 1840.
Greensberry Ellis and Rachell Summers, April 30, 1840.
Zachariah W. Summers and Eliza Gumm, May 3, 1840.
James A. Thompson and Sarah H. Frost, May 4, 1840.
Robert P. Ganaway and Mary A. Tarpley, May 7, 1840.
Robert A. Fagan and Margaret E. McKee, May 9, 1840.

William K. Ransom and Sarah A. Wilson, May 13, 1840.
Ambrose McKee and Susan Allen, May 12, 1840.
James M. Bobbitt and Matilda Denney, May 27, 1840.
Franklin Nash and Rebecka Raby, June 2, 1840.
Charles J. Williams and Sarah Felts, June 3, 1840.
William Rose and Ann Batson, June 6, 1840.
George W. Haston and Martha H. Yandell, June 6, 1840.
William C. Bowen and Mary C. Walkup, June 16, 1840.
Dawson Adcock and Fanny Johnson, June 29, 1840.
Edward Ford and Nancy Barnes, July 6, 1840.
Joel Read and Eliza Weatherford, July 9, 1840.
C. C. Ezell and Rebecca J. Mayfield, July 13, 1840.
Martin Edwards and Carolina Bullock, July 21, 1840.
Edward L. Jordan and Martha H. Fletcher, July 24, 1840.
Abram H. Helton and Rebecca L. Williams, July 31, 1840.
Richard M. Vaughan and Martha Posey, Aug. 1, 1840.
Jacob Hoover and Mary Baley, Aug. 4, 1840.
Hugh M. Bell and Margaret M. McCroken, Aug. 5, 1840.
David Summers and Jane Jones, Aug. 20, 1840.
Hugh W. Alexander and Mary A. Black, Aug. 29, 1840.
William Gasky and Margarett Rodgers, Aug. 31, 1840.
Walter T. Key and Eliza A. Berry, Sept. 1, 1840.
Franklin Hall and Elizabeth McCracken, Sept. 3, 1840.
William Miller and Willy Ann Moss, Sept. 30, 1840.
Absalom Soap and Elizabeth Warren, Sept. 7, 1840.
William Gobson and Margaret P. Freeman, Sept. 7, 1840.
Asa Coulter and Mary Allman, Sept. 7, 1840.
Bassel Jacobs and Biney Summers, Sept. 9, 1840.
P.M.C. Elliott and Caroline Taylor, Sept. 15, 1840.
James M. Routon and Tabitha Flowers, Sept. 15, 1840.
Albert Harris and Charlotte Ellison, Sept. 15, 1840.
James Johnson and Lucy Bashears, Sept. 16, 1840.
Alfred J. Mustain and Elizabeth F. Woodson, Sept. 16, 1840.
Peter Campbell and Elizabeth P. Furgerson, Sept. 17, 1840.
Joseph Traylor and Martha Williams, Sept. 18, 1840.
William S. Belts and Mary E. Swink, Sept. 28, 1840.
Benj. V. Rowland and Docy M. Swink, Sept. 28, 1840.
Alfred P. Low and Mary Kirk, Oct. 5, 1840.
Thomas D. Walpole and Mary T. James, Oct. 7, 1840.
Giles S. Harding and Mary H. Blackman, Oct. 7, 1840.
Elihu White and Mary Crocker, Oct. 12, 1840.
James Leehu and Mary Ellen Carpenter, Oct. 12, 1840.
Joseph Coleman and Margaret Hailey, Oct. 13, 1840.
Mathew Ligon and Ann E. Braksdale, Oct. 13, 1840.
John W. Mabry and Marinda B. Cook, Oct. 15, 1840.
Barnett Jackson and Ann C. Grimes, Oct. 14, 1840.
Thomas Robinson and Elizabeth Elliott, Oct. 14, 1840.
William T. Sudberry and Mary E. Sudberry, Oct. 16, 1840.
James Vaughan and Martha A. E. Elliott, Oct. 17, 1840.
Josephus Moore and Manervy Puckett, Oct. 22, 1840.
James A. Marr and Vavina Modrall, Oct. 24, 1840.

Walter S. Lowe and Amanda Norman, Oct. 28, 1840.
Richard Vaughan and Narcissa Johnson, Nov. 2, 1840.
Samuel H. McKnight and Isabella Neeley, Nov. 2, 1840.
Robert A. Read and Mary Smith, Nov. 10, 1840.
O. H. Wade and Catherine Wade, Nov. 12, 1840.
Edmund Goodrich and Letty Daniel, Nov. 24, 1840.
Josiah F. Penn and Mira M. Sneed, Nov. 26, 1840.
Garland E. Inglis and Jane Statum, Nov. 26, 1840.
Richard C. Jones and Theodica Jarratt, Nov. 28, 1840.
Israel P. Mayfield and Susan J. Feltcher, Nov. 30,1840.
Silas Tucker and Jane K. Moore, Dec. 1, 1840.
Pettis W. Norman and Tabitha E. Webb, Dec. 3, 1840.
William Wells and Mary Prewett, Dec. 2, 1840.
Hiram Rouse (free man of colour) and Nancy Jenkins (Col.)
    Dec. 3, 1840.
Asberru Underwood and Lucinda T. Smotherman, Dec. 7,
    1840.
Benjamine Underwood and Mary Spence, Dec. 17, 1840.
Nicholas H. Johns and Susannah T. Vaughan, Dec. 8,1840.
Thomas B. Lyons and Nancy C. Alexander, Dec. 8, 1840.
Richard Parker and Martha M. Sanford, Dec. 9, 1840.
Charles Watts and Margarett Lillard, Dec. 9, 1840.
Herrod Bruce and Nancy Bruce, Dec. 10, 1840.
Thomas G. Taylor and Elizabeth Goodrich, Dec. 14, 1840.
William Smith and Susan Tombs, Dec. 16, 1840.
William Parker and Mary Parrish, Dec. 17, 1840.
Walker Peek and Cynthia Dunn, Dec. 17, 1840.
William Hamilton and Martha J. Sneed, Dec. 17, 1840.
William Bozzell and Mary Adcock, Dec. 18, 1840.
James Burnett and Rebecca Petty, Dec. 22, 1840.
Lewis Graves and Nancy Warren, Dec. 24, 1840.
Jackson Stam and Elizabeth Smotherman, Dec. 24, 1840.
Armstead B. Worrel and Nancy C. Phelps, Dec. 28, 1840.
Jesse Smith and Cynthia Zachry, Dec. 30, 1840.
William D. Bradley and Frances Edwards, Dec. 31, 1840.
John A. Filker and Mary Louise Barley, Jan. 4, 1841.
Miles Halstead and Arenia C. McKean, Jan. 5, 1841.
Isaac McCullough and Nancy McFadden, Jan. 7, 1841.
Michael Inhoof and Nancy Harris, Jan. 9, 1841.
James Jamison and Sarah Lorance, Jan. 10, 1841.
James Daniel and Margaret A. Taylor, Jan. 11, 1841.
Barkley M. Fugett and Octavia P. Mayfield, Jan. 11,1841.

Section 3: 1841-1872

1841

Adams, John W. & Nancy Adams, Mar. 11, 1841.
Adkins, William & Elizabeth Aclin, Nov. 24, 1841.
Alexander, David & Elizabeth Howell, Sept. 21, 1841.
Arnett, William & Susannah C. Bivins, Dec. 14, 1841.
Arnold, Edwin & Harriet N. McClanahan, June 10, 1841.
Arnold, John B. & Rhoda H. Hill, Jan. 28, 1841.
Atkinson, William & Frances Batey, July 17, 1841.
Baker, Hiram B. & Mary Renshaw, Sept. 21, 1841.
Barnes, David & Sarah Hail, Aug. 25, 1841.
Barrett, Lawrence & Amanda Reynolds, May 4, 1841.
Battson, Phillip & Julia Rose, Jan. 21, 1841.
Baugh, Joseph W. & Cicely H. Jetton, Jan. 19, 1841.
Bell, Obediah & Lucy Farmer, Mar. 8, 1841.
Binford, Joseph W. & Margarett L. A. Calhoun, Nov. 17, 184]
Bivins, Fielder & Easter Lorance, Mar. 15, 1841.
Blankenship, Allen & Nancy Hoover, Jan. 23, 1841.
Blankenship, David B. & Frances E. Farriss, Dec. 27, 1841.
Bone, Henry F. & Margaret J. Ivie, May 18, 1841.
Braswell, William L. & Elizabeth James, Mar. 11, 1841.
Brewer, James & Rebecca Petty, Dec. 22, 1841.
Brewer, William & Elizabeth McPeak, Feb 22, 1841.
Burnett, James & Rebecca Petty, Dec. 22, 1841.
Brooks, Jordan & Jane W. Marlin, Dec. 15, 1841.
Carnahan, Newton C. & Pernelia I. Acres, Mar. 17, 1841.
Cates, Elza & Sarah H. Moore, Apr. 11, 1841.
Clark, Yandell & Caroline Bradfield, Dec. 23, 1841.
Clarke, Thomas G. & Elenor Patterson, June 21, 1841.
Cook, Robert & Nancy E. E. Posey, Aug. 11, 1841.
Corner, Adam & Susan Page, Dec. 21, 1841.
Dalton, James M. & Martha Powell, Jan. 30, 1841.
Daniel, James & Margarett A. Taylor, Jan. 11, 1841.
Davis, Anderson S. & Jane Church, Dec. 23, 1841.
Davis, Charles L. & Jane Simmons, May 19, 1841.
Davis, Richard & America Gregory, Mar. 30, 1841.
Davis, Samuel & Susan C. Lowe, Sept. 20, 1841.
Dean, E. H. & Temperance Acre, Oct. 14, 1841.
Denton, William & Elizabeth Bynum, Aug. 22, 1841.
Dwiggins, Robert S. & Locky A. Watkins, July 1, 1841.
Edwards, John A. & Elizabeth A. Alford, Nov. 11, 1841.
Edwards, Thomas & Martha J. Vaughan, May 10, 1841.
Elrod, Thomas S. & Mary Woosley, Feb. 19, 1841.
Estes, Coleman & Mary Barlow, Feb. 14, 1841.
Evans, John & Elizabeth Spence, May 27, 1841.
Felker, John A. & Louisa Bailey, Jan. 5, 1841.
Fields, Ira W. & Caroline Jones, Dec. 17, 1841.

Fletcher, Minos L. & Lucretia H. Overall, July 6, 1841.
Foster, Rufus H. & Sarah A. Spain, Nov. 12, 1841.
Fugett, Barkley M. & Octavia P. Mayfield, Jan. 11, 1841.
Goodman, Thomas H. & Martha A. Oliphant, Oct. 26, 1841.
Greer, John & Mary Meddling, Mar. 17, 1841.
Hall, Nathan A. & Mary A. McKinley, Mar. 31, 1841.
Halstead, Miles & Arenia C. McKean, Jan. 5, 1841.
Hamilton, Andrew M. & Elizabeth A. Anderson, Aug. 1, 1841.
Haynes, Harry H. & Mary Webb, Jan. 2, 1841.
Henderson, A. G. & Eveline M. Love, Mar. 25, 1841.
Henning, James G. & Rachel McKite, Nov. 4, 1841.
Hester, Alexander & Ann Finny, Apr. 7, 1841.
Hill, John & Susan Arnold, May 12, 1841.
Hoover, Benjamin S. & Sarah Dillard, Aug. 16, 1841.
Hoover, Isaac & Anny Hoover, May 8, 1841.
Hoover, Jacob & Elizabeth L. Rawlings, May 8, 1841.
Hoover, James & Elizabeth Renshaw, Apr. 12, 1841.
Howell, Alfred & Emaline Puckett, July 15, 1841.
Howland, William & Mary Nisbitt, Jan. 11, 1841.
Hudson, Alfred & Lucy Jane Smith, Nov. 1, 1841.
Hudson, William S. & Elizabeth Davis, Apr. 7, 1841.
Hunter, Robert & Florida Jackson, Dec. 31, 1841.
Inhoos, Michael & Nancy Harrison, Jan. 9, 1841.
Jacobs, William & Catharine Roberts, Mar. 19, 1841.
Jamison, James & Sarah Lorance, Jan. 9, 1841.
Jarratt, David M. & Charlotte Sanders, July 19, 1841.
Jernigan, William & Elizabeth Herrell, Jan. 21, 1841.
Johns, William & Selinia A. Wood, Dec. 10, 1841.
Jones, Pinkney & Sarah Curtis, Mar. 20, 1841.
Kelton, James H. & Martha J. Yardley, Mar. 10, 1841.
Kelton, William H. & Martha A. Cox, July 8, 1841.
Kester, Alexander & Ann Finney, Apr. 7, 1841.
Koonce, Owen & Arend Sims, June 11, 1841.
Lahn, William & Delilah I. Adams, Mar. 11, 1841.
Lantern, Thomas & Charlotte Collins (col), Dec. 20, 1841.
Lawrence, Edward & Nancy Cook, Dec. 30, 1841.
Lawrence, John D. & Mary J. F. Crockett, June 23, 1841.
Lawrence, John L. & Margarett I. Henderson, June 19, 1841.
Lillard, David W. & Sophronia Cock, Jan. 21, 1841.
Love, Hugh & Mary B. Dement, Jan. 19, 1841.
Maberry, Wilson & Rebecca Cates, Jan. 20, 1841.
Maney, Thomas H. & Fanny M. Bell, Oct. 12, 1841.
Miles, Thomas B. & Catharine E. Johns, June 9, 1841.
Mitchell, Stephen & Hannah M. Ralph, Mar. 29, 1841.
Moore, Thomas & Nancy J. Howse, June 9, 1841.
Morton, Joseph & Ruthy Garner, Nov. 4, 1841.
Moseley, Peter B. & Elinor J. Priestly, Mar. 20, 1841.
Mustain, Devrix & Susan L. Rutledge, Dec. 29, 1841.
McCroy, Reden M. & Nancy Randolph, Feb. 22, 1841.
McCullough, Isaac & Nancy McFadden, Jan. 7, 1841.
McFarlin, Henry & Catharine Twigg, May 29, 1841.
McKnight, David M. & Eliza Martin, Nov. 12, 1841.
Nance, William S. & Martha I. Wilson, Jan. 30, 1841.
Nash, George R. & Virginia Atkinson, July 22, 1841.
Newsom, Samuel & Catharine J. Hall, Dec. 13, 1841.

Oliphant, William C. & Elizabeth R. Lane, May 14, 1841.
Pafford, Wilie & Lucinda Freeman, Apr. 5, 1841.
Palmer, Greenville & Martha Sneed, Sept. 21, 1841.
Parker, Dorton & Mary C. Wilson, July 22, 1841.
Peach, Reuben R. & Mary Williams, Oct. 28, 1841.
Perry, Jessee & Eliza Bynum, Oct. 20, 1841.
Perry, John W. & Polly Higgin, Oct. 21, 1841.
Phelps, Joshua & Martha Jones, Jan. 27, 1841.
Poindexter, Daniel L. & Alpha Patterson, July 27, 1841.
Randolph, Samuel R. & Mary A. McCroy, Sept. 3, 1841.
Ridley, John C. & Nancy Ridley, Mar. 4, 1841.
Ritner, John & Kitturah Mosby, Aug. 9, 1841.
Robbins, Harmon & Lucinda Freeman, Mar. 23, 1841.
Robbins, James H. & Ann C. Fourmawalt, June 14, 1841.
Robert, John I. V. & Lucinda Lannom, Nov. 15, 1841.
Rodgers, James & Levina Featherstone, June 5, 1841.
Rushing, Joel & Mary A. Butler, Apr. 21, 1841.
Sanders, William A. & Cynthia A. Castleman, Aug. 28, 1841.
Shanklin, R. D. & Amanda Henley, June 3, 1841.
Shaw, Christopher G. W. B. & Martha Keyser, July 22, 1841.
Singleton, John & Margarett Denny, Feb. 3, 1841.
Smith, Dennis B. & Leah A. Overall, Dec. 22, 1841.
Smith, Jesse & Cynthia Zachry, Dec. 31, 1841.
Smith, Robert G. & America N. Smith, Nov. 23, 1841.
Smith, Robert M. & Mary J. Jamison, Mar. 10, 1841.
Smith, Robert H. & Elinor Russwurm, Aug. 11, 1841.
Smith, William & Eliza Ailor, Nov. 29, 1841.
Smithia, William & Susan Tombs, Dec. 10, 1841.
Smotherman, Francis & Elizabeth West, Nov. 15, 1841.
Smotherman, Isham & Charity Hester, Feb. 6, 1841.
Snell, James E. & Mary Wray, Oct. 20, 1841.
Snell, Theophulus B. & Mary E. Woods, Oct. 12, 1841.
Spain, John & Martha Parkman, Mar. 31, 1841.
Stem, James & Mary Smotherman, Sept. 9, 1841.
Stephenson, William M. & Margaret Kelton, Sept. 16, 1841.
Stewart, Anderson & Prudence Morris (col), Dec. 20, 1841.
Tatum, Absolum & Mary E. Jarratt, June 22, 1841.
Taylor, Robert H. & Matilda A. Bates, Dec. 30, 1841.
Taylor, William C. & Sarah J. Davidson, June 24, 1841.
Thompson, James & Beattus Shelton, July 5, 1841.
Thompson, William M. & Catherine B. Keeble, Nov. 22, 1841.
Threet, Harman & Mary A. Heath, Dec. 25, 1841.
Tilker, John A. & Louisa Bailey, Jan. 4, 1841.
Todd, Fielding & Elizabeth Summers, Dec. 18, 1841.
Trail, Felix G. & Martha A. Cosey, Dec. 16, 1841.
Traylor, Joseph & Martha Williams, Mar. 5, 1841.
Vaughan, John & Susan Neal, Sept. 29, 1841.
Vaughter, Thomas & Susan Bonds, Mar. 30, 1841.
Wade, John C. & Sarah Sperry, Aug. 12, 1841.
Walker, Charles B. & Jane O. Jetton, Nov. 4, 1841.
Walker, George & Ann E. Barkley, Dec. 20, 1841.
Ward, William & Mary E. Newgent, Dec. 1, 1841.
Warren, John T. & Ducenia A. Huggins, Feb. 23, 1841.
Whiteleau, James & Jane McKay, Sept. 11, 1841.
Wiley, John F. & Jane Dobson, May 3, 1841.

Williams, William B. & Nancy E. Ramsey, Apr. 15, 1841.
Williamson, Thomas S. & Margarett W. Ross, Dec. 6, 1841.
Wilson, John M. & Martha Furgerson, Dec. 18, 1841.
Wood, Joel & Mary J. Hailey, Feb. 15, 1841.
Woodfin, John J. & Elizabeth Smith, Dec. 18, 1841.
Worrel, John T. & Cintha Castleman, July 2, 1841.
Wrather, George W. & Elizabeth E. Jones, Dec. 22, 1841.
Yardley, Thomas N. & Elizabeth M. Lawrence, Feb. 10, 1841.

1842

Aclin, James W. & Elizabeth G. Sanford, Feb. 1, 1842.
Adcock, John & Elizabeth Johnson, Feb. 2, 1842.
Alexander, Martin L. & Sarah H. Ivy, June 9, 1842.
Alexander, P. M. & Martha L. Kimbro, Mar. 29, 1842.
Armstrong, John B. & Susannah M. Ready, May 21, 1842.
Arnold, Stephen & Lucinda Hunt, May 8, 1842.
Baker, George E. & Martha Underwood, Nov. 12, 1842.
Baldridge, Andrew J. & Jane Williams, June 30, 1842.
Barnwell, James M. & Matilda A. Roberts, Dec. 29, 1842.
Barton, Robert D. & Artillia P. Goodloe, Aug. 4, 1842.
Bell, George W. & Eveline Smith, Jan. 19, 1842.
Bell, Robert & Sarah A. Hancock, Mar. 24, 1842.
Bethshears, John & Mary T. Wilson, Feb. 19, 1842.
Bigham, Robert H. & Elizabeth C. Robinson, Jan. 14, 1842.
Bishop, John S. & Mary Freeman, Nov. 18, 1842.
Black, Lunsford P. & Elizabeth Rucker, June 1, 1842.
Blankenship, David B. & Frances E. Ferriss, Dec. 27, 1842.
Blankenship, James H. & Mary E. Beesley, Nov. 3, 1842.
Boaz, Josiah & Lucinda A. Sanford, Dec. 8, 1842.
Bobbitt, Thomas & Elizabeth Potts, June 28, 1842.
Bowles, James C. & Elizabeth Shacklett, Dec. 14, 1842.
Bowling, Matthew & Susan Yardley, Jan. 1, 1842.
Bragg, Joseph & Perrella E. Bowman, Mar. 1, 1842.
Brewer, James G. & Dicey Cunningham, Apr. 25, 1842.
Brewer, William & Elizabeth McPeak, Feb. 22, 1842.
Bryant, Thomas & Leviny Cunningham, Dec. 4, 1842.
Bryant, William & Nancy Poe, July 4, 1842.
Burnett, Woodson & Mary Pace, Sept. 9, 1842.
Cantrell, Tilmon & Jane B. Jamison, Aug. 16, 1842.
Cayce, William H. & Mary K. Boring, May 14, 1842.
Charlton, James H. & Mary Richardson, Sept. 26, 1842.
Childress, Thomas D. & Ann E. Wilson, Sept. 24, 1842.
Clark, Thomas W. & Arena Jourdan, Dec. 28, 1842.
Climer, Milton & Matilda Mackey, Dec. 28, 1842.
Conly, Alfred W. & Martha A. Hall, Oct. 24, 1842.
Connie, Willobe A. & Elizabeth Murry, Feb. 19, 1842.
Covington, Edwin J. & Lucinda Newgent, June 12, 1842.
Crainor, Thomas B. & Mary A. Alexander, June 29, 1842.
Cravens, Thomas & Sarah Esler, Feb. 7, 1842.
Crichlow, James & Martha M. Williams, Sept. 14, 1842.
Crocker, John C. & Mary E. Gooch, Mar. 10, 1842.
Davidson, Richard & Margarett Nickson, Mar. 10, 1842.
Dove, Stephen S. & Lucinda Hackett, May 31, 1842.
Dunaway, Archibald M. & Perlina W. Singleton, Oct. 3, 1842.

Ewes, Thomas & Sarah Perryman, June 8, 1842.
Fain, John & Emiley Ann Crowder, Nov. 21, 1842.
Farr, Joseph C. & Tabitha B. Cunningham, Sept. 26, 1842.
Faucett, Archibald & Lucinda Collins, July 26, 1842.
Floyd, George W. & Mary A. Allen, May 14, 1842.
Goodman, John & Mary Louisa Davis, Sept. 5, 1842.
Goss, Willis H. & Christina Singleton, Dec. 24, 1842.
Grimes, Robert B. & Mary F. Wood, Dec. 27, 1842.
Halleburton, John E. & Mary Bumpass, Jan. 26, 1842.
Harrison, James A. & Susan C. Dement, Nov. 22, 1842.
Harrison, Robert & Mary Sanders, Aug. 8, 1842.
Hartwell, John A. & Margaret C. Jones, June 30, 1842.
Haynes, William A. & Winaford Glymp, Aug. 27, 1842.
Higdon, Thomas C. & Elizabeth F. Robinson, Mar. 8, 1842.
Hodge, James & Eliza Neel, Apr. 4, 1842.
Holden, Jordan & Lousia Horton, Dec. 19, 1842.
Hooker, John & Sarah R. Arnold, Nov. 10, 1842.
Hoover, Jacob & Polly Bailey, Aug. 24, 1842.
Hoover, Martin V. & Martha C. Bailey, June 6, 1842.
Hoover, Mathias W. & Elizabeth J. Hall, June 6, 1842.
Horton, William & Susan Adcock, Jan. 4, 1842.
Howell, William G. & Francis Griffin, Feb. 16, 1842.
Hunt, John W. & Elizabeth Barber, Oct. 26, 1842.
Jackson, William P. & Elizabeth Carter, Mar. 12, 1842.
Jacobs, Alfred M. & Jane Roberts, Mar. 22, 1842.
Jarnagen, Kinchen & Hetta Best (or Bett), Aug. 10, 1842.
Jones, Charles & Elizabeth Cobb, Aug. 26, 1842.
Jones, John & Louisia Ferriss, Aug. 21, 1842.
Keele, Richmond & Louisa Hoover, Oct. 31, 1842.
King, Elias & Eveline T. Adams, Feb. 12, 1842.
Kirkpatrick, John C. & Narcissus F. Ridley, Oct. 4, 1842.
Koonce, John & Melvinia D. Anderson, June 28, 1842.
Lannom, Joseph N. & Sarah A. Sharp, Dec. 8, 1842.
Lannom, Levi & Jediah Fussell, Oct. 18, 1842.
Lannom, Tilman W. & Harriett Clardy, Dec. 27, 1842.
Lawrence, Edward & Nancy Cook, Dec. 30, 1842.
Lawrence, Thomas H. & Nancy L. W. Rogers, Jan. 3, 1842.
Lawrence, William & Agnes Dement, Jan. 17, 1842.
Lee, John S. & Sarah M. Barton, Oct. 17, 1842.
Lenoir, William B. & Cornelia Ann B. Moore, --------
Lillard, William B. & Delia E. Blackman, Apr. 27, 1842.
Lockard, Preston & Louisa Arnold, Nov. 29, 1842.
Love, James H. & Frances Rowlett, Oct. 24, 1842.
Lowe, William S. & Martha J. Youree, Oct. 25, 1842.
Lyell, Thomas A. & Martha D. Mustean, Mar. 15, 1842.
Lyon, Richard & Louisa Ruff, Dec. 4, 1842.
Mankin, Jesse W. & Sophia Jarratt, Dec. 19, 1842.
Mayfield, Fountain S. & Susan E. Henderson, Apr. 12, 1842.
McAdoo, Alfred P. & Christinia E. Spain, Oct. 26, 1842.
McClaron, Deniel C. & Susan H. Delbridge, Aug. 22, 1842.
McCulloch, Sam D. & Sarah A. Booker, Nov. 16, 1842.
McDowell, James & Harriett Petty, June 19, 1842.
McDowell, Wallace & Melissa Sherron, June 21, 1842.
McFadden, William R. & Clementine A. Brock, Mar. 22, 1842.
McKee, James & Mary A. McEwen, Mar. 1, 1842.

McMurry, George W. & Lavinia Swan, Jan. 6, 1842.
Miller, John & Nancy Gillispie, Nov. 28, 1842.
Mosley, Gilliam & Rebecca Felts, June 27, 1842.
Mosley, William & Elizabeth Beesley, Jan. 13, 1842.
Newman, John A. & Racheal Burks, Aug. 9, 1842.
Northern, Thomas Y. & Pallona Smith, Oct. 15, 1842.
Oakley, Stanford P. & Narcissa H. Edwards, Feb. 21, 1842.
Overall, Baxter D. & Martha A. Kerby, Feb. 28, 1842.
Overall, Nance S. & Parmelia Kerby, Feb. 25, 1842.
Owen, Charles E. & Eliza Fuller, Dec. 29, 1842.
Pace, Ezekiel & Susan Brown, June 6, 1842.
Parker, John & Mary A. Lisendy, Apr. 22, 1842.
Peebles, Robert R. & Ann E. Lewis, Dec. 12, 1842.
Penual, Tilford & Elizabeth H. Summers, Sept. 14, 1842.
Perry, Claibourn G. & Catharine Sanders, June 4, 1842.
Pitts, Matthew & Martha A. Nolen, Oct. 12, 1842.
Pyland, William & Martha J. Jordan, Aug. 18, 1842.
Ransom, William A. & Martha Kimbro, Apr. 25, 1842.
Rawlings, Martin H. & Polly T. J. Hoover, Mar. 24, 1842.
Read, William & Seabery Brewer, Dec. 13, 1842.
Robbins, Lemuel & Mary L. Brewer, Feb. 28, 1842.
Robinson, Willie G. & Mary A. Ricks, May 14, 1842.
Rogers, J. C. & H. E. Bullock, June 30, 1842.
Rogers, Nicholas & Jane Miller, June 21, 1842.
Rowton, Rulant & Sarah J. Loyd, Nov. 12, 1842.
Rucker, William H. & Matilda Elliott, July 27, 1842.
Sanford, John A. & Catharine C. Aclin, Feb. 1, 1842.
Scruggs, Gross & Mary S. Saunders, Oct. 12, 1842.
Seward, Edward S. & Clarkey Ward, Sept. 28, 1842.
Sikes, Robert M. & Anna C. Jones, Nov. 26, 1842.
Sims, George S. & Ellin Cunningham, Aug. 26, 1842.
Sloan, Joseph & Izbel P. Boyd, Dec. 19, 1842.
Smith, Ephraim F. & Nancy C. Miles, Oct. 5, 1842.
Smith, James & Lusinda Flowers, June 9, 1842.
Smotherman, Greenberry & Nancy Holden, Jan. 8, 1842.
Snell, Rodger D. & Martha Maxwell, Jan. 1, 1842.
Spain, John Q. & Sarah M. McKnight, Sept. 5, 1842.
Stamford, George W. & Elizabeth Y. Burge, Oct. 10, 1842.
Starnes, James & Jane McCrary, Oct. 25, 1842.
Stephenson, William M. & Margaret A. Kelton, Sept. 13, 1842
Stockard, James E. & Lucy B. McGowen, Feb. 16, 1842.
Summers, Zachariah & Elizabeth Newman, Aug. 13, 1842.
Tally, Peter C. & Jane Donoho, Nov. 27, 1842.
Tatum, William M. & Martha A. Landers, Dec. 22, 1842.
Thomas, William & Emaline Bates, Dec. 9, 1842.
Thompson, Phillip & Christina Bone, May 12, 1842.
Todd, Anderson & Mary F. Brown, Aug. 15, 1842.
Todd, William & Sarah Bates, Nov. 12, 1842.
Toombs, James W. & Martha A. Foster, Dec. 22, 1842.
Townsend, Thomas & Lucy J. Brothers, Feb. 9, 1842.
Travis, William & Sarah G. Butler, Feb. 9, 1842.
Tucker, Joshua & Caroline Roberts, Jan. 4, 1842.
Vaughan, William & Martha A. E. T. Payne, Mar. 21, 1842.
Vaught, Sam & Malinda Dickson, Nov. 16, 1842.
Vernon, James & Elizabeth Heath, Jan. 20, 1842.

RUTHERFORD COUNTY MARRIAGES

Viar, William & Sarah Ralph, Aug. 30, 1842.
Wadley, Daniel & Martha E. Ramsey, Feb. 2, 1842.
Walker, Iley & Martha Allman, Nov. 3, 1842.
Ward, James J. & Louisa Ward, Jan. 20, 1842.
Ward, Nicholas G. & Sarah A. Patillo, Oct. 2, 1842.
Watkins, Samuel B. & Mary Ann Wade, Dec. 21, 1842.
Watts, William E. & Elizabeth Neely, Oct. 5, 1842.
Weatherford, Allen S. & Mary E. Read, Oct. 12, 1842.
Welch, Benjamin F. & Mary M. Lannom, Oct. 8, 1842.
Williams, Isaac & Sally Holly, Mar. 2, 1842.
Winston, Walter & Mary Sanders, Oct. 20, 1842.
Wood, William T. J. & Louisa Crockett, Sept. 24, 1842.
Woodruff, Richard & Ann T. Arnold, Apr. 8, 1842.
Wright, Marcus N. & Mary Hallum, Dec. 30, 1842.
Yardley, John W. & Sarah Fulks, Dec. 15, 1842.

1843

Abernathy, Jesse J. & Mary M. Murfree, Oct. 17, 1843.
Adams, John Q. & Martha Ann Gillem, June 23, 1843.
Alexander, John S. & Lucinda P. Williams, Nov. 29, 1843.
Alsup, Elijah & Mary Dement, Dec. 20, 1843.
Armstrong, James M. & Lucinda Dyel, Aug. 30, 1843.
Ballentine, John M. & Martha A. Blair, May 8, 1843.
Barber, John M. & Ceily Wadley, Oct. 5, 1843.
Baskett, William T. & Melissa A. Ellis, Feb. 19, 1843.
Bennett, William D. & Martha A. Pearson, Jan. 17, 1843.
Blakely, William B. & Luzinda B. Jones, Feb. 6, 1843.
Boehms, Joseph A. & Ann E. Vaughan, Oct. 11, 1843.
Booker, Efford D. & Eliza Nash, Nov. 29, 1843.
Brewer, John & Mary A. Neely, ----------.
Brewer, Sterling & Hannah Denton, Dec. 23, 1843.
Brockman, Barney & Talithy C. T. Alandrom, Apr. 8, 1843.
Brown, Cornelius & Racheal Read, Mar. 21, 1843.
Bryan, William A. & Rebecca A. Blair, Aug. 11, 1843.
Burnett, Samuel & Elizabeth C. Alexander, Nov. 23, 1843.
Burnett, Thomas & Elizabeth J. Wray, Dec. 16, 1843.
Cardwell, Badoe W. & Eliza A. Doak, Apr. 11, 1843.
Carnahan, William & Elizabeth A. Whitfield, Mar. 8, 1843.
Cook, George S. & Mary J. Mabry, Jan. 12, 1843.
Cox, Joshua T. & Elizabeth Nance, Nov. 11, 1843.
Crawford, James & Susan F. Merritt, Sept. 9, 1843.
Crockett, Dandridge M. & Lucetta E. Harrison, Mar. 6, 1843.
Crockett, William G. & Elizabeth J. Jarratt, Dec. 27, 1843.
Davidson, James & Elizabeth Rich, Sept. 6, 1843.
Elam, George F. & Purlina E. Jarratt, Dec. 19, 1843.
Elliatt, Thomas J. & Rebecca E. Howland, Jan. 13, 1843.
Ellis, Radford G. & Sophia B. Anderson, Oct. 19, 1843.
Eskridge, William R. & Cyntha A. Neal, Sept. 29, 1843.
Fields, Bennett G. & Adala A. Clayton, Dec. 21, 1843.
Flowers, Cornelius J. & Margaret Miceall, Sept. 22, 1843.
Floyd, Josiah W. & Nancy E. Doak, Mar. 7, 1843.
Ford, Andrew M. & Mary Vernus, Nov. 15, 1843.
Gilliam, Jesse & Catharine Wright, Nov. 2, 1843.
Gilliam, Richard & Susan Adams, June 28, 1843.

Goodman, Edmund & Amanda Neal, Mar. 8, 1843.
Goss, Willis H. & Mary A. Ellison, Aug. 23, 1843.
Grimes, Robert B. & Mary F. Wood, Dec. 26, 1843.
Hale, William & Martha Hays, June 17, 1843.
Hall, Ferdinand P. & Elizabeth Youree, Jan. 19, 1843.
Harris, Lawson & Eliza Head, Mar. 30, 1843.
Harris, William H. & Manervia Mundy, May 20, 1843.
Helton, Joshua & Nancy Williams, Feb. 15, 1843.
Hendrix, Thomas & Mary May, Nov. 20, 1843.
Herrell, Noah & Mary Harris, Nov. 25, 1843.
Herrell, William & Martha Boling, June 20, 1843.
Holden, Jonathan & Mary Holden, Nov. 15, 1843.
Holden, William & Nancy Wyott, Dec. 9, 1843.
Holton, John R. & Jemima Jane Covington, June 10, 1843.
Hoover, John H. & Elizabeth E. Reece, Sept. 7, 1843.
Hoover, Julias & Martha Moreland, Jan. 25, 1843.
Ivey, Abram S. & Arabellah K. Donnell, Aug. 16, 1843.
Jackson, Giles & Mary Grimes, June 30, 1843.
Jackson, James W. & Eliza Hogwood, July 1, 1843.
Jackson, Richard & Elizabeth C. Clark, Nov. 27, 1843.
Jetton, William & Elizabeth Stroop, Dec. 14, 1843.
Johnson, James M. & Caroling Russ, Mar. 2, 1843.
Jones, Darling & Margaret E. Miller, Feb. 27, 1843.
King, Thomas R. & Frances A. G. Sutton, Jan. 16, 1843.
Lamb, Benjamin & Sophia Smotherman, July 22, 1843.
Lambert, Harrison & Susan Herrin, Dec. 27, 1843.
Lane, William T. & Martha J. Collier, Nov. 1, 1843.
Lanier, Nicholas S. & Mary Cavender, July 21, 1843.
Lasiter, James & Mary Bonds, Feb. 11, 1843.
Lee, William H. & Mary Sanders, Feb. 2, 1843.
Lively, David E. & Dorothy J. Neely, Nov. 21, 1843.
Lyche, William & Elizabeth Watson, June 29, 1843.
Lynch, Owen & Martha H. Puckett, Nov. 26, 1843.
Mankin, Charles & Mary E. Lowe, Sept. 18, 1843.
Maxwell, William & Susan Smotherman, Nov. 10, 1843.
Meredith, John D. & Mary L. Neely, Mar. 9, 1843.
Meredith, John D. & Tabitha B. Pullum, May 10, 1843.
Morrison, William G. & Ann Farr, Mar. 6, 1843.
Merritt, Samuel & Eliza Coulter, Nov. 14, 1843.
Mullins, John & Unity A. Harvey, Mar. 9, 1843.
Murfree, William L. & Fanny Pricilla Dickinson,
    Nov. 22, 1843.
Murray, Hiram W. & Nancy M. Lyon, Nov. 1, 1843.
McClaran, John D. & Saluda Vaughan, Oct. 2', 1843.
McCullough, Jamas M. & Nancy C. Zachery, Dec. 25, 1843.
McDonnell, James R. & Martha McRoy, July 14, 1843.
McElwrath, William C. & Martha Hall, Aug. 28, 1843.
McKee, Ambrose & Sally C. Read, Dec. 29, 1843.
McKnight, Andrew M. & Jemima J. Martin, Apr. 8, 1843.
Nelson, Evin & Jane A. Fulks, Jan. 2, 1843.
Newgent, David D. & Louisia A. McAllister, Oct. 22, 1843.
Newgent, William H. & Judith Brown, Sept. 22, 1843.
Newman, Allen & Elizabeth N. Freeman, July 31, 1843.
Norman, Carney & Mary A. Doak, June 12, 1843.
Northcutt, Robert S. & Mary M. Cunningham, Dec. 15, 1843.

Oakley, James W. & Jane Hester, Aug. 17, 1843.
Orr, Elezar A. & Sarah Brandon, June 17, 1843.
Overall, William S. & Frances Fletcher, Mar. 27, 1843.
Patterson, Amaziah C. & Nancy Allen, Feb. 2, 1843.
Phelps, Joshua & Martha Jones, Dec. 8, 1843.
Prater, John & Martha Zumbro, Nov. 8, 1843.
Price, John W. & Parthenia E. Donoho, May 19, 1843.
Pugh, Fletcher & America Anglin, Oct. 15, 1843.
Ramsey, Jesse & Catharine Stroop, Jan. 30, 1843.
Rawlings, John Marshall & Martha Bailey, Apr. 19, 1843.
Rice, James & Deborah Arnold, Aug. 12, 1843.
Rich, Jacob & Ann Lane, Aug. 19, 1843.
Richardson, James T. & Lucy A. Randolph, Aug. 14, 1843.
Richardson, Joseph & Sarah A. Clay, Mar. 28, 1843.
Rowland, Thomas T. & Elizabeth Smotherman, Sept. 29, 1843.
Rutledge, William A. & Sarah A. Lyell, Oct. 4, 1843.
Scales, William T. & Mary Hardeman, Oct. 21, 1843.
Shelton, Samuel & Emily A. Yardley, June 2, 1843.
Shelton, William H. & Rachel Gibson, Nov. 29, 1843.
Shelton, Wilson & Nancy A. Blaze, Oct. 5, 1843.
Shipp, William & Julia A. Pearce, Mar. 17, 1843.
Singleton, Howell & Sarah A. Holton, May 31, 1843.
Slater, Edwin C. & Ann E. Linster, Oct. 17, 1843.
Smith, James E. & Leanah Summer, Apr. 13, 1843.
Smith, John H. & Mary Ann Sanders, Jan. 25, 1843.
Smithey, Timothy & Susan Gates, Feb. 20, 1843.
Smotherman, Bartholomew & Mariah C. Sudberry,
     Aug. 19, 1843.
Smotherman, Thomas & Susan E. Sudberry, May 13, 1843.
Smothers, William & Nancy Todd, Feb. 17, 1843.
Spann, Richard H. & Lucretia Jarratt, Mar. 27, 1843.
Stovall, Joptha D. & Mildred B. Turner, Oct. 21, 1843.
Sudberry, Pattrick H. & Sarah Smotherman, May 13, 1843.
Summer, John & Louisa Adams, Jan. 26, 1843.
Summer, Moses & Eveline Smith, Feb. 22, 1843.
Summers, William & Martha Dooley, Aug. 30, 1843.
Swink, James H. A. & Judy Arnold, Aug. 22, 1843.
Thacker, Charles M. & Louisiana C. Merritt, June 7, 1843.
Thomas, Sampson & Lucretia Oakley, Jan. 7, 1843.
Thompson, Joseph & Susan Peck, Sept. 21, 1843.
Tindel, Furnery F. & Sarah Holt, July 3, 1843.
Todd, Frederick E. B. & Serenia Anderson, Feb. 18, 1843.
Travis, William & Mary A. Higenbothom, Dec. 25, 1843.
Travis, William A. & Martha B. Caldwell, Dec. 14, 1843.
Tredway, Henry H. & Tabitha Vaulx, Oct. 19, 1843.
Turner, Ephriham B. & Louisa Hall, Apr. 6, 1843.
Turner, Martin C. & Elizabeth A. Hall, June 12, 1843.
Underwood, Joseph M. & Frances Evans, Oct. 25, 1843.
Upchurch, James & Martha Bonds, July 18, 1843.
Vaughan, John S. & Elizabeth A. Jones, July 11, 1843.
Vaughan, William O. & Elizabeth H. Parker, Dec. 30, 1843.
Verdell, John D. & Elizabeth Lane, Jan. 10, 1843.
Vincent, John W. & Sarah A. Meridy, Nov. 4, 1843.
Walden, John W. & Martha Mitchell, Feb. 3, 1843.
Walden, Richard E. & Mary M. McLeek, Jan. 24, 1843.

Walpool, Benjamin H. & Elizabeth C. Walpool, Mar. 22, 1843.
Wasson, Logan A. & Sophia Lillard, Sept. 12, 1843.
Wasson, Richard & Frances L. Lillard, Aug. 30, 1843.
Welch, Nathan H. & Sarah T. Turner, Feb. 27, 1843.
Whiteman, James H. & Arena Helton, Apr. 29, 1843.
Williams, Locrick & Nancy Green, July 7, 1843.
Wills, John & Caroline E. Cox, Dec. 9, 1843.
Wooten, Henderson C. & Martha Pinkard, Oct. 12, 1843.
Wright, Stephen C. & Mary Flowers, Aug. 7, 1843.

1844

Abston, James & Martha J. Stovall, Sept. 10, 1844.
Adcock, Josiah & Tabitha Jacobs, Jan. 23, 1844.
Alford, William M. & Matilda W. Alexander, July 31, 1844.
Anderson, Patrick H. & Mary A. McGregor, Aug. 7, 1844.
Banks, William T. & Mary A. Robinson, July 24, 1844.
Bates, Jasper M. & Mary Olds (?) (Odle ?), Nov. 18, 1844.
Batey, Benjamin & Tabitha Jetton, Mar. 4, 1844.
Baucum, John & Nancy Crick, Nov. 22, 1844.
Beavers, David C. & Isabella Youree, Aug. 13, 1844.
Bell, Hezekiah & Catharine Swynk, Aug. 1, 1844.
Blake, James & Mary Ann Evans, July 1, 1844.
Boddie, Oliver B. & Josephine B. Rucker, Dec. 24, 1844.
Bostick, Jonathan & Margarett Elliott, Nov. 6, 1844.
Brandon, Robert W. & Mahala R. Ott, July 12, 1844.
Brandon, Thomas M. & Doci Ann Daniel, May 25, 1844.
Brown, John F. & Amanda Northcott, Sept. 9, 1844.
Brown, William H. & Lucinda E. Brown, Sept. 14, 1844.
Burks, James & Adaline Zackray, Mar. 11, 1844.
Burnett, Alexander M. & Cynthia Williford, July 31, 1844.
Caldwell, Thomas H. & Mary J. Hodge, Oct. 24, 1844.
Calhoun, Jefferson & Mary Davis, Aug. 7, 1844.
Campbell, Samuel & Elvira Eagleton, Aug. 7, 1844.
Carnahan, Andrew & Elizabeth McCrary, Feb. 19, 1844.
Chandler, John W. & Elizabeth J. Lawrence, July 15, 1844.
Chappell, Henry & Siothia Odell, June 29, 1844.
Chism, Davis & Mary J. Pugh, Jan. 3, 1844.
Clark, Isaiah & Elizabeth Johnson, Jan. 5, 1844.
Clark, Young & Indiana Simmons, Jan. 20, 1844.
Conley, Hardy S. & Martha E. Jones, Aug. 3, 1844.
Cook, Ellis E. & Camillia T. Hill, Dec. 28, 1844.
Cordell, Thomas M. & Mary E. Lawrence, July 16, 1844.
Cox, Samuel & Eliza Sanders, Aug. 8, 1844.
Crawford, William & Martha A. Brown, Dec. 16, 1844.
Crowder, John R. & Elizabeth E. King, Sept. 17, 1844.
Crowder, Stephen & Mary A. Rodgers, July 22, 1844.
Cruse, Beverly A. & Edy V. Webb, Aug. 10, 1844.
DeJarnatt, Daniel M. & Fanny Clayton, Apr. 11, 1844.
Denton, James & Nellie Benson, July 11, 1844.
Donaldson, Archibald Y. & Ann E. Ligon, May 23, 1844.
Douglass, George W. & Nancy K. Baugh, Jan. 23, 1844.
Drake, John P. & Melissa Hall, Dec. 24, 1844.
Drake, Mathew & Sarah Randolph, Dec. 20, 1844.
Edmonds, Thomas C. & Louisia McCray, Nov. 27, 1844.

Floyd, James H. & Martha Louisa Lawrence, Mar. 4, 1844.
Forbous, George W. & Mary Harris, Apr. 29, 1844.
Foster, James A. & Martha Wright, Jan. 5, 1844.
Foster, William & Elizabeth Coleman, Aug. 6, 1844.
Foster, William F. & Nancy Tombs, Dec. 28, 1844.
Gaines, Francis A. & Lucinda A. Whorton, Apr. 18, 1844.
Gilliland, Samuel E. & Violett B. Logan, Feb. 14, 1844.
Golliger, Michael & Levenia Cotton, Dec. 4, 1844.
Gregory, Richard & Rebecca J. Martin, Sept. 30, 1844.
Haines, Andrew J. & Lively Ann Coleman, Jan. 15, 1844.
Hale, James & Mary Hayes, Nov. 30, 1844.
Hall, Hansford R. & Orpha L. Conley, June 14, 1844.
Henry, Beverly W. & Rebecca L. Henley, Dec. 23, 1844.
Henry, Fantleroy & Sarah B. Elliott, Sept. 23, 1844.
Herrell, William F. & Mary Herrell, Feb. 7, 1844.
Higdon, William & Elizabeth Williford, May 24, 1844.
Hooberry, Jesse J. & Martha McLendon, June 10, 1844.
Howell, Alfred & Emaline Howell, Dec. 23, 1844.
Howell, William G. & Mary Catharine Revell, July 2, 1844.
Jacobs, Clinton & Mary Prewitt, Jan. 26, 1844.
Jacobs, Jackson & Sarah Rawlings, Sept. 3, 1844.
Jarratt, Sandy B. & Elizabeth E. Wheeler, Jan. 17, 1844.
Jerrell, Edmond T. & Emeline E. Nevill, July 9, 1844.
Johns, Paul V. & America C. Smith, Oct. 28, 1844.
Johnson, Benjamin & Areminta Wright, June 27, 1844.
Johnson, William E. & Nancy A. Blair, Aug. 19, 1844.
Jordan, Blount & Laura C. Brock, Sept. 28, 1844.
Jordan, Blanch & Sarah Quarles, Dec. 26, 1844.
Kelton, James L. & Eliza E. Martin, Dec. 9, 1844.
King, William & Nancy M. Bell, Oct. 3, 1844.
Knox, Joseph A. & Mary O. Elam, Jan. 22, 1844.
Lamb, Thomas & Sarah Lamb, Dec. 20, 1844.
Landrum, Merriman & Elizabeth Portis, Oct. 10, 1844.
Lawing, William & Sarah McEwin, Sept. 9, 1844.
Leath, John A. & Francis J. Gibson, May 13, 1844.
Leathers, Allen W. & Mary A. Vinson, Sept. 30, 1844.
Leigh, Daniel & Elizabeth Pugh, Mar. 11, 1844.
Lowe, James & Jane Newman, Dec. 23, 1844.
Lytle, Ephraim F. & Julia E. M. Searcy, June 12, 1844.
Martin, John D. & Mary A. Hunt, Feb. 15, 1844.
Mayfield, Isaac & Mary A. Baldridge, Oct. 9, 1844.
Mayfield, Jesse W. & Eliza Jane Bowman, Feb. 21, 1844.
Moore, James W. & Nancy Crowder, Nov. 15, 1844.
Morris, Henry & Julia Stewart, Feb. 17, 1844.
Mosley, James & Nancy C. Hogan, Dec. 7, 1844.
Mullins, Nelson & Susan A. Read, Jan. 3, 1844.
McClanahan, John B. & Hannah N. Zumbro, Apr. 10, 1844.
McCollom, Alexander & Racheal Burget, Dec. 17, 1844.
McCutchen, Fines & Joanah Summer (col), Jan. 4, 1844.
McFadden, James S. & Elizabeth A. Morgan, Mar. 11, 1844.
Nance, William W. & Theodocia B. Goodloe, Sept. 22, 1844.
Nelson, Drury D. & Elizabeth C. Nelson, Nov. 6, 1844.
Newman, John E. & Elizabeth Yearwood, Oct. 16, 1844.
Nurney, Nelson & Elizabeth Herrin, Aug. 17, 1844.
Oden, John A. & Levina S. Jarratt, Oct. 24, 1844.

Omohundro, William & Matilda Norvell, Oct. 2, 1844.
Ott, Anderson D. & Jane M. Kelton, Dec. 13, 1844.
Parsley, William N. & Manlind Sharber, Aug. 22, 1844.
Patrick, William & Jemima Smoot, Dec. 10, 1844.
Pearcy, John F. & Sarah Dunaway, Jan. 10, 1844.
Polk, Hiram & Mary Sims, July 20, 1844.
Pope, William & Clementine Rose, Jan. 12, 1844.
Powers, William D. & Nancy Davis, July 4, 1844.
Putman, James & Elizabeth Lamb, July 23, 1844.
Quarles, John W. & Frances C. Elam, Apr. 4, 1844.
Ransom, John & Nancy Crick, Nov. 21, 1844.
Reeves, Archibald F. & Virginia W. Smith, Feb. 21, 1844.
Revill, Wilson R. Y. & Elizabeth C. Howell, Mar. 27, 1844.
Richard, James & Mary Creech, Mar. 26, 1844.
Richards, William P. & Lucy J. Warpool, Dec. 13, 1844.
Roach, Neal & Missora Ann Newsom, Oct. 14, 1844.
Rooker, William & Nancy Farmer, June 18, 1844.
Ryan, Micheal T. & Rhebe Hayes, Dec. 22, 1844.
Ryan, Paterick & Mary Cotton, July 9, 1844.
Sanders, George & Martha W. Elliott, Oct. 19, 1844.
Sanders, James J. & Almira Read, Jan. 25, 1844.
Scruggs, William & Sarah W. C. Kimbro, Dec. 23, 1844.
Smith, John E. & Mary A. S. Davis, Dec. 16, 1844.
Smith, John W. & Elizabeth B. Williams, Nov. 23, 1844.
Smotherman, Barton & Terissa R. Acree, Apr. 11, 1844.
Smotherman, Eldridge & Susan T. Smith, July 15, 1844.
Spence, William & Matilda J. Wasson, Mar. 19, 1844.
Summers, Abner & Lucinda Todd, Dec. 13, 1844.
Summers, Alvin F. & Catharine Belt, July 9, 1844.
Summers, David & Malinda Summers, Oct. 28, 1844.
Tassey, David F. & Rosanah Boyd, Jan. 9, 1844.
Thompson, Eli N. & Matilda McElroy, Aug. 16, 1844.
Tiller, Henry & Elizabeth Carter, Nov. 23, 1844.
Todd, Caleb & Sarah Harrell, Oct. 23, 1844.
Todd, Jeremiah & Vicey Runnels, Oct. 26, 1844.
Tombs, William & Lavenia Nixon, July 5, 1844.
Vaughan, Robert J. & Harriett W. Winston, Dec. 17, 1844.
Vaughn, Thomas H. & Susan Lawing, Feb. 20, 1844.
Wade, Richard W. & Narcissa J. Neal, Apr. 10, 1844.
Waldron, John W. & Elizabeth A. Harman, Nov. 27, 1844.
Warren, Edwin & Cornelia A. Huggins, Feb. 1, 1844.
Webb, John F. & Sarah C. Landrom, Feb. 12, 1844.
West, Simpson & Martha Holden, Nov. 29, 1844.
Wheeler, E. D. & Margaret Eagleton, Aug. 17, 1844.
Wheeler, Hiram W. & Mary C. Jarratt, Feb. 15, 1844.
Wiggins, James D. & Mary Tutor, Dec. 16, 1844.
Wiley, Elvey & Mary Attwood, Dec. 7, 1844.
Willeford, Clabron H. & Mary E. Sanders, July 18, 1844.
Williams, James R. & Susannah Batey, May 1, 1844.
Wilson, William & Sally Rouse (col), Jan. 13, 1844.
Wood, George W. & Mary Posey, Jan. 30, 1844.
Wood, Thomas & Mary Ann Overall, Feb. 20, 1844.
Wright, John J. & Martha C. Batey, Jan. 15, 1844.
Yager, Edward & Mary A. Green, Oct. 29, 1844.
Youree, Francis O. & Matilda C. Patrick, Jan. 16, 1844.

Zumbro, William & Cyntha Yearwood, Oct. 13, 1844.

1845

Adams, Reubin & Elizabeth Bell, June 14, 1845.
Allen, Richard H. & Amanda M. Coleman, Aug. 25, 1845.
Alsup, Layfayett & Elizabeth J. Lannum, Nov. 4, 1845.
Anderson, James & Emily Beesley, Sept. 13, 1845.
Anderson, James & Docie Campbell, Oct. 14, 1845.
Archer, Samuel & Aberilla Collins (free of col),
   Feb. 1, 1845.
Baker, John L. & Sarah C. Renshaw, July 3, 1845.
Baley, Richard & Mahaley Jacobs, May 27, 1845.
Ballard, Riley & California A. Patterson, Nov. 19, 1845.
Baltimore, John & Phebe Todd, Sept. 11, 1845.
Barnes, Simmons & Mary J. Shaver, July 22, 1845.
Bass, Thomas & Nancy Avent, Jan. 15, 1845.
Bell, George D. & Nancy Trigg, Dec. 13, 1845.
Bell, John & Mary Mathews, Feb. 7, 1845.
Bennett, John & Elizabeth Cook, Feb. 19, 1845.
Bivins, Silas A. & Lucy W. Ganaway, Dec. 15, 1845.
Blackman, Lazrus & Virginia A. Smith, Oct. 6, 1845.
Boner, Michael J. & Martha A. Pugh, Sept. 11, 1845.
Bostick, James A. & Mary J. Elliott, Jan. 15, 1845.
Brinkley, Amos & Simme Herrod, Apr. 26, 1845.
Brown, Edmund D. & Mary E. Bowman, June 13, 1845.
Brown, Francis S. & Elizabeth A. Taylor, Aug. 15, 1845.
Brown, Joseph & Lamanda M. E. Martin, Mar. 1, 1845.
Brown, Phillip J. & Ana E. Reeves, Jan. 30, 1845.
Bumpass, Robert & Sarah Wood, July 30, 1845.
Burchett, William T. & Mary Johnson, Jan. 2, 1845.
Burk, James & Sarah E. Foster, May 16, 1845.
Burnes, William & Jana Cotton, Dec. 4, 1845.
Carnahan, Preston & Sarah B. McCrary, Aug. 21, 1845.
Carter, Culin & Ruth Hailey, Sept. 18, 1845.
Carter, Joseph & Susan R. Carnahan, Jan. 15, 1845.
Clark, Isaiah & Elizabeth Johnson, Jan. 3, 1845.
Clark, Newton & Elizabeth Morgan, Feb. 21, 1845.
Collier, James M. & Eliza L. McFadden, Nov. 6, 1845.
Cox, William & Permilia F. Sanders, May 30, 1845.
Craig, William B. & Mary J. Davis, July 1, 1845.
Crawford, Joseph G. & Mary A. Sage, Feb. 25, 1845.
Crichlow, James & Jane Sims, July 5, 1845.
Crichlow, Thomas H. & Helen M. Wasson, Oct. 15. 1845.
Crocker, Isaac & Elizabeth Jetton, Oct. 9, 1845.
Cross, George W. & Mary E. Flemming, Mar. 10, 1845.
Crutchfield, John & Mary Eastwood, Nov. 25, 1845.
Curtis, William & Lucy Cogburn, Dec. 31, 1845.
Dailey, Michael C. & Martha Cotton, Aug. 25, 1845.
Daniel, James E. & Susanah Helton, Jan. 14, 1845.
Daulton, William & Sarah M. Allen, July 3, 1845.
Davis, Drury & Lethsha Abbott, Aug. 7, 1845.
Davis, Phillip & Rebecca Smith, Jan. 27, 1845.
Davis, William & Melinda Ward, Sept. 19, 1845.
Davidson, Lewis & Zalpha Rogers, Aug. 7, 1845.

Dean, John W. & Adaline Wills, Oct. 10, 1845.
Dickey, William E. & Lidia Phelps, Sept. 11, 1845.
Dickson, John D. & Margaret McKissick, Aug. 28, 1845.
Dillon, John & Eleanor Knox, Apr. 22, 1845.
Doughtry, William & Nancy Howland, Dec. 23, 1845.
Eakes, Daniel & Mary M. Holt, Apr. 3, 1845.
Farliss, Elisha & Arcy A. Lyell, Oct. 10, 1845.
Flemming, George W. & Susan A. Cross, Apr. 10, 1845.
Flemming, William & Elizabeth Joy, Oct. 23, 1845.
Fletcher, John W. & Louisa E. Geanes, Apr. 10, 1845.
Fossett, James & Catharine C. Bowman, Sept. 18, 1845.
Foster, Chestine & Matilda Davidson, Dec. 24, 1845.
Foster, John & Marandy D. Sanders, Sept. 15, 1845.
Freeman, Daniel M. & Nancy E. Fulks, Sept. 8, 1845.
Freeman, William & Matilda Mearhead, Jan. 19, 1845.
Fretwell, Joshiah & Sarah Ann Mosley, May 27, 1845.
Gooden, John D. & Ladosha Thompson, Feb. 3, 1845.
Goodloe, William H. & Sarah P. Hall, Dec. 31, 1845.
Green, Joseph A. & Emily Smotherman, Dec. 29, 1845.
Green, Thomas J. & Ardenia F. Todd, Feb. 24, 1845.
Greer, Henry & Lucinda Bell, Dec. 27, 1845.
Gregory, Alexander & Frances May, Dec. 15, 1845.
Griffin, Andrew J. & Louisa Ferriss, July 26, 1845.
Hall, Jacob G. & Eliza A. McDaniel, Jan. 16, 1845.
Hardy, Samuel M. & Sarah A. Goss, Feb. 10, 1845.
Harris, Allen & Mary Smith, Aug. --, 1845.
Harris, John & Harriet T. Moore, June 7, 1845.
Henry, Joel G. & Mary Ann Sneed, Nov. 16, 1845.
Herndon, Samuel & Martha Batey, July 19, 1845.
Hoover, John P. & Susan A. McKee, Jan. 30, 1845.
Howse, Charles A. & Elizabeth Delbridge, Dec. 9, 1845.
Howse, George W. & Mary E. Burris, Feb. 12, 1845.
Hume, Jesse W. & Mary J. Weakley, Mar. 10, 1845.
Hutcherson, John L. & Ann W. Whitlow, Feb. 13, 1845.
Jacobs, John G. & Margaret A. Mathews, Aug. 21, 1845.
Jackson, James L. & Angeline Landrum, Aug. 28, 1845.
Jameson, Thomas & Catharine Donnelly, Sept. 9, 1845.
January, Robert W. & Martha A. Watts, Aug. 24, 1845.
Jetton, P. D. & Mary Stegar, Feb. 28, 1845.
Johnson, James N. & Martha Adcock, Mar. 30, 1845.
Johnson, William H. & Sarah Thompson, July 24, 1845.
Jones, Bedford C. & Louisa Fall Jones, Mar. 20, 1845.
Jones, Gaston & Frances C. Cothrin, Dec. 23, 1845.
Keeble, Walter & Eliza Edmondson, Mar. 12, 1845.
Keys, Erasmus S. & Nancy D. Todd, Aug. 19, 1845.
King, John & Elizabeth Ralph, Feb. 19, 1845.
King, Rufus & Eliza Sanford, Oct. 4, 1845.
Kirk, John J. & Nancy M. Brothers, Mar. 10, 1845.
Lamb, Benjamin & Sophia Smotherman, July 24, 1845.
Lambert, William C. & Harriett H. Grimes, Dec. 15, 1845.
Lassiter, William M. & Nancy G. Murphey, Feb. 17, 1845.
Lawhorn, Exum & Frances Anglin, Nov. 8, 1845.
Lawhorn, Thomas M. & Nancy Greer, Sept. 27, 1845.
Lawing, Robert & Elenor Ward, Apr. 20, 1845.
Lewis, Richard H. & Chelnisa D. Dickie, Sept. 24, 1845.

Lillard, George W. & Elmira Saunders, Nov. 30, 1845.
Luman, James J. & Martha E. Campbell, Apr. 22, 1845.
Marchant, Wilie & Eny Taylor, Dec. 19, 1845.
Mayfield, John C. & Catharine Arnold, Sept. 2, 1845.
Miller, Isaac L. & Sarah G. Hankins, Oct. 16, 1845.
Miller, James & Susan A. Nichols, Dec. 18, 1845.
Mitchell, Eli C. & Sarah A. Lively, Dec. 16, 1845.
Morgan, Wesley & Milly Summars, Jan. 18, 1845.
McDonald, James A. & Martha McRoy, --- --, 1845.
McIntire, James & Eveline Ward, Jan. 10, 1845.
McKee, Andrew & Catharine Martin, July 7, 1845.
McLaughlin, William H. & Margaret K. Edkridge, Apr. 19,
   1845.
McLean, Alney H. & Martha J. Moore, Nov. 25, 1845.
Nixon, William & Lucy Tombs, Apr. 8, 1845.
Omohundro, James Y. & Catharine Clark, Nov. 10, 1845.
Osment, Y. N. & Nancy Wooten, May 10, 1845.
Owen, John W. & Frances H. Tune, Oct. 8, 1845.
Owen, William E. & Martha Hoover, Oct. 1, 1845.
Patterson, Hillery & Susan Webb, Nov. 10, 1845.
Pearce, William & Mary Sexton, June 28, 1845.
Pearson, Joseph & Mary Newman, Aug. 11, 1845.
Pey, Thomas T. & Nancy S. Kelton, Feb. 19, 1845.
Pigg, James & Elizabeth Hamilton, Apr. 11, 1845.
Pinkard, William & Caroline E. Howell, June 18, 1845.
Powers, William B. & Nancy Davis, July 13, 1845.
Prater, Aaron & Mary Fulks, Mar. 8, 1845.
Primm, John G. & Mary E. Jackson, July 14, 1845.
Prince, Alfred & Elizabeth Tucker, May 15, 1845.
Putnam, Simpson & Emaline Webb, Jan. 22, 1845.
Ramsey, Samuel & Mary A. Clark, Feb. 4, 1845.
Ransom, William A. & Susan F. Johns, Feb. 19, 1845.
Rawlings, William & Rebecca Tribble, Mar. 5, 1845.
Richardson, Robert B. & Mary E. Avent, Nov. 18, 1845.
Ridley, James A. & Elmire Russwurm, Dec. 22, 1845.
Rodgers, George B. & Leann Miller, June 5, 1845.
Rowan, Stokely D. & Jane E. Grundy, Nov. 25, 1845.
Rucker, Robert B. & Mary Harrison, Feb. 25, 1845.
Sartor, William & Levy Ann Sanders, June 21, 1845.
Sarver, Jacob A. & Martha A. Jetton, Apr. 10, 1845.
Saunders, Jesse B. & Mary Lillard, July 10, 1845.
Seargint, Edward H. & Eliza Read, Jan. 9, 1845.
Simpson, David M. & Mary Ann S. Brooks, Mar. 13, 1845.
Smith, George S. & Elizabeth R. Dunlap, Feb. 1, 1845.
Smith, James & Luninda Summer (col), July 10, 1845.
Smith, Jonathan G. & Jane E. Mayfield, Oct. 22, 1845.
Smith, Morgan & Malinda Statham, Dec. 26, 1845.
Smith, William R. & Sarah S. Tatum, Dec. 25, 1845.
Smotherman, Elbert & Elmira Woodson, Mar. 10, 1845.
Smotherman, James F. & Virginia Johnson, Sept. 6, 1845.
Smotherman, Jonathan P. & Rebecca S. May, Apr. 16, 1845.
Stewart, William & Nancy Hill (col), Mar. 22, 1845.
Summers, Benjamin & Nancy Vandergriff, Apr. 9, 1845.
Taylor, Andrew J. & Martha A. Webb, Sept. 24, 1845.

Taylor, Joseph M. & Frances A. Holden, Apr. 2, 1845.
Taylor, Powell & Caroline Smith, Feb. 17, 1845.
Tucker, Gideon & Mary Tider, Mar. 31, 1845.
Tune, Travis H. & Mary E. Mullins, June 25, 1845.
Walden, Erastus S. & Paralee Leek, Sept. 6, 1845.
Waller, Benjamin P. & Elizabeth Miller, Nov. 4, 1845.
Williams, Isaac H. & Ailsy A. Crowder, Sept. 27, 1845.
Winston, Samuel & Ezabella E. Rucker, Oct. 18, 1845.
Wood, John & Rebecca Webb, June 28, 1845.
Wood, Johnson & Elizabeth Johnson, Nov. 1, 1845.
Wood, Robert H. & Amanda M. Nash, Aug. 25, 1845.
Woodliff, William L. & Elizabeth Trail, June 2, 1845.

1846

Adcock, William V. & Elenor Puckett, Mar. 25, 1846.
Allen, George W. & Lucy J. Pearson, Dec. 24, 1846.
Arnett, James & Martha McCullough, Feb. 19, 1846.
Baker, William H. & Mary E. Hester, June 5, 1846.
Ball, William J. & Mary Crowse, Sept. 5, 1846.
Barnes, Simmons & Mary J. Shaver, Aug. 7, 1846.
Barton, Bedford H. & Clementine Barnes, Dec. 17, 1846.
Batey, Henry H. & Judy A. Jarratt, Oct. 29, 1846.
Bell, John L. & Catharine Thomas, Jan. 1, 1846.
Bell, Zedick & Elizabeth C. Mathews, Sept. 11, 1846.
Belt, Dotson & Nancy Daughtery, Oct. 24, 1846.
Belt, Martin & Lurenia T. Luck, Sept. 15, 1846.
Bivins, Joseph & Elizabeth Goode, Aug. 16, 1846.
Black, Lunsford T. & Martha A. Nelson, Apr. 7, 1846.
Bond, Asaph & Mary A. Carnes, Feb. 24, 1846.
Bowen, John W. & Sarah J. Barkley, Oct. 10, 1846.
Bowling, James & Rebecca C. Herrod, Nov. 10, 1846.
Bowling, Joseph H. & Elizabeth E. Shipp, Dec. 9, 1846.
Bradley, William M. & Martha J. R. Barkley, Dec. 2, 1846.
Broiles, Mathias & Jemima Hoover, Jan. 30, 1846.
Bullard, John D. & Margaret Bruce, June 27, 1846.
Cheatham, William A. & Mary A. Ready, Oct. 20, 1846.
Clark, William A. & Margaret M. Lock, Dec. 23, 1846.
Cockreal, James & Sarah A. Cheatham, Dec. 21, 1846.
Coleman, James E. & Mary A. E. Nance, Jan. 15, 1846.
Coleman, William C. & Rebecca H. Coleman, Aug. 4, 1846.
Collins, Thomas & Micha McLaren, Oct. 26, 1846.
Dement, John B. & Nancy J. Morrow, June 16, 1846.
Dorsey, Alexander & Jane Fox, Jan. 12, 1846.
Douglas, James H. & Martha A. Kerby, Jan. 21, 1846.
Dunaway, Jacob & Elizabeth Dunaway, Feb. 2, 1846.
Edmonds, Henry L. & Sarah A. Stegall, Jan. 26, 1846.
Edwards, Thomas M. & Susan Henry, Dec. 24, 1846.
Elliote, Joseph & Harriett C. Daniel, Dec. 17, 1846.
Espey, John W. A. & Susan Parker, Nov. 26, 1846.
Evans, Riley & Mica P. Barker, Feb. 18, 1846.
Ewell, Jessee & Rebecca Hurse, Feb. 28, 1846.
Farless, Martin & Mary A. Daulton, Nov. 4, 1846.
Ford, Lewallen & Louisia M. Carson, Feb. 10, 1846.
Ford, Pleasant & Elizabeth Warrne, Apr. 22, 1846.

Floyd, William S. & Elizabeth S. Woosley, Apr. 14, 1846.
Freeman, James H. & Elizabeth Prater, Dec. 2, 1846.
Freeman, Robert W. & Loudicy K. Neal, Nov. 3, 1846.
Gallaway, Lewis G. & Martha Ella Dickinson, Sept. 10, 1846.
George, Robert S. & Mary E. Smith, Mar. 14, 1846.
Gowen, Kendrew & Lyda Williams, July 13, 1846.
Gregory, Henry & Mary G. Mason, Apr. 14, 1846.
Grogan, James H. & Adelane Lane, May 25, 1846.
Gum, John & Cynthia C. McCracken, Apr. 3, 1846.
Hall, W. C. & Elizabeth Dill, May 23, 1846.
Harris, James & Elizabeth J. Gambill, June 15, 1846.
Harrison, John H. & Julia F. Atkinson, Feb. 11, 1846.
Hart, Samuel & Edny M. Hedgepeth, Dec. 23, 1846.
Hawley, Joseph & Eliza Logan (col), Mar. 30, 1846.
Hayes, Newett & Nancy Gates, Nov. 2, 1846.
Haynes, Nicholas & Margaret J. Neal, Dec. 20, 1846.
Height, James W. & Nancy E. Neely, Nov. 20, 1846.
Henderson, Harmon L. & Louisia C. Henderson, Nov. 16, 1846.
Henry, William B. & Mary L. Kelton, Oct. 22, 1846.
Herrington, James & Nancy McKee, June 20, 1846.
Hill, James & Olevar A. Hutcherson, Nov. 23, 1846.
Hill, William H. & Minerva F. Vernon, Nov. 2, 1846.
Holden, James & Jane Smotherman, Jan. 6, 1846.
Hopkins, James C. & Nancy Adcock, Dec. 3, 1846.
Howland, John & Jane Waller, Apr. 15, 1846.
Hunter, James H. & Sarah Morrow, July 1, 1846.
Hutcherson, William S. & Rebecca Pearson, Sept. 23, 1846.
Jaunary, William H. & Matilda Hardeman, Apr. 11, 1846.
Johnson, Charles & Sally Summers, Jan. 10, 1846.
Johnson, Eakin & Sarah Rushing, Mar. 7, 1846.
Johnson, Joel & Martha Newman, Oct. 12, 1846.
Johnson, Joshua & Amanda C. C. Wright, Mar. 7, 1846.
Jones, George & Ann C. Smith (col), Nov. 17, 1846.
Jones, William A. & Mary S. Conley, July 22, 1846.
Kellough, William A. & Elizabeth P. Nash, Oct. 29, 1846.
Kelly, A. G. & Pauline J. Ramsey, Aug. 28, 1846.
King, Robert & Matilda Bell, Jan. 24, 1846.
Landrum, Azariah K. & Martha Tutor, Oct. 1, 1846.
Lane, William T. & Catharine Chisenall, Jan. 12, 1846.
Lannom, John M. & Mary B. Lannom, Dec. 15, 1846.
Lannom, Joseph & Jane Brewer, June 16, 1846.
Lenoir, Isaac P. & Mary C. Hogge, Apr. 7, 1846.
Logan, William C. & Martha Fields, June 6, 1846.
Lowe, Robert W. & Nancy N. Rawlings, Oct. 1, 1846.
Martin, Noah & Charlotte P. Howse, May 30, 1846.
Maxwell, Abner T. & Margaret C. Smotherman, Aug. 15, 1846.
Maxwell, James T. & Nancy Smotherman, Sept. 3, 1846.
Maxwell, John A. & Margaret J. Redding, Feb. 2, 1846.
Maxwell, William P. & Louisa Smotherman, May 4, 1846.
Milton, James & Mary Creek, June 10, 1846.
Milton, Newton & Louisia Milton, Sept. 30, 1846.
Morris, Robert & Martha A. Boatwright, Apr. 1, 1846.

Morrow, William T. & Eliza J. Moore, Mar. 7, 1846.
Morton, Jacob J. & Amanda G. Edwards, Jan. 28, 1846.
Mosley, Thomas G. & Mary Sikes, Dec. 16, 1846.
McCullough, Henry & Eliza W. Bigham, Sept. 1, 1846.
McCullough, Phillip D. & Lucy Burrus, Nov. 18, 1846.
McEntire, William & Nancy Ward, May 13, 1846.
McGill, Isaac & Elizabeth A. McCrary, Mar. 9, 1846.
McKee, Ambrose & Mary Crook, Nov. 3, 1846.
McKee, James H. & Elizabeth Martin, Jan. 20, 1846.
McKnight, James D. & Virginia F. Smith, Nov. 17, 1846.
McKnight, William W. & Eliza Y. McFarland, Jan. 23, 1846.
McLin, James S. & Sarah Earthman, Apr. 22, 1846.
Norman, Benjamin P. & Mary J. Gowan, Feb. 2, 1846.
Owen, Thomas & Prudence Hall, Dec. 17, 1846.
Parrish, William C. & Jane Allen, Apr. 16, 1846.
Pattrick, John G. & Elizabeth Sneed, Jan. 6, 1846.
Peel, George W. & Mahulda W. Winston, Jan. 8, 1846.
Phelps, James & Emeline Starkey, Nov. 3, 1846.
Phelps, Joshua & Martha Jones, Jan. 1, 1846.
Phelps, Wilson H. & Mary W. Tune, Apr. 6, 1846.
Pinson, Joel & Rebecca Wilkinson, June 22, 1846.
Pitts, Anderson & Martha M. Flemming, Oct. 20, 1846.
Posey, William Y. & Martha M. Bumpass, Nov. 12, 1846.
Priestly, John T. & Eliza B. Williams, Nov. 7, 1846.
Read, Clement T. & Rebecca L. Jackson, Dec. 26, 1846.
Read, William A. & Martha A. Major, Oct. 13, 1846.
Reed, George W. & Ann E. Brooks, Sept. 28, 1846.
Rowan, William B. & Susan Watkins, Feb. 25, 1846.
Rowland, William & Elizabeth Brown, July 18, 1846.
Rowlett, Edward A. & Rebecca Blankenship, Jan. 14, 1846.
Rowlett, Peter M. & Lovy Ann Cobler, Aug. 25, 1846.
Rucker, Samuel J. & Mary E. Mitchell, Sept. 29, 1846.
Rushing, Bartley M. & Nancy M. Butler, Mar. 14, 1846.
Rushing, John C. & Nancy Daughtry, Aug. 4, 1846.
Sanders, Marshall H. & Sarah Jamison, July 28, 1846.
Sanders, Richard B. & Mary K. Owen, Jan. 22, 1846.
Sanders, Samuel R. & Sarah A. Thompson, Mar. 31, 1846.
Saunders, Jarratt & Lydia R. Spickard, Aug. 20, 1846.
Saunders, Thomas S. & Lucinda Hedgpeth, Nov. 13, 1846.
Sewell, William & Mary Perryman, Mar. 26, 1846.
Shelton, James H. & Mary A. Hoover, Feb. 18, 1846.
Shelton, Liffus & Susannah M. L. Bowman, Dec. 11, 1846.
Sherrell, Alexander N. & Parthenia N. Mason, Jan. 12,
1846.
Singleton, Chappell H. & Martha J. Dunn, July 16, 1846.
Smith, Archibald N. & Sarah Farmer, Feb. 20, 1846.
Smith, John & Elizabeth Newgent, May 13, 1846.
Smith, Malcomb & Jane Moore, Jan. 24, 1846.
Smith, Robert & Susan Finney, Feb. 7, 1846.
Smith, William & Louvisa C. Aclin, Jan. 22, 1846.
Smith, William A. & Lucy F. Rucker, Feb. 11, 1846.
Spence, William J. & Amy L. Smotherman, Sept. 21, 1846.
Summers, William & Jane Patterson, Mar. 8, 1846.
Taylor, James & Ellen Thomas, Feb. 7, 1846.

Taylor, James P. & Margaret Ransom, Aug. 3, 1846.
Taylor, John & Frances Jackson, Sept. 3, 1846.
Thompson, Young & Elizabeth Woods, Mar. 19, 1846.
Tombs, Willie & Mary A. Hodge, Sept. 19, 1846.
Traylor, Edmund P. & Sarah W. H. Neely, May 16, 1846.
Traylor, Hilas & Catharine O. Beesley, Feb. 19, 1846.
Tucker, Granville T. & Matilda Claxton, Jan. 13, 1846.
Tudor, John & Sarah Thomas, Mar. 3, 1846.
Vardell, William & Lucinda E. Covington, Nov. 21, 1846.
Vaughan, Ambrose W. & Sarah W. Elliott, Aug. 17, 1846.
Vaughan, James R. & Michey F. Brown, May 15, 1846.
Vaughter, William B. & Amanda M. Goodman, Dec. 30, 1846.
Walker, James A. & Lucinda W. Sanders, Mar. 7, 1846.
Warren, John & Jane R. Cox, May 23, 1846.
Webber, Richard & Mary J. Arnold, July 25, 1846.
Western, James J. & Amanda Richardson, Oct. 24, 1846.
Wherry, Legrand & Lucinda Dunn, Sept. 30, 1846.
Williams, Benjamin & Mary Smotherman, Sept. 21, 1846.
Williams, James R. & Persila Davis, Mar. 4, 1846.
Williams, Robert B. & Ann E. Mullins, May 15, 1846.
Williams, William & Elizabeth Anderson, Jan. 2, 1846.
Winfrey, Allen & Susan Webb, Sept. 18, 1846.
Winsett, Abraham G. & Virginia Wood, June 29, 1846.
Winsett, John T. & Tempy Heath, Nov. 21, 1846.
Winsett, Jonas J. & Mary A. C. Landrum, May 15, 1846.
Winsett, Josiah F. & Evergreen A. Jackson, Sept. 30, 1846.
Wood, John H. & Nancy W. West, Apr. 22, 1846.
Wrather, Baker & Levenia Green, Nov. 24, 1846.
Wrather, William B. & Mary A. Kellough, Nov. 13, 1846.
Wray, James E. & Elizabeth E. Burns, Nov. 6, 1846.
Zumbro, George W. & Elvira E. Frost, Mar. 2, 1846.

1847

Albright, John & Catharine Waller, Aug. 16, 1847.
Allen, Samuel J. & Susan Prince, Apr. 19, 1847.
Allen, Tilford R. & Mary Kerby, Dec. 9, 1847.
Allison, Daniel & Elizabeth Green, Oct. 2, 1847.
Allman, Lemuel & Charity A. Allen, Oct. 18, 1847.
Anderson, Henderson & Nancy J. McGill, Aug. 18, 1847.
Arnette, John & Martha A. McEwing, Dec. 8, 1847.
Arnold, William & Eleanor Elliott, Jan. 30, 1847.
Avritte, Francis M. & Louisa E. Bishop, Oct. 24, 1847.
Barlow, Cyrus Y. & Nancy C. McDaniel, Oct. 6, 1847.
Barlow, Kendall H. & Nancy D. Garner, Aug. 12, 1847.
Barrett, Randolph C. & Julia H. Evans, May 31, 1847.
Bass, Isaac B. & Elen E. Hager, Mar. 20, 1847.
Beasley, James P. & Sarah Burnes, Apr. 5, 1847.
Bellah, William E. & Sarah G. Thompson, Aug. 31, 1847.
Biles, Obediah & Martha Keeble, Nov. 5, 1847.
Bishop, Abner & Sarah Forehand, Sept. 20, 1847.
Blakemore, Pleasant M. & Fanny Cook, July 13, 1847.
Blanton, Albert G. & Frances B. Yandell, Feb. 16, 1847.
Blithe, Moses & Barbary Helton, Aug. 3, 1847.

Bowerman, Milton & Jane Kelton, Dec. 8, 1847.
Brewer, John & Nancy M. Carter, Dec. 29, 1847.
Burns, Ivey P. & Julia Ann Boatwright, Jan. 12, 1847.
Butler, George C. & Mary I. Lyle, Dec. 28, 1847.
Carpenter, Charles & Lucinda Kennedy, Nov. 11, 1847.
Charlton, George W. & Mary H. Hannah, Mar. 22, 1847.
Chisenall, James & Susan Cox, Aug. 14, 1847.
Christopher, Thomas & Lucy Newsom, Nov. 3, 1847.
Claud, Frances N. & Amanda F. Smith, Mar. 9, 1847.
Clay, John A. & Susan Roberts, Jan. 20, 1847.
Cody, William S. & America Davis, Mar. 17, 1847.
Cole, William T. & Mary I. Mathews, Feb. 8, 1847.
Coleman, Edwin & Mary G. Wrather, June 21, 1847.
Coleman, James E. & Mary Jane Allen, Jan. 2, 1847.
Cone, George W. & Margaret Howland, June 29, 1847.
Cooke, Richard D. & Elizabeth Davis, Apr. 27, 1847.
Coulter, Sherley & Mary E. Mullins, Dec. 28, 1847.
Crick, Perry & Martha Trail, May 11, 1847.
Crick, James & Rebecca Mangrum, June 24, 1847.
Crockett, Overton W. & Caroline Ransom, Aug. 18, 1847.
Crutchfield, John H. & Nancy C. Bell, Nov. 4, 1847.
Curl, Andrew J. & Manervia Lorance, Dec. 11, 1847.
Curlee, John F. & Julia R. Jarratt, Dec. 2, 1847.
Davidson, George W. & Lucy Moore, Apr. 14, 1847.
Dement, David & Eliza E. Jordan, Aug. 5, 1847.
Dement, Joseph A. & Margaret J. Lackey, Mar. 25, 1847.
Douglass, Abram & Nancy Maxwell, Aug. 23, 1847.
Douglass, James & Elvira Stovall, June 12, 1847.
Drumright, Alexander J. & Rhonda Ann McDowell, Feb. 26,
    1847.
Eastwood, William & Nancy A. Johnson, Apr. 20, 1847.
Earthman, William W. & Elizabeth Bumpass, Oct. 26, 1847.
Edes, William & Susan Woods, Nov. 16, 1847.
Escue, Hardin (col) & Eliza A. Holly, Nov. 22, 1847.
Espey, George & Ann Wright, Apr. 3, 1847.
Floyd, Thomas A. & Lucinda Thomas, Dec. 29, 1847.
Forbs, William & Rebecca Williams, Aug. 31, 1847.
Fowler, John G. & Amanda E. Crocker, Nov. 22, 1847.
Furgerson, George W. & Sarah J. January, Nov. 7, 1847.
Fuller, Thomas & Margarett Ann Barnett, Feb. 25, 1847.
Garner, Nathan G. & Emily A. Blair, Dec. 20, 1847.
Gates, Joseph & Susan Eastwood, May 17, 1847.
Goss, Charles B. & Margaret J. Smith, Dec. 6, 1847.
Graham, Dudley J. & Elizabeth Goodloe, Nov. 30, 1847.
Gray, Abraham C. & Usley M. Espey, Dec. 27, 1847.
Greer, Stephen & Nancy Chestnut, Feb. 26, 1847.
Grimes, Richard & Airey Acree, Dec. 25, 1847.
Gumm, William N. & Margarett Ward, Jan. 3, 1847.
Hager, Peter J. & Sarah A. Rowlett, Dec. 15, 1847.
Hale, Wilson & Caroline Northcott, Dec. 6, 1847.
Hall, Seth J. & Martha E. Lewis, Jan. 25, 1847.
Halston, Benjamin & Casarinda Cullum, Dec. 11, 1847.
Hamilton, Thomas & Ester C. Miller, Jan. 5, 1847.
Hart, William & Mary E. Batey, Nov. 17, 1847.

RUTHERFORD COUNTY MARRIAGES

Hawkins, Alvin & Justina M. Ott, Aug. 16, 1847.
Hawkins, Elisha & Eleanor Wilson, Feb. 3, 1847.
Henderson, Albert G. & Elizabeth M. Love, Aug. 31, 1847.
Heugley, John & Malinda G. Brewer, May 17, 1847.
Hill, William G. & Emaline Patterson, May 10, 1847.
Holden, Joseph & Rachel A. Douglass, Nov. 8, 1847.
Hollowell, James J. & Cynthia A. McLean, July 19, 1847.
Hoover, Mathias W. & Martha Bailey, Nov. 16, 1847.
Hunt, Bennett S. & Sarah Arnett, Nov. 15, 1847.
Hunt, Thomas & Asenath Jacobs, Oct. 23, 1847.
Hunter, David & Rebecca Rowlett, Dec. 21, 1847.
Hutcherson, William & Nancy Hunt, Mar. 31, 1847.
Jackson, James & Zilpha Bolton, Mar. 10, 1847.
Jackson, Newton C. & Matilda J. Jackson, June 24, 1847.
Jackson, William H. & Elizabeth T. Edwards, Nov. 20, 1847.
Jamison, Henry & Leticher H. Jones, Oct. 23, 1847.
Jewell, William C. & Nancy Dunaway, Jan. 13, 1847.
Johns, Joseph B. & Margarett J. Wade, Jan. 12, 1847.
Johnson, James M. & Margarett Nichols, Oct. 25, 1847.
Johnson, James M. & Susan Price, Sept. 29, 1847.
Jolly, Thomas J. & Mary C. McCulloch, June 7, 1847.
Jordan, Constantine & Nancy N. Morton, Mar. 15, 1847.
Jordan, Isaiah & Frances Pyland, Mar. 10, 1847.
Jordan, James B. & Angelina A. Anderson, Mar. 15, 1847.
Jordan, Micheal B. & Sarah R. Jones, Oct. 25, 1847.
Jordan, Stephen & Margarette Blanch, Nov. 27, 1847.
Keeble, Horace P. & Cassndra C. Currin, June 22, 1847.
Kelton, Thomas C. & Sarah Dunn, Oct. 14, 1847.
Lewis, Abram & Nancy Mosley, Nov. 19, 1847.
Lewis, Joseph & Francis E. Dickie, Nov. 8, 1847.
Lorance, George W. & Rebecca E. Burchley, Dec. 2, 1847.
Love, Thomas B. & Frances A. Bethshares, Dec. 23, 1847.
Lynch, Andrew J. & Frances A. Edmonds, Nov. 10, 1847.
Lytle, John & Jane H. King, Apr. 7, 1847.
Manire, Edmund H. & Elizabeth J. Sharber, Mar. 3, 1847.
Martin, John & Elizabeth Kelton, Oct. 13, 1847.
Mason, Henry & Jane S. Haynes, June 25, 1847.
Maxwell, William A. & Sophia Whitelock, July 19, 1847.
Maxwell, William F. & Susan K. Butts, May 20, 1847.
May, William W. & Sarah J. Beesley, Aug. 26, 1847.
Miller, Felix G. & Sarah Given, Oct. 19, 1847.
Miller, James C. & Elizabeth M. Arnold, Dec. 15, 1847.
Miller, Joseph & Nancy W. Lewis, Dec. 21, 1847.
Milliken, George H. & Sonora T. Vaughan, Sept. 27, 1847.
Mitchell, Calvin G. & Sarah E. W. Gannaway, Jan. 19, 1847.
Mobbs, Jesse & Martha Merritt, May 7, 1847.
Morgan, William & Izabella C. Means, July 19, 1847.
Morrow, John H. & Mary E. Moore, Oct. 9, 1847.
Morton, Arbam W. & Martha A. Allen, Feb. 20, 1847.
McCabe, Joseph B. & Sarah M. Brown, June 5, 1847.
McCaul, James J. & Matilda C. Kelton, Sept. 2, 1847.
McClure, James R. & Lucinda Ellis, Dec. 21, 1847.
McDaniel, John & Elizabeth McElroy, Sept. 13, 1847.

113

McElroy, Newton A. & Susan Neely, Sept. 13, 1847.
McEntire, William & Nancy Ward, May 13, 1847.
McGill, James & Amanda M. N. Lowe, Nov. 25, 1847.
Mac Gowan, Thomas M. & Martha Rodgers, Nov. 20, 1847.
Mac Gowan, William & Rebecca J. Loyd, Feb. 6, 1847.
McKee, William P. & Elizabeth A. Fox, Nov. 9, 1847.
Neely, John D. & Matilda Read, Nov. 8, 1847.
Newsom, Balam & Ann Elizabeth McCray, Dec. 21, 1847.
Norman, Logan H. & Amanda R. Parker, Dec. 22, 1847.
Northcott, Andrew J. & Nancy R. Arnold, Feb. 6, 1847.
Northcott, James M. & Eliza McKee, Nov. 29, 1847.
Ott, J. N. & Mary A. Bishop, Dec. 17, 1847.
Owen, Thomas & Prudence Hall, Dec. 16, 1847.
Pace, William C. & Mary E. McCracken, Feb. 19, 1847.
Partlow, James W. & Sarah J. Arnold, July 3, 1847.
Peck, Josiah & Nancy E. Burchett, May 27, 1847.
Peck, William & Sarah A. Wheeler, Dec. 23, 1847.
Pendergrass, Pleasant & Amanda J. Stovall, Oct. 14, 1847.
Petty, Charles & Nancy P. Youree, Dec. 21, 1847.
Phillips, John M. & Margarett C. Pugh, Jan. 9, 1847.
Phillips, William R. & Elizabeth M. Conley, Oct. 5,
   1847.
Prater, Monroe & Caroline Knox, Aug. 27, 1847.
Raby, E. B. & Elizabeth Wood, Nov. 18, 1847.
Read, Richard G. & Nancy C. Sanders, Feb. 24, 1847.
Rowton, Ryland & Elizabeth J. Lewis, June 8, 1847.
Runnels, Pollard R. & Mary E. Maxwell, Dec. 8, 1847.
Sanders, Thomas L. & Margarett J. Ralph, Feb. 9, 1847.
Sanders, Whitfield & Elizabeth McCray, Feb. 22, 1847.
Segraves, William & Jane C. Brown, May 13, 1847.
Shelton, John & Elizabeth Bennett, Apr. 27, 1847.
Shofner, Hezekiah & Emily C. Pitt, Aug. 29, 1847.
Sinclair, Smith & Sarah Ann Thorn, Oct. 29, 1847.
Sikes, Green M. & Zilpha A. Jones, Feb. 22, 1847.
Smith, Jackson & Martha Hunt, Apr. 13, 1847.
Smith, James & Melvina Wilson, Mar. 23, 1847.
Smotherman, Alfred & Elizabeth Smotherman, Aug. 11,
   1847.
Snipes, John & Fanny Webb, Dec. 27, 1847.
Staten, Elijah & Frances Cavender, June 15, 1847.
Stewart, James W. & Mary M. Sublett, Nov. 30, 1847.
Sullivan, William G. & Mary J. James, Oct. 26, 1847.
Summer, Jackson & Penelope A. Smith (col), Jan. 9, 1847.
Tarpley, Cader D. & Holly A. Frost, Nov. 9, 1847.
Tarpley, James A. & Mary C. Mosley, Dec. 27, 1847.
Tatum, Jesse B. & Margarett E. Welch, Oct. 18, 1847.
Taylor, Charles T. & Elizabeth K. Ransom, Aug. 30, 1847.
Taylor, Thomas S. & Sarah O. Smith, July 29, 1847.
Templeton, Burgess & Elizabeth M. Kirk, May 13, 1847.
Thompson, David S. & Samantha A. Holden, July 27, 1847.
Trigg, Thomas B. & Susan N. Weakley, June 23, 1847.
Vincent, Alexander A. & Rhoda A. E. Lynch, May 3, 1847.
Vinson, Jackson & Sarah Williamson, Dec. 27, 1847.
Wade, Dabner & Caroline T. McKay, Aug. 4, 1847.

Wasson, Lasson M. & Martha E. Lillard, Dec. 22, 1847.
Webb, Benjamin & Margarett N. Jacobs, Dec. 13, 1847.
Webb, W. S. & Adelphia Wheeler, Mar. 13, 1847.
Webb, William & Rebecca Wilson, Nov. 29, 1847.
Webber, Richard & Deborah Green, July 26, 1847.
West, Alfred & Tabitha Tutor, Apr. 16, 1847.
West, Levi & Susan C. Holden, Sept. 22, 1847.
Wheeler, John A. & Drucilla Peek, Apr. 14, 1847.
Wheeler, William T. & Malinda C. Yandell, Oct. 23, 1847.
Whitmore, William & Susan C. Crutchfielf, Jan. 25, 1847.
Williams, William J. & Ester Martin, Dec. 16, 1847.
Williamson, H. G. & Lucy Shacklett, Sept. 6, 1847.
Wilson, George B. & Margarett Haynes, June 1, 1847.
Winston, Isaac & Mahala E. Hunt, Jan. 16, 1847.
Witherspoon, Alexander B. & Jane Neely, Nov. 22, 1847.
Witherspoon, Benjamin F. & Matilda E. Elder, Dec. 24, 1847.
Wood, James & Sarah McKay, May 29, 1847.
Wood, Layfayette & Mary E. Beasley, Feb. 26, 1847.
Wrather, Wesley S. & Susan S. Wrather, Feb. 24, 1847.
Wray, William & Parthenea Wilson, July 2, 1847.
Yearwood, James & Martha J. Hall, July 3, 1847.
Yearwood, James & Mary Johnson, Feb. 23, 1847.

1848

Alexander, John H. & Nancy N. Barrett, July 26, 1848.
Alsup, Elijah B. & Elizabeth Harshaw, Nov. 7, 1848.
Anderson, George W. & Julia Drake, Oct. 26, 1848.
Arnold, William & Eleanor Elliott, Jan. 4, 1848.
Ashley, Alexander & Mary Ann McCrary, Aug. 24, 1848.
Atkinson, James E. & Marinda J. Smith, Dec. 20, 1848.
Ballard, James & Ann Weatherford, Jan. 12, 1848.
Barkley, Henry B. & Mary H. Pritchett, Apr. 16, 1848.
Barkley, Samuel J. & Sarah C. Bivins, Dec. 14, 1848.
Barlow, Benjamin D. & Elvina Z. Brown, Aug. 24, 1848.
Barton, Robert & Catharine Thompson, Oct. 1, 1848.
Barton, Swinfield H. & Mary J. Barnes, Mar. 18, 1848.
Bates, John A. & Melissa Vaughan, Oct. 3, 1848.
Batey, Robert W. & Melvina White, Nov. 1, 1848.
Baukum, Mark L. & Louisa J. Little, Oct. 14, 1848.
Baxter, John D. & Ann A. Lackey, Mar. 23, 1848.
Beasley, John E. & Elizabeth C. Hall, Sept. 28, 1848.
Becton, George W. & Jane H. Mitchell, Oct. 17, 1848.
Bell, George & Margaret Anderson, Aug. 22, 1848.
Bennett, John W. & Nancy A. Lannom, May 22, 1848.
Bennett, Monroe & Margarett Renshaw, Sept. 7, 1848.
Bivins, B. R. & Eliza T. Adams, June 22, 1848.
Bivins, L. M. S. & Elizabeth Thompson, Nov. 16, 1848.
Bradley, William L. & Emaline Dunn, Dec. 12, 1848.
Brashears, Gilbert & Sarah Crick, Mar. 17, 1848.
Brashears, James L. & Mary Ann Bishop, Mar. 14, 1848.
Briggs, Samuel M. & Poline M. S. Kelton, Feb. 10, 1848.
Brothers, George P. & Joanna Smith, Jan. 20, 1848.

Brown, Joseph H. & Martha N. Barnes, July 7, 1848.
Bruce, Nehemiah & Rebecca J. Duggin, Dec. 16, 1848.
Bulloch, Joseph J. & Elizabeth Summers, Oct. 3, 1848.
Burnett, Monroe & Margaret Renshaw, Sept. 6, 1848.
Butler, Henry & Delilah Jerland, Sept. 12, 1848.
Carney, William & Eveline Sartin, Feb. 26, 1848.
Chandler, Robert B. & Nancy B. Freeman, Oct. 16, 1848.
Childress, Alfred & Martha E. Nichols, May 20, 1848.
Childress, Edward & Margaret Ann Nichols, July 19, 1848.
Compton, Elisha & Susan H. McDaniel, Jan. 11, 1848.
Coursey, John B. & Martha Heath, Jan. 27, 1848.
Coursey, Tyree & Mary Hogan, Dec. 7, 1848.
Crockett, Samuel O. & Rebecca C. Harrison, Oct. 18, 1848.
Crowse, Henry C. & Eliza A. Dickson, Jan. 13, 1848.
Daniel, Walter W. & Martha A. Maddox, Aug. 28, 1848.
Daniel, William & Caroline Moss, Oct. 20, 1848.
Davis, James A. & Elizabeth Rucker, Aug. 15, 1848.
DeJarnett, James G. & Sarah T. Alford, Mar. 28, 1848.
Dunn, William C. & Martha R. Smotherman, Feb. 5, 1848.
Edwards, Hughs & Elizabeth Puckett, Apr. 16, 1848.
Edwards, Sterling C. & Martha A. Hunt, Feb. 29, 1848.
Floyd, Thomas & Lucinda Thomas, Jan. 15, 1848.
Foster, John H. & Elizabeth M. Crocker, May 5, 1848.
Fox, John W. & Rebecca Drake, Jan. 12, 1848.
Gardner, Robert W. & Mary W. Hoskins, July 4, 1848.
Gates, Joseph A. & Malinda J. Taylor, Aug. 14, 1848.
Gilliam, James W. & Mary E. Bethshares, Sept. 2, 1848.
Goss, Thomas C. & Mary N. Miller, Sept. 11, 1848.
Gregory, Andrew & Temperance Ann Smith, Apr. 6, 1848.
Gregory, Josephus & Emeline Gilmore, Oct. 9, 1848.
Gregory, Abraham & Jane Whites, Apr. 6, 1848.
Griffin, Isaiah P. & Catherine Rich, July 8, 1848.
Haile, James & Jane Lenear, Sept. 14, 1848.
Hart, John & Elizabeth Batey, Jan. 22, 1848.
Hatchett, Preston & Mary M. Lawing, Sept. 5, 1848.
Hayes, Thomas P. & Mary E. Hutcherson, Mar. 11, 1848.
Heath, Wilson & Sarah E. Rowlett, Oct. 4, 1848.
Hendrix, W. P. & Mary L. Saunders, July 12, 1848.
Herrod, Edward & Sarah Webb, Sept. 16, 1848.
Hight, Robert A. & Martha Ann Jordan, Aug. 5, 1848.
Hill, William & Susan H. Graves, Aug. 2, 1848.
Holden, Jerdan & Martha R. Clanton, June 19, 1848.
Howland, James L. & Martha Waller, Mar. 15, 1848.
Jacobs, Houston & Elizabeth Brinkley, Feb. 25, 1848.
Jacobs, William & Nancy Haley, Dec. 26, 1848.
James, Allen W. & Elizabeth Sartan, Mar. 11, 1848.
Johnson, John B. & Martha Lackey, Aug. 16, 1848.
Johnson, John F. & Fanny M. Avent, Aug. 30, 1848.
Jones, Robert S. & Elizabeth Harris, Mar. 29, 1848.
Jones, Samuel & Elizabeth Thurman, Mar. 9, 1848.
Jones, Wilson Y. & Julia DeJarnett, Sept. 13, 1848.
Kerby, James H. & Laura A. Overall, Jan. 27, 1848.
Lackey, A. R. & Mary Ann Robinson, Sept. 28, 1848.
Lacy, Ebenezer & Elizabeth Jordan, Oct. 3, 1848.

Lamb, Willis & Naoimia Covington, Oct. 12, 1848.
Lawrence, Joseph & Elizabeth A. Baird, Nov. 25, 1848.
Lenear, James R. & Elenor E. Griffin, May 5, 1848.
Lewis, John W. & Elizabeth Miller, Dec. 11, 1848.
Lewis, Leven & Mariah Webber, Apr. 22, 1848.
Lewis, William A. & Sarah E. Spann, Aug. 9, 1848.
Love, Charles T. & Elizabeth B. Buchanan, Sept. 11, 1848.
Lyon, Anderson M. & Mary Caffy, Dec. 20, 1848.
Mankin, William & Elizabeth Howland, June 8, 1848.
Mankin, Welcome H. & Louisa J. Lamb, Jan. 27, 1848.
Maxwell, James H. & Amanda Mathews, July 8, 1848.
Miller, John R. & Aribella Jarratt, Sept. 25, 1848.
Miller, Riley & Mary Ann Roberson, Mar. 24, 1848.
Miller, Robert C. & Mary A. Burks, Nov. 28, 1848.
Miller, Samuel G. & Sarah C. Gilmore, Sept. 6, 1848.
Mitchell, James & Elizabeth Brent, Jan. 21, 1848.
Moore, Benjamin F. & Mary J. McFadden, Sept. 7, 1848.
Morris, Thomas W. & Julia Courtney, Oct. 4, 1848.
Morton, James W. & Ann E. Hicks, Jan. 21, 1848.
Mosley, Hartwell & Martha Singleton, Oct. 16, 1848.
Muerhead, William D. & Caroline R. Smith, Aug. 30, 1848.
Muirhead, John & Mary Birdsong, Jan. 13, 1848.
Mullins, Joel & Sarah E. Mullins, Feb. 3, 1848.
McBowen, William & Elizabeth A. Gooch, Nov. 25, 1848.
McCullough, Henry C. & Nancy A. Lewis, Jan. 10, 1848.
McDaniel, William A. & Sarah A. Lewis, Jan. 5, 1848.
McElroy, John C. & Nancy A. Neeley, Oct. 25, 1848.
McKay, Silas & Harriet J. Smotherman, Oct. 2, 1848.
Naylor, Calvin H. & Susan Black, Nov. 14, 1848.
Neely, David M. & Elizabeth Crutchfield, Nov. 15, 1848.
Nelson, George F. & Elizabeth L. Wade, Feb. 16, 1848.
North, Thordorick & Elizabeth E. Cook, Apr. 20, 1848.
Owen, David R. & Frusanah Wray, Jan. 24, 1848.
Owen, James A. & Lucy O. Tune, Oct. 9, 1848.
Parrish, Thomas L. & Sarah Jane McCoy, Jan. 3, 1848.
Pearson, William & Serenia Todd, Feb. 24, 1848.
Pendergrass, Charles & Bashiba Medley, Oct. 4, 1848.
Perry, Burrel B. & Nancy M. Leek, Dec. 27, 1848.
Phipher, James & Mathenia H. Sneed, Dec. 6, 1848.
Pitts, William & Amanda M. Sanders, Jan. 15, 1848.
Ransom, William A. & Sarah A. Gardner, June 20, 1848.
Rawlings, German D. & Sarah M. Jones, May 25, 1848.
Reeves, Thomas B. & Louisa E. Ford, Sept. 5, 1848.
Reynolds, Calvin & Ann Todd, Feb. 9, 1848.
Robinson, George W. & Mary E. Mankin, Aug. 5, 1848.
Rowland, John & Anna Brown, Nov. 1, 1848.
Rucker, William & Martha Lillard, Dec. 21, 1848.
Savage, Richard & Margaret Lattimore, May 22, 1848.
Seward, Warren B. & Martha S. Warren, Oct. 19, 1848.
Smith, James M. & Delitha Peck, Mar. 30, 1848.
Smith, Simeon & Amanda E. Blair, Jan. 24, 1848.
Smotherman, John & Leticia Grinage, Apr. 20, 1848.
Smotherman, John R. & Nigara A. Holden, Mar. 29, 1848.
Sullivan, John E. & Mary C. G. Martin, Apr. 29, 1848.

Summers, Davidson & Mary Ann Howland, July 25, 1848.
Summers, U. T. & Nancy A. Johnson, Oct. 3, 1848.
Summers, Uriah T. & Mahaley F. Bailey, Oct. 27, 1848.
Swink, William L. & Nancy A. Thompson, July 3, 1848.
Taylor, Thomas L. & Nancy Sharber, Mar. 6, 1848.
Thompson, Albert C. & Mary J. Ford, July 3, 1848.
Thompson, Nimrod & Nancy W. Alford, Nov. 1, 1848.
Todd, Reuben & K. Wilson, Aug. 31, 1848.
Traylor, E. P. & Elizabeth McDaniel, Apr. 22, 1848.
Tucker, Joseph M. & Julia Mullins, Dec. 20, 1848.
Vaughan, James D. & Mary Ann S. Parker, June 29, 1848.
Wadley, John W. & Caroline Patterson, Dec. 13, 1848.
Walsh, Thomas & Ann Elizabeth Sperry, May 30, 1848.
Wardlaw, James C. & Mary J. Holden, Sept. 16, 1848.
Warren, Peyton S. & Mary A. Howse, Dec. 12, 1848.
Weatherford, Charles M. & Mary A. Hoover, Jan. 26, 1848.
Webb, James F. & Elizabeth C. Smith, Jan. 11, 1848.
Webb, John L. & Susanah F. Harris, June 15, 1848.
Welch, Larkin & Nancy C. Richardson, Dec. 23, 1848.
Wheeler, Jesse M. & Purlina T. Woodson, Oct. 25, 1848.
White, James A. & Lucy E. Elder, Apr. 17, 1848.
Williford, Jesse W. & Lee Ann Ford, Oct. 5, 1848.
Wilson, John B. & Milly Deason, Sept. 20, 1848.
Wilson, William K. & Frances R. Sanders, Apr. 26, 1848.
Wright, James H. & Malinda Todd, May 24, 1848.
Wright, John & Martha J. Melton, Nov. 2, 1848.
Wright, William & Harriett E. Sanders, May 25, 1848.
Yeargan, Hilary H. L. & Elmira F. Jarratt, Jan. 6,
  1848.
Yearwood, William P. & Martha Ann Rodgers, July 20,
  1848.
Young, Isaac B. & Judy M. Jarratt, Feb. 25, 1848.
Youree, Francis H. & Elizabeth Lowe, Dec. 19, 1848.
Zumbro, Allen J. & Nancy Inhoof, Aug. 1, 1848.

1849

Alexander, Henry V. & Mary S. E. Webb, Aug. 14, 1849.
Alexander, James H. & Sarah Ann Coleman, Oct. 4, 1849.
Alexander, P. M. M. & Mary E. Kimbrough, Nov. 14, 1849.
Alford, John W. & Mary E. Bone, Dec. 31, 1849.
Armstrong, James P. & Cilista N. Black, Apr. 10, 1849.
Ashley, Arthur & Catharine Pruett, Nov. 5, 1849.
Baird, James P. & Sarah A. Ward, Sept. 11, 1849.
Ballard, Riley & Elizabeth Baukum, Dec. 31, 1849.
Banning, Thomas & Nancy Walkup, Mar. 27, 1849.
Barker, James B. & Sarah A. James, Sept. 8, 1849.
Barksdale, William H. & Mary H. Baskett, July 31, 1849.
Barnes, Bennett & Mary Moseley, Mar. 6, 1849.
Barratt, Jeremiah & Martha Ward, Aug. 13, 1849.
Bates, Thomas F. & Louisa H. Brook, Oct. 30, 1849.
Batey, James M. & Mary E. Howse, May 3, 1849.
Batten, John D. & Sarah H. Burks, Sept. 15, 1849.
Baucum, Willis & Emeline Wray, Feb. 10, 1849.

Beavers, Josiah P. & Eliza Whitsett, Sept. 11, 1849.
Bevel, James & Rebecca King, Mar. 14, 1849.
Bond, John & America Avarey, Aug. 7, 1849.
Bowen, Elijah R. & Emily M. Kelton, Mar. 7, 1849.
Bowman, David B. F. & Rebecca H. Brown, Feb. 26, 1849.
Brogain, Parson M. & Mary Garner, Feb. 15, 1849.
Brookshier, G. G. & Sally F. Bacon, June 26, 1849.
Brothers, Thomas & Martha J. Thomas, Jan. 10, 1849.
Brown, William H. & Martha A. Pierce, Sept. 25, 1849.
Brown, William L. & Cynthia P. Overall, Feb. 21, 1849.
Bryant, David O. & Sarah Melton, Feb. 28, 1849.
Burk, Nathaniel H. & Martha E. Moore, Dec. 11, 1849.
Burnett, Thomas & Lucinda Renshaw, Feb. 13, 1849.
Caldwell, John & Sarah J. Taylor, Apr. 12, 1849.
Carlton, Benajah & Clary Morris, Dec. 4, 1849.
Clark, Peyton & Rebecca Ballard, Mar. 31, 1849.
Clopton, B. N. & Mary E. McLin, Dec. 25, 1849.
Coleman, John & Mary Alexander, Sept. 29, 1849.
Coleman, Joshua & Nancy Coleman, Jan. 31, 1849.
Coleman, Samuel C. & Mary L. Dickie, Dec. 4, 1849.
Coleman, Sutton & Elmira S. McCray, Oct. 10, 1849.
Collins, Thomas & Susannah Watson, May 21, 1849.
Corder, Jackson & Frances J. Covington, Jan. 11, 1849.
Cornatz or, Thomas R. & Margaret S. Bowman, Dec. 14, 1849.
Crowder, George G. & Sarah E. Boyd, Jan. 9, 1849.
Crutchfield, Thomas N. & Sarah Noe, Dec. 10, 1849.
Davis, William E. & Sarah L. Lawrence, Aug. 22, 1849.
Dickie, William L. & Mary Nivins, Dec. 28, 1849.
Dickins, Ja. H. & Margaret M. McKnight, Jan. 22, 1849.
Dove, John & Jane Sackett, May 12, 1849.
Duffer, Edmund & Elmira Hancock, Dec. 11, 1849.
Edwards, George W. & Rebecca A. Bulloch, Feb. 21, 1849.
Elliott, Richard B. & Abigil Taliferro, Oct. 4, 1849.
Ferrell, Stephen & Rebecca H. Jolly, Feb. 17, 1849.
Fleming, Peter E. & Lavinia Shipp, Dec. 5, 1849.
Floyd, Benjamin W. & Mary C. Dyer, Nov. 5, 1849.
Frazier, Isaac & Amanda Kimbro, July 19, 1849.
Freas, Jacob W. & Beatins Thompson, Dec. 17, 1849.
Furgerson, Jordan & Margaret E. Anderson, Jan. 1, 1849.
Garner, John H. & Martha E. Blair, Dec. 3, 1849.
Garner, Larner B. & Rebecca Hoover, Sept. 26, 1849.
Geirs, Jean Joseph & Mary L. Gooch, May 2, 1849.
Grigg, Lewis M. & Mary Beaty, Sept. 27, 1849.
Guest, John M. & Eliza R. Dennison, May 4, 1849.
Hall, Gideon B. & Narcissa R. Abernathy, Mar. 17, 1849.
Hall, Henry & Sarah Crockett, Mar. 8, 1849.
Hall, James C. & Elizabeth L. Harrell, June 15, 1849.
Harriford, Jacob H. & Josephine Brown, Dec. 20, 1849.
Harrison, William L. & Pamela A. Ellis, June 5, 1849.
Haynes, Nicholas S. & Sarah A. Goodman, Oct. 22, 1849.
Heath, Thomas J. & Mary A. Winsett, Sept. 11, 1849.
Hendricks, David B. & Jennetta Taylor, Aug. 6, 1849.
Hendrix, William W. & Margaret J. Reed, Oct. 3, 1849.

Henry, Mathews & Elizabeth D. Smith, Jan. 16, 1849.
Hill, D. F. & Isabella J. Graham, Dec. 18, 1849.
Hogan, Thomas & Narcissa Ward, Jan. 16, 1849.
Holden, C. W. & Rachel Holden, Dec. 19, 1849.
Holden, James M. & Elizabeth C. Leathers, Oct. 24, 1849.
Hopkins, Samuel & Mary J. Ferris, Sept. 7, 1849.
Howse, John C. & Martha Finney, Nov. 19, 1849.
Hunt, Andrew J. & Mary M. Kerby, Sept. 8, 1849.
Jarman, George W. & Isabella W. Fletcher, July 18, 1849.
Jarman, Robert H. & Christina J. Jones, Oct. 15, 1849.
Jarratt, Benjamin F. & Elizabeth A. Posey, Aug. 9, 1849.
Johnson, George E. & Judith M. Lawrence, Jan. 22, 1849.
Johnson, William A. & Elizabeth A. Waller, May 25, 1849.
Jones, James E. & Cecelia S. Overall, May 10, 1849.
Jones, Richard C. & Mary Cock, Dec. 18, 1849.
Joy, Robert C. & Mariah Wilson, June 16, 1849.
Keeble, Walter & Frances M. Rucker, May 17, 1849.
Kirk, John J. & Nancy Parker, July 31, 1849.
Koonce, Lemuel G. & Rebecca M. Tucker, Dec. 22, 1849.
Landers, Nathaniel W. & Mary E. Hester, Jan. 17, 1849.
Lawrence, George W. & Martha A. Howse, May 31, 1849.
Lewis, Benjamin & Sarah Ann Haynes, Feb. 6, 1849.
Loftin, William L. & Margaret H. Wray, Oct. 1, 1849.
Loven, Edmond & Mary Ann E. Maxwell, Dec. 10, 1849.
Lowe, Calvin C. & Elizabeth M. Kelton, Jan. 27, 1849.
Lowery, Alvin & Frances Owen, Nov. 17, 1849.
Lyon, John B. & Rebecca M. Flemming, July 9, 1849.
Maney, David D. & Mary E. Bell, Oct. 10, 1849.
Mangrum, Jesse W. & Louisa Prince, Jan. 24, 1849.
Manor, David M. & Susan E. Ezzell, Mar. 21, 1849.
Martin, Lewis H. & Eliza B. Leath, Jan. 27, 1849.
Mason, William N. & Martha J. Hoover, Sept. 20, 1849.
Mathews, John & Nancy K. Beavers, June 2, 1849.
Miller, Robert & Sarah A. Nichols, Jan. 31, 1849.
Moody, Daniel & Martha A. Benson, Dec. 5, 1849.
Morris, Jackson & Jane E. Kerby, Sept. 18, 1849.
Moseley, Albert & Mary Smith, June 18, 1849.
Murry, Lemuel G. & Rebecca Hays, Jan. 29, 1849.
McCandless, James T. C. & Susan A. Lovell, July 28, 1849.
McCoy, Andrew A. & Martha L. Webb, Aug. 6, 1849.
McCracken, Joseph T. & Druziller E. Wheeler, Feb. 22, 1849.
McCrary, Robert & Jane Fleming, Nov. 28, 1849.
McCullough, James D. & Elizabeth M. Loftin, Aug. 18, 1849.
McGill, David & Isabellah Neisbett, Oct. 11, 1849.
McGinnis, Andrew & Sophia A. M. Ward, Jan. 12, 1849.
McHenry, John & Mary A. Reeves, Dec. 4, 1849.
McKee, William & Jane Martin, Nov. 16, 1849.
McKnight, Enos & Rosanna McCombs, Dec. 11, 1849.
McKnight, William J. & Martha J. Covington, Nov. 8, 1849.
Newman, John A. & Martha Foster, Aug. 20, 1849.
Newman, William M. & Rebecca Summers, May 30, 1849.
Nichols, James A. & Marvann Dove, July 17, 1849.

RUTHERFORD COUNTY MARRIAGES

Norvell, Abram & Emily Harrell, Jan. 22, 1849.
O'Bryant, David & Sarah Melton, Feb. 26, 1849.
Overall, Robert A. & Amanda D. Hutcherson, Dec. 6, 1849.
Parker, John A. & Margaret S. Alexander, Aug. 18, 1849.
Patterson, Isaac & Susan E. Winston, Jan. 22, 1849.
Patterson, L. B. & Louisa Burks, Feb. 10, 1849.
Patterson, Thomas H. & Ellen B. McCullough, Dec. 26, 1849.
Patterson, William K. & Samuel J. Ridley, Nov. 27, 1849.
Peek, James M. & Martha W. DeJarnett, Jan. 23, 1849.
Perkins, Peter A. & Sarah Ann McCullough, Oct. 16, 1849.
Piercy, Robert R. & Nancy J. Harshaw, Jan. 29, 1849.
Pinkston, William B. & Mary Ann Jerland, Apr. 16, 1849.
Pitts, Benjamin E. & Mary McGinnis, Apr. 7, 1849.
Prater, Austin & Martha F. Woodfin, Dec. 24, 1849.
Prewitt, Larry E. & Harriet J. Brothers, Dec. 8, 1849.
Prince, -----, & Rebecca Ann Barber, Oct. 1, 1849.
Raney, John E. & Gibernia E. Vernon, Jan. 29, 1849.
Ray, John C. & Aeriadne T. Pritchett, May 1, 1849.
Reeves, John A. & Susan C. McCullough, Jan. 18, 1849.
Roberts, Henry & Susan J. Stovall, Mar. 23, 1849.
Roberts, William J. & Elmira F. Baldridge, Jan. 10, 1849.
Robinson, Calvin & Hannah Langstaff, Oct. 23, 1849.
Robinson, Samuel & Elizabeth Brown, July 18, 1849.
Sanders, Stephen C. & Nancy E. Caraway, Oct. 13, 1849.
Sanford, Willis & Elizabeth Helton, Sept. 11, 1849.
Sellers, Wesley M. & Mary E. McAdoo, Oct. 3, 1849.
Skeen, D. H. & Rose J. Dillard, June 13, 1849.
Smith, Hardy & Rebecca Mosley, Mar. 27, 1849.
Smith, John H. & Harriett Johnson, Sept. 18, 1849.
Smith, John J. & Mary Hall, Apr. 25, 1849.
Smith, Robert & Cueley Smith, July 19, 1849.
Smith, Taswell S. & America E. Kerby, May 1, 1849.
Smotherman, William & Nancy Pope, Feb. 7, 1849.
Spencer, William R. & Rebecca J. Lee, Apr. 28, 1849.
Summerhill, A. H. & Catherine Parrish, July 25, 1849.
Swiney, Calvin & Elizabeth C. Parrish, Nov. 20, 1849.
Tassey, Alexander & Elizabeth Gumm, Oct. 20, 1849.
Taylor, James & Dimeda Caldwell, June 14, 1849.
Taylor, Daniel W. & Mary J. Shanklin, Mar. 13, 1849.
Thompson, Joseph M. & Sarah Helton, Mar. 3, 1849.
Thompson, Thomas B. & Anna Clay, June 15, 1849.
Todd, Walker & Juliann Painter, Apr. 12, 1849.
Todd, Walker & Mary Ann Summers, Sept. 27, 1849.
Toliver, William & Mahala Brinkley, Dec. 22, 1849.
Trail, Wiley & Sarah Lamb, Sept. 26, 1849.
Vaught, James & Mary S. Blackwood, Feb. 26, 1849.
Wade, Robert & Esther S. Peak, Feb. 13, 1849.
Walker, James & Louisa Martin, Dec. 24, 1849.
Walls, Thomas & Mary Grogan, June 7, 1849.
Ward, Harrison & Elizabeth A. Merritt, Mar. 5, 1849.
Warren, William & Susan C. Glenn, May 28, 1849.
Washington, Francis W. & Sarah C. Crockett, Oct. 18, 1849.

RUTHERFORD COUNTY MARRIAGES

Watts, William E. & Mary Read, Mar. 19, 1849.
Webb, Francis M. & Mary S. Fowler, June 21, 1849.
Williams, Addison H. & Martha G. Blaze, Oct. 30, 1849.
Wilson, James E. & Margaret E. Deasont, Apr. 21, 1849.
Wilson, William M. & Elizabeth Crouse, Dec. 19, 1849.
Woods, John, Jr. & Lucinda A. Richardson, Nov. 28, 1849.
Woods, Stephen H. & Elizabeth L. Lyon, Feb. 21, 1849.
Word, John C. & Caroline M. Wade, Jan. 16, 1849.
Wright, Thomas C. & Sarah Wade, Jan. 17, 1849.
Yardley, Thomas & Martha Evans, Mar. 24, 1849.

1850

Adams, Edward & Elizabeth Hughes, Nov. 23, 1850.
Adams, William & Elizabeth Crouse, Dec. 19, 1850.
Arnold, David L. & Margaret Bell, Aug. 15, 1850.
Arnold, Robert & Elizabeth Bell, Oct. 8, 1850.
Bailey, George W. & Johanah Carrick, Dec. 12, 1850.
Bailey, Thomas & Mary Ann Simpson, Jan. 23, 1850.
Baird, William D. & Amanda V. Jarratt, Oct. 14, 1850.
Ballentine, Charles & Louisa Conley, Oct. 31, 1850.
Barnwell, William E. & Martha A. Glimp, Sept. 9, 1850.
Bayless, Thomas H. & Martha A. M. Smith, Sept. 17, 1850.
Bone, James & Jane Rankin, Oct. 16, 1850.
Bowman, Henry & Mary J. Johnson, Mar. 7, 1850.
Bumpass, John & Julia A. Averitt, Dec. 10, 1850.
Burger, Samuel N. & Sarah A. Kelton, Oct. 17, 1850.
Burk, Thomas M. L. & Clementine L. Petty, June 20, 1850.
Burkhart, Alexander & Ava Ann Revel, Nov. 12, 1850.
Burkhart, James & Margaret Ballard, Feb. 5, 1850.
Burnett, Benjamin J. & Martha Vardell, Jan. 8, 1850.
Campbell, Peter & Mary Daniel, Nov. 6, 1850.
Cheatham, A. J. & Permelia Sanders
    (Free man of color & free woman of color), Nov. 8,
    1850.
Coleman, James A. & Mary L. Blair, Jan. 8, 1850.
Connelly, James B. & Ann Waits, July 4, 1850.
Coppage, William & Obedience Taylor, Sept. 26, 1850.
Cotten, James & Ann E. Dement, July 21, 1850.
Courts, George W. & Mary A. E. Gingary, Mar. 17, 1850.
Covington, Joseph & Emily Fuller, Nov. 23, 1850.
Covington, Joseph A. & Sarah Ann Furguss, Dec. 31, 1850.
Crick, William M. & Mary Crick, Nov. 9, 1850.
Crocker, Thomas B. & Elizabeth M. Thompson, Sept. 18,
    1850.
Daughtry, Jesse & Mary J. Jacobs, June 27, 1850.
Dickie, William L. & Mary Nivins, Jan. 3, 1850.
Dodson, Paul W. & Sarah M. Burton, July 23, 1850.
Drennon, Andrew J. & Sarah P. Smart, Sept. 23, 1850.
Espey, Robert & Mary C. Wade, Oct. 10, 1850.
Felps, William C. & Cintha O. Sinkler, Nov. 23, 1850.
Fleming, Jacob M. & Adaline Bulloch, July 18, 1850.
Ford, Abram & Clementine Swink, Nov. 10, 1850.
Foster, Elliott R. & Caladonia Neal, Oct. 1, 1850.
Foster, Richard H. & Elizabeth Revel, Oct. 31, 1850.

Freeman, Marshall & Sarah Foster, Oct. 7, 1850.
Gardner, A. B. & America R. Elam, Mar. 7, 1850.
Gibson, George E. & Martha Ann Brown, June 10, 1850.
Gibson, John M. & Mary C. McKee, Sept. 26, 1850.
Gilliam, Anderson & Catharine Causey, Oct. 2, 1850.
Gilmore, Peter & Elenor Marlin, Nov. 8, 1850.
Green, William T. & Narcissus A. Yeager, Nov. 5, 1850.
Groom, Thomas & Elizabeth Martin, May 5, 1850.
Gullett, Henry & Susan Winfrey, Aug. 3, 1850.
Harrison, Joseph & Mary J. McDowell, Dec. 15, 1850.
Haynes, Isaac & Tabitha Beesley, Aug. 27, 1850.
Hazelwood, Benjamin F. & Margaret S. Tucker, July 17, 1850.
Hendrix, Nathan W. & Julia Ann Jones, Nov. 5, 1850.
Hicks, William & Sarah C. Rick, June 16, 1850.
Hill, Thomas M. & Susan G. C. Wade, Oct. 8, 1850.
Hoover, A. H. & Lucy A. Rawlings, May 7, 1850.
Hoover, Henry J. & Adaline V. Rex, Sept. 24, 1850.
Hoover, Martin & Nancy Bingham, Feb. 21, 1850.
Hopkins, William & Sabry L. Welch, Dec. 25, 1850.
Howse, Leander J. & Ann Bivins, May 29, 1850.
Hutchinson, James M. & Elizabeth R. Overall, Sept. 19, 1850.
Inglish, Elihu & Elizabeth Cook, Aug. 29, 1850.
Insell, Thomas S. & Mary Rolins, Nov. 18, 1850.
Jackson, William J. & Judith Ann Primm, Apr. 4, 1850.
Jacobs, Alfred & Emeline Cates, Oct. 10, 1850.
Jacobs, Alvin & Melvinia Bowerman, May 29, 1850.
Jacobs, Jeremiah & Rebecca Auberry, Aug. 28, 1850.
Jacobs, William & Ritta Auberry, Aug. 10, 1850.
Jarratt, Thomas L. & Louisa Murphey, Oct. 17, 1850.
Jetton, Robert B. & Joanna L. Rucker, Nov. 6, 1850.
Jones, Sterling B. & Locky Prewett, Jan. 1, 1850.
Kennedy, John & Elizabeth S. Thurman, July 26, 1850.
Knox, John W. A. & Elizabeth Hoover, Sept. 19, 1850.
Lamb, Jonathan & Nancy Hendrix, Nov. 7, 1850.
Lamb, William & Tempeance Pope, Apr. 4, 1850.
Lambert, Edmond & Leathy Eaks, June 10, 1850.
Lannon, William D. & Milbry J. McGregor, Mar. 26, 1850.
Lewis, James A. & Susan Lane, Oct. 17, 1850.
Luster, John & Mary J. J. C. McCallister, Oct. 2, 1850.
Lytle, Franklin & Sophia E. Burrus, Jan. 31, 1850.
Marable, Silas S. & Mary E. Lewis, Feb. 14, 1850.
Martin, James B. & Lucinda B. Holmes, Oct. 31, 1850.
Martin, Joseph G. & Mary J. Wright, Aug. 27, 1850.
Miller, Isaac & Rebecca O. Elam, Nov. 14, 1850.
Miller, James R. & Cassay N. Howland, Nov. 14, 1850.
Mitchell, Robert & Mary J. Gilliam, Aug. 1, 1850.
Mitchell, William & Priscilla Dennis, Oct. 5, 1850.
Moore, Albert M. & Elizabeth Peck, Nov. 7, 1850.
Morton, John B. & Mary J. Cook, Jan. 9, 1850.
Morton, Robert H. & Mary Nash, Oct. 5, 1850.
Mosley, Chesley & Martha Curl, Jan. 29, 1850.
Mount, John T. W. & Narrissa Thomas, Dec. 30, 1850.

RUTHERFORD COUNTY MARRIAGES

Mullins, Franklin & Elizabeth B. Perry, Oct. 29, 1850.
Mulloy, Arthur & Mary Brown, July 30, 1850.
McCaslin, William & Miss Emmeline J. Herrell, Oct. 8, 1850.
McClanahan, Ezekiel W. & Louisa F. Leath, Feb. 26, 1850.
McCrary, James F. & Sarah E. J. Donnell, Feb. 7, 1850.
McKnight, William W. & Margaret J. Martin, Jan. 1, 1850.
Neal, Phillip & Ann Green, Dec. 5, 1850.
Neely, John C. & Adaline Rowlett, Mar. 6, 1850.
Newman, Allen & Isabella Youree, June 30, 1850.
Newman, William & Serenia S. Clemons, Oct. 31, 1850.
Norman, Henry & Sarah O. White, Nov. 12, 1850.
Northcott, John W. & Mary H. Read, Aug. 22, 1850.
Northcott, William J. & Sarah J. Barker, May 14, 1850.
Osborn, Caleb & Elizabeth V. Rankin, July 24, 1850.
Overall, P. N. & Miss S. E. Cartwright, Apr. 4, 1850.
Phillips, James & Sarah Rucker, Nov. 6, 1850.
Porter, William & Martha A. Pigg, Sept. 26, 1850.
Porterfield, Leonidus F. & Eliza A. Brown, Jan. 25, 1850.
Pulley, Richard & Mary S. Rowlett, Nov. 14, 1850.
Pulley, William R. & Mary A. Crary, Oct. 17, 1850.
Rains, John & Ticey J. Stephens, Aug. 12, 1850.
Reed, Ezra & Nancy Webb, Aug. 8, 1850.
Revel, John & Lucy E. Puckett, Nov. 28, 1850.
Revis, Lewis W. & Mary Ann Mathews, Apr. 1, 1850.
Richardson, John G. & Elizabeth Allen, Sept. 11, 1850.
Roberts, George W. & Elmira Covington, Aug. 11, 1850.
Robinson, Uriah & Jane Bonds, May 7, 1850.
Rodgers, James & Elizabeth Saunders, Dec. 22, 1850.
Rowlett, John & Sarah Ann Cobler, Jan. 13, 1850.
Sanders, Mankin S. & Tabitha Compton, Aug. 29, 1850.
Sanders, Thomas W. & Margaret A. Smotherman, Oct. 17, 1850.
Shelton, Lifus & Sarah Hoover, May 7, 1850.
Sims, William A. & Nancy T. Young, Aug. 12, 1850.
Sled, Etheldred & Elizabeth Burkhart, Oct. 1, 1850.
Smotherman, John & Cyntha Ann Foster, July 4, 1850.
Smotherman, Joseph & Balinda Smotherman, Aug. 22, 1850.
Sneed, Dabney & United America Thompson, Dec. 5, 1850.
Sneed, James B. & Martha Ward, Jan. 7, 1850.
Spain, Stephen R. & Caroline M. Sanford, Mar. 7, 1850.
Stewart, James W. & Sarah A. Sublett, Nov. 28, 1850.
Stewart, Joseph H. & Lavinia E. Burton, June 4, 1850.
Summers, Milus & Louisa Morgan, June 4, 1850.
Taylor, Vincent & Tabitha Cary, June 17, 1850.
Thompson, Azariah & Mary Harris, Sept. 5, 1850.
Tines, Charles M. & Elizabeth Stegar, Dec. 23, 1850.
Toombs, Joel & Mary V. Jackson, Nov. 12, 1850.
Thraer, Reece & Nancy C. E. C. Wooten, Dec. 4, 1850.
Trailor, Isham & Vicey Phelps, Oct. 5, 1850.
Trigg, Samuel S. & Sarah Ann E. Hazelwood, Oct. 24, 1850.
Tucker, A. K. & Tabitha Pope, Aug. 11, 1850.
Tucker, George M. & Martha P. Swink, Jan. 2, 1850.
Tucker, Silas & Ellen M. Clark, Feb. 8, 1850.

RUTHERFORD COUNTY MARRIAGES

Tucker, Thomas C. & Martha E. Shanklin, Dec. 31, 1850.
Underwood, Miles & Elizabeth Lovin, Sept. 26, 1850.
Uselton, Christopher & Harriett E. Taylor, Oct. 22, 1850.
Vaughan, James & Mary L. Elliot, Jan. 3, 1850.
Vaughan, Peter T. & Mary A. Robinson, Nov. 28, 1850.
Wall, Alexander A. & Elizabeth C. Harrison, Oct. 3, 1850.
Ward, James I. & Mary J. Leath, June 18, 1850.
Watkins, Abasalom & Roxanna Hancock, May 23, 1850.
Watson, Pleasant A. & Elizabeth L. Williamson, Oct. 16, 1850.
Weatherford, Stephen D. & Sarah Hooper, Apr. 15, 1850.
Webb, Thomas & Caroline Morris, June 24, 1850.
Welch, W. L. & Amanda Shumake, Nov. 11, 1850.
White, William B. & Martha C. Peebles, June 5, 1850.
Whitson, William & Maria E. Philips, Nov. 6, 1850.
Williams, Nicholas, H. & Sarah Stegar, Mar. 7, 1850.
Wilson, William N. & Nancy G. Read, Feb. 12, 1850.
Winsett, David G. & Catharine Ryon, May 23, 1850.
Woodfin, Jasper N. & Sarah Ann M. Yakes, Jan. 16, 1850.
Wrather, John B. & Mary E. U. Lannom, July --, 1850.
Wright, Henry C. & Susan C. Fletcher, Sept. 17, 1850.

1851

Adkinson, F. M. & Susan G. Phillips, June 23, 1851.
Anderson, Henry C. & Catharine Horton, Jan. 22, 1851.
Anthony, Casper N. & Mary E. Pitts, Oct. 11, 1851.
Bates, Aaron & Eliz. Hopkins, June 9, 1851.
Batey, Jasper N. & Isabel N. Tassy, Nov. 5, 1851.
Batey, Wm. P. & Eliz. M. Hoskins, Dec. 1, 1851.
Bell, Hezikiah & Permelea M. Mathis, July 26, 1851.
Bell, Jos. T. & Hannah H. Mathis, July 8, 1851.
Bemus, Wm. & Eliz. J. Dill, Dec. 2, 1851.
Bird, Wm. & Lavina C. Williams, Sept. 17, 1851.
Blair, Geo. S. & Purlina N. Noe, Dec. 20, 1851.
Bond, John & Eliz. Luster, Jan. 23, 1851.
Boring, Sterling B. & Martha S. Edwards, Nov. 25, 1851.
Bowne, Wm. H. & Margaret A. Dobbins, Sept. 3, 1851.
Bowman, Bedford C. & Martha Denson, Jan. 20, 1851.
Bradford, James & Maria Martin, May 30, 1851.
Brandon, Geo. N. & Eliz. McGregory, Nov. 29, 1851.
Broady, Alexander & Narcissa J. Floyd, Dec. 25, 1851.
Brooks, Jordan & Rebecca Johnson, Jan. 28, 1851.
Brown, James & Mary M. Fleming, July 30, 1851.
Brown, John W. & Eliz. McCracken, Mar. 26, 1851.
Brown, Benj. & Jane Taylor, June 21, 1851.
Brown, Thomas P. & Julia F. Gannon, Mar. 7, 1851.
Bryant, James R. & Nancy E. Hood, Jan. 15, 1851.
Burnett, Thomas & Rachel Cantrell, Oct. 22, 1851.
Cannon, Abram W. & Mary E. Huggins, Feb. 27, 1851.
Castleman, Joseph R. & Sarah E. Pugh, Feb. 26, 1851.
Charlton, George W. & Mary A. Hannah, Mar. 25, 1851.
Childress, John W. & Mary E. Phillips, Oct. 15, 1851.

Clopton, John A. & Lucy W. Martin, Sept. 25, 1851.
Cobb, S. J. & Jane Alba, Aug. 12, 1851.
Coleman, Jesse A. & Mary J. Newsom, Jan. 2, 1851.
Colman, Walter E. & Fanny J. Black, Sept. 2, 1851.
Collier, John A. & Susan F. Brewer, Aug. 21, 1851.
Cook, Wm. D. & Margaret J. Hunter, Dec. 26, 1851.
Corder, John & Margaret J. Morton, Nov. 26, 1851.
Cotton, John H. & Nancy J. McMurry, Nov. 22, 1851.
Coughanour, David & Eliz. Grimes, Nov. 20, 1851.
Covington, Larkin M. & Sarah E. Fagan, June 12, 1851.
Crick, Richard & Martha Mangrum, Sept. 11, 1851.
Crockett, Allen B. & Louisa Hall, Apr. 17, 1851.
Cummings, Alfred M. & Lucinda T. Daniel, Jan. 16, 1851.
Cunningham, George & Melissa Taylor, Dec. 24, 1851.
Curlee, Calvin D. & Emely Lyon, Apr. 25, 1851.
Daughtry, Jeremian & Eliza Belt, May 18, 1851.
Drenon, Thomas & Raymeth S. Smart, Sept. 27, 1851.
Drumwright, Alexander J. & Rhoda Ann McDowell, Feb. 25, 1851.
Duncan, Robert L. & Mary Ann Wyatt, Jan. 23, 1851.
Dunlap, Jacob H. & Nancy C. Sage, Oct. 15, 1851.
Dowling, John M. & Mary W. Smith, Oct. 28, 1851.
Doyle, Wm. H. & Adeline Grogan, June 6, 1851.
Ellis, Hicks, & Sarah Jackson, Jan. 21, 1851.
Evans, Peter, & Phebe F. Smotherman, Sept. 23, 1851.
Farless, Obediah & Sarah V. Brook, Aug. 20, 1851.
Farmer, Wm. & Martha Wade, May 29, 1851.
Fears, Prier & Armenia Covington, Jan. 8, 1851.
Finch, Adam & Casha R. Jarratt, Jan. 7, 1851.
Frasier, Wm. & Eliz. Thurman, May 22, 1851.
Freeman, Joshua & Martha Cherry, Oct. 15, 1851.
Fugett, Mathew S. & Ann Eliaz Jones, Oct. 24, 1851.
Fowler, James B. & Melissa Tucker, May 16, 1851.
Gilbert, Charles & Eliz. Ann Tudor, Nov. 19, 1851.
Gilchrist, Philip P. & Ellen A. Phillips, Dec. 16, 1851.
Gooch, J. C. & Martha J. Randolph, June 18, 1851.
Green, Joseph J. & Mariah E. H. Hyde, May 29, 1851.
Gullett, Henry & Susan Winfrey, July 31, 1851.
Gum, Alexander & Martha Wade, Nov. 25, 1851.
Hall, Alexander & Jane M. Fletcher, Nov. 17, 1851.
Harrell, Layman & Mary C. Harrell, July 21, 1851.
Herrod, Right & Hannah Eades, Oct. 17, 1851.
Hill, Samuel M. & Clementine Dailey, Aug. 21, 1851.
Hope, James W. & Clementine Burnett, Oct. 28, 1851.
Hoover, Benj. F. & Susan J. Marlen, Dec. 17, 1851.
Horton, John N. & Sarah Ann Fowler, Feb. 26, 1851.
Horton, Wm. J. & Martha A. Smotherman, May 29, 1851.
Houston, Wm. & Eliz. C. Clark, June 3, 1851.
Jackson, John F. & Sarah C. Lawrence, Dec. 12, 1851.
Jackson, Thomas M. & Mary Hendricks, Dec. 11, 1851.
James, John A. & Oliver F. D. Smith, Nov. 24, 1851.
Johnson, Granville & Frances M. Foster, Sept. 11, 1851.
Johnson, S. H. & Sarah A. Gum, Aug. 6, 1851.
Johnson, Wm. & Nancy J. Posey, Feb. 6, 1851.
Jones, John & Lucy A. Richardson, Oct. 28, 1851.

Jordan, James M. & Sarah Petillo, June 5, 1851.
Kidd, G. W. & Martha A. Brittain, Dec. 15, 1851.
Kirk, F. G. & Rozetta Norman, July 15, 1851.
Knight, Lewis W. & Eliza Eagleton, May 20, 1851.
Knox, James C. & Sarah A. Ryon, Oct. 6, 1851.
Knox, John & Manervia Waller, Jan. 23, 1851.
Lane, James & Mary A. McCrea, June 7, 1851.
Lantern, Henry & Lucretia Collins, Aug. 29, 1851.
Lee, James M. & Martha A. Blair, Oct. 13, 1851.
Lewis, Wm. J. & Lutha Ann Glenn, Dec. 10, 1851.
Livings, Allen G. & Susan C. Waller, May 28, 1851.
Loughry, J. N. & Miss A. A. Brown, Apr. 17, 1851.
Malone, Andrew J. & Amanda F. Peyton, Sept. 16, 1851.
Mangrum, Joshua & Sarah Crick, July 22, 1851.
Mathis, David C. & Nancy E. Serrell, May 5, 1851.
Meredeth, Joseph & Rhuah A. Fleming, July 3, 1851.
Miles, Caswell M. & Nancy W. Gentry, June 11, 1851.
Miller, Edward S. & Mary Miller, Oct. 27, 1851.
Moorehead, Wm. & Nancy Smith, Nov. 26, 1851.
Morgan, Wm. & Louisa Ann Caston, Mar. 1, 1851.
Moore, James B. & Andromedia Grisham, Dec. 17, 1851.
Mullins, John & Emeline Crosthwaite, Sept. 23, 1851.
McBride, Willis H. & Malinda Holden, Sept. 3, 1851.
McElroy, Wm. E. & Margarett A. Neely, Nov. 23, 1851.
McFadden, Candor & Sarah L. Stroop, Apr. 24, 1851.
McMurray, Geo. W. & Margarett J. Clark, May 10, 1851.
McRea, Wm. D. & Frances E. Threatt, Oct. 29, 1851.
Newman, John D. & Martha Elliott, Mar. 3, 1851.
Northcott, John & Eliza McKee, July 4, 1851.
Odeneal, T. J. & Catharine Martin, Nov. 8, 1851.
Overall, John W. & Mary McCullough, Nov. 25, 1851.
Ozment, Henry H. & Mary A. Wrather, Dec. 18, 1851.
Patterson, John & Julia A. Lytle, July 31, 1851.
Patton, Joseph C. & Judith C. Edwards, June 23, 1851.
Peyton, Thomas B. & Mary E. Sanders, Oct. 7, 1851.
Pinkston, Hugh & Mary McKee, Nov. 29, 1851.
Pope, Christopher & Tabitha Lamb, Nov. 11, 1851.
Pryor, James L. & Mary E. Winston, Dec. 22, 1851.
Pugh, Edmund B. & Hettie A. E. McClendon, Nov. 26, 1851.
Ransom, Richard P. & Frances Bass, Nov. 17, 1851.
Rich, Robert & Mary L. Neely, Jan. 27, 1851.
Richardson, Harry P. & Nancy E. Devault, May 21, 1851.
Robertson, Green B. & Mary F. Parrish, Dec. 14, 1851.
Rodgers, Robert & Sally Hooker, Aug. 4, 1851.
Rodgers, Ranzel H. & Mary C. Bivins, Aug. 7, 1851.
Rucker, Bennett & Mary Mathis, Oct. 10, 1851.
Rucker, Samuel & Mary T. Wright, Dec. 16, 1851.
Ruffner, John F. & Margaret T. L. Hopkins, Mar. 17, 1851.
Rouse, Isaac & Louisa Wilson, Jan. 2, 1851.
Rouse, Richard & Manervia Wilson, Feb. 20, 1851.
Sanflor, Candor & Sarah J. McCullough, Sept. 11, 1851.
Scales, Daniel R. & Susan Whigby, Mar. 30, 1851.
Scales, Joseph H. & Mary E. Hickman, Dec. 3, 1851.
Simmons, Wm. W. & Louisa L. Thornton, Oct. 3, 1851.

Sivily, Wm. H. & Frances H. Lawing, Oct. 8, 1851.
Slanter, Spencer S. & Alline Koonce, Mar. 8, 1851.
Smith, Geo. W. & Eliz. Henderson, May 15, 1851.
Smith, Henry B. & Sarah E. Finch, June 5, 1851.
Smith, James & Lavicy Todd, Aug. 5, 1851.
Smith, James M. & Frances P. Becton, Dec. 16, 1851.
Smith, Jesse B. & Joicy Cavinder, Sept. 12, 1851.
Smith, John T. & America Johnson, Jan. 5, 1851.
Smotherman, Elmore & Mary Smotherman, Aug. 14, 1851.
Stovall, Jephtha & Harriet Fields, Sept. 8, 1851.
Summers, Lafayette & Nancy Morgan, Oct. 14, 1851.
Summers, U. T. & Nancy A. Johnson, Oct. 17, 1851.
Thomas, Robert G. & Sarah Ann Vaught, Sept. 6, 1851.
Thomas, Sampson & Suraney Williams, Sept. 30, 1851.
Towns, Wm. C. & Lucinda Covington, Dec. 19, 1851.
Vaughan, Edward J. & Mary Ann E. Thornton, Sept. 30, 1851.
Vaughn, Thomas J. & Priscilla Cooke, Oct. 7, 1851.
Vernon, Wm. T. & Martha S. Floyd, Dec. 7, 1851.
Wadley, John W. & Cynthia A. Hollowell, Nov. 30, 1851.
Wallace, A. M. & Sarah Reed, Dec. 23, 1851.
Walpole, Chas H. & Catherine J. Walpole, June 9, 1851.
Warren, James & Sarah J. Cook, Nov. 27, 1851.
Warren, Wm. & Charloote J. May, Jan. 25, 1851.
Watkins, Joseph & Margaret H. Linster, Dec. 23, 1851.
Watkins, W. S. & Adeline W. Wilkinson, Jan. 15, 1851.
Weatherly, P. W. or W. P. & Julia Bishop, June 18, 1851.
Webb, Thomas L. & Sarah A. Lee, Dec. 24, 1851.
Webb, W. S. & Adelphia Wheeler, Mar. 14, 1851.
Webber, Edward & Jane Green, Oct. 6, 1851.
Williams, Henry J. & Susan E. Sumner, May 28, 1851.
Wingo, T. R. & Eliza R. Smith, July 10, 1851.
Winsett, Robert W. & Mary Crick, Oct. 15, 1851.
Wood, Johnson & Amanda F. Claud, Sept. 18, 1851.
Woodruff, John M. & Eliza. J. Todd, June 1, 1851.
Wood, Lafayette & Mary E. Beasley, Feb. 27, 1851.
York, Uriah & Mahala P. Batey, Feb. 26, 1851.
Youree, Wm. F. & Angeline T. Richardson, Mar. 13, 1851.

1852

Adcock, Henry W. & Margaret Odel, Nov. 18, 1852.
Alexander, John D. & Violet L. Baird, Dec. 10, 1852.
Anderson, Chas. W. & Martha Ann Love, Sept. 10, 1852.
Andrews, Wm. & Nancy J. S. Nance, Feb. 5, 1852.
Armstrong, Wm. A. & Sarah A. Wright, July 22, 1852.
Askew, Aaron O. & Susan C. Read, Dec. 9, 1852.
Barkley, Samuel Y. & Catharine J. Harrison, Oct. 12, 1852.
Barkley, Thomas C. & Nancy J. Wilson, July 17, 1852.
Barnes, Thomas F. & Siota Patterson, July 28, 1852.
Barnes, Thomas P. & Lavinia F. Coleman, Jan. 19, 1852.
Batten, Wm. S. & Nancy Ann Winston, Apr. 21, 1852.
Beesley, James & Sarah C. Anderson, Nov. 9, 1852.
Bennett, Zachariah & Lucinda Fleming, Nov. 3, 1852.

RUTHERFORD COUNTY MARRIAGES

Blackman, C. A. & Mickey W. Smith, June 30, 1852.
Bowman, Francis M. & Mary E. Know, Jan. 19, 1852.
Bracken, Richard H. & Caroline A. Tucker, Dec. 15, 1852.
Brewer, Henry J. & Martha Ann Vaulx, Jan. 29, 1852.
Brothers, Andrew W. & Sarah G. Crockett, July 27, 1852.
Brown, Felix & Nancy Slinkard, Aug. 22, 1852.
Brown, Ross O. & Mary A. Smith, Dec. 8, 1852.
Burk, Thomas & Mary H. Wright, July 21, 1852.
Burks, Romulus & Eliz. McNabb, Aug. 13, 1852.
Bush, Jesse W. & Melvinia Whitfield, Jan. 29, 1852.
Bushley, James & Sarah C. Anderson, Nov. 10, 1852.
Butler, James & Jane Stevenson, Oct. 10, 1852.
Campbell, Josiah E. & Martha J. Macgowan, Feb. 13, 1852.
Castleman, James H. & Mary Castleman, Feb. 21, 1852.
Cates, John A. & Elizabeth Ann Benson, Aug. 12, 1852.
Cole, John H. & Sarah C. Floyd, Oct. 20, 1852.
Coleman, Wm. D. & Angeline E. Caldwell, Nov. 24, 1852.
Caldwell, Thomas M. & Margaret J. B. Cannon, Sept. 28, 1852.
Cooke, John H. & Lucinda Noe, June 17, 1852.
Cooke, Wm. L. & Mary A. E. McClaren, Feb. 25, 1852.
Cooksey, W. H. & Miss M. A. Hester, Apr. 12, 1852.
Couch, Isaac M. & Sarah E. Rushing, Nov. 22, 1852.
Coulter, Manning & Mary Sifers, July 16, 1852.
Crocker, Thomas B. & Eliza J. Holden, Aug. 17, 1852.
Crockett, A. S. & Octavia Miller, Dec. 21, 1852.
Cromer, Joseph H. & Evelina D. May, Nov. 29, 1852.
Dalton, Fountain & Mahulda Allen, July 12, 1852.
Donnell, John W. & Susan Bowman, Mar. 31, 1852.
Doyl, Patrick & Jane Webb, Oct. 25, 1852.
Drake, Thomas & Sarah J. Mierhead, Apr. 25, 1852.
Dunaway, Drury & Caudis F. Patterson, Jan. 30, 1852.
Duncan, Patrick L. & Judy Ann Hall, Oct. 9, 1852.
Elder, Wm. K. & Eveline Batey, Mar. 4, 1852.
Fanning, A. J. & Susan P. Blackman, Aug. 23, 1852.
Featherston, Prestley & Mary Blessing, Mar. 12, 1852.
Fleming, Samuel & Jane C. Maxwell, Apr. 14, 1852.
Freeman, Thomas R. & Margaret R. Bingham, Mar. 31, 1852.
Fry, John & Neaty C. Moss, Dec. 28, 1852.
Furgason, Samuel D. & Margaret T. Thompson, Jan. 17, 1852.
Galaway, John B. & Rebecca Beasley, Sept. 25, 1852.
Garner, Thomas C. & Virginia Hughes, Mar. 15, 1852.
Gibbs, James H. & Cornelia M. Welden, Dec. 25, 1852.
Gillespie, Daniel J. & Amanda Willeford, June 30, 1852.
Gilliam, Richard & Emeline Cantrell, Jan. 23, 1852.
Gosney, Richard C. & Manervia Shields, May 21, 1852.
Graham, John & Sarah Snadridge, Apr. 22, 1852.
Gramps, John & Mary S. H. Smith, July 21, 1852.
Greer, Andrew & Eliz. Brown, July 3, 1852.
Greer, Thomas & Manervia A. F. Brown, Dec. 15, 1852.
Grimes, James M. & Balsonia Patterson, Feb. 21, 1852.
Hall, Thomas & Mary J. Ward, Feb. 13, 1852.
Hancock, Benj. C. & Sarah N. Revell, Nov. 30, 1852.
Harpins, Patrick & Rebecca Cotton, Jan. 29, 1852.

Harris, Elgin & Mary E. Crocker, Nov. 15, 1852.
Hastings, Giles P. & Rhoda Ann Jarrett, Feb. 24, 1852.
Hays, Wm. & Martha E. Hays, Feb. 17, 1852.
Herrod, Rubin & Mary J. Armstrong, Jan. 2, 1852.
Hill, Wm. & Sarah Butler, Feb. 26, 1852.
Holden, Goodman & Dorinda S. Smotherman, June 2, 1852.
Horton, James H. & Amanda Smith, Sept. 9, 1852.
Howland, Leroy D. & Eliz. C. Waller, Jan. 6, 1852.
Hughes, Thomas F. & Milly E. Shockler, Nov. 24, 1852.
Isom, Absalum & Emeline McCaslin, June 24, 1852.
Jarratt, James A. & Caroline V. Johnson, Dec. 29, 1852.
Jones, James H. & Hester A. R. May, Dec. 1, 1852.
Jones, Richard C. & Mary J. McHenry, Jan. 22, 1852.
Jordan, M. D. & Hardenia Dumpus, Jan. 6, 1852.
Jordan, Wm. A. & Martha H. Crouse, Sept. 21, 1852.
Kellough, Samuel & Margaret Williams, Feb. 9, 1852.
Lasiter, Wm. & Susan M. Rodgers, July 10, 1852.
Laughlin, Joseph Y. & Mary L. Sneed, Feb. 10, 1852.
Layne, Alfred J. & Harriett N. McRae, Dec. 1, 1852.
Loven, James A. & Polita Ann Douglass, June 26, 1852.
Lyell, Robert B. & Eliz. Crick, June 21, 1852.
Manire, Philip H. & Homora T. Donnelly, May 11, 1852.
Mankin, Welcome H. & Tabitha Deason, Dec. 22, 1852.
Manley, Wm. R. & Malinda R. Welch, Dec. 18, 1852.
Martin, Wm. C. & Lockey J. Donnell, Apr. 6, 1852.
Medling, Wm. A. & Eliz. H. Lasiter, Oct. 18, 1852.
Moore, Peter W. & Margaret L. Dickinson, Apr. 19, 1852.
Mooney, Jonathan A. & Martha Jane Seay, Oct. 20, 1852.
Moore, Samuel & Malinda Todd, Nov. 20, 1852.
McCaslin, Hugh R. & Rebecca Ann Youree, Dec. 16, 1852.
McCoy, John T. H. & Sarah C. A. Swink, Oct. 28, 1852.
McFarlin, M. P. & Emila McKinley, Aug. 5, 1852.
McKissick, Hugh L. W. & Milbra J. McGrigor, Jan. 4, 1852.
Newman, Anderson & Minerva Insell, Jan. 14, 1852.
Nisbett, Ephraim & Naoma Swan, Sept. 28, 1852.
O'Callaghan, W. A. & Frances McDowell, Apr. 28, 1852.
Owens, James F. & Mary E. Drumwright, Dec. 23, 1852.
Parker, Alfred K. & Margaret S. Johnson, Dec. 25, 1852.
Parker, John & Mary Taylor, July 7, 1852.
Patterson, R. H. & Mary Smith, Mar. 1, 1852.
Pearson, John M. & Mary Prewett, Aug. 31, 1852.
Phillips, Richard S. & Margaret C. Turner, Sept. 29,
    1852.
Pinkard, Wm. & Susan Halliburton, Mar. 3, 1852.
Powell, Robert J. & Susannah D. Bingham, Sept. 27, 1852.
Prater, Wm. H. & Mary A. Jacobs, Feb. 3, 1852.
Pyland, ---- & Susan Lassater, July 5, 1852.
Rather, Wm. & Martha Cawthorn, Mar. 16, 1852.
Robertson, Higdon J. & Martha A. Waller, Feb. 24, 1852.
Rogers, Benj. F. & Louisa Lockard, Apr. 23, 1852.
Rogers, John & Mary J. Lasiter, Aug. 2, 1852.
Rushing, John C. & Mary Stephenson, Apr. 14, 1852.
Russell, Newton & Eliz. Hutson, Nov. 3, 1852.
Ryan, Newton & Sarah J. Foster, Nov. 23, 1852.

Shelton, Geo. A. & Tabitha Eaton, Sept. 11, 1852.
Shelton, Wm. & Sarah A. Cates, Dec. 3, 1852.
Shelton, Wilson & Lucy Moore, Aug. 7, 1852.
Smart, Gideon & Areanah Freeman, Oct. 18, 1852.
Smith, Clemons M. & Marg. Dalton, Feb. 12, 1852.
Smith, Henry P. & Martha A. Waller, Mar. 8, 1852.
Smith, Sherwood W. & Eliz. Doring, Nov. 30, 1852.
Sneed, Charles & Ann B. Haines, Apr. 5, 1852.
Stem, Asa L. & Eliz. M. Birdwell, Feb. 22, 1852.
Summer, Mathew & Manerva J. Kelby, Jan. 5, 1852.
Thomas, John A. & Mary Reed, Aug. 19, 1852.
Thomas, John W. & Eliz. J. Thomas, July 8, 1852.
Todd, Jackson & Margaret Cox, June 26, 1852.
Trail, Valentine & Eliz. Ann Russell, Aug. 18, 1852.
Turner, Wm. G. & Isabelah Hisbett, Dec. 8, 1852.
Waldron, Charles H. & Ann E. Buchanan, June 28, 1852.
Wale, George W. F. & Nancy J. Wood, Mar. 7, 1852.
Ward, Kinchen & Eliz. Barrett, Aug. 17, 1852.
Warren, Edwin & Eliz. C. Henry, Apr. 1, 1852.
Watkins, Joseph & Margaret Linster, Dec. 23, 1852.
Webb, E. J. & Mary E. Daniel, Oct. 4, 1852.
Wendel, Robert S. & Emma C. James, Nov. 3, 1852.
White, Charles T. & Mary Elliott, Dec. 30, 1852.
Wilkerson, D. F. & Mary A. E. Sanders, Sept. 13, 1852.
Wilson, Joseph & Sarah E. Bishop, Sept. 28, 1852.
Wilson, Washington & Ann E. Burgess, Nov. 22, 1852.
Wimberly, Henry O. Catherine E. Bowman, Dec. 20, 1852.
Wright, Emuel & Johannah Smith, May 3, 1852.
Wood, A. J. & Ann M. Beasley, Feb. 3, 1852.
Woods, Nathan A. & Mary Jane Brewer, Aug. 28, 1852.
Young, Wm. & Lucinda J. Mangrum, Sept. 11, 1852.
Youree, James F. & Harriett E. Lancaster, Jan. 6, 1852.

1853

Adams, John W. & Mary J. Murry, Jan. 25, 1853.
Ailor, Joseph & Mary Ann D. Summers, Aug. 1, 1853.
Alexander, Robert M. & Amanda M. F. Dennison, Sept. 15, 1853.
Allen, Lunsford E. & Martha Hood, Jan. 15, 1853.
Andrews, Alphonso & Sallie D. Seward, Jan. 20, 1853.
Armstrong, John J. & Catharine Summers, Sept. 8, 1853.
Baird, Wm. D. & Catharine O. Ready, June 21, 1853.
Ball, Thomas W. & Mary Crouse, Jan. 8, 1853.
Barnes, Wm. & Mary Williams, Oct. 27, 1853.
Bates, Robert F. & Mary James, July 4, 1853.
Bearkley, Benj. F. & Emily Hall, May 15, 1853.
Bennett, James M. & Susanah M. Walden, June 17, 1853.
Bennett, Joseph M. & Jane K. Hall, Jan. 10, 1853.
Blackwood, John T. & Mary E. Good, Apr. 12, 1853.
Boring, Sterlins R. & Martha L. Edwards, Nov. 24, 1853.
Bounds, George W. & Mary Pope, Nov. 16, 1853.
Bowen, James A. & Eliz. Kelton, Apr. 6, 1853.
Bowling, Henry G. & Martha Parker, Jan. 20, 1853.

Boyd, Nathan A. & Martha A. S. Vaughn, Mar. 19, 1853.
Bradshaw, Sandiford & Susa E. Smith, Jan. 24, 1853.
Brown, J. D. T. & Mary J. Pukett, Aug. 6, 1853.
Brunson, Isaac & Harriet N. Weakley, July 3, 1853.
Bryant, Emanuel A. & Eliza. M. Donnell, Sept. 12, 1853.
Bryant, Henry W. & Margaret Cole, Dec. 27, 1853.
Burchett, Andrew J. & Mary E. Rogers, Sept. 13, 1853.
Burnett, Brookin J. & Martha S. Perry, Dec. 13, 1853.
Burnett, George M. & Emily J. Elder, Jan. 12, 1853.
Burnett, Wm. & Narcissa Beasley, July 25, 1853.
Burnett, Wm. C. & Mary C. McKee, Sept. 3, 1853.
Burns, Wm. R. & Mary J. Evins, July 28, 1853.
Burton, James A. & Stacy Ann Burk, Feb. 14, 1853.
Cain, Thomas M. & Cornelia A. Mullins, July 27, 1853.
Carter, John W. & Mary A. Todd, Nov. 4, 1853.
Charlton, Joseph & Sapronia A. Gregory, Mar. 14, 1853.
Childress, John & Eliza Greer, Sept. 24, 1853.
Clay, Theordrick S. & Jane E. Crutcher, Nov. 30, 1853.
Coleman, John & Lucinda Blari, Feb. 4, 1853.
Conner, Thomas W. & Palmyra A. Dethel, Jan. 12, 1853.
Corbin, Christopher C. & Susan D. White, June 30, 1853.
Cotton, Manaus C. & Martha Carter, Dec. 6, 1853.
Crenshaw, John W. & Elen L. Campbell, Dec. 8, 1853.
Curlee, Cullin & Margaret E. Lyon, Feb. 8, 1853.
Dane, Drury & Mary J. Abbott, Dec. 17, 1853.
Davis, Young & Queen E. Patterson, Mar. 10, 1853.
Delbridge, Edward H. H. & Frances Miles, Jan. 3, 1853.
Dunaway, Daniel J. & Nancy C. Kellow, Sept. 29, 1853.
Eagleton, Wm. C. & Mary A. Green, July 20, 1853.
Ellis, Edward N. & Lucy M. McKinney, Nov. 14, 1853.
Ewing, John A. & Caroline E. Buchanan, July 4, 1853.
Finch, James A. & Louisa R. Huggins, Feb. 2, 1853.
Fleming, Wm. & Eliza. A. Johnson, Sept. 29, 1853.
Floyd, James P. & Martha W. Rion, Mar. 4, 1853.
Freeman, Marshall & Eliz. J. Hall, Dec. 9, 1853.
Frost, Natha A. & Caladonia C. Prichett, May 2, 1853.
Fugett, Benj. & Jane H. Becton, Dec. 1, 1853.
Garrett, Wm. G. & Phebe Cunningham, Jan. 12, 1853.
Gilliam, Thomas & Malissa Stone, Mar. 3, 1853.
Grey, Joel A. & Cary Ann Winsett, Oct. 31, 1853.
Gwin, Alexander H. & Sarah C. Crichlow, Oct. 26, 1853.
Hailey, Wm. D. & Nancy E. Webb, Oct. 25, 1853.
Hale, Joseph P. & Eliz. C. Vaughan, Dec. 14, 1853.
Hall, John & Mary L. Finch, Dec. 6, 1853.
Hartman, John & Eliz. Leek, Sept. 1, 1853.
Hatfield, James & Tinzey Dickerson, Jan. 22, 1853.
Hayes, Thomas H. & Lucy Ann Clemons, Mar. 12, 1853.
Haynes, John W. & Margaret A. Datey, Jan. 18, 1853.
Henry, Washington C. & Amanda C. Elliott, Dec. 8, 1853.
Hickman, John H. & Milley F. Glymp, Apr. 2, 1853.
Holden, Benj. H. & Permelia A. Vaughn, Feb. 16, 1853.
Holden, Granville C. & Manirva Crocker, Mar. 15, 1853.
Holden, Thomas J. & Hannah V. Nash, Sept. 13, 1853.
Holmes, J. T. & Miss P. L. Hill, May 2, 1853.
Hooberry, Finus & Sallina A. Wall, Oct. 22, 1853.

RUTHERFORD COUNTY MARRIAGES

Hoover, Jasper N. & Sarah M. Dunn, Sept. 8, 1853.
Huddleston, George M. & Eliz. J. Durk, Apr. 5, 1853.
Hughes, James & Amanda Douglass, Aug. 20, 1853.
Hunt, Hustus & Eliz. Winston, Nov. 15, 1853.
Ivins, Albert P. & Martha Ann Pearcy, Feb. 21, 1853.
Jacobs, John W. & Amanda Howland, Jan. 27, 1853.
January, Joseph A. & Virginia Henry, Feb. 3, 1853.
Johnson, James P. & Sarah J. Sikes, May 24, 1853.
Jordan, Joshua & Locky F. Vaughan, June 29, 1853.
King, Benj. S. & Mary M. Neal, Apr. 11, 1853.
Knox, Franklin & Nancy D. Leach, Feb. 9, 1853.
Lamb, David & Almary Westbrooks, May 30, 1853.
Lannum, Alfred T. & Melvina Mullins, Feb. 30, 1853.
Lassiter, John & Eliz. E. Mayfield, Sept. 28, 1853.
Leathers, Theophilus H. & Martha J. Dunn, May 9, 1853.
Lillard, Thomas W. & Mary E. P. Howard, Aug. 3, 1853.
Lockard, Elijah & Fanny Dove, Aug. 23, 1853.
Lomx, Wm. C. & Harriet Cowger, Nov. 28, 1853.
Lyell, Wm. T. & Mary J. Tudor, Aug. 11, 1853.
Lyon, John B. & Bratha M. Caffy, Oct. 26, 1853.
Mallard, John W. & Parthenia Bell, Feb. 22, 1853.
Manire, David C. & Martha Read, Dec. 22, 1853.
Manor, James W. & Charity Hunt, Feb. 23, 1853.
Mathews, Wm. H. & Isabella M. Pasley, Mar. 3, 1853.
Miles, John Z. & Sarah A. Tutor, Aug. 9, 1853.
Miller, Durrel G. & Hannah E. Miller, Oct. 4, 1853.
Miller, Daniel R. & Nancy A. Jones, Jan. 3, 1853.
Morgan, Anderson & Eliz. Rushing, May 26, 1853.
Mullins, Radford L. & Martha E. Rowlett, June 30, 1853.
Myrick, Francis A. & Eliza Summerhill, Sept. 15, 1853.
McClaran, Daniel & Lucinda Potts, Oct. 15, 1853.
McCombs, John R. & Sane Stewart, Feb. 16, 1853.
McDowell, Joseph F. & Sarah McClannahan, July 27, 1853.
McKnight, James G. & Lucy M. Johns, July 20, 1853.
McKnight, Wm. T. & Virginia Johnson, Dec. 14, 1853.
McMillion, Franklin P. & Jane Robinson, Sept. 10, 1853.
Nance, James A. & Susan C. Neal, Jan. 24, 1853.
Neal, Thomas & Tabitha Merideth, May 7, 1853.
Northcott, Benj. F. & Mary R. Rucker, Sept. 1, 1853.
Oden, Thomas M. & Roxana J. Sims, Dec. 22, 1853.
Owen, Sandifer H. & Lucy J. Owen, May 9, 1853.
Page, Jesse T. & Eliz. Richardson, Sept. 28, 1853.
Pickett, Joseph T. & Sarah Bowman, Feb. 21, 1853.
Reynolds, Alfred & Catharine Wright, Dec. 27, 1853.
Rhodes, Albert W. & Martha J. Crawley, Mar. 21, 1853.
Robason, James M. & Mary E. Adcock, May 30, 1853.
Robinson, Alexander & Mary Brinkley, June 7, 1853.
Ross, Felix G. & Nancy E. Buchanan, Sept. 7, 1853.
Rouse, Joseph & Matilda Watkins, Dec. 15, 1853 or Apr.
  ?, 1853.
Sanders, Hiram & Margaret Brown, Aug. 5, 1853.
Sanford, John A. & Nancy Northcott, Sept. 15, 1853.
Settle, Seth D. & Ann Ledbetter, Jan. 19, 1853.
Simmons, Wm. J. & Ann M. Graves, Oct. 22, 1853.
Smith, Daniel J. & Matilda A. Tines, Dec. 6, 1853.

Smith, Daniel G. & Susan D. McLean, Dec. 19, 1853.
Smotherman, Dennis W. & Ruthy C. McCoy, Sept. 1, 1853.
Smotherman, James A. & Mary Douglass, May 30, 1853.
Snell, Thomas A. & Elvira J. Haynes, Dec. 14, 1853.
Spann, Thomas W. & Mary McDaniel, Jan. 12, 1853.
Spense, Abner & Lucinda Daniel, Jan. 1, 1853.
Spence, Joseph & Margaretta D. Wendel, Mar. 11, 1853.
Summerhill, Norvel R. & Martha E. Mathis, Oct. 18, 1853.
Tanner, Robert & Harriett Furguson, Nov. 1, 1853.
Taylor, Joseph M. & Nancy O. Lamb, Mar. 23, 1853.
Thomas, Gideon W. & Nancy A. McEwen, Dec. 14, 1853.
Thompson, Eli N. & Mary A. E. Zumbro, Mar. 9, 1853.
Tucker, Nathaniel B. & Louisa Tucker, Sept. 22, 1853.
Vaughan, Wm. L. & Sarah Allman, Apr. 28, 1853.
Vinson, Wm. & Mary Ann Cogburn, Nov. 15, 1853.
Ward, Benj. & Malinda F. Holden, Aug. 11, 1853.
Waters, Elisha E. & Mary D. Hamilton, Dec. 14, 1853.
Watson, John M. & Mary Ann Haynes, Feb. 21, 1853.
Weatherly, John B. & Nelly Ann Arnold, Apr. 19, 1853.
Webb, Isaac S. & Mary Ann Seay, Aug. 15, 1853.
White, James P. & Johanna Hutson, July 9, 1853.
White, Wm. L. & Mary Jarman, Aug. 10, 1853.
Wilkinson, John H. & America Bailey, Apr. 28, 1853.
Wilson, James & Louisa Datey, Sept. 27, 1853.
Wilson, Wm. J. & Nancy J. Fain, June 20, 1853.
Woodruff, James T. & Lucretia E. Ring, Nov. 5, 1853.
Wright, Nathaniel & Eliz. P. Lewis, Aug. 11, 1853.

1854

Adkerson, John J. & Sarah Sneed, Jan. 20, 1854.
Allen, Valentine S. Nancy A. Ridley, Aug. 31, 1854.
Arnett, Samuel & Sarah Stone, Jan. 21, 1854.
Arnold, Alexander & Eliz. Knox, Aug. 10, 1854.
Arnold, Granville & Eliz. J. Revis, Jan. 24, 1854.
Barnes, Elizah & Mary Mitchell, Sept. 22, 1854.
Barnes, Geo. A. & Lucretia Bottom, Mar. 8, 1854.
Baugh, Joseph L. & Anna Butterworth, Oct. 11, 1854.
Bell, Robert F. & Susan E. Neal, Sept. 30, 1854.
Brantly, E. L. & Mary E. McKnight, Oct. 9, 1854.
Brewer, Thomas & Eliz. Stephens, May 1, 1854.
Bright, Robert S. & Lavina Kerby, Nov. 4, 1854.
Brinkley, James & Sarah Auberry, Oct. 5, 1854.
Brittain, Pleasant H. & Sarah A. Neal, Mar. 11, 1854.
Brittain, Wm. W. & Sarah H. N. Blair, Oct. 23, 1854.
Brown, Archibald S. & Mary Sparks, Dec. 27, 1854.
Brown, Henry & Isora H. Walden, June 19, 1854.
Brown, Samuel M. & Amanda A. Taylor, Aug. 21, 1854.
Brookshire, Nathaniel & Nancy E. Brown, Jan. 4, 1854.
Brothers, Benj. & Susan Elliott, Jan. 19, 1854.
Buchanan, Alexander D. & Louisa A. Buchanan, July 17, 1854.
Burkett, Wm. H. & Nancy D. Walden, June 21, 1854.
Burnett, John W. & Martha A. McKee, Aug. 29, 1854.

RUTHERFORD COUNTY MARRIAGES

Bynum, Geo. & Lucy Ann Eaks, Aug. 25, 1854.
Carothers, Robert B. & Martha Fletcher, May 3, 1854.
Caruthers, John F. & Mary J. Puckett, Apr. 1, 1854.
Clark, A. W. D. & Eliz. J. Smith, Dec. 7, 1854.
Clark, Joseph & Louisa Ellis, Sept. 6, 1854.
Cobb, Reuben W. & Sarah G. Arnold, Sept. 11, 1854.
Coleman, John & Sarah J. Pope, June 14, 1854.
Coleman, Wm. F. T. & Judith A. Miller, May 25, 1854.
Collins, James & Eveline Hickins, Sept. 13, 1854.
Covington, Larkin A. & Emely E. Covington, Nov. 21, 1854.
Crick, Merriman & Virginia C. Winsett, Nov. 14, 1854.
Curlee, Thomas G. & Mary S. McKnight, Nov. 7, 1854.
Curtis, Wm. D. & Mary Barnes, Apr. 22, 1854.
Daniel, Henry T. & Martha M. Brown, Dec. 11, 1854.
Daniel, Icabud & Judith D. Daniel, May 4, 1854.
Davis, Wm. K. & Mary E. Allen, Jan. 17, 1854.
Edwards, Wm. & Mary J. Fleming, May 18, 1854.
Elder, James G. & Susan C. Harris, Sept. 5, 1854.
Farmer, E. J. & Mary E. Hicks, Oct. 2, 1854.
Farmer, George J. & Harriett R. Woodfin, May 4, 1854.
Felts, Richard & Mary Sherron, Oct. 14, 1854.
Fletcher, James M. & Susannah Jeans, Dec. 23, 1854.
Floyd, Joshua A. & Mary J. Jones, Aug. 28, 1854.
Fowler, John G. & Amanda Tucker, Dec. 11, 1854.
Fox, Isaac W. & Eliz. Major, Aug. 15, 1854.
Frizzell, John & Matilda Winford, July 22, 1854.
Garrett, Thomas & Lucinda C. Arnold, Feb. 1, 1854.
Gaskey, Garrett D. & Frances A. A. Hooper, Jan. 12, 1854.
Hallyburton, James O. & Nancy Clemons, Sept. 11, 1854.
Harrell, Franklin & Sarah Burks, Mar. 21, 1854.
Harrison, Lewis & Rebecca B. Loyd, June 1, 1854.
Harrison, Wm. C. & Martha J. Davis, Sept. 4, 1854.
Hayes, John & Eliz. W. Smith, Apr. 19, 1854.
Helton, Anderson P. & Mary M. Arnett, Aug. 17, 1854.
Hicks, Henry H. & Mary W. Ward, Nov. 3, 1854.
Hills, Charles J. & Mary M. Todd, July 26, 1854.
Holden, James P. & Mary J. Read, Aug. 26, 1854.
Holt, John H. & Rebecca S. Smotherman, Jan. 5, 1854.
Hyde, Hartwell B. & Malissa A. Morton, Dec. 5, 1854.
Jarratt, Alexander W. & Eliz. M. Fleming, Dec. 30, 1854.
Jarratt, Levi D. & Susan Brown, Jan. 16, 1854.
Jenkins, Nimrod & Jane W. Moore, Jan. 18, 1854.
Jetton, John D. & Margaret J. Warren, Dec. 21, 1854.
Johnson, C. M. & Mary C. Davis, Oct. 19, 1854.
Johnson, Edward & Nancy J. Brown, Oct. 9, 1854.
Jones, John & Eliza L. Booker, May 12, 1854.
Jones, Richard H. & Martha J. Patterson, Nov. 27, 1854.
Landrum, John & Peney Winsett, Nov. 2, 1854.
Lannon, Wm. A. & Rachel W. Thorn, Jan. 3, 1854.
Layne, Robert & Flora McRae, Nov. 1, 1854.
Lee, Robert A. & Mary T. Nance, Aug. 29, 1854.
Lewis, Benj. & Martha A. E. Watson, Jan. 6, 1854.
Logan, Samuel F. & C. Virginia Welch, Dec. 5, 1854.
Lowe, Walter & Martha S. Kelton, Sept. 13, 1854.

RUTHERFORD COUNTY MARRIAGES

Mangrum, Joseph & Louisa Vaughan, Sept. 13, 1854.
Maddox, Thomas F. & Amanda L. Nance, Sept. 16, 1854.
Mangrum, Jesse & Mary Jackson, Oct. 28, 1854.
Mason, Martin S. & Nannetta S. Hamilton, Jan. 17, 1854.
Mathis, Wm. T. & Susanah Wade, Oct. 5, 1854.
Merritt, George R. & Nancy M. Allen, July 3, 1854.
Mitchell, Wm. & Maryann Higgenbotham, Aug. 27, 1854.
Moore, Leroy & Mary Armstrong, Dec. 11, 1854.
Moore, Leroy & Rebecca Trolander, Oct. 3, 1854.
Morris, Joseph & Mary J. Vaughan, Nov. 20, 1854.
Morton, John W. & Lillian E. C. Glass, Nov. 17, 1854.
Mullins, Andrew J. & Mary A. Shannon, Dec. 5, 1854.
Myrick, Alvis & Nancy Jones, Sept. 11, 1854.
McCoy, James P. & Sarah J. Yews, Nov. 15, 1854.
McFarlin, John A. & Nancy E. Nichols, Nov. 6, 1854.
McGinnis, Joseph & Catharine Read, Feb. 1, 1854.
MacGowen, Geo. W. & Catura J. White, Jan. 18, 1854.
McGowan, Isaac W. & Nancy Harris, Apr. 29, 1854.
McGrigor, Clinton & Mary V. Reece, Dec. 30, 1854.
McGuire, Thomas J. & Martha J. Ferris, Dec. 25, 1854.
McKee, James & Sarah Vaughan, Oct. 31, 1854.
McRea, Thomas R. & Martha J. Fleming, Dec. 23, 1854.
Nations, Christopher & Jane Adams, Jan. 10, 1854.
Norman, Granville L. & Catharine E. Cowen, Nov. 23, 1854.
Orr, Wm. C. & Temperance Miller, Jan. 5, 1854.
Overall, Perilous N. & Louisa M. Kerby, Oct. 19, 1854.
Palmer, Joseph D. & Ophelia M. Durris, Feb. 14, 1854.
Parker, Isaac P. & Margaret J. Mullins, July 19, 1854.
Parsley, James J. & Martha E. V. T. Mathews, Dec. 18, 1854.
Partee, Rodolphus G. & Polemna T. Miles, Feb. 13, 1854.
Patton, Samuel M. & Nancy J. McCloud, Oct. 18, 1854.
Perryman, Wm. F. & Susan C. Sewell, Aug. 16, 1854.
Posey, Wm. S. & Mary J. Anderson, Nov. 9, 1854.
Prater, Philip J. & Isabella Kelton, Sept. 4, 1854.
Quigley, James P. & Mary E. Hall, Mar. 23, 1854.
Randolph, Wm. W. & Mary A. Morton, July 25, 1854.
Rankin, Franklin W. & Martha P. McKnight, Nov. 15, 1854.
Ransom, Robert N. & Isabella S. Huggins, Dec. 13, 1854.
Reed, Marvin & Julia E. Brown, Feb. 28, 1854.
Ring, Joseph F. & Levetha Burks, Nov. 6, 1854.
Rion, Thomas D. & Nancy A. Jones, Jan. 4, 1854.
Sage, Wm. F. & Corinda A. Felts, Mar. 1, 1854.
Sanders, John C. & Sophia W. Wasson, May 24, 1854.
Sanders, Samuel R. & Henrietta S. Thompson, Jan. 3, 1854.
Shuttleworth, Wlizah M. & Martha E. Jamison, Dec. 20, 1854.
Smith, James A. & Rebecca J. Taylor, June 29, 1854.
Smith, John D. & Missouri O. T. A. Pogue, Mar. 2, 1854.
Smith, Josiah L. & Ann M. Smith, May 2, 1854.
Smotherman, Joseph & Mary A. Smotherman, Sept. 11, 1854.
Sneed, John W. & Miss A. L. C. Farmer, Mar. 9, 1854.
Snell, James C. & Malissa J. Kirk, Nov. 2, 1854.
Spann, Richard R. & Eliz. Murphey, Mar. 6, 1854.

RUTHERFORD COUNTY MARRIAGES

Spann, Wm. R. & Rebecca Hays, Oct. 25, 1854.
Sugg, Wm. & Delitha Smothers, Apr. 12, 1854.
Summers, John W. & Laura A. Kerby, Jan. 5, 1854.
Swan, Lunsford Y. & Harriett C. Elliott, Feb. 8, 1854.
Talbert, Wm. T. & Martha E. Read, July 30, 1854.
Tappan, James C. & Mary E. Anderson, June 26, 1854.
Tatum, Wm. M. & Rebecca E. Swan, June 2, 1854.
Taylor, John H. & Sarah V. Dove, Aug. 10, 1854.
Thewer, Reese & Dovy Auberry, Sept. 20, 1854.
Thweatt, Joseph O. & Eliz. Welch, Jan. 17, 1854.
Thomas, Stephen & Eliz. Naron, Sept. 16, 1854.
Thompson, Albert C. & Eliz. C. Northcott, Feb. 11, 1854.
Thompson, George W. & Eliz. R. Sanford, Mar. 7, 1854.
Walton, Willis R. & Mary P. Ellis, Feb. 28, 1854.
Ward, Benj. F. & Evelina Hicks, Sept. 13, 1854.
Ward, James R. & Jane A. Baird, Dec. 19, 1854.
Ward, John P. & Ailey F. Walpole, Feb. 14, 1854.
Ward, Milton Y. & Caroline Ward, June 20, 1854.
Ward, Raford C. & Melisa M. Bone, Nov. 28, 1854.
Warren, Robert & Eliz. K. Snell, Nov. 27, 1854.
Williams, Wm. M. & Lucinda Covington, Jan. 16, 1854.
Wilson, James T. & Martha Lane, Sept. 27, 1854.
Winn, E. P. & Lucy Bellenfant, Aug. 11, 1854.
Wood, Andrew J. & Lodica Tucker, Dec. 21, 1854.
Wood, Joseph & Susan C. Wood, Jan. 9, 1854.
Wood, Obediah & Caroline M. Lane, Apr. 8, 1854.
Yearwood, Jacob S. & Martha J. Yearwood, Jan. 13, 1854.

1855

Abernathy, Jesse J. & Susan E. Williams, Jan. 16, 1855.
Alexander, Henry V. & Sarah J. Holden, Sept. 30, 1855.
Anderson, Charles & Martha J. Burge, Sept. 22, 1855.
Batey, David & Mary P. Hallyburton, Feb. 12, 1855.
Bell, Noah C. & Martha A. Oliphint, June 18, 1855.
Benson, John W. & Eliz. A. Mitchell, Feb. 21, 1855.
Blakemore, Wm. H. & Mary E. Ridley, May 8, 1855.
Blake, John R. & Josephine Murphey, Feb. 19, 1855.
Booker, Geo. W. & Catharine L. Dill, Oct. 11, 1855.
Boring, Sterling D. & Eliz. Edwards, Nov. 21, 1855.
Bowen, John A. & Juliann L. Dowman, May 10, 1855.
Boyce, Joseph A. & Louisa F. Dunn, Jan. 18, 1855.
Boyd, Wm. B. & Narcissa Dill, Sept. 18, 1855.
Bradford, Wm. & Pamelia Spain, Mar. 27, 1855.
Brothers, Jesse & Susan Ann Powell, Sept. 1, 1855.
Brown, Wm. D. & Mundora Rucker, May 9, 1855.
Bruce, Wm. M. & Nancy C. Smith, Feb. 3, 1855.
Bryant, Wm. F. & Margaret Johnson, Mar. 21, 1855.
Burton, Thomas & Martha Batey, Nov. 22, 1855.
Caffy, James N. & Mary H. Youree, Dec. 20, 1855.
Christopher, Martin A. & Rhoda A. Threat, Feb. 12, 1855.
Chumby, David A. & Frances Staton, June 2, 1855.
Craig, F. D. & Roxannah S. Fletcher, May 13, 1855.
Crockett, Wm. M. & Sallie C. Hollowell, Oct. 17, 1855.
Daniel, James M. & Martha D. Clement, Mar. 12, 1855.

Daniel, Lucious & America W. Hughes, June 19, 1855.
Davis, Able & Eliz. Johnson, Aug. 30, 1855.
Dement, Wilson Y. & Mary B. Harrison, Dec. 6, 1855.
Dillion, James A. & Nancy J. Johnson, Nov. 24, 1855.
Douglas, Thomas & Sarah Williford, Feb. 12, 1855.
Drake, Francis M. & Martha A. Walker, Nov. 25, 1855.
Edwards, Isaac S. & Sarah A. E. Pully, Dec. 4, 1855.
Elam, Daniel F. & Ellen P. Crawford, June 24, 1855.
Embry, Edmund & Martha Rouse, Sept. 14, 1855.
Evans, William & Mary Pearcy, June 5, 1855.
Ewing, Josiah W. & Ada Byron Hord, Nov. 21, 1855.
Farmer, James A. & Nancy J. Runnells, Feb. 1, 1855.
Fletcher, James F. & Mary Moore, Oct. 9, 1855.
Fox, Wm. & Jane E. Prewitt, Mar. 29, 1855.
Frost, John W. & Susan M. Rather, Oct. 23, 1855.
Gilmore, Wm. M. & Eliz. C. Naylor, Dec. 19, 1855.
Glymp, George W. & Lucinda Ryon, Jan. 15, 1855.
Gordon, Wm. & Mary Jane Thompson, July 19, 1855.
Gotcher, Henry P. & Julia G. Anderson, Jan. 8, 1855.
Grant, James T. & Martha A. Hill, Nov. 24, 1855.
Hale, Joseph P. & Eliz. C. Vaughan, Dec. 14, 1855.
Hall, Wm. J. & Susan Gambill, Oct. 20, 1855.
Harney, Andrew T. & Susanah J. McCrary, Dec. 26, 1855.
Harney, George W. & Jane J. M. Witherspoon, Dec. 22,
  1855.
Harris, James R. & Tennessee A. Crutcher, Apr. 10, 1855.
Henley, Richard L. & Lucretia Henry, Aug. 30, 1855.
Herrod, Rubin & Mary A. Brinkley, July 19, 1855.
Herrall, Calvin C. & Nancy Brown, Jan. 5, 1855.
Herrell, John T. & Martha J. Sherrell, July ?, 1855.
Hibbett, James R. & Isabella W. Burnett, Jan. 1, 1855.
Higgenbotham, John & Martha Renshaw, Jan. 30, 1855.
Hightower, W. W. & Armilda D. Blanton, Oct. 23, 1855.
Hoover, Byron & Euphemia E. Hodge, Sept. 19, 1855.
Hoover, Daniel D. & Mary E. Burks, Sept. 19, 1855.
Hoover, Joab & Eliz. Prewitt, Jan. 10, 1855.
Huggins, Camillus D. & Sallie E. Ridley, Jan. 3, 1855.
Hutcherson, Jos. & Martha Ann Horton, Dec. 19, 1855.
Hutcherson, Thomas & Sarah N. Yardley, May 30, 1855.
Isham, Absalom & Martha Winfrey, Mar. 5, 1855.
Jackson, John C. & Mary J. Covington, Dec. 19, 1855.
Jacobs, Stokley & Susan Anglin, Dec. 5, 1855.
Jacobs, Thomas H. & Margaret S. Parker, Oct. 7, 1855.
James, John W. & Mary J. Vaught, June 13, 1855.
Jetton, John H. & Isabella Mason, Feb. 20, 1855.
Jones, Geo. L. & Emily Owen, Jan. 18, 1855.
Jones, Wm. E. & Eliz. Wade, Sept. 5, 1855.
Jordan, James F. & Eliza G. Spain, Jan. 10, 1855.
Kerby, Christopher A. & Mary D. Vaughan, Jan. 20, 1855.
Kirk, Alexander M. & Sarah A. Brothers, Nov. 27, 1855.
Lawrence, John B. & Roberta S. Mason, Oct. 10, 1855.
Lawrence, Munroe & Parthenia E. Jones, May 10, 1855.
Lovin, Hugh F. & Angline Evans, Sept. 24, 1855.
Lowe, Milton M. & Mary A. Patton, Jan. 9, 1855.

RUTHERFORD COUNTY MARRIAGES

Lyon, Elijah & Mary J. McCrary, Mar. 27, 1855.
Mankin, James A. & Susan C. Pinkard, Jan. 16, 1855.
Miller, Mathew C. & Zilphia C. Johnson, Sept. 3, 1855.
Miller, M. C. & Harriett C. Tucker, Nov. 13, 1855.
Miller, Henry & Mary J. Cobb, Oct. 10, 1855.
Mitchell, Calvin G. & Mary O. Gannaway, Oct. 2, 1855.
Moore, Thomas Y. & Lavinia Anglin, Mar. 8, 1855.
Morton, Robert H. & Frances McCoy, Feb. 9, 1855.
Mosely, Henry & Holly Robertson, Dec. 19, 1855.
Murphey, James P. & Mary E. T. Wood, Aug. 6, 1855.
McBroom, Abel & Elmena Hoskins, Apr. 17, 1855.
McCann, John J. & Juliet S. Chamberlain, Dec. 10, 1855.
McCrary, Alex E. & Dorothy Youree, Jan. 24, 1855.
McKnight, John P. & Mary Neeley, Dec. 24, 1855.
McKnight, James N. & Martha A. Alexander, Nov. 20, 1855.
McLaughlin, George W. & Tennessee L. Morton, Sept. 15,
    1855.
Neeley, Joshua R. & Sarah Ann Smith, May 7, 1855.
Nelson, Isaac R. & Harriet V. Haynes, Dec. 7, 1855.
Nolan, Martin & Maranda D. Cochran, Nov. 7, 1855.
Norvell, Charles W. & Sarah A. Tennison, Oct. 24, 1855.
Pearcy, John J. & Eliza Jane Herbert, Nov. 13, 1855.
Perkins, John D. & Eliz. Tatum, Mar. 13, 1855.
Pierson, Richmond & Sarah N. Summers, June 27, 1855.
Pinion, Augustus & Nancy S. Harris, July 3, 1855.
Pinkston, James D. & Eliz. J. Mankin, Oct. 8, 1855.
Porter, James M. & Jennie T. Hannah, Apr. 25, 1855.
Portis, Joseph H. & Sarah E. McCullough, Aug. 25, 1855.
Pride, John S. M. & Sallie E. Morgan, Jan. 11, 1855.
Puckett, Benj. & Eliz. H. Ridout, Oct. 11, 1855.
Ralston, Alexander H. & Harriet R. Thompson, June 5,
    1855.
Rice, W. F. & Mary A. Sanders, Jan. 15, 1855.
Richardson, Wm. T. & Sallie J. Majors, Sept. 6, 1855.
Ridley, James B. & Mary J. Ridley, Nov. 8, 1855.
Ridley, Wm. A. & Nancy L. Haynes, Dec. 4, 1855.
Rucker, Samuel J. & Ada Mitchell, Feb. 15, 1855.
Runnells, James D. & Polly H. Todd, Nov. 30, 1855.
Rutledge, Benj. & Sarah Webb, Jan. 15, 1855.
Ryan, James M. & Elvey Winsett, Dec. 4, 1855.
Sanders, Andrew T. & Martha J. Semmons, Oct. 17, 1855.
Searcy, Anderson & Amanda E. Batey, Apr. 25, 1855.
Shelton, Thomas & Sarah E. Naron, Feb. 21, 1855.
Shilcutt, Thomas A. & Henrietta M. Buchanan, Feb. 13,
    1855.
Shipp, Joseph E. & Martha Ann Lewis, Dec. 19, 1855.
Shlaffer, Mathias & Martha Ehrenseller, Oct. 31, 1855.
Smith, Nepoleon B. & Mary D. Fletcher, Nov. 26, 1855.
Smith, W. W. & Julia Ann McLean, Nov. 26, 1855.
Smotherman, Bartholemew & Judith C. Wood, May 12, 1855.
Smotherman, James A. & Mary A. Douglass, Jan. 23, 1855.
Smotherman, Wm. & Mary J. Love, Feb. 15, 1855.
Snell, Jonathan L. & Martha E. Harris, Dec. 19, 1855.
Span, Hartwell & Eliz. Ryan, July 21, 1855.
Statler, Samuel & Mary Ann Lillard, June 26, 1855.

Stephens, Geo. M. & Sarah Ann Koonce, Aug. 16, 1855.
Sullivan, Robert J. & Sarah E. Barr, Oct. 18, 1855.
Tarpley, John A. & Indiana Jackson, Oct. 9, 1855.
Tassey, John W. & Esther A. Daniel, Feb. 1, 1855.
Thomas, Robert & Sarah E. Johnson, Oct. 2, 1855.
Thompson, Dela F. & Zusilla E. Watson (Halsen), May 14, 1855.
Todd, John & Rhoda Trolinger, Oct. 15, 1855.
Todd, Jacob M. & Mary A. Nichols, Jan. 6, 1855.
Toliver, Wm. & Martha Brinkley, Oct. 1, 1855.
Tompkins, D. C. & Louisa A. Jones, Nov. 14, 1855.
Underwood, Wm. & Nancy H. Barber, Oct. 23, 1855.
Vaughan, Isaac & Susan H. Taylor, Dec. 27, 1855.
Vawter, Jesse R. & Virginia A. Blackman, Jan. 9, 1855.
Walden, John & Eliz. Bishop, Apr. 7, 1855.
Westbrooks, Wm. C. & Julia A. Smotherman, Sept. 4, 1855.
Wiggs, Thomas W. & Martha E. Smith, Dec. 6, 1855.
Wilson, Wm. & Martha Ann Benson, Oct. 25, 1855.
Windrow, Travis & Catherine E. Pate, Jan. 1, 1855.
Woolen, Geo. W. & Josephine Zachry Smith, Nov. 27, 1855.
Wrather, Enoch D. & Ellen V. Robinson, Feb. 9, 1855.
Wright, Thompson J. & Eliz. A. Barker, Nov. 26, 1855.

1856

Alexander, W. T. & Euphemia L. Travis, Sept. 30, 1856.
Alford, Thomas W. & Athelia H. Bone, Feb. 11, 1856.
Allen, James A. & Eliz. D. Christopher, Dec. 14, 1856.
Anderson, Henry R. & Nancy E. Baxter, Mar. 31, 1856.
Armstrong, J. H. & Mary A. Roberts, May 17, 1856.
Arnett, Henry & Martha A. Burnett, July 29, 1856.
Arnold, Wm. J. & Sarah A. Rice, Feb. 25, 1856.
Alsup, E. B. & Susan F. Pearcy, Oct. 1, 1856.
Askew, Aaron O. & Susan C. Read, Dec. 9, 1856.
Baird, Thomas A. & Lucy A. Perry, Sept. 17, 1856.
Baker, James F. & Amanda Evans, Feb. 19, 1856.
Barnes, John H. & Martha Ivey, Jan. 27, 1856.
Barnett, G. F. & Eliz. Sanders, Aug. 20, 1856.
Baskette, James B. & Martha E. Neal, Jan. 24, 1856.
Baskette, W. T. & Hellin M. Crichlow, Oct. 8, 1856.
Batey, James M. & Harriette C. Morton, July 25, 1856.
Batson, Madison F. & Mary E. Ransom, Dec. 17, 1856.
Beatey, James M. & Mahaly C. Briant, Oct. 21, 1856.
Bell, John & Sarah M. McKee, Jan. 30, 1856.
Bell, Robert F. & Eliz. Major, Nov. 10, 1856.
Belt, William & Celia Howland, Jan. 17, 1856.
Bibb, A. S. & Sarah Ann Hord, Sept. 20, 1856.
Bigham, Robert H. & Lucy Ann Duncan, Jan. 26, 1856.
Bingham, John D. & Nancy C. Pearson, Oct. 31, 1856.
Birdwell, Samuel & Amanda L. Naylor, Jan. 9, 1856.
Blackman, Raiford C. & Ann B. Ridout, Oct. 4, 1856.
Bone, D. P. & Sarah L. Rankin, June 7, 1856.
Boyd, John & Martha S. North, Mar. 22, 1856.
Boyd, Nathan A. & Mary E. Marable, July 14, 1856.

RUTHERFORD COUNTY MARRIAGES

Bradford, W. H. & S. E. Perry, Nov. 4, 1856.
Brooks, H. J. & Isabella Miles, Apr. 30, 1856.
Brown, Geo. A. & Susan A. Sublett, Mar. 12, 1856.
Brown, Repps O. & Mary E. McAdoo, Jan. 28, 1856.
Bryant, Wm. O. & Mossouria A. Hedgepath, Nov. 8, 1856.
Buckner, Marian L. & Sarah J. Brinkley, Sept. 25, 1856.
Burlinson, Isaac & Julia Holloway, July 16, 1856.
Bumpass, Wm. M. & Hannah E. Nash, Jan. 14, 1856.
Cabler, James F. & Martha J. Dickie, Dec. 17, 1856.
Caldwell, Robert R. & Tennessee L. Buchanan, Mar. 29, 1856.
Carlton, John A. & Louisa A. Haynes, Aug. 25, 1856.
Carney, Wm. J. & Mariah L. Butler, May 14, 1856.
Cole, James H. & Mary F. Taylor, Jan. 14, 1856.
Coursey, Joseph & Amanda M. Lamb, Oct. 1, 1856.
Cross, John C. & Catharine Newget, Oct. 16, 1856.
Dickie, James H. & City M. Rowlett, July 11, 1856.
Dillon, Wm. H. & Martha A. Hill, Feb. 11, 1856.
Dunaway, Drury & Parlee Smith (Garrison), Sept. 29, 1856.
Dunaway, Thomas & Nancy Moore, June 9, 1856.
Dunn, Bolin H. & Catharine Summerhill, Apr. 30, 1856.
Dunn, Nuton C. & Cathrine Blagg, Dec. 18, 1856.
Eagleton, John A. & Mary A. J. Bethel, Dec. 17, 1856.
Elder, Elias A. & Eliz. C. Wilson, Dec. 29, 1856.
Elrod, Adam & Eliz. W. Good, Sept. 18, 1856.
Fields, Joseph H. & Mary J. Blair, Mar. 6, 1856.
Fletcher, Wm. C. & Sarah A. Edwards, Jan. 9, 1856.
Furgason, Beriman & Susan Hubbard, May 12, 1856.
George, Wm. P. & Chancy Etter, June 28, 1856.
Glenn, Stephen M. & Lucie W. Searcy, July 2, 1856.
Glenn, Wm. T. & Louisa Glimp, Dec. 16, 1856.
Gooch, James H. & Mary Jane Harris, June 21, 1856.
Gorden, John B. & Mary Eliz. Ealy, June 28, 1856.
Graves, Joseph L. & Amanda Robertson, May 5, 1856.
Greer, Elijah V. & Sarah Primm, Nov. 24, 1856.
Hail, Baxter W. & Rebecca M. Smith, Mar. 6, 1856.
Haley, James A. & Eliz. E. Robertson, Apr. 10, 1856.
Heraldston, Joseph S. & Sarah A. Sanders, Nov. 17, 1856.
Harrison, David A. & Sarah H. Huggins, Oct. 1, 1856.
Harrison, Duke W. & Addie Sublett, Oct. 6, 1856.
Haynes, Harvy J. & Julia Ann L. Posey, Nov. 8, 1856.
Hays, Thomas H. & Ann Newman, Feb. 20, 1856.
Hays, Wm. J. & Martha J. Weatherly, Feb. 8, 1856.
Higginbotham, M. L. & Margarett Jane Louis (Lewis), Aug. 21, 1856.
Hill, Wm. & Priscilla J. Baker, Aug. 27, 1856.
Hockins, Elisha & Mary L. Powell, Sept. 24, 1856.
Hodge, Wm. L. & Sarah O. Tombs, Mar. 8, 1856.
Holden, Geo. W. & Martha Jarratt, Mar. 17, 1856.
Hoover, Wm. F. & Martha A. Halton, Dec. 4, 1856.
Hoover, James M. & Martha J. Barker, Oct. 9, 1856.
Holmes, Charles R. & Sally S. Wade, Dec. 4, 1856.
House, James & Nancy G. Wilson, Jan. 24, 1856.

Howland, Lewis H. & Izabel Daughtery, Oct. 2, 1856.
Huitt, Wm. N. & America Roling, Nov. 26, 1856.
Irwin, George T. & Mary J. Cates, Jan. 23, 1856.
Jacobs, Alfred & Mary M. Creasy, Jan. 10, 1856.
Jackson, Mead H. & Sarah A. Nance, Jan. 1, 1856.
James, J. F. D. & Susan Batey, Oct. 9, 1856.
Jamison, John W. & Sarah Ann Colman, Nov. 12, 1856.
Jarratt, Robert & Cyntha Hewitt, July 18, 1856.
Johnston, Wm. A. & Jane E. Smith, Nov. 22, 1856.
Karney, Charles & Josephine Clark, Sept. 27, 1856.
Keller, James M. & Margaret L. Parker, Feb. 14, 1856.
Kirby, Smith & Violet Harris, Sept. 25, 1856.
Kirk, Wm. C. & Eliz. Smothers, May 12, 1856.
Lackey, W. K. & Lucy A. Felts, May 29, 1856.
Lamb, Thomas & Martha J. Westbrooks, Jan. 7, 1856.
Lyon, G. W. & M. D. Fagan, Aug. 12, 1856.
Maberry, W. Y. & Sarah McCalister, Dec. 24, 1856.
Mankin, Welcome & Sarah Lyon, Feb. 23, 1856.
Marable, Isaac L. & Eliz. Ward, Jan. 22, 1856.
Marshall, Wm. A. & Sarah J. Tully, Apr. 14, 1856.
Meadows, John A. & Amanda F. Barlow, Jan. 27, 1856.
Medlin, John M. & Eliz. C. Hood, Sept. 9, 1856.
Miers, Samuel & Eliz. Harris, Apr. 21, 1856.
Minter, John M. & Symantha A. Hendrix, Apr. 21, 1856.
Mooney, Wellborn & Susan F. Dromgool, Apr. 15, 1856.
Moore, Wm. M. & Margaret Heasbitt, Apr. 15, 1856.
Mullins, Thomas J. & Paralee F. McMinn, Jan. 24, 1856.
McCullough, R. C. & Catharine Ledbetter, Jan. 7, 1856.
McElroy, A. M. & Mary Weaver, June 28, 1856.
McKnight, D. M. & Eliza J. Herncon, Sept. 2, 1856.
McKnight, Iverson W. & Amanda E. Lyon, Sept. 2, 1856.
McKnight, Robert J. & Lucy A. Black, Sept. 18, 1856.
McKnight, Wm. T. & Pamela Jones, Sept. 18, 1856.
O'Briant, Wm. & Mossouria A. Hedgepeth, Dec. 10, 1856.
Osborn, Reps T. & Darthula A. McAdoo, Aug. 26, 1856.
Ozment, Thomas J. & Eliz. J. Osment, Dec. 9, 1856.
Parish, Samuel A. & Louisa A. Arthis, May 29, 1856.
Pfaff, Edward & Catharine Lyon, Feb. 14, 1856.
Phillips, Benj. F. & Eliz. H. Eillon, Dec. 27, 1856.
Pilkerton, Henry L. & Mary Benson, Dec. 17, 1856.
Pilkerton, Benj. F. & Malinda Gum, Mar. 24, 1856.
Prater, Austin & Harriett Brinkley, Aug. 26, 1856.
Prater, John & Sarah F. More, Jan. 5, 1856.
Pryor, Wm. & Mary A. Byers, June 18, 1856.
Puckett, David L. & Mariah M. Beesley, Mar. 22, 1856.
Raborn, R. D. & Mary J. McGill, Nov. 12, 1856.
Randolph, Peyton & Sarah J. Sanford, Mar. 19, 1856.
Reed, John W. & Miss A. E. Alexander, Feb. 26, 1856.
Rhodes, James H. & Martha J. Dill, Mar. 13, 1856.
Ring, M. L. & Letty M. Benson, Dec. 3, 1856.
Roberts, C. A. & Mary E. Putman, Dec. 1, 1856.
Shelton, Lewellen W. & Ann C. Bennett, Jan. 17, 1856.
Simmons, Wm. H. & America E. Graves, Mar. 3, 1856.
Sinclair, John M. & Sarah D. Flowers, Mar. 28, 1856.

Singleton, S. H. & Sarah M. Tompkins, Dec. 11, 1856.
Smith, J. B. & M. E. Davis, Dec. 17, 1856.
Smith, John G. & Eliz. Johns, Nov. 18, 1856.
Smotherman, Henry & Martha J. Smotherman, May 21, 1856.
Smotherman, John & Francis Loving, Dec. 16, 1856.
Smotherman, Wm. & Amanda Smotherman, June 17, 1856.
Sneed, Alexander & Mary M. Fulton, Oct. 14, 1856.
Spann, Benj. & Mary J. Hester, July 14, 1856.
Stafford, John A. & Barbary Teal, Dec. 23, 1856.
Summers, Wm. & Margarett Painter, Mar. 7, 1856.
Thompson, David & Emma H. Crutcher, Mar. 7, 1856.
Thorn, Thomas D. & Cornelia A. Underwood, Mar. 3, 1856.
Threet, Joseph M. & Caroline Evins, Apr. 7, 1856.
Todd, Harrison & Sarah E. Armstrong, Nov. 6, 1856.
Travis, Benj. & Francis K. Howse, Oct. 16, 1856.
Trigg, John S. & Lucy A. T. Walden, Jan. 16, 1856.
Turner, W. G. & Rosannah Nesbitt, Nov. 4, 1856.

1857

Acre, Levi F. & Louisiana Dunn, Jan. 20, 1857.
Alexander, H. V. & Samantha A. Thompson, Aug. 29, 1857.
Alexander, J. D. & Emeliza Moore, Jan. 14, 1857.
Anderson, W. L. & N. M. McHenry, July 16, 1857.
Avent, James M. & Mary Childress, Feb. 24, 1857.
Barnes, James D. & Luvicia Jane Bethel, Apr. 11, 1857.
Batey, James & Mary Walker, Sept. 5, 1857.
Batey, W. O. & Mary C. Hollowell, Nov. 25, 1857.
Bell, Benj. H. & Eliz. Richards, Nov. 29, 1857.
Bell, Obediah & R. E. Stephens, July 21, 1857.
Bench, W. M. & A. M. Keys, Dec. 2, 1857.
Bennett, E. G. & Jane E. Colman, Feb. 12, 1857.
Bingham, Columbus & Jane A. Sugg, Sept. 20, 1857.
Bivins, A. J. & Mary A. Lawrence, Jan. 15, 1857.
Blair, Solomon & Nancy E. Cates, May 23, 1857.
Bone, Henry C. & Martha E. Rankins, Sept. 7, 1857.
Bone, Wm. D. & C. V. Smith, Nov. 2, 1857.
Bostick, T. K. & M. H. Peay, Sept. 21, 1857.
Bottoms, John A. & Jane Crouse, Sept. 23, 1857.
Bridges, Henry & Lucy White, Mar. 18, 1857.
Brinkley, Lewis & Sarah A. Early, June 2, 1857.
Brown, E. T. & Louiza J. Bowman, Jan. 5, 1857.
Brown, James & Sarah W. Hamilton, Oct. 4, 1857.
Brown, John C. & A. P. Jarratt, Nov. 2, 1857.
Burgess, James N. & Eliza Lovel, June 28, 1857.
Burnett, W. W. & Mary Ann Graves, May 20, 1857.
Caffy, Thomas A. & Mary E. Dunn, Jan. 24, 1857.
Carney, John L. & Amanda W. Turner, May 27, 1857.
Charlton, James H. & Virginia P. Burt, July 27, 1857.
Cobb, G. L. & Susan Clemens, Apr. 15, 1857.
Cook, James H. & Martha A. McHenry, Feb. 16, 1857.
Cook, Samuel W. & Mary C. Hunter, Sept. 7, 1857.
Cosby, W. M. & Eliz. F. Ott, Jan. 28, 1857.
Coulter, S. & A. H. Morton, Mar. 30, 1857.

RUTHERFORD COUNTY MARRIAGES

Creech, John W. & Amanda Swann, July 2, 1857.
Crichlow, W. D. & L. J. Stevens, July 16, 1857.
Crouse, H. A. & Isabella C. McCullough, Sept. 30, 1857.
Daughtry, John & Nancy Pitts, Feb. 21, 1857.
Davis, A. P. & Mary J. Oliphint, Feb. 16, 1857.
Davis, W. L. & S. E. Searcy, Feb. 24, 1857.
Delbridge, James T. & Eliz. J. Howell, Mar. 14, 1857.
Dill, J. M. & J. P. Kelton, Aug. 10, 1857.
Dillon, R. A. & Eliz. A. Martin, Mar. 7, 1857.
Dobbins, D. P. & Sallie A. Rollins, Dec. 3, 1857.
Dobrowsky, P. M. & C. H. Gilliam, Jan. 8, 1857.
Donnell, S. C. & S. F. McAdoo, Feb. 16, 1857.
Drennon, J. N. & M. J. Thorn, June 6, 1857.
Drenon, D. C. & Elvina M. C. Lannom, Dec. 15, 1857.
Duglass, James J. & Francis E. Keel, May 20, 1857.
Edwards, Jarman B. & Jane Manning, Dec. 31, 1857.
Elam, K. E. & Lucinda E. Pearcy, Sept. 18, 1857.
Elliott, Archibald & Catharine Drake, Dec. 16, 1857.
Elliott, Milton M. & Margarett C. Lynch, Dec. 29, 1857.
Ellis, Zachariah W. A. & Susannah McKinney, Dec. 29,
  1857.
Engleman, Geo. F. & Mary W. Clay, Jan. 1, 1857.
Espy, Samuel E. & Nancy M. Powel, Feb. 28, 1857.
Farmer, James A. & Lucinda Bell, July 16, 1857.
Farmer, James C. & Judith E. Hicks, Feb. 18, 1857.
Finny, G. P. & Eliza H. Robb, Dec. 5, 1857.
Fitzjarrald, Wesley & Margarett J. Donaho, May 27, 1857.
Fleming, P. E. & Mary Shipps, Nov. 23, 1857.
Fletcher, Thomas H. & Isabella Hall, Apr. 11, 1857.
Ford, Henry & Margarett Vaughan, Dec. 21, 1857.
Foster, James E. & Susan Alexander, July 30, 1857.
Foster, Wm. & Eliz. Tombs, Nov. 17, 1857.
Gambill, John & Ann Adcock, Dec. 30, 1857.
Gibson, W. F. & Manerva Gibson, June 27, 1857.
Gilbert, James & Mary Ann Morton, June 1, 1857.
Gilbert, John F. & V. W. Kerr, July 22, 1857.
Gillespie, W. C. & Eliz. C. Puckett, Dec. 22, 1857.
Glimp, John H. & M. Lee, Nov. 23, 1857.
Goodlow, John W. & Margaret J. Thompson, May 28, 1857.
Goodman, Samuel H. & Amanda H. Speer, Sept. 14, 1857.
Haley, James W. & Tabitha Haley, Jan. 13, 1857.
Haley, John Will & Fanny Mitchell, Apr. 19, 1857.
Hamilton, James & Laura C. Jordan, Jan. 12, 1857.
Hart, Wm. & Sarah J. Modrall, Oct. 29, 1857.
Haynes, John W. & Sarah E. Snell, Feb. 11, 1857.
Helton, James N. & Susan Ann E. Johnson, Nov. 26, 1857.
Herrell, Ruben & Mary E. Brown, Aug. 6, 1857.
Hesbroner, Jacob A. & Julia D. Hall, June 4, 1857.
Hicks, John M. & Sarah Ann Murfree, Dec. 22, 1857.
Hill, Wm. & Eliz. Parker, May 14, 1857.
Hooper, W. J. & M. P. Hallyburton, Dec. 14, 1857.
Hoover, Julius & Mary Hockett, Feb. 8, 1857.
Hunt, John P. & Luanna Hall, Dec. 29, 1857.
Hutcherson, John & Tabitha Lamb, Jan. 12, 1857.
Ivey, Burrell & Sallie Bryant, Dec. 24, 1857.

Jackson, John W. & Lemiza S. Glenn, Nov. 11, 1857.
Jakes, Geo. & Mary E. Fox, Dec. 7, 1857.
Jamison, Wm. R. & Martha Arnett, July 29, 1857.
Jarmon, Wm. R. & Lucinda C. Crouse, Feb. 9, 1857.
Jetton, Robert B. & Esther L. Murfree, Jan. 27, 1857.
Johns, Wm. & Mary A. Hubbard, Aug. 19, 1857.
Johnson, James W. & Eliz. J. McNeal, Jan. 20, 1857.
Johnson, John S. & Martha Carter, Dec. 24, 1857.
Johnson, Robert & Martha McDaniel, Feb. 11, 1857.
Johnson, Wm. & Anna Jackson, July 1, 1857.
Johnson, Wm. W. & Eliza. J. Bowman, Feb. 2, 1857.
Jones, G. M. C. & Louisa Murphey, Feb. 19, 1857.
Kelton, Robert E. & Mary Brothers, May 15, 1857.
Kelton, Robert J. & Nancy S. Clark, Oct. 26, 1857.
Kimbro, W. L. & Susan Sanford, June 15, 1857.
Kirk, Samuel D. H. & Louisa M. Roberts, Mar. 21, 1857.
Ledbetter, Wm. Jr. & M. C. Lytle, May 6, 1857.
Lyon, A. M. & Martha A. Caffey, Mar. 19, 1857.
Major, John W. & Lucie W. Harris, Dec. 2, 1857.
Malone, R. D. & Harriett H. Major, Mar. 4, 1857.
Marlin, Isaac & Martha Elliott, May 13, 1857.
Marlin, John P. & Eliz. E. Knox, Sept. 16, 1857.
Martin, Matt & Amelia E. Henkle, Oct. 15, 1857.
Mitchell, James M. & Catherine T. Buchanan, Sept. 5, 1857.
Mitchell, Samuel A. & Emily L. Warren, Aug. 8, 1857.
Mitchell, W. B. & C. R. Blair, Jan. 16, 1857.
Moore, James E. & Nancy Pickett, Sept. 26, 1857.
Morton, Hiram & Sarah F. Nash, July 23, 1857.
Mullins, James P. & Louisa A. Mullins, Feb. 26, 1857.
Mullins, John & Sophia Pope, Mar. 7, 1857.
McClanahan, E. W. & Amanda Leath, Jan. 20, 1857.
McClanahan, John D. & Judy Ann Phelps, Sept. 19, 1857.
McCrae, Wm. A. & Eliz. E. Edmonds, Feb. 11, 1857.
McCulloch, G. J. & Martha Meritt, Sept. 7, 1857.
McDowell, David & Lucinda E. Heaton, Dec. 28, 1857.
McGuire, John W. & Mary Jane Clanton, Jan. 9, 1857.
McHenry, Henry & Sarah T. Dill, Jan. 20, 1857.
McKee, Wm. A. & Margarett J. McKee, Feb. 7, 1857.
McKnight, K. P. E. & Hannah K. Hogwood, Jan. 27, 1857.
Nance, John W. & Julia A. Jackson, Dec. 14, 1857.
Nash, Geo. N. & Virginia Nash, Mar. 17, 1857.
Nealy, Wm. W. & Mary F. Sulivan, Apr. 8, 1857.
Neely, M. H. & Nancy J. Aylor, Aug. 20, 1857.
Neill, James F. & Josephine A. Rucker, Nov. 12, 1857.
Newman, Gabrial & Mary E. Nichols, July 13, 1857.
Northcutt, Geo. N. & Margarett Miller, Dec. 2, 1857.
Owen, E. M. & Susan A. Mason, Feb. 12, 1857.
Owen, Nathaniel & Mary E. McNiel, Dec. 23, 1857.
Overall, Isaac R. & Martha D. Jones, Jan. 20, 1857.
Overstreet, John T. & Margarite C. Reed, Feb. 23, 1857.
Parrent, Louis & Cornelia A. Brown, Nov. 23, 1857.
Pate, Henry H. & Levina F. Dyer, Oct. 26, 1857.
Peyton, G. W. L. & L. A. Clayton, May 19, 1857.
Peyton, John W. & Julia A. Malone, Mar. 4, 1857.

RUTHERFORD COUNTY MARRIAGES

Pope, John W. A. & Mary M. Spence, Nov. 11, 1857.
Posey, P. F. & Martha A. Speer, June 13, 1857.
Prater, David & Mary E. Moore, Nov. 24, 1857.
Prater, John & Sarah F. More, Jan. 5, 1857.
Price, Wilson B. & M. C. Barton, Dec. 23, 1857.
Raines, John & Margarett Sikes, Nov. 30, 1857.
Rainey, John W. & Margarett C. Howse, Apr. 21, 1857.
Reed, David & Julia Ann Jones, Nov. 2, 1857.
Reeves, Wm. T. & Mary F. Nolen, Mar. 9, 1857.
Richmon, John D. & Mary A. E. Mathews, Dec. 1, 1857.
Roane, J. H. & Sallie R. Holden, Nov. 30, 1857.
Robb, W. W. & H. T. House, Nov. 4, 1857.
Rose, Robert & Brina Batson, Mar. 2, 1857.
Ryan, John W. & Sarepta E. Stack, Dec. 14, 1857.
Saffill, Andrew J. & Martha J. Singleton, Jan. 7, 1857.
Sanders, A. B. & M. A. E. Cradock, Jan. 7, 1857.
Sanders, J. P. & America Price, June 15, 1857.
Sanders, W. D. & Nancy Ann Vaughan, July 17, 1857.
Shannon, Finas E. & Rosannah A. Hunt, Aug. 19, 1857.
Sharber, J. M. & Isabella Trale, Feb. 4, 1857.
Sharber, Wm. C. & Mary A. Morris, Feb. 26, 1857.
Shingleton, John W. & Sarah Guest, Dec. 15, 1857.
Sirls, James & Nancy M. Todd, Apr. 14, 1857.
Smith, Charles P. & Ann Morton, Mar. 17, 1857.
Smith, Robert P. & Lizza McGill, Nov. 17, 1857.
Smith, S. W. & Arlamissa Wetherly, Oct. 27, 1857.
Smotherman, Uriah & Eliz. R. H. Simpson, Dec. 7, 1857.
Sneed, D. H. & Martha E. James, Jan. 1, 1857.
Spain, Thomas & Lucy A. Davis, Feb. 10, 1857.
Spangler, James & Martha Jane Tucker, Nov. 9, 1857.
Spence, James D. & Eliz. J. Williams, Mar. 10, 1857.
Stafford, John A. & Barbary Teal, Jan. 8, 1857.
Stanton, Pickney & Marandy E. Sanders, Nov. 11, 1857.
Stacey, David & Louisa Travis, Dec. 30, 1857.
Stewart, Richard & Martha Stewart, Nov. 11, 1857.
Taylor, Creed & Sarah L. Yearwood, Dec. 17, 1857.
Thompson, F. C. & M. J. Sanders, Sept. 2, 1857.
Toliver, Henry & Mary Ann Young, Apr. 19, 1857.
Tuttle, Solomon & Violett J. Burgett, July 26, 1857.
Upchurch, James A. & Eliza A. Jourden, Sept. 18, 1857.
Wade, Julius C. & Margaret H. Cowan, Mar. 3, 1857.
Waldran, James W. & S. D. Guthrie, July 5, 1857.
Wallace, W. H. & Caroline Smith, July 7, 1857.
Walls, Robert & Catherine Hunt, Nov. 5, 1857.
Warren, Joseph N. & Sarah J. McFadden, Nov. 5, 1857.
Watts, J. H. & Nancy A. Crowse, May 5, 1857.
Welch, Thomas & M. A. Mankin, Aug. 20, 1857.
White, John D. & Mary Allen, Nov. 5, 1857.
Wiggs, John M. & Mary E. Rosborough, Aug. 13, 1857.
Williams, Henry R. & Julia S. Pillow, Feb. 2, 1857.
Williams, Samuel M. & Sarah Burnett, Dec. 29, 1857.
Woods, Robert H. & Cicila Pinkard, July 23, 1857.
Wright, James W. & Martha A. Sanders, Sept. 29, 1857.
Yearger, Edmon & America Jarratt, Dec. 22, 1857.

RUTHERFORD COUNTY MARRIAGES

Adcock, Thomas J. & Levina J. Adcock, July 8, 1858.
Alford, John B. & Martha E. Ward, June 1, 1858.
Alford, Thomas J. & Mahulda Sanders, Mar. 25, 1858.
Arbuckel, C. F. L. & Mary I. Mann, Dec. 2, 1858.
Arnold, C. C. A. & L. C. Kirby, Sept. 23, 1858.
Arnold, Wm. & Jane Carter, Dec. 23, 1858.
Barber, John A. L. & Martha A. Ward, Dec. 28, 1858.
Barger, Isaiah & Martha E. Hayes, July 20, 1858.
Barton, T. S. & Mendozia Bivins, Nov. 24, 1858.
Benson, W. I. & Sarah E. Wisen, Apr. 6, 1858.
Bivens, David M. & Susan E. Johnson, Sept. 26, 1858.
Bivens, W. D. & Mary R. Barton, Nov. 23, 1858.
Black, James F. & N. C. Alexander, Nov. 4, 1858.
Bomar, A. J. & L. M. Janusary, June 22, 1858.
Bowman, D. S. & Caroline Gill, June 10, 1858.
Brothers, George & Oelvia Holder, Nov. 29, 1858.
Bryant, Wm. H. & Sarah Baker, Apr. 8, 1858.
Burgett, James & Eliz. Parris, Mar. 9, 1858.
Burrows, Thomas W. & M. C. Henry, Dec. 23, 1858.
Bush, J. W. & Martha E. Coleman, June 1, 1858.
Cates, John A. & Mary Benson, May 2, 1858.
Coleman, Daniel & Mary Hunt, Aug. 24, 1858.
Cook, David Jr. & Margarett Wade, Feb. 23, 1858.
Cook, Elbert & Sarah Ann Cotton, Aug. 12, 1858.
Cook, James P. & Cenia Ann Bailey, Aug. 6, 1858.
Cooke, Thomas M. & Dorothy A. White, Nov. 11, 1858.
Corben, John & Ellen E. Adcock, Mar. 3, 1858.
Covington, T. H. P. & Malisa A. Hendrix, Oct. 5, 1858.
Covington, Wm. & R. F. C. Hendrick, June 22, 1858.
Cowan, Joseph D. & Lucy F. Brown, Aug. 31, 1858.
Cox, Elisah & Eliza A. Jetton, Jan. 13, 1858.
Crawley, M. D. & M. P. Wilson, Jan. 26, 1858.
Cunningham, John & Margarett Moss, Jan. 9, 1858.
Daniel, Wm. R. & Sarah A. Ethredge, May 31, 1858.
Davis, A. J. & N. A. Edwards, Oct. 14, 1858.
Doak, J. M. & Mary A. Seay, July 31, 1858.
Doughlass, Asa & Nancy J. Anderson, July 11, 1858.
Downing, Andrew L. & Sarah Hoover, Jan. 5, 1858.
Downing, Melton & Milly W. Brooks, Sept. 8, 1858.
Eades, Samuel A. & Edy E. McCoy, July 27, 1858.
Eades, Wm. & Julia F. Barrett, Feb. 16, 1858.
Eads, Solomon & Nancy Pullon, Jan. 8, 1858.
Edward, Thomas & Martha A. E. Vaughan, Oct. 13, 1858.
Elliot, Wm. G. & Louisa F. M. Elliot, Mar. 28, 1858.
Fergus, James L. D. E. & Susan A. F. Neely, Jan. 11, 1858.
Floyd, D. D. & Sara J. Dyer, Jan. 6, 1858.
Garner, Wm. & Matilda Jane Herndon, June 17, 1858.
Gay, Dempsey & Mary McKinney, Nov. 3, 1858.
George, Wm. R. & Rebecca Mullins, Nov. 11, 1858.
Haley, W. W. & Eliza G. McFarlin, Sept. 23, 1858.
Hall, Drury & Eliz. John, Dec. 23, 1858.
Harris, Elgin G. & Nancy T. Spence, Jan. 17, 1858.
Harris, Richard O. & Martha A. Mainor, Dec. 16, 1858.

RUTHERFORD COUNTY MARRIAGES

Haynes, Abram & Rebecca E. Pope, Nov. 17, 1858.
Henderson, Wm. P. & Louisiana Pruett, Apr. 28, 1858.
Henry, Benj. F. & Sarah L. Pritchitt, Oct. 14, 1858.
Herron, Frederick & L. A. (Liddie) Goodman, Aug. 14, 1858.
Hoover, W. M. & Manerva Fox, Jan. 26, 1858.
Huchens, John W. & Lucy M. Daniel, July 15, 1858.
Hughes, Francis W. & Adaline E. Alexander, Oct. 12, 1858.
Hunt, E. D. & A. P. Hutcherson, Aug. 31, 1858.
Hutcherson, Joseph & Mary E. Evans, July 15, 1858.
Insell, George & Jane Price, Sept. 16, 1858.
Jenkins, E. M. & Nancy A. Victory, Apr. 7, 1858.
Johnson, Albert A. & Eliz. Mayfield, Feb. 16, 1858.
Johnson, Wm. A. & Eliza Suggs, Oct. 15, 1858.
Jolly, John J. & Susan W. Richardson, Apr. 8, 1858.
Jones, W. A. & V. G. Brown, July 14, 1858.
Jordan, J. R. & Susan C. Snell, Oct. 11, 1858.
Justice, James C. & Martha Mankins, Sept. 7, 1858.
Kellow, James M. & Martha Parker, Oct. 18, 1858.
Kimbro, Isaac N. & Sarah A. Eskredge, Jan. 28, 1858.
Kirby, Thomas D. & Eliz. Northcutt, Sept. 9, 1858.
Lamb, Wm. M. & Nancy T. Lawrence, June ?, 1858.
Lanier, Geo. W. & Ameliza Jennings, Nov. 28, 1858.
Lasiter, Wm. M. & Eliz. Witherspoon, Nov. 30, 1858.
Lillard, James M. & Sarah Greer, Dec. 22, 1858.
Linebaugh, B. F. & Martha V. Miller, July 28, 1858.
Lynch, M. S. & Drucilla A. Newman, May 19, 1858.
Manire, Amasa & Julia A. White, Mar. 11, 1858.
Mason, Luke T. & Myrtilla M. Burnitt, June 8, 1858.
Manier, Lemuel & Mary N. Hendrix, July 15, 1858.
Moore, John A. & Amanda Adams, Sept. 11, 1858.
McCrary, Arthur A. & Mary A. Gumm, Apr. 15, 1858.
McDonough, J. P. & Ann Clark, June 3, 1858.
McKay, Silas H. & Mary R. Ralston, May 25, 1858.
McLean, Joseph M. & Temperance C. McClean, Mar. 13, 1858.
McNabb, C. A. & Serena Burks, Aug. 12, 1858.
McNabb, James M. & Susan F. Mayfield, May 27, 1858.
Neal, John E. & Martha A. Coleman, Jan. 4, 1858.
Neely, John J. & Louisa J. Naylor, Apr. 4, 1858.
Newsom, James R. & Mary A. Vaughn, Mar. 10, 1858.
Nice, John W. & Jane Welch, Feb. 9, 1858.
O'Brien, John & M. J. Fuller, Jan. 26, 1858.
Old, John H. & Mary Noe, May 31, 1858.
Overall, L. D. A. & Lucinda J. Bates, Apr. 22, 1858.
Powell, Joseph & Margaret E. Brothers, Nov. 30, 1858.
Prewett, David L. & Susan Hickmon, Mar. 9, 1858.
Puckett, Robert D. & Mary E. Palmer, July 22, 1858.
Pugh, George W. & Eliza Castleman, Aug. 31, 1858.
Rather, Daniel & Sallie Tucker, Mar. 3, 1858.
Reeves, Daniel L. & Mary L. Garner, Oct. 12, 1858.
Renshaw, James J. & Mary D. Youree, Aug. 4, 1858.
Rice, James D. & Ann Welch, Aug. 4, 1858.
Rice, John W. & Jane Welch, Feb. 5, 1858.

Robinson, G. W. & Nelly Jane Williams, Dec. 30, 1858.
Rucker, D. L. & H. J. Adkerson, Dec. 14, 1858.
Russworm, Samuel C. & Virginia C. Green, Feb. 22, 1858.
Smith, Hiram & Eliz. Slaughter, Mar. 2, 1858.
Smith, Joseph B. & Mary ---- Alexander, Dec. 13, 1858.
Snider, Wm. Riley & Nancy W. Murry, Oct. 10, 1858.
Speer, W. S. & Julie S. Huff, May 24, 1858.
Thurman, N. F. & Lucy Wyatt, Nov. 10, 1858.
Todd, Aaron & Milly Eads, Aug. 22, 1858.
Toombs, James W. & Mary C. Robertson, Oct. 22, 1858.
Vardell, John T. & Catharine Elliot, Nov. 29, 1858.
Wadley, C. M. & Miss Cato Garner, Aug. 5, 1858.
Walden, James A. & Rebecca P. Duncan, Oct. 21, 1858.
Walker, Lewis & Mary Goober, June 10, 1858.
Weakley, J. P. H. & Lucy A. Muse, Nov. 17, 1858.
Webb, Aden & Delitha Mauberry, Dec. 13, 1858.
Welch, Nicholas & Malisa Tilford, June 30, 1858.
Welchance, Simon & Martha Barrett, Apr. 14, 1858.
Williams, Edmond P. & Savannah Whitworth, July 18, 1858.
Williams, James A. & Ann Roberty Short, Aug. 24, 1858.
Wilson, John W. & Tabitha Hoover, Apr. 9, 1858.
Winsett, J. F. & Sarah F. Butts, Dec. 14, 1858.
Whitson, Nathaniel & Rebecca Ann Hendrix, Sept. 29, 1858.
Word, T. C. & Sarah E. Jones, June 23, 1858.
Wray, G. C. & Julie Ann Murphy, Aug. 28, 1858.

1859

Andleton, W. W. & Rebecca Eaton, Jan. 6, 1859.
Ashley, John & Julia Tarlton, Dec. 14, 1859.
Bain, Peter H. F. & Sarah Rose, Nov. 22, 1859.
Barton, J. H. & Docia Bethshears, Oct. 20, 1859.
Batey, Wm. D. & Tabitha J. Searcy, Nov. 28, 1859.
Batey, W. F. M. & Sophia B. Rucker, Oct. 9, 1859.
Beasley, G. W. & Martha K. Neely, Jan. 20, 1859.
Beasley, T. J. & Frances E. Lewis, June 30, 1859.
Bedford, John N. & A. C. Smith, July 12, 1859.
Bethel, R. H. & Eliz. G. House, Dec. 22, 1859.
Blackman, James A. & Mary C. Richardson, Mar. 15, 1859.
Blair, Joseph M. & Martha Jane Philpott, Mar. 29, 1859.
Braden, Thomas J. & Nancy A. Daniel, May 4, 1859.
Brady, William & Susan McGowan, Apr. 27, 1859.
Brewer, Elisha & Susan Coleman, July 24, 1859.
Briles, Wm. T. & Thankful E. Tribble, Dec. 15, 1859.
Brown, Thomas F. & Martha W. Wharton, Oct. 6, 1859.
Bryant, Lorenzie & Stansheary Morris, Oct. 13, 1859.
Bryant, Zebadiah & Sarah A. Jones, Apr. 21, 1859.
Burton, Peyton S. & Lucy F. Lawrence, Oct. 12, 1859.
Butler, Wm. R. & Isadora Smith, Nov. 1, 1859.
Caldwell, John G. & Mary A. Holden, July 21, 1859.
Carlton, Benj. & Eliz. E. Crick, Sept. 30, 1859.
Carter, James C. & Margarett Jane Smith, Jan. 27, 1859.
Childress, J. K. P. & Ellen W. Avent, Dec. 20, 1859.
Childress, James N. & Rebecca Greer, Mar. 27, 1859.

Clark, H. W. & Miss E. R. Kelton, Apr. 14, 1859.
Clark, James A. & Mary A. Clark, Dec. 14, 1859.
Clinard, Andrew D. & Mary A. Wharton, Nov. 10, 1859.
Cole, Geo. W. & Sarah A. Haynes, Dec. 20, 1859.
Coleman, John H. & Sarah A. Shelton, Feb. 7, 1859.
Coleman, Patrick H. & Elmina Jane Bone, Jan. 20, 1859.
Cook, Geo. C. & Susan C. Reeves, Dec. 21, 1859.
Cooke, James R. & Harriet C. Batey, July 19, 1859.
Cooper, John A. & Mary E. Mason, Apr. 13, 1859.
Cotter, James L. & Mary J. Hays, July 7, 1859.
Craddock, G. G. & Eliza A. Jennings, Sept. 4, 1859.
Crockett, Robert P. & Mary E. Watkins, Oct. 12, 1859.
Cunningham, C. P. & Amanda C. Ross, Mar. 3, 1859.
Cunningham, Moses & Martha Morse, Oct. 6, 1859.
Daniel, R. D. & Rebecca R. M. Batey, Mar. 10, 1859.
Davis, A. T. & A. E. Boring, Dec. 7, 1859.
Davis, Constant H. & America Ann E. Mullins, Dec. 4,
    1859.
Deason, D. G. & Sarah J. Powell, Dec. 6, 1859.
Dill, Thomas & Eliza Dill, Sept. 10, 1859.
Dill, W. C. & Margaret J. Maberry, Dec. 1, 1859.
Dill, Wm. & Nancy M. Greer, Jan. 11, 1859.
Drake, Thomas & Eliz. Newman, Aug. 25, 1859.
Dunn, John L. & Mary Davidson, Oct. 20, 1859.
Eads, Mathew W. & Parthenia Avery, Jan. 3, 1859.
Eaton, Newton J. & Sarah F. White, June 16, 1859.
Elder, Levi W. & Mary E. T. McGowan, Apr. 27, 1859.
Eshredge, Wm. D. & Nancy C. Eshredge, Jan. 9, 1859.
Farmer, Thomas & Mary Jane Corder, Feb. 22, 1859.
Fletcher, D. D. & E. A. Alexander, May 10, 1859.
Fox, Wm. & Tinnie Rowden, Aug. 30, 1859.
Gannaway, R. D. & Sarah Davis, Aug. 9, 1859.
Garrett, G. C. & Nancy R. Arnold, Nov. 16, 1859.
Garrett, J. F. & M. C. Arnold, July 27, 1859.
Garrett, Wm. & Nancy A. Lannom, Aug. 1, 1859.
Gibson, Robert D. & Mary F. Miller, Mar. 8, 1859.
Graham, M. V. & S. C. Puckett, Mar. 28, 1859.
Graves, Richard R. & Eliz. Osment, Aug. 31, 1859.
Hall, John W. & Mary Jane Shelton, Feb. 7, 1859.
Hall, Wm. & America McDaniel, Feb. 23, 1859.
Hancock, E. D. & Fannie D. Murfree, Oct. 18, 1859.
Hallyburton, J. O. & L. M. Johnson, Nov. 21, 1859.
Harel, P. Y. & Nancy Brown, Oct. 22, 1859.
Harris, W. T. & E. E. Dill, Sept. 12, 1859.
Henry, Fontain J. & Sarah E. Osborn, May 19, 1859.
Herron, B. F. & Mecca H. Dunnaway, Oct. 6, 1859.
Hill, Samuel & Clementine Bailey, Sept. 29, 1859.
Hobson, H. H. & M. N. Williams, Dec. 7, 1859.
Hooper, Wm. J. & Eliz. A. White, Dec. 22, 1859.
Hoover, Mathias & Margarit Rollins, Aug. 17, 1859.
House, J. W. & S. J. Dunn, Mar. 10, 1859.
Howell, Wm. & Frances Williams, Dec. 29, 1859.
Howland, Ephraim & Malinda Todd, Nov. 23, 1859.
Howland, R. L. & Martha M. Baugh, Mar. 1, 1859.
Howse, G. A. & Mary E. White, Dec. 27, 1859.

Hughes, Thomas F. & Sarah J. Mayfield, May 12, 1859.
Hunt, John & Luzanna Miers, Jan. 13, 1859.
Jarratte, L. J. & Catherine Haynes, Nov. 3, 1859.
Jarrell, James W. & Mary A. Hevel, May 19, 1859.
Jernigan, J. W. & Mary M. Todd, Apr. 3, 1859.
Johns, Paul V. & Margarett E. Pearson, Jan. 26, 1859.
Johnson, J. N. & Catharine C. Faucett, Feb. 17, 1859.
Jordan, E. L. & Mildred Williams, Sept. 28, 1859.
Kirby, John & Nancy J. White, Dec. 14, 1859.
Koger, J. M. & Lucretia Barnes, Mar. 17, 1859.
Lannom, A. T. & Mary E. Clark, May 31, 1859.
Leath, John W. & Mary E. Ward, Nov. 1, 1859.
Lewis, J. M. & M. J. Fletcher, July 19, 1859.
Lewis, M. & Mary A. Hickman, Jan. 5, 1859.
Long, James & Ann Robb, Jan. 25, 1859.
Lowe, Hugh K. & Virginia Green, Nov. 27, 1859.
Mainor, D. S. & Eliz. Brady, Apr. 27, 1859.
Marable, Fountain & Martha L. Lester, Dec. 29, 1859.
Marshall, Geo. & Martha Brown, Mar. 29, 1859.
Mathews, John K. & Martha E. Johns, Oct. 13, 1859.
Matthews, N. J. & P. A. E. Logon, Apr. 4, 1859.
Mattox, Albert & Mary C. Sanders, Dec. 27, 1859.
Maxwell, J. L. & Susan C. Wood, Dec. 6, 1859.
Miles, C. M. & Sarah Russworm, Aug. 10, 1859.
Miller, James R. & Rebecca R. Rowlett, Mar. 1, 1859.
Modral, R. N. & Rody A. Tucker, Mar. 9, 1859.
Molden, W. E. & Mary F. Fox, Dec. 15, 1859.
Moore, John E. & Martha Ann Overall, Mar. 9, 1859.
Moore, W. F. & Sarah Tuder, June 5, 1859.
Morton, J. D. & F. E. Cook, Dec. 8, 1859.
Morton, Samuel T. & Rachel Jacobs, Sept. 6, 1859.
Mullins, John & Lovy O. J. Robertson, Mar. 15, 1859.
Mullins, W. L. & Mary H. Philpott, Jan. 2, 1859.
McCanlis, John & Martha J. Millins, Mar. 22, 1859.
McClain, J. H. & Lucy Wade, Sept. 9, 1859.
McDaniel, Wm. & Lucretia Elliott, Apr. 10, 1859.
McKee, James & Laura Pully, Sept. 8, 1859.
McKinley, John T. & Lizzie A. Ivie, June 9, 1859.
Nance, D. F. & Nancy Night, Dec. 1, 1859.
Heal, J. W. & Mary A. Mobs, Jan. 29, 1859.
Nesbit, Ephram & Susan H. Nelson, Oct. 11, 1859.
Norman, E. A. & Mary E. Miller, Sept. 25, 1859.
Northcott, D. P. & S. J. Thompson, Dec. 29, 1859.
Page, John E. & Eliz. Rutledge, July 26, 1859.
Parker, John W. & Mary A. L. Oslin, Oct. 20, 1859.
Parker, Joseph & Louisa H. Bailey, Feb. 10, 1859.
Patterson, Beverly D. & Maxmilly Patterson, July 21, 1859.
Payne, Geo. W. & Ellen Watts, July 9, 1859.
Pearcy, James & Martha Howell, Sept. 13, 1859.
Phillips, John & Lockey E. Crawford, Oct. 18, 1859.
Pitts, James J. & A. H. Green, July 27, 1859.
Prater, Henry & Mary E. Farmer, Mar. 1, 1859.
Prater, Phillip G. & Mary A. Fulks, Sept. 8, 1859.

Ray, Wm. R. & Eliz. J. Covington, Jan. 28, 1859.
Reed, T. J. & Louise J. Stitt, Jan. 26, 1859.
Renshaw, John A. & I. C. Myers, Oct. 5, 1859.
Rieves, Ira O. & Mary L. Nelson, Oct. 17, 1859.
Rutledge, Albert & Rachel Pogue, Dec. 22, 1859.
Rutledge, Richard & Elenor Gilmore, Dec. 27, 1859.
Ryan, C. F. & Martha A. E. Lee, Jan. 12, 1859.
Ryan, John R. & Sarah L. Sanders, Mar. 30, 1859.
Searcy, W. W. & Mattie Buchanan, Nov. 26, 1859.
Sikes, W. H. & Martha T. Gooch, Dec. 22, 1859.
Simpson, John T. & Mary J. Hood, Dec. 22, 1859.
Sims, E. S. & C. P. Randolph, Jan. 20, 1859.
Smith, James D. P. & Lockey C. Suggs, Oct. 13, 1859.
Smith, Joseph H. & Arabella McMurry, Nov. 24, 1859.
Snell, James H. & Louisa Y. Howse, Dec. 20, 1859.
Sudberry, John H. & C. T. Smotherman, Jan. 31, 1859.
Swan, Moses & Tabitha Neely, Jan. 23, 1859.
Swanger, David & Mary M. Bowman, Aug. 25, 1859.
Swett, Henry & Eliz. Kellow, Apr. 13, 1859.
Spence, Beverly D. & Maxmilly Patterson, July 21, 1859.
Tarpley, Henry L. & Arsenath L. Barr, Jan. 13, 1859.
Thomas, Benj. & Margaret Miller, July 25, 1859.
Thomas, James & Catharine Miller, Nov. 18, 1859.
Tilford, Henry W. & Eliza J. Ivie, Jan. 27, 1859.
Tribble, F. D. & Ann Kelton, Nov. 30, 1859.
Turner, Thomas & Manerva Haynes, Feb. 23, 1859.
Vaughan, Richard R. & Sallie N. Cooke, Aug. 14, 1859.
Waller, John B. & Mary E. Clements, Sept. 15, 1859.
Watkins, James & Mary A. Nickens, Nov. 10, 1859.
Wharton, Robert N. & Martha J. Mullins, Nov. 17, 1859.
White, Hugh L. & Matilda Elder, Feb. 23, 1859.
White, Thomas D. & Lizzie White, Mar. 8, 1859.
Williams, Thomas J. & Eliz. C. Nivins, Dec. 13, 1859.
Williams, Wm. D. & Virginia Powell, Dec. 12, 1859.
Wilson, W. L. & M. H. Carney, Jan. 18, 1859.
Woolfendon, Henry & A. E. Todd, Apr. 5, 1859.
Youree, John & Eliz. Lyon, Jan. 27, 1859.

1860

Allen, James H. & Sarah E. Lane, Feb. 2, 1860.
Averett, James H. & B. R. Phillips, July 16, 1860.
Averett, Wm. R. & M. T. Windrow, June 20, 1860.
Batey, T. J. & J. L. Smith, Feb. 13, 1860.
Baugh, J. M. M. & Mariah L. Murfree, May 3, 1860.
Beasley, John & Martha A. J. Dell, Dec. 25, 1860.
Benson, Argile & Mary A. Jones, Aug. 8, 1860.
Blanton, N. C. & Emma Peak, Feb. 14, 1860.
Brogan, John A. & Jemima Owen, Oct. 14, 1860.
Buchanan, J. A. & N. A. Ridley, Mar. 21, 1860.
Burkhart, A. & Martha Beasley, July 2, 1860.
Burkhart, Alexander & Hiley Bryan, Oct. 30, 1860.
Caraway, S. C. & Mary J. Blair, Nov. 28, 1860.
Carlton, Kinion & Margaret A. Holden, Dec. 18, 1860.
Carlton, Wm. J. & Sarah J. Spence, Aug. 29, 1860.

Carter, H. H. T. & Margaret Goodman, Feb. 22, 1860.
Carter, J. H. & M. J. Ricketts, Feb. 6, 1860.
Carter, John & Crecy M. Williams, Dec. 2, 1860.
Carter, John F. & Sallie G. Jamison, Dec. 26, 1860.
Cawthorn, J. T. & Eliz. J. Jackson, Nov. 28, 1860.
Clardy, N. L. & Ellen Lillard, July 3, 1860.
Cone, J. J. & V. P. Rowton, Apr. 8, 1860.
Conley, J. A. & Permelia Holden, Nov. 22, 1860.
Cook, D. L. W. & Martha T. Carter, June 15, 1860.
Cook, John S. & Isabella Thompson, Aug. 13, 1860.
Cook, Joseph H. & Emily C. Lamb, Sept. 9, 1860.
Cooper, Caleb & Isabella Smith, Nov. 14, 1860.
Corbett, Richard & Jane Ornean, Jan. 25, 1860.
Couch, R. W. & Lucy W. Tucker, May 26, 1860.
Counsel, Jacob W. & Caroline E. Newsom, Dec. 2, 1860.
Covington, James N. & Susan Foster, Nov. 6, 1860.
Crick, F. G. & Mary A. Patterson, Oct. 5, 1860.
Crosslin, A. M. & Permelia R. Gibson, Oct. 3, 1860.
Crouse, Thomas & Mary G. Dill, Aug. 7, 1860.
Curl, Portland I. & Susan D. Marshall, Oct. 23, 1860.
Davidson, W. M. & M. S. Warren, Oct. 24, 1860.
Davis, James N. & Mary E. Barkley, Jan. 2, 1860.
Davis, John W. & Mary J. Hume, May 1, 1860.
Dobbins, Wm. & Mary J. Rawlings, Sept. 18, 1860.
Donnell, James & Arminda Jacobs, Oct. 6, 1860.
Dowell, Gideon M. & Ellen Isham, Dec. 7, 1860.
Dromgoole, Geo. C. & Mamie R. Gibson, Jan. 10, 1860.
Dunn, G. M. & Sarah E. Helton, Feb. 2, 1860.
Dunnevan, W. H. & Mary B. Fleming, Jan. 5, 1860.
Dyer, J. W. & Martha A. F. Glenn, Jan. 23, 1860.
Elrod, James M. & Parlee Thomas, Jan. 9, 1860.
Farmer, Benj. F. & Nancy L. Garrett, Mar. 1, 1860.
Featherstone, Calvin & Nancy J. Lamb, Oct. 17, 1860.
Featherstone, Oliver P. & M. J. North, June 26, 1860.
Fergason, Levi W. & Josephine W. Mitchell, Mar. 1, 1860.
Flowers, A. J. & Elmira Rose, Jan. 18, 1860.
Flowers, J. A. & Ann Cawthorn, Feb. 1, 1860.
Fox, Samuel & Mary A. Kelton, Dec. 20, 1860.
Freeman, Levander & Mary Yearwood, Feb. 2, 1860.
Freeman, W. F. & Mary F. Sanders, Oct. 13, 1860.
Fuquay, Joel & Eliz. America Sanders, Dec. 5, 1860.
Goodwin, J. D. & S. A. Mabry, Mar. 21, 1860.
Gorden, A. W. & Amanda J. Nelson, Mar. 20, 1860.
Gresham, A. G. & J. W. Jenkins, Feb. 2, 1860.
Hais, Washing F. & Malinda L. Taylor, Mar. 14, 1860.
Harris, E. G. & Eliz. Dickerson, Apr. 1, 1860.
Haynes, I. J. C. & July A. Warren, Apr. 25, 1860.
Henry, John L. & Cornelia Jamison, Dec. 26, 1860.
Herrell, Miles & Delila Burks, July 29, 1860.
Hight, Archy & Ann A. Mathes, Feb. 28, 1860.
Hill, Wm. A. & Martha Miller, Dec. 19, 1860.
Holden, Jordan & Ann Clanton, Mar. 7, 1860.
Hollowell, R. T. & Mattie Patterson, Dec. 10, 1860.
Hunt, Wm. & T. J. Barlow, Dec. 4, 1860.
Inglish, Thomas N. & Frances E. Johnson, Dec. 11, 1860.

RUTHERFORD COUNTY MARRIAGES

Inman, P. H. & Sallie J. Cowan, May 15, 1860.
Ivie, John G. & Spicy G. Parker, Aug. 8, 1860.
Jackson, James H. & Louisa Wright, Oct. 22, 1860.
Jamerson, Robert & Miss Camelia Patterson, Dec. 26, 1860.
Jamison, B. H. & Martha Cox, Feb. 8, 1860.
Jarrett, D. M. & Nancy D. Ivie, Feb. 28, 1860.
Jennings, C. A. & S. E. Hill, Sept. 5, 1860.
Johns, John D. & M. L. Mason, Nov. 27, 1860.
Johnson, I. H. & M. M. Glenn, Nov. 6, 1860.
Jones, Enoch H. & Caroline Hancock, Nov. 22, 1860.
Jones, Samuel & Nancy Warren, July 19, 1860.
Jones, Wm. & Mary Jane Moss, Apr. 5, 1860.
Knight, John & Eliza C. Reed, May 17, 1860.
Lamb, C. H. & Fannie Williams, June 27, 1860.
Lamb, J. M. & Mary Cole, Oct. 1, 1860.
Lamb, Willis H. & Sarah Mead, Apr. 8, 1860.
Lattemore, B. F. & Jenny Hoskins, Dec. 25, 1860.
Lawrence, J. S. & S. A. Brandon, Oct. 25, 1860.
Lee, E. E. B. & M. C. Ralston, July 11, 1860.
Leek, John & B. L. Neal, Feb. 7, 1860.
Lovericke, Fredrick & Jane Powell, Sept. 4, 1860.
Lovorn, H. F. & T. A. Underwood, Mar. 31, 1860.
Lowe, Thomas F. & Margaret E. McCrary, Mar. 15, 1860.
Madox, Alfred & Mary Jane Tucker, Aug. 10, 1860.
Mann, Aaron & Nannie C. Rucker, Sept. 18, 1860.
Marshal, Jasper & Susan H. McFadden, Dec. 4, 1860.
Martin, Wm. & Matilda Goodner, May 25, 1860.
Meadows, Geo. W. & Judeth W. Sharp, Apr. 18, 1860.
Miller, I. J. & Nancy A. Johnson, Nov. 27, 1860.
Miller, Sylvanus & Mary White, Apr. 9, 1860.
Moore, John M. & Myra L. Moore, Feb. 29, 1860.
Mullins, H. A. & Matilda J. Jones, Dec. 16, 1860.
McFarlin, R. B. & Mary Tilford, Jan. 12, 1860.
McGowen, C. E. & Josephine Mason, Nov. 12, 1860.
Nelson, L. & Evie B. Weakley, May 19, 1860.
Nelson, P. M. & Miss Nannie Peebles, May 15, 1860.
Noe, Geo. W. & Eliz. Mathews, April 11, 1860.
Owen, John W. & Eliz. A. Hunter, Oct. 7, 1860.
Parker, Nehemiah & Harriett Pruett, Jan. 24, 1860.
Peyton, James H. & Mary A. Sanders, Mar. 21, 1860.
Phelps, Samuel C. & Eliz. Jernigan, Aug. 14, 1860.
Pilkinson, Thomas W. & Nancy P. Benson, Apr. 3, 1860.
Poindexter, W. H. & I. L. Nelson, Feb. 26, 1860.
Powell, Joseph & Mary E. Corder, Oct. 3, 1860.
Pratt, Baldwin & Betty Elder, Mar. 6, 1860.
Price, James & Eliz. Brown, Apr. 11, 1860.
Price, R. L. & Mary L. Cook, Jan. 5, 1860.
Price, T. J. & Eliz. Ann Guy, Sept. 20, 1860.
Puckett, Wm. M. & Mary T. McElrath, June 17, 1860.
Ransom, Lemuel & Isabella J. Clark, May 17, 1860.
Ransom, Medicus & Temperance A. Peck, Nov. 28, 1860.
Robinson, Jacob & Mary L. Hoover, July 25, 1860.
Robinson, Phillip O. & Moriah L. Wrather, July 19, 1860.
Ross, Geo. W. & Margaret J. Putman, Feb. 2, 1860.
Rucker, M. & Mildred Rebecca Revie, Feb. 23, 1860.

Runnels, Calvin & Sarah E. Sadler, Aug. 18, 1860.
Rushing, J. C. & Mary Jane Daniel, Sept. 18, 1860.
Russel, Chesley B. & Matt M. Brooks, Dec. 18, 1860.
Sanders, Samuel R. & C. Crockett, Jan. 24, 1860.
Schiff, A. & Hellen Rosenfield, Sept. 3, 1860.
Sexton, M. L. & Elender Bond, Jan. 4, 1860.
Sharber, J. A. & Lucretia Jackson, Mar. 7, 1860.
Simpson, F. M. & N. R. Leathers, Dec. 14, 1860.
Smith, James M. & Mary Hutton, Oct. 8, 1860.
Smotherman, Joshua & Mary F. Leathers, July 16, 1860.
Snell, F. M. & Lavinia V. Murfree, Mar. 8, 1860.
Snell, Robert & Mary E. Greer, Jan. 19, 1860.
Spain, Thomas & Narcissa Cawthorn, Mar. 13, 1860.
Speer, E. A. & N. E. H. Lyon, Jan. 31, 1860.
Stanburg, Lewis & Catherine Coleman, Sept. 4, 1860.
Straughter, Spence S. & America Summers, June 5, 1860.
Swancey, Cataline & Rebecca Simmons, June 12, 1860.
Taylor, Henry & Mary J. Dement, May 31, 1860.
Taylor, Wm. & Martha J. White, Sept. 3, 1860.
Tennison, A. J. & Sarah Owen, Jan. 31, 1860.
Thomas, Sawney & July E. Winn, Apr. 27, 1860.
Thomas, Wm. & Mary Jane Miller, Apr. 27, 1860.
Timms, C. W. & Amanda E. Nash, July 17, 1860.
Townsend, D. C. & E. E. Lowe, May 1, 1860.
Vaughan, David A. & America C. Smith, Dec. 18, 1860.
Waters, James & Letitia Pendleton, Jan. 3, 1860.
Webb, David & Susan Beasley, Nov. 17, 1860.
Webb, Robert & Morenda Horton, Dec. 23, 1860.
West, Stephen & Eliz. Snow, Aug. 23, 1860.
White, R. M. & Bettie Baugh, Apr. 10, 1860.
Williams, Henry & Francis W----, Feb. --, 1860.
Williams, Henry & Harriet Y. Williams, Nov. 20, 1860.
Williams, Jesse W. & Fannie E. Alford, Sept. 27, 1860.
Williams, John N. & Louvina Byrd, Nov. 6, 1860.
Williams, Richard & Sallie Holden, Sept. 26, 1860.
Williford, R. P. & Mary A. Caldwell, Sept. 27, 1860.
Willis, C. J. & Mary D. Arzeno, June 27, 1860.
Wilson, John B. & Mary E. Hickman, Dec. 31, 1860.
Wilson, John W. & Eliza Ford, May 21, 1860.
Winfrey, Alfred & Lylia M. Haggett, Nov. 8, 1860.

1861

Alexander, James & Martha Howland, Jan. 3, 1861.
Allen, F. L. & Josephine C. Sullivan, Sept. 17, 1861.
Arnett, John & Martha J. Arnett, Apr. 17, 1861.
Bailey, Newton & Melissa Campbell, Nov. 15, 1861.
Baird, John & Marthenia Bales Barrett, Jan. 15, 1861.
Batey, D. D. & S. W. Hunt, Dec. 26, 1861.
Batey, Henry & Eliz. Foster, Jan. 11, 1861.
Batey, James G. & Cathrine Walker, Apr. 2, 1861.
Bell, James & P. J. Wyatt, Aug. 17, 1861.
Bell, John & Louisana Thomas, Jan. 1, 1861.
Bell, John H. T. & Rody Coffett, Sept. 17, 1861.

Bilbro, B. H. & S. J. Sublett, Jan. 14, 1861.
Bivins, H. F. & Dotia T. Adams, Jan. 14, 1861.
Brady, W. F. & Martha E. Magowan, Jan. 2, 1861.
Branon, John A. R. & Dona Burchett, Sept. 3, 1861.
Brown, W. H. G. & F. A. Brown, Apr. 2, 1861.
Burkett, W. H. & Anne Elder, Apr. 24, 1861.
Butler, W. E. & America E. Crouse, Sept. 5, 1861.
Carter, Joseph E. & Pricilla D. Burton, May 14, 1861.
Carter, W. R. & Eliz. Durks, Jan. 17, 1861.
Clayton, B. T. & Rebecca F. Sharp, Jan. 7, 1861.
Clifton, John C. & Lucinda Clifton, Sept. 20, 1861.
Colman, Daniel & Mary E. Batey, Jan. 22, 1861.
Comer, Michael & Sarah Johnson, Oct. 21, 1861.
Cook, James & R. A. Cuthchens, June 24, 1861.
Cook, Stephen & Margaret Baxter, Oct. 30, 1861.
Cox, E. C. & Addie Todd, July 16, 1861.
Dunn, J. A. & M. P. Smotherman, Feb. 17, 1861.
Dunn, J. N. & Nancy Stone, Aug. 21, 1861.
Elam, Thomas J. & Sallie E. Snell, Nov. 11, 1861.
Elder, John S. & Zinia Overall, Feb. 14, 1861.
Ellington, Wm. & Maggie A. Lackey, Jan. 31, 1861.
Farmer, Willis H. & Julia Lasiter, Apr. 9, 1861.
Floyd, A. H. & Sarah C. Windrow, Apr. 2, 1861.
Gambille, J. G. & M. A. Furgus, Dec. 24, 1861.
Graham, John A. & Carrie Hollowell, Apr. 2, 1861.
Hall, Lion D. & Serena McDaniel, Feb. 21, 1861.
Harris, John C. & Jane H. Peyton, Mar. 5, 1861.
Haynes, Thomas K. & Manerva V. Winsett, Mar. 28, 1861.
Hays, Thomas H. & Margaret C. Burgess, Feb. 17, 1861.
Herron, John S. & Nancy C. Benson, Mar. 18, 1861.
Holden, Wm. S. & Eliz. Comer, Dec. 28, 1861.
Hoover, Joseph P. J. & Nancy E. Drake, Jan. 22, 1861.
Jamison, Wm. R. & Mary J. Sheton, Nov. 2, 1861.
Jenkins, David & Susan Norman, Aug. 22, 1861.
Jennings, James H. & Lucinda F. McEwing, Feb. 12, 1861.
Jones, John L. & L. C. Hood, Jan. 15, 1861.
Jordan, John W. & Cordelia Crockett, Feb. 14, 1861.
Kerr, Stephen & Annie Thompson, Oct. 23, 1861.
Kimbro, N. G. & H. L. Goodman, Jan. 15, 1861.
Lovvorn, John W. & Sarah E. Stem, June 24, 1861.
Mabry, John H. & Mar. E. Brown, Feb. 25, 1861.
Massey, T. J. & Mary J. Scales, Mar. 21, 1861.
Miles, P. P. & Mary E. Thomas, Feb. 10, 1861.
Miller, Sylvanius S. & Viola Bowman, Jan. 29, 1861.
Moore, Charles F. & M. H. Totty, Jan. 10, 1861.
Morton, Wm. & Caroline Bell, Dec. 28, 1861.
McGowan, Samuel W. & Mary E. Cook, Apr. 17, 1861.
Owen, M. P. & Amanda Travis, Jan. 19, 1861.
Parker, Albert Y. & Martha J. Shepherd, Feb. 19, 1861.
Price, R. C. & Sarah C. Northcutt, Sept. 28, 1861.
Ransom, S. H. & Bettie King, Nov. 23, 1861.
Roberts, Jack & Julia A. Summer, Jan. 1, 1861.
Robinson, Thomas J. & N. J. Broiles, Jan. 2, 1861.
Ryan, James M. & Louisa C. Edmunds, Jan. 15, 1861.
Sanders, D. J. & Fannie J. Stockard, Nov. 12, 1861.

Sanders, J. C. & Sarah Mitchell, Oct. 15, 1861.
Sergeant, John W. & Annie Cowen, Feb. 26, 1861.
Sharber, M. K. & M. J. Morris, July 23, 1861.
Shepherd, Benj. F. & Louisa J. Hoover, Feb. 12, 1861.
Simmons, Wm. & Nancy M. Noland, Feb. 14, 1861.
Smith, S. W. & Lizzie Kellough, Dec. 16, 1861.
Stevens, J. B. & Nancy R. Northcutt, Oct. 12, 1861.
Thornhill, W. L. & H. M. A. Jones, Jan. 2, 1861.
Tompkins, James E. & Viola Bowman, Jan. 30, 1861.
Tucker, Lewis & Mary Jane Winston, Dec. 21, 1861.
Wade, T. C. & Sarah E. Cothran, Sept. 16, 1861.
Walker, Wm. & Martha Couch, Mar. 27, 1861.
Westbrooks, J. H. W. & E. J. Reid, Jan. 30, 1861.
Willard, S. D. & Susan E. Spence, Mar. 4, 1861.
Williams, W. N. & Mary J. Comer, Jan. 21, 1861.
Willson, John & Sarah Eliz. Benson, Oct. 3, 1861.
Winn, Jordan A. & Frances A. McAdoo, Jan. 28, 1861.
Wray, Thomas J. & E. J. Snell, Apr. 28, 1861.
Young, Wm. C. & Parlena F. Caldwell, Feb. 15, 1861.

1862

Adams, F. M. & Susan C. Morton, Oct. 27, 1862.
Burnett, T. S. & Catharine Bethell, Dec. 25, 1862.
Carter, D. C. & Angeline Stem, Mar. 8, 1862.
Chamberlin, J. D. & Miss Ellen Spence, Nov. 30, 1862.
Cook, Wm. C. & Mary Osborn, Mar. 14, 1862.
Covington, Thomas & Jane Colman, Mar. 11, 1862.
Curlee, Dalis & Mary Carter, July 14, 1862
Eastice, John & Mary Jane Mount, Nov. 11, 1862.
Elgin, F. G. & Ann Coleman, Feb. 26, 1862.
Fields, Richard & Mary F. Grimes, Mar. 31, 1862.
Gandy, Wm. A. & Maria J. McBroom, Sept. 25, 1862.
Glymp, W. T. & Emily Jane Lester, Sept. 10, 1862.
Gordon, J. B. & Lucinda Davis, Jan. 29, 1862.
Hamby, J. G. & Nancy Pruett, Jan. 29, 1862.
Haynes, W. A. & Sarah W. Vaughan, Aug. 29, 1862.
Johnson, M. & Frances Swink, Nov. 26, 1862.
Jones, Abner & Mary Fry, Nov. 22, 1862.
Jones, J. W. & Mary Mathews, Jan. 28, 1862.
Jones, T. A. & Pink Covington, Dec. 3, 1862.
Kimbro, John & Emma F. Shacklett, Dec. 25, 1862.
Miller, J. F. & S. E. Greer, Mar. 28, 1862.
Morgan, John H. & Miss Mattie Ready, Dec. 13, 1862.
Mosley, Wm. & Millie A. Smith, Mar. 15, 1862.
Murfree, James B. & Ada J. Talley, Jan. 14, 1862.
Neal, W. P. & Nancy Noe, Mar. 11, 1862.
Nichol, J. Y. & Eliz. Bivins, Jan. 4, 1862.
Noe, W. R. & Nancy Noe, Mar. 11, 1862.
Oren, Thomas & Mary Jones, Dec. 15, 1862.
Patten, James & Nancy Irvin, Dec. 16, 1862.
Phelps, Wm. & Sarah N. Prater, July 1, 1862.
Phipps, E. H. & Manirva Williams, Jan. 2, 1862.
Porterfield, D. H. & Mary E. Carter, Sept. 29, 1862.
Roberson, Isiah & Mary A. Drennon, Nov. 28, 1862.

Robinson, Wm. A. & Hellen E. C. Dromgoole, Dec. 18, 1862.
Rogers, W. W. & Fannie M. Leatherman, May 24, 1862.
Short, Anderson & Martha White, Mar. 24, 1862.
Span, James T. & Harriett V. McCrea, Aug. 15, 1862.
Statland, Walter H. & Eliza T. Duncan, July 5, 1862.
Upchurch, Abner & Melissa N. Williams, Mar. 10, 1862.
Valentine, P. J. & Catharine R. Baird, Nov. 17, 1862.
Vantriece, S. J. & Sarah Jane Parrish, Oct. 2, 1862.
Ward, L. J. & C. M. Nash, July 17, 1862.
Weaver, Rev. J. P. & Miss Bells Bolls, Dec. 16, 1862.
White, Charles H. & Mary A. Rutledge, Dec. 23, 1862.
Winfrey, Alfred & Susan English, Mar. 8, 1862.
Winsett, J. J. & A. Seay, Oct. 27, 1862.
Woodroff, Richard & Rebecca A. Hamilton, May 29, 1862.

1863

Arnold, H. & Mary Mosbey, Oct. 2, 1863.
Benton, W. I. & Mary E. McCrary, Sept. 7, 1863.
Bowling, M. W. & Nancy Sanders, Nov. 19, 1863.
Brown, Robert F. & Susan Smith, Dec. 14, 1863.
Brown, Wm. D. & Lucinda M. Herrod, Oct. 26, 1863.
Burton, F. M. & Eliz. Rutledge, Nov. 2, 1863.
Campbell, I. G. & Drucilla Turner, Sept. 18, 1863.
Carlisle, James M. & Rebecca Prewett, Oct. 26, 1863.
Clemens, M. T. S. & Sarah Gibson, Nov. 10, 1863.
Davidson, Stephen & Eliz. J. Alexander, Sept. 17, 1863.
Dill, John & Sarah E. Hopkins, Dec. 24, 1863.
Dunaway, Drewry & Salle Patterson, Aug. 26, 1863.
Dunn, James & Martha Earley, Mar. 1, 1863.
Farmer, James A. & Eliz. Sanders, Aug. 2, 1863.
Floyd, James P. & Celia Jones, Sept. ?, 1863.
Gaity, Wm. W. & Sarah J. Clark, Mar. 11, 1863.
Grant, James M. & Isabella Cothran, Dec. 4, 1863.
Halstead, Calvin & Evergreen Dorrell, Dec. 24, 1863.
Hamilton, Lucian & R. F. Mullins, Dec. 2, 1863.
Johnson, Joel & Marye E. Dill, Nov. 17, 1863.
Johnson, T. B. & Lottie Hobbard, Nov. 7, 1863.
Kelton, John T. & Amanda E. Prater, Nov. 6, 1863.
Layne, Geo. M. & Nancy Crick, Dec. 22, 1863.
Lesetter, James & Eliz. L. Marable, Nov. 23, 1863.
Lindsay, Joseph & Mary A. Mitchell, Sept. 14, 1863.
Malone, A. J. & Didie Brothers, Nov. 4, 1863.
McGowan, Thomas M. & Susan C. BArnett, Dec. 2, 1863.
Northcott, G. N. & Nancy C. Coonce, Sept. 18, 1863.
O'Dell, Hiram F. & Harriett E. Taylor, Nov. 4, 1863.
Powell, W. M. & E. J. Maberry, Sept. 7, 1863.
Putman, Wm. & Charlotte Mayberry, Oct. 21, 1863.
Richardson, Isaac & Thankful Mankins, Oct. 10, 1863.
Rucker, J. N. & M. K. M. T. Hill, Oct. 20, 1863.
Sanders, Leonard W. & Mattie I. Walker, Sept. 8, 1863.
Shelton, Meredith & Judith Childress, Apr. 20, 1863.
Snow, F. M. H. & Miss Jane Ingram, June 8, 1863.
Thompkins, Geo. I. & Eliz. Prewett, Oct. 8, 1863.

Thompson, John A. & Rachel I. Hensley, Sept. 22, 1863.
Wade, Levi & Catherine E. Thompson, Jan. 7, 1863.
Williford, James & Mary Whillock, June 10, 1863.

1864

Abernathy, Charles & Fanny Jones, Apr. 13, 1864.
Allen, S. J. & Miss Emeline Sharp, Nov. 5, 1864.
Allison, W. T. & Mary W. Jordan, Sept. 14, 1864.
Arnold, James & Susan Murry, Oct. 30, 1864.
Arnold, R. T. & Maria Thompson, Jan. 7, 1864.
Barnett, Levi & Miss Panola Daniel, July 17, 1864.
Batey, J. S. & Mary Hutchens, Feb. 3, 1864.
Bell, Wm. T. & Ruthanna Gibson, July 15, 1864.
Bivins, James & Eliz. Boid, June 19, 1864.
Bradbery, John M. & Susan Hill, Sept. 19, 1864.
Brewer, John C. & Rebecca Ann Bell, Feb. 27. 1864.
Bright, L. & Jane Owens, Sept. 7, 1864.
Brown, I. E. & Clem C. Rino, Aug. 17, 1864.
Brown, Thomas & Lidia A. Smith, Oct. 29, 1864.
Burnett, John G. & Dolley Vardell, Mar. 1, 1864.
Cain, John I. & Maggie Smith, Sept. 12, 1864.
Carleton, Thomas H. & Sarah C. Jackson, Mar. 9, 1864.
Carpenter, Syrus W. & Martha Alison, Feb. 28, 1864.
Carter, Peyton & Martha Jurnigan, Oct. 6, 1864.
Cawthan, Alfred M. & V. R. Manor, Oct. 6, 1864.
Cawthron, Dabney & Eliz. Sanders, Aug. 2, 1864.
Charlton, James D. & Bettie Hunter, Nov. 10, 1864.
Cockran, David & Rebecca Lester, Nov. 14, 1864.
Comer, Charles & Eliz. M. Underwood, Sept. 14, 1864.
Cosbey, W. M. & Thenia Watts, June 26, 1864.
Council, J. L. & R. A. Dickey, Sept. 15, 1864.
Crawfoed, Preston & Mary E. Johnson, July 10, 1864.
Crews, John W. & Louisa J. Boswell, Feb. 25, 1864.
Crick, Wm. H. & Eliz. Lamb, May 22, 1864.
Damron, M. B. & A. M. Vincent, Nov. 24, 1864.
Davenport, J. C. & Tanson Sneed, Aug. 9, 1864.
Davis, Charles T. & Martha A. Baldridge, Feb. 22, 1864.
Davis, Geo. W. & Malinda F. Hall, Dec. 20, 1864.
Davis, S. B. & Sarah E. McDaniel, June 12, 1864.
Delyell, Nathan & S. J. Cross, Oct. 21, 1864.
Dolton, Wm. & Mary Bowman, July 26, 1864.
Fane, E. L. & Eliz. Olds, Aug. 10, 1864.
Ferrill, Charles & Eliz. Carnahan, Nov. 23, 1864.
Fink, A. C. & Mattie A. Chamberlin, Jan. 21, 1864.
Floyd, J. H. & Lizzie T. Floyd, May 9, 1864.
Ford, Wm. & Louisa Clinton, July 4, 1864.
Forsythe, E. M. & Susan Brady, Jan. 7, 1864.
Freeman, W. M. & Delong Northcott, Apr. 5, 1864.
Garnagan, Nedham & Clary Clark, Oct. 4, 1864.
Garrett, Milton & Lucinda E. Sage, Jan. 26, 1864.
Gooch, I. S. & Evalina B. Hume, Oct. 4, 1864.
Gordan, J. B. & Vanda E. Stovall, Aug. 24, 1864.
Gowan, James & Sarah Parker, Feb. 30, 1864.
Green, Irvin & Sallie Elliott, Jan. 10, 1864

Gregory, W. A. & Laura Smith, Feb. 26, 1864.
Griffis, John P. & Louisa Brown, Mar. 13, 1864.
Hall, A. E. & Eliz. J. Hoover, Dec. 21, 1864.
Harrison, C. D. Capt. & Sophia R. Lyth, June 27, 1864.
Hawkins, I. D. & Sarah Lawrence, Mar. 10, 1864.
Haynes, W. H. & Louisa Rowland, Feb. 15, 1864.
Herrod, M. N. & Frances Shepherd, Aug. 7, 1864.
Herron, Michael & Nancy Jane Arnett, Feb. 25, 1864.
Hickman, Geo. W. & Mary J. Nokes, Apr. 6, 1864.
Higgins, John & Lavina Brown, Nov. 21, 1864.
Higgins, John & Sarah Brown, Sept. 17, 1864.
Hill, Luther & Mary Roberson, Dec. 25, 1864.
Holden, J. M. & S. A. Garrett, Oct. 6, 1864.
Holden, Jordan & Harriet M. Holden, --------, 1864.
Holden, T. W. & Mary J. Underwood, Oct. 3, 1864.
Hoover, J. C. & Mary E. Lowe, Sept. 8, 1864.
Hope, Alexander & P. T. Rollins, Oct. ?, 1864.
Horton, G. B. & Nigary Holden, July 19, 1864.
Jackson, J. N. & Ada Stone, Sept. 1, 1864.
Jacobs, T. B. & S. A. Todd, July 12, 1864.
Johnson, W. W. & Sarah Marlin, Sept. 26, 1864.
Johnson, Wm. & Clary Ann Reed, Nov. 16, 1864.
Jordan, Holden & Harriet M. Holden, Apr. 16, 1864.
Jordan, Wm. N. & Mary E. Thompson, June 15, 1864.
King, G. S. & Judeth A. Manor, July 15, 1864.
Lamb, A. J. & Sophia W. Lane, Sept. 11, 1864.
Lambert, Henry A. & L. P. Sampler, July 9, 1864.
Laudmilk, James & Laura A. Bell, Apr. 28, 1864.
Lish, D. A. (David) & Eliza Johnson, Oct. 6, 1864.
Lorance, J. E. & Mary A. Creson, Mar. 30, 1864.
Lowe, W. E. & Mattie E. Prater, June 18, 1864.
Lyon, T. A. & Mary J. Lowe, Apr. 3, 1864.
Mankin, James H. & Sallie Hutchison, Apr. 30, 1864.
Manning, Joseph S. & Eliz. Castleman, Aug. 23, 1864.
Mason, Wm. N. & Frances J. Sanders, Sept. 5, 1864.
Morison, Thomas & Lucy A. Bell, Mar. 1, 1864.
Mullins, Jonas & Sarah A. Pearey, July 26, 1864.
Murphey, James K. & Louisa Moss, Oct. 30, 1864.
McBroom, Alexander & Rachel A. Hope (Rebecca), July 5, 1864.
McCorkle, Geo. W. & Nancy A. Bush, July 14, 1864.
McCullough, Joseph & Rachel C. Barber, Feb. 9, 1864.
McDowel, J. P. & Nancy J. Eaton, Aug. 10, 1864.
McGoughey, J. L. & A. M. Alexander, Sept. 7, 1864.
Newman, J. W. & J. W. Howland, Nov. 26, 1864.
Oliver, Wm. & Mary Bond, Jan. 17, 1864.
Overall, L. D. & Fronia E. Farmer, June 15, 1864.
Owen, Dr. I. R. (USA) & Albin I. Smith, May 5, 1864.
Owen, I. W. & M. E. A. Hegdon, Feb. 22, 1864.
Owen, M. P. & E. A. Travis, Jan. --, 1864.
Palmore, Wm. & Louisa M. Christopher, Dec. 1, 1864.
Parker, Thomas & H. J. Hays, Jan. 2, 1864.
Parnell, John S. & Judeth S. Holsted, Nov. 23, 1864.
Patton, Geo. E. & Pricilla P. Creson, Feb. 4, 1864.
Pitts, Anderson & Eliz. North, Mar. 1, 1864.

Powell, Dallis & Virginia Williams, Sept. 24, 1864.
Quest, Charles & Lucinda Brown, June 23, 1864.
Rankin, James H. & Sallie Hutchison, May 1, 1864.
Rasson, Geo. & Sarah Harris, Dec. 21, 1864.
Reed, James B. & Amanda V. Williams, May 23, 1864.
Roberts, D. M. & Mary R. Hite, June 25, 1864.
Rollins, Joseph & Susan Keel, Nov. 17, 1864.
Roulett, Major & Liza Wood, May 9, 1864.
Rowlett, Benj. F. & Susan A. Hudson, Feb. 10, 1864.
Rowlett, T. N. & Anne Woods, May 22, 1864.
Sadler, F. E. & M. E. Arnold, Sept. 10, 1864.
Sanford, James H. & Susan A. Helton, June 8, 1864.
Sanford, Peyton & Louisa E. Edmondson, Sept. 20, 1864.
Sauls, Henry & Louisa Summers, Feb. 4, 1864.
Shinn, J. D. & S. E. Baldridge, Feb. 22, 1864.
Ship, Wm. & Sallie Cotton, Nov. 2, 1864.
Smith, John B. & Sarah E. Turner, Nov. 1, 1864.
Smith, Thomas J. & Tinnier Weeden, June 25, 1864.
Smotherman, James & Mary H. Holden, Mar. 2, 1864.
Smotherman, R. H. & M. A. Vincent, Oct. 8, 1864.
Spray, W. W. & Lavinia E. Lynch, July 6, 1864.
Stone, James G. & Miss Eliz. Smith, Nov. 23, 1864.
Sullivan, H. R. & Martha E. Sanders, Mar. 23, 1864.
Summers, John W. & Susan A. Kirby, Jan. 5, 1864.
Taylor, W. C. & Amanda Powell, Aug. 10, 1864.
Thomas, James & Aurelia (Annette Brothers), June 14, 1864.
Thompson, Franklin & Lockey Tarpley, Oct. 17, 1864.
Thrailkill, Henry H. & Mary A. Morton, May 25, 1864.
Travis, Wm. A. & Mary J. Warren, Aug. 23, 1864.
Tucker, John H. & Lucy R. Rowlett, May 22, 1864.
Vardell, John & Rebecca E. Watkins, Oct. 25, 1864.
Vaughan, John B. & Mary E. Haynes, Mar. 9, 1864.
Vaughan, M. R. & Mary A. Lester, Apr. 2, 1864.
Wade, Levi & Catherine Thompson, Jan. 6, 1864.
Ward, Spious & Virginia Arthur, Feb. 10, 1864.
Watson, J. M. & Matilda A. Windrow, July 17, 1864.
Webb, James H. & C. T. McCrea, June 2, 1864.
Williams, Benj. & Eliz. McHenry, Aug. 3, 1864.
Williams, Charles & Annie Furgeson, Nov. 21, 1864.
Williams, H. G. & Frances R. Shacklett, Mar. 14, 1864.
Winsett, James J. & Margaret Marshall, Aug. 3, 1864.
Winsett, W. W. & Sarah F. Robertson, Sept. 12, 1864.
Wood, Thomas & Louisa Alexander, Apr. 11, 1864.
Woodruff, John & Susan J. Metter, Jan. 7, 1864.
Woods, J. N. & Mary Johnson, Mar. 1, 1864.

1865

Abernathy, Emanuel & Ellen Winrow, Nov. 15, 1865.
Abernathy, Franklin & Martha Alexander, Nov. 15, 1865.
Adams, Henry & Nancy Wright, Sept. 17, 1865.
Adams, Wm. & Julia Pope, Jan. 26, 1865.
Adams, W. J. & Miss Amanda B. Crouse, Apr. 6, 1865.
Adkerson, Jacob & Tennessee Coleman, Aug. 26, 1865.

Adkinson, Dick & Jane Scott, Aug. 26, 1865.
Adkinson, Emanuel & Ailsey Adkinson, Aug. 28, 1865.
Adkinson, Frank & Charlotte Adkinson, Aug. 30, 1865.
Adkinson, Jerry & Patsey Adkinson, Aug. 26, 1865.
Adkinson, Philip & Lucinda Bridges, Sept. 9, 1865.
Adkinson, Rufus & Rechel Lannom, Aug. 28, 1865.
Alexander, Abe & Lucinda Wright, Aug. 25, 1865.
Alexander, Alfred & Easter Alexander, Sept. 9, 1865.
Alexander, Anderson & Matilda Randolph, Sept. 9, 1865.
Alexander, Anthony & Dolly Alexander, Aug. 19, 1865.
Alexander, Christopher & Winney Alexander, Aug. 31,
    1865.
Alexander, David & Lorena McQuirter, Aug. 19, 1865.
Alexander, Ephraim & Aggy Webb, Dec. 15, 1865.
Alexander, Ezekiah & Celia Winston, Aug. 19, 1865.
Alexander, Henry & Matilda Alexander, Sept. 10, 1865.
Alexander, Isaac & Milinda Alexander, Aug. 19, 1865.
Alexander, James & Mallissa Summers, Aug. 23, 1865.
Alexander, Jeff & Meriah Wright, Aug. 22, 1865.
Alexander, Jessee & Mariah Alexander, Aug. 19, 1865.
Alexander, Jessee & Nancey Bethshares, Aug. 19, 1865.
Alexander, Job & Ellen Alexander, Asept. 16, 1865.
Alexander, John & Fanny Winston, Aug. 19, 1865.
Alexander, John W. & Martha B. Daniel, Sept. 5, 1865.
Alexander, Joseph & Amanda Whitson, July 4, 1865.
Alexander, Nelson & Jinny Nisbett, Aug. 20, 1865.
Alexander, Poney & Isabella Norman, Aug. 20, 1865.
Alexander, Samuel & Miss Barbary Winston, May 13, 1865.
Alexander, Taswell & Eliza Alexander, Sept. 8, 1865.
Alexander, Wm. & Easter Alexander, Oct. 14, 1865.
Alford, Frank & Adaline Peek, Aug. 20, 1865.
Alford, Henry & Malinda Hunt, Dec. 27, 1865.
Alford, James & Johanna S. Rucker, July 18, 1865.
Alford, John & Ellen Clayton, Aug. 19, 1865.
Alford, Ned & Hannah Waller, Aug. 26, 1865.
Allen, George & Barbery Reed, Sept. 10, 1865.
Allen, James & Adeline Allen, Aug. 26, 1865.
Allen, Milton & Martha Ann Clopton, Aug. 26, 1865.
Allen, Peter & Evelina Lark, Sept. 3, 1865.
Ambrose, Merida & Sarah Ambrose, Aug. 20, 1865.
Anderson, Alfred & Caroline Lytle, Aug. 29, 1865.
Anderson, Alfred & Margaret Hill, Sept. 17, 1865.
Anderson, Andrew & Ellen Hicks, Aug. 26, 1865.
Anderson, Ben & Syntha Miles, Sept. 10, 1865.
Anderson, David & Hannah Davis, Sept. 3, 1865.
Anderson, Ellis & Lavania Anderson, Aug. 26, 1865.
Anderson, Henry & Dicey Mitchell, Aug. 20, 1865.
Anderson, Henry & Sarah Espy, Nov. 10, 1865.
Anderson, Lewis & Narcissa Johns, Aug. 23, 1865.
Anderson, Richard & Fannie Winston, Aug. 20, 1865.
Anderson, Richard & Willis Drake, Aug. 20, 1865.
Anderson, Sam & Mary Jane Miller, Aug. 26, 1865.
Anderson, Wm. & Beckey Anderson, Aug. 23, 1865.
Anderson, Wm. & Mary Eliza Delbridge, Nov. 11, 1865.
Anthony, Charles & Mary Nelson, Aug. 26, 1865.

Arbuckle, J. K. & Mary E. Thompson, Nov. 28, 1865.
Armstrong, Elmore & Minerva Armstrong, Aug. 28, 1865.
Arnold, Berry & Silva Arnold, Aug. 31, 1865.
Arnold, Moses & Syntha Arnold, Sept. 2, 1865.
Arnold, Robert & Amanda Johnson, Nov. 10, 1865.
Arnold, Toliver & Nancy Cluck, June 20, 1865.
Ashley, Richard & Dolly Pearson, Sept. 1, 1865.
Ashley, Wm. T. & E. A. Newman, Mar. 15, 1865.
Austin, Jackson & Laura Austin, Aug. 28, 1865.
Baird, Andy & Jane DeJarnatt, Aug. 20, 1865.
Baird, Anthony & Amanda Jordan, Aug. 26, 1865.
Baker, Henry & Victoria Robertson, Jan. 1, 1865.
Baker, Sterling & Rose Ann Goodwin, Oct. 5, 1865.
Balentine, J. W. & Eliza Richards, Apr. 20, 1865.
Balentine, James & Margaret Philpot, Mar. 16, 1865.
BArker, Roger & Annie Wright, Aug. 23, 1865.
Barkley, Isaac & Susan Barkley, Aug. 26, 1865.
Barnes, Alexander & Lucy Smith, Aug. 23, 1865.
Barnes, Benj. & Betsy Jones, Oct. 7, 1865.
Barnes, Geo. & Christina Barnes, Aug. 31, 1865.
Barnum, E. T. & Amy B. Greenlee, Oct. 17, 1865.
Barrett, Sam & Sue Hood, May 26, 1865.
Barton, Bob & Tenny Smith, Aug. 19, 1865.
Baskett, Ben & Martha Baskett, Aug. 27, 1865.
Baskette, Claiborn & Lucinda Oden, Aug. 10, 1865.
Bass, Henry & Mary Bass, Aug. 22, 1865.
Bass, James & Lucinda Bass, Sept. 2, 1865.
Bass, Jesse & Hannah Bass, Sept. 23, 1865.
Bass, Mark & Matilda Bass, Aug. 19, 1865.
Bass, Shed & Minerva Bass, Aug. 26, 1865.
Batey, Abram & Sophia Shelton, Aug. 3, 1865.
Batey, Dick & Clarissa Batey, Aug. 26, 1865.
Batey, Herbert & Jane Batey, Aug. 26, 1865.
Batey, Isaac & Ailsey House, Aug. 27, 1865.
Batey, Isaac & Anaky Batey, Aug. 27, 1865.
Batey, James & Martha Coleman, Dec. 23, 1865.
Batey, Jerry & Tildy Batey, Aug. 20, 1865.
Batey, Lawrence & Matilda Smith, Aug. 26, 1865.
Batey, Mark & Lilly Tilghman, Sept. 8, 1865.
Batey, Mat & Rebecca Weatherly, Aug. 23, 1865.
Batey, Moses & Susan Kirby, Aug. 19, 1865.
Batey, Rial & Nicey Batey, Aug. 26, 1865.
Batey, Sam & Dicy Batey, Aug. 26, 1865.
Batey, Willis & Jane Batey, Aug. 24, 1865.
Battle, Green & Winnie Bradford, Oct. 8, 1865.
Battle, Thomas & Salley King, Sept. 10, 1865.
Battle, Young & Mary Williams, Oct. 19, 1865.
Baugh, Alfred & Ailsey Baugh, Aug. 26, 1865.
Baugh, Geo. & America Baugh, Aug. 26, 1865.
Baugh, Horace & Delitha Hoover, Aug. 27, 1865.
Baugh, John & Celia Wright, Nov. 1, 1865.
Baugh, Willis & Harriet Howland, Aug. 26, 1865.
Beasley, Britor & Judeth Beasley, Aug. 25, 1865.
Beasley, Horace & Winnie Beasley, Aug. 18, 1865.
Beasley, Scott & Sophia Jarratt, Aug. 21, 1865.

Beasley, Willis & Lizzie Jackson, Nov. 11, 1865.
Beaty, Jordan & Harriett Batey, Aug. 26, 1865.
Bedford, Enos & Adline Bedford, Aug. 27, 1865.
Beedle, John & Mary A. Warrin, Dec. 17, 1865.
Beemer, Alexander & Hannah Tuxby, Oct. 7, 1865.
Beesley, Geo. & Patsy Jones, Aug. 29, 1865.
Belcher, Frank & Ann Belcher, Aug. 19, 1865.
Bell, Allen & Martha Crutcher, Oct. 21, 1865.
Bell, Jim & Effie Holden, Aug. 19, 1865.
Bell, Jim & Emlfry Tilghman, Sept. 3, 1865.
Bell, Thomas & Lizzie Henderson, Oct. 26, 1865.
Bell, W. J. & N. J. Eaton, Nov. 2, 1865.
Bellah, Daniel & Caroline Kelton, Aug, 23, 1865.
Belleford, Reuben & Mary Barnes, Aug. 26, 1865.
Bellephant, Emanuel & Rachel Bellephant, Aug. 28, 1865.
Bennett, Burton & Agnes Bennett NS, ------, 1865.
Bennett, Hilliard & Paralee Caldwell, Aug. 30, 1865.
Bethshares, Samuel & Frances Barker, Aug. 13, 1865.
Bilbro, Samuel & Mary Trimble, Aug. 21, 1865.
Binford, Tom & Mary Binford, Aug. 26, 1865.
Black, Houston & Diana Crawford, Sept. 8, 1865.
Black, Jack & Charity Coleman, Aug. 26, 1865.
Black, Joshua & Eliza Black, Aug. 19, 1865.
Black, Rufus & Martha Crawford, Aug. 29. 1865.
Black, Wiley & Nancy Black, Aug. 26, 1865.
Blackman, Allen & Vina Blackman, Aug. 21, 1865.
Blackman, Anthony & Charity House, Aug. 23, 1865.
Blackman, charles & Caroline Blackman, Sept. 17. 1865.
Blackman, Charles & Lucy Windrow, Aug. 26, 1865.
Blackman, Tom & Lucy Blackman, Aug. 23, 1865.
Blackwell, Shederick & Caroline Hall, Sept. 24, 1865.
Blair, Amos & Margaret McGlothlin, Oct. 22, 1865.
Blair, Austin & Lee Smith, Dec. 26, 1865.
Blair, James H. & Betty Coleman, Sept. 21, 1865.
Blair, Martin & Mary Tilghman, Sept. 16, 1865.
Blair, Sirous & Melly Mason, Dec. 29, 1865.
Bokum, Samuel & Melvina Webb, Oct. 17, 1865.
Bond, Robert & Mary Dunn, Sept. 1, 1865.
Bond, Robert & Mary Jane Bond, Aug. 20, 1865.
Boren, John & Lemiza Boren, Sept. 3, 1865.
Bowles, Pleasant & Mariah Edwards, Aug. 5, 1865.
Bowman, Geo. & Betty Jones, Aug. 31, 1865.
Boyce, W. M. & Manerva Cook, June 27. 1865.
Boyd, Aaron & Mariah Smotherman, Aug. 8. 1865.
Bracken, Andrew & Mariah Davis, Oct. 26, 1865.
Bracken, Haywood & Dicy Bracken, Nov. 12, 1865.
Bracken, Sandy & George Ann Chamberlin, Sept. 10, 1865.
Bracken, Zacheriah & Fanny Bracken, Aug. 26, 1865.
Bracy, Brite & Malinda Wilson, Mar. 17, 1865.
Bracy, James & Eliza Jane Jackson, Aug. 12, 1865.
Bracy, John & Amanda Smith, Sept. 2, 1865.
Bradbury, Thomas L. & Sarah E. Harris, Nov. 13, 1865.
Brannon, Wm. & Ally Wright, Aug. 25, 1865.
Brashears, Jo & Julia A. Sanders, Aug. 26, 1865.
Brewer, Enoch & Ada Pace, Sept. 1, 1865.

Bridges, Bob & Frances Richardson, Aug. 26, 1865.
Bridges, Henry & Caroline Walden, Aug. 26, 1865.
Bridges, Matt & Nicy Tucker, Aug. 26, 1865.
Britton, Bob & Lucinda Seward, Sept. 2, 1865.
Brock, James & Nancy Brock, Aug. 19, 1865.
Brook, Arnold & Agnes Brooks, Aug. 24, 1865.
Brooks, Jim & Unity Smith, Aug. 19, 1865.
Brookshier, J. C. & America Kirkland, Feb. 19, 1865.
Brothers, Charles & Lizzie Peyton, Oct. 1, 1865.
Brothers, Geo. & Nancy Bradley, Oct. 20, 1865.
Brown, Aaron & Dinah Brown, Aug. 19, 1865.
Brown, Anthony & Ruthey Ann Taylor, Aug. 23, 1865.
Brown, Benj. & Loretta Brown, Aug. 29, 1865.
Brown, Booker & Frances Brown, Aug. 19, 1865.
Brown, Charles & Nancy Brown, Aug. 21, 1865.
Brown, Cole & America Dement, Aug. 18, 1865.
Brown, Geo. & Mary Brown, Aug. 24, 1865.
Brown, Geo. & Mary Ann Brown, Aug. 26, 1865.
Brown, Henry & Julia Brown, De.c 16, 1865.
Brown, Isaac & Dicy Brown, Aug. 26, 1865.
Brown, Jeffery & Eliza Burrow, Aug. 22, 1865.
Brown, John & Kate Nelson, Oct. 22, 1865.
Brown, Joseph & Amanda Brown, Dec. 23, 1865.
Brown, Joseph & Lucy Smith, Aug. 19, 1865.
Brown, Moses & Meriah Brown, Aug. 21, 1865.
Brown, O. P. & Miss Jane Johnson, Feb. 26, 1865.
Brown, Ples & Mary Davis, Dec. 28, 1865.
Brown, Sipio & Lucinda Carter, Oct. 16, 1865.
Brown, Steven & Partenia Overall, Aug. 19, 1865.
Brown, Thomas & Ann Norton, Aug. 24, 1865.
Brown, Tom & Nonan Sanders, Sept. 3, 1865.
Bruer, Sterling & Indiana Dunn, Jan. 4, 1865.
Bryant, John & Matilda Reed, Oct. 14, 1865.
Bryson, Nathan & Eliza Smith, July 21, 1865.
Buchanan, Braddock & Elvira Cochran, Oct. 8, 1865.
Buchanan, Grundy & Margaret Buchanan, Dec. 12, 1865.
Buchanan, Mark & Jane Buchanan, Sept. 9, 1865.
Buchanan, Nicholas & Mary Buchanan, Oct. 8, 1865.
Burem, Newton & Louisa Rogers, Sept. 4, 1865.
Burk, Alexander & Doshia H. Fleming, Aug. 28, 1865.
Burke, Milton & Charity Pritchett, Aug. 19, 1865.
Burleson, Edmond & Caroline Burleson, Aug. 26, 1865.
Burleson, Isaac & Jane Wade, Sept. 10, 1865.
Burleson, Sam & Lila Burleson, Aug. 19, 1865.
Burleson, Wm. & Harriett Burleson, Aug. 26, 1865.
Burlison, Edmond & Caroline Burlison, Aug. 26, 1865.
Burlison, Peter & Jane Miles, Sept. 2, 1865.
Burnett, Daniel & Dorcas Burnett, Aug. 23, 1865.
Burnett, L. G. & Isabella Hunter, Aug. 30, 1865.
Burnett, Wm. W. & Eliza A. Phillips, July 26, 1865.
Burrow, Jeffery & Eliz. Burrow, Aug. 22, 1865.
Burrow, Stephen W. & Harriett Rollins, Sept. 14, 1865.
Burrus, Cizar & Cornelia Smith, Aug. 20, 1865.
Burrus, David & Mary House, Aug. 27, 1865.
Burrus, Fordy & Lucinda Garrett, Aug. 20, 1865.

Burrus, Jesse & Hettie Lytle, Aug. 26, 1865.
Burrus, Sterling & Mahildy Burrus, Jan. 22, 1865.
Burton, Benj. & Eliz. Burton, Aug. 22, 1865.
Burton, Tony & Martha Lindsey, Dec. 27, 1865.
Bush, Joe & Margaret Baker, Aug. 16, 1865.
Butler, Edwin & Eliz. Butler, Aug. 31, 1865.
Butler, J. H. & Mary E. Murphey, May 17, 1865.
Butler, Jack & Lorenda Kimbro, Sept. 14, 1865.
Butler, John & Mary Fletcher, Aug. 26, 1865.
Butler, Nathan & Martha Della Hubbard, Aug. 20, 1865.
Butler, Osborn & Lucinda Butler, Sept. 2, 1865.
Butler, Wm. & Hannah Yearwood, Sept. 6, 1865.
Butler, Wm. & Matilda Adkinson, Aug. 30, 1865.
Byars, Henry & Caroline Roberts, Aug. 19, 1865.
Cain, Frank & Harriet Cain, Aug. 26, 1865.
Calhoun, Amamuel & Nancy Davis, Dec. 9, 1865.
Campbell, Ceasar & Sarah Campbell, Aug. 24, 1865.
Campbell, Robert & Ann Spence, Aug. 26, 1865.
Cannon, Carroll & Mary Furgeson, Sept. 3, 1865.
Cannon, Hardin & Fannie Cannon, Sept. 4, 1865.
Cannon, John & Mariah Cannon, Sept. 3, 1865.
Cannon, Scipia & Mary Cannon, Sept. 3, 1865.
Cannon, Wm. & Mary Bracken, Aug. 26, 1865.
Cantrell, Martin & Nancy Jane Webb, Aug. 19, 1865.
Caperton, Jesse & Deanna Allen, Aug. 11, 1865.
Carlton, Wm. & Laura Jackson, Dec. 23, 1865.
Carney, Duncan & Caroline Murfree, Sept. 1, 1865.
Carney, Monday & Sarah Cooper, Aug. 25, 1865.
Carson, Geo. & Ann Carson, Aug. 26, 1865.
Carter, Lewis & Aggie Charlton, Sept. 20, 1865.
Carter, Israel & Tempy Carter, Sept. 20, 1865.
Carter, R. K. & Margaret Cathey, Nov. 22, 1865.
Caruthers, Lewis & Sarah Stephens, Oct. 8, 1865.
Cason, Peter & Mary Huddleston, Oct. 21, 1865.
Caswell, Henry & Sylva Jarrett, Aug. 19, 1865.
Cavin, David & Amanda Swan, Aug. 19, 1865.
Chaffin, Charles Edward & Sabrien Miller, Aug. 15, 1865.
Chaffin, Geo. & Sylla Chaffin, Aug. 22, 1865.
Chaffin, Minos & Alice Hoover, Aug. 22, 1865.
Charles, Nicholas & Martha Charles, Aug. 25, 1865.
Charlton, Henry & Caroline Finney, Sept. 2, 1865.
Charlton, Stephen & Caroline Grigory, Dec. 3, 1865.
Chears, John & Peggy Brothers, Dec. 19, 1865.
Childress, Henry & Rose Childress, Aug. 31, 1865.
Childress, Jack & Sarah Childress, Aug. 23, 1865.
Childress, Joe & Amanda Childress, Aug. 23, 1865.
Childress, Paul & Nancy Childress, Sept. 7, 1865.
Childress, Washington & Eliza Jane Avent, Aug. 26, 1865.
Christian, James W. & Amanda Christian, Aug. 26, 1865.
Christian, Wm. & Malvina Christian, Aug. 26, 1865.
Clayton, Sipeo & Roxanna Clayton, Aug. 27, 1865.
Clem, Wilson & Polly Jacobs, Aug. 13, 1865.
Clopton, Samuel & Fanny Patterson, Aug. 28, 1865.
Clusky, Frederick & Jenny Deahne, June 13, 1865.

Cocks, Cosby M. & Martha Bruice, Jan. 26, 1865.
Colbert, David & Emaly Alexander, Aug. 26, 1865.
Colbert, Lewis & Nancy Smith, Aug. 9, 1865.
Cole, Nelson & Emeline Maberry, Aug. 15, 1865.
Coleman, Bartlett & Harriett Bennett, Aug. 28, 1865.
Coleman, Claiborne & Harriett Ann Allen, Sept. 17, 1865.
Coleman, Fayett & Amanda Malone, Oct. 1, 1865.
Coleman, Green & Tennessee Martin, Aug. 26, 1865.
Coleman, Houston & Elvira Crawford, Aug. 22, 1865.
Coleman, John & Rebecca Coleman, Aug. 22, 1865.
Coleman, Mat & Lilly Ann Coleman, Aug. 31, 1865.
Coleman, Robert B. & Mary L. Coleman, Nov. 7, 1865.
Coleman, Spencer & Margaret Coleman, Sept. 17, 1865.
Collier, Henry & Sarah Miles, Oct. 7, 1865.
Collier, Lindsay & Margaret Hoover, Sept. 2, 1865.
Collins, Hill & Adeline Collins, Aug. 26, 1865.
Collins, John & Mary McCrea, Dec. 26, 1865.
Collins, Joseph & Prudy Jarratt, Oct. 23, 1865.
Colman, Isaac M. & Eliz. Prater, Dec. 18, 1865.
Colman, James K. & Miss Millie J. Fleming, Nov. 20, 1865.
Colman, N. A. & Cicely A. Bush, Dec. 14, 1865.
Colman, Toney & Eliz. Mason, Aug. 26, 1865.
Colman, Walter P. & Sallie Neilson, July 11, 1865.
Comer, Alexander & Mariah Nance, Aug. 5, 1865.
Comer, Jerry & Milinda Jackson, Aug. 30, 1865.
Cooper, Geo. & Emma Jarratt, Sept. 23, 1865.
Cooper, James & Alvin Cooper, Aug. 28, 1865.
Cooper, M. T. & Lavinia Minter, Dec. 28, 1865.
Corbin, H. B. & Lily E. Brown, Dec. 18, 1865.
Corble (Corbitt), Peter & Charlott Loughry (Langley), Aug. 26, 1865.
Coulter, Aaron & Amanda Coulter, Aug. 12, 1865.
Covington, Tom & Narcissa Covington, Aug. 26, 1865.
Cowan, Calip & A. Ginkins, Sept. 9, 1865.
Cowan, Martin & Citty Hannah, Oct. 21, 1865.
Cowan, Nelson & Milley Palmer, Aug. 27, 1865.
Cowan, Slartin & Celly Flenaman, Oct. 12, 1865.
Coyne, John & Ellen Rine, Feb. 7, 1865.
Cram, John & Henrietta Miller, Aug. 23, 1865.
Criswell, R. T. & Janette F. Brewer, Oct. 2, 1865.
Critchlow, Joseph E. & Eliz. E. Nelson, Oct. 9, 1865.
Crockett, Harry & Patience Crockett, Oct. 28, 1865.
Crockett, Nathan & Keshiah Fletcher, Aug. 21, 1865.
Crouse, John & Mary Dillon, Aug. 19, 1865.
Crowell, Moses & Ann Corwell, Nov. 8, 1865.
Crump, W. B. & Agatha Ann Stovall, Oct. 12, 1865.
Crutcher, Brown & Zelia Smith, Oct. 12, 1865.
Crutcher, Richard & Tennessee Crutcher, Aug. 26, 1865.
Culp, Charles & Winney Johnson, Dec. 2, 1865.
Cummings, Jacob & Lidy Martin, Sept. 1, 1865.
Cunningham, Jesse & Susan Reeves, Aug. 21, 1865.
Curren, Abraham & Nancy Farris, Dec. 26, 1865.
Currin, Horace & Clarissa Barton, Aug. 23, 1865.

RUTHERFORD COUNTY MARRIAGES

Currin, Sam & Rose Keeble, Sept. 10, 1865.
Dalton, John & Miss N. E. Nash, Apr. 18, 1865.
Dance, Jim & Minty Dance, Aug. 21, 1865.
Daniel, Andy & Pleas Ann Ridout, Aug. 22, 1865.
Daniel, Geo. A. & Miss Martha E. Walker, Jan. 8, 1865.
Daniel, Richard & Fanny Dobbins, Aug. 26, 1865.
Darcas, Rowland & Adeline Duncan, Aug. 21, 1865.
Darragh, Thomas B. & Lucy E. Leiper, Nov. 7, 1865.
Davis, Anthoney & Eliza Wilson, Aug. 19, 1865.
Davis, Anthony & Mariah Davis, Sept. 9, 1865.
Davis, Charles & Julia Davis, Oct. 10, 1865.
Davis, Ed. & Jane Kimbro, Oct. 8, 1865.
Davis, Edmund & Amanda Eskredge, Dec. 28, 1865.
Davis, Frank & Maria Peebles, Aug. 26, 1865.
Davis, George & Minerva Walker, Oct. 16, 1865.
Davis, Harry & Louiza Caldwell, Sept. 8, 1865.
Davis, Jacob & Sally Davis, Sept. 10, 1865.
Davis, James & Susan King, Oct. 15, 1865.
Davis, Joseph & Syrenia Davis, Aug. 18, 1865.
Davis, Lewis & Fanny Bass, Sept. 16, 1865.
Davis, Miles & Sallie Furgeson, Sept. 16, 1865.
Davis, Perry & Lottie Batey, Sept. 22, 1865.
Davis, Simon & Jane Bennett, Sept. 11, 1865.
Davis, Tom & Jane Davis, Sept. 24, 1865.
Dawson, Washington & Ann Dawson, Aug. 26, 1865.
Daysey, Wm. & Mary Ann Daysey, Aug. 26, 1865.
Deason, Wm. & Isabel Deason, Aug. 27, 1865.
Deckard, Henry & Syntha Wesner, Dec. 5, 1865.
Dejarnatt, Bill & Annis Dejarnatt, Aug. 26, 1865.
Dejarnatt, Tobe & June Spence, Aug. 26, 1865.
Dejarnette, Edmund & Jane Quarles, Aug. 19, 1865.
Dejarnett, Jack & Vicey Dejarnett, Aug. 25, 1865.
Dejarnett, Moses & Martha Dejarnett, Sept. 9, 1865.
Dejarnett, Reuben & Martha Hall, Aug. 26, 1865.
Delbridge, Fred & Ann Patton, Sept. 30, 1865.
Delbridge, Jerry & Tishey McClareb, Aug. 27, 1865.
Dement, Charles L. & Mary Lewis, Dec. 28, 1865.
Dement, Wilson & Nancy Lewis, Dec. 22, 1865.
Derly, Wm. & Lucy A. Brown, Aug. 27, 1865.
Dickens, John & Rebecca Wright, Sept. 17, 1865.
Dickinson, Wm. & Sarah Dickinson, Aug. 18, 1865.
Dickson, John & Tempy Carney, Dec. 27, 1865.
Dillow, Jacob & Harriet Crouse, Sept. 8, 1865.
Doak, Sam & Phebe Loften, Aug. 19, 1865.
Donnell, Charles & America Martin, Aug. 20, 1865.
Donnell, Daniel & Martenia Donnell, Aug. 19, 1865.
Donnell, Wesley & Sally White, Aug. 26, 1865.
Dorson, Warren & Martha Alsup, Oct. 18, 1865.
Downing, John & Miss Sarah A. Stone, Feb. 25, 1865.
Drake, Ben & Lizzie Watkins, Oct. 7, 1865.
Drake, Henry & Martha Johns, Aug. 20, 1865.
Drake, Thomas & Martha Sparks, Nov. 2, 1865.
Drennon, George & Eliz. Sneed, Sept. 3, 1865.
Drennon, Lewis & Mary Jane Brown, July 29, 1865.

Drennon, Osborn & Martha Peyton, Aug. 30, 1865.
Drennon, Phillip & Mima Sanders, Sept. 4, 1865.
Dromgoole, Albert & Eveline Watkins, Aug. 11, 1865.
Dromgoole, Philip & Mahaly Jamison, Aug. 14, 1865.
Dudley, R. U. & Mattie L. Ross, Sept. 18, 1865.
Dunaway, John W. & Martha Pearcy, Dec. 21, 1865.
Dunaway, Phil & Mary McKee, Aug. 28, 1865.
Duncan, James K. & Mary Orzey, Sept. 30, 1865.
Dunn, Charles & Lucy Dunn, Aug. 29, 1865.
Dunn, J. A. & Eliz. Vaught, Oct. 26, 1865.
Dunnaway, Cumby & Ann Johns, Aug. 25, 1865.
Dwiggins, Wm. & Martha Seward, July 22, 1865.
Dyer, James & Edny Childress, Dec. 26, 1865.
Dyer, John & Dicy Keeble, Dec. 4, 1865.
Eads, A. J. & Miss Judeth J. McCoy, May 22, 1865.
Eagleton, Young & Fanny Eagleton, Aug. 19, 1865.
Eakin, Abraham & Mindo Eakin, Aug. 31, 1865.
Earp, E. J. & Ledea J. Guess, July 1, 1865.
Edmondson, Baldy & Caroline Weakley, Oct. 22, 1865.
Edmondson, Baldey & Lucinda Weakley, Oct. 22, 1865.
Edmondson, Ed. & Tabitha Goodwin, Aug. 26, 1865.
Edmondson, Henry & Isabella Watkins, Aug. 2, 1865.
Edmondson, Peyton & Queen Gooden, Sept. 9, 1865.
Edmondson, Solomon & Celia Weakley, Sept. 9, 1865.
Edmondton, John James & Sarah Jane Barnes, May 12, 1865.
Edward, Daniel & Jean Boren, Sept. 10, 1865.
Edwards, Daniel & Mary Irby, Dec. 27, 1865.
Edwards, Harrison & Susan Johnson, Aug. 26, 1865.
Edwards, Henry & Jane Ditto, Aug. 30, 1865.
Edwards, Henry & Susan Edwards, Aug. 26, 1865.
Edwards, Henry & Susan Nelson, Aug. 30, 1865.
Edwards, Jack & Lockey Jennings, Aug. 20, 1865.
Edwards, John W. & Vilet Davis, Sept. --, 1865.
Edwards, Moses & Sylva Edwards, Aug. 24, 1865.
Edwards, Nat & Mary J. Patton, Aug. 21, 1865.
Edwards, Nathan & Charlotte Traylor, Aug. 26, 1865.
Edwards, Sam & Caroline Batey, Sept. 9, 1865.
Edwards, Thomas & Louiza Honeycutt, Aug. 15, 1865.
Edwards, Wm. & Sarah Price, July 19, 1865.
Elam, Tom & Roberta House, Aug. 19, 1865.
Elder, George W. & Amanda Richardson, Sept. 3, 1865.
Elkin, Shedrich W. & Mary J. Ivie, Nov. 25, 1865.
Elliott, Glasgow & Isabel House, Sept. 3, 1865.
Elliott, Nelson & Mary Snell, Sept. 4, 1865.
Elliott, Wm. & Eliza Fletcher, Dec. 29, 1865.
Ellis, Albert & Frances Calhoun, Dec. 23, 1865.
Elseback, Wilson & Jane Frye, Sept. 7, 1865.
Espy, Moses & Rebecca Bell, Aug. 27, 1865.
Estes, Andrew & Dicey Estes, Aug. 24, 1865.
Estes, J. K. & Mary J. Scarberry, Oct. 6, 1865.
Etta, Ben & Jane Etta, Oct. 7, 1865.
Etta, Nathan & Arabella Etta, Sept. 2, 1865.
Etta, Tom & Milly Etta, Sept. 2, 1865.
Evans, Jim & Florida Gentry, Aug. 25, 1865.

Farmer, Washington & Nancy Adkerson, Sept. 11, 1865.
Farris, Wm. & Josephine N. Jackson, Dec. 19, 1865.
Fathera, N. R. & Charlotte F. Barker, Nov. 28, 1865.
Fergason, Gran & Harriett Ridley, Sept. 3, 1865.
Fergason, Sam & Lucy Fergason, Sept. 3, 1865.
Ferguson, Jim & Mary Jones, Sept. 1, 1865.
Feris, Lewis & Rosetta Faris, Aug. 12, 1865.
Feris, R. W. & Eliz. Jackson, Sept. 24, 1865.
Fields, Richard & Martha Fields, Sept. 5, 1865.
Fisher, Isaac & Fanny Vaughan, Aug. 18, 1865.
Fisher, John & Lou C. Baird, Nov. 14, 1865.
Fleming, Austin & Ditcy Fleming, Aug. 25, 1865.
Fleming, G. D. & Martha Fleming, Oct. 5, 1865.
Fleming, Wm. & Harriet Yearwood, Aug. 22, 1865.
Fletcher, Boney & Beckey Fletcher, Aug. 22, 1865.
Fletcher, Dock & Amanda Norman, Aug. 22, 1865.
Fletcher, Jack & Martha Thompson, Aug. 18, 1865.
Fletcher, Mat & Sophronia Ransom, Sept. 2, 1865.
Fletcher, Moses & Margaret Fletcher, Aug. 19, 1865.
Fletcher, Nelson & Tempy Nichol, Aug. 23, 1865.
Fletcher, Sterling & Jane Webb, Aug. 21, 1865.
Floyd, Edward & Nancy Snell, Aug. 26, 1865.
Floyd, Jacob & Sallie P. Tucker, Jan. 14, 1865.
Floyd, Jason & Judy Glenn, Aug. 27, 1865.
Floyd, John & Angeline Yeargan, Sept. 3, 1865.
Floyd, Moses & Beckey Stroop, Aug. 18, 1865.
Floyd, Nelson & Rachel Byer, Aug. 22, 1865.
Floyd, Tom & Hannah Haley, Sept. 3, 1865.
Foltheringham, Alex. & Miss Elender J. Rogers, Apr. 13, 1865.
Foote, Willis & Sarah Alsup, Oct. 14, 1865.
Forbish, Albert A. & Martha J. Moore, July 11, 1865.
Francis, Henry & Eliz. Francis, Aug. 20, 1865.
Frazier, Adam & Charlotte Miller, Aug. 21, 1865.
Frazier, Harrison & Amanda Baugh, Aug. 26, 1865.
Frazier, Ross & Elisa Richardson, Nov. 4, 1865.
Freeling, Abraham & Anna Brown, Dec. 26, 1865.
Freeman, Robert & Edith Jakes, Sept. 7, 1865.
Frierson, Napoleon & Epheba Frierson, Aug. 14, 1865.
Fugatt, Albert & Jane Clark, Dec. 5, 1865.
Fulks, John W. & Mar. Jane Fox, Aug. 24, 1865.
Fulton, Jerry & Mary Alley, Aug. 26, 1865.
Fuquay, Harrison H. & Nancy Mitchell, Dec. 12, 1865.
Furgeson, Alfred & Sallie Haker, Oct. 8, 1865.
Furgeson, Frank & Sarah Maberry, Sept. 3, 1865.
Furgeson, Green & Susan Buchanan, Sept. 16, 1865.
Furgeson, Jim & Mary Jones, Sept. 1, 1865.
Furgeson, Lewis & Frances Clemons, Sept. 3, 1865.
Furgeson, Ransom & Kenira Davis, Dec. 28, 1865.
Furgeson, Sam & Lucy Furgeson, Apr. 26, 1865.
Galphin, Hezekiah & Betsy Presly, Aug. 23, 1865.
Gannaway, Daniel & Roanna Avent, Dec. 28, 1865.
Garner, Geo. & Rose Garner, Aug. 31, 1865.
Garner, Hardy & Winney Garner, Aug. 23, 1865.

Garner, Harry & Alexa White, Sept. 4, 1865.
Garner, Hilliard & Emily Fox, Sept. 1, 1865.
Garner, Jackson & Lear Brown, Aug. 26, 1865.
Garner, Jordan & Melissa Childress, Aug. 24, 1865.
Garner, Luke & Harriett Mankin, Sept. 1, 1865.
Garrett, Jerry & Susan Short, Oct. 25, 1865.
Garrett, Wm. G. & Miss Kate Puckett, Mar. 1, 1865.
Gentry, Harry & Ann Miles, Aug. 26, 1865.
Gibson, Joe & Becky Gibson, Dec. 31, 1865.
Gibson, C. L. & Narcissa Norman, Oct. 17, 1865.
Gibson, Wm. & Jane Gibson, Aug. 28, 1865.
Gilden, Peyton & Sally Gilden, Sept. 1, 1865.
Gilden, Peyton & Sally Gilden, Aug. 20, 1865.
Gilliam, Julous & Abbey Gilliam, Aug. 16, 1865.
Gillis, John F. & Nancy C. Welch, Aug. 31, 1865.
Gilly, J. R. & Miss M. M. McCrary, Dec. 14, 1865.
Glenn, Luke & Eliza Graves, Aug. 28, 1865.
Glenn, Wm. & Minty Ross, Nov. 18, 1865.
Gooch, Aaron & Adeline Kimbro, Sept. 11, 1865.
Gooch, Dick & Angeline Kimbro, Sept. 14, 1865.
Gooch, Jim & Missouri Sanders, Sept. 2, 1865.
Gooch, Lucas & Martha Weakley, Sept. 5, 1865.
Gooch, Monroe & Catherine Espey, Sept. 26, 1865.
Gooch, Thomas Romind & Lucinda Logue, Nov. 13, 1865.
Goodloe, Caleb & Patsey Bradley, Aug. 26, 1865.
Goodloe, Reuben & Eliz. Narkley, Aug. 26, 1865.
Goodwin, Alred & Harriet Goodwin, Nov. 12, 1865.
Goodwin, Isaac T. & Eveline Harrison, Aug. 9, 1865.
Goodwin, Jim & Mimah Furgeson, Sept. 3, 1865.
Goodwin, Sam & Cresia Goodwin, Nov. 26, 1865.
Gorden, W. A. & Margaret P. Modrall, Nov. 10, 1865.
Grason, Isham & Angeline Webb, June 3, 1865.
Green, Wray & Sallie Green, Aug. 29, 1865.
Green, Geo. & Martha Green, Nov. 4, 1865.
Green, Henry W. & Mahaly Nord, Sept. 4, 1865.
Green, Hilliard & Mariah Black, July 31, 1865.
Green, Isaac & Margaret Green, Aug. 23, 1865.
Green, Jefferson & Julia Ann Green, Sept. 3, 1865.
Green, King & Flora Rodgers, Aug. 31, 1865.
Green, Santee & Rose Thompson, Aug. 21, 1865.
Green, W. W. & Miss Sophia McKee, Jan. 19, 1865.
Gregory, Nathan & Martha Gregory, Dec. 3, 1865.
Gregory, Nelson & Catherine Gregory, Sept. 3, 1865.
Gregory, Wyatt & Eliza Weakley, Sept. 9, 1865.
Gresham, Edmond & Sylva Gresham, Aug. 26, 1865.
Gresham, Harrison & Lucy Hall, Aug. 29, 1865.
Gresham, James & Martha Smith, Aug. 18, 1865.
Gresham, Sam & Amanda Ridley, Oct. 15, 1865.
Griffin, Elija & Fanny Griffin, Aug. 30, 1865.
Griffin, John & Arey Gooch, Aug. 28, 1865.
Grimes, Sam & Celia McCullough, Aug. 23, 1865.
Grundy, Ephraim & Louisa Grundy, Aug. 26, 1865.
Guidon, Jim & Emily Guidon, Sept. 19, 1865.
Guilford, Rufus & Sarah Fulton, Aug. 7, 1865.

Guthra, Edmond & Catharine Owen, Aug. 19, 1865.
Guy, Peter & Martha McLean, Aug. 8, 1865.
Guy, Quince & Milly Watkins, Aug. 19, 1865.
Guy, Thomas & Eliz. Guy, Aug. 23, 1865.
Hall, Albert E. & Emily C. Herod, Nov. 16, 1865.
Hall, Alfred & Julien Hall, Aug. 22, 1865.
Hall, Dick & Milly Crockett, Aug. 29, 1865.
Hall, Drury & Martha Short, Apr. 4, 1865.
Hall, Gordan & Sylva Baird, Aug. 19, 1865.
Hall, Jo & Charlotte Barker, Aug. 26, 1865.
Hall, Jo & Louzana Vaught, Aug. 23, 1865.
Hall, John A. & Catherine Polk, June 20, 1865.
Hall, John & Dianna Hall, Aug. 29, 1865.
Hall, Ralph R. & Eliz. C. Blackman, Nov. 13, 1865.
Hall, Richard & Alsey Moore, Aug. 19, 1865.
Hall, Spencer & Epheba Hall, Aug. 23, 1865.
Hall, Tom & Betsy Todd, Nov. 10, 1865.
Hall, Wm. A. & Frances Somers, Sept. 17, 1865.
Hall, Wm. T. & Sylva N. Baker, July 29, 1865.
Halliburton, Jim & Lucretia Wade, Aug. 12, 1865.
Halliburton, Wm. & Tilla Alexander, Aug. 21, 1865.
Hallyburton, Hampton & Synthia Smith, Dec. 16, 1865.
Hallyburton, Solomon & Jane Hamilton, Dec. 11, 1865.
Ham, Robert & Susan Collier, Aug. 24, 1865.
Hamilton, Berry & Nancy Sanford, Sept. 17, 1865.
Hamilton, Jesse & Charity Mitchell, Sept. 3, 1865.
Hancock, Edm. & Mariah Miller, Aug. 23, 1865.
Hancock, Tom & Venus Hancock, Aug. 21, 1865.
Hanesay, Jesse & Margaret Burger, Aug. 26, 1865.
Hardin, Jim & Patsy Cowan, Aug. 27, 1865.
Harkins, Samuel & Milley Harkins, Aug. 26, 1865.
Harmon. Bradley & Emily Prince, Dec. 6, 1865.
Harrell, A. J. & E. E. Arnold, July 16, 1865.
Harris, Benj. & Lucy Bigham, Aug. 5, 1865.
Harris, Claiborne & Vera McAdoo, Aug. 24, 1865.
Harris, Crawford & Mary J. England, Aug. 26, 1865.
Harris, Granville & Harriet Alexander, Sept. 2, 1865.
Harris, John & Sallie Gambill, Dec. 11, 1865.
Harris, Wm. & Clara Harris, Sept. 10, 1865.
Harrison, Jesse & Lilly Burton, Nov. 20, 1865.
Hartwell, Darius & Melinda Hartwell, Aug. 19, 1865.
Hartwell, Harry & Amanda Bedford, Aug. 27, 1865.
Hartwell, Pompy & Mary J. Hicks, Aug. 27, 1865.
Hartwell, Willis & Ellen Thompson, Aug. 23, 1865.
Hash, Charles & Matilda Clark, Aug. 31, 1865.
Hastings, James & Eliza Ann Lawten, Dec. 23, 1865.
Hawes, Andrew J. & Kate Baker, Jan. 26, 1865.
Hawkins, Frank & Catherine Lillard, Dec. 17, 1865.
Haynes, Geo. & Martha Blackman, Sept. 9, 1865.
Haynes, Henry & Josephine Buchanan, Sept. 15, 1865.
Haynes, Jefferson & Caroline Childress, Sept. 1, 1865.
Haynes, Jesse & Ritta Haynes, Aug. 28, 1865.
Haynes, Lewis & Ann Haynes, Aug. 26, 1865.
Haynes, Ned & Rose Ann Haynes, Aug. 26, 1865.
Haynes, Reuben & Betty Manson, Aug. 26, 1865.

Haynes, Sandy & Sarah Jane Seay, Aug. 26, 1865.
Haynes, Simon & Catey Haynes, Aug. 26, 1865.
Haynes, Wiley & Mary Vaughan, Sept. 17, 1865.
Haynes, Wm. & Elender Gregory, Aug. 28, 1865.
Haynes, Willis & Jennie Hollowell, Aug. 26, 1865.
Heffling, Joseph & Permelia Fulton, Dec. 31, 1865.
Helton, A. P. & Nancy L. Jamison, Feb. 6, 1865.
Helton, Pompey & Lucinda Cook, Aug. 17, 1865.
Helton, W. N. & Jennie Sanders, Nov. 1, 1865.
Henderson, Alexander & Lou Sikes, Sept. 2, 1865.
Henderson, Edward & Meriah Henderson, Aug. 25, 1865.
Henderson, Joe & Syrena Halliburton, Aug. 22, 1865.
Henderson, Robert & Mitty White, Aug. 26, 1865.
Henisy, Jessee & Mar. Burgess, Aug. 26, 1865.
Henly, James & Harriet Spence, Dec. 28, 1865.
Henly, Wm. & Martha Henly, Aug. 26, 1865.
Henry, B. T. & Miss M. G. Ridout, Nov. 28, 1865.
Henry, Bill & Lucinda Prater, June 25, 1865.
Henry, Overton & Miss Caroline Walpool, Dec. 4, 1865.
Henry, Thomas & Martha Henry, Aug. 21, 1865.
Hensley, Alfred & Hannah Hensley, Oct. 3, 1865.
Heuett, Leander & Mary E. Simpson, Jan. 15, 1865.
Hibbetts, Fayett & Martha Charlton, Dec. 5, 1865.
Hickerson, Isaac & Matilda Jacobs, Aug. 14, 1865.
Hicks, Albert & Ann Haynes, Sept. 10, 1865.
Hicks, Allen & Rose Telman, Aug. 28, 1865.
Hicks, Ben & Frances Hicks, Aug. 21, 1865.
Hicks, Henry & Nicey Trigg, Sept. 1, 1865.
Hicks, John & Cena Walden, Aug. 26, 1865.
Hicks, Silas & Isabella Reid, Sept. 10, 1865.
Higgins, John & Laura Brown, Nov. 21, 1865.
Hill, Alex & Louisa Cannon, Sept. 3, 1865.
Hill, Jesse & Ann Alexander, Aug. 27, 1865.
Hill, John & Jane Davis, Dec. 25, 1865.
Hill, Isaac & Betsy Wright, Oct. 8, 1865.
Hill, Presly & Manerva Mason, Dec. 25, 1865.
Hill, Preston & Minerva Miller, Aug. 26, 1865.
Hill, Sandy & Kitty Hill, Aug. 28, 1865.
Hill, Toney & Manerva Malone, Aug. 24, 1865.
Hill, W. S. & Maggie T. Davis, Aug. 25, 1865.
Hill, Wm. & Catharine Ginnings, Nov. 25, 1865.
Hodge, Geo. & Mary Spence, Aug. 30, 1865.
Hoggatt, Ben & Judy Hoggatt, Oct. 3, 1865.
Hoggatt, Isham & Rachel Hogatt, Aug. 26, 1865.
Hoggatt, Squire & Esther Hoggatt, Aug. 26, 1865.
Hoggatt, Watt & Louisa Hoggatt, Aug. 26, 1865.
Hoggett, Dick & Lucinda Hoggett, Aug. 28, 1865.
Hoggett, Phil & Amanda Jarratt, May 24, 1865.
Hoggett, Spencer & Matilda Hoggett, Aug. 28, 1865.
Hoggett, Toney & Rhoda Hoggett, Sept. 18, 1865.
Hogwood, Henry & Rebecca Taylor, Aug. 23, 1865.
Holbert, Alexander & Penny Marshall, Aug. 28, 1865.
Holbert, Wm. & Sarah Cain, Sept. 14, 1865.
Holbrooks, Andrew & Henrietta Hogett, Aug. 15, 1865.
Holden, Anthoney & Minerva Holden, Aug. 8, 1865.

Holden, Levi & Martha J. Holden, Aug. 19, 1865.
Holden, Philip & Mary Woods, Aug. 12, 1865.
Holland, Michael & Josephine Roberts, Dec. 21, 1865.
Hollowell, Henry & Mary Anderson, Aug. 26, 1865.
Hollowell, Solomon S. & Sallie K. Edwards, Sept. 6, 1865.
Holmes, Arthur & Critty Holmes, Oct. 17, 1865.
Holt, Daniel & Lilly Ann Booth, Nov. 25, 1865.
Holt, Wm. T. & Sylva R. Baker, Jan. 25, 1865.
Hooberry, Jacob S. & Salina A. Hoobery, June 21, 1865.
Hood, John & Roxie Ann Putnam, Sept. 7, 1865.
Hoover, Isaac & Milly Hoover, Aug. 19, 1865.
Hopkins, Sam & Polly Hopkins, Aug. 26, 1865.
Hord, Brice & Levina Hord, Aug. 26, 1865.
Hord, Thomas & Julia Ann Hord, Aug. 29, 1865.
Hoskins, Adam & Jane Hoskins, Aug. 26, 1865.
Hoskins, Samuel & Milly Hoskins, Aug. 26, 1865.
Hoskins, Simon & Emily Rucker, Aug. 21, 1865.
Hotchfield, Jacob & Mary Stanley, Aug. 19, 1865.
House, Claiborn & Charlotte King, Aug. 19, 1865.
House, Edmond & Judy House, Aug. 26, 1865.
House, John & Lizzie Washington, Aug. 26, 1865.
House, Peter & Liza House, Aug. 19, 1865.
House, Robert & Narcissa Marable, Aug. 19, 1865.
House, Woodly & Sally House, Aug. 18, 1865.
House, Woodley & Martha McClaren, Aug. 27, 1865.
Houston, R. W. & Miss Blanch Venable, Jan. 10, 1865.
Houston, Samuel & Rody Fannell, Nov. 25, 1865.
Howell, Andrew & Candice Richardson, Sept. 10, 1865.
Howland, Burrel & Mary Ridley, Sept. 3, 1865.
Howland, Dock & Mittie McMurray, Aug. 23, 1865.
Howland, Gloster & Harriett Lowe, Aug. 20, 1865.
Howland, R. L. & Mollie Paugh, July 19, 1865.
Howland, Wm. & Cherry Rollins, Aug. 26, 1865.
Howse, Henry & Jane Bass, Sept. 16, 1865.
Howse, Jack & Lucinda Marable, Aug. 26, 1865.
Howse, Nelson & Lucinda Vawter, Aug. 27, 1865.
Howse, Nicholas & Darcas Richardson, Aug. 26, 1865.
Howse, Tom & Kiner McClaren, Aug. 27, 1865.
Howse, Washington & Caroline Cannon, Sept. 9, 1865.
Howse, Washington & Martha Rowan, Sept. 8, 1865.
Hubanks, Sandy & Amanda Kelly, Sept. 2, 1865.
Hubbard, Geo. & Miss M. Jarrett, Apr. 14, 1865.
Huddleston, Coleman & Indy Huddleston, Aug. 19, 1865.
Huddleston, Henry & Milly Martin, Aug. 26, 1865.
Huddleston, Henry & Lucy Putnam, Oct. 4, 1865.
Huddleston, Mat & Milly Buckner, Aug. 15, 1865.
Huddleston, Nelson & Emilin Lassiter, Aug. 19, 1865.
Hudson, James & Miss Martha Beasley, Mar. 18, 1865.
Huff, John & Eliz. Huff, Aug. 19, 1865.
Huggins, James & Tempey Huggins, Dec. 26, 1865.
Huggins, Luke & Martha Huggins, Aug. 19, 1865.
Hunnicut, John & Louisa Pilkerton, July 3, 1865.
Hunt, Henry & Charity Hunt, Sept. 2, 1865.
Hutcherson, Wm. M. & Miss Eliza Earley, Feb. 1, 1865.

Hutchfield, James & Mary Stanley, Aug. 19, 1865.
Hutchison, Zack & Martha Owen, Aug. 29, 1865.
Irby, Sam & Harriet Irby, Sept. 4, 1865.
Irwin, Jack & Ellen Modreall, Aug. 17, 1865.
Isbell, George & Sylvia Windman, Aug. 27, 1865.
Ivey, Anthoney & Francis Wright, Aug. 23, 1865.
Jackson, Charles & Hannah Reed, Aug. 23, 1865.
Jackson, Charles & Martha Hearden, Aug. 21, 1865.
Jackson, Hardy & Violett Downing, Aug. 27, 1865.
Jackson, Henry & Sciota Jane Ransom, Aug. 26, 1865.
Jackson, Jessee & Mary Bracey, Aug. 12, 1865.
Jackson, Moses & Nancy Jackson, Aug. 19, 1865.
Jackson, Richard & Roxana Faris, Sept. 9, 1865.
Jackson, T. M. & Eliz. Carlton, Nov. 16, 1865.
James, Braxton & Charlotte Thompkins, Aug. 20, 1865.
James, Charles & Louisa Sims, Aug. 25, 1865.
James, Edm. & Harriet Lytle, Aug. 24, 1865.
James, Geo. & Henrietta Lytle, Aug. 26, 1865.
James, John & Lucinda John, Aug. 30, 1865.
James, John & Rachel Brown, Dec. 15, 1865.
James, Wm. & Mary Lewis, Dec. 15, 1865.
Jameson, Gus & Harriett Jamison, Aug. 18, 1865.
Jameson, John & Phillis Jamison, Aug. 18, 1865.
Jamison, Cook & Hattiet Batton, Aug. 18, 1865.
Jamison, Edm. & Mary Jamison, Aug. 23, 1865.
Jamison, Entram & Nancy White, Aug. 11, 1865.
Jamison, Isaac & Jane Tucker, Aug. 26, 1865.
Jamison, King & Sarah Jamison, Aug. 26, 1865.
Jamison, Nelson & Fannie Kimbro, Aug. 20, 1865.
January, Wm. & Agnes Smith, Aug. 19, 1865.
Jarman, Richard & Ann Johnson, Aug. 19, 1865.
Jarman, Will & Fanny Dillon, Sept. 17, 1865.
Jarratt, Andrew & Julia Kennedy, Nov. 22, 1865.
Jarratt, George & Easter Jordan, Aug. 12, 1865.
Jarratt, Jacob & Susan Jarratt, Aug. 12, 1865.
Jarratt, Manuel & Harriett Jarratt, Aug. 18, 1865.
Jarratt, Nelson & Jenny Eaton, Sept. 9, 1865.
Jarratt, Peter & Haly McKay, Aug. 21, 1865.
Jarratt, Sandy & Phillis Jarratt, Sept. 2, 1865.
Jasper, David & Patsey Jasper, Aug. 27, 1865.
Jefferson, Thomas & Mary Thomas, Aug. 18, 1865.
Jenkins, Randal & Ellen Jenkins, Oct. 5, 1865.
Jenkins, Sam & Louisa Jenkins, Sept. 18, 1865.
Jenkins, Wesley & Julia Jenkins, Sept. 3, 1865.
Jennings, Robert & Amanda Hopkins, Aug. 22, 1865.
Jett, Andrew & Hannah Jett, Aug. 20, 1865.
Jetton, Albert & Fannie Jones, Sept. 22, 1865.
Jetton, Bob & Beckey Wright, Aug. 23, 1865.
Jinkins, Anderson & Liddy Jenkins, Sept. 10, 1865.
Johns, Ed & Martha Ann Johns, Aug. 19, 1865.
Johns, Henry & Caroline Sanders, Sept. 10, 1865.
Johns, Henry & Lucinda Robertson, Aug. 26, 1865.
Johns, James & Lucinda Johns, Aug. 30, 1865.
Johns, Jefferson & Lucinda Merritt, Aug. 20, 1865.
Johns, Richard & Mary Johns, Sept. 8, 1865.

RUTHERFORD COUNTY MARRIAGES

Johns, Robert & Ellen Kirby, Aug. 19, 1865.
Johnson, Andrew & Lucinda Johnson, Aug. 29, 1865.
Johnson, D. H. & Sallie J. Scott, July 20, 1865.
Johnson, Frank & Jane Robertson, Dec. 27, 1865.
Johnson, Gabriel & Mary Ann Thompson, Oct. 30, 1865.
Johnson, Geo. & Melinda Morgan, Aug. 19, 1865.
Johnson, Geo. & Louisa Collins, Sept. 4, 1865.
Johnson, Gideon & Mary A. Smith, Dec. 30, 1865.
Johnson, Grandison & Sallie Jordan, Dec. 7, 1865.
Johnson, Harry & Nancy Johnson, Aug. 20, 1865.
Johnson, James & Fanny Moore, Aug. 26, 1865.
Johnson, John & Emiline Johnson, Aug. 19, 1865.
Johnson, Larkin & Nicy Hartwell, Aug. 20, 1865.
Johnson, Moses & Martha Bivins, Aug. 27, 1865.
Johnson, Patrick & Alimedia Johnson, Aug. 26, 1865.
Johnson, Peter & Sarah Johnson, Aug. 26, 1865.
Johnson, Robert & Malinda Jones, Aug. 26, 1865.
Johnson, Squire & Fannie Smith, Aug. 19, 1865.
Johnson, Steven & Melissa Hartwell, Aug. 19, 1865.
Johnson, Thomas & Jemimah Johnson, Aug. 26, 1865.
Johnson, Tillman & Nancy Chaffin, Aug. 20, 1865.
Johnson, Wash & Rhoda Hoggatt, Oct. 5, 1865.
Joiner, Wiley & Charlott Joiner, Aug. 19, 1865.
Jones, A. P. & Miss Mary Ross, Mar. 30, 1865.
Jones, Anthony & Susan Childress, Aug. 19, 1865.
Jones, Arthur & Isabella Jones, Oct. 8, 1865.
Jones, Barber & Clarissa Rucker, Aug. 26, 1865.
Jones, Bob & Judy C. Wright, Aug. 23, 1865.
Jones, Charles & Matilda Alexander, Aug. 23, 1865.
Jones, Edward & Harriet Childress, Dec. 2, 1865.
Jones, Frank & Jemima Cotten, Sept. 14, 1865.
Jones, Harrison & Mira Jones, Sept. 1, 1865.
Jones, Harrison & Matilda Malone, Sept. 10, 1865.
Jones, Henry & Jane Span, Aug. 29, 1865.
Jones, Henry & Mary Jones, Aug. 31, 1865.
Jones, Henry & Sally Lyons, Aug. 23, 1865.
Jones, Iverson & Sophia V. Wright, Dec. 29, 1865.
Jones, James & Joanna Jones, Aug. 26, 1865.
Jones, Jo & Hannah Peyton, Aug. 29, 1865.
Jones, John & Betty Jones, Sept. 3, 1865.
Jones, John & Lucinda Span, Sept. 3, 1865.
Jones, Lewis & Emily Gilliam, Aug. 16, 1865.
Jones, Lewis & Mariah Fletcher, Aug. 21, 1865.
Jones, Ned & Sarah Miller, Sept. 9, 1865.
Jones, Samuel P. & Miss Mattie P. McCulloch, Oct. 17, 1865.
Jones, Thomas & Eliza Scruggs, Dec. 17, 1865.
Jones, Thomas & Lea Johnson, Dec. 5, 1865.
Jones, Turner & Lucinda Quarles, Aug. 26, 1865.
Jones, Wilburn & Nancy Smith, Aug. 22, 1865.
Jordan, Anderson & Mary Jane Huddleston, Aug. 27, 1865.
Jordan, Ed & Frotia House, June 24, 1865.
Jordan, Harvey & Sarah Jordan, Aug. 31, 1865.
Jordan, Jeff & Mason Jordan, Aug. 22, 1865.
Jordan, Jim & Amanda Haley, Sept. 3, 1865.

RUTHERFORD COUNTY MARRIAGES

Jordan, John & Cladonia Kirby, June 15, 1865.
Jordan, Kincheon & Mason Bostick, Sept. 24, 1865.
Jordan, Lewis & Amy Jordan, Aug. 30, 1865.
Jordan, Maryland & Sophia Murfree, Aug. 14, 1865.
Jordan, Tom & Ruthey Jordan, Aug. 26, 1865.
Jordan, Richard & Rosa Jordan, Aug. 18, 1865.
Jordan, Rufus & Lucinda Jordan, Aug. 18, 1865.
Keeble, Baldy & Penny Ridley, Sept. 10, 1865.
Keeble, Billy & Betsy Keeble, Sept. 9, 1865.
Keeble, Jordan & Amanda Kirk, Sept. 10, 1865.
Keeble, Mack & Frissa Keeble, Aug. 22, 1865.
Keeble, Thomas & Maria Bridges, Sept. 10, 1865.
Keith, Charles L. & Susan J. Prater, Dec. 23, 1865.
Kellis, Haywood & Malinda Buchanan, Nov. 26, 1865.
Kelly, Edm. & Clarissa Turner, Sept. 2, 1865.
Kelton, Wm. A. & Mary P. Jacobs, Aug. 9, 1865.
Kerr, Saml. & Sarah M. Thompson, Dec. 8, 1865.
Killough, Harry & Easter Killough, Sept. 11, 1865.
Kimbro, Andrew & Matilda Kimbro, Oct. 15, 1865.
Kimbro, Hal & Mary L. Kimbro, Aug. 20, 1865.
Kimbro, Joseph & Ellen Maddox, Dec. 10, 1865.
Kimbro, Stephen & Amy Bryson, Nov. 18, 1865.
Kimbro, Toney & Sophia Alexander, Aug. 12, 1865.
King, Anthony & Jane Hoggatt, Sept. 18, 1865.
King, Calvin & Francis Wade, Sept. 16, 1865.
King, Charles & Maria King, Sept. 2, 1865.
King, Fed & Jennie Smith, Nov. 18, 1865.
King, Hardy & Mary Simmons, Aug. 26, 1865.
King, Isiah & Charlott Anderson, Aug. 26, 1865.
King, John & Julia Puckett, Aug. 31, 1865.
King, Robert & Martha Mason, Oct. 8, 1865.
King, Steven & Ellen King, Aug. 21, 1865.
King, Thomas M. & Miss Mary A. Turner, Dec. 20, 1865.
Kirby, Geo. & Ann Kirby, Aug. 29, 1865.
Kirby, Jack & Sarah Yearwood, Aug. 22, 1865.
Kirk, Lemuel & Anna Kirk, Aug. 19, 1865.
Kirk, Matthew & Sylvia Goss, Sept. 24, 1865.
Law, Tom & Louiza Jordan, Aug. 17, 1865.
Lawrence, Felix & Caroline Snell, Sept. 17, 1865.
Lawrence, George & Rebecca Snell, Aug. 25, 1865.
Lawrence, John W. & Sophronia W. Mankins, Dec. 5, 1865.
Lawrence, Lemon & Maria Lawrence, Aug. 30, 1865.
Lawrence, Nathaniel & Laura Ann Knight, Aug. 25, 1865.
Lawrence, Samuel & Maria Fagett, Sept. 9, 1865.
Lawrence, Wm. & Phillis Gooch, Aug. 25, 1865.
Lawson, Nathan & Eliza Jane Nash, Oct. 10, 1865.
Leathers, Jonathan & Chaney Holden, Aug. 7, 1865.
Lee, James M. & Miss M. E. Fleming, Jan. 10, 1865.
Lee, Jerry & Mary Ann Swan, Aug. 26, 1865.
Lee, R. H. & Matilda C. Carter, Mar. 20, 1865.
Lee, Thomas J. & Sarah E. Brannon, Sept. 12, 1865.
Leftrich, John & Cornelia Bryant, Aug. 21, 1865.
Leigh, Allen & Lucy Faulkner, Aug. 27, 1865.
Leith, Spencer & Nancy Welsh, Oct. 1, 1865.

RUTHERFORD COUNTY MARRIAGES

Lewis, A. A. & Mary Burnett, Aug. 13, 1865.
Lewis, Henry & Clara Lewis, Sept. 3, 1865.
Lewis, John & Ellen Reeves, Aug. 18, 1865.
Lewis, Samuel & Rachel Robertson, Aug. 30, 1865.
Lickens, James & Selia Castleman, Feb. 18, 1865.
Lillard, Alex & Judy Ward, Aug. 26, 1865.
Lillard, David & Mary Jordan, Dec. 21, 1865.
Lillard, Sam & Matilda Lillard, Aug. 26, 1865.
Lindsey, Bob & Rose Ann Rooker, Sept. 30, 1865.
Lindsey, Garriel & Arey Watkins, Sept. 30, 1865.
Lindsey, Solomon & Charlotte Lindsay, Sept. 3, 1865.
Linster, Tom & Fanny Smith, Nov. 19, 1865.
Lockard, Newton & Sarah Daughtery, Mar. 4, 1865.
Loftin, Lewis & Chancy Butts, Aug. 23, 1865.
Long, Clinton & Nancy A. Woodward, Dec. 19, 1865.
Long, John & Minerva Puckett, Aug. 12, 1865.
Love, John R. & Sarah C. Davis, Aug. 9, 1865.
Love, Reuben & Harriet Love, Aug. 18, 1865.
Love, Wesley & Harriet Brawdin, Oct. 8, 1865.
Lovel, Wm. A. & Mary Jane Stem, Dec. 20, 1865.
Lowry, Charles & Louisa Lowry, Aug. 29, 1865.
Lyon, Stephen & Sarah Maury, Aug. 19, 1865.
Lytle, Dennis & Axey Morgan, Aug. 27, 1865.
Lytle, Ed & Mariah Kade, Dec. 25, 1865.
Lytle, Geo. & Sylva Murfree, Aug. 27, 1865.
Lytle, Harry & Nancy Dartis, Aug. 18, 1865.
Lytle, Isaac & Maria Spence, Aug. 26, 1865.
Lytle, Jerry & Hetty Hoggatt, Aug. 26, 1865.
Lytle, Randal & Melinda Lytle, Aug. 26, 1865.
Lytle, Robert & Kate Lytle, Sept. 12, 1865.
Lytle, Sam & Susan Perry, Aug. 27, 1865.
Maberry, Edm. & Frankie Maberry, Nov. 12, 1865.
Mabry, Wm. & Anne E. Sloan, Dec. 26, 1865.
Mack, Thomas & Lucinda Smith, Aug. 15, 1865.
Madaris, Green & Sally Gant, Aug. 29, 1865.
Madison, Fielding & Lucy Madison, Aug. 18, 1865.
Madison, James & Ailsey Madison, Aug. 18, 1865.
Madison, James & Margaret Owen, Sept. 10, 1865.
Majors, James & Polly Hoggett, Aug. 26, 1865.
Majors, Wm. & Abigail Vancleve, Nov. 23, 1865.
Malone, Barrister & Manerva Wilderson, Sept. 9, 1865.
Malone, Jack & Rachel Malone, Oct. 1, 1865.
Malone, John & Harriet Childress, Aug. 8, 1865.
Malone, Luke & Louiza Keeble, Oct. 14, 1865.
Malone, Thomas & Mary Harris, Nov. 11, 1865.
Maneever, Solomon & Charlotte Hendricks, Aug. 12, 1865.
Maney, Anthoney & Henrietta Jones, Aug. 20, 1865.
Maney, Geo. & Hester Bell N.S., Dec. 5, 1865.
Maney, Henry & Marg. Dickerson, Aug. 20, 1865.
Maney, Nathan & Nancy Maney, Aug. 19, 1865.
Maney, Riley & Harriet Maney, Aug. 19, 1865.
Maney, Tom & Peggy Crowford, Aug. 22, 1865.
Manley, Isaac & Edith Frizzell, Aug. 23, 1865.
Manson, Adam & Cinthia Washington, Aug. 26, 1865.
Marable, Albert & Lucinda Sikes, Aug. 25, 1865.

Marable, Allen & Martha Berlason, Aug. 26, 1865.
Marable, Anthony & Ellen Smith, Aug. 27, 1865.
Marable, Clem & Louisa Smith, Aug. 26, 1865.
Marable, Daniel & Nancy Davis, Aug. 26, 1865.
Marable, Daniel & Sarah Hollowell, Aug. 26, 1865.
Marable, Jerry & Ellen Marable, Aug. 26, 1865.
Marable, Jerry & Julia Lane, Sept. 3, 1865.
Marable, Philip & Luckey Berlerson, Aug. 26, 1865.
Marable, Taswell & America Sikes, Nov. 4, 1865.
Marlin, T. C. & America T. Painter N.S., Dec. 9, 1865.
Marshall, James & Sallie Pruett, Nov. 5, 1865.
Martin, Charles & Elvira Furgeson, Aug. 22, 1865.
Martin, Charles & Mary Martin, Aug. 23, 1865.
Martin, Henry & Arsey Harriet Webb, Aug. 29, 1865.
Martin, Henry & Eliza Jones, Aug. 18, 1865.
Martin, Henry & Irene Brantly, Oct. 21, 1865.
Martin, Jesse & Mary Jennings, Aug. 19, 1865.
Martin, Jim & Mary Martin, Aug. 25, 1865.
Martin, Richard & Amanda Davis, Aug. 27, 1865.
Martin, Sam & Fannie Martin, Aug. 17, 1865.
Martin, Wm. & Jane Duncan, Aug. 20, 1865.
Mason, Ellis & Harriet Stone, Aug. 28, 1865.
Mason, John & Adeline Mason, Oct. 8, 1865.
Mason, John & Clarissa Mason N.S., Sept. 2, 1865.
Mason, Luke & Margaret Mason, Feb. 4, 1865.
Mason, Philip & Winnie Mason, Oct. 8, 1865.
Mason, Richard & Caroline Puckett, June 26, 1865.
Masten, Peter & Mary Ann Coleman, Aug. 26, 1865.
Mathews, Charles & Mima Mathews, Aug. 19, 1865.
Mathews, John & Lavina Jenkins N.S., Sept. 2, 1865.
Mathews, L. H. & Mildred R. Rucker, June 11, 1865.
May, Abram & Matilda Webb, Mar. 4, 1865.
May, Domina & Zeina May, Aug. 19, 1865.
Mayfield, Daniel & Mary Agnes Floyd, Sept. 1, 1865.
Mayfield, J. W. & Mary E. Pinkard, Mar. 27, 1865.
Merefee, John & Ellen Rivers N.S., Aug. 25, 1865.
Merritt, Charles & Mary Owens, Sept. 23, 1865.
Merritt, Samuel & Mariah Vaughan, Aug. 19, 1865.
Messick, Richard & Catharine Pruitt, Aug. 17, 1865.
Miles, Dock & Julia Russwurm (Issued 1865, not sol.
  until 1871).
Miles, Green & Mahaly Miles, Sept. 9, 1865.
Miles, Jack & Lucy Miles N.S., Aug. 30, 1865.
Miles, Philip & Teller Miles, Sept. 10, 1865.
Miller, Bate & Mariah Lytle, Sept. 15, 1865.
Miller, Dick & Nicy Wade, Nov. 11, 1865.
Miller, F. G. & Kate E. Wadley, Dec. 14, 1865.
Miller, Fountain H. & Sarah L. Davis, Dec. 5, 1865.
Miller, Geo. & Sophia Norman, Oct. 22, 1865.
Miller, H. N. & Miss Mary Robinson, Apr. 28, 1865.
Miller, Isaac & Minerva Miller, Aug. 26, 1865.
Miller, Jackson & Aneca Duncan, Aug. 30, 1865.
Miller, John & Fanny Wade, Nov. 11, 1865.
Miller, Jos. & Milley Maloy, Aug. 27, 1865.
Miller, Lawson & Mira Fletcher, Aug. 15, 1865.

RUTHERFORD COUNTY MARRIAGES

Miller, Madison & Hettie Howland, Sept. 3, 1865.
Miller, Robert & Ruth Hutton, Dec. 9, 1865.
Miller, Scott & Josephine Alexander, Dec. 29, 1865.
Miller, Solomon & Marg. Howland, Sept. 3, 1865.
Miller, Thomas & Harriet Miller, Aug. 15, 1865.
Miller, Thomas J. & Sarah N. McMurray, Nov. 21, 1865.
Miller, W. I. & Parmentine A. Gordon, Nov. 10, 1865.
Mills, Benj. & Rachel Jackson, Aug. 26, 1865.
Minter, Harry & Nancy Vaughan, Aug. 26, 1865.
Mitchell, Mark & Patsey Drake, Aug. 27, 1865.
Mitchell, Simon & Jane Drake, Dec. 2, 1865.
Mitchell, Zachariah & Salley Mitchell, Sept. 2, 1865.
Molloy, Samuel & Silvy Gentry, Aug. 20, 1865.
Molloy, Simon & Flora Henry, Aug. 31, 1865.
Moore, Davis & Amanda Whitecer, Aug. 21, 1865.
Moore, Francis & Nancy Brown, Aug. 10, 1865.
Moore, Geo. & Melinda Lewis, Oct. 12, 1865.
Moore, Joseph & Julia A. Travis, Dec. 3, 1865.
Moore, Milford & Lyrena McLean, Oct. 5, 1865.
Moore, Nathan & Minerva Lillard, Aug. 5, 1865.
Moore, Meekin & Lucinda Baird, Aug. 19, 1865.
Moore, Robert & Roxana Parish, July 16, 1865.
Moore, Stephen & Caroline Moore, Mar. 24, 1865.
Moore, Wm. & Malinda Moore N.S., Aug. 29, 1865.
Morgan, Daleem & Louiza Jamison, Aug. 20, 1865.
Morgan, Jack & Louisa Fletcher, Aug. 27, 1865.
Morris, Wm. & Martha Fulton, Aug. 7, 1865.
Morton, John & Eliz. Snell, Aug. 21, 1865.
Morton, Joshua & Aggy Peebles, Aug. 26, 1865.
Morton, Henry & Malvina Henderson, Sept. 2, 1865.
Morton, Levi & Mariah Morton, Aug. 26, 1865.
Morton, Matt & Margaret A. Morton N.S., Nov. 24, 1865.
Mosley, J. C. & Minnie L. Cain N.S., Nov. 21, 1865.
Mount, Simon & Mary Smith, Aug. 5, 1865.
Mozer, Chesterfield & Rachel Lusk, Aug. 27, 1865.
Mullins, Edm. & Hannah Mullins, Oct. 8, 1865.
Mullins, Wm. & Evaline Espy, Sept. 24, 1865.
Murfree, Dread & Mary Ann Booker, Aug. 28, 1865.
Murfree, Ephraim & Milly Snell, Sept. 17, 1865.
Murfree, Henny & Mary T. Lytle, Sept. 12, 1865.
Murfree, John & Leanna Murfree, Aug. 25, 1865.
Murfree, Robert & Sarah Murfree, Aug. 19, 1865.
Murfree, Thadeous & Adaline Murfree N.S., Dec. 16, 1865.
Murfree, Toney & Viney Murfree, Aug. 18, 1865.
Murfree, Washington & Hannah Stevens, Aug. 19, 1865.
Murray, Asa & Martha Murray, Aug. 29, 1865.
Murray, Gabriel & Lizzie Maney N.S., Aug. 29, 1865.
Murray, Joseph & Harriett Hall, Aug. 29, 1865.
Murray, Leonard & Ellen Carter, Oct. 28, 1865.
Murray, Stephen & Nancy Dolly, Aug. 29, 1865.
Murry, Anthoney & Caroline Murry, Aug. 26, 1865.
McAdoo, Calvin & Elmira Donnell, Aug. 26, 1865.
McAdoo, Dick & Viney Rucker, Aug. 20, 1865.
McAdoo, Gabriel & Hetty Toney (Jones)?, Aug. 19, 1865.
McAdoo, George & Amanda Floyd, Aug. 19, 1865.

McAdoo, Jackson & Nicy Ann McAdoo, Aug. 23, 1865.
McAdoo, James & Harriet McAdoo, Aug. 23, 1865.
McAdoo, Joseph & Harriett White, Aug. 26, 1865.
McAdoo, Randel & Martha Ivey N.S., Aug. 26, 1865.
McAdoo, Solon H. & Sallie Weaver, Nov. 13, 1865.
McAfee, James T. & Sylva Wilson N.S., Aug. 30, 1865.
McCarden, James & Matilda Moore, Aug. 30, 1865.
McCauly, Henderson & Mary McCauly, Aug. 19, 1865.
McCathey, Edm. & Ann Spellings, Aug. 23, 1865.
McClaren, Rolly & Patsey Johnson N.S., Aug. 30, 1865.
McClarin, Lewis & Sally Spann, Aug. 27, 1865.
McCollum, John & Sarah Jane Ross, June 17, 1865.
McCord, Wm. & Ruthey Ann Rucker N.S., Sept. 29, 1865.
McCullough, Daniel & Isabella Cowan, Sept. 23, 1865.
McCullough, D. S. & Miss Mattie J. Jordan, July 18,
1865.
McCullough, Philip & Susan Ellis, Aug. 26, 1865.
McCullough, Wesly & Catharine McCullough, Nov. 25, 1865.
McElroy, A. M. & Mrs. Mary Jane Tucker, Dec. 19, 1865.
McFadden, James & Manerva McFadden, Aug. 26, 1865.
McFadden, Wm. & Beckey Jones, Aug. 30, 1865.
McFerrin, Wm. & Mary Young, Apr. 13, 1865.
McGill, Alfred & Isabella Wooten, Sept. 1, 1865.
McGill, George & Jane Dillon, Sept. 19, 1865.
McGill, Harvy & Jane Sullens, Aug. 23, 1865.
McGill, Henry & Caroline McGill, Aug. 26, 1865.
McGill, Lewis & Joanna McGill N.S., Aug. 28, 1865.
McGill, Robin & Delphia McGill, Aug. 22, 1865.
McGowan, Ceazar & Judy McGowen, Aug. 19, 1865.
McGowan, W. F. & Nancy Morton, May 7, 1865.
McHenry, Phil & Miranda McHenry, Aug. 27, 1865.
McHenry, Geo. & Susan Reeves, Sept.7, 1865.
McKay, C. W. & Miss E. Harris (Ella Maria), June 1,
1865.
McKever, Robert & Betty Gregory, Apr. 14, 1865.
McKnight, John R. & Christian Trimble, Dec. 15, 1865.
McKnight, Joshua & Clarissa Hall, Aug. 19, 1865.
McLaughlin, Frank & Sallie Morton N.S., Dec. 23, 1865.
McLean, Bob & Matilda Webb, Mar. 4, 1865.
McLean, Henry & Mallinda McLean, Apr. 8, 1865.
McLean, Solomon & Fanny McLean, Aug. 8, 1865.
McMurray, Nelson & Caroline Jamison, Aug. 18, 1865.
McNichol, Barney & Amanda Horton, Oct. 28, 1865.
McRunnels, Charles & Eliza McRunnels, Aug. 17, 1865.
Nance, Isaac N. & Eliza Hunt, Feb. 15, 1865.
Neal, Charley & Amanda Neal, Sept. 4, 1865.
Neal, Claiborne & Susan Jetton, Sept. 4, 1865.
Neal, Lewis & Argan Duncan, Apr. 31, 1865.
Neal, Salem & Poley Whitworth N.S., Aug. 15, 1865.
Neal, Sam & Lavinia Furgeson, Oct. 5, 1865.
Neel, Philip & Mima Neel N.S., July 8, 1865.
Neely, Jackson & Kisey House, Dec. 16, 1865.
Neely, J. H. & Miss Bettie Nesbett, Oct. 25, 1865.
Neely, James Q. E. & Susan E. Witherspoon, June 9, 1865.

Neely, W. W. & Mary E. Palmer, Sept. 5, 1865.
Nelson, Geo. & Mary Nelson, Sept. 17, 1865.
Nelson, Hal & Milly Childress, Sept. 17, 1865.
Nelson, Marshal & C. Hoover, June 10, 1865.
Nelson, Minter & Anamda Denny, Jan. 3, 1865.
Nelson, Ralph & Jean Sanders, Aug. 19, 1865.
Nelson, Simon & Angeline Clark, Nov. 18, 1865.
Nelson, Tom & Nancy Hill, Sept. 17, 1865.
Nevels, Hamton & Sarah Wilman, Aug. 22, 1865.
Newman, Charles & Melinda Newman, Aug. 19, 1865.
Newman, G. J. & Mahala Yearwood, Nov. 9, 1865.
Newman, George & Doritha Gibson, Aug. 20, 1865.
Night, Isaac & Sarah Night, Aug. 27, 1865.
Noland, Robert C. & Drucie A. Davis, Jan. 3, 1865.
Nolen, Lewis & Lizean Clayton, Aug. 19, 1865.
Nolin, Moses T. & Sallie A. Owen, Nov. 23, 1865.
Norfleet, Nelson & Nelly Jordan, Aug. 29, 1865.
Norman, Bradley & Emily Prince, Dec. 6, 1865.
Norman, Joe & Lucy Bouse, Sept. 19, 1865.
Norman, Joseph & Ann Caldwell, Oct. 30, 1865.
Norman, Thomas & Caroline Norman, Aug. 20, 1865.
North, David & Susan Bracey, Sept. 17, 1865.
North, Davy & Katy Ransom N.S., Sept. 9, 1865.
North, Nathan & Mary North, Aug. 30, 1865.
Oden, Edm. & Melissa Lane, Aug. 18, 1865.
Oliver, John A. & Anacy Leonard, Feb. 15, 1865.
Oliver, Wm. & Mary Bonds, Jan. 18, 1865.
Overall, Aaron & Harriet Overall N.S., Aug. 18, 1865.
Overall, Buck & Louisa Settle N.S., Aug. 26, 1865.
Overall, Geo. & Rachel Kirby, Dec. 28, 1865.
Overall, Geo. & Harriet Overall, Aug. 25, 1865.
Overall, Geo. & Rachel Yearwood, Dec. 28, 1865.
Overall, Roger & Malinda Overall, Aug. 22, 1865.
Overall, Solomon & Mary Overall N.S., Aug. 18, 1865.
Owen, Geo. & Susan Owens N.S., Aug. 19, 1865.
Owens, Henry & Fanny Owens, Sept. 16, 1865.
Owens, Jim & Emiline Rucker, Sept. 16, 1865.
Owens, Starks & Eliza Overall, Aug. 28, 1865.
Pace, Jacob & Louisa Blackburn, Aug. 27, 1865.
Painter, John F. & Margaret Goss, Oct. 10, 1865.
Parker, A. Y. & Nancy W. Lawing, Oct. 10, 1865.
Parker, Wm. & Amanda Jetton, May 8, 1865.
Pate, Houston & Martha Pate, Sept. 16, 1865.
Patterson, Frelingheison & Susan Parish, Sept. 5, 1865.
Patterson, Lewis & Queen Windrow, Jan. 5, 1865.
Patterson, Robert W. & Sallie B. McKee, Nov. 17, 1865.
Patterson, Taylor & Hannah Goss, Sept. 8, 1865.
Patton, James & Minirva Haynes, Sept. 9, 1865.
Paxton, James M. & Mary J. Harpol, July 12, 1865.
Pearce, Geo. & Polly Pearce, Sept. 2, 1865.
Pearce, John & Mary Pearce, Sept. 9, 1865.
Pearson, Squire & Rose Rucker, Dec. 30, 1865.
Peebles, Adam & Nancy Batey, Aug. 26, 1865.
Peebles, Ben & Lavina Mitchell, Aug. 26, 1865.

RUTHERFORD COUNTY MARRIAGES

Peebles, Geo. & Ann Davis, Aug. 26, 1865.
Peebles, John & Necy Craddick, Sept. 13, 1865.
Peebles, Moses & Dianna Batey, Sept. 2, 1865.
Peebles, Sandy & Martha Smith, Aug. 26, 1865.
Perry, Anderson & Eliza Carter, Dec. 29, 1865.
Perry, Edw. & Martha Perry, Aug. 22, 1865.
Perry, Henry & Martha E. Tucker, Dec. 4, 1865.
Peyton, Geo. & Peggy Malone, Sept. 30, 1865.
Peyton, Geo. & Maria Sneed, Dec. 11, 1865.
Peyton, Peyton & Ann Peyton, Aug. 27, 1865.
Philips, Jessee & Harriet Coppage, Aug. 25, 1865.
Philips, Joe & Jane Childress N.S., Aug. 23, 1865.
Philips, Osborne & Louisa Philips, Aug. 26, 1865.
Philips, Wm. & Liana Armstrong, Nov. 12, 1865.
Phillips, Davis & Eliza Robertson, Aug. 24, 1865.
Phillips, Grant & Annis Brown, Aug. 22, 1865.
Phillips, J. E. & M. A. Thacker, Oct. 17, 1865.
Phillips, James B. & Mary E. Murphrey, Aug. 10, 1865.
Phillips, Wm. & Miss Martha Burton, Apr. 18, 1865.
Philpott, Simon M. & Miss Jane Bell Blair, July 25,
 1865.
Pickett, Rufus & Dicey Pickett, Aug. 30, 1865.
Pinckard, James & Susan Besham, Aug. 19, 1865.
Pinkard, Lewis & Rosa Jane Norman, Aug. 19, 1865.
Pitts, Andrew & Amanda Kendell, Dec. 29, 1865.
Pitts, Isaac & Sarah Pitts, Aug. 23, 1865.
Poindexter, John R. & Malinda L. Lawrence, Sept. 25,
 1865.
Pope, J. J. & Emily Mathews N.S., Dec. 18, 1865.
Pope, Moses & Mary Ann Lamb, Aug. 7, 1865.
Posey, Green & Patsey Hord, Sept. 5, 1865.
Posey, Richard & Martha Miles, Aug. 26, 1865.
Prater, W. I. & G. E. Kelton N.S., Aug. 7, 1865.
Preston, Alfred & Carolone Summer, Aug. 10, 1865.
Prewitt, Clard & Susan Prewitt, Sept. 8, 1865.
Prim, James & Miss R. A. Rowett, Feb. 16, 1865.
Primm, Frank & Mary Primm N.S., Aug. 21, 1865.
Proctor, Joe & Eliza Proctor, Sept. 14, 1865.
Pruitt, Clark & Susan Pruitt, Sept. 8, 1865.
Puckett, James N. & Mary F. White N.S., Nov. 27, 1865.
Puckett, Joe & Mary Ransom N.S., Aug. 28, 1865.
Puckett, Virgil & Ann Puckett, Aug. 21, 1865.
Purdy, Robert & Mary Lytle, Aug. 25, 1865.
Quarles, Emanuel & Minirva Harris, Aug. 25, 1865.
Quarles, Henry & Rutha Quarles, Aug. 26, 1865.
Ragland, Henry & Pricilla Ragland, Sept. 17, 1865.
Ralston, Ephriam & Martha Ralston, Sept. 10, 1865.
Ralston, Rankin & Martha Ralston N.S., Aug. 26, 1865.
Randal, Geo. & Lucretia Randal, Sept. 18, 1865.
Randolph, Augustus & Polly Wade, Sept. 9, 1865.
Randolph, Beverly, Jr. & Bettie C. Wade, Dec. 19, 1865.
Randolph, Buck & Sally Bell N.S., Aug. 26, 1865.
Randolph, Calvin & Ara Bell, Dec. 9, 1865.
Randolph, James & Jennie Randolph, Sept. 2, 1865.
Randolph, Joseph & Martha Alford, Sept. 9, 1865.

RUTHERFORD COUNTY MARRIAGES

Randolph, Nathaniel & Maria Miller, Sept. 10, 1865.
Rankin, E. E. & E. J. Broiles, Sept. 19, 1865.
Rankin, Edmond & Jane Spence N.S., Aug. 19, 1865.
Ransom, Alexander & Louisa Lawrence, Aug. 9, 1865.
Ransom, Daniel & Mary Ransom N.S., Aug. 28, 1865.
Ransom, Geo. & Mickey Brooks, Aug. 29, 1865.
Ransom, Green & Einey Ransom, Sept. 1, 1865.
Ransom, Henry & Cornelia Turner N.S., Nov. 18, 1865.
Ransom, James & Cinthia Ransom, Aug. 27, 1865.
Ransom, Peter & Jemima Lillard, Nov. 5, 1865.
Ransom, Samuel & Hettie Reeves, Sept. 6, 1865.
Ransom, Simon & Amanda Ransom, Aug. 29, 1865.
Ransom, Tom & Mariah Woodson N.S., Aug. 28, 1865.
Rayburn, French & Hollie A. McFadden (Also Raborn),
    Mar. 20, 1865.
Ready, Thomas & Luviny Rory, Aug. 28, 1865.
Reece, Eggleston & Clarissa Green, Sept. 9, 1865.
Reed, Emanuel & Betsy Reed, Sept. 10, 1865.
Reed, Caswell & Becky Sims N.S., Nov. 11, 1865.
Reed, Jack & Matilda Reed, Sept. 10, 1865.
Reese, Joseph & Amy Ricks, Aug. 26, 1865.
Reeves, Ben & Allis McFadden, Sept. 9, 1865.
Reeves, Benjamin & Sarah Ransom, Aug. 19, 1865.
Reeves, James L. & Annie Graham, Dec. 15, 1865.
Reeves, Washington & Harriet James, Aug. 26, 1865.
Renfro, Geo. & Julia A. Ashley N.S., Nov. 11, 1865.
Reynolds, James & Jane Derbin N.S., Nov. 18, 1865.
Rhodes, Green & Margaret McDonald, Aug. 27, 1865.
Rice, Nelson & Ann McLean, Aug. 8, 1865.
Richardson, Charles & Harriet Kimbro, Sept. 17, 1865.
Richardson, Clem & Mary Richardson, Aug. 26, 1865.
Richardson, Edmund & Amanda Batey, Sept. 2, 1865.
Richardson, Gains & Louisa Richardson, Aug. 26, 1865.
Richardson, Mat & Edith Richardson, Aug. 24, 1865.
Richardson, Pat & Emily Tucker, Aug. 25, 1865.
Richardson, Reuben & Narcissa Newman, Aug. 21, 1865.
Richardson, Sandy & Harriet Walden, Sept. 2, 1865.
Ridley, Burrell & Patty Ridley, Dec. 26, 1865.
Ridley, Claiborne & Lucy Ridley, Sept. 10, 1865.
Ridley, Edward & Malinda Ridley N.S., Dec. 16, 1865.
Ridley, Emmanuel & Serena Ridley, Aug. 26, 1865.
Ridley, George W. & Melinda Ridley, Aug. 26, 1865.
Ridley, Hannibal & Mary Jane Ridley, Sept. 10, 1865.
Ridley, Selestia Ridley, Sept. 17, 1865.
Ridley, Henry & Laura Ridley N.S., Aug. 26, 1865.
Ridley, Jackson & Lizzie Ridley, Sept. 10, 1865.
Ridley, Jim & Minerva Haynes, Sept. 4, 1865.
Ridley, Joseph & Louisa Ridley, Nov. 20, 1865.
Ridley, Mat & Sophia Thompson N.S., Sept. 20, 1865.
Ridley, Virgil & Betsey Ridley, Aug. 28, 1865.
Ridley, Washington & Maria Keeble, Sept. 8, 1865.
Ridley, York & Molly Reed, Sept. 10, 1865.
Ridout, John & Caroline Ransom N.S., Sept. 9, 1865.
Robert, James & Mary Frazer N.S., Dec. 18, 1865.
Roberts, Wm. & Eliza Ann Jordan, Sept. 4, 1865.

Robertson, Adam & Amanda Robertson, Aug. 26, 1865.
Robertson, Charles & Ailsey Dunnaway, Aug. 26, 1865.
Robertson, Chester & Milly Robinson, Aug. 27, 1865.
Robertson, Greef & Eda Hall, Aug. 25, 1865.
Robertson, James M. & Mary J. Sanders, June 12, 1865.
Robertson, Pompy & Lytle -----, May 14, 1865.
Robertson, Peter & Eliza Jane Huddleston, Aug. 15, 1865.
Robertson, Tom & Ann Wrather, Nov. 25, 1865.
Robins, Joseph & Eliz. Williams, N.S., June 20, 1865.
Robinson, John & Ellis Robinson, Sept. 14, 1865.
Robinson, John & Ensey Robinson, Aug. 19, 1865.
Robinson, Joe & Cinthia Robinson, Aug. 27, 1865.
Rooker, David & Martha Sanders, Oct. 21, 1865.
Ross, Amos & Susan Wade N.S. Aug. 26, 1865.
Ross, Peter & Harriett Ross, Aug. 19, 1865.
Ross, Richard & Ellen Peebles, Aug. 26, 1865.
Ross, Sam & Sylvia Peebles, Aug. 26, 1865.
Ross, Sterlin & Mary Nelson, Aug. 19, 1865.
Roulet, Wm. & Mary E. Spence, Oct. 2, 1865.
Rouse, Edmond & Sarah Roy, Sept. 19, 1865.
Rowland, L. B. & Sarah A. Winsett, Sept. 27, 1865.
Rowlett, Benj. & Susan A. Henderson N.S., Feb. 8, 1865.
Rowlett, Joseph W. & Fannie Vaughan N.S., Nov. 15, 1865.
Rucker, Anderson & Harriett Rucker, Aug. 20, 1865.
Rucker, Catesby & Thelia Rucker, Aug. 27, 1865.
Rucker, Clinton & Lidia Rucker, Aug. 20, 1865.
Rucker, David & Cloa Rucker, Aug. 20, 1865.
Rucker, Dick & Adaline Rucker, Aug. 27, 1865.
Rucker, Elizah & Jane Rucker, Aug. 20, 1865.
Rucker, Frank & Viney Miller N.S., Aug. 29, 1865.
Rucker, Glasgow & Mariah Rucker, Aug. 19, 1865.
Rucker, Hancie & Jean Rucker, Sept. 2, 1865.
Rucker, Harry & Mahala Jane Jordan, Sept. 2, 1865.
Rucker, Henry & Mariah Rucker, Aug. 20, 1865.
Rucker, Henry & Sophia Kirby, Aug. 19, 1865.
Rucker, Isaac & Rebecca Cook, Aug. 20, 1865.
Rucker, Isaac & Winney Rucker, Aug. 19, 1865.
Rucker, Ishmael & Easter Rucker, Aug. 22, 1865.
Rucker, Jesse & Margaret Hoskins, Aug. 27, 1865.
Rucker, Jim & Mary Rucker, Aug. 20, 1865.
Rucker, Jim & Phelis Rucker, Aug. 20, 1865.
Rucker, Kebber & Amelia Rucker, Aug. 20, 1865.
Rucker, Nathan & Jenetta McAdoo, Aug. 21, 1865.
Rucker, Ned & Tildy Rucker, Aug. 20, 1865.
Rucker, Ned & Catey Rucker, Aug. 19, 1865.
Rucker, Nelson & Anna McAdoo, Aug. 20, 1865.
Rucker, Nelson & Charity Rucker, Aug. 20, 1865.
Rucker, Osborn & Minda Rucker, Aug. 20, 1865.
Rucker, Peter & Patience Childress N.S., Aug. 26, 1865.
Rucker, Philip & Eliza Rucker, Aug. 27, 1865.
Rucker, Richard & Cornelia Sharp, Aug. 20, 1865.
Rucker, Sidney & Eliza Holmes, Aug. 22, 1865.
Rucker, Washington & Frances Hare, Aug. 25, 1865.
Rucker, Washington & Harriett Jetton, Aug. 20, 1865.
Rucker, Wm. & Katey Rucker, Aug. 28, 1865.

RUTHERFORD COUNTY MARRIAGES

Rucker, Wm. & Matilda Adkinson, Sept. 10, 1865.
Rucker, Zacheriah & Amanda Sanders N.S., Aug. 15, 1865.
Runnels, H. A. & Sarah A. Miller, Oct. 29, 1865.
Runnels, John & Jenny Runnels, Aug. 19, 1865.
Runnels, Sam & Clara Runnels N.S., Aug. 27, 1865.
Runnels, Wm. & Meriah Dervin, Sept. 7, 1865.
Russell, Jasper H. & Sallie A. Neely, July 4, 1865.
Russell, Jefferson & Matilda Warren, Aug. 27, 1865.
Russell, L. & Martha L. House, Feb. 1, 1865.
Russell, Robert & Cloa Hedge, Aug. 28, 1865.
Ryan, Charles & Milly Ryan N.S., Aug. 19, 1865.
Sage, John W. & Fannie Haynes, Dec. 24, 1865.
Sanders, Anderson & Mariah Sanders, Aug. 27, 1865.
Sanders, David & Eliza Sanders, Sept. 17, 1865.
Sanders, George & Celia Ann Hooker, Aug. 24, 1865.
Sanders, Phillip & Hannah Coleman, Aug. 19, 1865.
Sanders, Phillip S. & Mary M. Sanders, Jan. 30, 1865.
Sanders, Ransom & Harriett Sanders, Sept. 16, 1865.
Sanders, Sam & Charlotte Welch, Aug. 27, 1865.
Sanders, Wm. & Jane Sanders, Sept. 3, 1865.
Sanford, Peck & Betsy Sanford, Aug. 25, 1865.
Sanford, Rial & Emma Spence, Aug. 19, 1865.
Sanford, Willis & Eliz. Sanford, Aug. 21, 1865.
Saunders, Samuel & Usler Saunders, Aug. 23, 1865.
Sawyer, Edward & Margaret C. Goodwin, Mar. 15, 1865.
Sawyers, Hiram & Mahala Sawyers, Aug. 30, 1865.
Sawyers, Peter & Martha Sawyers, Aug. 23, 1865.
Scales, David & Minerva Smith, Sept. 4, 1865.
Schofflin, Archer & Julia Schofflin, Aug. 11, 1865.
Scroggins, Squire Henry & Rethenia Posey, Sept. 5, 1865.
Scruggs, Wm. & Polly Scruggs, Sept. 9, 1865.
Searcy, Tarlton & Lucinda Searcy, Aug. 27, 1865.
Sears, Dennis & Cinthia Ann Sears, Nov. 18, 1865.
Seat, James G. & Sarah Tucker, N.S., Apr. 15, 1865.
Seay, Franklin & Jane Edwards Bracey, Aug. 12, 1865.
Seay, Mark & Caroline Ferris, Aug. 12, 1865.
Seay, Riley & Sarah Ferris, Aug. 12, 1865.
Sellars, Cumley & Vicy Johns, Sept. 11, 1865.
Seward, Abram & Harriet Seward, Aug. 22, 1865.
Seward, Harrison & Amanda Lillard, Dec. 1, 1865.
Seward, Martin & Melinda Carter, Aug. 26, 1865.
Shannon, Martin & Emeline Manson, Aug. 26, 1865.
Sharber, Wm. & Hager Seay, Aug. 10, 1865.
Sharp, Andrew & Eliza Clayton, Aug. 28, 1865.
Sharp, John & Sylva Molloy, Aug. 20, 1865.
Sharp, Ned & Betsey Sharp, Aug. 20, 1865.
Shaver, Isham & Francis Shaver, Aug. 23, 1865.
Shelton, Smith Allen & Nancy Shelton, Nov. 20, 1865.
Sherron, Gilbert & Harriet Gant, Aug. 24, 1865.
Sherron, Thomas & Laura Bass, May 20, 1865.
Short, James & Paralee Hoover, Nov. 15, 1865.
Shuffield, Jon & Harriet Isabella Shuggied, Aug. 19, 1865.
Shute, Jim & Victoria Wade, Aug. 28, 1865.

Sikes, Joseph & Hannah Esby, Sept. 16, 1865.
Simmons, John & Jane Harris, Aug. 24, 1865.
Simmons, Ned & Rina Simmons, Sept. 9, 1865.
Simpson, Lewis & Mariah White, Aug. 20, 1865.
Sims, Geo. & Nancy Alexander, Aug. 19, 1865.
Sims, Lewis S. & Sarah June Snell, Dec. 13, 1865.
Sims, Peter & Amanda Bivins, Dec. 25, 1865.
Sims, W. H. & Mrs. M. L. Moore, May 23, 1865.
Sloan, Andrew T. & Mary F. Wilson, Aug. 20, 1865.
Sloss, Henry & Clarisa Pennal, Aug. 26, 1865.
Small, James & Sally Small, Oct. 8, 1865.
Smith, Albert & Ginny McHenry, Aug. 19, 1865.
Smith, Aaron & Nancy Smith, Aug. 21, 1865.
Smith, Albert & Laura Ann Smith, Sept. 10, 1865.
Smith, Ananias & Julia Hall, Aug. 23, 1865.
Smith, Anthony & Mariah Smith, Aug. 20, 1865.
Smith, Arthur & Ann Smith, Sept. 19, 1865.
Smith, Booker & Nelly Thompson, Aug. 24, 1865.
Smith, Charles & Lucinda Smith, Aug. 28, 1865.
Smith, David & Minerva Smith, Sept. 4, 1865.
Smith, E. & Melvina Winfrey N.S., Aug. 19, 1865.
Smith, Edm. & Martha Edmondson, Dec. 9, 1865.
Smith, Edm. & Patience Smith, Aug. 20, 1865.
Smith, Frank & Mary Washington, Sept. 2, 1865.
Smith, Geo. & Easter Davis, Aug. 26, 1865.
Smith, Geo. & Harriet Bass, Dec. 31, 1865.
Smith, Golden L. & Eliz. Rice, Oct. 26, 1865.
Smith, Granderson & Betsey Jetton, Aug. 26, 1865.
Smith, Green & Caroline Davis, Aug. 26, 1865.
Smith, Harrison & Eliza Baird, Aug. 26, 1865.
Smith, Henry & Esabella Black, Dec. 2, 1865.
Smith, Iley & Ellen Smith, Aug. 27, 1865.
Smith, J. E. & Ozella J. Smith, Aug. 25, 1865.
Smith, Jack & Dinah Donnell, Aug. 21, 1865.
Smith, Jack & Harriet Williamson, Aug. 29, 1865.
Smith, Jack & Jane Kimbro, Oct. 21, 1865.
Smith, Jessee & Sarah Smith, Aug. 19, 1865.
Smith, Jim Polk & Minerva Smith, Sept. 2, 1865.
Smith, John & Martha Rideout, Aug. 28, 1865.
Smith, John & Matilda Garrett, Oct. 7, 1865.
Smith, Joseph P. & Lockie Weatherly, Nov. 18, 1865.
Smith, Joshua & Louisa Smith, Aug. 19, 1865.
Smith, Julius & Anna Smith, Aug. 26, 1865.
Smith, Julous & Catherine Smith, Aug. 29, 1865.
Smith, Lamb & Angess Baird, Sept. 16, 1865.
Smith, Levi & Louisa House, Aug. 31, 1865.
Smith, Marshall & Luvenia Smith N.S., Dec. 22, 1865.
Smith, Martin & Mary Sanders, Sept. 3, 1865.
Smith, Nat & Becky Smith, Sept. 16, 1865.
Smith, Ned & Mariah Ridout, Sept. 17, 1865.
Smith, Peter & Priscilla Smith, Aug. 20, 1865.
Smith, Sam & Emily Huddleston, Aug. 26, 1865.
Smith, Sam Houston & America Smith, Sept. 16, 1865.
Smith, Simon & Nancy Smith, May 18, 1865.

Smith, Steben & Christina Smith N.S., Aug. 19, 1865.
Smith, Thomas & Pallina Reed N.S., Aug. 19, 1865.
Smith, Warren & Martina Smith, Aug. 19, 1865.
Smith, Warren & Mary Smith, Nov. 4, 1865.
Smith, Watson & Minerva Buchanan, Sept. 10, 1865.
Smith, Wm. & Celia Peebles, Sept. 2, 1865.
Smith, Wm. & Miss Rachel Williams, -- ---, 1865 (issued
    1865 Sol. 1867).
Smith, Wm. & Sarah J. Farr, Nov. 23, 1865.
Smotherman, Frank & Ann Nance, Aug. 8, 1865.
Smotherman, James M. & Sarah Smotherman, Dec. 10, 1865.
Smotherman, Samuel & Sophronia Smotherman, Aug. 12,
    1865.
Smotherman, Solomon & Emily Smotherman, Aug. 8, 1865.
Sneed, David & Mary Brittain, Sept. 4, 1865.
Sneed, Henry & Sally Reed, Dec. 23, 1865.
Sneed, Joshua & Beckey Sneed, Sept. 10, 1865.
Sneed, Mat & Angeline Sanders, Aug. 24, 1865.
Sneed, Milton & Dilcey Batey, Sept. 4, 1865.
Snell, Abram & Easter Ransom, Sept. 23, 1865.
Snell, Ezekiel & Sarah Spence, Aug. 15, 1865.
Snell, James T. & Sallie P. Avaritt, Nov. 23, 1865.
Spain, Geo. & Parthenia Martin, Aug. 20, 1865.
Span, Harrison & Marcena Span, Sept. 3, 1865.
Span, Jim & Amanda Haynes, Aug. 29, 1865.
Spence, David & Caroline Spence, Aug. 23, 1865.
Spence E. M. & Miss Melissa A. Mallard, Apr. 16, 1865.
Spence, Jim & Louiza Spence, Sept. 23, 1865.
Spence, John & Narcissa Spence, Aug. 29, 1865.
Spence, M. V. & Miss Mary E. Patterson, Jan. 31, 1865.
Spence, Peter & Matilda Marshall, Aug. 23, 1865.
Spence, Philip & Eliza Spence, Sept. 2, 1865.
Spencer, Belvin R. & Clemmontine F. Dillon, May 18,
    1865.
Springer, Robert & Martha White, Dec. 27, 1865.
Stansler, Harvey & Malissa Sanders, Nov. 10, 1865.
Stattens, Joseph & Mary J. Fox, Mar. 16, 1865.
Steele, Calvin & Ann Clarity, Aug. 27, 1865.
Stegall, Lewis & Eliz. Woods, Dec. 18, 1865.
Stevans, Alexander & Selina Hartwell, Aug. 20, 1865.
Stewart, Jack & Judy Wade, Aug. 28, 1865.
Stewart, Wm. & Nancy Stewart, Aug. 30, 1865.
Stewart, Wm. & Tennessee Collins, June 3, 1865.
Stokes, Robert & Betty Stokes N.S., Feb. 22, 1865.
Stover, Geo. W. & Eliza C. Aylor, Sept. 21, 1865.
Strickland, Mathew & Lucy Jane Scales, Aug. 27, 1865.
Sturdephant, Stephen & Mary J. Watson, Aug. 25, 1865.
Sublett, Albert & Harriet McAdoo, Aug. 20, 1865.
Sublett, Jasper & Ann Henry, Aug. 23, 1865.
Sublett, Jim & Susan Brown, Aug. 18, 1865.
Sublett, John & Miss Lucy McAdoo, Aug. 20, 1865.
Sublett, Sam & Marg. Rucker, Aug. 27, 1865.
Suggs, Isham & Amanda Turrentine, Aug. 26, 1865.
Sullivan, Calvin & Anna Weedon, Jan. 10, 1865.
Sullivan, Peter & Nancy Ann Sullivan, Sept. 5, 1865.

RUTHERFORD COUNTY MARRIAGES

Sumner, Lewis & Cloie Kirk, Aug. 26, 1865.
Suttle, Elbert & Priscilla Smith, Sept. 2, 1865.
Sutton, John & Charlott Henderson, Aug. 28, 1865.
Swift, John & Eliz. Blackman, Dec. 9, 1865.
Swink, Thomas & Lucinda Mullen, Mar. 3, 1865.
Sykes, Joseph & Hannah Espy, Sept. 16, 1865.
Talley, John & Ann Tally, Aug. 21, 1865.
Talley, Rufus & Marg. Barkley, Aug. 26, 1865.
Talley, Will & Emma McKnight, Aug. 24, 1865.
Tankert, Harbet & Lucy Richards, Mar. 8, 1865.
Taylor, E. E. & Susana Hendrix, Oct. 15, 1865.
Taylor, J. W. & R. A. Anderson N.S., May 22, 1865.
Taylor, Sam & Henryetta Taylor, Aug. 19, 1865.
Taylor, Tom & Lurenia Taylor (Lorena), Aug. 19, 1865.
Thomas, C. E. & Mary A. Maberry, July 3, 1865.
Thomas, Charles A. & Eliza R. Williams, Dec. 18, 1865.
Thomas, Harchas & Jinnie Thomas, Sept. 2, 1865.
Thomas, Henry & Lavinia Thomas, Sept. 12, 1865.
Thomas, Joe & Martha Nelson, Aug. 12, 1865.
Thomas, John & Judy Williamson, Sept. 4, 1865.
Thompson, Amanuel & Caroline Lipscomb, Aug. 22, 1865.
Thompson, Arehy & Anelza Lyon N.S., Oct. 30, 1865.
Thompson, Bill & Milly Thompson, Aug. 24, 1865.
Thompson, Burton & Vilet Thompson, Aug. 19, 1865.
Thompson, Cal & Peggy Thompson, Aug. 23, 1865.
Thompson, Granklin & Miss Lockey Tarpley, Oct. 18, 1865.
Thompson, Jessee & Eliza Bone, Aug. 20, 1865.
Thompson, Jim & Mira Baird, Aug. 24, 1865.
Thompson, John & Mary Holdin, Aug. 19, 1865.
Thompson, John S. & Mary I. Kerr, Dec. 7, 1865.
Thompson, Ples & Martha Letherman, Aug. 27, 1865.
Thompson, Sam & Milly Spence N.S., Aug. 19, 1865.
Thompson, Sam & Rachel Thompson, Sept. 9, 1865.
Throer, Harry & Adeline Swense, Aug. 28, 1865.
Tilghman, Dasey & Ann Bell N.S., Sept. 2, 1865.
Tillman, Henry & Angeline Tillman N.S., Aug. 19, 1865.
Tillman, Jim & Patience Rooker, Sept. 2, 1865.
Tilman, James & Cely Tilman, Aug. 20, 1865.
Todd, Henry & Mariah Goodwin, July 25, 1865.
Todd, Thomas A. & Susan M. Freeman, July 13, 1865.
Tompkins, Henry & Lavinia Tompkins, Aug. 21, 1865.
Tompkins, Robert & Martha Windrow, Aug. 26, 1865.
Toombs, John & Harriet Toombs, Aug. 28, 1865.
Townsend, Abram & Liza Townsend, Aug. 26, 1865.
Traylor, Berry & Minerva Jobe, Aug. 26, 1865.
Trigg, Weldon & Evelina Davis, Sept. 8, 1865.
Trimble, Amanuel & Lucretia Alexander, Sept. 2, 1865.
Trimble, Geo. & Mary McKnight, Aug. 22, 1865.
Trimble, Lewis & Nelly Lorance N.S., Aug. 10, 1865.
Trimble, Russell & Isabella Trimble, Oct. 10, 1865.
Tucker, Fred & Eliza Tucker, Aug. 27, 1865.
Tucker, Tobe & Phillis Davis, Nov. 13, 1865.
Tucker, Warrick & Jennet Tucker, Oct. 14, 1865.
    (license 1866).

RUTHERFORD COUNTY MARRIAGES

Tucker, Washington & Jane Tucker, Aug. 26, 1865.
Tucker, Wm. B. & Miss Mattie J. Hobbs, Nov. 1, 1865.
Tucker, Wm. & Syrena Tucker N.S., Nov. 14, 1865.
Tucker, Willis & Sarah Tucker, Nov. 12, 1865.
Tune, D. N. & Martha Cotten (Daniel), Nov. 14, 1865.
Turner, Aaron & Narcissa Turner, Aug. 26, 1865.
Turner, Bob & Minty Turner, Sept. 17, 1865.
Turner, John & Jane Snell, Aug. 24, 1865.
Turner, Milton & Eliz. Ledbetter, Aug. 19, 1865.
Turner, Moses & Eliza Winfree N.S., Aug. 19, 1865.
Turner, Tom & America Turner, Aug. 27, 1865.
Upcher, Daniel & Lucinda Upcher N.S., Oct. 7, 1865.
Ustus, Charles & Caroline Ustus, Aug. 23, 1865.
Van Buren, Martin & Amanda Fite, Aug. 31, 1865.
Vaughan, Anderson M. & Martha J. Webb, Dec. 22, 1865.
Vaughan, Claiborne & Fanny Vaughan, Sept. 10, 1865.
Vaughan, Thomas & Ellen Clay, Mar. 31, 1865.
Vernon, Harrison & Melvina Roberts, Oct. 5, 1865.
Vernon, Jack & Julia Ann Jones, Sept. 3, 1865.
Vernon, Samuel & Martha Jones, Aug. 29, 1865.
Wade, Alexander & Ellen Black, Aug. 20, 1865.
Wade, Archie & Betsy Wade, Aug. 20, 1865.
Wade, Charles & Mary Wade N.S., Aug. 26, 1865.
Wade, Caliborn & Mary Wade, Aug. 26, 1865.
Wade, Dick & Martha Wade, Sept. 16, 1865.
Wade, Dick & Mary Wade, Aug. 26, 1865.
Wade, Drew & Eliz. Richardson, Sept. 2, 1865.
Wade, Green & Eliz. Lindsley, Sept. 9, 1865.
Wade, Hal & Rose Ann Wade, Oct. 17, 1865.
Wade, Henry & Mary Black, Aug. 26, 1865.
Wade, Jerry & Nancy Wade, Aug. 26, 1865.
Wade, John & Evelin Wade, Sept. 9, 1865.
Wade, John & Martha Anderson, Aug. 17, 1865.
Wade, John & Sarah Wade, Sept. 9, 1865.
Wade, Joshua & Sarah Wade, Aug. 27, 1865.
Wade, Littleton & Eliz. Wade, Sept. 10, 1865.
Wade, Littleton & Lavinia Moore, Aug. 26, 1865.
Wade, Moses & Eliz. Wade, Dec. 10, 1865.
Wade, Phil & Marg. Wade, Aug. 30, 1865.
Wade, Philip & Milly Wade, Aug. 26, 1865.
Wade, Sam & Eliza Miller, Sept. 10, 1865.
Wade, Sam & Mariah Wade, Sept. 23, 1865.
Wade, Sam & Mary Wade, Aug. 24, 1865.
Wade, Spencer & Sally Wade, Oct. 28, 1865.
Wade, Thomas J. & Olivia A. Jarrett, Dec. 14, 1865.
Wade, Titus & Harriet Snell N.S., Aug. 15, 1865.
Wade, Washington & Violet Anderson N.S., Sept. 13, 1865.
Wade, Wat & Sallie Wade, Aug. 26, 1865.
Wadley, Isaac & Julia Wadley N.S., Aug. 18, 1865.
Walden, Gran & Sarah Sikes, Sept. 2, 1865.
Walden, Henry & Harriet Smith, Dec. 2, 1865.
Walden, Sam & Mary Jane Sikes, Sept. 2, 1865.
Walker, George & Mary Goodwin, Nov. 26, 1865.
Walker, Moses & Harriett Baker, Aug. 29, 1865.
Walker, Wm. & Tabitha Beasley, Aug. 19, 1865.

Wallace, Geo. W. & Salley A. Powel, Aug. 27, 1865.
Waller, Benj. & Maria Clayton, Sept. 24, 1865.
Wammuck, James & Liddy Tolds, Aug. 24, 1865.
Ward, Albert & Celia Keeble, Sept. 10, 1865.
Ward, Albert & Lavinia Bell, Sept. 2, 1865.
Ward, F. C. & Eliz. Dalton, Dec. 13, 1865.
Ward, Daniel & Cilla Ward, Sept. 10, 1865.
Ward, George & Laura Brooks, Aug. 24, 1865.
Ward, James B. & Susan Ann Arnold, Aug. 5, 1865.
Ward, John & Rhody Ann Lillard, Aug. 24, 1865.
Ward, Julius & Betsy Ward, Oct. 14, 1865.
Ward, Louis (Lewis) & Caley (Katey) Ward, Aug. 19, 1865.
Warren, Abram & Dilley Carney N.S., Aug. 19, 1865.
Washington, David & Isabella Smith, Sept. 2, 1865.
Washington, George & Martha Washington, Sept. 3, 1865.
Washington, George & Melinda Buchanan, Sept. 10, 1865.
Washington, Randolph & Eliza Jinkins, Aug. 26, 1865.
Washington, Sam & Hannah Washington, Aug. 26, 1865.
Waterhouse, Alex & Sarah Waterhouse N.S., Nov. 22, 1865.
Waters, Prince & Arpha Waters, Aug. 21, 1865.
Watkins, Charles & Emily Patton, Aug. 28, 1865.
Watkins, Henry & Salley Lindsey, Sept. 9, 1865.
Watkins, Richard & Amy Watkins, Aug. 26, 1865.
Watson, Davis & Catharine Burleson N.S., Aug. --, 1865.
   (bride died).
Watson, George & Sallie Wade, Aug. 14, 1865.
Watson, John & Clara Anderson, Sept. 20, 1865.
Watterson, Nelson & Susan Norman, Sept. 19, 1865.
Weakley, Albert & Caroline Goodwin, Nov. 12, 1865.
Weakley, Albert & Sallie Buchanan, Oct. 4, 1865.
Weakley, Anderson & Tabby Furgeson, Sept. 3, 1865.
Weakley, Daniel & Eliza Russworm, Aug. 26, 1865.
Weakley, Harvey & Bell Carter N.S., Sept. 20, 1865.
Weakley, Horace & Martha White, Nov. 12, 1865.
Weakley, Messech & Ruth Woods, Dec. 31, 1865.
Weakly, Billy & Louisa Weakly, Sept. 9, 1865.
Weakly, Bob & Amanda Walker, Jan. 6, 1865.
Weakly, Edm. & Batsy Gooch, Sept. 9, 1865.
Weakly, Garland & Nancy Weakly, Sept. 9, 1865.
Weakly, Henry & Dorcas Weakly, Oct. 22, 1865.
Weakly, Joe & Jane Furgeson, Sept. 3, 1865.
Weakly, Lewis & Harriet Weakly, Sept. 9, 1865.
Weakly, Sam & Betty Muse, Oct. 22, 1865.
Weakly, Wm. & Betsy Weakly, Oct. 1, 1865.
Weaver, Mat & Hannah Weaver, Aug. 27, 1865.
Webb, Geo. & Clarissa Webb, Sept. 6, 1865.
Webb, Geo. & Emiline Drake, Aug. 19, 1865.
Webb, Levi & Milly Woods, Aug. 16, 1865.
Webb, Samuel & Harriet McLean, Aug. 23, 1865.
Webster, Alexander & Mariah Golden, Apr. 6, 1865.
Webster, Wesley & Chaney House, Oct. 28, 1865.
Welch, Jeptha F. & Martha L. Todd, Aug. 29, 1865.
Welch, Squire & Maria Smith, Oct. 23, 1865.
Welkerson, Griffin & Levanna Maney N.S., Oct. 14, 1865.

Welkerson, Travis & Levina Ransom, Oct. 16, 1865.
Wendel, Charles & Eliz. Bivins (Burrus)?, Aug. 19, 1865.
Wendell, Andy & Nancy Morton N.S., May 6, 1865.
Wendell, Davy & Jane Ransom, Aug. 26, 1865.
White, Abe & Martha Buchanan, Oct. 5, 1865.
White, Ben & Sarah White N.S., Aug. 17, 1865.
White, Dick & Alice White, Aug. 26, 1865.
White, Edward S. & Emma M. Spence, Dec. 9, 1865.
White, Essex & Rose White N.S., Aug. 26, 1865.
White, Gilbert & Mariah Bracken, Aug. 29, 1865.
White, Gilbert & Paralee Lytle, Aug. 29, 1865.
White, Henry & Mira Davis, Sept. 9, 1865.
White, Isaac & Victoria Bridges, Nov. 25, 1865.
White, Joe & Emiline Baker, Oct. 8, 1865.
White, John & Eliza Goodwin, Oct. 8, 1865.
White, Lewis & Lorenia Jarmon, Oct. 21, 1865.
White, Peyton & Cornelia Henderson N.S., Aug. 26, 1865.
White, R. H. & Nannie R. James, Aug. 8, 1865.
White, Richard & Julia A. West, Dec. 22, 1865.
White, Spencer & Rose Harris, Sept. 11, 1865.
White, Wadley & Oney Johns N.S., Sept. 2, 1865.
White, Wm. & Jane White, Sept. 4, 1865.
Whitson, Daniel & America Benson, Aug. 12, 1865.
Wiggs, Daniel P. & Mary J. Nevins, N.S., Sept. 28, 1865.
Wilkinson, Ceazer & Minerva Patillo, Sept. 4, 1865.
Wilkinson, Jessee & Delia Wilkinson N.S., Aug. 19, 1865.
Wilkinson, Sam & Carolin Black, Sept. 1, 1865.
Wilkinson, W. A. & Nanie L. Black, Dec. 6, 1865.
Williams, Andrew & Levina Kirk, Mar. 16, 1865.
Williams, Austin & Martha Merton, Dec. 2, 1865.
Williams, C. H. & Miss A. Newsom, June 21, 1865.
Williams, Daniel & Bell Kelley, Aug. 18, 1865.
Williams, David & Demerris Henderson, Nov. 17, 1865.
Williams, Edmund & Malenda McElroy N.S., Jan. 11, 1865.
Williams, Gilbert & Eveline Vaulx N.S., Aug. 23, 1865.
Williams, Harry & Jane Reed, Sept. 19, 1865.
Williams, John & Eliz. Williams N.S., Nov. 27, 1865.
Williams, John N. & Nancy E. Baily, June 20, 1865.
Williams, John Watson & Ann Buckett, Sept. 13, 1865.
Williams, Nelson & Flora Neal N.S., May 21, 1865.
Williams, Philip & Nancy McGill N.S., Aug. 26, 1865.
Williams, Richard & Lucy Quarles (Watkins?), Dec. 29,
  1865.
Williams, S. J. & Martha J. Nevins N.S., Nov. 4, 1865.
Williams, Thomas G. & Eliz. M. Jordan, May 23, 1865.
Williamson, Albert & Betsy Williamson, Sept. 3, 1865.
Williamson, James & Sally Jones N.S., Aug. 28, 1865.
Williamson, John A. & Eliz. Farris N.S., Nov. 27, 1865.
Willis, Henderson & Rhoda Willis, Aug. 5, 1865.
Wills, Benj. & Rachel Jackson, Aug. 26, 1865.
Wilman, Westly & Susan Miller, May 18, 1865.
Wilson, American & Cherokee Wilson, Nov. 16, 1865.
Wilson, Ben & Malinda Davis N.S., Dec. 23, 1865.
Wilson, Thomas & Catherine Archias, Sept. 22, 1865.

Windrow, Nelson & Matilda Collier, Dec. 30, 1865.
Winrow, Geo. & Vilet Moore, Aug. 31, 1865.
Winrow, Wyatt & Harriet Thomas, Sept. 17, 1865.
Winsett, Billy & Dilcey Marshall, Aug. 9, 1865.
Winsett, Jack & Nancy Winsett N.S., Aug. 28, 1865.
Winston, Andy & Betsy Nisbett, Aug. 15, 1865.
Winston, Isaac & Lucinda Jaratt, Aug. 19, 1865.
Winston, Thompson & Martha Black, Aug. 25, 1865.
Woldridge, Nelson & Rachel Woldridge, Aug. 16, 1865.
Wood, Sam & Harriet Floyd, Aug. 19, 1865.
Woodrough, John & Susan J. Miller, Jan. 7, 1865.
Woodruff, Hall & Lucy Woodruff, Apr. 28, 1865.
Woods, Edm. & Jane Woods, Aug. 26, 1865.
Woods, Gabriel & Aggie Woods, Aug. 22, 1865.
Woods, Jasper N. & Mary Johnson, Mar. 1, 1865.
Woods, Joseph & Jane Smith, Aug. 23, 1865.
Woods, Ned & Caroline Woods, Aug. 27. 1865.
Woods, Peyton & Susan Woods, Aug. 23, 1865.
Woods, Russell & Lucy Woods, Aug. 26, 1865.
Woods, Wesley & Marg. Woods, Aug. 17, 1865.
Woods, Wm. & Maria Anderson, Sept. 4, 1865.
Woodson, Albert & Mariah Jarratt N.S., Aug. 12, 1865.
Wooten, B. P. & Julia Lawrence, Dec. 11, 1865.
Wooten, Carney H. & Nancy C. Reed, Oct. 24, 1865.
Wooten, Isaac & Phillis Prewitt, Aug. 9, 1865.
Wooten, Wm. N. & Susan Nesbitt, Dec. 15, 1865.
Wormack, Monroe & Harriet Wormack, Aug. 30, 1865.
Wrather, Ned & Maria Wrather, Aug. 29, 1865.
Wright, Alfred & Martha A. Wright, Aug. 23, 1865.
Wright, Allen & Matilda Wright N.S., Aug. 18, 1865.
Wright, B. & Amanda McKnight, Dec. 14, 1865.
Wright, Isaac & Eliza Wright, Dec. 2, 1865.
Wright, James & Mary Ryan, Dec. 31, 1865.
Wright, John & Milly Overall, Aug. 23, 1865.
Wright, Lewis & America Jetton, Dec. 31, 1865.
Wright, Lewis & Lucretia Wright, Aug. 23, 1865.
Wright, Simon & Sarah Fulks, Aug. 23, 1865.
Yeargan, Ferrill & Milly McClaren, Sept. 3, 1865.
Yeargan, Jim & Caroline Rowlett, Aug. 3, 1865.
York, Geo. & Dianna Douglass, Aug. 19, 1865.
York, Ralph & Harriett Smiley, Aug. 26, 1865.
York, Tom & Ann Bright, Aug. 26, 1865.
York, Tom & Malinda Simpson, Aug. 27, 1865.
Young, Cardy & Fanny Harris N.S., Oct. 23, 1865.
Youngblood, Syrus & Jane Newman N.S., Aug. 19, 1865.
Zumbro, W. F. & Miss L. D. Fuquay, Dec. 25, 1865.

1866

Abernathy, Frank & Martha Scruggs, June 10, 1866.
Adams, James & Sue Hubbard, Mar. 2, 1866.
Adoc, John E. & Kate Newman W., June 11, 1866.
Adoway, Andrew & Sally Davis, Oct. 27, 1866.
Alexander, Isaac & Louisa King, Mar. 3, 1866.

Alexander, J. T. & Sally B. White, Dec. 24, 1866.
Alexander, Nathan & Sarah Rucker, Dec. 26, 1866.
Alexander, W. H. & Louisa McDaniel, Dec. 17, 1866.
Alford, Wm. & Eliza Corns, Mar. 8, 1866.
Allen, Benjamin & Frances Fisher N.S., Nov. 17, 1866.
Allen, Nathan & Delany Rucker, Sept. 16, 1866.
Allen, Thomas & Alsy Searcy, Nov. 29, 1866.
Allen, Thomas D. & Celia Prater, Oct. 7, 1866.
Alsup, Riley & Eliza Pearce, June 30, 1866.
Anderson, Ben & Ellen Patterson (James Henry?) N.S.,
    Feb. 17, 1866.
Anderson, Burton & Susan Fletcher, Feb. 9, 1866.
Anderson, David & Tinny Burlerson, Aug. 11, 1866.
Anderson, Moses & Charlotte Summers, Mar. 24, 1866.
Anderson, Wm. & Harriet Scales, Nov. 15, 1866.
Arnhart, Pleasant & Lavina Daniel, Sept. 28, 1866.
Arnold, Alexander & Martha Arnold, Jan. 1, 1866.
Augustus, Aaron & Malina A. Smith N.S., Feb. 11, 1866.
Avaritt, Albert & Bettie Webb, Jan. 27, 1866.
Averette, Freeman & Fanny Williams, Nov. 1, 1866.
Banks, James & Margaret Weakley, June 30, 1866.
Barns, T. P. & Eliz. S. Hodge, Jan. 21, 1866.
Basman, John & Adelaide Lytle N.S., Sept. 1, 1866.
Bass, James & Virginia Solomon, June 21, 1866.
Batey, Benj. & Kitty Miller, Mar. 1, 1866.
Batey, Isaiah & Lov Smith, Feb. 3, 1866.
Battle, Frank & Bettie House, Jan. 1, 1866.
Batton, Lewis & Catherine Lowe, Apr. 21, 1866.
Beasley, John & Mattie A. Jones, Dec. 17, 1866.
Beaty, Meredith & Lucindy Briley N.S., Aug. 6, 1866.
Becton, Benj. M. & Mary McGill, Aug. 6, 1866.
Bell, Solomon & Marg. Tilmon, Dec. 26, 1866.
Bennefield, Henry & Julia Harris, Jan. 29, 1866.
Bennett S. B. & Mary E. Forbs, Sept. 7, 1866.
Benson, George W. & Matilda Jones, Jan. 17, 1866.
Berner, Nathan & Sarah Butler, Dec. 28, 1866.
Betty, Edmond & Caroline Smith, Sept. 22, 1866.
Binns, John E. & Lou Wood, Sept. 13, 1866.
Bivins, Burt & Jenny Hames, Mar. 22, 1866.
Black, Reuben & Cynthia Black, Mar. 16, 1866.
Blackman, Alfred & Mary A. Bass, Dec. 11, 1866.
Blair, Isaac & Charlotte Snell N.S., Feb. 16, 1866.
Bolds, Jeffrey & W. Bolds, Feb. 21, 1866.
Bonds, Calvin & Clacy Irby N.S., Dec. 8, 1866.
Bonner, Bill & Malinda Mitchell, June 9, 1866.
Bowling, Jessee S. & Edy E. Douglass, Jaq. 4, 1866.
Bowman, Benj. & Sallie D. Petty, Dec. 24, 1866.
Bowman, Robert & Judith B. Daniel, Feb. 14, 1866.
Bracken, Ephraim & Mariah Randal, Aug. 4, 1866.
Bradford, Henry & Caroline Henderson, Oct. 15, 1866.
Brady, John & Louiza Bane, May 20, 1866.
Brady, Thomas W. & Rebecca Howland, June 18, 1866.
Brandon, Andrew J. & Melissa Lowe, Jan. 25, 1866.
Brandon, Noah A. & Martha F. Holden, Nov. 15, 1866.

RUTHERFORD COUNTY MARRIAGES

Brewster, John W. & Anna Reed, July 11, 1866.
Bridges, Henry & Nancy N. M. B. Smith, Mar. 1, 1866.
Bridges, Henry & Peggy Peebles, Sept. 15, 1866.
Brinklye, John & Louisa Rogers, Nov. 22, 1866.
Brooks, Albert & Malissa Wade, Oct. 27, 1866.
Brooks, Joseph S. & E. E. Lasiter, Dec. 18, 1866.
Brooks, Joseph F., Jr. & Hester A. G. Hendrix, Feb. 16, 1866.
Brown, D. S. & Bell V. Owens, Oct. 28. 1866.
Brown, James A. & Mary Ann Traysull, Dec. 11, 1866.
Brown, John & Jane Brown, June 6, 1866.
Brown, Jordan & Francis Ross, Jan. 6, 1866.
Brown, Lewis & Luvenia Bass, Dec. 29, 1866.
Brown, Wm. & Syliva Baugh, Oct. 6, 1866.
Bumpas, Henry H. & Josephine Smith, Nov. 28, 1866.
Burleson, Ben & Hariette Davis, Oct. 27, 1866.
Burnitt, Henry J. & Louise J. Haynes, Aug. 9, 1866.
Burns, Henry & Mar. Woods, Sept. 20, 1866.
Burrus, Billy & Sarah McGregor, Apr. 9, 1866.
Burton, D. W. & Sarah Eliz. Philpot, Dec. 20, 1866.
Butler, Henry & Rutha Woods, Dec. 27, 1866.
Butler, John & Mary Beasley, Nov. 27, 1866.
Byers, Henry & Margarett Woods, Sept. 29, 1866.
Bryant, John A. & M. A. E. Woods, Nov. 27, 1866.
Campbell, John & Narcissa Neal, Feb. 23, 1866.
Cantral, John & Louisa Gilliam, Feb. 10, 1866.
Capland, Joseph & Tempy Jordan, Oct. 13, 1866.
Carlton, Wm. J. & Nannie V. Williamson, Dec. 19, 1866.
Carmack, David & Ann Coffee, Apr. 29, 1866.
Carneghan, J. M. & Sue A. Lyons, May 18, 1866.
Carr, McLin & Sarah Scott, May 20, 1866.
Carroll, Charles & Rebecca Hoggett, Nov. 24, 1866.
Carter, John & Malinda Carter, Mar. 2, 1866.
Cates, Joe & Sarah Burks, Sept. 29, 1866.
Cathey, John N. & Mary Hoover N.S., Apr. 5, 1866.
Cavanaugh, James & Mary Malinda Bruce N.S., Sept. 11, 1866.
Chambers, J. M. & Nannie Gregory N.S., Dec. 24, 1866.
Childress, Andrew & Sarah Brown, Jan. 20, 1866.
Childress, Carroll & Mary Fletcher, Dec. 13, 1866.
Childress, Eli & Rachel Johnson N.S., May 10, 1866.
Childress, Henry & Adaline Mathews N.S., Oct. 13, 1866.
Childress, Lysander & Keton Childress N.S., May 5, 1866.
Christenberry, Silas & Malinda R. Manly, July 30, 1866.
Clayton, Wm. & Evy Bedford, Sept. 15, 1866.
Clements, R. P. & S. H. E. Wood, Nov. 27, 1866.
Coleman, Robert B. & Mary L. Coleman, Nov. 7, 1866.
Comer, Jim & Martha Hopkins, Jan. 21, 1866.
Compton, Richard H. & Emma H. Vaught (Compton?), Dec. 3, 1866.
Cooper, James & Elvira Cooper, May 11, 1866.
Cooper, John & Susan Wortham, Sept. 9, 1866.
Cooper, M. T. & L. A. R. Ransom N.S., Nov. 7, 1866.
Corbin, H. B. & Lilly E. Brown, Dec. 18, 1866.

Cothran, A. H. & Sallie Bodily (Barnett?), Feb. 25, 1866.
Couch, Thomas J. & Anna Adcock, Aug. 10, 1866.
Covington, L. A. & Deanna Smotherman, Apr. 17, 1866.
Covington, Thomas & Abedia Hancock, Nov. 5, 1866.
Cowan, Joseph & Celia Warren, June 23, 1866.
Cox, Michael & Julia Smith, Mar. 10, 1866.
Craner, Moses & Mary A. Furgason, Oct. 23, 1866.
Critts, Sebastian & Francis Mullins, Sept. 24, 1866.
Crockett, Calvin & Frusanna House, Feb. 25, 1866.
Crockett, Nathan & Nancy Floyd, June 11, 1866.
Crouse, Joseph L. & Mary Jane Bruch, Dec. 4, 1866.
Crump, M. R. R. M. & Addie Rankin N.S., May 15, 1866.
Cunningham, Samuel & Isabella Bass, Apr. 20, 1866.
Dallis, Geo. M. & Eliza Jane Sanderson, Dec. 27, 1866.
Daniel, Geo. & Emaline Hannah, Jan. 6, 1866.
Danile, John & Adelphia Campbell, June 23, 1866.
Davenport, Isaac & Louisa Philips, July 15, 1866.
Davis, D. C. & E. L. Palmore, Sept. 6, 1866.
Davis, Henry & Emily Davis, Sept. 30, 1866.
Davis, John A. & Sophronia Smith, July 22, 1866.
Davis, Robert J. & Adeline Wade, Dec. 3, 1866.
Dickey, W. P. & Sarah E. Holowell, Jan. 4, 1866.
Dickson, Geo. & Viney Jacobs, Jan. 19, 1866.
Dill, James & Sarah A. Juell, Jan. 18, 1866.
Dillon, R. J. & A. ''. Thompson, Nov. 14, 1866.
Doke, T. J. & E. H. Lyon, Feb. 22, 1866.
Douglass, W. T. & Mary A. Vaughan, June 25, 1866.
Douglas, Wm. & Mary Moore, Nov. 12, 1866.
Dowell, Presly & Rebecca Crutchfield, Dec. 22, 1866.
Drake, Willis & Nancy Williams, Nov. 15, 1866.
Dunaway, D. I. & Frances I. Barr, Jan. 24, 1866.
Duncan, Alfred H. & Amanda J. Alexander N.S., June 1, 1866.
Dunkin, Charles & Mary Scruggs, Nov. 1, 1866.
Dunn, Mathew & Sarah A. Brown, Feb. 4, 1866.
Dyer, B. W. & Miss R. D. Sawyers, Nov. 20, 1866.
Ealon, Samuel & Laura Bass, Dec. 7, 1866.
Early, Jessee & Medoria O. Bivins, Apr. 25, 1866.
Edmondson, John James & Sarah J. Burns, May 2, 1866.
Elder, Benj. A. & Mary Hegdon, Nov. 20, 1866.
Elmore, Lucian C. & Louisa A. Pope N.S., Dec. 17, 1866.
Evans, Isaham & Mary Avant, Mar. 17, 1866.
Ferrill, James R. & Luvenia McDaniel, Dec. 13, 1866.
Finney, Milton & Mariah Goodwin, Mar. 11, 1866.
Fips, Edmond & Milly Mason N.S., Apr. 21, 1866.
Fisher, Isaac & Ellen Childress, Dec. 15, 1866.
Fleming, Joseph & Dicy Pearson, Apr. 17, 1866.
Flemister, Mack & Meseah Gooch, Mar. 10, 1866.
Fletcher, Andrew J. to Florence Ewing, Oct. 2, 1866.
Flutral, Reubin & Eliza Ralston, Mar. 26, 1866.
Foot, Peter & Louisa Foot, June 20, 1866.
Fortner, Joshua & Celia Fortner, Dec. 28, 1866.
Foster, Geo. & Mary Ann Moseley, Mar. 17, 1866.

Fowler, Wm. R. & Sue Smith, Sept. 6, 1866.
Fox, John E. & Susan Prater, Aug. 22, 1866.
Fox, John M. & Harriet A. Dunn, Jan. 14, 1866.
Francis, John & Elementine Thomas, Feb. 27, 1866.
Franklin, Nathan & Tennessee Kelly, Dec. 27, 1866.
Franklin, Thomas & Sarah J. Coleman N.S., Mar. 12, 1866.
Frizell, H. H. & Sarah C. Taylor, Dec. 11, 1866.
Freeman, Mayfield & Malinda Haynes, July 11, 1866.
Fugett, Benj. & C. G. White, Mar. 6, 1866.
Garrett, Thomas W. & Eleanor H. Jackson, Jan. 25, 1866.
Garrison, Jacob & Sarah Snow N.S., Feb. 13, 1866.
Gifford, Joseph G. & Lockey W. Buffer, Mar. 6, 1866.
Gilly, J. A. & N. J. McCrary, May 8, 1866.
Gilmon, Herbert & Martha N. McElroy, Dec. 13, 1866.
Glover, Joe & Sarah Toney, Mar. 27, 1866. (not issued)
Gooch, Elis & Martha A. Ross, Apr. 28, 1866.
Goodman, Jack & Edith Gooch, Oct. 1, 1866.
Gordan, Samuel & Eliza Vaughan, Mar. 17, 1866.
Goss, John W. & Mary R. Martin, July 4, 1866.
Gosset, Lavander & Caroline Morgan, Dec. 15, 1866.
Graham, John L. & Martha I. Crouse, Dec. 11, 1866.
Graham, Wm. & Josephine Smith, Mar. 24, 1866.
Griggs, Fountain & Martha J. Winfrey, July 1, 1866.
Gum, Wilson A. & Martha A. Bowman, Feb. 15, 1866.
Hackett, Taylor & Julia Puckett, May 21, 1866.
Hadley, Isaac & Delly Warson, Aug. 12, 1866.
Hale, T. P. & E. A. Kelton, Nov. 13, 1866.
Haley, J. W. & Eliz. Colman, Jan. 23, 1866.
Hall, Bob & Betsy Jones, Oct. 24, 1866.
Hall, Drury & July Jones N.S., Apr. 11, 1866.
Hall, John & Catharine Brown, Dec. 30, 1866.
Hall, Joseph & Frances Jones, Oct. 14, 1866.
Hallyburton, D. F. & Mary A. Batey, Jan. 6, 1866.
Hallyburton, Milton & Mary Chaffin, Jan. 28, 1866.
Hamilton, Henry & Agness Lock N.S., Feb. 9, 1866.
Hamilton, Isaac & Lucy J. Smith, July 13, 1866.
Hamilton, Thomas N. & Bettie Woods, June 19, 1866.
Hammond, H. C. & Mary W. Wisner, Nov. 8, 1866.
Harding, Alfred & Maria Barkley, Jan. 26, 1866.
Harding, George & Millie Sneed, Dec. 15, 1866.
Harding, Samuel & Sally Harding, Dec. 29, 1866.
Harpool, Andrew J. & Caroline Lockard, Aug. 30, 1866.
Harris, John C., Jr. & Anna M. Breen, Dec. 6, 1866.
Harris, Marian & Kitty Murfree, Dec. 21, 1866.
Harrison, Neale & Sarah Crutchfield, Oct. 7, 1866.
Hawkins, Henry & Matilda Johnson, May 27, 1866.
Haynes, Geo. & Sarah Sikens, Jan. 18, 1866.
Haynes, Henry & Malinda Furgason, July 28, 1866.
Haynes, Silas & Mary Murray, Sept. 16, 1866.
Haynes, Zachary & Eliz. F. Crouse N.S., Feb. 14, 1866.
Hays, John P. & Eliz. Yates, July 2, 1866.
Headley, John W. & Miss Mary P. S. Overall, Dec. 18, 1866.
Heath, Robert & Matilda A. Holden, June 18, 1866.
Hedgpeth, Elisha & Mary E. McPeak, Mar. 24, 1866.

Helton, A. P. & Nancy L. Jamison, Feb. 6, 1866.
Henderson, Nelson & Julia Ward, Jan. 1, 1866.
Henderson, R. K. & Mollie Young, Dec. 19, 1866.
Hendrix, Jack & Martha Farris, July 14, 1866.
Henry, B. W. & Mary Ann Mathews, Oct. 28, 1866.
Hibits, Ira & Jane Cook, May 12, 1866.
Hight, Henry & Florinda Lowery, Aug. 8, 1866.
Hill, Henry H. & Sallie L. Mabry, Sept. 6, 1866.
Hoggett, Jacob & Dorcas Hoggett, Dec. 29, 1866.
Hoggett, Rodney & Mary King, Dec. 1, 1866.
Hoggett, Umphrey & Anna Evans, Sept. 19, 1866.
Hollowell, Ed & Martha Rankin, Dec. 31, 1866.
Hollowell, James P. & Allzaera Jarratt N.S., Dec. 4,
    1866.
Holmes, Joseph & Lititha Winsett, Jan. 26, 1866.
Honeycutt, James & Mary Pearson, Mar. 13, 1866.
Hooker, James & Louvenia King N.S., Feb. 10, 1866.
Hoover, B. S. & Mary F. Herrod, Feb. 23, 1866.
Hoover, Filmore & Eliz. Finey, Mar. 12, 1866.
Hoover, Geo. & Leah Hoover, Mar. 19, 1866.
Hopkins, Samuel & Jane Leach, Mar. 18, 1866.
Hopkins, W. H. & Lavenia Dill, Jan. 18, 1866.
Horton, John & Harriet Taylor, July 15, 1866.
House, Henry & Sally Spann, DEc. 2, 1866.
House, Wesley & Martha House N.S., June 16, 1866.
Howard, Giles & Ann Kimbro, Jan. 19, 1866.
Howell, A. W. & Mary M. Revis N.S., Dec. 11, 1866.
Hudson, Wm. & Mar. Joyner, Aug. 10, 1866.
Huff, Alexander & Catharine Smith, Oct. 21, 1866.
Hunt, Aupha & Louisa Baird, Dec. 29, 1866.
Ingleburger, Wm. & Louisa Williams, July 31, 1866.
Jackson, George & Eliza Butler, Feb. 12, 1866.
Jackson, Isaac & Eliza Howse, Oct. 21, 1866.
Jackson, James H. & Deratha F. Polk, May 19, 1866.
Jackson, Jim & Sally Garner, Feb. 10, 1866.
Jackson, Thomas J. & Martha E. Winsett, Aug. 31, 1866.
Jackson, Wm. & Sylva Jackson, Jan. 19, 1866.
Jacobs, James & Jane Kelly, July 5, 1866.
Jacobs, Pinkney & Emaline Kelly, Nov. 24, 1866.
Jacobs, W. P. & Bettie D. Lowe, Oct. 18, 1866.
James, W. F. & Miss H. C. Campbell, July 8, 1866.
Jamison, Mac & Lucy Johns, May 19, 1866.
Jarratt, Levi & Eliza Lester, Jan. 2, 1866.
Jarratt, Martin & Susan Jarratt, July 14, 1866.
Jarratt, Nelson & Harriet Keeble, Dec. 10, 1866.
Jenkins, Henry & Caroline Smith, Dec. 28, 1866.
Jenkins, James & Sarah Rouse, July 14, 1866.
Jennings, Lafayett & Sally Vaught, Dec. 20, 1866.
Jetton, Lafayett & Mariah McGill, Jan. 6, 1866.
Jinkins, Calvin & Lucy Smith, Dec. 28, 1866.
Jinkins, John & Caroline Newman, Aug. 29, 1866.
Johns, B. H. & Mary McCullough, Sept. 15, 1866.
Johns, Joseph & Laura Batey, Dec. 27, 1866.
Johnson, Hiram & Parny Baugh, Dec. 12, 1866.

Johnson, James & Harriet Miller, June 2, 1866.
Johnson, Samuel & Eliz. Richardson, Mar. 8, 1866.
Johnson, Sherrod & Tennessee Johnson, June 2, 1866.
Johnson, Snep & Francis McGill, Aug. 10, 1866.
Jones, Andrew & Eliz. Lee, Feb. 27, 1866.
Jones, B. A. & Mollie Sue Richardson, Jan. 19, 1866.
Jones, Granderson & Harriet Crouse, Dec. 31, 1866.
Jones, John C. & Nancy C. Smith, Jan. 11, 1866.
Jones, Lewis & Jane Haynes, Sept. 26, 1866.
Jones, Robert & Miss J. E. Hall, Jan. 20, 1866.
Jordan, Edward L. & Miss Sue A. Farris, Mar. 19, 1866.
Jordan, Garner M. Dr. & Miss Susan J. McClaren, Nov. 26, 1866.
Jordan, Jacob & Levina Gooch, Aug. 19, 1866.
Jordan, John A. & Martha Winsett, Jan. 8, 1866.
Jordan, Richard & Mary J. Haynes, Dec. 16, 1866.
Kerr, M. M. & Alice Jenkins, Dec. 20, 1866.
Kimmons, Isaac & Rachel A. Spence, July 14, 1866.
King, C. M. & Ann Wood, July 12, 1866.
King, Moses & Milly Mullins, Aug. 20, 1866.
Kirby, Henry R. & Mahala P. York, July 10, 1866.
Knott, John B. & Martha Russell, Apr. 18, 1866.
Knox, Peter & Rebecca Dillin, July 15, 1866.
Land, Philip & Angeline Hill, Mar. 20, 1866.
Langlin, Tom & Syntha Martin, July 4, 1866.
Lannom, Robert T. & Martha E. Barrett, Dec. 2, 1866.
Lannom, Thomas E. & Mary A. Welch, Feb. 20, 1866.
Lawrence, Wm. H. & Miss M. R. Stanfield, Jan. 18, 1866.
Leathers, J. T. H. & Miss M. C. Holden, Dec. 5, 1866.
Ledbetter, Jordan & Maggie James, Jan. 3, 1866.
Ledbetter, Wm. & Mary C. Lytle, Apr. 1, 1866.
Legg, Harrison & Jemima Legg, June 18, 1866.
Lewis, Wm. & Arena Miller, Nov. 24, 1866.
Lillard, Geo. & Milly Henderson, Dec. 25, 1866.
Lillard, John & Charlott Robertson, Dec. 31, 1866.
Lindsey, Elijah & Fanny Tucker, Mar. 11, 1866.
Long, Jessee & Susan Hines, June 18, 1866.
Lorance, Isaac & Frances Davis, May 24, 1866.
Love, Jeffery & Helly Stockard, Sept. 23, 1866.
Love, John & Betty Reed, Sept. 22, 1866.
Loyd, Jenry F. & Mollie J. Champion, Nov. 22, 1866.
Lynch, E. C. & Tabitha B. Jacobs, Aug. 3, 1866.
Lynn, Albert H. & T. E. Swane, Dec. 18, 1866.
Lyons, Geo. & Amanda Ovell, Sept. 23, 1866.
Lyons, Wm. & Margaret Ezell, Sept. 1, 1866.
Lytle, Albert & Henrietta Butler, May 27, 1866.
Lytle, Cezer & Cena Jones, May 6, 1866.
Mabes, Philip N. & Eliza J. Pearcy, July 31, 1866.
Major, John & Sarah E. Dobson, Apr. 1, 1866.
Majors, A. W. & Lavicy Miller, July 4, 1866.
Mallard, John & Julia A. Spence, Sept. 3, 1866.
Malone, Sanders & Amanda Malone, June 18, 1866.
Maney, Giles & Lizza James, July 25, 1866.
Maney, Riel & Sarah Humbel, Dec. 26, 1866.

Mankin, Welcome & Louisa Harrison, Oct. 9, 1866.
Marlin, Joseph & Martha J. Oakley, Dec. 15, 1866.
Marlin, Samuel & Mollie J. Gum, Sept. 11, 1866.
Marshall, Edmond & Amanda White, Dec. 27, 1866.
Martin, Ezekiel & Caty Carney, Dec. 26, 1866.
Martin, Joseph L. & Nora Hawkins, July 22, 1866.
Martin, Spencer & Adaline Ott, Dec. 26, 1866.
Martin, W. D. & Mary A. Baird, Nov. 28, 1866.
Mason, Luke & Margaret Mason, Feb. 4, 1866.
Mathews, James T. & Nancy A. Howell, Dec. 11, 1866.
Mathews, Samuel & Martha Lahue, Mar. 30, 1866.
Matlock, Julian J. & Miss Tennessee Nevins, Dec. 2, 1866.
May, G. W. & Margaret J. Edwards, July 13, 1866.
May, John C. & Amanda Shelton, Nov. 20, 1866.
Mayfield, Geo. M. & Susan Wetherford, Aug. 2, 1866.
Mayfield, J. S. & Mary E. Pinkard, Mar. 26, 1866.
Maxwell, R. D. & Mary A. Burkitt, Dec. 12, 1866.
Mazy, Joseph & Alibella Fields, Mar. 3, 1866.
Mercer, Wm. & Julia Slaughter, July 27, 1866.
Merrett, Charles & Harriett Hutchison, May 19, 1866.
Miles, Geo. & Caroline Wade, Oct. 27, 1866.
Miliner, Mike & Hannah Lindsey, Aug. 18, 1866.
Miller, Hannibal & Mary Moore, Jan. 30, 1866.
Miller, Thomas & Amanda Ward, Dec. 15, 1866.
Millhouse, Millman & Amanda Harris, Aug. 11, 1866.
Mitchell, Henry & Mary Ann Jordan, Dec. 30, 1866.
Mitchell, Littleton & Manerva Wilkerson, Dec. 27, 1866.
Moon, John & Polly Summers, Apr. 10, 1866.
Moore, Americus & Retha Smith, Aug. 11, 1866.
Moore, Jacob & Fanny McHenry, July 21, 1866.
Morgan, James & Sally Amos, June 16, 1866.
Morris, James H. & Mary E. Underwood, Jan. 10, 1866.
Morse, Henry & Fanny Lehue, Feb. 14, 1866.
Morton, George & Oney Warmoth, Feb. 3, 1866.
Mulky, Dr. Wm. L. & Geneveeve Smith, Apr. 28, 1866.
Mullins, J. V. & Kitturia Ann Cook, Sept. 18, 1866.
Munday, Wm. S. & Virginia James, Jan. 17, 1866.
Murfree, Felix & Dicy McClure, Nov. 1, 1866.
Murfree, James & America Hallyburton, Feb. 21, 1866.
Murfree, Stephen & Judy Ann Bowman, Dec. 27, 1866.
Murphey, Clay T. & Jane Sullivan, Jan. 7, 1866.
Murry, Nathan & Jane Murry, Apr. 1, 1866.
Muse, Howard & Cath. Peg, Jan. 6, 1866.
McAdoo, Albert & Fanny Dunaway, Jan. 8, 1866.
McDaniel, Nelson & Jane McDaniel, Oct. 20, 1866.
McDonnell, Geo. & Isabella Ward, Feb. 5, 1866.
McDowell, Richard & Fanny James, Dec. 27, 1866.
McGehe, Joseph & Martha Glass, May 20, 1866.
McGehe, Samuel & Eliza J. Purser, May 20, 1866.
McGill, A. M. & Eliz. Youree, June 2, 1866.
McGill, Ned & Louisa Lytle, Jan. 9, 1866.
McHugh, James & E. K. Winsett, July 16, 1866.
McKever, Robert & Milly Gregory, Apr. 14, 1866.
McKnight, F. A. & Isabella Caffy, Dec. 6, 1866.

McKnight, Thomas & Jane Parker, May 12, 1866.
McLaughlin, Henry & Harriett Edmondson, June 14, 1866.
McLean, Solomon & Myra Jackson, Aug. 12, 1866.
McLilland, Wm. N. & Betsy Vaulx, Nov. 17, 1866.
McMilon, John & Eliz. Robertson, Mar. 1, 1866.
McNamara, Edward W. & Kate M. Baker, Aug. 13, 1866.
McTaggart, Daniel & Maggie A. Beigle, June 4, 1866.
Neal, J. E. & Edna Mullins, Dec. 11, 1866.
Neal, Napoleon & Sarah F. Partee, Feb. 6, 1866.
Nelson, Allen & Rosabella Nelson, Nov. 15, 1866.
Nelson, Geo. & Nancy Lindsey, Aug. 10, 1866.
Nelson, Geo. & Nancy Todd, May 5, 1866.
Nelson, Logan & Hally Campbell, Oct. 9, 1866.
Nesbitt, Ephriam & Eliz. P. Hallyburton, June 26, 1866.
Noe, Aquilla & Martha J. Sanford, July 12, 1866.
Noland, John L. & Je. E. Rankin, Apr. 18, 1866.
Norman, H. H. & Mollie A. Watkins, Nov. 13, 1866.
North, Anthony & Susan Smotherman, Dec. 30, 1866.
Northcott, V. H. H. H. & Mary M. V. Northcott, Aug. 28,
   1866.
Norwood, Wm. & Henrietta Young, May 4, 1866.
Oaff, James & Nellie Turner, Dec. 5, 1866.
Odom, Wm. F. & Anna Hutchison, Dec. 30, 1866.
Overall, Braxton & Nancy Donnell, Apr. 13, 1866.
Overall, Fountain & Ann Partee, Dec. 27, 1866.
Overall, Will & Jane Woods, May 9, 1866.
Owen, J. M. & A. E. Puckett, Sept. 26, 1866.
Owen, Oscar & Ann Owen, June 18, 1866.
Owen, Wm. & Mariah Barlow, Jan. 22, 1866.
Owens, John & Fanny Russell, July 29, 1866.
Page, Jordan & Minerva Sparkman, Sept. 15, 1866.
Parker, Benj. & Mary Melton, Mar. 14, 1866.
Parris, W. B. & Amanda L. Burch, Jan. 23, 1866.
Patterson, Bob & Cilla Bennett, Mar. 17, 1866.
Patterson, Samuel G. & Lizzie Harding, Dec. 19, 1866.
Paton, Lewis & Queen Windrow, July 15, 1866.
Payne, Andrew B. & Ada Buchanan, Sept. 13, 1866.
Peak, James & Milly Leakray, Apr. 26, 1866.
Peak, Marshall & Mary Vickery, Mar. 29, 1866.
Peak, Solomon B. & Eliz. Vickery, Mar. 29, 1866.
Pearce, Charles & Jane Jinkins, July 14, 1866.
Pearce, Henry & Julia A. Hunt, Dec. 29, 1866.
Perkins, Henry & Margaret Hopkins, Dec. 29, 1866.
Perkins, Samuel & Jane Manear, May 13, 1866.
Peyton, Geo. & Lizzie Burton, Apr. 28, 1866.
Philips, Henry & Julia Simmons, June 14, 1866.
Philips, Primas & Louiza Coppage, July 7, 1866.
Phillips, Henry & Jane Hoover, July 5, 1866.
Phillips, John & Minty Fuller, Dec. 19, 1866.
Phillips, Wm. Mitchell & Jinny Fletcher, Aug. 18, 1866.
Pilkerton, L. B. & Mary L. Benson, July 4, 1866.
Poindexter, Joseph W. & Mary White Sloan, Sept. 13, 1866.
Pope, Francis K. & Martha A. Young, Nov. 3, 1866.
Pope, J. K. & Louisa Neal, Nov. 16, 1866.

Pope, Wm. & Anne Richards, Jan. 3, 1866.
Porter, Burton & Agga Porter, Nov. 8, 1866.
Proffit, Isiah & Louisa King, Aug. 4, 1866.
Pruitt, Harry & Melinda Rucker, Apr. 4, 1866.
Puckett, Albert & Elzira King, Nov. 25, 1866.
Rabern, G. V. & Christina Scruggs, July 30, 1866.
Ragland, Hosea & Eliza J. Cannon, July 15, 1866.
Ralston, Rankin & Martha Ralston, Apr. 13, 1866.
Ransom, Robert & Dilsey Lillard, July 16, 1866.
Rawlings, R. L. & I. A. Lawing, Sept. 29, 1866.
Ray, J. H. & Miss T. A. Vaughan, Nov. 20, 1866.
Ready, Albert & Marion Leeper, June 26, 1866.
Redby, Claiborn & Ann Tucker, Jan. 4, 1866.
Reed, Claxton & Nancy P. Todd, Jan. 15, 1866.
Reed, Wash & Frankie Hicks, Jan. 28, 1866.
Renfro, Geo. & Martha C. Taylor, Jan. 7, 1866.
Ridley, Clayborn & Ann Tucker, Jan. 4, 1866.
Ridley, G. C. & Betty Jones, June 6, 1866.
Ridley, Hense & Polly Wrather, Apr. 5, 1866.
Roads, Robert & Mary Cason, Sept. 3, 1866.
Roberson, A. J. & Bettie Chandler, Feb. 28, 1866.
Roberson, Robert & Amanda Hastings, Sept. 28, 1866.
Roberts, Allen & Mary Bennis, May 31, 1866.
Robertson, A. M. & Fanny Hunter, Dec. 20, 1866.
Robertson, Geo. & Amanda Johnson, Nov. 11, 1866.
Robertson, Hiram & Anna Rogers, July 14, 1866.
Ross, Caswell & Levina Betty, May 14, 1866.
Rouse, James & Jane Norman, Oct. 29, 1866.
Rouse, James & Polly Rouse, Dec. 20, 1866.
Rouse, Thomas & Martha Ann Stewart, Dec. 20, 1866.
Rucker, Charley & Eliza Rucker, Dec. 15, 1866.
Rucker, Edmond & Lina Jordan, Jan. 29, 1866.
Rucker, Madison & Molly Phillips, Sept. 8, 1866.
Runnels, Wm. & Leana Mancy, Nov. 2, 1866.
Sanders, Mark & Matty P. Adkerson, Sept. 26, 1866.
Sanders, Robert A. & Mattie E. L. Crawford, Mar. 6, 1866.
Sanders, Squire & Mariah Morgan, June 12, 1866.
Sanders, Wm. & Nancy Sanders, Jan. 6, 1866.
Sanford, J. W. & Sarah Crutchfield, Dec. 6, 1866.
Sanford, Willis & Mary Jane Cooper, Aug. 25, 1866.
Scott, Crockett & Adaline Worley, Mar. 8, 1866.
Scott, John A. & Eliz. J. Byer, May 20, 1866.
Scruggs, W. M. & A. T. Jarratt, May 9, 1866.
Sharpe, Jessee & Marg. Wright, Mar. 27, 1866.
Sherron, Isaac W. & Salena Ann Bowman, May 3, 1866.
Sims, Wesly & Malenda Fisher, Aug. 18, 1866.
Sims, Willis & Easter Turner, Feb. 1, 1866.
Singleton, James & Jane Jenkins, June 15, 1866.
Slakes, Robert & Betty Slakes, Feb. 22, 1866.
Slawter, Thomas & Rachel Allen, Mar. 17, 1866.
Sloss, Daniel & Easter Sloss, Feb. 20, 1866.
Sloss, Jackson & Harriett Sloss, Jan. 26, 1866.
Small, Edm. & Julia Small, Aug. 11, 1866.

Smith, Anthony & Anna North, July 14, 1866.
Smith, Burrel & Fann McDermott, Sept. 22, 1866.
Smith, C. H. & N. J. Smith, Feb. 18, 1866.
Smith, Daniel & Betsy Randolph, Nov. 10, 1866.
Smith, Edmund & Teney Wright, Dec. 19, 1866.
Smith, Geo. & Roxana Morton, Mar. 17, 1866.
Smith, Jackson & Matilda Dickerson, Feb. 2, 1866.
Smith, John & Dilcy Jarratt, Dec. 22, 1866.
Smith, John & Isabella Hoggett, Dec. 29, 1866.
Smith, Moses & Eliz. Smith, Oct. 20, 1866.
Smith, Newton & Sarah E. Todd, Dec. 27, 1866.
Smith, Stephen & Emaline Jones, Sept. 26, 1866.
Smith, Solomon & Eliza Leakray, Sept. 6, 1866.
Smith, Tarlton & Lizzie Suggs, Nov. 18, 1866.
Smith, Washington & Mariah Bunkins, May 16, 1866.
Smith, Wm. & Nancy A. Colbert, Aug. 3, 1866.
Smotherman, John W. & Nancy M. E. Smotherman, Dec. 12, 1866.
Smotherman, Robert M. & Margaret E. Carlton, Dec. 20, 1866.
Snell, Ambrose & Macy Carney, Jan. 20, 1866.
Snell, Lewis & Carney Lawrence, Dec. 30, 1866.
Spain, Charles G. & Mary E. Huddleston, Feb. 17, 1866.
Spain, W. M. & Miss M. E. Palmer, Nov. 8, 1866.
Span, F. M. & M. F. Span, Jan. 23, 1866.
Sparks, Jessee W. & Josephine Bivins, Apr. 18, 1866.
Sparks, Matthew & Louisa Hubbard, Jan. 24, 1866.
Spence, Thomas & Nancy T. Spence, Sept. 11, 1866.
Stamper, Wm. & Mary Parker, Oct. 17, 1866.
Starvens, Geo. & Parthenia Settle, Mar. 3, 1866.
Stevenson, Ephraim & Julia Ann Haley, July 4, 1866.
Stevenson, Simon & Caroline Heaventon, Apr. 3, 1866.
Stewart, Cezar & Nancy Sikes, Aug. 18, 1866.
Stokes, Robert & Molly Green, Aug. 3, 1866.
Stone, H. B. & M. C. Neal, Dec. 9, 1866.
Stoner, John M. & Martha Leakray, July 25, 1866.
Stovall, Bill & Lizzie McMurray, Feb. 4, 1866.
Sublett, Norance A. & Virginia C. McAdoo, Dec. 11, 1866.
Sublett, Joseph & Marg. Philips, May 23, 1866.
Sudberry, Wm. & M. A. Smotherman, May 31, 1866.
Sullivan, Wm. B. & Mary E. Jetton, May 31, 1866.
Summerhill, T. A. & Mary E. Rankin, Feb. 14, 1866.
Summers, Lewis & Abigail Jones, Jan. 4, 1866.
Sutherds, Monroe & Eliza Goodman, Oct. 13, 1866.
Suttle, Ben & Mary White, Oct. 6, 1866.
Sutton, J. P. & Mary E. Bestie, Jan. 17, 1866.
Sutton, Joseph & Julia Ann Todd, Jan. 11, 1866.
Swink, John & Mary A. Weatherford, Apr. 3, 1866.
Tarpley, Geo. W. & Ann E. Ott, Nov. 21, 1866.
Taylor, James M. & Lucy J. Webb, Jan. 24, 1866.
Teate, Wm. & Sarah Fulton, Oct. 27, 1866.
Terry, Walter & Julia Ezell, Mar. 17, 1866.
Thompson, Abram & Ellen Scruggs, Jan. 5, 1866.
Thompson, Eli N. & Fannie E. Inhoff, July 5, 1866.

Thompson, Geo. W. & Charlott Sneed, Mar. 4, 1866.
Thompson, Mizakiah & Rachel Reeves, Mar. 17, 1866.
Thompson, Richard & Malinda Jane Thompson, Dec. 27, 1866.
Thompson, M. P. & Sarah Ann Dillin, Oct. 25, 1866.
Todd, Aaron & Eliz. Prater, Oct. 25, 1866.
Todd, Wm. & Mary J. Campbell, Dec. 20, 1866.
Todd, Wm. & Mamie Todd, Oct. 13, 1866.
Travis, Robert & Nancy M. Hughes, Feb. 27, 1866.
Tucker, David & Midy Smith, Sept. 22, 1866.
Tucker, Ransom & Mary E. Featherston, Feb. 15, 1866.
Turman, Sac & Kate N. Brown, July 12, 1866.
Turner, Dr. A. J. & Miss Laura Butler, Oct. 31, 1866.
Valentine, Edward & Mary Smith, Apr. 13, 1866.
Vandagriff, John B. & Miss E. M. Farr, Sept. 13, 1866.
Vannerson, Clinton & Emily Thomas, Mar. 20, 1866.
Vaughan, Isaac & Louisa Snell, Dec. 20, 1866.
Vaughan, R. B. & V. T. Snell, Jan. 24, 1866.
Vaughan, R. H. & M. T. McCowan, Dec. 1, 1866.
Vaughan, Thomas & Ellen Clay, Mar. 31, 1866.
Vickers, Wm. & Sarah Mitchell, Apr. 8, 1866.
Wade, Isaac & Eliza Wade, Nov. 25, 1866.
Wade, James & Catherine Lindsey, Feb. 14, 1866.
Wade, Moses & Eliz. Wade, Jan. 16, 1866.
Wade, Nelson & Angeline Cates, Oct. 7, 1866.
Walace, Richard W. & Mrs. Susan Smiddy, July 22, 1866.
Walker, Allen & Fanny Walker, Sept. 25, 1866.
Walker, Cezar & Mary Balejack, Dec. 26, 1866.
Walker, Lewis & Rosa Smith, May 10, 1866.
Walker, Samuel & Myra Lytle, June 21, 1866.
Waller, Geo. R. & Miss Kate Garner, May 12, 1866.
Wallis, Robert & Minerva Thompson, Sept. 8, 1866.
Walter, Lewis & Rosa Smith, May 10, 1866.
Ward, James H. & Nancy S. Vaughan, Sept. 18, 1866.
Ward, Jerry & Caroline Stevens, Mar. 22, 1866.
Ward, Robert N. & Anna W. Howard, Sept. 26, 1866.
Ward, Solomon & Susan Stockard, Feb. 8, 1866.
Warmuth, H. J. & Mollie W. Peebles, Jan. 24, 1866.
Warson, Taylor & Hannah Searcy, Dec. 28, 1866.
Watkins, James & Tonny Bennett, Aug. 11, 1866.
Watson, Wm. & Estha Harris, Dec. 28, 1866.
Weakley, David & Mary Woods, Oct. 6, 1866.
Weakley, Horace & Martha White, Nov. 12, 1866.
Webb, John & Mittie Webb, Apr. 3, 1866.
Webb, Monroe & Ann Floyd, Nov. 24, 1866.
Webb, Richard & Easter Murry, Feb. 10, 1866.
Webster, Alexander & Mariah Golden, Apr. 16, 1866.
Welch, Hampton & Sarah J. Hines, Mar. 21, 1866.
Wems, Alfred & Elisa Irvin, Dec. 16, 1866.
Wendel, Baker & Partneia Reeves, May 21, 1866.
Wendel, Joshua & Mary C. Morn, Feb. 13, 1866.
White, Frank & J. E. Miller, Mar. 6, 1866.
White, James & Mary Taylor, Sept. 8, 1866.
White, Luke & Eliza Nelson, Aug. 11, 1866.

White, Wm. N. & L. C. White, Mar. 26, 1866.
Wilkerson, Anderson & Sarah Wilkerson, June 20, 1866.
Wilkerson, Isaac M. & Mrs. Casandra McGill, Oct. 10, 1866.
Williams, Henderson & Margaret Ezell, Sept. 1, 1866.
Wills, John & Betty Fletcher, Aug. 5, 1866.
Wood, Davis T. & Amanda P. Cafton, Dec. 12, 1866.
Woodfin, James G. & Mary Jane Clark, Nov. 28, 1866.
Woods, Aaron & Catharine Anthony, Dec. 25, 1866.
Woods, Alfred & Nelly Haynes, Nov. 25, 1866.
Woods, Henry & Sarah Bedley, Feb. 28, 1866.
Woods, Ned & Nicy Smith, Feb. 3, 1866.
Woods, Thomas T. & Mary J. Woods, Jan. 15, 1866.
Woods, Washington & Violet Fisher, Mar. 24, 1866.
Woods, Zachariah & Anne Jetton, Dec. 27, 1866.
Worke, Henry & Fanny Donnell, Dec. 31, 1866.
Worke, Henry & Harriett Worke, Oct. 19, 1866.
Yearwood, Wm. & Sarah J. Sloan, Jan. 11, 1866.

1867

Abernatha W. M. & Mrs. L. M. Ward, July 20, 1867.
Alexander, G. A. & N. A. Moore, Oct. 17, 1867.
Alexander, George & Ann Barnes, July 5, 1867.
Alexander, Lewis & Aggy Snell, Jan. 6, 1867.
Alexander, Nathan & Sarah Rucker, Jan. 3, 1867.
Alexander, Presly & Amanda Ward, July 27, 1867.
Alexander, Robert & Charlotte Davis, Feb. 6, 1867.
Alexander, Safe & Martha Alexander, Mar. 1, 1867.
Alford, Thomas & Rachel Colman, Dec. 28, 1867.
Allen, Frances A. D. & Nancy K. Overall, Jan. 9, 1867.
Allen, Granville G. & Fanny L. Tune, Sept. 4, 1867.
Allen, Henry & Louisa Mathews, June 16, 1867.
Allen, T. J. & Harriet N. Koonce, Aug. 18, 1867.
Allen, Thomas & Lucy J. Patton, Jan. 11, 1867.
Alsup, Taylor & Charlotte Brown, Aug. 8, 1867.
Anderson, Roid & Mariah Avant, Nov. 8, 1867.
Anderson, Wm. & Mary Wilson, June 16, 1867.
Anderson, Wm. & Nancy Ann Driver, Oct. 23, 1867.
Anderson, Wm. & Nancy Wilson, June 14, 1867.
Anderson, Wm. L. & J. A. Crouse, Dec. 30, 1867.
Angleman, Albert & Eliz. J. F. Dungeon, Jan. 18, 1867.
Armstrong, Houston & Fanny Mathews, Aug. 30, 1867.
Arnold, R. M. & Lucinda Green, Sept. 30, 1867.
Arnold, Thomas B. & Margaret S. Primm, Apr. 25, 1867.
Augustus, Julius & Ann Patton, Feb. 15, 1867.
Averett, Freeman & Fanny Walker, June 21, 1867.
Averett, Fountain & Francis Phillips, Nov. 18, 1867.
Averett, Taylor & Roxanna Holden, May 1, 1867.
Avery, M. E. & Jane Bence, Jan. 15, 1867.
Baird, Philip & Clemmy Meritt, Sept. 12, 1867.
Baker, Bill & Frances Gooch, June 15, 1867.
Baker, Ezekiel & Martha Alsop, Mar. 23, 1867.
Banks, Henry & Eliz. Ryan, Jan. 6, 1867.

Barksdale, Wm. M. & Lucy Donoho, July 1, 1867.
Barlow, John J. & Sophronia McKee, Sept. 9, 1867.
Barnes, Jackson & Margaret Barton, Sept. 1, 1867.
Barnett, Clabourn & Malenda Sikes, July 8, 1867.
Barr, H. J. & E. A. Parker, Nov. 6, 1867.
Barton, George & Fanny Brown, May 18, 1867.
Baskette, G. H. & Anna McFadden, Sept. 24, 1867.
Bass, Allen & Tennessee Jones, Dec. 10, 1867.
Bass, Hartwell P. & Charlotte A. Sims, Nov. 21, 1867.
Bass, James & Harriet Coldwell, Oct. 6, 1867.
Bass, Samuel & Lucy Hoover, Feb. 21, 1867.
Baucum, James & Julia Ann Posey, Sept. 14, 1867.
Baugh, B. M. & L. M. Childress, Jan. 8, 1867.
Baugh, Gilbert & Nancy Garner, Dec. 27, 1867.
Beasley, James & Eliz. Heath, Oct. 31, 1867.
Beesley, J. M. & Bettie Vaughan, June 21, 1867.
Bell, J. L. & L. A. Stell, Sept. 19, 1867.
Bell, John H. & Mary Odum, Jan. 7, 1867.
Bellifant, ---- & Malissa A. Seay, Feb. 1, 1867.
Bellifant, Amanuel & Lucy Chambers, Apr. 14, 1867.
Bellifant, Hiram & Jinny Gentry, Feb. 13, 1867.
Best, Burton & Milly Grisham, June 20, 1867.
Bethell, R. K. & Elvina House, May 24, 1867.
Betty, Cary & Raner Corder, Dec. 18, 1867.
Bibb, Wm. & Martha Watkins, Mar. 27, 1867.
Black, Hanibal & Eliz. Garrett, Jan. 2, 1867.
Black, Robert & Molly Mathews, Dec. 25, 1867.
Blackman, Titus & Amanda Elliott, Aug. 7, 1867.
Boles, Charley & Jane Gannoway, Feb. 16, 1867.
Bond, Bonner Bill & Malinda Mitchell, Jan. 9, 1867.
Booth, Solomon & Killy Black, Jan. 12, 1867.
Bostick, Starlin & Martha Edwards, June 29, 1867.
Bowen, W. M. & Susan F. Kelton, Apr. 14, 1867.
Bowling, Bailey & Lorinda E. Smotherman, June 25, 1867.
Boyd, John & Easter McDaniel, July 14, 1867.
Boyd, John W. & Susan N. Pitts, Oct. 29, 1867.
Boyd, Marian & Lucinda Harris, Dec. 30, 1867.
Brandon, G. T. & Margaret J. Helton, Oct. 2, 1867.
Brooks, Sam & Laura Crutcher, July 13, 1867.
Brown, John & Jane Brown, June 6, 1867.
Brown, John & Alsey McAdoo, Dec. 19, 1867.
Brown, Joseph T. & Colly F. Mabry, July 17, 1867.
Brown, Wm. & Eliz. Thompson, July 20, 1867.
Buchanan, John P. & Fannie L. McGill, Oct. 24, 1867.
Burchett, James & Clary A. Reed, Jan. 22, 1867.
Burton, Frank & Mariah Jordan, May 20, 1867.
Butler, Wm. & Nancy Calhoun, Mar. 16, 1867.
Caldwell, Charles & Mary Bennett, Jan. 17, 1867.
Calhoun, Washington & Aller Jane Seward, Aug. 16, 1867.
Camus, Emile F. & Mollie W. McWhorter, Oct. 29, 1867.
Cannon, Andrew & Polina Reeves, Apr. 30, 1867.
Cannon, Nicholas & Amy Martin, Feb. 24, 1867.
Carney, Granville & Susan Rideout, Dec. 29, 1867.
Carney, Joseph & Louisa Butler, Jan. 3, 1867.

Carroll, Benj. & Sallie Taylor, July 7, 1867.
Carter, F. M. & Salina Shook, Nov. 6, 1867.
Cathey, J. N. & H. C. Dill, Jan. 23, 1867.
Childress, Aaron & Milly Jakes, Oct. 28, 1867.
Childress, Edmund & Dolly Phillips, Dec. 30, 1867.
Childress, Eli & Rachel Johnson, May 12, 1867.
Childress, Geo. & Louiza Duffer, Jan. 26, 1867.
Childress, Henry & Adaline Mathews, Oct. 13, 1867.
Childress, Henry & Jane McConnell, June 15, 1867.
Childress, Nichodemus & Emaline Lytle, July 15, 1867.
Clark, W. F. & N. J.McMurray, Jan. 2, 1867.
Clayton, Samuel & Sallie Ward, Dec. 10, 1867.
Colman, Edmund & Martha Howse, Sept. 29, 1867.
Colman, James & Caroline Thompson, Sept. 13, 1867.
Colman, John C. & Eliz. Bowman, July 18, 1867.
Cook, J. P. & Susan Fergason, Dec. 20, 1867.
Cook, R. A. & Susan I. Noe, Sept. 8, 1867.
Cooper, Henry & Mary Brazelton, Jan. 8, 1867.
Cooper, Robert & Miss Mary Johns, Dec. 12, 1867.
Cooper, Thomas & Sallie Crockett, Dec. 26, 1867.
Copeland, Lewis & Ann Lee, Dec. 26, 1867.
Corbett, Henry & Phillis Haynes, May 25, 1867.
Couch, Thomas J. & Mary C. Vickery, Mar. 25, 1867.
Cowan, Joseph & Louisa Butler, Jan. 3, 1867.
Cox, George & Bell Baskett, Sept. 2, 1867.
Cox, Michael & Julia Smith, Mar. 10, 1867.
Cozart, John & Mary J. Rowland, Nov. 22, 1867.
Crockett, Dr. F. P. & Virginia A. Orgain, Feb. 14, 1867.
Crockett, W. C. & Sallie Lawrence, Dec. 5, 1867.
Crowe, Daniel & Mary F. Watts, Nov. 3, 1867.
Crowse, B. S. & Mary Jane Cleche, Feb. 19, 1867.
Crutcher, Neal & Isabella McClure, Sept. 19, 1867.
Cunningham, S. P. & Lou Haskins, May 8, 1867.
Curlee, Robert & Charlott Fletcher, May 18, 1867.
Dale, Robert & Mary E. Span, Jan. 14, 1867.
Dassey, James & Fanny Pate, Sept. 29, 1867.
Davis, Isaac & Peggy Rucker, Jan. 9, 1867.
Davis, Mosbey & Emily G. Goodman, Jan. 15, 1867.
Davis, Robert I. & Adaline Wade, Dec. 3, 1867.
Davis, Wm. & Eliz. E. Pitters, Jan. 17, 1867.
Davenport, Garrison & Aggy Jamison, Aug. 15, 1867.
Dokes, Jordan & Sarah Moore, Jan. 2, 1867.
Donaldson, J. W. & Harriett Hall, Apr. 25, 1867.
Donnell, Calvin & Lucretia Allen, Aug. 17, 1867.
Donnell, Jack & Martha Ann Donnell, May 15, 1867.
Donnell, John & Puss McAdoo, Jan. 16, 1867
Douglass, Fred & Ellen Phillips, Jan. 4, 1867.
Drennon, Joby & Clarkey Ann Oliver, Mar. 24, 1867.
Drennon, Philip & Louisa Smith, Dec. 26, 1867.
Dromgoole, George & Lucy Newman, Jan. 4, 1867.
Dromgoole, Jerry & Jemima Dromgoole, Dec. 25, 1867.
Dunaway, Sandy & Ellen Searcy, June 15, 1867.
Dunaway, Thomas & Elizabeth Fletcher, Dec. 4, 1867.
Dunn, T. F. & Lavica E. Nelson, Feb. 7, 1867.

RUTHERFORD COUNTY MARRIAGES

Eakin, Nelson & Dolly Espey, June 8, 1867.
Eakin, W. G. & Bettie Eskridge, June 20, 1867.
Edmondson, Charles & Martha Ross, Nov. 12, 1867.
Edwards, Henry & Lucretia Rucker, Dec. 26, 1867.
Edwards, Hiram G. & Philonica Ann Smith, Oct. 24, 1867.
Estus, John & Malinda Estus, Aug. 18, 1867.
Evans, James & Roxanna Holden, Dec. 31, 1867.
Evett, Wm. & Catharine Vickory, July 3, 1867.
Fanning, A. J. & E. R. Hill, Aug. 19, 1867.
Fletcher, Sarlin & Jane Webb, Apr. 7, 1867.
Floyd, W. H. & Miss Lou Johnson, Nov. 10, 1867.
Foster, Isaac & Susan F. Barnett, Oct. 9, 1867.
Fox, James F. & Sally Pruett, Feb. 14, 1867.
Frazier, Marshal & Martha Edwards, Feb. 17, 1867.
Freeman, John M. & Miss Mary A. Green, Mar. 15, 1867.
Freeman, Mayfield & Melinda Haynes, July 11, 1867.
Fuquay, Samuel & Mary Baker, Dec. 28, 1867.
Gaines, B. N. & Sallie J. Sharp, June 12, 1867.
Garner, Lewis & Ellen H. Mankin, Nov. 5, 1867.
Garner, Ned & Caroline Miller, Mar. 24, 1867.
Garner, Philip & Cassandra Lowe, Nov. 4, 1867.
Garvin, James & Mary E. Beasley, Dec. 23, 1867.
Garvin, Thomas & Martha A. Rowlett, Nov. 5, 1867.
Gault, Joseph H. & Martha J. Williamson, Dec. 10, 1867.
Gelbert, John E. (Capt.) & Addie Sikes, Nov. 19, 1867.
George, Albert & Amanda L. Stewart, Dec. 24, 1867.
Gibson, Edwin & Mary J. Rollins, Aug. 3, 1867.
Gibson, John N. & Eliz, Dowing, Sept. 1, 1867.
Gillis, John F. & Mariah Rollins, Dec. 19, 1867.
Gillmore, Robert & Fanny Smith, July 16, 1867.
Glenn, Daniel & Eliza Floyd, Dec. 18, 1867.
Gober, Samuel & Manerva Jordan, Dec. 18, 1867.
Gooch, Allen T. & Sallie Goodwin, May 15, 1867.
Gooch, Jerry & Charity Gooch, Mar. 30, 1867.
Gooch, Joseph & Clarah A. Kimbro, Dec. 26, 1867.
Goodman, David & Caroline Ellis, Oct. 1, 1867.
Gordan, Wm. & Emaline Wilburn, May 13, 1867.
Gordan, Wm. & Maria Young, Jan. 8, 1867.
Gray, Freemon & Rose Foster, Apr. 3, 1867.
Greenlief, Julius & Elender Baugh, June 1, 1867.
Greer, Charles & Susan Dement, Oct. 5, 1867.
Gregory, Green & Josephine White, Jan. 19, 1867.
Gregory, John H. & Nannie Martin, Mar. 9, 1867.
Gregory, Thomas & Josephine Smith, Sept. 10, 1867.
Gregsley, Samuel & Stacy T. Span, Jan. 22, 1867.
Grisham, Henry & Hannah Grisham, July 6, 1867.
Groghan, Franklin M. & Susanna Morris, Nov. 29, 1867.
Hall, Col. Alexander & Mrs. L. J. Watkins, Dec. 18, 1867.
Hall, Benj. & Jane Anderson, Mar. 16, 1867.
Hall, David & Amanda Jarratt, Dec. 28, 1867.
Hall, Jacob & Martha Hall, Mar. 31, 1867.
Hall, Sam & Tabitha Peebles, Jan. 8, 1867.
Hall, Wm. & Lucy McMinn, Nov. 1, 1867.

RUTHERFORD COUNTY MARRIAGES

Hamilton, Henry & Bettie McHenry, Aug. 3, 1867.
Hamilton, Isaac & Sarah Gamble, Dec. 14, 1867.
Hampton, Wade & Kitty Lytle, Dec. 26, 1867.
Harding, James H. & Esther J. Eades, Jan. 22, 1867.
Hargrove, Alfred & Mary McDermott, Apr. 20, 1867.
Harper, Elliott & Rosanna Mickey, Jan. 6, 1867.
Harris, Henry & Celia Malone, Sept. 21, 1867.
Harris, Richard A. & Miss Martha E. Fain, Nov. 10, 1867.
Harrison, Wm. & Dinah Pariker, May 4, 1867.
Harrison, Wm. H. & Isabella Carter, Mar. 24, 1867.
Hart, Thomas & Rebecca Johnson, July 19, 1867.
Haywood, Wm. & Ann Neal, Dec. 28, 1867.
Haynes, J. W. A. & D. E. Reed, Jan. 16, 1867.
Haynes, James J. & Permelia J. Creek, Aug. 22, 1867.
Hays, Harmon & Mary Jane Burt, Jan. 30, 1867.
Hays, John R. & Sarah E. Glimp, Oct. 6, 1867.
Henderson, Isaac & Lucinda Warmuth, Feb. 7, 1867.
Henderson, John P. & Miss Lou C.McFaddin, Sept. 11, 1867.
Henderson, Marshall & Amanda White, Feb. 2, 1867.
Henderson, Syrus & Nelly Bagby, June 15, 1867.
Hensley, Peter & Mary J. Owens, Sept. 7, 1867.
Herald, J. S. F. & Jane Adams, Sept. 13, 1867.
Herrin, Washington & Amanda Ezell, Feb. 9, 1867.
Herrod, David & Margaret Hoover, Oct. 18, 1867.
Hicks, J. H. & Molly White, July 29, 1867.
Higdon, John A. & Cary A. Cunningham, May 1, 1867.
Hinsee, Jessie & Jemima Armstead, Apr. 20, 1867.
Holdcomb, Geo. & Oma Doyle, Oct. 13, 1867.
Holden, F. C. & Martha J. Wadley, Oct. 13, 1867.
Holden, Thomas & Julia Ann Leathers, Feb. 7, 1867.
Holden, Wm. & Eliz. Smotherman, June 1, 1867.
Hollowell, L. R. & Miss Nannie P. Jobe, Dec. 15, 1867.
Holmes, Harry & Josephine Dean, Dec. 9, 1867.
Holt, W. G. & Nettie Arnold (Corrected to Eliza B.),
    Dec. 6, 1867.
Hoover, R. L. & E. R. Smith, Apr. 18, 1867.
Hord, Briden & Mary Anderson, June 23, 1867.
Howland, David & Susan Mankin, Oct. 31, 1867.
House, Nicks & Susan Simmons, Jan. 7, 1867.
House, Thomas & Mary Vaughan, Jan. 30, 1867.
Hueston, Hartwell & Deanna Rucker, June 22, 1867.
Huggins, A. D. & Sallie H. Harrison, Nov. 7, 1867.
Hugh, Nathan & Mary Reed, Apr. 4, 1867.
Hunt, Frank & Barbary Hunt, July 9, 1867.
Hunt, Joe & Paralee Johns, Apr. 1, 1867.
Hutcherson, Isaac & Lucinda Warmuth, Feb. 7, 1867.
Jackson, Jessie & Martha Jane Comer, Aug. 31, 1867.
Jackson, Wm. R. & Mary A. Posey, Jan. 3, 1867.
Jacobs, D. P. & F. V. Baugh, Jan. 8, 1867.
Jakes, Wimon & Anna Moore, Oct. 26, 1867.
James, Isaac & Emeline Etter, Nov. 9, 1867.
James Jsper N. & Mary Jane Hoover, Sept. 25, 1867.
James, John & Flora Currin, Dec. 9, 1867.
Jamison, A. & Esther G. Brandon, Sept. 24, 1867.

RUTHERFORD COUNTY MARRIAGES

Jarratt, Nelson & Caroline Kelso, Aug. 28, 1867.
Jarratt, Richard & Mary Ann Morton, Mar. 7, 1867.
Jenkins, Jones & Matty May, Jan. 17, 1867.
Jenkins, Wm. C. & Martha Jane Mallard, Nov. 29, 1867.
Jetton, Albert & Emma Tally, Nov. 20, 1867.
Jetton, Auston & Mary Jones, Dec. 31, 1867.
Johns, Daniel & Jenny Lockard, Jan. 31, 1867.
Johns, Wm. R. & Julia Allen, Sept. 12, 1867.
Johnson, Charles & Sarah Jane Johnson, June 22, 1867.
Johnson, Joseph & Angeline Ridley, Feb. 4, 1867.
Johnson, Taylor & Caty Smith, Jan. 2, 1867.
Joiner, Victoria & Bell Ralston, Jan. 25, 1867.
Jones, Wm. R. & Sue C. Johnson, Sept. 26, 1867.
Jones, Willis N. & Martha J. Benson, Jan. 10, 1867.
Jordan, Richard & Sallie Jordan, Sept. 7, 1867.
Keeble, Forbs & Lucinda Cooper, Feb. 14, 1867.
Keeble, Mack & Mary Nelson, Feb. 6, 1867.
Kenady, John C. & Bette Carson, Dec. 18, 1867.
Kerr, Thomas & Amanda Hutchison, July 5, 1867.
Killingsworth, J. C. & Margaret A. Holder, May 29, 1867.
Kimbro, Anthony & Mary Vincent, June 1, 1867.
King, Andy & Prusana Hoggett, Jan. 3, 1867.
King, David & Amanda Johns, Mar. 22, 1867.
Kirby, Preston & Sarah Ledbetter, Nov. 25, 1867.
Kirk, J. P. & Miss Mollie Modrall, Sept. 9, 1867.
Lackard, Wm. & Rebecca Cates, Sept. 9, 1867.
Lakemore, W. A. & Marilda J. Lillard, Dec. 15, 1867.
Landis, Jackson & Ellen Anderson, Jan. 31, 1867.
Landon, Jack & Lidia Lawrence, Dec. 15, 1867.
Lane, Moses & Lucinda Ransom, June 29, 1867.
Larkins, Lewis & Chaney Tucker, Feb. 20, 1867.
Lavender, Samuel & Julia Adkerson, Jan. 28, 1867.
Layne, A. J. & Mary A. Layne, Jan. 28, 1867.
Ledbetter, Raford & Elvira Smith, Dec. 24, 1867.
Lenore, John W. & Miss Bettie Waller, Oct. 31, 1867.
Lenore, Licurgus & Miss Lucy M. Colman, Dec. 17, 1867.
Levy, Henry & Miss Pertha Hines, Mar. 4, 1867.
Lewis, Franklin & Martha R. Earps, Nov. 14, 1867.
Lewis, Wm. & Eliz. Mullins, June 22, 1867.
Lillard, Jack & Caroline Haynes, Feb. 8, 1867.
Lillard, Robert & Emaline Black, Oct. 12, 1867.
Lillard, Shepherd & Nelly Hackett, Aug. 28, 1867.
Lincoln, W. H. & Miss M. L. Moore, Nov. 21, 1867.
Loften, Washington & Kitty Keeble, May 23, 1867.
Lokely, John W. & Charity Sidberry, Dec. 24, 1867.
Love, Ruben & Mary J. Searcy, Feb. 15, 1867.
Love, Rubin & Betty Sikes, Oct. 14, 1867.
Lowe, Claborne & Phillis Ott, Jan. 7, 1867.
Lowe, Stephen & Eliz. Daniel, Feb. 24, 1867.
Luster, James & Marnada A. Farr, Jan. 3, 1867.
Lytle, Frank & Julia Overall, Aug. 24, 1867.
Lytle, Geo. & Martha Sims, Oct. 12, 1867.
Lytle, Lafayett & Emily Jordan, Dec. 18, 1867.
Lytle, Peter & Lucy Davidson, Nov. 28, 1867.
Lytle, Willis & Ellen Rucker, May 11, 1867.

RUTHERFORD COUNTY MARRIAGES

Lytle, Zachary & Sally Murfree, Nov. 16, 1867.
Macon, H. H. & Miss Fannie Seward, Dec. 31, 1867.
Magatee, Charley & Eliza Bostick, June 29, 1867.
Malone, Fred & Edy Hannah, Nov. 2, 1867.
Maney, Frank & Mariah Maney, -----, 1867.
Mankin, A. J. & Miss Fanny Miller, Aug. 20, 1867.
Marable, Robert & Mary J. Ruker, Aug. 22, 1867.
Martin, Ive & Amanda Owen, Mar. 6, 1867.
Martin, Jessee & Lucy Farmer, Dec. 31, 1867.
Martin, Joe & Amanda Owen, Mar. 6, 1867.
Mason, J. H. & M. A. Fox, Aug. 8, 1867.
Mason, John B. & America A. Hoover, Jan. 28, 1867.
Mason, L. H. & Mary McDaniel, Oct. 30, 1867.
Mason, Lafayett & Martha Goodwin, Dec. 27, 1867.
Mathews, Frank & Eliza Rowton, Mar. 1, 1867.
Mathews, Joseph & Sarah Rose, Feb. 24, 1867.
Mathews, S. H. & Media G. Davis, Sept. 26, 1867.
Mathews, Wm. G. & Fanny L. Overall, July 12, 1867.
Maxwell, Edw. L. & Josephine Mathews, Feb. 3, 1867.
Maxwell, Jeffry & Charlott Wright, May 5, 1867.
Maxwell, Wm. T. & Malessa J. Span, Jan. 14, 1867.
May, Thomas & Judith Ross, Mar. 18, 1867.
Mayfield, Freeman & Malinda Haynes, Aug. 12, 1867.
Meshaw, Henry & Ann Anderson, Feb. 23, 1867.
Miles, Ben & Mary Watkins, Aug. 27, 1867.
Miles, Franklin & Levina Wade, Jan. 12, 1867.
Milican, John & Samantha E. Brown, Aug. 27, 1867.
Miller, Bill & Martha Nelson, Jan. 5, 1867.
Miller, Cole & Fanny Garner, Feb. 6, 1867.
Miller, J. R. & Miss Eliz. M. Finger, Oct. 17, 1867.
Miller, Jack & Harriett Turner, Jan. 15, 1867.
Miller, Levi & Tennessee McCullough, Oct. 14, 1867.
Miller, Madison & Dorinda Miller, Feb. 23, 1867.
Miller, Richard & Alsey Batey, Sept. 26, 1867.
Mitchell, Littleton & Manerva Wilkerson, Dec. 26, 1867.
Mitchell, Pompy & Mary Sanford, Dec. 25, 1867.
Modrel, John A. & Pernada A. Tucker, Sept. 23, 1867.
Montgomery, Jerry & Amanda Smith, Jan. 15, 1867.
Moore, Bird & Adelade Brown, Oct. 12, 1867.
Moore, Edm. & Lucretia Alexander, Dec. 21, 1867.
Moore, Jessee & Jane Wilson, Jan. 16, 1867.
Moore, Wm. & Mary Moore, Apr. 18, 1867.
Morris, G. W. & Mary Floyd, Dec. 29, 1867.
Morris, Joseph & Martha Wilson, Feb. 7, 1867.
Morton, W. Henry & Cath. Wilson, Dec. 25, 1867.
Mosly, Washington & Marg. Jones, Sept. 6, 1867.
Mullins, Robert & Henrie Buchanan, Nov. 15, 1867.
Murfree, John & Marg. Jordan, Aug. 30, 1867.
Murfree, S. H. & Rebecca S. Haynes, Jan. 25, 1867.
Murry, Charley & Martha Jane Todd, Sept. 28, 1867.
Murry, Frank & Sella Nelson, Feb. 7, 1867.
McAdoo, Noah & Louisa McAdoo, Feb. 27, 1867.
McAdoo, Robert & Mary Jenkins, July 18, 1867.
McAdoo, Wm. & Ellen Floyd, Apr. 1, 1867.

McAdoo, Wm. & Larecia Pickin, Dec. 30, 1867.
McCullough, Mas. R. & Nancy J. Earls, Dec. 31, 1867.
McDaniel, A. J. & Mary Howland, July 1, 1867.
McDaniel, G. W. & Miss M. A. Lawrence, Jan. 17, 1867.
McFadden, Jack & Paralee Hoover, Aug. 18, 1867.
McFadden, Wm. H. & Miss Mary C. Davis, Nov. 26, 1867.
McFadden, Wm. & Mariah Preston, July 22, 1867.
McFarlin, John & Miss Bettie Hollowell, Oct. 2, 1867.
McFerrin, Henry & Mary McFerrin, Jan. 24, 1867.
McGaughey, Geo. B. & Miss Lizzie Alexander, June 19, 1867.
McKnight, Wm. T. & Miss Fanny Jones, Dec. 24, 1867.
McLane, John & Mrs. Eliz. C. Smith, June 11, 1867.
McLean, Bob & Matilda Webb, Mar. 24, 1867.
McMahan, A. D. & Lucy Jones, Dec. 5, 1867.
McManton, Henry & Martha Colman, Nov. 20, 1867.
McNary, Henry & Rebecca Abernatha, Jan. 1, 1867.
McWilliams, J. H. & Emily Glymp, June 2, 1867.
Nabers, James W. & Martha L. Primm, Apr. 25, 1867.
Nance, Joseph & Mary Miller, Jan. 16, 1867.
Neal, Charley & Catharine Slakes, June 8, 1867.
Neal, R. J. & Miss R. J. Walker, Dec. 23, 1867.
Neely, Wm. & Fanny Smotherman, Apr. 6, 1867.
Nelson, F. & Miss C. J. Davis, Jan. 26, 1867.
Nesbett, N. C. & Mattie J. Knox, Oct. 17, 1867.
Newman, Thomas & Fanny Jenkins, June 22, 1867.
Nichols, Isaac D. & P. A. Miller, Dec. 10, 1867.
Noe, Benj. & Martha Noe, Oct. 22, 1867.
Norman, Allen & Polly Simpson, July 20, 1867.
Norman, Calvin & Lurinda Henderson, June 13, 1867.
Odem, B. F. & Miss Callie Sanders, Sept. 1, 1867.
Oliver, Ben & Angeline Overall, Dec. 18, 1867.
Overall, Albert H. & Harriet F. Mathis, Mar. 12, 1867.
Overall, G. R. & Maggie A. Rucker, May 18, 1867.
Overall, Robert & Harriet Price, Jan. 29, 1867.
Overall, W. T. & Rosanna C. Baird, Oct. 9, 1867.
Owen, Wm. & Caroline Rannaway, Aug. 1, 1867.
Owen, Mike & Susan Comer, Nov. 15, 1867.
Parsley, M. C. & S. R. Elliott, Nov. 20, 1867.
Patterson, Rev. D. R. & Anna V. Brown, Jan. 15, 1867.
Patterson, J. A. & Mary Goodrich, June 6, 1867.
Patterson, Moses & Rhoda Robertson, June 15, 1867.
Patterson, S. A. & Miss Fannie S. Sims, Oct. 17, 1867.
Pearce, John & Hannah Miller, Dec. 23, 1867.
Pearcy, Geo. W. & Sarah E. Ha----, Dec. 30, 1867.
Peebles, Tom & Lizzie Red, Apr. 27, 1867.
Persons, Geo. J. & Nancy Jones, Mar. 26, 1867.
Phillips, Alford & Julia Peters, Apr. 1, 1867.
Phillips, Averett & Mary Henderson, Aug. 10, 1867.
Phillips, Hartless & Sally Jarratt, Nov. 25, 1867.
Phillips, John & Mary Jane Hinson, June 9, 1867.
Pinkerton, Lewis & Matilda Daniel, Apr. 18, 1867.
Pollard, J. M. & Mrs. Permilia E. Bond, Sept. 22, 1867.
Pope, B. F. & Mary Jane Mullins, Oct. 30, 1867.

RUTHERFORD COUNTY MARRIAGES

Posey, Martin & Elvira Summerhill, Dec. 27, 1867.
Powers, Augustus & Candis Batey, Apr. 7, 1867.
Prater, Jerry & Jane Baird, Apr. 15, 1867.
Prater, Monroe & Marg. Crowder, Feb. 6, 1867.
Price, Preston G. & Marg. B. Brothers, Feb. 28, 1867.
Proby, Burrow & Eliz. Brousman, June 21, 1867.
Profitt, Isiah & Louisa King, Apr. 20, 1867.
Pruett, John M. & Miss Eliza A. Baugh, Sept. 17, 1867.
Puckett, Mr. A. P. & Miss M. E. Turner, Dec. 31, 1867.
Puckett, M. L. & L. A. Graham, Apr. 17, 1867.
Qualt, Jos. F. & Martha J. Williams, Dec. 10, 1867.
Quarles, G. N. & Miss M. A. Stroop, Feb. 12, 1867.
Quarles, Millus & Hannah Hodge, Feb. 23, 1867.
Quener, W. H. & Miss Jemima Parrish, Sept. 4, 1867.
Randal, Geo. & Kiziah Hoggett, Aug. 3, 1867.
Randolph, Isham & Susan Sanders, Feb. 12, 1867.
Rather, Peter & Malissa Jakes, Oct. 2, 1867.
Read, Wm. R. & Ruby E. Northcott, Jan. 15, 1867.
Ready, Albert & Maria Leiper, Jan. 26, 1867.
Reed, Philip & Ann White, July 13, 1867.
Reid, James & Sarah Thomas, Apr. 1, 1867.
Rhodes, Peter & Ellen Collins, Aug. 31, 1867.
Rice, Lewis & Rhoda Welch, Sept. 8, 1867.
Richardson, G. W. & Miss M. H. Becton, Dec. 24, 1867.
Richardson, Henry & Laney Sanders, Jan. 26, 1867.
Richardson, James M. & Harriett R. Prater, Feb. 12, 1867.
Ridley, Hershal & Mary A. Miller, Jan. 10, 1867.
Ridley, James & Clarisa Ridley, June 16, 1867.
Ridley, Polk & Hannah Thompson, June 17, 1867.
Roan, Charles H. & Peline Ready, Jan. 31, 1867.
Roberts, C. J. & Winney A. Green, Oct. 31, 1867.
Roberson, Alex & Edna Cates, June 2, 1867.
Rogers, W. M. & Miss Fannie Peck, Nov. 1, 1867.
Roges, Felix & Malinda McFadden, July 28, 1867.
Roland, T. M. & Judy A. Primm, Apr. 14, 1867.
Rollins, James & Anna Dowell, July 6, 1867.
Rorister, Geo. & Sallie Smith, May 19, 1867.
Rose, B. & S. J. M. Donnell, May 19, 1867.
Rostetter, Thomas & Miss Mattie M. Guailbreath, May 27, 1867.
Rouse, Wm. & Charlotte M. Gaines, June 15, 1867.
Rowen, Valentine & Chaney Harmon, Sept. 29, 1867.
Rowland, James C. & Polina J. Smotherman, Nov. 21, 1867.
Rucker, Albert & Milly A. Rucker, July 7, 1867.
Rucker, James & Hannah Brown, Jan. 1, 1867.
Rucker, Joseph A. & Amelia K. Overall, Jan. 29, 1867.
Rucker, R. M. & Anna L. Cowen, July 24, 1867.
Rucker, Samuel & Mary Pitts, Oct. 30, 1867.
Rucker, Samuel & Mary Richmond, Oct. 30, 1867.
Runnels, Jack & Matilda Hargrove, Dec. 19, 1867.
Runnels, Jack & Pathenia Fearguson, Dec. 19, 1867.
Russell, Clayborn & Cath. Marlin, Dec. 24, 1867.
Sadler, John & Marg. Benson, Nov. 21, 1867.
Sanders, Rich. & Caroline Stockard, Dec. 14, 1867.

RUTHERFORD COUNTY MARRIAGES

Sanders, Solomon & Paralee Alexander, Nov. 9, 1867.
Sandwich, Westey & Gracy Lytle, Aug. 10, 1867.
Scales, Jessee & Mary Patton, Apr. 15, 1867.
Schorn, Wm. & Fanny Ferrill, Jan. 20, 1867.
Scruggs, B. C. & Miss M. A. McCollock, Dec. 10, 1867.
Scruggs, Peter & Amanda Buchanan, Feb. 9, 1867.
Scruggs, Spencer & Molly Clark, Dec. 30, 1867.
Scruggs, W. T. & Miss L. J. Watkins, Dec. 24, 1867.
Shanks, Wm. & Sallie Jewell, June 9, 1867.
Sharber, Wm. J. & Anna Alexander, Feb. 13, 1867.
Sharp, Henry & Fanny Eagleton, May 1, 1867.
Shelton, Isaac & Drucilla M. Alford, Dec. 19, 1867.
Shelton, Jackson & Lucinda Upchurch, Feb. 15, 1867.
Shelton, John & Amy Walden, June 11, 1867.
Shelton, John A. & Mary E. Helton, Feb. 27, 1867.
Shepherd, Thomas H. & Mary E. Thompson, Feb. 25, 1867.
Sherrell, Tilman & Sarah Jane Cloud, Aug. 25, 1867.
Short, George & Charlott Boyd, June 29, 1867.
Sims, Bartlett E. & Nannie B. Patterson, Mar. 7, 1867.
Sims, Wesley & Malinda Fisher, Aug. 18, 1867.
Slaughter, Jacob & Mantania Hendrix, Jan. 17, 1867.
Smith, Amanuel & Tenia Thompson, Jan. 16, 1867.
Smith, Burrell & Fanny McDermott, Sept. 22, 1867.
Smith, Green & Fanny Knox, Apr. 19, 1867.
Smith, David M. & Mrs. Fannie Minor, Sept. 2, 1867.
Smith, J. E. & Tennie Knox, May 9, 1867.
Smith, John & Sarah Baldredge, Sept. 24, 1867.
Smith, S. B. & Maggie A. McAdoo, Jan. 15, 1867.
Smith, Theo & Matilda Bedford, Oct. 22, 1867.
Smith, Thomas & Margaret Ford, Aug. 29, 1867.
Smith, W. A. J. & Mary J. Stafford, Aug. 6, 1867.
Smith, Wm. & Margaret Davis, Jan. 4, 1867.
Smith, Wm. E. & Eliz. Suggs, Oct. 3, 1867.
Smotherman, Turman & M. E. Long, Dec. 18, 1867.
Sneed, H. H. & Quimona Allen, Sept. 11, 1867.
Snell, Thomas H. & Katharine R. Williams, Jan. 15, 1867.
Spain, John W. & Mary Ann Towns, Sept. 18, 1867.
Spain, Thomas & Mary D. Smith, Nov. 12, 1867.
Span, John W. & Mary Ann Gosos (Cross?), Sept. 18, 1867.
Spence, John & Narcissa Spence, May 6, 1867.
Steel, Robert & Lucinda Neal, June 2, 1867.
Steinhagan, R. T. & Mary E. White, Aug. 5, 1867.
Sterchie, F. P. & Mary M. Sanders, Dec. 18, 1867.
Stevenson, Jerry & Kitty Alford, Jan. 3, 1867.
Stoball, Samuel & Manerva Hall, May 18, 1867.
Stockel, Charles & Clarinda Gotto, July 29, 1867.
Stovall, Joseph & Lucy Ross, July 30, 1867.
Strickland, Alfred & Lizzie Strickland, June 19, 1867.
Strickland, Wiley & Louisa Childress, Dec. 31, 1867.
Sublett, Houston & Harriett Anderson, Dec. 26, 1867.
Sublett, John & Johanna Jones, Aug. 1, 1867.
Summers, John W. & Martha E. Guise, Jan. 22, 1867.
Swafford, John & Mary Jane Foster, Sept. 28, 1867.
Swan, Wm. R. & Mary A. Seagrove, Jan. 10, 1867.

214

Swater, Henry & Tabitha White, Jan. 26, 1867.
Tabern, Cornelius & Bettie Snell, Sept. 23, 1867.
Tally, Robert & Harlow Ready, Dec. 29, 1867.
Tally, Thomas & Sarah Brown, Jan. 26, 1867.
Tarpley, Burton & Ann Fitzgerald, Jan. 19, 1867.
Tarver, Lewis & Prudy Word, Mar. 27, 1867.
Taylor, Ned & Johannah Smith, Aug. 23, 1867.
Taylor, Uriah & Lizzie Miller, Jan. 12, 1867.
Terry, D. P. & S. F. Burge, Apr. 18, 1867.
Tilly, Joseph & Ann Turner, Jan. 26, 1867.
Thomas, James H. & Rachel Wharton, Nov. 7, 1867.
Thomas, Johnathan & Charlott Jordan, Sept. 10, 1867.
Thompson, Abram & Ellen Scruggs, Jan. 5, 1867.
Thompson, Isham & Emily Hall, June 22, 1867.
Thompson, Samuel & Judeth Huggins, Jan. 23, 1867.
Tompkins, A. G. & Lizzie January, Feb. 3, 1867.
Towsend, Martin & Harriet Manly, Jan. 22, 1867.
Troxler, S. W. & Catherine Sparks, June 20, 1867.
Tune, W. B. & M. A. Brewer, Oct. 10, 1867.
Turner, Dock & Harriet Rucker, Dec. 7, 1867.
Turner, Wm. & Fanny Morgan, Jan. 6, 1867.
Underwood, James & Jane Barrett, Apr. 6, 1867.
Underwood, Joseph & Susan M. Halstead, Apr. 24, 1867.
Upchurch, C. G. & Eliz. Chumly, Feb. 13, 1867.
Valentine, Edward & Mary Smith, Apr. 13, 1867.
Vance, John W. & Catherine Gilmore, Apr. 15, 1867.
Vandergriff, J. W. & Sarah A. Lahue, Aug. 1, 1867.
Vaughan, Robert & Julia Blackman, May 27, 1867.
Vaughan, Gus & Clarisa Roberts, Aug. 16, 1867.
Vaught, Thomas B. & Mary Knox, Sept. 21, 1867.
Vaught, Wm. & Sallie Lorance, Dec. 18, 1867.
Vawter, Moses & Catherine Haynes, Aug. 24, 1867.
Veal, Joseph & Emma Hicks, May 19, 1867.
Wagoner, Nelson & Emalene Shofner, Feb. 22, 1867.
Wail, J. L. D. & Eliz. Sullivan, Jan. 22, 1867.
Walker, J. T. & Sue F. Bell, Nov. 13, 1867.
Walkup, R. O. & Susan Rucker, Dec. 10, 1867.
Waller, Ephriam & Fanny Mitchell, Nov. 7, 1867.
Wallin, J. E. & Araminda R. Adcock, Aug. 15, 1867.
Walters, Geo. & Miss Kate Ross, Dec. 31, 1867.
Ward, James & Lizzie Nipper, Aug. 5, 1867.
Ward, James N. & Jennie Nichols, Jan. 1, 1867.
Ward, Sam & Mary Hall, Mar. 27, 1867.
Ward, Thomas & Betty Thorn, Apr. 5, 1867.
Warner, Joseph H. & Miss Allis G. Hord, June 21, 1867.
Warnick, Martin & Sarah Jarratt, Mar. 23, 1867.
Warren, John A. & Miss Bettie A. W. Vaught, Oct. 26, 1867.
Washington, Albert & Margaret Suttle, Aug. 10, 1867.
Watkins, W. D. & Josephine C. Dennis, Dec. 17, 1867.
Weatherford, Richard & Eliza Fuller, Oct. 26, 1867.
Webb, Harrison & Mary Smith, Jan. 6, 1867.
Webb, M. H. & Jane E. Elam, Dec. 11, 1867.
Wendel, Charley & Jane Rich, Aug. 6, 1867.

RUTHERFORD COUNTY MARRIAGES

Whitby, Wm. & Matilda F. Colman, Nov. 11, 1867.
White, Benj. & Patsy White, July 16, 1867.
White, L. B. & Mrs. Kate Mays, July 28, 1867.
Whitfield, Pilgrim & Sarah Gilliam, Dec. 12, 1867.
Whitis, R. L. & J. A. Carlton, Dec. 11, 1867.
Williams, Andrew & Isabella Kelly, Aug. 10, 1867.
Williams, G. & Mary J. Floyd, Dec. 29, 1867.
Williams, Henry & Nancy Tune, Sept. 18, 1867.
Williams, Henry & Susan Thomas, June 3, 1867.
Williams, J. S. & Emma A. Sellars, Dec. 13, 1867.
Williams, James L. & Rebecca J. Heath, Sept. 10, 1867.
Williams, Moses & Lucy Avant, Oct. 24, 1867.
Wilson, Geo. & Tennessee Colman, Dec. 31, 1867.
Wilson, Joseph & Sylva Lowe, Nov. 28, 1867.
Winn, Cader & Mary Winn, Feb. 18, 1867.
Winn, Henderson & Rachel Winn, Feb. 18, 1867.
Wood, A. T. & Mary Jane Wood, Nov. 22, 1867.
Wood, R. H. & Sallie E. Wooten, Dec. 12, 1867.
Woodfin, H. W. & M. E. Clark, Sept. 5, 1867.
Woodfin, S. C. & Eliz. F. Clark, Nov. 7, 1867.
Woodston, Jerry & Margaret Miller, Dec. 27, 1867.
Wooten, Charles B. & Mary C. Knox, Sept. 26, 1867.
York, Moses & Julia McLean, Dec. 22, 1867.
Youlett, James & Mariah Smith, June 1, 1867.
Zachary, Nathan & America Patton, Jan. 25, 1867.

1868

Adams, J. N. & Mary Ott, Feb. 4, 1868.
Addams, Wm. H. & Nannie Adkerson, Jan. 2, 1868.
Alexander, John H. & Virginia Burton, Dec. 26, 1868.
Alexander, Joseph & Amanda Whitson, July 4, 1868.
Alexander, Rufus & Mariah Pearce, Jan. 11, 1868.
Alexander, Solomon & Lucy Shuss, Dec. 30, 1868.
Alexander, Stephen & Martha Smotherman, Jan. 18, 1868.
Alexander, Wm. & Emeline McKnight, Dec. 24, 1868.
Allen, M. G. & Bell Dillon, Feb. 25, 1868.
Anderson, Aaron & Sue Manson, Mar. 16, 1868.
Anderson, Geo. & Charlotte McGlothan, Oct. 4, 1868.
Arledge, H. M. & N. C. Bivins, May 26, 1868.
Avant, Albert & Minnie Codwell, Apr. 24, 1868.
Baker, Anderson & Miss Minasey Barnette, Sept. 10, 1868.
Bailey, Alfred A. & Nancy Jane Bush, Apr. 12, 1868.
Baltimore, Charles & Nancy Dobson, Mar. 28, 1868.
Barber, Thomas & Miss Lulia Swain, Sept. 23, 1868.
Barfield, Sim & Jane Smith, Nov. 13, 1868.
Barrett, Nathan T. & Fannie Leonard, May 9, 1868.
Barrett, Tom & Sue Hood, June 26, 1868.
Barton, Robert & Tenney Smith, Jan. 18, 1868.
Barton, W. A. & Miss Laura Jones, Feb. 13, 1868.
Baksette, Wm. & Lizzie Smith, Nov. 19, 1868.
Bass, Jerry & Emaline Kennedy, May 23, 1868.
Bass, Sandy & Arie Stockard, Dec. 15, 1868.
Batey, John B. & Mary H. Richardson, May 6, 1868.

Baxter, B. F. & Miss Molly E. Thomas, Sept. 30, 1868.
Beard, William & Netty Patillow, Feb. 19, 1868.
Becton, Geo. & Minervy Alford, Dec. 24, 1868.
Bedford, Alex & Jane Hennicy, July 28, 1868.
Bell, Marshal & Julia Brown, Dec. 24, 1868.
Bell, W. A. & Mary Webb, May 10, 1868.
Bellefont, Hiram & Betsy Gooch, Oct. 17, 1868.
Benson, M. L. & Sallie Poindexter, Dec. 1, 1868.
Black, Henry & Matilda Black, Jan. 8, 1868.
Black, Horace & Lucy Morton, Dec. 16, 1868.
Blake, J. R. & Josephine Blake, June 17, 1868.
Bonner, Andy & Mary Randolph, Dec. 23, 1868.
Boone, Daniel & Emily Garner, Sept. 17, 1868.
Booth, Soloman & Kittie Black, Apr. 25, 1868.
Brooks, E. W. & Miss T. M. Rucker, Nov. 28, 1868.
Brown, J. T. & Miss D. F. Smith, Aug. 18, 1868.
Brown, John E. & Rhodie E. Eads, Apr. 7, 1868.
Brown, Samuel & Mollie Boyd, Jan. 31, 1868.
Brown, Wesley & Angeline Fletcher, Dec. 23, 1868.
Buchanan, Aaron & Isabella Neal, July 19, 1868.
Buchanan, Washington & Catharine Goodwin, Sept. 26, 1868.
Burk, Adam & Jane Cook, May 17, 1868.
Burkett, Stephen & Lizzie Pike, Sept. 15, 1868.
Burros, Nathan & Caroline Woods, Mar. 8, 1868.
Buross, Cesar & Annie Burross, June 27, 1868.
Burrus, Jackson & Clary Knox, Feb. 29, 1868.
Burten, Sam & Margaret Smith, Feb. 22, 1868.
Bush, W. A. & Mollie Peak, Dec. 2, 1868.
Butler, Geoge & Dilsie Butler, Dec. 16, 1868.
Butler, Hutson & Sarah Wade, Jan. 21, 1868.
Butler, John & Eliz. Smith, Oct. 10, 1868.
Caffy, M. F. & Mattie Carnahan, Nov. 19, 1868.
Calhoun, Milton & Eliza Norman, Dec. 31, 1868.
Cannon, John A. & Susan Malone, Jan. 20, 1868.
Cannon, Nicholas & Mary I. Ferguson, Sept. 11, 1868.
Carlton, J. N. & S. A. R. Patterson, Dec. 23, 1868.
Carter, Henry & Angeline Perry, Dec. 4, 1868.
Carter, Henry & Martha Moore, Sept. 4, 1868.
Carter, James H. & Callie Burnette, Sept. 15, 1868.
Carter, John & Brunette Polk, Feb. 6, 1868.
Carter, Perry & Minny Batey, Nov. 8, 1868.
Carter, W. A. & Peggy Barnatt, Jan. 7, 1868.
Caruthers, Moses & Amanda Wadley, March 3, 1868.
Chambers, Sandiford & Emaline Parmer, Mar. 30, 1868.
Childress, Isaac & Caroline Fletcher, Sept. 20, 1868.
Chrisman, Aaron & Susan Chrisman, Sept. 20, 1868.
Clark, E. M. & Annie M. Boles, May 28, 1868.
Collins, Simeon & Lourany Temples, Sept. 29, 1868.
Colman, Geo. & Doriny Bennett, Sept. 18, 1868.
Colman, Isham & Allice Johnson, Nov. 29, 1868.
Compton, Maj. Banister & Miss Sudie Duncan, Oct. 16, 1868.
Copeland, George & Eliza Belifant, July 9, 1868.
Cornwell, Eli & Eliza Foster, Jan. 3, 1868.

RUTHERFORD COUNTY MARRIAGES

Coursey, W. J. & F. A. Smotherman, Aug. 2, 1868.
Craddock, Nathaniel & N. V. McKnight, Dec. 2, 1868.
Crawford, Joshua & Ludia Woods, Oct. 15, 1868.
Crockett, Charles A. & Mollie Lawrence, Dec. 24, 1868.
Crockett, O. W. & Alice B. Crockett, Dec. 24, 1868.
Daniel, John M. & Sarah E. Shepherd, Jan. 14, 1868.
Darbley, Elijah & Eliza Darbley, Feb. 16, 1868.
Davidson, Jacob & Susan Williams, Feb. 27, 1868.
Davis, Edward & Rose Harris, Nov. 12, 1868.
Davis, I. L. & Miss M. N. Gregory, Jan. 22, 1868.
Davis, Turner & Sindy Thompson, Jan. 8, 1868.
Delbridge, E. W. & Mattie F. Pruett, Nov. 10, 1868.
Dennis, William & Lizzie Ryan, May 2, 1868.
Dickinson, M. A. & Martha V. Crews, July 25, 1868.
Dicus, W. D. & Nancy J. Ship, Apr. 22, 1868.
Dill, Joseph & M. R. Saunders, Dec. 21, 1868.
Dillard, John & Sallie Reeves, Dec. 1, 1868.
Dillin, Albert & Mary Sheppard, Dec. 24, 1868.
Doty, W. E. & Eliza Nelson, Oct. 10, 1868.
Douglass, Fred & Ellen Phillips, Jan. 4, 1868.
Douglass, John W. & Miss Mary F. R. Hill, May 4, 1868.
Dowdy, G. W. & S. G. Hendrix, Nov. 19, 1868.
Downing, Wm. & Nancy Moore, Dec. 5, 1868.
Drake, Willis & Rose Sanders, Sept. 26, 1868.
Drumwright, Wm. B. & Mattie F. Rather, Nov. 15, 1868.
Dudley, R. H. & Mattie E. Beasley, Apr. 9, 1868.
Dun, Wm. & Eliza Burleson, Nov. 5, 1868.
Dunaway, Sandy & Ellen Searcy, Feb. 26, 1868.
Duram, Henry & Margaret Gilbert, Mar. 13, 1868.
Eagleton, Alex & Lizzie Scruggs, Mar. 28, 1868.
Edwards, J. W. & Miss Laura Howse, Sept. 11, 1868.
Edwards, Thomas G. & Eliz. Mullins, June 6, 1868.
Edwards, L. H. & Mattie E. Elam, Dec. 24, 1868.
Ellington, Wm. & Mattie Smith, Feb. 26, 1868.
Elliott, James & Sarah Ann E. Morgan, July 10, 1868.
Embry, Charles & Ann White, May 23, 1868.
Emory, James K. & Adaline Morris, Nov. 14, 1868.
Eperson, Carson & Miss Narcissa C. Wilson, Sept. 17, 1868.
Etter, Jack & Sarah Tucker, Sept. 18, 1868.
Evans, Isham & Julia Ann Winston, Dec. 22, 1868.
Fain, R. W. & M. E. Nance, Feb. 20, 1868.
Fleming, Thomas & Rosanna Norman, Jan. 5, 1868.
Fletcher, Reuben & Lucinda Fletcher, Oct. 30, 1868.
Floyd, W. J. & Mary J. Carlton, Dec. 7, 1868.
Ford, Wm. & Malinda Ford, Nov. 18, 1868.
Forrester, J. E. & Mary E. Underwood, Jan. 5, 1868.
Fover, James H. & Martha Alman, Jan. 26, 1868.
Fowler, Thomas B. & Mrs. Sallie Richardson, Feb. 6, 1868.
Franklin, Doctor & Lou Brown, Feb. 27, 1868.
Frierson, Ballam & Mary Pitman, Oct. 10, 1868.
Frilus, Charlie & Mary Bush, Jan. 29, 1868.
Furgeson, Yateman & Dilcy Richardson, Sept. 26, 1868.
Gandy, W. A. & S. A. Hogwood, Dec. 7, 1868.
Garnette, Isaac & Nancy Johnson, Dec. 30, 1868.

Gilmore, J. D. & Mary L. Edwards, Dec. 24, 1868.
Golden, Josias & Nancy Drake, Dec. 26, 1868.
Gooch, Add & Caroline Hays, June 15, 1868.
Gooch, George & Mary Gooch, Dec. 28, 1868.
Gooch, Joseph & Sarah A. Kimbro, Dec. 26, 1868.
Gooch, Monroe & Casie Brown, Oct. 10, 1868.
Gooch, Wm. & Harriet Murray, Apr. 30, 1868.
Graham, Robert & Adline Davis, Dec. 28, 1868.
Gray, Charlie & Kitty Jameson, Jan. 25, 1868.
Green, Richard & Lindy Sanders, July 3, 1868.
Guffy, James C. & Miss S. E. Jones, Mar. 4, 1868.
Halbert, Edmund & Susan Wetherly, Jan. 2, 1868.
Hales, Jake & Lilly Jarrett, Mar. 22, 1868.
Hall, Henderson & Clovia Banks, Dec. 17, 1868.
Hall, John & Chisen & Louticia Allen, July 30, 1868.
Hall, Joseph & Angeline Irvin, Jan. 15, 1868.
Hall, Samuel & Anna Barton, Jan. 1, 1868.
Halstead, Benj. & Amanda Smotherman, Oct. 25, 1868.
Halstead, Benj. & Evergreen Halstead, Nov. 11, 1868.
Hamilton, Andrew & Elmira Calhoun, Dec. 31, 1868.
Hamilton, J. W. & Miss L. H. Still, Sept. 22, 1868.
Hamilton, John & Frances Ransom, Apr. 10, 1868.
Hamilton, R. J. & Miss Susan Donnell, July 6, 1868.
Hare, James & Luvery Johnson, Dec. 16, 1868.
Harris, Thomas & Perlina Span, Aug. 6, 1868.
Harrod, Edward & Eliza Jane Fletcher, Sept. 16, 1868.
Haynes, Wm. & Malinda Brock, Oct. 4, 1868.
Hays, Ned & Lizzie Williamson, Jan. 12, 1868.
Heath, David & Mrs. M. J. Jones, Jan. 12, 1868.
Helton, J. B. & Eliz. Eastwood, Jan. 30, 1868.
Henderson, Eli & Eliza Norton, Dec. 25, 1868.
Henderson, Richard & Alice Robison, Oct. 15, 1868.
Hibbett, George & Kitty Goodman, Dec. 24, 1868.
Hibbett, Thomas C. & Miss Sue Tommie Johns, Feb. 4, 1868.
Hill, Emanuel & Ruth Ann Snell, June 22, 1868.
Hirshbrunner, Jacob & Margaret Angeline Northcott, Nov. 21, 1868.
Hobbs, Jefferson & Miss Josephine Bona, Oct. 1, 1868.
Hockett, Anthony & Eliza Hockett, June 2, 1868.
Hodge, J. F. & Julia A. Colman, Dec. 26, 1868.
Hodge, S. H. & Emma Smith, Dec. 24, 1868.
Hogs, Geo. W. & Susan Spann, June 14, 1868.
Hogwood, J. F. & S. F. Cain, July 16, 1868.
Holden, Wm. M. & Isabella Holden, Nov. 5, 1868.
Hoover, Levi & Ann Gillerease, Feb. 12, 1868.
Hope, Wm. & Nancy A. Fleming, Mar. 12, 1868.
Hops, Sip & Eliz. Cox, Jan. 14, 1868.
Horton, Isaac W. & Melissa H. Talley, Aug. 31, 1868.
Hoskins, George & Ann Walker, Apr. 4, 1868.
Howland, Wilson & Amanda Norman, Jan. 18, 1868.
Hudson, Alex & Jane Anderson, Apr. 30, 1868.
Huddleston, Bos & Alice Carney, Aug. 10, 1868.
Hughs, Orange & Jane Grays, Aug. 8, 1868.
Hunt, Simon & Mollie Jarratt, Feb. 8, 1868.

Huston, Wm. & Martha Pate, Dec. 25, 1868.
Ivie, Patrick & Emily Muckelbatten, July 28, 1868.
Irvin, Robert S. & Miss E. A. Lackey, Dec. 2, 1868.
James, Gilbert & Mary Morton, Oct. 29, 1868.
Jameson, Allen & Susan Brown, Mar. 6, 1868.
Jarratt, Snow S. & Jinnia A. Howard, May 4, 1868.
Jenkins, W. R. & Miss Texie Wade, Nov. 10, 1868.
Jernigan, Reuben & Kitty Anderson, Jan. 17, 1868.
Jetton, R. B. & Miss Nancy Borring, Dec. 1, 1868.
Jetton, Wm. & Agnes Smith, Aug. 24, 1868.
Johns, Edmund G. & Anna M. Barlow, Oct. 13, 1868.
Johns, George & Rachel Black, Jan. 11, 1868.
Johnson, Eugene M. & Martha E. Norman, July 20, 1868.
Johnson, John & Ellen V. Reeves, Apr. 25, 1868.
Joiner, Tucker & Fanny Scruggs, Jan. 8, 1868.
Jones, Elihu & Mrs. Cassie Newman, Sept. 22, 1868.
Jones, F. M. & N. N. Hall, Aug. 25, 1868.
Jones, Janus & Falonie Buchanan, Feb. 1, 1868.
Jones, M. H. & M. E. Yearwood, Nov. 5, 1868.
Jones, Matt & Catherine Poser, Dec. 25, 1868.
Jones, Sam & Eliz. Lawrence, Dec. 25, 1868.
Jordan, James & Martha Crichlow, Dec. 25, 1868.
Jude, Ellis & Ann North, Nov. 24, 1868.
Keeble, Armstead & Ellen Mathews, July 7, 1868.
Keeble, Clem & Josephine Gooch, Dec. 18, 1868.
Keeble, Wm. G. & Nannie Yeargan, Dec. 2, 1868.
Kennedy, Washington & Mahala Washington, Feb. 16, 1868.
Kerr, Phillip & Violet Walker, Feb. 14, 1868.
King, Alfred & Mary Pearcy, May 30, 1868.
King, Jack & Vina Randolph, Jan. 4, 1868.
Knox, Robert & Mariah Thompson, Dec. 26, 1868.
Lamb, J. A. & Malissa E. Smotherman, Nov. 6, 1868.
Lamb, W. R. & Emaline Cole, May 8, 1868.
Lamey, S. J. & Mary R. McCoy, Feb. 26, 1868.
Lane, Purnal & Lucy Harshaw, Sept. 1, 1868.
Lane, P. & Margaret Lawrence, Jan. 15, 1868.
Lannis, Wm. N. & Sallie T. Sanders, Dec. 9, 1868.
Lannom. Joseph W. & Virginia W. Welch, Nov. 24, 1868.
Latimore, Geo. & Ann Rucker, Jan. 9, 1868.
Lawrence, Geo. & Eliza Span, Mar. 4, 1868.
Lawrence, Harrison & Sarah Bracy, Mar. 5, 1868.
Ledbetter, N. C. & Miss N. R. Lytle, Mar. 23, 1868.
Peiper, Wm. F. & Mary LaFon, Sept. 22, 1868.
Lester, C. S. & Catherine C. Marable, Sept. 24, 1868.
Lester, J. H. & Queen E. Smith, Dec. 16, 1868.
Lewis, Frank & Silla Malone, Nov. 2, 1868.
Lewis, J. W. & Camarius Rachels, Feb. 21, 1868.
Lewis, Abraham & Ellen Miles, Feb. 13, 1868.
Lillard, Jack & Tempy Kelton, Feb. 6, 1868.
Lillard, Jim & Victoria Williams, July 30, 1868.
Lillard, Robert & Lavinia Hanner, Mar. 4, 1868.
Lillard, Spencer & Kate Sawyers, Jan. 4, 1868.
Lockard, Wm. & Mary J. Zumbro, Sept. 24, 1868.
Long, James & Evelina Marlin, Oct. 15, 1868.
Love, Bunyan & Harriet Davis, July 7, 1868.

Love, Henderson & Jane Wrather, July 7, 1868.
Love, Peter & Jane Martin, Nov. 17, 1868.
Lyon, Edward & Mary Harris, Jan. 1, 1868.
Lytle, Andrew & Malinda Johnson, Aug. 1, 1868.
Maney, Henry & Ella Wade, Aug. 11, 1868.
Maney, Spencer & Matilda White, July 1, 1868.
Marable, J. R. & Oliver H. Smith, Dec. 28, 1868.
March, Moses & Margaret Hollis, Dec. 16, 1868.
Marlin, Edward & Laura J. Russworm, June 5, 1868.
Martin, Andrew B. & Miss C. Alice Ready, May 6, 1868.
Martin, H. C. & Maggie Jamison, Oct. 30, 1868.
Martin, John & Ann Roans, Jan. 29, 1868.
Martin, Richard & Martha Black, May 2, 1868.
Martin, Thomas & Melviny Maberry, Dec. 30, 1868.
Matthews, Nathan & Caldoin Bridges, July 4, 1868.
Maxwell, John A. & Queen E. Smith, Dec. 20, 1868.
May, J. H. & M. J. Goodman, Dec. 16, 1868.
Meeky, Edmond & Harriet Jordan, Aug. 1, 1868.
Miller, E. S. & Mrs. Q. E. Davis, Oct. 29, 1868.
Miller, John & Sallie E. Miller, Mar. 19, 1868.
Miller, P. C. F. & M. J. Gordon, Dec. 23, 1868.
Miller, Rolly H. & Zedda Parker, Apr. 7, 1868.
Mills, James & Ginny Lytle, Dec. 27, 1868.
Modrall, John & Miss Atelia F. White, ------, 1868.
Moore, Eli & Nelly Rogers, Jan. 6, 1868.
Moore, C. F. & Julia Arbuckle, Dec. 16, 1868.
Moore, John G. & Sue P. Haliburton, Jan. 23, 1868.
Moore, Joseph & Mandy Woods, Mar. 10, 1868.
Morton, Wm. H. & Sallie Douglass, Sept. 3, 1868.
Moxby, James C. & Mary Etta Hall, Feb. 23, 1868.
Mosley, John W. & Belle Byers, July 28, 1868.
Montgomery, James B. & M. F. Noe, Jan. 15, 1868.
Murphry, Nat & Loucinda Vaughan, Oct. 12, 1868.
Murphy, Harrison & Amy Smith, June 26, 1868.
Murray, Reubin & Susan Childress, Nov. 24, 1868.
Muse, J. W. & Bell Sumler, June 25, 1868.
McAdoo, Ed & Lucy Frazier, Oct. 30, 1868.
McAdoo, Green & Vina Robertson, Jan. 10, 1868.
McAdoo, Isham & Bettie Rucker, Jan. 9, 1868.
McAlister, Ben & Diner Dollan, June 17, 1868.
McClarrin, T. J. & Anna Vaughan, Jan. 12, 1868.
McCord, W. H. & S. Macon Williams, Dec. 18, 1868.
McCullough, J. F. & Annie Alford, Mar. 3, 1868.
McCullough, J. W. & S. E. Owen, May 29, 1868.
McCullough, R. T. & Miss S. A. Jordan, Aug. 14, 1868.
McGhee, Nelson & Rachel Parks, Mar. 16, 1868.
McGill, Pleasant R. & Amelia Williams, Sept. 5, 1868.
McGill, Wm. & Amanda Alexander, Apr. 4, 1868.
McGucken, George & M. F. Wyatt, June 14, 1868.
McKnight, John A. & Lucy M. Barker, Mar. 31, 1868.
McKnight, R. M. & S. F. Bivins, Apr. 16, 1868.
McLain, J. H. & Missouri Thorn, Aug. 20, 1868.
McLean, John C. & Sallie Hutton, Jan. 20, 1868.
McMeekin, Wm. & Ann E. Jordan, Nov. 7, 1868.

Nance, Burrel & Roxanna Butler, Feb. 7, 1868.
Neil, J. F. & Lucy A. Rucker, Sept. 17, 1868.
Nelson, Ed & Lucy Colman, Dec. 24, 1868.
Nelson, F. & Miss C. J. Davis, Jan. 26, 1868.
Nelson, Jerry & Sindy Woods, Mar. 29, 1868.
Nevins, Wm. & Josette Gooch, Dec. 29, 1868.
Newman, Albert & Harriett Lawrence, Mar. 8, 1868.
Newman, Andrew & Lucinda Kelly, Nov. 19, 1868.
Newman, Dick & Sophia Snell, Oct. 23, 1868.
Newman, J. T. & Ellen Todd, Sept. 28, 1868.
Newman, Wm. & Mollie Drake, Dec. 22, 1868.
Nichol, James & Julia Palmer, Jan. 16, 1868.
Nolen, James & Jane Trimber, Mar. 13, 1868.
Norman, Wm. & Mary A. Howland, Jan. 29, 1868.
North, J. A. & Nannie E. Williamson, Dec. 3, 1868.
Ott, J. T. & Levenia Baxter, Feb. 25, 1868.
Overall, James R. & Artelia Fathera, Feb. 24, 1868.
Overall, Solomon & Louisa Allen, Jan. 21, 1868.
Overall, W. F. & M. L. Jetton, Jan. 1, 1868.
Owens, C. J. & Tennessee A. Reeves, Mar. 4, 1868.
Paneely, John F. & Nancy A. Mathews, Apr. 7, 1868.
Parker, A. B. & Emily Bryant, Nov. 3, 1868.
Parker, Ben & Mary Patterson, June 13, 1868.
Parsley, J. A. & Sarah Span, Dec. 27, 1868.
Pate, George & Betty Redman, Dec. 18, 1868.
Patterson, Everard & Narcissa Winn, Oct. 13, 1868.
Peeble, Joshua & Hager Hill, Oct. 25, 1868.
Peden, Isaac N. & Mary Jane Burnett, Nov. 29, 1868.
Phillips, Andrew & Sophia E. Farris, June 16, 1868.
Phillips, Charlie & Violet Wallis, Feb. 14, 1868.
Phillips, Rev. J. M. & Miss Augusta Smith, Dec. 22, 1868.
Pickett, Charles & Margarette Phillips, July 2, 1868.
Pierce, John D. & Mary B. Grant, Feb. 13, 1868.
Pinkleton, Henry & Mary Jane Hall, June 12, 1868.
Piper, James & Susan Osborn, Mar. 31, 1868.
Pollard, Moses & Jennie Croswaite, Oct. 31, 1868.
Ponder, Anthony & Pelina Reed, Dec. 12, 1868.
Powell, W. O. & Mary A. McDowell, Feb. 11, 1868.
Poterfield, C. M. & Ann Hogwood, Nov. 18, 1868.
Price, Benj. & Eliza King, Aug. 10, 1868.
Price, Henry & Martha McKnight, Dec. 30, 1868.
Ralston, Ephraim & Susan Tucker, Jan. 24, 1868.
Ransom, C. & Frances Davis, Dec. 18, 1868.
Ray, Wm. Y. & Narcissa Lawrence, Feb. 17, 1868.
Reeves, Frank & Mattie Tucker, Aug. 23, 1868.
Rideout, Thomas & Jenny Murfree, Apr. 1, 1868.
Ridley, Boyd & Margaret Garrett, Jan. 30, 1868.
Ridley, Dick & Puss Davis, Apr. 19, 1868.
Ridman, Wm. & Jane Daniel, May 17, 1868.
Roads, Armon & Mary Trigg, Mar. 1, 1868.
Roberts, Abram & Sally Sims, Feb. 1, 1868.
Robertson, Burgus & Mandy Roberson, Dec. 31, 1868.
Robertson, Solomon & Margaret Overall, Jan. 26, 1868.
Robison, Calvin & Eliza Bly, June 13, 1868.
Rowden, Thomas & Ann C. Flowers, Aug. 8, 1868.

Rutledge, R. P. & Lucy Lockard, July 7, 1868.
Sadler, Wm. & Lou Maloan, Apr. 11, 1868.
Sanders, Abram & Ann Hatten, Nov. 11, 1868.
Sanders, Thomas & Miss Symantha Sanders, Sept. 13, 1868.
Sartin, James R. & Miss Bettie Mankin, Oct. 6, 1868.
Sawyers, David & Jennet McDowell, Sept. 8, 1868.
Sawyers, James C. & Eliza Massey, Aug. 6, 1868.
Sawyers, White & Margaret Ann Jordan, Aug. 23, 1868.
Scales, Isaac & Daphney Sawyers, Dec. 18, 1868.
Seay, John W. & Nancy B. Bellephant, Aug. 6, 1868.
Settle, Flem & Nancy Hooker, Jan. 4, 1868.
Seward, Abe & Emma Turner, May 2, 1868.
Seward, James & Eliz. Walden, Feb. 6, 1868.
Seward, Tobias & Martha Moore, Jan. 18, 1868.
Shaper, Isham & Martha Anderson, Dec. 15, 1868.
Shelton, Jesse & Martha Jane Eaton, Nov. 24, 1868.
Shelton, John B. & Susan E. Howse, Nov. 25, 1868.
Sikes, Harry & Joanna Ridley, Nov. 27, 1868.
Sims, L. G. & Miss Sallie E. Cooper, Oct. 24, 1868.
Singleton, Wm. L. & Miss Mary J. Swain, Aug. 23, 1868.
Sivley, Herman H. & Miss Katey Bohems, Mar. 31, 1868.
Sloan, Frank & Easter Youngblood, Nov. 9, 1868.
Smiley, Geo. & Violet Daniel, Jan. 25, 1868.
Smith, Benj. & Miss Susan Jordan, Nov. 20, 1868.
Smith, Buck & Sallie Smith, Feb. 13, 1868.
Smith, Gabe & Milly York, Feb. 23, 1868.
Smith, Granderson & Mahaly Vaughan, Jan. 2, 1868.
Smith, Henry & Eliza Watkins, June 20, 1868.
Smith, J. F. & Susan Insell, Sept. 29, 1868.
Smith, Jacob & Josephine Miller, Jan. 13, 1868.
Smith, James H. & Jane Insell, Dec. 31, 1868.
Smith, Joshua & Lavina Holt, Jan. 18, 1868.
Smith, Lenius & Fanny Jordan, Feb. 11, 1868.
Smith, Peter & Pricilla White, Jan. 10, 1868.
Smith, Thomas & Eliz. Irvin, Feb. 13, 1868.
Smith, Thomas & Eliz. Travis, Feb. 16, 1868.
Smith, Washington & Mira Perry, Oct. 3, 1868.
Smith, Zack & Lucy Stamper, July 13, 1868.
Smithey, Joseph & Margaret Lay, Jan. 20, 1868.
Smotherman, Robert & Martha E. Holt, Aug. 4, 1868.
Snider, Wm. & Rutha Jane Morgan, May 10, 1868.
Stem, Huriah & Eliz. Smotherman, Sept. 3, 1868.
Stewart, Alfred & Queen Windrow, Jan. 16, 1868.
Stewart, Elias & Lucy Welch, Jan. 7, 1868.
Stockard, Wm. S. & Lockie A. Russworm, Apr. 23, 1868.
Suggs, G. L. R. & M. J. Edwards, Feb. 13, 1868.
Suggs, Harvey & Alemede Hickenbottom, Sept. 4, 1868.
Sullivan, C. T. A. & Miss M. N. Sanders, Sept. 8, 1868.
Sullivan, Rufus D. & Sarah Eliz. Fox, Nov. 18, 1868.
Swink, Geo. W. & Gerusia Maxwell, Oct. 29, 1868.
Talley, D. H. & Frankie Henderson, Dec. 16, 1868.
Tallon, John L. & Martha J. Burkett, Mar. 19, 1868.
Tey, Zachariah & Ellen Holoway, July 3, 1868.
Thomas, Wiley Jefferson & Susanah Stem, Oct. 21, 1868.

Thompson, P. P. & Maggie Mabry, Feb. 20, 1868.
Tiller, George A. & Cordelia Miles, Nov. 9, 1868.
Tolliver, Wm. & Eliz. Collier, Sept. 17, 1868.
Traylor, H. F. & Miss Amanda Williams, Oct. 8, 1868.
Tucker, Thomas J. & Dovie E. Sanders, Dec. 1, 1868.
Trigg, John H. & Mrs. Lucy White, Apr. 4, 1868.
Turner, E. L. & Fanny Maney, Nov. 19, 1868.
Vaughan, Moses & Victoria Sanders, Apr. 8, 1868.
Vaught, Wm. & Sally Lorance, Dec. 18, 1868.
Vaulks, Carey & Charlotte Sublett, Nov. 7, 1868.
Wade, Robert & Minerva Russworm, Nov. 14, 1868.
Wade, Watson & Huldy Drake, Mar. 6, 1866.
Walker, Matt & Malindy Goodin, Sept. 14, 1868.
Walker, W. D. & Josephine Dennis, Jan. 18, 1868.
Ward, L. A. & Mrs. M. A. Farmer, Dec. 20, 1868.
Ward, Levi & Minny Turner, Aug. 22, 1868.
Washington, Henry & Mary Little, Dec. 26, 1868.
Watkins, Daniel & Fanny Sanford, Jan. 13, 1868.
Watson, Cap & Donia Rucker, Oct. 3, 1868.
Webster, Daniel & Mary Clark, Apr. 22, 1868.
Wells, J. A. & Miss M. E. Smith, Nov. 26, 1868.
Welsh, G. R. & Fanny Lannom, Nov. 5, 1868.
Wendel, Dr. J. E. & Miss Jane C. Eakin, Aug. 18, 1868.
White, Henry & Manie Davis, Dec. 28, 1868.
White, Stephen & Lucy Buchanan, Nov. 11, 1868.
Whitman, W. S. & Miss Kate Marchbanks, Jan. 13, 1868.
Whitson, Lorenza & Miss Tenny Fly, Aug. 6, 1868.
Whitworth, Lee & Bettie Ransom, Dec. 1, 1868.
Wilkinson, George & Miss Octie Henderson, Oct. 20, 1868.
Wilkinson, James R. P. & Miss Anna E. Crawford, Nov. 20,
   1868.
Wilkinson, Peter & Sarah Whaley, Aug. 30, 1868.
Williams, Andrew & Manervay Phipps, Jan. 26, 1868.
Williams, Austin & Eliza Wade, Nov. 28, 1868.
Williams, Daniel & Laura Turner, July 2, 1868.
Williams, Geo. & Charlotte Lowe, Dec. 17, 1868.
Williams, Haywood & Angeline Lawrence, Dec. 23, 1868.
Williams, J. D. & Mary A. Brothers, Oct. 11, 1868.
Williams, John A. & Miss A. B. Spence, Nov. 4, 1868.
Williams, John & Lucy Fletcher, Nov. 11, 1868.
Willoughby, J. M. & Mary Brothers, Nov. 19, 1868.
Wilson, J. B. & A. R. Kirk, Aug. 13, 1868.
Wilson, Robert & Nancy Jenkins, Jan. 2, 1868.
Winfrey, James A. & Eliz. Brown, Nov. 10, 1868.
Witherspoon, J. M. & Miss Henry, July 26, 1868.
Witt, Lucius & Leoma Reed, May 15, 1868.
Wood, Sam & Nancy McGill, Nov. 18, 1868.
Wood, W. C. & Amanda M. Howell, Jan. 12, 1868.
Woodard, Cornelius & Margaret A. Smith, Sept. 17, 1868.
Word, Thomas & Eliza Mason, Feb. 13, 1868.
Works, John & Frances McGill, Dec. 7, 1868.
Wright, John L. & Eliz. Hamilton, July 21, 1868.
Yell, John C. & Sarah E. Jacobs, Apr. 17, 1868.
York, Mitchell & Susan Beesley, June 7, 1868.
Young, John L. & Mrs. Nannie E. McAdoo, Nov. 8, 1868.

1869

Abernathy, Anderson & Sarah Harris, Jan. 21, 1869.
Adams, J. H. & M. S. Bryant, Jan. 12, 1869.
Allen, Wm. & Bettie Howell, July 13, 1869.
Alsup, James & Josie McGowen, May 11, 1869.
Alsup, Jasper & Martha Wrather, May 15, 1869.
Anderson, Benj. & Ella Black, Dec. 13, 1869.
Arnold, Thomas & Richard Ann Jacobs, Jan. 20, 1869.
Arthur, J. R. & D. A. Williams, Nov. 21, 1869.
Arthur, B. F. & P. J. Williams, Sept. 30, 1869.
Ashley, George & Catharine Norman, Dec. 16, 1869.
Auberry, J. G. & Mary Jane Newman, Mar. 11, 1869.
Bailey, J. S. & Rebecca M. Prater, Sept. 5, 1869.
Baird, H. P. & Victoria Ward, Feb. 25, 1869.
Baker, Henry & Rachel Davis, Nov. 6, 1869.
Ballentine, John H. & Melissa H. Batey, Jan. 26, 1869.
Barber, Joseph & Jennie Butler, Oct. 28, 1869.
Barlow, Wm. N. & Mary Ann Walls, Jan. 28, 1869.
Barton, George & Sarah Reeves, Mar. 31, 1869.
Bass, Austin & Milly Wade, Feb. 12, 1869.
Bass, Edmund & Adelaide Jarratt, Dec. 1, 1869.
Bass, Hartwell P. & Jennie S. Sims, Nov. 9, 1869.
Batey, Booker & Lovenia Childom, Mar. 7, 1869.
Batey, Edm. & Caroline Vawter, Sept. 4, 1869.
Batey, J. W. & Mary E. Foster, Jan. 15, 1869.
Batey, Martin & Joanna Haynes, Apr. 29, 1869.
Baty, David & Lizzie McDowell, Sept. 28, 1869.
Baugh, Wm. & Chaney Floyd, Dec. 28, 1869.
Belk, John A. & Martha Jane Barrett, Aug. 13, 1869.
Bellow, Jenry & Parthena Davis, Dec. 27, 1869.
Berry, Peter & Roxana Moore, June 5, 1869.
Bety, Col. W. F. M. & Laura Miller, Aug. 19, 1869.
Bird, Frank & Tempy Anderson, Jan. 14, 1869.
Blackman, Robert & Minerva Wade, Oct. 7, 1869.
Blackenship, Burrel & Arann Sharp, Apr. 20, 1869.
Blair, Jacob & Mary Ann York, Apr. 3, 1869.
Bock, Adam & Jennie Jordan, Feb. 3, 1869.
Bostick, Boson & Emma Banks, July 17, 1869.
Bowers, J. A. & Annie M. Dunn, Dec. 25, 1869.
Bowman, James C. & Josephine Jacobs, Aug. 6, 1869.
Boykin, W. O. & Lou Batey, Dec. 22, 1869.
Bratcher, B. F. & Mary Thompson, Aug. 11, 1869.
Bratey, Marshal & Leny Wright, Jan. 7, 1869.
Brittain, Columbus L. & Mary L. Brothers, Nov. 24, 1869.
Brooks, Henry & Ann Eliza Rucker, Oct. 27, 1869.
Brown, Cole & Nicey Bell, Feb. 18, 1869.
Brown, George & Betsy Jane Todd, June 10, 1869.
Brown, Isaac & Lucinda Green, May 7, 1869.
Brown, Jack & Laura Gooch, Apr. 3, 1869.
Brown, Jordan A. & W. A. Sanders, Oct. 19, 1869.
Brown, Ross M. & Alice K. Edwards, Feb. 25, 1869.
Brown, Samuel & Mollie Boyd, Jan. 31, 1869.
Broyles, John & Margaret Ransom, Mar. 1, 1869.

Buchanan, Anthony & Nannie Drennon, Sept. 3, 1869.
Burkett, Ellett & Melviny Pitman, Jan. 5, 1869.
Burns, Albert & Jane McGrefor, Feb. 10, 1869.
Burnett, John G. & Mary E. Miller, Sept. 23, 1869.
Burnett, John T. & Maggie Goodwin, Mar. 5, 1869.
Burris, Henry & Francis Wright, Jan. 6, 1869.
Butler, G. W. & Lizzie B. Manor, Sept. 8, 1869.
Butler, John & Martha Bailey, Oct. 5, 1869.
Butler, John & Milly Alford, Sept. 11, 1869.
Butts, Abner & Celia Lawrence, May 8, 1869.
Byers, Robert M. & Fanny Massey, Jan. 27, 1869.
Byford, John & Jane Couch, Dec. 17, 1869.
Caldwell, Anderson & Easter Pigg, July 3, 1869.
Campbell, D. S. & E. A. Batey, Oct. 28, 1869.
Cannon, E. C. & Sallie E. Lytle, June 22, 1869.
Cantrell, L. G. & S. A. Tucker, Dec. 12, 1869.
Carney, John & Josephine Sublett, Dec. 28, 1869.
Carney, Legrand V. & M ary Overall, Feb. 21, 1869.
Carothers, Moses & Lucy Parker, Dec. 16, 1869.
Carrol, Wm. & Mrs. Emeline Taylor, July 9, 1869.
Carson, W. H. & Mary Jane Taylor, Dec. 23, 1869.
Cathey, Josiah & Exeline Johnson, Apr. 3, 1869.
Cato, Daniel & Ellen Wade, Sept. 18, 1869.
Cauley, Wm. & Martha Gibbs, Aug. 14, 1869.
Champion, James A. & Nannie P. Davidson, Jan. 20, 1869.
Charles, Sam & Mary Lytle, Oct. 3, 1869.
Childress, Dempsy & Louisa Smith, Jan. 13, 1869.
Childress, Harvey & American Webb, Dec. 3, 1869.
Christy, S. B. & Mrs. S. M. Frost, Feb. 11, 1869.
Clark, G. N. & Mollie J. Crosslin, Dec. 19, 1869.
Claxton, A. J. & Melissa McElroy, Nov. 9, 1869.
Clayton, Wm. & Fanny Ross, Dec. 24, 1869.
Coleman, Charles & Eliza Ann Henderson, Jan. 13, 1869.
Coleman, John & Isabella Thorn, Feb. 25, 1869.
Collins, David R. & Addie B. Braswell, Nov. 16, 1869.
Comer, Geo. M. D. & Emeline Jenkins, Dec. 13, 1869.
Cook, J. G. & Martha A. Hale, Oct. 30, 1869.
Crawford, Bedford & Fannie Rogers, Jan. 30, 1869.
Crawford, Gid & Isabella Rucker, Dec. 18, 1869.
Critchlow, Thomas N. & Idella Clark, Nov. 24, 1869.
Crockett, Henry & Catherine Harris, June 16, 1869.
Crockett, G. H. & M. J. Smotherman, Feb. 2, 1869.
Crouse, Alfred & Caroline Burns, Dec. 26, 1869.
Crutchfield, B. J. & Sarah Catherine Elmore, Nov. 5,
    1869.
Currin, Henry & Lou Sanders, June 18, 1869.
Currin, Luke & Caroline Ivie, July 1, 1869.
Davis, Alfred & Sarah Martin, Feb. 7, 1869.
Davis. Richard & Laura Phelps, Nov. 13, 1869.
Davis, Turner & Sissy Thompson, Jan. 8, 1869.
Day, J. I. & Susie C. Halstead, Nov. 14, 1869.
Deckerd, Henry & Ann Roberts, Oct. 31, 1869.
Denny, B. R. & Rachel Jackson, Jan. 3, 1869.
Drake, Isaac & Etta Burton, Oct. 1, 1869.

RUTHERFORD COUNTY MARRIAGES

Driggins, Hugh & Amanda Caldwell, Aug. 20, 1869.
Dromgoole, Geo. C. & M. F. Duffer, May 25, 1869.
Dunn, A. P. & Alice A. Friffin, Dec. 23, 1869.
Dunn, Daniel & Cynthia Goodman, Dec. 23, 1869.
Eatherly, Patrick A. & Fannie E. Sanders, Jan. 20, 1869.
Edwards, Dennis & Marg. Vaughan, Oct. 22, 1869.
Edwards, Jeff & Nannie Gordon, Apr. 21, 1869.
Elder, Wm. & Sindy Randolph, Dec. 30, 1869.
Etheridge, Jerry & Sarah Cluck, Feb. 23, 1869.
Eustice, Charles & Hannah Beesley, July 17, 1869.
Evans, James & Helen Dromgoole, May 13, 1869.
Featherston, W. G. & Sarah F. North, July 14, 1869.
Fletcher, Henry & Hannah Sharp, Feb. 18, 1869.
Fletcher, James B. & Martha T. Shelton, Apr. 14, 1869.
Fletcher, Thomas & Susan Hines, Aug. 11, 1869.
Fletcher, Washington & Millie Fletcher, May 29, 1869.
Fletcher, Wm. & Sarah Miller, Apr. 11, 1869.
Floyd, L. H. & Martha O. Wilson, Dec. 23, 1869.
Floyd, Ned & Jane Haynes, Dec. 12, 1869.
Floyd, Thomas & Melissa Sawyers, Jan. 28, 1869.
Ford, Harrison & Sallie Thompson, Jan. 30, 1869.
Frierson, Porter & Martha Huggins, Dec. 30, 1869.
Fuller, John N. & Ann Travis, Dec. 20, 1869.
Furgeson, Philip & Anne White, July 24, 1869.
Garner, Adam & Amanda Clemens, Sept. 16, 1869.
Gibson, Joseph & Margaret Jane Frizzell, June 24, 1869.
Gilchrist, Carter & Lucy Garrett, Jan. 25, 1869.
Gooch, Jesse & Harriet Hill, Dec. 29, 1869.
Goodloe, R. M. & Emma Hall, Mar. 25, 1869.
Green, Joseph & Amelia Crawford, Dec. 24, 1869.
Griffin, George & Priscilla West, July 29, 1869.
Griffin, James T. & Virginia E. Lillard, July 1, 1869.
Grisham, Edm. & Susan Smith, Mar. 20, 1869.
Grisham, Rufus & Martha Young, Dec. 30, 1869.
Gwin, John & Martha Batey, Oct. 7, 1869.
Hatchett, George W. & Frony Mankin, -----, 1869.
Hadchett, Nathan C. S. & Susan E. Mankins, Mar. 24, 1869.
Haley, J. R. & E. Smotherman, Sept. 1, 1869.
Hall, John N. & American A. Patterson, Feb. 11, 1869.
Hall, Nat & Amanda Irvin, May 19, 1869.
Harris, Jefferson & Eveline Skinner, June 2, 1869.
Harvey, Dick & Mary Seekers, Mar. 25, 1869.
Haynes, Christopher & Leanna M. Floyd, Nov. 11, 1869.
Haynes, Geo. & Harriet Haynes, Sept. 4, 1869.
Haynes, John & Frances Washington, Mar. 4, 1869.
Haynes, John A. & Martha E. Taylor, Dec. 31, 1869.
Hays, Geo. W. & Tempie Ann Towns, Apr. 1, 1869.
Hays, Louis & Sarah Rayborn, Dec. 16, 1869.
Hazelwood, W. R. & Mrs. Isabella B. Cheek, June 3, 1869.
Hedgepath, A. W. & M. A. E. Carter, June 3, 1869.
Helton, John B. & Hetty Sheppard, Sept. 30, 1869.
Hendon, J. R. & Mattie Campbell, Oct. 19, 1869.
Hendricks, Wm. & Martha Haley, Dec. 30, 1869.
Hendrix, J. G. & Tennie P. Elliott, Sept. 3, 1869.

Henry, John & Isabella Murfree, Dec. 30, 1869.
Hert, John & Julia Keeble, Feb. 23, 1869.
Hibbett, Joseph C. & T. Carrie James, Mar. 16, 1869.
Higdon, Francis & Anna E. Farr, Oct. 3, 1869.
Hill, Alexander & Neely Ann Walpole, Dec. 24, 1869.
Hill, C. A. & Elvy Winsett, Feb. 25, 1869.
Hill, J. A. & E. B. Smith, Dec. 9, 1869.
Hockett, Van & Ellen Hockett, Nov. 1, 1869.
Hollowell, J. W. & Mollie I. Lytle, Nov. 25, 1869.
Hooker, James & Mary -----, June 16, 1869.
Hoover, Geo. & Jemima Neal, Dec. 27, 1869.
Hoover, Henry & Melinda Goodman, Oct. 8, 1869.
Hoover, W. H. & Hannah Herof, Nov. 4, 1869.
Hoover, Wm. & Aremita Lowe, Dec. 27, 1869.
Horton, James J. & Laura Elliott, Feb. 11, 1869.
Howland, Clinton & Winnie Alexander, June 2, 1869.
Howse, John R. & Josie Turner, Nov. 11, 1869.
Howse, Robert & Serry Golston, Dec. 30, 1869.
Hubbard, W. H. & Eliz. Chumley, Sept. 23, 1869.
Huggins, Weakley & Fannie Ridley, Sept. 25, 1869.
Hughes, Jacob & Louisa Hughes, Sept. 5, 1869.
Hunt, Howard & Ellen Malone, Oct. 2, 1869.
Hutchins, Henry N. & Kate Huggins, Apr. 29, 1869.
Jackson, Thomas & Caroline Roy, Feb. 14, 1869.
Jacobs, Alfred & Bettie Fox, Feb. 10, 1869.
Jamison, Joseph & Lucinda Burns, Feb. 18, 1869.
Jarratt, Benj. A. & Sarah J. Moss, Apr. 9, 1869.
Jarratt, Daniel & Mary Murphy, Feb. 3, 1869.
Jarratt, Patrick & Caroline Lyons, Nov. 30, 1869.
Jarratt, Wm. R. & Gertrude M. Woolbridge, Dec. 22, 1869.
Jenkins, Peter & Mollie Montgomery, July 25, 1869.
Jennings, Jerry & Nancy Jones, Mar. 21, 1869.
Jetton, Buck & Maria Woods, Feb. 27, 1869.
Jetton, John & Pricilla Childress, Oct. 28, 1869.
Johns, Nelson & Mintie White, Aug. 12, 1869.
Johnson, B. P. & E. P. Norman, Feb. 22, 1869.
Johnson, F. R. & Miss Serena B. Elder, May 20, 1869.
Johnson, Joseph & Nancy Gentry, Oct. 16, 1869.
Johnson, Mike & Mary Deaton, May 29, 1869.
Johnson, W. T. & Jemsha T. Read, Feb. 5, 1869.
Jones, E. H., Jr. & Ophelia Wasson, July 17, 1869.
Jones, Frank & Channy Phillips, Jan. 13, 1869.
Jones, Wm. & Lizzie Nelson, Dec. 3, 1869.
Jordan, Harrison & Violet Haley, Apr. 27. 1869.
Jordan, John & Martha McLean, Sept. 4, 1869.
Keeble, Henry & Eliza Stoves, Apr. 9, 1869.
Kelly, John & Mattie Brooks, Oct. 13, 1869.
Kelton, Adolphus A. & Mary A. Barker, Sept. 12, 1869.
Kidd, Thomas & Sallie Butler, Aug. 25, 1869.
Kimbro, George & Alice Rucker, Aug. 13, 1869.
King, Henry & Annie Howard, Aug. 21, 1869.
King, Isaiah & Parlee McFadden, Marc. 13, 1869.
King, John & Mary Lillard, Dec. 8, 1869.
King, Wm. & Frances C. Massey, Jan. 28, 1869.
Kirby, David & Martha Smith, Sept. 23, 1869.

Knight, Edw. & Jennie Dickinson, Nov. 25, 1869.
Knight, James & Caroline Runnels, Feb. 20, 1869.
Kirkman, Lewis & Lizzie Hall, Aug. 19, 1869.
Knox, Peter & Emeline McKnight, Feb. 12, 1869.
Lamb, James K. & Melissa F. Jorton, Nov. 28, 1869.
Lasater, Basil B. & Sarah Ann Cluck, June 15, 1869.
Lawrence, David & Jane Redmon, Dec. 29, 1869.
Lawrence, Walker & Georgiana Jordan, Nov. 3, 1869.
Leath, W. J. & Eliza June Barmer, Oct. 3, 1869.
Leatherman, D. M. & Bettie Snell, Jan. 28, 1869.
Lee, W. D. & Rebecca McKee, Jan. 9, 1869.
Leiper, James A. & Alice Kimbro, Mar. 13, 1869.
Lewis, Allen & Martha Bell, Oct. 16, 1869.
Lewis, N. M. & Josephine Alice Ward, Nov. 24, 1869.
Lillard, W. G. & Bettie Crockett, Feb. 25, 1869.
Lillard, Wesley & Sally Seward, Mar. 12, 1869.
Lipscomb, James & Rachel Wilson, Dec. 30, 1869.
Lofton, Lewis & Marg. Rucker, Dec. 26, 1869.
Lorance, Wright & Nancy Alexander, Dec. 7, 1869.
Love, Reuben & Sina Gooch, Dec. 29, 1869.
Love, Sumner & Mittie Alford, July 10, 1869.
Lowe, James G. & Rachel Kelton, Jan. 20, 1869.
Lowe, W. S. & Sarah Ashley, June 15, 1869.
Lowe, Willis & Mary Newman, June 18, 1869.
Lytle, Eva der & Mary Chath. Bibb, Jan. 13, 1869.
Lytle, Frank & Lucinda Spence, Aug. 11, 1869.
Lytle, Geo. & Sallie Ann Cason, Jan. 11, 1869.
Lytle, Granison & Caroline Martin, July 3, 1869.
Lytle, John & Mary Nelson, July 25, 1869.
Maberry, Cadimis & Sarah Ann Paris, Dec. 30, 1869.
Malone, Preston & Harriet Coleman, Dec. 17, 1869.
Maney, David & Lucy Burke, Dec. 1, 1869.
Maney, Nathan J. & Alice Yeargan, Feb. 13, 1869.
Mankins, Newton F. & Vinie Prater, Jan. 15, 1869.
Mankins, W. P. & Phebe Jane Runnels, Jan. 30, 1869.
Mankins, Wm. & Alice J. Kelton, July 13, 1869.
Manson, Mat & Oliva Snell, Oct. 31, 1869.
Marable, J. R. & Olivia Smith, Dec. 20, 1869.
Marlin, B. M. & Rebecca Johnson, Jan. 4, 1869.
Martin, G. W. & Sallie J. White, Sept. 2, 1869.
Mayne, John J. & Ellen Holden, Jan. 20, 1869.
Miles, Marshal & Amanda Miles, Jan. 28, 1869.
Miller, Benj. & Mollie Webb, Feb. 6, 1869.
Miller, Henry & Sarah Youree, Jan. 19, 1869.
Miller, John & Agatha Crawford, Feb. 24, 1869.
Miller, Matt & Mirandy Baugh, Jan. 17, 1869.
Miller, Taylor & Viny Minter, Jan. 14, 1869.
Miller, Wilson B. & Dellie Z. Cowan, Aug. 23, 1869.
Minter, Wm. & Ella Hill, June 3, 1869.
Mitchell, James & Melinda Burlason, Dec. 17, 1869.
Mitchell, Tony & Bettie Trimble, Mar. 15, 1869.
Moore, Jacob & Luncinda Davis, May 7, 1869.
Moore, Zack & Ann Scruggs, Dec. 30, 1869.
Morgan, John H. & Sue F. Fletcher, June 17, 1869.
Morrow, Jerry & Emma Miller, Dec. 20, 1869.

Morton, Anderson & Lexie Hickerson, Mar. 13, 1869.
Mount, John B. & Eliz. J. Arnold, Dec. 14, 1869.
Mullins, Andrew & Catherine Smith, Jan. 23, 1869.
Mullins, Jacob & Ellen Marlin, Dec. 31, 1869.
Mullins, Nelson W. & Eliz. D. Cook, Feb. 2, 1869.
Murfree, Henry & Grace Trimble, Nov. 11, 1869.
Murfree, Marcus & Matilda Reeves, Aug. 16, 1869.
Murhead, John & E. M. Brothers, Aug. 30, 1869.
Murphey, H. G. & Lou Miles, Dec. 9, 1869.
Murphy, James K. P. & Fannie J. Edwards, Dec. 16, 1869.
Murphy, Miles P. & Isabella Miles, Feb. 16, 1869.
Murray, Leonard & Jacky Haley, Oct. 1, 1869.
Murray, Thomas & Annie Thompson, Jan. 23, 1869.
Murry, Turner & Ellen Baskette, Jan. 9, 1869.
McAdoo, Henry & Puss Davis, Mar. 4, 1869.
McAdoo, Henry & Lutetia Huddleston, Sept. 2, 1869.
McAdoo, Jerry & Catherine Vaught, Aug. 30, 1869.
McCrary, G. N. & Lizzie Lowe, Feb. 16, 1869.
McDermott, John & Narcissa Scruggs, --------, 1869.
McIntyre, Geo. & Julia Reed, Dec. 31, 1869.
McKay, Martin & Ellen Farris, Apr. 3, 1869.
McKee, Ambrose & Susan Bell, June 30, 1869.
McKee, Rufus R. & Susannah F. Ott, --------, 1869.
McKnight, John N. & Nannie A. McKee, Mar. 3, 1869.
McLaughlin, A. E. & Annie T. Morton, Nov. 18, 1869.
Nance, J. N. & Mrs. L. P. Sampley, Nov. 10, 1869.
Napper, James W. & Margaret Clark, Feb. 2, 1869.
Neal, Grant & Louisa Rouse, Jan. 5, 1869.
Nelson, Geo. & Martha Randolph, Feb. 25, 1869.
Newman, James K. & Mary E. Prater, Sept. 29, 1869.
Newsom, Thomas & Mattie Caldwell, Jan. 26, 1869.
Nolen, Daniel & Eliz. Jones, Feb. 14, 1869.
North, David & Lucinda Burrus, Jan. 30, 1869.
Nuckolls, Dr. Garret S. & Mary E. Jordan, Aug. 15, 1869.
O'Neal, James A. & Vilett Clarinda Dunn, May 13, 1869.
Odell, R. S. & N. C. Gregory, Sept. 2, 1869.
Osborn, Henry & Melinda Jenkins, June 10, 1869.
Overall, Asbury & Louisa Allen, --------, 1869.
Owen, Israel & Susan Barlow, Dec. 6, 1869.
Owens, Joseph N. & Rebecca Arnett, Nov. 15, 1869.
Owens, W. G. & Mary E. Young, Mar. 13, 1869.
Palmer, Jacob & Amanda Brown, Jan. 29, 1869.
Parks, Lewis & Catty Anderson, Feb. 1, 1869.
Patterson, Charley & Josie Huff, Apr. 7, 1869.
Patterson, Frank & Emma Mathews, Nov. 17, 1869.
Patton, Wm. & Lizzie Sikes, Feb. 24, 1869.
Peay, Thomas T. & Miss Nancy Jarratt, Apr. 19, 1869.
Perry, Elec & Narcis Cannon, Apr. 24, 1869.
Petty, John Calvin & Susan Adeline Caffy, Dec. 14, 1869.
Petty, Thomas A. & Mary Jane Johnson, Dec. 15, 1869.
Phillips, Henry & Frances Crawford, June 12, 1869.
Phillips, Luke & Jennie Rucker, Aug. 17, 1869.
Phillips, Wm. H. & Sallie Jarratt, Feb. 12, 1869.
Phoenix, Samuel H. & Nancy L. Birdsong, Mar. 3, 1869.

RUTHERFORD COUNTY MARRIAGES

Pinkard, George & Creasy Rather, Jan. 6, 1869.
Pitman, Monroe & Josephine Talbert, Jan. 14, 1869.
Pittard, John H. & Mary Sheppard, Nov. 4, 1869.
Pitts, M. E. & E. L. Helton, Jan. 19, 1869.
Price, Jesse P. & Lizzie Dickson, May 25, 1869.
Price, Wesley & Lacey Ann Cotton, June 13, 1869.
Puckett, A. J. & E. R. Jones, June 21, 1869.
Randolph, Anderson & Isabella Malone, Jan. 12, 1869.
Randolph, Jacob & Amanda Hohn, Dec. 29, 1869.
Ransom, Harry & Mary Tapley, Dec. 28, 1869.
Reeves, John & Amanda Miller, Feb. 18, 1869.
Rhodes, Andrew J. & Nannie Donnell, Dec. 28, 1869.
Ridley, Stewart & Eliz. Hunt, Sept. 25, 1869.
Ridout, Braxton & Crene Smith, Dec. 23, 1869.
Roberts, Wm. Jr. & Mary Watkins, May 20, 1869.
Robertson, D. M. & Nancy C. Talant, Sept. 29, 1869.
Robison, James R. & Maggie C. McGill, Oct. 13, 1869.
Robison, Col. W. D. & Fannie D. Rice, Sept. 15, 1869.
Robison, Wm. & Mantie Hackett, June 22, 1869.
Rock, Stephen & Eliza Spence, Apr. 7, 1869.
Rogers, L. A. & Mattie A. Cates, Dec. 9, 1869.
Rogers, S. M. & Lucy S. Nesbitt, Nov. 24, 1869.
Ross, Frank E. & Mary L. Riddle, Oct. 14, 1869.
Ross, Thomas & Adaline Perkins, Dec. 28, 1869.
Rowland, Samuel & Isabella Slate, Nov. 8, 1869.
Rucker, Handy & Fanny Hall, July 2, 1869.
Rucker, Samuel & Rosie Carney, Dec. 16, 1869.
Rucker, Wm. & Harriett Rogers, Jan. 12, 1869.
Rushing, W. P. & Mary Spray, May 23, 1869.
Russell, Wm. & A. C. Manire, Mar. 7, 1869.
Rylee, J. E. & Bettie Warren, Jan. 15, 1869.
Salscorter, Meyer & Rachel Essinger, Jan. 28, 1869.
Sanders, Geo. & Caroline Claiborne, Aug. 24, 1869.
Scovel, Arthur & Dianna Covington, Apr. 20, 1869.
Scruggs, Joshua & Eliza Rogers, Jan. 6, 1869.
Shane, Samuel & Lucy Maney, Aug. 11, 1869.
Sharber, Benj. & Jane Kelson, Sept. 6, 1869.
Sheppard, Peyton & Nancy Ann Thompson, Dec. 13, 1869.
Sheppard, Dr. W. C. & Idell Jones, Dec. 2, 1869.
Sherrill, Dr. Llewellen & Julia Emma Mason, Oct. 21, 1869.
Shelton, W. P. & Rebecca Lee, Jan. 5, 1869.
Shipp, J. G. & Martha Jane Eastwood, Feb. 4, 1869.
Sikes, James & Marg. Shannon, Dec. 27, 1869.
Sikes, Jesse & Mary Garden, Feb. 27, 1869.
Simpson, Wm. T. & Frances L. Parker, Dec. 28, 1869.
Sims, James & Laura Elkins, Feb. 4, 1869.
Slaughter, Robert & Eliza Malone, Jan. 6, 1869.
Smith, Gran & Atlanta Smith, May 30, 1869.
Smith, Harvey & Miss Mary F. Welch, Jan. 14, 1869.
Smith, Martin & Susan Jarratt, Feb. 25, 1869.
Smith, Robert A. & Florence McLain, Nov. 9, 1869.
Smith, S. Hardy & Dora L. Wade, June 8, 1869.
Smith, W. J. & Lautrusy Castleman, Dec. 22, 1869.
Smith, Wm. & Mintie Harris, July 29, 1869.

RUTHERFORD COUNTY MARRIAGES

Smotherman, Barton & Eliz. Smotherman, Jan. 14, 1869.
Sneed, Wm. H. & Fruzanna Jane Anderson, Oct. 14, 1869.
Snell, Wm. & Adeline Lytle, Nov. 18, 1869.
Span, Cato & Martha Ann McLaren, Sept. 4, 1869.
Spence, Henderson & Isabella Anderson, Jan. 21, 1869.
Stanton, Joseph & Sarah Miller, Feb. 1, 1869.
Stearns, D. & Melvinia Childress, Dec. 30, 1869.
Stephens, George Washington & Harriet Neal, Jan. 14, 1869.
Stewart, Andrew & Charlotte Woods, Nov. 19, 1869.
Stockard, James E. & Mary L. Russworn, Feb. 17, 1869.
Stokes, John & Aury Orange, Jan. 1, 1869.
Sublett, Campbell & Rose Turner, Dec. 21, 1869.
Sublet, Washington & Martha Moore, ---- ----, 1869.
Sugs, Isham & Sallie Woods, Feb. 6, 1869.
Summers, Wm. A. & Melvina Milligan, Feb. 10, 1869.
Tallant, Wm. & Lutetia Allen, Dec. 27, 1869.
Taylor, John M. & Queen Victoria A. Syllivan, Nov. 17, 1869.
Taylor, R. W. & N. D. F. Rutledge, Jan. 12, 1869.
Terry, John & Sallie Bet Smith, Dec. 21, 1869.
Terry, Willis & American Jackson, Sept. 4, 1869.
Thomas, James & Sarah Hoagland, Mar. 7, 1869.
Thomas, James & Nicey Garner, Feb. 6, 1869.
Thompson, G. R. H. & Susan J. Hight, Feb. 7, 1869.
Thompson, Simon & Fanny Jefferson, Feb. 8, 1869.
Thompson, Stephen & Ann Brown, Aug. 28, 1869.
Thompson, Wm. W. & Sarah Patterson, Oct. 7, 1869.
Todd, C. W. & Lou M. Compton, Aug. 26, 1869.
Todd, J. T. & Martha Read, Jan. 20, 1869.
Todd, Samuel & Nancy McCullough, Apr. 18, 1869.
Tolbert, John & Adeline Johns, Sept. 8, 1869.
Toliver, Henry & Susan Ann Hays, July 27, 1869.
Tompkins, R. T. & Jennie Clark, June 1, 1869.
Townson, Stafford & Hannah Setton, Dec. 23, 1869.
Trimble, Lewis & Emily Barr, Nov. 19, 1869.
Trimble, Russell & Ann Terry, Sept. 22, 1869.
Tucker, L. G. & Miss S. A. Tucker, Dec. 12, 1869.
Underhill, Alex I. & Kate LeMay, Sept. 2, 1869.
Ursery, John & Nancy Susan Smiddy, Nov. 3, 1869.
Vaughan, J. F. & Miss M. C. Gannaway, Apr. 15, 1869.
Vaughan, J. L. & Fannie A. Lane, Feb. 17, 1869.
Vaughan, J. T. & Betty Haynes, Oct. 17, 1869.
Vaughan, John B. & Mary E. Maxwell, Mar. 7, 1869.
Vaughan, Joseph & Nancy Dunn, Feb. 7, 1869.
Vaughan, Wm. & Nancy Haley, Sept. 30, 1869.
Vaught, G. T. & Mary J. Bradley, Feb. 18, 1869.
Vaughter, D. R. & Miss Eldora Nashv, Dec. 15, 1869.
Vaughter, John B. & Sarah Jane Evins, Dec. 7, 1869.
Vickey, Daniel G. & Lucy J. Gannaway, June 16, 1869.
Voris, Thomas & Harriet Buchanan, Apr. 6, 1869.
Wade, John & Christina Smith, Dec. 22, 1869.
Wade, John W. & Miss Fannie Ransom, Dec. 28, 1869.
Wade, Israel & Theny Wade, Mar. 1, 1869.
Wade, M. B. & Miss Fannie Black, Mar. 30, 1869.

RUTHERFORD COUNTY MARRIAGES

Wade, Nathan & Addie Lipscomb, Dec. 9, 1869.
Wade, Robert & Adline Alford, Jan. 7, 1869.
Wagner, G. W. & Lizzie Clark, Mar. 10, 1869.
Wagner, Wm. & Martha Jane Tennyson, Nov. 23, 1869.
Walden, Daniel & Dosia Bell, June 6, 1869.
Walden, David & Ellen Hise, Apr. 24, 1869.
Walker, J. W. & Miss Painlee Willoughby, Nov. 11, 1869.
Walkup, John D. & Eliza J. Yearwood, Aug. 31, 1869.
Wallace, Wm. & Eliz. Riley, Feb. 23, 1869.
Ward, Andrew & Julia Cowans, June 27, 1869.
Warren, Gabriel & Abby Broiles, Nov. 23, 1869.
Warren, Henry & Pimmy Boner, Oct. 7, 1869.
Warren, J. P. & Nancy M. Crabtree, May 10, 1869.
Washington, James & Fannie Baugh, Nov. 27, 1869.
Waterson, Nelson & Julia Ann Covington, Nov. 4, 1869.
Watson, Jerry & Viola Smith, Mar. 5, 1869.
Weakley, Sandy & Samella Neal, Feb. 8, 1869.
Webb, Crockett & Rachel Williams, Aug. 8, 1869.
Webster, Daniel T. & Mattie C. Thompson, Apr. 29, 1869.
Wheeler, T. C. & Martha L. Swan, Sept. 16, 1869.
White, Marion W. & Mary E. Barlow, Dec. 30, 1869.
White, Robert L. C. & Miss Ella Wade, May 26, 1869.
Whitby, W. W. & S. E. Coleman, Feb. 9, 1869.
Whitemore, C. P. & Jemima Robison, July 20, 1869.
Wilkison, Cessar & Sallie Killough, Jan. 28, 1869.
Williams, Billy & Fannie Barton, Apr. 26, 1869.
Williams, F. B. & Miss Sarah R. Wiggs, Aug. 10, 1869.
Williams, George & Jane Baker, Sept. 18, 1869.
Williams, John Bell & Mary Virginia Williams, Apr. 19, 1869.
Williamson, Robert J. & Mary J. Johnson, May 13, 1869.
Wilson, Thomas & Harriet Wilson, Feb. 10, 1869.
Woods, Dock & Caroline Rudder, Dec. 28, 1869.
Woods, John W. & Elleanor Thompson, Dec. 22, 1869.
Wootson, Perry & Maria Windrow, Oct. 21, 1869.
Work, Henry & Nancy Smith, Aug. 13, 1869.
Woods, Wm. & Milly Webb, Sept. 30, 1869.
Wright, Mason & Mary Woods, Mar. 3, 1869.
Young, B. C. & Miss A. E. Hall, Dec. 8, 1869.
Young, Davis & Manervy Brown, Jan. 6, 1869.
Young, Emanuel & Susan Harrison, Mar. 7, 1869.
Young, Harry & Charity White, Jan. 9, 1869.
Young, Henry & Eliza Bryson, June 9, 1869.
Young, Samuel & Martha S. McDonald, Jan. 14, 1869.
Zumbro, Adam J. & Mary M. Hall, Oct. 17, 1869.

1870

Abernathy, Wash & Lotta Williams, Feb. 24, 1870.
Adams, Henry & Sally Bedford, Jan. 26, 1870.
Adkerson, Mark & Rachel Hutcherson, Dec. 30, 1870.
Adkins, J. M. & Miss Ella Ward, Dec. 24, 1870.
Adkinson, Irvin & Jane Edwards, Apr. 6, 1870.
Akin, John & Minerva Mayfield, May 30, 1870.
Aldridge, Thomas J. & Lou A. Espey, Feb. 1, 1870.

RUTHERFORD COUNTY MARRIAGES

Allen, M. P. G. & Miss Mary A. Harding, Apr. 19, 1870.
Allen, Thomas & Martha Mullins, Nov. 27, 1870.
Alstin, Wm. & Missouri V. Cole, June 2, 1870.
Anderson, B. F. & Miss Sallie E. Lee, Feb. 20, 1870.
Andrews, James J. & Miss Virginia L. Reeves, Dec. 21, 1870.
Arnold, N. A. & Miss M. A. Bates, Apr. 3, 1870.
Arnold, W. A. & Miss Mary C. Lockard, Nov. 23, 1870.
Arthor, Howard & Malinda Alford, Nov. 29, 1870.
Avent, George & Lucy Nevils, Apr. 2, 1870.
Baker, W. S. & M. J. A. Hunt, June 15, 1870.
Barbor, J. H. & Miss Sophronia Drumwright, Jan. 5, 1870.
Barlow, James H. & Miss Margarett Gray, Nov. 10, 1870.
Baskett, W. E. & Lizzie B. Reed, May 29, 1870.
Batey, Isiah & Vinie Freeman, July 16, 1870.
Batts, Wm. & Harriet Smith, Jan. 6, 1870.
Beard, Albert & Lizzie Jordan, May 14, 1870.
Beard, Richard & Maria Dromgoole, Feb. 15, 1870.
Bedord, Pat & Anna Smith, Dec. 29, 1870.
Beesley, Durant & Miss Willie A. Elliot, Aug. 30, 1870.
Beesley, Joel & Patsey McGee, Dec. 28, 1870.
Bell, Anderson & Fannie Johnson, Dec. 29, 1870.
Bell, Clinton & Julia Rucker, Oct. 12, 1870.
Bennett, Taylor & America Saver, Dec. 28, 1870.
Black, Thomas & Lizzie Sikes, Nov. 15, 1870.
Blair, Isaac & Winnie Beesley, Jan. 1, 1870.
Blankenship, G. W. & Miss Eliz. A. Barrett, Dec. 28, 1870.
Bowling, J. S. & Miss Mary Jane Peyton, Oct. 25, 1870.
Bowman, D. B. F. & Lucy J. Brown, Apr. 19, 1870.
Brantly, Appollo & Judy Barkly, Jan. 12, 1870.
Broiles, Frances & Miss Hattie E. Price, Nov. 8, 1870.
Brown, Abram & Candes Smith, Dec. 11, 1870.
Brown, Charles & Celia Davis, Aug. 26, 1870.
Brown, Thomas F. & Miss Margaret Mankins, Oct. 11, 1870.
Brown, Wm. & Tennessee Williams, Dec. 30, 1870.
Bunting, Daniel & Joanna Mitchell, Apr. 3, 1870.
Burnett, A. M. & Miss Sarah J. Dunn, Apr. 6, 1870.
Burnett, John & Miss Isabel E. Winston, Dec. 21, 1870.
Burns, Rens & Jennyling Jordan, Dec. 2, 1870.
Burrel, Stephen W. & Louisa Sanders, Apr. 10, 1870.
Butler, Perry & Alice Henderson, Jan. 6, 1870.
Butler, Randal & Bettie Jordan, Feb. 13, 1870.
Campbell, Wm. & Miss Nora Taylor, Feb. 6, 1870.
Carney, Isaac & Louisa Carney, Feb. 6, 1870.
Carter, Edward & Miss Nanne E. McElroy, Sept. 22, 1870.
Carver, G. W. & Mrs. M. E. Stanton, Dec. 15, 1870.
Caswell, Henry & Vinnie Murphy, Jan. 11, 1870.
Cates, J. B. & Adie C. McNeil, Jan. 4, 1870.
Cawley, James & Miss Naw Fletcher, Dec. 29, 1870.
Cheer, John & Bettie Johnson, Dec. 19, 1870.
Christman, W. D. & Miss Eliz. Hartman, Feb. 12, 1870.
Cloudy, Henry & Miss Martha Edmonds, June 4, 1870.
Cloud, Jackson & Sallie McGill, Dec. 2, 1870.
Cockran, Dr. G. W. & Miss A. V. Holden, Sept. 23, 1870.
Cody, Isham & Lydia Rowlett, Mar. 5, 1870.

Colbert, R. A. & Vinnie E. Rucker, Jan. 28, 1870.
Cole, Thomas & Susan Frazier, Jan. 22, 1870.
Comer, C. R. & Miss Mary Jane Garrett, Dec. 9, 1870.
Cooper, Anderson & Tennessee Alexander, Nov. 28, 1870.
Couch, H. C. & Miss M. E. Davis, Aug. 19, 1870.
Cox, T. W. & Miss Emma Overall, Feb. 1, 1870.
Crick, Jesse A. & Amanda E. Green, May 28, 1870.
Cunningham, W. & Mary Peebles N.S., Dec. 17, 1870.
Curlee, C. D. & Miss Margaret Arnold, Dec. 7, 1870.
Cutchen, W. M. & Miss S. J. Goodman, Nov. 15, 1870.
Daniel, Henry & Ellen Sanders, Dec. 29, 1870.
Daniel, Joseph & Jennie Fletcer, Aug. 23, 1870.
Daniel, Robert & Chris Davis, Nov. 1, 1870.
Davis, Thomas & Agnes Caldwell, Feb. 10, 1870.
Davis, Turner & Mary Gray, Nov. 12, 1870.
Davis, W. T. & Miss Nannie DeJarnett, Oct. 6, 1870.
DeJarnett, John & Sally Crockett, Jan. 10, 1870.
Dement, Abner & Miss Sallie Barker, Dec. 10, 1870.
Dill, James & Miss Harriet Butler, July 31, 1870.
Douglass, P. & R. C. Knox, July 13, 1870.
Dowell, James & Bettie Randolph, May 14, 1870.
Downing, Edmund & Minerva Jane Copeland, May 12, 1870.
Duncan, John & Emily Ryan, Mar. 10, 1870.
Edwards, Granville & Fannie Rankin, Aug. 27, 1870.
Epps, Wm. & Miss Amanda Neal, Dec. 27, 1870.
Etheridge, Matthew & Dithula Wetherly, Feb. 17, 1870.
Everett, Taylor & Lizzie Wadley, Apr. 3, 1870.
Evans, Jacob & Laura Johns, Aug. 27, 1870.
Farless, Washington & Minta Reed, May 29, 1870.
Fite, Arthur & Adeline Datriss, Aug. 6, 1870.
Fleming, James & Miss Martha A. Hoover, Aug. 18, 1870.
Fletcher, James F. Jr. & Miss Medora Henderson, Nov. 3,
    1870.
Floyd, Luke & Susan McClary, June 15, 1870.
Floyd, Wiley & Pylin Tally, Sept. 22, 1870.
Foster, John & Mary Ann Crick, Aug. 11, 1870.
Foster, Lewis & Josephine Alexander, Mar. 6, 1870.
Frazier, Sandy & Lou Fletcher, Dec. 28, 1870.
Free, Joseph & Mary E. Davis, Mar. 27, 1870.
Frierson, Porter & Nancy Martin, Feb. 2, 1870.
Fugitt, Albert & Tennessee Jordan, Sept. 10, 1870.
Garrett, Charlie & Bettie Johnson, Dec. 27, 1870.
Gentry, Robert & Abby Henderson, Feb. 2, 1870.
Gilchrist, Abram & Tely Smith, Sept. 1, 1870
Golfin, Hezdkiah & Jane Hoover, Oct. 2, 1870.
Gooch, Alexander & Lucy Alexander, Aug. 22, 1870.
Gooch, Anderson & Isabella Sanders, Oct. 22, 1870.
Gooch, Edmund & Ellen Davidson, Oct. 22, 1870.
Gooch, Egbert & Betty Cooper, May 6, 1870.
Gooch, Nathaniel & Miss Maggie Ridley, Apr. 14, 1870.
Green, Joseph & Ellen Ready N.S., July 19, 1870.
Green, King & Kate Thompson, Sept. 1, 1870.
Green, M. F. & Miss Lizzie Batey, Dec. 15, 1870.
Greer, Henry & Miss Mahala Swain, Apr. 14, 1870.

RUTHERFORD COUNTY MARRIAGES

Greer, Samuel & Julia Lillard, Jan. 31, 1870.
Grigg, A. P. & Miss R. I. Lowe, July 6, 1870.
Hale, J. R. & Miss Ada E. Jarman, Oct. 19, 1870.
Hall, J. T. & Cora E. Jones, Dec. 18, 1870.
Hall, John & Jenny Lytle, Feb. 5, 1870.
Hall, T. F. & Miss Bettie Brandon, Mar. 23, 1870.
Harlin, Davy & Winny Webb, Dec. 31, 1870.
Harris, Charlei & Lucy McLean, Dec. 25, 1870.
Harris, Richard A. & Miss J. M. Reed, Dec. 8, 1870.
Harris, Sam & Betsey Carney, Sept. 7, 1870.
Harris, Wm. & Esther Jones, Jan. 3, 1870.
Harrison, Henry & Fanny Blackman, Feb. 12, 1870.
Hartwell, John C. & Susan A. Compton, Dec. 18, 1870.
Hartwell, Wilis & Amanda Hartwell, Jan. 1, 1870.
Haynes, G. C. & Miss S. R. W. Vaughan, Sept. 1, 1870.
Haynes, Robert & Dorcas Moseley, Aug. 7, 1870.
Haynes, Wm. & Celia A. Keeble, Feb. 12, 1870.
Heath, Wm. H. & Mary Crick, Aug. 21, 1870.
Henderson, Patrick & Julia A. Batson, Dec. 18, 1870.
Henderson, Alec & Louvinia Davis, Oct. 22, 1870.
Hendrix, Elisha W. & Sarah Jane Rowland, Mar. 29, 1870.
Hendrix, Tom & Emily Wiggins, Aug. 19, 1870.
Henry, Reuben & Feeby Hicks, Jan. 14, 1870.
Henry, W. C. & Mrs. E. A. Fletcher, Apr. 26, 1870.
Hill, Isaac & Susan Mason, Aug. 21, 1870.
Holden, John & Jincy Ann West, Dec. 14, 1870.
Holden, John B. & Martha Holden, Nov. 30, 1870.
Hood, John F. & Miss Julia S. Warren, Oct. 25, 1870.
Hoover, B. A. & Judith A. C. Richardson, Mar. 2, 1870.
Hoover, J. A. & Emily Jane Herod, Nov. 13, 1870.
Hoover, Jasper & Tennessee Fox, Nov. 9, 1870.
Hord, Pary & Elixa Youman, July 17, 1870.
Howse, Clem & Louisa Johnson, June 5, 1870.
Hughes, Rev. John F. & Mrs. Helen M. Baskett, Apr. 6, 1870.
Hughes, Hardin & Martha Matilda Williamson, Jan. 2, 1870.
Hyde, John & Lizzie Jordan, Dec. 11, 1870.
Ivie, Thomas & Miss Sallie Lawing, Dec. 19, 1870.
James, Charles & Mary Ganaway, Aug. 19, 1870.
James, Robert & Jemima Wendel, Mar. 16, 1870.
Jarmon, L. B. & Fannie McLean, Mar. 23, 1870.
Jenkins, Albert & Josephine Wilson, Dec. 27, 1870.
Jernigan, J. S. & N. L. Arnold, Nov. 23, 1870.
Jett, Thomas D. & Tabitha A. Kirkendall, Feb. 14, 1870.
Jetton, J. F. & Mollie J. Todd, Nov. 23, 1870.
Jetton, Taylor & Martha Spann, Nov. 12, 1870.
Johnson, B. T. & Alta Brandon, Dec. 7, 1870.
Johnson, Dallas & Mary Hood, Dec. 27, 1870.
Johnson, James Wm. & Virginia Russell, July 10, 1870.
Johnson, R. L. & J. Ella Martin, Mar. 8, 1870.
Jordan, E. B. & Mollie Posey, Nov. 1, 1870.
Keeble, Green & Narcissa Gooch, Sept. 24, 1870.
Keeble, Joseph & Filey A. Rowan, May 4, 1870.
Keele, G. W. & L. S. Stovall, Oct. 18, 1870.
Kelton, Thomas N. & Mary Mankins, Dec. 28, 1870

Kerr, Wilson & Ella A. Mitchell, May 4, 1870.
Key, Alexander W. & Hattie A. Jarratt, Dec. 1, 1870.
Lannon, J. T. & Sallie Barber, Dec. 18, 1870.
Lannon, Thomas E. & Mary Smith, Sept. 14, 1870.
Lawrence, Walker & Georgiana Jordan, Nov. 10, 1870.
Layhew, Joseph B. & Miss Sarah V. Bennett, Oct. 13, 1870.
Leath, Lewis & Lucy Russworm, Feb. 3, 1870.
Lee, Wm. & Emma Davidson, June 9, 1870.
Legg, Allen & Lucinda Alford, Jan. 9, 1870.
Lillard, Henry & Polly Jordan, Jan. 14, 1870.
Lillard, Mordecia & Sue P. Hallyburton, Sept. 20, 1870.
Lillard, T. O. & Hattie Hill, Feb. 1, 1870.
Lockard, Preston & Mrs. Mary Wilkerson, Dec. 19, 1870.
Loughry, W. D. & Miss S. E. McAdoo, Sept. 27, 1870.
Love, F. P. & Miss M. P. Ransom, Oct. 13, 1870.
Lowe, F. P. & Miss M. P. Ransom, Oct. 13, 1870.
Lowe, G. N. & Ella Clark, Sept. 29, 1870.
Lowe, R. L. & Miss Sophia Williams, Nov. 30, 1870.
Lytle, Carrol & Roxana Grisham, Aug. 21, 1870.
Lytle, Henry & Maria Jetton, Mar. 26, 1870.
Lytle, Parker & Judy Minter, Jan. 21, 1870.
Malone, George & Sallie McLine, Mar. 21, 1870.
Malone, John & Martha Magills, Apr. 22, 1870.
Malone, Jordan & Bettie Ross, Jan. 6, 1870.
Maney, Nathan J. & Caroline Thomas N.S., Jan. 27, 1870.
Mankin, G. R. & Miner Todd, Oct. 7, 1870.
Martin, Essick & Onie Martin, Oct. 8, 1870.
Martin, Levi & Jennie Brown, Jan. 27, 1870.
Martin, Nicholas & Amanda Wilson, Jan. 11, 1870.
Matthews, Isham & Malinda Winsett, Oct. 5, 1870.
Maxwell, Green P. & Mary A. E. Lewis, May 22, 1870.
Maxwell, John & Mary E. Vaughan, Feb. 4, 1870.
Mays, Greenberry & Tennessee Batey, Mar. 20, 1870.
Mays, J. E. & Nannie Floyd, Sept. 22, 1870.
Mercer, Alexander & Hannah McLaren, Aug. 26, 1870.
Miles, Charlie & Sallie Miles, Oct. 29, 1870.
Miller, Henry & Ann Stroud, Jan. 7, 1870.
Miller, Henry & Josephine Grim, Dec. 28, 1870.
Miller, Thomas J. & Mollie Johnson, Sept. 2, 1870.
Minter, Samuel & Mary Minter, Dec. 28, 1870.
Moody, John & Sarey McDermott, Dec. 31, 1870.
Moore, C. W. & M. F. Burgess, Jan. 5, 1870.
Moore, James A. & Rosie Carney, Jan. 17, 1870.
Morgan, Monteville L. & Mrs. Eliza S. Jones, Jan. 27, 1870.
Mullenax, L. S. & Nancy Davis, Apr. 30, 1870.
Mullins, Martin H. & Sallie J. Mason, Mar. 3, 1870.
Murfree, Nat & Addie Jordan, Sept. 7, 1870.
Murrell, Pleasant & Lizzie Duffer, Jan. 9, 1870.
McAdoo, J. P. & Miss M. E. Pitts, Dec. 13, 1870.
McAdoo, Major & Tena Keeble, Mar. 9, 1870.
McCrary, Joseph N. & Mary A. Carnahan, Jan. 25, 1870.
McDowell, Richard & Vinie McCullough, June 11, 1870.
McGill, John & Bettie Mankin, June 12, 1870.

RUTHERFORD COUNTY MARRIAGES

McKee, James & Emeline F. Upchurch, Jan. 16, 1870.
McKnight, John & Line Jones, July 24, 1870.
McLean, Geo. & Martha Jarratt, Feb. 29, 1870.
McLean, Wesley & Lavina Simons, May 21, 1870.
McLemore, Charles & Artimtia Alford, Oct. 29, 1870.
McNairy, John & Mary Ross, Jan. 5, 1870.
Nelson, Adam & Caroline Webb, Dec. 15, 1870.
Northcott, G. N. & Jane Batson, Dec. 15, 1870.
Odell, J. A. & Mrs. Nancy G. Doyle, July 6, 1870.
Oden, John & Sally Rouse, Jan. 20, 1870.
Odom, Walter & Sarah Wallace, Apr. 24, 1870.
Oliver, James & Mary Thomas, Mar. 15, 1870.
O'Neil, James & Mrs. Nancy Morgan, Jan. 5, 1870.
O'Neil, Joseph & Jane Pitman, Nov. 26, 1870.
O'Neil, Thomas Park & Mrs. Emeline Driver, Sept. 8, 1870.
Ore, Richard & Abitha Gaiter, Jan. 20, 1870.
Overall, F. M. & Miss Amanda Sanders, Nov. 11, 1870.
Overall, Nathan & Polly Ryan, Jan. 23, 1870.
Owen, J. H. & F. J. Pogue, Jan. 19, 1870.
Ozment, James T. & Charity A. Phelps, Dec. 29, 1870.
Parker, Joseph A. & Fannie Howland, Aug. 22, 1870.
Patterson, George & Lucy Graves, Dec. 28, 1870.
Patterson, J. L. & E. T. Shannon, Jan. 7, 1870.
Patterson, John W. & Mollie E. Jordan, Jan. 27, 1870.
Patterson, Silas & Jane Stroud, Mar. 3, 1870.
Patterson, Wm. & Mintie Batts, Nov. 4, 1870.
Patton, W. L. & Mary J. Prater, Oct. 25, 1870.
Philips, Andrew & Laura Henderson, Dec. 29, 1870.
Pirtle, J. P. & Martha Summers, Dec. 22, 1870.
Potts, Wm. & L. J. Coleman, Mar. 15, 1870.
Price, Jessie & Emma Parmer, Oct. 29, 1870.
Ransom, O. W. & Fannie J. Oden, Dec. 28, 1870.
Ransom, Reuben & Nancy Hawkins, May 14, 1870.
Read, R. W. & Mary Hill, Jan. 23, 1870.
Ready, John & Lucy Miller, July 13, 1870.
Reese, Joseph & Kittie Rucker, Jan. 9, 1870.
Reeves, M. P. & Miss M. E. Burks, Dec. 3, 1870.
Rhodes, Henry & Ann Owens, Aug. 26, 1870.
Richards, David & Sarah Thompson, Dec. 15, 1870.
Roberson, Pompy & Meriky Crawford, Nov. 5, 1870.
Robinson, Martin & Catherine Woods, Feb. 8, 1870.
Rogers, Jerry & Sue Jordan, July 3, 1870.
Rose, Jacob B. & Harriett E. Alsup, Sept. 18, 1870.
Ross, Abram & Susan Bennett, Jan. 1, 1870.
Ross, Henry & Lucinda Miller, Dec. 28, 1870.
Ross, John & Mandy Dunaway, Dec. 25, 1870.
Ross, Oscar & Addie Puckett, June 2, 1870.
Rowan, Robert & Lizzie Anderson, Mar. 2, 1870.
Rucker, James & Martha America Ragin, July 24, 1870.
Rucker, Stephen & Peachie Ann Kerr, Dec. 21, 1870.
Runnels, Aaron & Jane Pearson, Jan. 11, 1870.
Sanders, George & Fannie Webb, Jan. 12, 1870.
Sanders, J. E. & S. E. McMinaway, Dec. 22, 1870.
Sanders, Robert A. & Miss Alice M. McAdoo, Sept. 10, 1870.
Sanders, T. M. & M. A. Gregory, Dec. 1, 1870.

RUTHERFORD COUNTY MARRIAGES

Satterwhite, S. T. & Lucy Butler, Dec. 7, 1870.
Sawyers, Andrew C. & Mary L. Bain, Mar. 8, 1870.
Scruggs, Edmond & Alder Williams, Apr. 14, 1870.
Searcy, Charles & Francis Wrather, Jan. 10, 1870.
Seward, Charles & Bettie Spence, May 26, 1870.
Shannon, Sydna & Dora Smith, Oct. 9, 1870.
Sharp, F. J. & Martha E. Lawrence, Sept. 11, 1870.
Sharpe, Alexander & Margaret A. Jones, Sept. 22, 1870.
Shelton, W. B. & Mary S. A. Richardson, Apr. 16, 1870.
Sherrill, Henry & Mary Smith, Apr. 16, 1870.
Short, John & Mrs. E. J. Alford, Dec. 24, 1870.
Simpson, John & Sarah Henderson, Dec. 25, 1870.
Sims, John & Jane Spence, Dec. 27, 1870.
Sinn, John & Sarah A. J. Wormington, Mar. 14, 1870.
Smith, A. T. & Lou A. Ott, Jan. 12, 1870.
Smith, Alex & Minerva Scales, Oct. 5, 1870.
Smith, Elias & Matilda Butler, Feb. 12, 1870.
Smith, Elijay & Sarah Jane Owens, Sept. 17, 1870.
Smith, Geo. & Fanny Brown, Oct. 2, 1870.
Smith, Henderson & Anna Davis, Mar. 12, 1870.
Smith, Rufus & Eliz. Minter, Oct. 6, 1870.
Smith, Wm. & Sarah Vaughan, Apr. 28, 1870.
Smithy, Wm. & Mintie Cutchin, Jan. 5, 1870.
Smotherman, Parton & Q. F. Reed, June 16, 1870.
Smotherman, C. C. & Mrs. M. A. Loven, Dec. 31, 1870.
Snell, Jack & Robertine Harvey, Feb. 11, 1870.
Snell, John & Emma Tennon, July 14, 1870.
Spence, Alson & Mary Jane Dunn, Feb. 28, 1870.
Stanford, Lafayette & Jennie Carter, Mar. 3, 1870.
Stephenson, John L. & Rebecca E. Eaton, Dec. 20, 1870.
Stovers, George W. & Susan Seward, May 20, 1870.
Sublett, Joseph & Myra Bilbro, Dec. 26, 1870.
Talley, Reuben & Susan Wright, Sept. 15, 1870.
Tally, Jake & Ruthy Woods, Nov. 24, 1870.
Taylor, Creed & Mary E. Beazley, June 27, 1870.
Teasley, Alexander & Maria Knight, Jan. 13, 1870.
Teete, David J. & Mahala Colwell, Feb. 20, 1870.
Thom, James & Unity V. Sanders (Thorn?), Mar. 2, 1870.
Thomas, Sandy & Patsy Ledbetter, Jan. 27, 1870.
Thomas, Wm. & Tena Lytle, Mar. 3, 1870.
Thompson, Samuel & Abbie Gaylord, June 20, 1870.
Tilford, Monroe & Becca Henderson, Dec. 18, 1870.
Tillman, James & Polly Jordan, Feb. 12, 1870.
Travis, B. F. & Nannie A. Warren, Dec. 15, 1870.
Travis, J. Z. & T. C. Batey, Sept. 29, 1870.
Trimble, Daniel & Dicy Ann Thompson, Aug. 11, 1870.
Tucker, B. R. & Josie Neal, Dec. 27, 1870.
Tucker, Haywood & Laura Gooch, July 2, 1870.
Underwood, Alex & Eliz. Towns, July 27, 1870.
Vaughan, Robert & Lindy McHenry, Dec. 28, 1870.
Vaughan, Wm. L. & Francis E. McRae, Apr. 10, 1870.
Vaught, Robert D. & Virginia McKnight, Sept. 8, 1870.
Wade, Ben & Nancy Chase, June 19, 1870.
Wade, Joe & Lucinda McDaniel, Jan. 13, 1870.
Waller, Ben & Harriet Robison, Apr. 12, 1870.

RUTHERFORD COUNTY MARRIAGES

Waller, James R. & Sarah P. Robertson, Dec. 8, 1870.
Warpool, Wm. P. & Mary J. Williams, June 30, 1870.
Watson, David C. & A. C. Haynes, Dec. 22, 1870.
Weakley, John & Lucinda Scruggs, Aug. 12, 1870.
Webb, John W. & Sarah Webb, Jan. 11, 1870.
White, Archy & Carherine Alexander, Jan. 11, 1870.
White, Henry & C. A. Larkin, Jan. 13, 1870.
White, Mason & Lizzie Ransom, Mar. 3, 1870.
White, W. H. & Sarah C. Barnes, Jan. 13, 1870.
Whitworth, J. E. & Miss J. L. Pope, Dec. 27, 1870.
Wilburn, Robert & Mary Alexander, Dec. 29, 1870.
Williams, Geo. & Matilda Nelson, Feb. 4, 1870.
Williams, Nick & Sarah Cooper, Nov. 30, 1870.
Williams, Stephen & Martha Parker, Jan. 6, 1870.
Wilson, Alex & Narcissa Cannon, Sept. 24, 1870.
Wilson, Sam & Anna Stokes, Oct. 31, 1870.
Wilson, Wesley & Margaret Pearson, Aug. 1, 1870.
Windrow, John W. & Susan E. Watson, Mar. 27, 1870.
Winn, George & Maggie Ledbetter, Oct. 21, 1870.
Wise, Charles & Mary E. Cheatham, Jan. 9, 1870.
Witt, A. T. & Sarah E. Richards, Aug. 19, 1870.
Woods, Wm. & Keziah Howse, Aug. 12, 1870.
Yeargan, Gilbert & Ann Newsom, Mar. 9, 1870.
Yearwood, John & Mary Ann Jernigan, Mar. 31, 1870.
Young, Peter & Mrs. Eliza M. Davis, May 11, 1870.

1871

Adams, James & Caldonis Hubbard, Oct. 19, 1871.
Adcock, J. W. & Jane Corlile, June 7, 1871.
Adkerson, Alfred & Eveline Weakley, Oct. 25, 1871.
Adkerson, Geo. & Rebecca Batey, Dec. 15, 1871.
Adkerson, Henry & Sallie Mullins, Dec. 16, 1871.
Adkins, Wm. & Sarah Hollis, Aug. 2, 1871.
Alexander, Bob & Rena Alexander, May 10, 1871.
Alexander, Charlie & Puss Jackson, Apr. 10, 1871.
Alexander, Dick & Della Smith, May 17, 1871.
Alexander, W. F. & Ermina Caldwell, May 11, 1871.
Alford, Levi & Susan Coleman, Jan. 13, 1871.
Allen, Jesse & America A. Smith, Feb. 21, 1871.
Anderson, Daniel & Lucy Lewis, Aug. 24, 1871.
Anderson, Green & Susan Davis, Sept. 30, 1871.
Anderson, Moses & Jennet Jordan, Dec. 26, 1871.
Asher, Sam & Amy Alexander, Sept. 5, 1871.
Bagwell, Henry B. & Anna E. Welch, Aug. 30, 1871.
Baird, Benj. & Mollie Weaver, Nov. 29, 1871.
Barret, John & Martha Eads, July 11, 1871.
Barrett, Wm. & Nancy Templeton, Nov. 10, 1871.
Bass, Emanuel & Nancy Vawter, Jan. 6, 1871.
Batey, John W. & E. L. Potts, May 23, 1871.
Beasley, L. M. & S. J. Sandford, Sept. 20, 1871.
Bell, J. F. & Angeline Bell, May 31, 1871.
Bell, J. S. & Lou Boyd, Dec. 14, 1871.
Bell, Joseph & Adline Miller, May 25, 1871.
Bellenfant, John & Sallie Webb, Sept. 4, 1871.

Bennett, Hardy & Mandy Owen, Dec. 13, 1871.
Bennett, Dr. Thomas J. & Sallie P. Jarrett, Apr. 11, 1871.
Bennett, Wyatt & Mollie Britton, Jan. 6, 1871.
Bigham, Steve & Mary McGill, Aug. 15, 1871.
Black, Cornelius & Angleine Marable, Dec. 27, 1871.
Black, Henry & Adline Hunt, Dec. 3, 1871.
Bostick, Barton & Ada Bostick, Dec. 28, 1871.
Brannon, W. H. & Sarah White, Apr. 12, 1871.
Bradford, Robert & Ella Hibbits, Dec. 25, 1871.
Brewer, W. H. & Martha Barrett, Nov. 14, 1871.
Britt, J. R. & S. J. Lenoir, Sept. 14, 1871.
Brown, E. G. & Miss M. L. McAdoo, May 9, 1871.
Brown, King & Angline Thompson, Dec. 25, 1871.
Brown, Lewis & Mollie Webb, Oct. 11, 1871.
Bryant, S. R. R. & Marg. Evans, Mar. 16, 1871.
Bryson, Samuel & Fannie McGill, Dec. 19, 1871.
Buchanan, Jess & Sarah Kimbro, Jan. 8, 1871.
Burnett, George & Emeline Burch, Sept. 14, 1871.
Burt, Wm. H. & Fannie E. Walker, Oct. 14, 1871.
Caito, Daniel & Annie Webb, Oct. 5, 1871.
Campbell, J. A. & Sa Wadley, Apr. 13, 1871.
Carter, J. W. J. & Nannie H. Crutcher, Sept. 26, 1871.
Cartwright, Joseph & Sallie Buntin, Dec. 16, 1871.
Cherry, J. B. & M. W. Marshall, Oct. 19, 1871.
Childress, Dennis & Adline Alford, May 5, 1871.
Childress, J. P. & Mary B. Keeble, Dec. 6, 1871.
Coles, Harrison & Maggie Grisham, July 19, 1871.
Collier, David & Celia Rather, Dec. 1, 1871.
Copeland, J. M. & Anna V. Kinnard, Dec. 19, 1871.
Copeland, Tom & Bettie Bennett, Dec. 13, 1871.
Couch, Henry & Nancy A. Medfrey, June 22, 1871.
Cowan, Nelson & ---- Mitchell, Nov. 26, 1871.
Crockett, Frank & Amanda Delbridge, Oct. 29, 1871.
Crutcher, J. A. & S. F. Cromer, Oct. 12, 1871.
Cruchway, Wm. & Emily Jackson, Dec. 7, 1871.
Dement, John & Miss Christine E. Overall, Oct. 30, 1871.
Denham, A. E. & Martha E. Reeves, Jan. 19, 1871.
Denham, Esquire W. & Louisa York, Aug. 9, 1871.
Denton, James & Susan Frier, Apr. 30, 1871.
Douglass, M. J. & S. A. Posey, Sept. 28, 1871.
Douglass, Wm. P. & Smanda Summar, Mar. 16, 1871.
Dunkin, Harrison & Chany Drake, Mar. 18, 1871.
Dunnaway, Joseph & Dora Elam, Dec. 25, 1871.
Eatherly, Martin A. & Lucinda C. Foster, Dec. 6, 1871.
Edmondson, T. P. & Josephine Sanders, July 13, 1871.
Edwards, J. W. & Bettie Miller, Jan. 4, 1871.
Edwards, J. W. & Hattie ----, Jan. 11, 1871.
Ensley, Allen & Sarah J. Lawrence, Dec. 28, 1871.
Epps, F. R. & Sarah E. Braden, Oct. 22, 1871.
Epps, Lawrence & M. E. Smith, Dec. 1, 1871.
Erwin, James A. & Sue Broiles, Sept. 12, 1871.
Farlar, Ed & Emerline Arnold, Apr. 20, 1871.
Fletcher, John & Martha E. Lewis, Aug. 20, 1871.
Fletcher, Samuel & Ailcy Hines, Nov. 27, 1871.
Floyd, Charles & Millie Jordan, Mar. 18, 1871.

Floyd, Nelson & Malinda Patterson, Oct. 7, 1871.
Forgus, John F. & Sarah J. Finch, Jan. 26, 1871.
Fox, Sam & Eady Mason, Oct. 22, 1871.
Frazier, Ephraim & Nancy Mosely, Apr. 4, 1871.
Freas, Dr. S. H. & Mary F. Byrn, Dec. 28, 1871.
Freeman, R. C. & Mrs. E. A. Thompson, Feb. 8, 1871.
Fugitt, David & Hester Chafin, Dec. 3, 1871.
Gannaway, J. W. & Mary F. Martin, Aug. 31, 1871.
Garner, Johnson & Mary Miles, Nov. 27, 1871.
Gee, James M. & Miss Jane Edwards, June 12, 1871.
Gibson, Wm. & Mary Jane Settle, Feb. 24, 1871.
Gooch, James & Bettie Goodman, Nov. 7, 1871.
Gooch, Joe & Nancy Bowring, Jan. 19, 1871.
Good, J. N. & Martha A. Mesbitt, Sept. 6, 1871.
Goodman, Wm. A. & Laura Allen Charlton, Dec. 21, 1871.
Goodwin, G. M. & S. A. Mabry, June 11, 1871.
Green, G. J. & Mary Douglas, Mar. 1, 1871.
Green, J. & Ellen Dromgoole, Jan. 14, 1871.
Green, Jessie & Matilda Randolph, Jan. 10, 1871.
Green, Wm. & Susan Green, Dec. 3, 1871.
Gresham, Zach & Sarah Ransom, Feb. 23, 1871.
Haley, John R. & Mary A. Smotherman, June 25, 1871.
Hall, Hilry & Jennie Hutcherson, Mar. 12, 1871.
Hall, J. C. & Susan Bowman, May 14, 1871.
Harlin, Wm. & Ruthy Miller, Sept. 9, 1871.
Harp. J. W. & Mattie Zumbro, May 4, 1871.
Harris, Albert & M. E. Spence, Jan. 8, 1871.
Harris, Ben & Martha Wood, May 19, 1871.
Harrison, Daniel & Jennie Wade, Feb. 16, 1871.
Haynes, James J. & Miss Emiline Hutson, Nov. 22, 1871.
Hays, James & Clemmie West, Oct. 7, 1871.
Hedgpeth, Houston & Alice Griffin, Dec. 28, 1871.
Hendrix, Isaac & Mollie Anderson, Jan. 5, 1871.
Herral, J. T. & Miss Nancy Dunnaway, Oct. 25, 1871.
Herrod, M. N. & Melissa J. Sullivan, Oct. 24, 1871.
Hicks, Henry N. & S. R. Nance, Mar. 8, 1871.
Hill, A. G. & Ellen Amy Harding, Nov. 9, 1871.
Hill, Charlie & Ann Cradick, Dec. 14, 1871.
Hockett, Lewis & Ellen Jarrett, Aug. 26, 1871.
Hodge, Wm. & Lou Randles, Dec. 25, 1871.
Honeycutt, Rufus M. & Isabel Insell, Aug. 23, 1871.
Hooker, John P. & Sophia McAdoo, Oct. 24, 1871.
Hoover, Sam & Milly Smith, Oct. 5, 1871.
Hoover, Van & Jane Baugh, Aug. 13, 1871.
Hopkins, Henry & Amanda Dill, Dec. 10, 1871.
Horton, Henry & Isabella Allen, Feb. 15, 1871.
Howland, John F. & Francisco Brown, Oct. 25, 1871.
Howland, John F. & Mary S. Ford, July 19, 1871.
House, George & Ennen Leatherwood, Dec. 17, 1871.
Hudson, J. C. & Amanda J. Wilson, July 27, 1871.
Hunt, Aaron & Martha Jackson, Dec. 4, 1871.
Hunt, Samuel G. & Dennie Arnold (Mary Dean), Oct. 31, 1871.
Hunter, Dennie & Susan Cunigan, Dec. 28, 1871.
Hunter, R. L. & Mary Ann Walker, Jan. 10, 1871.

Insell, George & Amanda Newman, Nov. 14, 1871.
Jackson, Moses & Mary Jackson, Nov. 30, 1871.
Jacobs, Lawyer & Martha Teel, Mar. 28, 1871.
Jamison, Entram & Mary Davis, June 24, 1871.
Jarrett, Jim & Pheby McCullough, Oct. 26, 1871.
Jency, Fleming & A. W. O'Neal, Oct. 10, 1871.
Jenkins, Sam & Diner Cage, Mar. 18, 1871.
Jernigan, Wm. & Paralee Yearwood, Aug. 17, 1871.
Jetton, Walkup & Sallie Page, Feb. 23, 1871.
Johns, B. H. & Eliza Puckett, Nov. 24, 1871.
Johns, Jefferson & Narcissa Smith, Sept. 21, 1871.
Johns, Joseph & America Rucker, Oct. 12, 1871.
Johns, Joseph B. & D. L. Pierce, Mar. 30, 1871.
Johnson, Lafayette & L. J. Swink, Aug. 27, 1871.
Jones, G. W. & Emeline Coleman, Nov. 16, 1871.
Jones, R. C. & Amanda McHenry, Feb. 26, 1871.
Jones, Wm. & Frances Baugh, Jan. 2, 1871.
Jordan, Tom & Julia Fearn, Dec. 23, 1871.
Keeble, T. M. & Eliza J. Wright, June 28, 1871.
Kellow, N. J. & Mrs. Sallie Patterson, May 3, 1871.
Kelton, S. T. & M. F. Lowe, Feb. 5, 1871.
Keys, John & Elizabeth Kelly, Jan. 24, 1871.
Kimmons, Jack & Maggie C. Shannon, Nov. 12, 1871.
King, Aaron & Jane Smith, Dec. 25, 1871.
King, James M. Jr. & Sallie Alexander, Aug. 30, 1871.
King, John H. & Hattie Gooch, Apr. 5, 1871.
King, Wm. H. & Oliver Jamison, Nov. 29, 1871.
Knox, R. N. & Cattie Fox, Jan. 4, 1871.
Lamb, G. H. & Nancy A. Smotherman, Aug. 17, 1871.
Lawrence, Walker & Judy Ann Willianson, Dec. 3, 1871.
Lewis, Henry & Cassie Sikes, Oct. 22, 1871.
Love, Dock & Martha Works, Feb. 28, 1871.
Lowe, John W. & Tennie Brown, Oct. 29, 1871.
Lowry, Henry D. & Dora F. White, July 2, 1871.
Lynch, G. T. & Delila Elliott, Oct. 4, 1871.
Lynch, Lewis & Nancy J. Brothers, Oct. 8, 1871.
Lyon, Nathan & Mary C. Donnel, Jan. 5, 1871.
Lytle, John & Colan Haynes, Oct. 1, 1871.
Malery, John & Miss Alice J. Sutton, Jan. 9, 1871.
Manier, Jake & Susan Jordan, Feb. 2, 1871.
Mankin, W. C. & Ada Lee Jones, Jan. 24, 1871.
Manley, W. R. & Ella J. Mankin, Dec. 21, 1871.
Marlin, W. B. & Nannie E. Jacobs, Jan. 10, 1871.
Marshall, Alexander & Patsy Cowan, Dec. 2, 1871.
Maupin, W. C. & Miss Ida Lee Jones, Jan. 24, 1871.
Maxwell, A. T. & M. J. Smotherman, Oct. 11, 1871.
Merritt, Franklin & Harriet Reeves, Jan. 13, 1871.
Miles, Dock & Julia Russworm, Jan. 10, 1871.
Miller, E. L. & Miss Rebecca A. Miller, Oct. 11, 1871.
Miller, F. H. & Mrs. Lou Jones, Aug. 3, 1871.
Miller, Peter & Augusta Patton, Jan. 19, 1871.
Miller, Wm. & Netty Huggins, Jan. 19, 1871.
Mintor, Jim & Jane Frazier, Jan. 15, 1871.
Mitchell, Wm. & Miss M. E. House, May 17, 1871.
Mitchell, Zack & Fannie Harris, Jan. 4, 1871.

Morris, P. A. & Miss Jane Yancy, June 22, 1871.
Morris, Robert & Adalade Dickson, Dec. 26, 1871.
Morton, Henry & Catherine Sanders, Sept. 29, 1871.
Mount, R. L. & Miss A. E. Alsup, Dec. 26, 1871.
Moxley, J. W. & Miss Bettie Robinson, Dec. 5, 1871.
Murfree, Washington & Pleasant Ann Beasley, May 4, 1871.
Murry, Tobe & Callie Hockett, Dec. 30, 1871.
McAdoo, Tom & Phillis Overall, Oct. 19, 1871.
McClaren, Alexander P. & Mrs. Melissa Welch, Oct. 11, 1871.
McCord, John & Mary Jordan, Dec. 28, 1871.
McGill, Robert & Amanda Overall, Dec. 12, 1871.
McGregor, Alford & Bell Cox, May 8, 1871.
McKee, Robert & Miss Calfernia Hubbard, Oct. 4, 1871.
McKnight, Will T. & Miss Mary A. R. Lawrence, Jan. 25, 1871.
McLean, Anderson & Lizzie Davis, Feb. 28, 1871.
McMason, Wm. & Miss P. A. Hoover, Feb. 28, 1871.
McPeak, Richard & Miss Nancy F. Arnold, Jan. 12, 1871.
Neely, Dr. D. M. & Miss Mary A. Lewis, Oct. 31, 1871.
Nelson, J. S. & Miss Fannie Davidson, Oct. 4, 1871.
Nesbitt, Julius & Ann Hord, Jan. 13, 1871.
Nettle, George & Mentdora Arnold, Nov. 7, 1871.
Newson, Henry & Miss Sarah Winfre, Nov. 23, 1871.
Noland, David & Rachel Johns, Dec. 29, 1871.
Norman, C. W. & Cassie Newman, Nov. 9, 1871.
Norman, Thomas & Nancy Duncan, Sept. 11, 1871.
North, W. J. & Miss Mary E. Jones, Dec. 20, 1871.
Northcutt, G. N. & Miss Arrena F. Batson, Aug. 10, 1871.
Northcutt, S. K. & Miss Martha Lewis N.S., Aug. 19, 1871.
Odom, Sherman & Ann Byrn, Sept. 21, 1871.
Oglevie, Jasper & Miss Josephine A. Smith, Dec. 6, 1871.
Overall, Burton & Laurena Brown, Nov. 18, 1871.
Owen, Jesse & Sallie James, Feb. 8, 1871.
Owens, James & Narcissa Williams, Apr. 13, 1871.
Owens, John & Aggie Moore, Feb. 19, 1871.
Pass, D. M. & Mrs. Margaret McDaniel, Jan. 7, 1871.
Parish, Jack & Easter Culf, Nov. 29, 1871.
Patrick, Wm. & Miss Mary Jane Scott, Apr. 27, 1871.
Patterson, C. A. & Miss Isabella Dunnaway, Dec. 22, 1871.
Patterson, E. E. & Miss Tabitha Hunter, Jan. 4, 1871.
Patterson, Taylor & Caroline Jordan, Dec. 20, 1871.
Patton, John & Miss Martha Jones, Oct. 24, 1871.
Patton, Miles & Eliza Patton, Aug. 11, 1871.
Patey, B. F. & Miss Flora Lillard, June 6, 1871.
Pearcy, J. G. & Miss Martha A. Jordan, Aug. 9, 1871.
Pearcy, Wm. F. & Miss Lucy H. Jewel, Mar. 9, 1871.
Percy, Thomas J. & Miss Sarah E. Tune, Feb. 2, 1871.
Prater, W. P. & Miss Letty Pruett, Mar. 7, 1871.
Pinchard, G. W. & Miss Mattie S. Lowe, May 10, 1871.
Pruett, Mark & Miss Tabitha Vaughan, Aug. 6, 1871.
Quackenbass, J. A. & Miss Ida L. Wade, Oct. 17, 1871.
Quinn, Thomas B. & Miss Betsy Batey, Jan. 18, 1871.
Ralston, Wm. & Miss S. N. R. Hendrix, Dec. 14, 1871.
Raney, Isham & Miss Ony W. Taylor, Sept. 7, 1871.

RUTHERFORD COUNTY MARRIAGES

Rankin, Jerry & Malinda Fry, Sept. 16, 1871.
Rankin, John A. & Nelly Oden, Jan. 13, 1871.
Ransom, Ed & Sallie Miller, Jan. 2, 1871.
Ransom, Sam & Eliza Frazier, Jan. 21, 1871.
Ready, Tony & America Jones, Feb. 1, 1871.
Reece, George E. & Miss Lutitie E. Pruett, Feb. 15, 1871.
Reic, E. C. & Miss S. L. Ralston, Jan. 23, 1871.
Rhodes, Robert & Addrana McAdoo, Nov. 1, 1871.
Rion, Francis P. & Miss Josephine Sullivan, Nov. 2, 1871.
Roberson, Lee & Mary Jones, Sept. 7, 1871.
Roberts, Warren & Tennie Stroop, Dec. 7, 1871.
Robinson, Lee & Mary Jones, Sept. 7, 1871.
Ross, Henry & Mary Mullins, Dec. 14, 1871.
Rowland, F. M. & Miss Mary Sullivan, Dec. 6, 1871.
Rowland, M. P. & Mrs. Melissa Lamb, Aug. 3, 1871.
Rucker, Handy & Bettie Mitchell, Apr. 28, 1871.
Rucker, James & Lucy Arnold, May 5, 1871.
Runnels, P. R. & Mrs. Martha E. Manley, June 10, 1871.
Sanders, John & Miss Mahana Talent, Apr. 12, 1871.
Sanders, Isaac & Miss Tennie L. Goodwin, Nov. 22, 1871.
Sanders, W. L. & Miss Sallie L. Sanders, Apr. 6, 1871.
Savage, G. M. & Miss Fannie F. Williams, July 26, 1871.
Seay, Frank & Eliza Bracey, Oct. 5, 1871.
Sherron, Elijah & Hettie Lingo, Jan. 21, 1871.
Short, Daniel & Bell Robinson, Dec. 27, 1871.
Shriver, D. W. & Miss Catherine Runnels, Aug. 1, 1871.
Simmons, Bennett & Dolly Couch, Dec. 25, 1871.
Sledge, J. W. & Miss Mary E. Russell, Mar. 29, 1871.
Sloan, W. A. & Miss Millie Jones, Oct. 12, 1871.
Smith, Berry & Ella Ready, Mar. 27, 1871.
Smith, Jack Woods & Miss M. W. Vawter, Feb. 7, 1871.
Smith, Robert A. & Miss Bettie B. Lannon, Aug. 31, 1871.
Smith, Thaddeus & Elina Cage, Dec. 30, 1871.
Smotherman, Azariah & Miss Dorinda Smotherman, Aug. 17, 1871.
Smotherman, Elbert & Miss Lizzie Williams, Sept. 21, 1871.
Smotherman, W. L. & Miss Sarah E. Spence, Dec. 4, 1871.
Snell, Aaron & Violet ----, Dec. 9, 1871.
Snell, Dock & Unis McLean, Mar. 16, 1871.
Snell, Henry & Eliz. Trimble, Jan. 3, 1871.
Snell, Wm. & Miss Mollie J. Kirk, Feb. 14, 1871.
Speakard, Bartley & Martha Harris, Oct. 14, 1871.
Spence, James H. & Miss M. A. Talley, Dec. 18, 1871.
Spencer, W. J. & Miss Jane Holden, July 17, 1871.
Spray, Abram & Miss Mary M. Brown, Feb. 2, 1871.
Spray, John & Miss Susan Peerson, July 27, 1871.
Stainback, J. M. & Miss M. E. Boran, Nov. 28, 1871.
Staton, Charles W. & Miss Ellennora Mosbey, Jan. 31, 1871.
Sublett, George & Rebecca Spain, Jan. 31, 1871.
Summers, Abner & Miss H. N. Chadwick, Feb. 8, 1871.
Summers, John & Jennie Leathers, Jan. 30, 1871.
Swan, Albert & Mary Gannaway, Oct. 14, 1871.

Talley, James S. & Miss Martha Cantrell, Aug. 17, 1871.
Tatum, J. H. & Mrs. Mary Jane Thomas, Aug. 22, 1871.
Taylor, S. H. & Miss Mattie Presley, Nov. 18, 1871.
Tharp, David & Miss Mary Pilkenton, Aug. 8, 1871.
Thomas, J. M. & Miss Eliza J. Powell, Mar. 9, 1871.
Thompson, Eldridge & Ann James, Dec. 28, 1871.
Thompson, Pleas & Lucinda Thompson, Jan. 2, 1871.
Todd, Tobe & Rose Ann Lyon, July 13, 1871.
Tucker, Anderson & America Kelly, Mar. 14, 1871.
Tucker, Lee S. & Miss Lizzie C. Davis, Oct. 11, 1871.
Tucker, Wm. & Miss Zillie Arnos, Aug. 15, 1871.
Underwood, M. C. & Miss Lucinda West, Sept. 13, 1871.
Underwood, W. A. & Miss S. J. Eastwood, Dec. 10, 1871.
Upchurch, Wm. & Miss Lucy R. Hunt, Sept. 27, 1871.
Vawter, Edmond & Winny Leathwood, Nov. 20, 1871.
Vawter, Jo & Adline Digins, Jan. 4, 1871.
Wade, Adam & Mary Calhoun, Nov. 3, 1871.
Wade, Aron & Sallie Webb, Apr. 14, 1871.
Wade, John & Chany Frazier, June 30, 1871.
Wade, Quill & Caroline Clayton, Jan. 25, 1871.
Wade, Washington & Hettie Buchanan, May 29, 1871.
Wafer, Dick & Lou Brown, Nov. 18, 1871.
Walker, Sam & Sue Truner, July 13, 1871.
Walls, G. W. & Miss Francis A. West, Sept. 13, 1871.
Ward, Marshall & Mallie Satten, Nov. 4, 1871.
Washington, George & Rosana Dickson, Mar. 23, 1871.
Washington, John & Emma Cummings, July 9, 1871.
Watkins, A. G. & Miss Lottie Batton, Feb. 14, 1871.
Weakley, Anderson & ----, Aug. 7, 1871.
Weatherly, Bob & Lucy Alexander, July 15, 1871.
Webb, Robert & Miss Lou Body, Jan. 10, 1871.
Wheeler, James A. & Miss Anna E. Sneed, Dec. 27, 1871.
White, Dennis & Minty White, Feb. 19, 1871.
White, Peter & Phillis Gibson, July 3, 1871.
Whitlock, H. H. & Miss S. E. Pearcy, Feb. 7, 1871.
Wigg, J. W. & Miss Rosie E. Howland, Sept. 17, 1871.
Wilhoite, J. T. & Miss M. E. Johnson, Jan. 31, 1871.
Wilkinson, Alzy & Miss F. C. Ward, Apr. 25, 1871.
Williams, Billy & Wilmoth Proby, July 13, 1871.
Williams, W. B. & Miss Nancy M. Summers, Nov. 9, 1871.
Wilson, D. W. & Miss Mattie D. Welch, Feb. 2, 1871.
Wilson, Jim & Henrietta Gooch, Aug. 5, 1871.
Wooten, Wm. & Eliza Ralston, Apr. 1, 1871.
Work, J. L. & Miss Susan R. Reeves, Dec. 18, 1871.
Works, Sidney & Mariah Fletcher, Jan. 13, 1871.
Wrather, T. P. & Miss I. M. Robinson, Dec. 19, 1871.
Wright, Augustus & Miss Julia Hickman, Mar. 26, 1871.
Yeargan, James & Dicy Pickett, July 21, 1871.
Young, Emanuel & Ann Spence, Aug. 8, 1871.
Young, George & Polly Rather, Nov. 10, 1871.
Ytth, Ransel & Ann Spence, Aug. 8, 1871.

Adkins, George & Martha Ward, Nov. 30, 1872.
Alexander, Henry & Ada Moore, Dec. 24, 1872.
Allen, J. W. & Miss Josephine Parsley, Mar. 20, 1872.
Anderson, George & Jemima Clift, June 12, 1872.
Anderson, John & Josephine Avent, Aug. 8, 1872.
Anderson, John C. & Miss C. J. Bellefant, Aug. 7, 1872.
Anderson, Miles & Lizzie Leath, Apr. 25, 1872.
Anderson, Sam C. & Mrs. Francis L. Bush, Nov. 3, 1872.
Arbuckle, J. K. P. & Miss M. J. Crouch, Dec. 26, 1872.
Armistead, J. M. & Nancy Besheres, Nov. 21, 1872.
Avent, Daniel & Adaline Butler, Nov. 7, 1872.
Auberry, Logan & Miss Mary Kelton, Dec. 25, 1872.
Baker, Wm. & ---- Frazier, Sept. 19, 1872.
Barette, Wm. R. & Miss Georgeanna Leonard, Jan. 7, 1872.
Barnett, Samuel T. & Miss Ella Heriford, July 14, 1872.
Barns, Frederic & Adaline Hinds, Dec. 8, 1872.
Bass, Frank & Cora Richardson, Jan. 12, 1872.
Batey, Allen & Charlotte Jobe, Jan. 11, 1872.
Batey, Ambrose & Eliza Richardson, Nov. 14, 1872.
Batey, Burton & Lou Bennett, Jan. 7, 1872.
Batey, Green & Mattie Miller, Oct. 12, 1872.
Batey, Santana & Laura McLaughlin, Jan. 1, 1872.
Beasley, George & Miss E. A. Jordan, Oct. 18, 1872.
Beasley, J. B. & Mary S. Cabler, Dec. 17, 1872.
Beavers, F. Y. & Miss M. M. Witherspoon, Jan. 31, 1872.
Beller, William & Emma Veels, Nov. 10, 1872.
Berry, Peter & Roxana Parrish, Aug. 10, 1872.
Blackman, Frank & Annie Miller, Oct. 27, 1872.
Blanton, D. N. & Miss Alice Parsley, Mar. 20, 1872.
Blanton, Henson & Emma Lee, Aug. 19, 1872.
Braden, M. M. & Miss Anna E. J. Holton, Nov. 28, 1872.
Bradford, Robert & Marina Martin, Oct. 12, 1872.
Brancen, J. W. & Miss E. P. Pinkston, Aug. 8, 1872.
Bratcher, J. P. & Miss Sallie Taylor, Sept. 15, 1872.
Brooks, Elisha W. & Miss Sallie E. Yearwood, Dec. 18, 1872.
Brooks, Pempy & Harriet Roberson, Jan. 20, 1872.
Brown, Elup & Mary Young, Dec. 31, 1872.
Brown, John J. & Miss Harriett T. Johnson, Aug. 19, 1872.
Brown, Thomas L. & Miss A. A. Barton, Oct. 31, 1872.
Bruer, Sandy & Jane Ready, Oct. 31, 1872.
Buchanan, Frank & Melvina Shelbin, Apr. 10, 1872.
Buchanan, Grundy & Drucilla Butler, Jan. 18, 1872.
Burk, Ransom & Elmira Brown, Dec. 21, 1872.
Bush, U. A. & Miss A. J. Campbell, Feb. 28, 1872.
Butler, Aaron & Katie Butler, Feb. 16, 1872.
Butler, Johnson & Josephine Turner, June 19, 1872.
Caffee, Isahm & Harriet McLean, Sept. 30, 1872.
Caldwell, T. H. & Miss M. E. Jordan, Sept. 4, 1872.
Campbell, Henry & Kittie Patton, Aug. 22, 1872.
Cantrell, N. R. & Miss S. A. Lowderwilk, Oct. 13, 1872.
Carlton, J. W. & Miss E. J. Elmore, Feb. 5, 1872.
Childress, Wash & Jane Childress, Dec. 12, 1872.

RUTHERFORD COUNTY MARRIAGES

Coleman, Guy & Cinda Weakley, Feb. 21, 1872.
Coleman, James & Adelphia Coleman, Jan. 28, 1872.
Covington, Robert & Miss Siotia Putman, Sept. 22, 1872.
Cozart, J. W. & Miss M. M. Daniel, Jan. 25, 1872.
Cozart, W. J. & Miss Lemmie Helton, Feb. 11, 1872.
Crawford, Essex & Chatarine Smith, Oct. 13, 1872.
Cross, M. & Miss Nancy C. Mann, Dec. 4, 1872.
Crosslin, J. S. & Miss M. W. Mosbey, Nov. 28, 1872.
Crouse, George J. & Miss Mary A. V. Blackwood, Dec. 19, 1872.
Cunningham, Wm. & Isabella Ready, Apr. 11, 1872.
Currin, Luke & Dilcie Ward, Oct. 11, 1872.
Davidson, James & Miss Nancy Benson, Nov. 24, 1872.
Davis, Alexander & Lizzie Haywood, Mar. 14, 1872.
Davis, Joe & Narcissa Weakley, Aug. 5, 1872.
Dean, Wm. & Martha Jarrett, Feb. 1, 1872.
DeJarrett, Gabe & Susan Cross, Aug. 3, 1872.
Dickson, Henry & Addie Wade, Oct. 19, 1872.
Dillard, John & Emily Gregory, Dec. 27, 1872.
Dillon, W. E. & Miss H. L. Furguson, Jan. 19, 1872.
Dismukes, Z. T. & Miss S. A. Stockard, Dec. 12, 1872.
Doak, J. M. & Miss L. F. Brothers, Nov. 20, 1872.
Douglass, B. H. & Miss Sarah Summers, Feb. 29, 1872.
Drew, W. F. & Catharine A. Majors, Mar. 19, 1872.
Duffel, Benj. & Miss Francis Williams, Dec. 29, 1872.
Duncan, Alfred & Mary Ready, Jan. 11, 1872.
Dunn, G. H. & Miss Tennessee Smotherman, Aug. 31, 1872.
Durden, Alfred & Mollie Hibbitts, June 22, 1872.
Eastwood, John & Miss Jennie Zumbro, Jan. 14, 1872.
Edwards, J. W. & Miss Bettie Miller, Jan. 4, 1872.
Ellis, Neal & Lucy Hithe, Dec. 27, 1872.
Erp, Claiburn & Miss Eliz. Painter, Jan. 12, 1872.
Esco, George & Miss Eliz. Bower, July 4, 1872.
Espey, Jo & Mary Miller, Mar. 28, 1872.
Featherstone, Press & Miss Fannie Gates, Mar. 10, 1872.
Floyd, Jake & Susan Marable, Feb. 15, 1872.
Fox, John & Margaret Howland, Sept. 20, 1872.
Frazier, Henry & Sallie Work, Aug. 12, 1872.
Frazier, Simon & Caroline Sherrill, Mar. 9, 1872.
Frazier, Wm. E. & Mattie Vaughan, May 4, 1872.
Frierson, R. M. & Miss Lizzie McDermott, Oct. 10, 1872.
Furgason, Andrew & Lucinda Work, Mar. 21, 1872.
Gardener, James & Amanda Davis, Oct. 6, 1872.
Gilliam, M. G. & Mary A. Ryan, Dec. 2, 1872.
Goodloe, J. Camp & Miss M. C. White, Jan. 16, 1872.
Grant, Henry & Mary Jane Miles, Nov. 17, 1872.
Green, Jo & Pheraby Sims, Jan. 19, 1872.
Greer, Nelson & Creasy Overall, Oct. 9, 1872.
Grigg, J. P. & Miss M. J. McElroy, Jan. 22, 1872.
Guy, Andrew Jackson & Mrs. Sallie McCauley, Apr. 14, 1872.
Hager, Samuel E. & Miss Eliza J. Balentine, Oct. 29, 1872.
Hall, L. C. & Miss Martha P. Bivins, May 26, 1872.

RUTHERFORD COUNTY MARRIAGES

Hall, Zachariah & Miss Melissa D. Datson, Apr. 23, 1872.
Hammond, J. N. & Miss B. C. Harrison, Dec. 24, 1872.
Harding, Gus & Dinah Overall, Oct. 26, 1872.
Hargrove, H. C. & Miss Margaret W. Braden, Jan. 3, 1872.
Harmon, J. W. & Miss S. E. Bunch, Dec. 19, 1872.
Harris, Henry & Fannie Brown, June 22, 1872.
Harrison, G. W. & Miss Mary Mason, July 11, 1872.
Harrison, J. S. Jr. & Miss S. E. Lytle, Oct. 2, 1872.
Hartman, C. R. & Miss Catherine Warpole, Apr. 10, 1872.
Henry, Thomas & June Davenport, Sept. 24, 1872.
Herrod, J. T. & Miss Martha J. Fleming, Dec. 22, 1872.
Hickman, Thomas G. & Miss Eugenia Anderson, Apr. 30,
    1872.
Hicks, Henry & Mary Ann Bridget, Dec. 25, 1872.
Hicks, Madison & Lizzie Emory, Dec. 19, 1872.
Hodge, J. J. & Miss U. E. Coleman, Jan. 2, 1872.
Hogg, Andrew J. & Sophia House, Dec. 6, 1872.
Hoggett, Rodney & Jane Haynes, Aug. 8, 1872.
Holden, Thomas C. & Mary Scott, Apr. 13, 1872.
Holden, Winston & Alsey Batey, Dec. 17, 1872.
Hollins, Sam & Catherine Ridley, Jan. 24, 1872.
Holmes, Wm. F. & Miss Mintie Hall, Nov. 26, 1872.
Hooker, Abram & Ellen Brittain, Dec. 26, 1872.
Hoover, Martin & Miss Sallie Pilkerton, Mar. 19, 1872.
Hopkins, John L. & Miss N. A. Arnold, Jan. 1, 1872.
Horton, Jefferson & Fanny Royster, Sept. 1, 1872.
House, Lit & Patience Vaughter, Oct. 6, 1872.
House, Wm. & Ellen Miller, May 16, 1872.
Howard, John & Susan Simpson, Dec. 12, 1872.
Howland, John & Susan Simpson, Dec. 11, 1872.
Huddleston, Frank & Anna Johnson, Aug. 20, 1872.
Huggins, Harrison & Ellen Sublett, Sept. 13, 1872.
Hunt, Edmund & Nannie Alford, Apr. 13, 1872.
Hunt, Frank & Sallie Randolph, Sept. 14, 1872.
Hunter, H. T. & Miss M. L. Rucker, Feb. 15, 1872.
Hutchinson, G. W. & Miss Sarah Ann Kerr, Dec. 19, 1872.
Hutson, Alex & Katie Owens, Dec. 24, 1872.
Jackson, Francis M. & Miss Sue A. Covington, Feb. 20,
    1872.
Jackson, James & Mariah Jamison, Oct. 2, 1872.
Jackson, John Stonewall & Margaret Beard, Oct. 27, 1872.
Jackson, Robert & Eliza Jones, Mar. 3, 1872.
Jackson, T. M. & Miss Sallie M. North, Oct. 26, 1872.
Jacobs, James H. & Miss Mollie Green, Sept. 19, 1872.
Jacobs, Lawyer & Martha Teel, Mar. 26, 1872.
Jakes, Ben & Rebecca Teel, Sept. 3, 1872.
James, G. T. & Miss L. Lluella White, June 4, 1872.
Jamison, E. D. & Miss P. E. Powling, Dec. 5, 1872.
Jarman, J. H. & Miss Callie Allen, Dec. 11, 1872.
Jarrett, Dennis & Willie Wood, Jan. 4, 1872.
Jewel, I. C. & Miss Francis James, Aug. 3, 1872.
Johns, Frank & Jennie Drake, Dec. 1, 1872.
Johns, L. W. & Miss Mintie M. Rankin, Sept. 22, 1872.
Johnson, Ephraim & Emma McKnight, June 26, 1872.
Johnson, Isaiah & Malissa Walden, Oct. 25, 1872.

Johnson, J. B. & Miss Mary E. Wilkinson, May 9, 1872.
Johnson, John & Lucinda Robinson, Feb. 23, 1872.
Johnson, Nelson & Lizzie Black, Aug. 3, 1872.
Johnson, Wm. & Lanora Hoggatt, Nov. 30, 1872.
Johnson, Wm. A. & Miss Jennie Roberson, May 2, 1872.
Jones, J. M. & Miss Christina Thompson, Apr. 21, 1872.
Jones, J. M. & Miss Alexander Traylor, Oct. 14, 1872.
Jones, James H. & Miss Ella Green, Dec. 25, 1872.
Jones, Jo & Lillie Betty, Sept. 14, 1872.
Jones, Jo & Miss Sallie M. North, Oct. 26, 1872.
Jones, Lewis & Mariah Jones, Jan. 15, 1872.
Jordan, Bill & Alice Yeargan, Aug. 1, 1872.
Jordan, Isam & Elmira Jordan, Nov. 29, 1872.
Jordan, J. M. & Miss L. C. Lee, Sept. 3, 1872.
Jordan, Leland & Miss Ella L. Ready, Dec. 21, 1872.
Jordan, Wilson & Tilla Manear, Feb. 8, 1872.
Keeble, Clem & Bell Miles, Feb. 24, 1872.
Keeble, E. A. & Miss Tennie Easley, Dec. 26, 1872.
Keeble, Marshall & Hattie Smith, Dec. 26, 1872.
Keele, James W. & Miss Z. C. Miller, Sept. 1, 1872.
Key, Ben & Mariah Brown, Nov. 6, 1872.
Kimbro, Harvey & Anna Leath, Dec. 20, 1872.
King, G. W. & Miss Mattie S. Mason, Apr. 11, 1872.
Kirby, John C. & Mrs. Sarah Squarberry, June 2, 1872.
Kirby, LB. F. & Miss Julia F. Travis, Jan. 10, 1872.
Kirkpatrick, Dr. John O. & Miss Izora Wade, May 23, 1872.
Lambeth, Anthony & Mary Holloway, Nov. 28, 1872.
Lane, James B. & Miss Lizzie McLin, May 29, 1872.
Lannom, A. R. & Miss Laura A. Rose, Jan. 31, 1872.
Lannom, H. C. & Miss F. E. Rose, Feb. 6, 1872.
Lewis, G. B. & Miss Judith C. Johnson, Dec. 4, 1872.
Lillard, Charlie & Sallie Davis, Jan. 27, 1872.
Lillard, Jack & Lattie Walker, Dec. 14, 1872.
Lillard, Jones & Indiana Russell, Mar. 18, 1872.
Lillard, Pierce & Mollie Jackson, Nov. 10, 1872.
Little, Richard & Mary Floyd, Dec. 24, 1872.
Long, Luther & Josephine House, Jan. 4, 1872.
Lowe, Nathan & Sievy Lowe, Mar. 21, 1872.
Lyon, David & Ferby Maney, Apr. 5, 1872.
Lyon, Steve & Harriet Davis, Sept. 24, 1872.
Lytle, John & America E. Floyd, Dec. 31, 1872.
Lytle, Robert & Ellen Baskett, Oct. 24, 1872.
Lytle, Sam & Fannie Floyd, Jan. 3, 1872.
Lytle, Wm. & Mary Blackman, Apr. 5, 1872.
Mabry, Henry & Cordelia Martin, Jan. 13, 1872.
Maney, Joseph & Narcissa Smith, Dec. 26, 1872.
Manier, John H. & Adaline Owens, Dec. 26, 1872.
Manor, David & Sarah Davidson, Oct. 24, 1872.
Marlin, B. W. & Miss Mattie Bradford, Dec. 18, 1872.
Marlin, Matthew & Mary J. Weaver, June 25, 1872.
Marritt, Albert & Lizzie Suggs, Dec. 18, 1872.
Miles, Harden & Eliz. Ridley, July 20, 1872.
Miller, H. H. & Miss Hattie Gregory, Feb. 21, 1872.
Miller, James & Frances Lannom, Feb. 9, 1872.
Miller, Wm. & Sarah Rinkard, Dec. 19, 1872.

Mitchell, Green & Matilda Cove, Apr. 5, 1872.
Mitchell, Simon & Jane Key, Dec. 6, 1872.
Mitchem, W. E. & Miss Mickie Bumpus, Dec. 18, 1872.
Moore, Edmund & Martena Smith, Dec. 18, 1872.
Moore, T. J. & Nettie G. Wade, Nov. 13, 1872.
Muse, Ned & Nancy Bank, July 1, 1872.
Myers, G. W. & Miss S. V. Meredith, July 14, 1872.
McAdoo, Russell & Crecy Truner, Nov. 21, 1872.
McAdoo, Anderson, & Lucinda Turner, Feb. 2, 1872.
McClaren, James P. & Miss Martha J. Stokes, Jan. 17, 1782.
McGaughey, W. G. & Miss Cora R. Alexander, July 30, 1872.
McGill, John & Margaret Knight, Dec. 14, 1872.
McKinney, Joe & Martha Baird, May 18, 1872.
McPeak, Wm. & Miss Mary F. Foster, Feb. 9, 1872.
Nelson, J. A. & Miss F. H. Melchor, July 14, 1872.
Newman, John & Mira Jordan, Dec. 20, 1872.
Newsom, Sugar & Susan Nevels, Jan. 11, 1872.
Norman, Henry & Miss Maggie J. Anderson, Nov. 21, 1872.
North, Richard & Lottie Burger, July 18, 1872.
Norton, Jefferson & Fannie Royster, Aug. 21, 1872.
O'Neal, W. S. & Miss M. J. Quite, Aug. 15, 1872.
O'Neil Rufus & Roena Williams, Mar. 28, 1872.
Orman, Freeman L. & Miss Susan F. Braden, Jan. 5, 1872.
Osborn, Caleb & Miss Adalaide Smith, June 4, 1872.
Overall, Ben & Mariah Barkley, Mar. 27, 1872.
Overall, John & Eliza Smith, Apr. 24, 1872.
Overall, Rochard D. & Miss Martha A. Hill, Oct. 8, 1872.
Overall, Robert & Patsey Overall, Jan. 19, 1872.
Owen, W. J. & Miss Kizzie E. Burnett, Apr. 4, 1872.
Paskel, Wm. & Mellie Bennett, Dec. 6, 1872.
Patton, John & Amanda Woodward, Dec. 19, 1872.
Peebles, Adam & Melie Ann Ross, Dec. 31, 1872.
Perkins, Levi & Ellen Hall, May 11, 1872.
Pilkerton, Nathan & Miss Sarah E. Knight, Dec. 18, 1872.
Pool, Benj. & Miss Mary L. Thompson, Dec. 24, 1872.
Pope, A. J. & Miss Sarah L. Richards, Jan. 20, 1872.
Posey, Green & Malinda Burleson, Sept. 12, 1872.
Puckett, B. A. & M. J. Parsley, Oct. 22, 1872.
Pryor, John Randal & Ann Vawter, Apr. 13, 1872.
Randolph, Wm. & Bettie Clark, Dec. 27, 1872.
Rankin, A. W. & Miss Cora Scules, Oct. 8, 1872.
Rankin, Henry & Lou Norris, Dec. 24, 1872.
Rankin, Lewis & Bettie Standord, Sept. 6, 1872.
Rannols, Charlie & Josephine Miles, Sept. 12, 1872.
Ransom, James & Lottie Howland, Feb. 8, 1872.
Ransom, Jerry & Nancy McGill, Jan. 7, 1872.
Rayborn, Charles & Miss Fannie Burton, June 23, 1872.
Rayborn, Samuel & Miss Kate Green, Sept. 11, 1872.
Reeves, Henderson & Minervy McGill, Dec. 27, 1872.
Reeves, Marion & Philis DeJarnett, Dec. 13, 1872.
Ridley, Moses & Ellen Martin, Mar. 1, 1872.
Rion, C. J. & Miss Martha A. Baldridge, Jan. 4, 1872.
Robertson, Barney & Julia Green, Oct. 12, 1872.
Ross, Booker & Jane Puckett, Oct. 3, 1872.

Rowan, James & Fruzana Owens, Dec. 19, 1872.
Rucker, Butler & Julia Ganson, Aug. 22, 1872.
Rucker, Elijah & Mary Ransom, Dec. 26, 1872.
Rucker, Felix & Cinda Blair, Dec. 26, 1872.
Rucker, Isaac & Mary Hodge, June 6, 1872.
Rucker, Isham & Martha Ransom, Dec. 26, 1872.
Rucker, James & Mary Hooker, July 13, 1872.
Runnels, Charles & Josephine Miles, Sept. 12, 1872.
Russell, Albert F. & Sallie E. Johnson, Dec. 24, 1872.
Russell, Henry & Mary Clardy, Sept. 24, 1872.
Russell, John & Sylva Johnson, Dec. 27, 1872.
Ryan, C. J. & Miss Martha A. Baldridge, Jan. 4, 1872.
Sanders, Houston & Mary Brandon, Dec. 13, 1872.
Sanders, James M. & Miss Sue Weaver, Nov. 21, 1872.
Sanders, Mason & Rebecca Hall, Jan. 1, 1872.
Sanford, Thomas & Candis Lindsay, Jan. 3, 1872.
Scrugg, Henry & Louisa Weakley, May 29, 1872.
Shannon, W. R. & Miss N. A. Garner, Dec. 20, 1872.
Shaw, D. W. & Miss M. A. Brown, Mar. 12, 1872.
Shines, Parker & Cornelia Shines, Mar. 22, 1872.
Sikes, Alfus & Mary Salone, Dec. 23, 1872.
Sikes, Henry & Adelia Burleson, Aug. 31, 1872.
Simmons, Alex & Addie Turner, Nov. 22, 1872.
Sims, George & Nancy Hicks, Feb. 17, 1872.
Sims, James Jr. & Miss Alice Pruett, Jan. 9, 1872.
Sims, John P. Jr. & Miss Martha E. Rutherford, Oct. 2, 1872.
Smith, Green & Jane House, Dec. 12, 1872.
Smith, Jonas & Darcus Manson, Jan. 18, 1872.
Smith, Nathan & Frankie Jackson, Dec. 28, 1872.
Smith, Sanders & Francis Henderson, Nov. 23, 1872.
Smith, Simon & Delfey Hartwell, Dec. 25, 1872.
Smith, Wm. & Lishy Smith, Sept. 24, 1872.
Smith, Wm. M. & Miss Tempie B. Lillard, Dec. 26, 1872.
Smithy, Jim & Clara Ridley, Dec. 27, 1872.
Smotherman, Eldridge & Miss Martha T. Crick, Nov. 27, 1872.
Sullivan, Richard & Kit Randolph, May 11, 1872.
Sumner, Osborn & Mary Jane Dunnaway, Oct. 21, 1872.
Sutton, Ed. & Bettie Gentry, Apr. 7, 1872.
Sutton, John & Nellie Harding, Oct. 26, 1872.
Stewart, Harrison & Ann Scisom, Feb. 10, 1872.
Stone, James P. & Mary Maney, June 19, 1872.
Swain, D. F. & Miss Callie Lenoir, Feb. 13, 1872.
Tallent, Wm. & Miss Sarah Todd, Oct. 27, 1872.
Talley, Martin & Maria Martin, Nov. 27, 1872.
Tarver, Lewis & Kittie Black, Oct. 2, 1872.
Taylor, Stacker J. & Miss Emma Ledbetter, Feb. 21, 1872.
Terry, John & Caroline Scott, Feb. 25, 1872.
Thompson, Eli N. & Martha Fathera, July 11, 1872.
Thompson, Wm. & Jane Smith, Dec. 31, 1872.
Thorn, W. T. & Miss Julia Tucker, Jan. 10, 1872.
Tidball, John & Narcissa Roberson, Aug. 3, 1872.
Todd, James C. & Miss Sophia T. Pearson, Mar. 27, 1872.
Todd, W. N. & Sarah Isabella Lowe, Feb. 21, 1872.

RUTHERFORD COUNTY MARRIAGES

Temple, Hiram James & Tennessee Collins, Mar. 6, 1872.
Trigg, Alexander & Winnie Brashears, Mar. 11, 1872.
Tucker, Thadius & Lucinda Spence, Jan. 24, 1872.
Tune, Alexander & Miss Lizzie Ervin, Oct. 24, 1872.
Turner, H. C. & Miss F. A. Williams, Jan. 22, 1872.
Turner, William & Charity Nelson, Jan. 4, 1872.
Ulist, James & America Rucker, Mar. 2, 1872.
Upchurch, Robert L. & Miss Mary E. Temple, Aug. 21, 1872.
Vantrease, Stephen & Mollie Jennings, Dec. 26, 1872.
Vardell, John T. & Mrs. Martha Marshall, Feb. 6, 1872.
Vaughn, Andrew D. & Miss Nellie Buchanan, Sept. 4, 1872.
Vaughn, John R. & Ellen Prater, Jan. 6, 1872.
Vaughn, L. H. & Nancy Davis, Feb. 1, 1872.
Vicary, Wm. G. & Miss Eliz. Brown, Oct. 16, 1872.
Wade, Jacob & Mary Sims, Dec. 10, 1872.
Wade, L. D. & Miss Violet Lytle, May 29, 1872.
Walden, David & Francis Bridges, May 18, 1872.
Walden, Weldon & Catherine Bridges, Dec. 30, 1872.
Walker, James & Martha Baskett, June 1, 1872.
Ward, W. W. & Betsy Sikes, Jan. 3, 1872.
Warner, Bob & Ellen Chancy, Dec. 30, 1872.
Watkins, S. S. & Miss Maggie Turner, May 15, 1872.
Watson, T. W. & Miss M. L. Windrow, Oct. 8, 1872.
Watts, L. C. & Miss Mollie Brown, Dec. 22, 1872.
Weaver, Frank & Miss Mattie Billes, Dec. 26, 1872.
Weaver, L. J. & Miss S. A. Edwards, Aug. 13, 1872.
Webb, Alex & Fannie Childress, Jan. 12, 1872.
Webb, Randel & Amanda Batey, Feb. 8, 1872.
Wesley, Fletcher & Amanda Prater, Dec. 14, 1872.
Wharton, Aaron W. & Miss Tennie V. Hallyburton, Jan. 10, 1872.
White, Samuel & Mattie Davis, Jan. 25, 1872.
Whitsworth, John & Nancy Chafin, Feb. 24, 1872.
Willard, Jones & Indiana Russell, Mar. 18, 1872.
Williams, Edmond & Miss Ellen Rawlings, Mar. 10, 1872.
Williams, George & Edy Jordan, June 23, 1872.
Williams, W. N. & Miss R. J. Simpson, July 4, 1872.
Williams, Wiley & Chaney Sanford, Dec. 23, 1872.
Williamson, Robert & Martha Duncan, Oct. 24, 1872.
Wilson, J. H. & Miss R. E. Bowling, Nov. 28, 1872.
Womack, John K. & Mary Jane Scales, Mar. 31, 1872.
Woodruff, Isham & Lockie Garner, Dec. 25, 1872.
Woods, Henry & Jennie Davis, Mar. 10, 1872.
Woods, Wm. & Mariah Carney, Jan. 18, 1872.
Yancy, W. P. & Miss A. M. Johnson, Oct. 23, 1872.
Yearwood, W. A. & Miss Sarah J. Brown, Aug. 2, 1872.
Young, D. C. & Miss M. S. Jackson, Nov. 10, 1872.
Young, R. H. & Mrs. Sarah F. Gannaway, Mar. 19, 1872.
Zumbro, John A. & Miss Eliz. Travis, Oct. 8, 1872.

Alexander, (cont.)
Hugh W. 90
Isaac 162, 193
J. D. 143
J. T. 194
James 1, 63, 155, 162
James A. 88
James H. 2, 17, 118
Jane 26
Jeff 162
Jesse 1, 3
Jessee 162
Job 162
John 1, 3, 162
John D. 1, 128
John H. 115, 216
John S. 99
John W. 162
Jonathan 2
Jonathan H. 84
Joseph 162, 216
Josephine 180, 235
Levi 2
Lewis 205
Miss Lizzie 212
Louisa 161
Lucinda A. 62
Lucretia 189, 211
Lucy 235, 246
Madison H. 34, 69
Margaret S. 121
Mariah 162
Martha 161, 205
Martha A. 139
Martin L. 96
Mary 119, 240
Mary ---- 149
Mary A. 96
Matilda 162, 176
Matilda W. 102
Milinda 162
N. C. 147
Nancy 46, 187, 229
Nancy C. 91
Nathan 194, 205
Nelson 162
P. M. 96
P. M. M. 118
Paralee 214
Parker 37
Poney 162
Presly 205
Pritchard 2, 14
Pritchett 53
Rena 240
Robert 205
Robert M. 131
Rufus 216
Safe 205
Sallie 243
Samuel 162
Solomon 216
Sophia 177
Stephen 216
Susan 144
Taswell 162
Tennessee 235
Tilla 172
W. F. 240
W. H. 194
W. T. 140
William 2, 162, 216
Wm. H. 2
Winney 162
Winnie 228
Alford, Adline 233, 241
Annie 221

Alford, (cont.)
Artimtia 238
Drucilla M. 214
Mrs. E. J. 239
Elizabeth 2
Elizabeth A. 93
Fannie E. 155
Frank 162
Harriett 84
Henry 162
James 162
John 162
John B. 147
John W. 118
Kitty 214
Levi 240
Lucinda 237
Malinda 234
Martha 183
Milly 226
Minervy 217
Mittie 229
Nancy W. 118
Nannie 249
Ned 162
Sarah T. 116
Thomas 205
Thomas J. 147
Thomas W. 140
Wm. 194
William M. 102
Alfred, Harriett 84
Alison, Martha 159
Allen, Adeline 162
Benjamin 194
Benjamine 2
Miss Callie 249
Charity A. 111
David L. 2
Deanna 166
Elizabeth 25, 124
F. L. 155
Frances A. D. 205
George 162
George W. 108
Granville G. 205
Harriet 48
Harriett Ann 167
Henry 205
Isabella 242
J. W. 247
James 162
James A. 140
James H. 152
Jane 110
Jesse 240
John 2, 72
Julia 210
Louisa 222, 230
Louticia 219
Lucretia 207
Lunsford E. 131
Lutetia 232
M. G. 216
M. P. G. 234
Mahulda 129
Martha A. 113
Mary 146
Mary A. 97
Mary E. 135
Mary Jane 112
Matilda 2
Milton 162
Nancy 101
Nancy M. 136
Nathan 194
Peter 162

Allen, (cont.)
Quimona 214
R. B. 2
Rachel 202
Rebecca 23
Reuben 2, 25
Richard H. 105
S. J. 159
Samuel J. 111
Sanford G. 54
Sarah M. 105
Susan 90
T. J. 205
Thomas 194, 205, 234
Thomas D. 194
Tilford R. 111
Valentine S. 134
William 2, 225
Alley, Arena 38
Ezekiel T. 2
Isaac 78
Mary 170
Allison, Daniel 111
Mathias H. 2
Richard D. 19
W. T. 159
Allman, Lemuel 111
Martha 89, 99
Mary 90
Richard 2, 28, 41
Sarah 134
Allmon, Hardin 54
Allsup, Abigail 18
Alman, Martha 218
Richard 12
Alrid, Hannah 69
Alsop, Martha 205
William 2
Alstin, Wm. 234
Alsup, Miss A. E. 244
E. B. 140
Elijah 99
Elijah B. 115
Elizabeth 18
Harriett E. 238
James 225
Jasper 225
Layfayett 105
Martha 168
Polly 78
Riley 194
Sally 18
Sarah 170
Taylor 205
Ambrose, Merida 162
Sarah 162
Amos, Sally 200
Anberry, Noland 60
Anderson, Aaron 216
Alfred 162
Andrew 162
Angelina A. 113
Ann 211
B. F. 234
Bartlett 25
Beckey 162
Ben 162, 194
Benj. 225
Burton 194
Catty 230
Charles 2, 137
Charles M. 2
Chas. W. 128
Charlott 30, 177
Clara 191
Daniel 240
David 162, 194

Anderson, (cont.)
Edmund R. 2
Elizabeth 111
Elizabeth A. 94
Ellen 210
Ellis 162
Miss Eugenia 249
Frances 58
Fruzanna Jane 232
Gabriel 2
Garland 85
George 216, 247
George W. 2, 115
Green 240
Harriett 214
Henderson 111
Henry 162
Henry C. 125
Henry R. 140
Isabella 232
Jackson 2
James 105
James Henry ? 194
James M. 2
Jane 208, 219
John 2, 247
John C. 247
Julia Ann 78
Julia G. 138
Kitty 220
Lavania 162
Levi C. 2
Lewis 162
Lizzie 238
Miss Maggie J. 251
Margaret 115
Margaret E. 119
Margaret W. 84
Maria 193
Martha 190, 223
Mary 174, 209
Mary E. 137
Mary J. 136
Melvinia D. 97
Miles 247
Mollie 242
Moses 194, 240
Nancy 15
Nancy E. 58
Nancy J. 147
Patrick H. 102
Patsey 54
Patton 72
R. A. 189
Richard 162
Robert 3, 4
Roid 205
Sally 41
Sam. 162
Sam. C. 247
Samuel 3
Sarah C. 128, 129
Serenia 101
Sophia B. 99
Tempy 225
Violet 190
W. L. 143
Wm. 162, 194, 205
Wm. L. 205
William W. 58
Andleton, W. W. 149
Andres, James 20
Jane 20
Andrews, Alphonso 131
Elizabeth Julia 26
James J. 234
Mary M. 19

Andrews, (cont.)
Samuel H. 79
Wm. 128
Angel, Julia 28
Angleman, Albert 205
Anglen, Anglen 16
Anglin, America 101
Anderson 3, 16
David W. 3
Frances 106
Lavinia 139
Martha 67
Peyton 3
Sarah J. 88
Susan 16, 138
Thomas 3
Anthony, Casper N. 125
Catharine 205
Charles 162
Elizabeth M. 49
Frances B. 44
Arbuckel, C. F. L. 147
Arbuckle, J. K. 163
J. K. P. 247
Joseph 3
Polina 24
Ralston 3
Archer, Samuel 105
Archias, Catherine 192
Arledge, H. M. 216
Armistead, J. M. 247
Armstead, Jemima 209
Armstrong, Elmore 163
Ezekiel 3
Houston 205
J. H. 140
James M. 99
James P. 118
John B. 96
John J. 131
Knox 3
Liana 183
Martin W. 3
Mary 136
Mary J. 130
Mary M. 3
Minerva 163
Sarah E. 143
Wm. A. 128
Zenas 3
Arnett, Henry 140
James 108
John 44, 155
Martha 145
Martha J. 155
Mary M. 135
Nancy Jane 160
Rebecca 230
Samuel 134
Sarah 113
William 93
Arnette, John 111
Arnhart, Pleasant 194
Arnold, Alexander 134, 194
Ann T. 99
Asa 3
Becker 3
Berry 163
C. C. A. 147
Catharine 107
David L. 122
Deborah 101
Dennie 242
E. E. 172
Edmund 69
Edwin 93

Arnold, (cont.)
Eliz. J. 230
Eliza B. 209
Elizabeth M. 113
Emerline 241
Enoch 3, 76
Ezekiel 3
Granville 134
H. 158
Hubert 3
James 3, 159
James G. 3
John 3
John B. 93
John W. 66
Judy 101
Levi 38
Louisa 97
Lucinda C. 135
Lucy 245
M. C. 150
M. E. 161
Miss Margaret 235
Martha 194
Mary J. 111
Mentdora 244
Milly 46
Moses 163
N. A. 234
Miss N. A. 249
N. L. 236
Nancy 27, 38
Miss Nancy F. 244
Nancy R. 114, 150
Nelly Ann 134
Nettie 209
O. 30
Peter 3, 69, 76
R. M. 205
R. T. 159
Robert 122, 163
Sally 19
Sarah G. 135
Sarah J. 114
Sarah R. 97
Silva 163
Stephen 96
Susan 26, 94
Susan Ann 191
Syntha 163
Thomas 86, 225
Thomas B. 205
Thomas M. 85
Toliver 163
W. A. 234
William 3, 21, 111, 115, 147
William J. 140
Arnos, Miss Zillie 246
Arthor, Howard 234
Arthur, B. F. 225
J. R. 225
Virginia 161
Arzeno, Mary D. 155
Asberry, Noland 60
Asby, Amelia 76
Asher, Sam. 240
Ashford, Michael 3
Michaell 88
Ashley, Alexander 115
Arthur 118
George 225
James 3
John 149
Julia A. 184
Richard 163
Sarah 229

Ashley, (cont.)
Wm. T. 163
Askew, Aaron O. 128, 140
Arthis, Louisa A. 142
Atkinson, Frances 71
Grace 52
James E. 115
James H. 4
Julia F. 109
Virginia 94
William 93
Attwood, Mary 104
Auberry, Dovy 137
J. G. 225
Logan 247
Martha 84
Rebecca 123
Ritta 123
Sarah 134
Augustus, Aaron 194
Julius 205
Austin, Jackson 163
Laura 163
Lucinda 76
Martha J. W. 70
Owen E. 4
Avant, Albert 216
Lucy 216
Mariah 205
Mary 196
Avarey, America 119
Avaritt, Albert 194
Littleton 4
Sallie P. 188
Aveant, Benjamine W. 4
Avent, Ann 51
B. W. 6
Benj. W. 18
Daniel 247
Eliza Jane 166
Ellen W. 149
Eveline T. 6
Fanny M. 116
George 234
James M. 143
Josephine 247
Mary E. 107
Nancy 105
Roanna 170
Averett, Fountain 205
Freeman 205
James H. 152
Taylor 205
Wm. R. 152
Averette, Freeman 194
Averitt, Julia A. 122
Nancy 8
Avery, M. E. 205
Parthenia 150
Avritte, Francis M. 111
Aylor, Eliza C. 188
Nancy J. 145
Aymett, William 30
Aymette, William 4
Babbett, Elizabeth 68
Bacchus, John 4
Bacon, Sally F. 119
Bagby, Nelly 209
Bagwell, Henry B. 240
Bailey, Alfred A. 216
America 134
Campain 4
Campion 4
Cenia Ann 147
Clementine 150
George W. 122
Hannah 88

Bailey, (cont.)
J. S. 225
Jamison 4
Louisa 93
Louisa H. 151
Mahaley F. 118
Martha 101, 113, 226
Martha C. 97
Newton 155
Patsey 38
Polly 97
Thomas 52, 122
Baily, Nancy E. 192
Bain, Mary L. 239
Peter H. F. 149
Bainbridge, Alexander M. 60
Baird, Andy 163
Angess 187
Anthony 163
Benj. 240
Catharine R. 158
Eliza 187
Elizabeth A. 117
H. P. 225
J. M. 4
James P. 4, 118
James W. 4, 49
Jane 213
Jane A. 137
John 155
Lemuel M. 4
Lou C. 170
Louisa 198
Lucinda 180
Martha 251
Martin 4
Mary A. 200
Mary R. 1
Mira 189
Philip 205
Rosanna C. 212
Sylva 172
Thomas A. 140
Violet L. 128
William D. 122, 131
Baker, Anderson 216
Bill 205
Delila 11
Emiline 192
Ezekiel 205
G. 4
George E. 96
Hampton A. 4
Harriett 190
Henry 163, 225
Hiram B. 93
Jacob 4
James F. 140
Jane 233
John L. 105
Joseph D. 4
Kate 172
Kate M. 201
L. D. 23
Margaret 47, 166
Mary 208
Priscilla J. 141
Sarah 147
Sterling 163
Susanna 18
Sylva Ann 174
Sylva N. 172
W. S. 234
William 4, 247
William D. 4
William H. 108

Baksette, (See also
Baskett, Baskette)
Wm. 216
Baldredge, Sarah 214
Baldridge, Andrew J. 96
David C. 4
Elmira F. 121
Francis 4
James 14
Martha A. 159
Miss Martha A. 251,
252
Mary 26
Mary A. 103
Matthew 4
Nelson W. 48
S. E. 161
Balejack, Mary 204
Balentine, Miss Eliza J.
248
J. W. 163
James 163
Baley, Hannah 64
Mary 90
Richard 105
Ball, Thomas W. 131
William J. 108
Ballard, Avery 4
James 115
Lewis 4
Margaret 122
Matilda 38
Rebecca 119
Riley 105, 118
William 4
Willie 4
Ballentine, Charles 122
Eliza 57
Jesse 4
John 57
John H. 225
John M. 99
Lydia 4
Ballew, Aaron 4
Caleb 15
Baltimore, Charles 216
John 105
Bane, Louiza 194
Banes, Rebecca 7
Bangston, Caroline 49
Bank, Nancy 251
Bankhead, Polly 5
Banks, Anne 72
Charity 72
Clovia 219
David 4
Emma 225
George F. 4
Henry 205
James 194
William T. 102
Banning, Alexander 4
Thomas 118
Banton, Elizabeth A. 27
Barber, Eliza 40
Elizabeth 58, 71, 97
James 4
Joel 4
John A. L. 147
John M. 99
Joseph 225
Margaret 4
Nancy 58
Nancy H. 140
Rachel 39
Rachel C. 160
Rebecca Ann 121

Barber, (cont.)
  Sallie 237
  Thomas 4, 216
  William 4, 71
Barbery, Frances 40
Barbor, J. H. 234
Barbour, John A. 5
  Jonah L. 5
Barchlay, Mary 57
Barette, Wm. R. 247
Barfield, Sally 42
  Sim 216
Barger, Isaiah 147
Barker, Charlotte 172
  Charlotte F. 170
  Dollarson 53
  Eliz. A. 140
  Eliza 86
  Frances 164
  Frances M. 53
  James B. 118
  Lucy M. 221
  Martha J. 141
  Mary 30
  Mary A. 228
  Mica P. 108
  Patsey 8
  Roger 163
  Miss Sallie 235
  Sarah J. 124
Barkley, Ann E. 95
  Henry 64
  Henry B. 115
  Isaac 163
  Jane K. 87
  Jane P. 61
  Marg. 189
  Maria 197
  Mariah 251
  Martha J. R. 108
  Mary 57
  Mary E. 153
  Samuel J. 115
  Samuel Y. 128
  Sarah J. 108
  Susan 163
  Thomas C. 128
Barkly, Judy 234
Barksdale, Catherine 7
  Martha 67
  Mary 59
  Mildred Ann 77
  Randolph 5
  William 2, 5
  William H. 118
  Wm. M. 206
Barley, Mary Louise 91
Barlow, Alfred 5
  Amanda F. 142
  Anna M. 220
  Benjamin D. 115
  Benjamine D. 5
  Cyrus M. 111
  Harriet 62
  James H. 234
  John J. 206
  Kendall H. 111
  Kendrick 27
  Mariah 201
  Mary 93
  Mary E. 233
  Nancy 59
  Susan 230
  T. J. 153
  William 5
  Wm. N. 225
Barmer, Eliza June 229

Barnatt, Peggy 217
Barndon, William G. 86
Barnes, Alexander 163
  Ann 205
  Benj. 163
  Bennett 118
  Catherine 62
  Christina 163
  Clementine 108
  Daniel T. 5
  David 93
  Elizah 134
  Geo. 163
  Geo. A. 134
  Henry 87
  Jackson 206
  James D. 143
  John H. 140
  Lucretia 151
  Martha N. 116
  Mary 135, 164
  Mary J. 115
  Nancy 45, 90
  Pamelia 26
  Rebecca 7
  Saluda M. 46
  Sarah 40
  Sarah C. 240
  Sarah Jane 169
  Simmons 105, 108
  Thomas F. 128
  Thomas P. 128
  Wm. 131
Barnett, Ambrose 5
  Clabourn 206
  Clara 14
  G. F. 140
  Henrietta S. 52
  John 14
  Levi 5, 159
  Margarett Ann 112
  Peggy 77
  Sally Bodily ? 196
  Samuel T. 247
  Susan 62
  Susan C. 158
  Susan F. 208
Barnette, Miss Minasey
    216
Barnhill, Bachel 5
  James M. 5
Barns, Frederic 247
  T. P. 194
Barnum, E. T. 163
Barnwell, James M. 96
  Mariah 80
  William E. 122
Barpo, Joseph 11
Barr, Arsenath L. 152
  Delemore 5
  Emily 232
  Frances I. 196
  H. J. 206
  Mary 69
  Sarah E. 140
Barratt, Jeremiah 118
Barret, John 240
Barrett, Eliz. 131
  Miss Eliz. A, 234
  Jane 215
  Julia F. 147
  Lawrence 93
  Levi 5
  Martha 149, 241
  Martha E. 199
  Martha Jane 225
  Marthenia Bales 155

Barrett, (cont.)
  Nancy N. 115
  Nathan T. 216
  Randolph C. 111
  Sam 163
  Tom 216
  Wm. 240
Barrington, Washington 5
  (See Harrington,
    Washington 5), 26
Barry, J. M. 5, 27
  John M. 31
Barton, Miss A. A. 247
  Anna 219
  Bedford H. 108
  Bob 163
  Clarissa 167
  Elizabeth 70
  Elizabeth A. 5, 87
  Fannie 233
  George 206, 225
  Hale 5
  J. H. 149
  Joshua 5, 7
  M. C. 146
  Margaret 206
  Martha V. 23
  Mary R. 147
  Miriam H. 28
  Robert 5, 25, 115, 216
  Robert D. 5, 96
  Ruthey 5
  Sarah M. 97
  Swinfield H. 115
  T. S. 147
  W. A. 216
  William 23
Basey, Frances 74
Basham, Joseph E. 13
  Mourning 26
Bashears, Lucy 90
Baskett, (See also Bak-
    sette)
  Bell 207
  Ben 163
  Ellen 250
  Mrs. Helen M. 236
  Martha 163, 253
  Mary H. 118
  W. E. 234
  William T. 99
Baskette, Claiborn 163
  Ellen 230
  G. H. 206
  James B. 140
  W. T. 140
Basman, John 194
Bass, Allen 206
  Austin 225
  Benjamine F. 5
  Edmund 225
  Emanuel 240
  Fanny 168
  Frances 127
  Frank 247
  Hannah 163
  Harriet 187
  Hartwell P. 206, 225
  Henry 163
  Isaac B. 111
  Isabella 196
  James 163, 194, 206
  James, Jr. 5
  Jane 174
  Jerry 216
  Jesse 163
  Laura 186, 196

259

Beasley, (cont.)
Scott 163
Susan 155
T. J. 149
Tabitha 190
Taylor 87
Thomas W. 87
Willis 164
Winnie 163
Beatey, James M. 140
Beaty, Allen 46
James 6
Jordan 164
Mary 119
Meredith 194
Nancy 35
Nathaniel 6
Beavers, Abraham 6
Anne 59
David C. 102
F. Y. 247
Josiah P. 119
Nancy K. 120
Beazley, Mary E. 239
Becton, Benj. M. 194
F. E. 25
Frances P. 128
Frederick E. 6
Fredk. B. 36
Fredk. E. ,Jr. 24
Geo. 217
George W. 6, 115
Jane H. 132
John M. 6
Miss M. H. 213
Nancy 23
William J. 6
Bedford, Adline 164
Alex. 217
Amanda 172
Enos 164
Evy 195
Fanny A. 49
John N. 149
John R. 6
Mary A. P. 74
Mary Coleman 6
Matilda 214
Robert 6
Sally 233
Thomas 6, 69
Bedley, Sarah 205
Bedord, Pat 234
Beedle, John 164
Beemer, Alexander 164
Beesley, Anna 11
Catharine O. 111
Christopher 6
Durant 6, 234
Elizabeth 78
Emily 105
Geo. 164
Hannah 227
J. M. 206
James 128
Jane 33
Joel 234
John P. 6
L. Christopher 32
Levica 16
Louiza 34
Lucinda 19
Major P. 6
Mariah M. 142
Martha 78
Mary A. 88
Mary E. 96

Beesley, (cont.)
Menervia 85
Rebecca 98
Sarah 38
Sarah J. 113
Sol. 44
Susan 61, 224
Tabitha 70, 123
Winnie 234
Beigle, Maggie A. 201
Belcher, Ann 164
Frank 164
Belieu, Celia 46
Belifant, Eliza 217
Belk, John A. 225
Bell, Alfred 14
Allen 164
Anderson 234
Angeline 240
Ann 189
Anne 17
Ara 183
Benj. H. 143
Benjamine H. 6
Caroline 156
Catherine E. 87
Clinton 234
Dosia 233
Elizabeth 105, 122
Esther 34
Fanny M. 94
George 115
George D. 105
George W. 96
Hester 178
Hezekiah 102
Hezikiah 125
Hugh M. 90
J. F. 240
J. L. 206
J. S. 240
James 34, 87, 155
Jim 164
John 6, 105, 140, 155
John H. 206
John H. T. 155
John L. 108
Jos. T. 125
Joseph 240
Joseph W. 6
Laura A. 160
Lavinia 191
Lucinda 106, 144
Lucy A. 160
Margaret 122
Marshal 217
Martha 229
Mary E. 120
Matilda 109
Nancy 17, 43
Nancy C. 112
Nancy M. 103
Nicey 225
Noah C. 137
Obediah 93, 143
Parthenia 133
Peggy 71
Rebecca 169
Rebecca Ann 159
Robert 96
Robert F. 134, 140
Sally 19, 183
Samuel 6
Samuel P. 6
Sarah 84
Solomon 194
Sue F. 215

Bell, (cont.)
Susan 230
Thomas 164
W. A. 217
W. J. 164
Wm. T. 159
Zachariah P. 6, 18
Zadock 6
Zedick 108
Zedock C. 89
Bellah, Daniel 164
Elizabeth 76
John 6
William E. 111
Bellefant, Miss C. J. 247
Bellefont, Hiram 217
Belleford, Reuben 164
Bellen, Reuben 6
Bellenfant, John 240
Lucy 137
Bellephant, Emanuel 164
Nancy B. 223
Rachel 164
Beller, William 247
Bellifant, ---- 206
Amanuel 206
Hiram 206
Bellow, Jenry 225
Belt, Arthur 7
Arthur H. 7
Benjamine 7
Catharine 104
Dotson 108
Eliza 126
Hyram 7
Martin 108
Rebecca 39
William 140
Belts, William S. 90
Bemus, Wm. 125
Bence, Jane 205
Bench, W. M. 143
Bendles, John 6
Benge, O. M. 22
Bennefield, Henry 194
Bennett, Agnes 164
Ann C. 142
Bettie 241
Burton 164
Cilla 201
Doriny 217
E. G. 143
Elizabeth 114
Fredonia 30
Hardy 241
Harriett 167
Hilliard 164
James M. 131
Jane 88, 168
John 105
John W. 115
Joseph M. 131
Lou 247
Mary 206
Mellie 251
Monroe 115
S. B. 194
Sarah 64
Miss Sarah V. 237
Susan 238
Taylor 234
Dr. Thomas J. 241
Tonny 204
William 7, 65
William D. 99
Wyatt 241
Zachariah 128

Botts, Aaron 88
Botyer, Henry 13
Bounds, George W. 131
Bouse, Lucy 182
Bowen, Abner 9, 59
　Charles 9
　Daniel 41
　Elijah R. 119
　James 9
　James A. 131
　John A. 137
　John W. 108
　Thomas 9
　W. M. 206
　William C. 90
Bower, Miss Eliz. 248
Bowerman, Melvinia 123
　Milton 112
Bowers, J. A. 225
Bowes, Ledy 86
Bowles, James C. 96
　Mary 52
　Pleasant 164
Bowling, Bailey 206
　Henry G. 131
　James 108
　Jessee S. 194
　John 9
　Joseph H. 108
　Levi 34
　M. W. 158
　Matthew 96
　Miss R. E. 253
Bowman, Bedford C. 125
　Benj. 194
　Catharine C. 106
　Catherine E. 131
　D. B. F. 234
　D. S. 147
　David B. F. 119
　Eliz. 207
　Eliza. J. 145
　Eliza Jane 103
　Elizabeth 58
　Elmira F. C. 73
　Francis M. 129
　Geo. 164
　Henry 122
　James 9
　James C. 225
　James P. 9
　John 9
　Judy Ann 200
　Louiza J. 143
　Malissa A. 73
　Margaret 31
　Margaret S. 119
　Martha A. 197
　Mary 159
　Mary E. 105
　Mary M. 152
　Nancy 61
　Patrick H. 74
　Perrella E. 96
　Priscilla 25
　Robert 194
　Salena Ann 202
　Samuel P. 9
　Sarah 133
　Susan 1, 129, 242
　Susannah M. L. 110
　Viola 156, 157
　Viola A. 6
　William H. 34, 43, 49,
　　76
Bowne, Wm. H. 125
Bowring, Nancy 242

Box, Henry F. 85
Boyce, Joseph A. 137
　W. M. 164
Boyd, Aaron 164
　Charlott 214
　Elizabeth E. 9
　Isabella 9
　Izbel P. 98
　James H. 9
　John 9, 140, 206
　John W. 206
　Lou 240
　Mack 9
　Marian 206
　Mollie 217, 225
　Nathan A. 132, 140
　Paul W. 9
　Robert 9
　Rosanah 104
　Rosannah E. 9
　Sarah E. 119
　Thomas 17
　Wm. 9
　Wm. B. 137
　William M. 9
Boyer, Elizabeth 13
Boykin, W. O. 225
Boyles, Obadiah 9
Bozzell, William 91
Bracey, Eliza 245
　Jane Edwards 186
　Mary 175
　Susan 182
Bracken, Andrew 164
　Dicy 164
　Ephraim 194
　Fanny 164
　Haywood 164
　Mariah 192
　Mary 166
　Richard H. 129
　Sandy 164
　Zacheriah 164
Bracy, Brite 164
　James 164
　John 164
　Sarah 220
Bradberry, John M. 159
Bradbury, Thomas L. 164
Braddy, Benjamine 9
Braden, M. M. 247
　Miss Margaret W. 249
　Sarah E. 241
　Miss Susan F. 251
　Thomas J. 149
Bradfield, Caroline 93
　Daniel 43
　Martha 58
Bradford, Ann 38
　Henry 194
　Henry C. 28
　James 125
　Miss Mattie 250
　Millanda D. 17
　Narcissa 87
　Robert 241, 247
　W. H. 141
　Wm. 137
　Winnie 163
Bradley, Edmond S. 9
　Elizabeth 50
　Isabel 66
　John 58
　Mary 75
　Mary J. 232
　Nancy 165
　Patsey 171

Bradley, (cont.)
　William D. 91
　William L. 115
　William M. 108
Bradshaw, Levina 44
　Sandiford 132
Brady, Eleanor 35
　Eliz. 151
　Frederick 9
　John 194
　Mary 1, 22
　Mathew H. 87
　Susan 159
　Thomas W. 194
　W. F. 156
　William 9, 22, 149
Bragg, Joseph 96
　Thomas 9, 13
Braksdale, Ann E. 90
　Ann G. 83
　Virginia A. 88
Brancen, J. W. 247
Brandon, Alta 236
　Andrew J. 194
　Betsy 28
　Miss Bettie 236
　Cornelius 9
　Esther G. 209
　G. T. 206
　Geo. N. 125
　George 9, 66, 71
　James 9
　Jane 65
　Mary 252
　Noah A. 194
　Polly E. 59
　Robert W. 102
　S. A. 154
　Sarah 101
　Thomas 37
　Thomas M. 102
Brannon, Sarah E. 177
　W. H. 241
　Wm. 164
Branon, John A. R. 156
Brantly, Appollo 234
　E. L. 134
　Irene 179
Brashear, Elizabeth 79
　Jesse 84
Brashears, Gilbert 115
　Isaac W. 9
　James L. 115
　Jo. 164
　Nathan 9
　Sally 32
　Winnie 253
Brasher, Elizabeth 79
　Jesse 28
　Leodocia 7
　Rebecca 37
Braswell, Addie B. 226
　William L. 93
Bratcher, B. F. 225
　J. P. 247
Bratey, Marshal 225
Brawdin, Harriet 178
Brawley, Hugh 9
　Levi 9
　Martha 41
　Thomas 41
Braynt, Sam'l. P. 80
Brazelton, Mary 207
Breen, Anna M. 197
Brent, Elizabeth 117
Brewer, Elisha 149
　Elizabeth 14

264

Brewer, (cont.)
Enoch 164
Henry J. 129
James 93
James G. 96
Jane 109
Janette F. 167
John 99, 112
John C. 159
M. A. 215
Malinda G. 113
Mary Jane 131
Mary L. 98
Seabery 99
Sterling 99
Susan F. 126
Thomas 134
W. H. 241
William 93, 96
Brewster, John W. 195
Briant, Elizabeth 35
Mahaly C. 140
Mary M. 17
Bridges, Bob 165
Caldoin 221
Catherine 253
Francis 253
Henry 143, 165, 195
Lucinda 162
Maria 177
Matt 165
Victoria 192
Bridget, Mary Ann 249
Briggs, Samuel M. 115
Bright, Ann 193
L. 159
Robert S. 134
Briles, Wm. T. 149
Briley, Lucindy 194
Brinkley, Amelia 85
Amos 105
Elizabeth 116
Harriett 142
James 134
Lewis 143
Mahala 121
Martha 140
Mary 133
Mary A. 138
Sarah J. 141
Brinklye, John 195
Britt, J. R. 241
Britt, Mills A. 43
Brittain, Columbus L. 225
Ellen 249
Evaline M. 42
Martha A. 127
Mary 188
Pleasant H. 134
Wm. W. 134
Brittenham, John 9
Britton, Bob 165
John 9
Mollie 241
William T. 9
Broady, Alexander 125
Brock, Clementine A. 97
James 165
Laura C. 103
Malinda 219
Melissa 85
Nancy 165
Brockman, Barney 99
Elizabeth 87
John 10, 51
Brogain, Parson M. 119
Brogan, John A. 152

Broiles, Abby 233
E. J. 184
Frances 234
Mathias 108
N. J. 156
Sue 241
Susan 75
Broils, Nancy 29
Polly 30
Brook, Arnold 165
Louisa 118
Sarah V. 126
Brooks, Agnes 165
Albert 195
Ann E. 110
E. W. 217
Elisha W. 247
Elizabeth 58
Elizabeth Jane 80
H. J. 141
Henry 225
Jim 165
Jordan 93, 125
Joseph F. , Jr. 195
Joseph S. 195
Laura 191
Mary Ann S. 107
Matilda 50
Matt M. 155
Mattie 228
Mickey 184
Milly W. 147
Pempy 247
Sam 206
Brookshier, G. G. 119
J. C. 165
Brookshire, Benjamine 10
Mannering 10
Martha 36
Milly 78
Nathaniel 134
Broomfield, Elizabeth 54
Sarah 54
Brothers, Andrew W. 129
Annette 161
Aurelia 161
Benj. 134
Benjamine 85
Burton D. 54
Charles 165
Didie 158
E. M. 230
Elizabeth 37, 69
Geo. 165
George 147
George P. 115
Harriet J. 121
Jackson C. 89
James 10
Jesse 137
John 37, 85
Miss L. F. 248
Lucy J. 98
Marg. B. 213
Margaret E. 148
Mary 145, 224
Mary A. 224
Mary L. 225
Nancy Ann 72
Nancy J. 243
Nancy M. 54, 106
Peggy 166
Sarah A. 138
Thomas 10, 40, 119
William T. 69
Broughton, Ruth W. 55
Thomas 10, 24

Brousman, Eliz. 213
Brown, Miss A.A. 127
Aaron 165
Abram 234
Adelade 211
Alexander 10
Amanda 165, 230
Ann 232
Anna 117, 170
Anna V. 212
Annis 183
Anthony 165
Archibald S. 134
Benj. 125, 165
Booker 165
Casie 219
Catharine 197
Charles 165, 234
Charlotte 205
Cole, 165, 225
Cornelia A. 145
Cornelius 99
D. S. 195
David C. 10
Dicy 165
Dinah 165
E. G. 241
E. T. 143
Edmund D. 105
Elisha 10
Eliz. 129, 154, 224
Miss Eliz. 253
Eliza 84
Eliza A. 124
Elizabeth 34, 110, 121
Elmira 247
Elup 247
Elvina Z. 115
F. A. 156
Fannie 249
Fanny 206, 239
Felix 129
Frances 165
Francis 65
Francis S. 105
Francisco 242
Geo. 165
Geo. A. 141
George 10, 34, 225
George H. 10
Hannah 213
Henry 134, 165
I. E. 159
Isaac 165, 225
Isaac C. 10
J. D. T. 132
J. T. 217
Jack 225
James 10, 23, 125, 143
James A. 10, 195
James M. 10
Jane 195, 206
Jane C. 114
Jeffery 165
Jennie 237
Jeremiah 29
Jesse 10
John 10, 165, 195, 206
John B. 83
John C. 143
John E. 217
John F. 102
John J. 247
John W. 125

265

Brown, (cont.)
Jordan 195
Jordan A. 225
Joseph 105, 165
Joseph H. 116
Joseph T. 206
Josephine 119
Judith 100
Julia 165, 217
Julia E. 136
Kate N. 204
King 241
Laura 173
Laurena 244
Lavina 160
Lear 171
Lewis 195, 241
Lilly E. 195
Lily E. 167
Loretta 165
Lou 218, 246
Louisa 160
Lucinda 161
Lucinda E. 102
Lucy A. 168
Lucy F. 147
Lucy J. 234
Miss M. A. 252
Manervia A. F. 129
Manervy 233
Mar. E. 156
Margaret 133
Mariah 250
Martha 151
Mrs. Martha 47
Martha A. 102
Martha Ann 123
Martha M. 135
Mary 9, 43, 63, 124, 165
Mary Ann 165
Mary E. 144
Mary F. 98
Mary Jane 168
Miss Mary M. 245
Matilda 79
Meriah 165
Michey F. 111
Miss Mollie 253
Moses 165
Nancy 14, 21, 138, 150, 165, 180
Nancy E. 134
Nancy J. 135
O. P. 165
Phillip J. 105
Ples 165
Rachel 45, 175
Rebecca H. 119
Repps O. 141
Richard 10, 86
Robert 10
Robert F. 158
Robert M. 87
Ross M. 225
Ross O. 129
Sally 64
Samantha E. 211
Samuel 217, 225
Samuel M. 134
Sarah 160, 195, 215
Sarah A. 196
Sarah Ann 84
Miss Sarah J. 253
Sarah M. 113
Sipio 165
Steven 165

Brown, (cont.)
Susan 98, 135, 188, 220
Tennie 243
Thomas 10, 159, 165
Thomas F. 149, 234
Thomas L. 247
Thomas P. 125
Tom 165
V. G. 148
W. H. G. 156
Wesley 217
Wm. 10, 195, 206, 234
Wm. D. 137, 158
William H. 102, 119
William L. 119
William S. 10
William T. 10
Willie 10
Broyles, Alfred 10, 53
Eleanor 21
Elizabeth 53
Jemimah 25
Joel 10
John 225
Brubker, Garrett 10
Bruce, Herrod 91
James H. 10
John 10
John F. 85
Lethey 30
Margaret 108
Mary Malinda 195
Nancy 91
Nehemiah 116
Patsy 10
Wm. M. 137
Bruch, Mary Jane 196
Bruer, Sandy 247
Sterling 165
Bruice, Martha 167
Brumfield, Anne D. 22
Martha J. 79
Brunson, Isaac 132
Bryan, Hiley 152
Mary 30
Susan D. 15
Bryant, Amanda 14
Cornelia 177
David O. 119
Elizabeth 14
Emanuel A. 132
Emily 222
Henry W. 132
James R. 125
John 165
John A. 195
Lorenzie 149
M. S. 225
Oney 13
S. R. R. 241
Sallie 144
Samuel H. 10
Thomas 96
William 10, 96
Wm. F. 137
Wm. H. 147
William L. J. 11
Wm. O. 141
William T. 11, 28
Zebadiah 149
Bryson, Amy 177
Eliza 233
Nathan 165
Samuel 241
Buchanan, Aaron 217

Buchanan, (cont.)
Ada 201
Alexander D. 134
Amanda 214
Ann E. 131
Anthony 226
Braddock 165
Caroline E. 132
Catherine T. 145
Elizabeth B. 117
Falonie 220
Frank 247
Grundy 165, 247
Harriet 232
Henrie 211
Henrietta M. 139
Hettie 246
J. A. 152
James 11
Jane 165
Jas. B. 28
Jess 241
John P. 206
Josephine 172
Louisa A. 134
Lucy 224
Malinda 177
Margaret 165
Mark 165
Martha 192
Mary 165
Mattie 152
Melinda 191
Minerva 188
Nancy E. 133
Miss Nellie 253
Nicholas 165
Sallie 191
Susan 170
Tennessee L. 141
Washington 217
Buckett, Ann 192
Buckner, Marian L. 141
Milly 174
Permelia Ann 70
William B. 30
Buffer, Lockey W. 197
Buford, John 11
Thomas A. 86
Bugg, Benjamine 39
Bugs, Willeby 11
Bulla, James 11
Bullard, John 11
John D. 108
Peter H. 11
Unice 70
Bulloch, Adaline 122
Joseph J. 116
Rebecca A. 119
Bullock, Carolina 90
H. E. 98
Thomas 11
Bumgarner, Peter 11
Rebecca 11
Bumpas, Henry H. 195
Bumpass, Elizabeth 112
John 122
Martha M. 110
Mary 97
Robert 105
Robert H. 11
Wm. M. 141
Bumpus, Miss Mickie 251
Bunch, Miss S.E. 249
Bunkins, Mariah 203
Bunny, Samuel 11
Buntin, Sallie 241

Bunting, Daniel 234
Burch, Amanda L. 201
  Emeline 241
Burchett, Anderson 11
  Andrew J. 132
  Bradley 11
  Dona 156
  James 206
  Leonard 55
  Mary 49
  Nancy 85
  Nancy E. 114
  Susan 14
  Thos. 11
  William T. 105
Burchley, Rebecca E. 113
Burem, Newton 165
Burge, Elizabeth Y. 98
  Henry 11
  Jeremiah 11
  Martha J. 137
  Richard 11
  S. F. 215
Burger, Lottie 251
  Margaret 172
  Samuel N. 122
Burgess, Ann E. 131
  Edward 11
  Elizabeth 11
  James N. 143
  John 11
  Lucretia 38
  M. F. 237
  Mar. 173
  Margaret C. 156
  Nancy 13
  Thomas 11
Burget, Racheal 103
Burgett, James 147
  Violett J. 146
Burk, Adam 217
  Alexander 165
  James 105
  Nathaniel H. 119
  Ransom 247
  Stacy Ann 132
  Thomas 129
  Thomas M. L. 122
Burke, John H. 49
  Lucy 229
  Martha 47
  Milton 165
  Samuel 55
Burkes, Willis 11
Burkett, Ellett 226
  Martha J. 223
  Stephen 217
  W. H. 156
  Wm. H. 134
Burkhart, A. 152
  Alexander 122, 152
  Elizabeth 124
  James 122
Burkitt, Mary A. 200
Burkly, Priscilla 34
Burks, Delila 153
  Herod 57
  James 102
  Leroy 11, 14, 54
  Levetha 136
  Louisa 121
  Miss M. E. 238
  Mary A. 117
  Mary E. 138
  Nelly 14
  Racheal 98
  Romulus 129

Burks, (cont.)
  Sarah 54, 135, 195
  Sarah H. 118
  Serena 148
  Sheriba 62
  Willis 11
Burlason, Melinda 229
Burlerson, Tinny 194
Burleson, Adelia 252
  Ben 195
  Caroline 165
  Catharine 191
  David 11
  Edmond 165
  Eliza 218
  Harriett 165
  Hilkey 11
  Isaac 165
  Joseph 11
  Lila 165
  Malinda 251
  Sam 165
  Usley 63
  Wm. 165
Burlinson, Isaac 141
Burlison, Caroline 165
  Edmond 165
  Ersula 7
  Isaac 11
  Peter 165
  Sally 59
Burnes, Sarah 111
  William 105
Burnett, Miss---- 49
  A. M. 234
  Alexander M. 102
  Ann 49
  Benjamin J. 122
  Brookin J. 132
  Brooking 60
  Clementine 126
  Daniel 165
  Dorcas 165
  Elizabeth 89
  George 241
  George M. 132
  Harriet 48
  Isabella W. 138
  James 91, 93
  John 2, 84, 234
  John G. 159, 226
  John T. 226
  John W. 134
  Joseph 11
  Miss Kizzie E. 251
  L. G. 165
  Lewis G. 11
  Margaret C. 61
  Martha A. 140
  Mary 178
  Mary Jane 222
  Monroe 116
  Nathaniel 88
  Samuel 11, 99
  Sarah 146
  T. S. 157
  Thomas 99, 119, 125
  W. W. 143
  William 83, 89, 132
  Wm. C. 132
  Wm. W. 165
  Woodson 96
Burnette, Callie 217
Burnitt, Henry J. 195
  Myrtilla M. 148
Burns, Albert 226
  Caroline 226

Burns, (cont.)
  Elizabeth E. 111
  Henry 195
  Ivey P. 112
  Jesse 11
  Louisa 10
  Lucinda 228
  Rens 234
  Sarah J. 196
  Wm. R. 132
Buross, Cesar 217
Burrel, Stephen W. 234
Burris, Henry 226
  Mary E. 106
Burros, Nathan 217
Burross, Annie 217
Burrow, Eliz. 165
  Eliza 165
  Jeffery 165
  Stephen W. 165
Burrows, Thomas W. 147
Burrus, Billy 195
  Cizar 165
  David 165
  Eliz. ? 192
  Elizabeth 3
  Fordy 165
  Jackson 217
  James R. 37
  Jesse 166
  Lucinda 230
  Lucy 110
  Mahildy 166
  Phillip J. 11
  Sophia E. 123
  Sterling 166
  William C. J. 18
Burt, Mary Jane 209
  Virginia P. 143
  William 11
  William H. 241
Burten, Sam 217
Burton, Benj. 166
  D. W. 195
  Edney 63
  Eliz. 166
  Elizabeth 86
  Etta 226
  F. M. 158
  Miss Fannie 251
  Frances E. 17
  Frank 206
  James A. 132
  Lavinia E. 124
  Lilly 172
  Lizzie 201
  Miss Martha 183
  Mary M. 28
  Peyton S. 149
  Pricilla D. 156
  Richard 12
  Sarah M. 122
  Thomas 137
  Tony 166
  Virginia 216
Bush, Cicely A. 167
  Mrs. Francis L. 247
  J. W. 147
  Jesse W. 129
  Joe 166
  John H. 12, 49
  Mary 218
  Nancy A. 160
  Nancy Jane 216
  U. A. 247
  W. A. 217
  Zachariah 12

Chaffin, (cont.)
  Minos 166
  Nancy 176
  Sylla 166
Chafin, Hester 242
  Nancy 253
Chamberlain, Juliet S.
  139
Chamberlin, George Ann
  164
  J. D. 157
  Mattie A. 159
Chambers, J. M. 195
  Lucy 206
  Sandiford 217
Champion, James A. 226
  James N. 85
  Mollie J. 199
Chancy, Ellen 253
Chandler, Bettie 202
  John W. 102
  Robert B. 116
Chappell, Henry 102
  John 13
Charles, Martha 166
  Nicholas 166
  Sam 226
Charlton, Aggie 166
  George W. 112, 125
  Henry 166
  James A. 36
  James D. 159
  James H. 42 , 96, 143
  Joseph 132
  Laura Allen 242
  Martha 173
  Stephen 166
Chase, Nancy 239
Chears, John 166
Cheatham, A. J. 122
  John A. 13
  Mary E. 240
  Sarah A. 108
  William A. 108
Cheek, Mrs. Isabella B.
  227
Cheer, John 234
Cherry, Catherine 9
  J. B. 241
  John 13
  Martha 126
  Mary 55
Cheshier, John 41
Chestnut, Nancy 112
Childers, William 13
Childom, Lovenia 225
Childress, Aaron 207
  Alfred 116
  Amanda 166
  Andrew 195
  Caroline 172
  Carroll 195
  David 13
  Dempsy 226
  Dennis 241
  Edmund 207
  Edny 169
  Edward 116
  Eli 195, 207
  Elizabeth 7
  Ellen 196
  Fannie 253
  Geo. 207
  Harriet 176, 178
  Harvey 226
  Henry 13, 25, 166,
    195, 207

Childress, (cont.)
  Isaac 217
  J. K. P. 149
  J. P. 241
  Jack 166
  James 14
  James N. 149
  Jane 183, 247
  Joe 166
  John 14, 132
  John W. 11, 61, 62,
    125
  Joseph 14
  Judith 158
  Keton 195
  L. M. 206
  Logan 14
  Louisa 214
  Lysander 195
  Martha 23
  Mary 143
  Mary S. 88
  Melissa 171
  Melvinia 232
  Milly 182
  Nancy 166
  Nichodemus 207
  Patience 185
  Paul 166
  Pleasant 7
  Pricilla 228
  Rose 166
  Sarah 166
  Susan 56, 62, 176,
    221
  Thomas D. 96
  Wash 247
  Washington 166
  William 14
Chisa, Anne 57
Chisenall, Catharine 109
  James 112
Chisenhall, Elizabeth 17
  Rebecca W. 17
Chism, Clarissa 26
  David 102
  Susannah 78
Chissenhall, Elizabeth
  51
Chizenhall, John 14
Choate, John J. 26
Chrisman, Aaron 217
  Susan 217
Crisp, William 14, 29
Christenberry, Silas 195
Christian, Amanda 166
  James W. 166
  Malvina 166
  Peyton 14
  Wm. 166
Christman, W. D. 234
Christopher, Eliz. D.
  140
  John 14
  Joshua 14
  Louisa M. 160
  Martin A. 137
  Thomas 112
Christy, James C. 38, 44
  S. B. 26, 226
  William T. 5, 10, 16,
    21, 22
Chumby, David A. 137
Chumley, Eliz. 228
Chumly, Eliz. 215
Church, Jane 93
  John A. 14

Church, (cont.)
  Mary K. 71
  Rebecca J. 87
  Robert 14
  Cl----, B. J. 64
Clack, John 14
Claiborne, Caroline 231
Claiton, William B. 57
  Zilpha 57
Claitor, William C. 85
Clanton, Ann 153
  Martha R. 116
  Mary Jane 145
Clardy, Harriett 97
  Mary 252
  N. L. 153
Clarity, Ann 188
Clark, A. W. D. 135
  Anderson A. 14
  Angeline 182
  Ann 148
  Bettie 251
  Calvin T. 45
  Catharine 107
  Clary 159
  E. M. 217
  Elisha B. 14
  Eliz. C. 126
  Eliz. F. 216
  Eliza 58
  Elizabeth C. 100
  Ella 237
  Ellen M. 124
  G. N. 226
  Gilbert B. 6, 8
  H. W. 150
  Idella 226
  Isabella J. 154
  Isaiah 102, 105
  James 14
  James A. 150
  James M. 14
  James W. 89
  Jane 170
  Jennie 232
  Jerusha M. 69
  John N. 14
  Joseph 135
  Josephine 142
  Jourdin 14
  Lizzie 233
  M. E. 216
  Malinda 64
  Margaret 230
  Margarett J. 127
  Mariah 15
  Martha 65
  Martin 22, 26, 61, 73,
    80
  Mary 224
  Mary A. 107, 150
  Mary C. 35
  Mary E. 151
  Mary Jane 205
  Mary O. 76
  Matilda 172
  Molly 214
  Nancy A. 43
  Nancy S. 145
  Newton 105
  Peyton 119
  Sam 24, 43, 56
  Sam'l. 56
  Samuel 66
  Sarah J. 158
  Susan 40
  Thos. P. 14

Clark, (cont.)
Thomas W. 96
W. F. 207
William 14
William A. 108
William D. 52, 76, 83
Yandell 93
Young 102
Clarke, Elisha B. 62
George 14
Lewhanna 3
Nancy 45
Sarah 40
Thomas G. 93
Clater, Elizabeth 53
Claud, Amanda F. 128
Frances N. 112
Claxton, A. J. 226
Matilda 111
Clay, Anna 121
Christiana H. 24
Elizabeth W. 38
Ellen 190, 204
John A. 112
Joseph W. 1
Mary W. 144
Melison E. 38
Samuel T. 14
Sarah A. 101
Sydney 14
Telitha P. 55
Theordrick S. 132
Claybrook, Patsy 42
Clayton, Adala A. 99
B. T. 156
Caroline 246
Eliza 186
Elizabeth 39
Ellen 162
Fanny 102
L. A. 145
Lizean 182
Maria 191
Mary I. 17
Roxanna 166
Samuel 207
Sipeo 166
William 14, 195, 226
Wm. B. 57
William C. 14
Zilpha 57
Cleche, Mary Jane 207
Clem, Wilson 166
Clemens, Amanda 227
M. T. S. 158
Susan 143
Clement, Martha D. 137
Clements, John G. 14
Mary E. 152
R. P. 195
Clemmons, U. S. 56
Zibeath 11
Clemons Frances 170
Lucy Ann 132
Nancy 135
Serenia S. 124
Clendenan, John 14
Clendennon, John 14
Clift, Jemima 247
Clifton, Elizabeth 27
Henry 27
John C. 156
Lucinda 156
Climer, Milton 96
Clinard, Andrew D. 150
Clinton, Louisa 159
Cloddy, Mary P. 41

Clopton, B. N. 119
John A. 126
Martha Ann 162
Samuel 166
Walter, Jr. 14
Cloud, Jackson 234
Sarah Jane 214
Cloudy, Henry 234
Clough, Joseph 80
Clouse, Mary 59
Cluch, Adam 39
Cluck, Nancy 163
Sarah 227
Sarah Ann 229
Clusky, Frederick 166
Coats, Armstead 14
Paiton H. 70
Peyton H. 14
Cobb, Darky 2
Elizabeth 97
G. L. 143
Mary J. 139
Reuben W. 135
S. J. 126
Thomas 14
William 21
Cobler, Lovy Ann 110
Sarah Ann 124
Coburn, Nancy 66
Cochran, Edward A. 14,
74
Elvira 165
James 30
Maranda D. 139
Mary 7
Nathan W. 85
Cock, Mary 120
Nelly Glass 73
Sophronia 94
Cocke, Elizabeth G. 34
James W. 15
Mary 45
Cockran, David 159
Dr. G. W. 234
Cockreal, James 108
Cocks, Cosby M. 167
Codwell, Minnie 216
Cody, Isham 234
William S. 112
Coffee, Ann 195
Coffett, Rody 155
Cogburn, Lucy 105
Mary Ann 134
Coggins, Dan'l. 69
Colbert, David 167
Lewis 167
Nancy A. 203
R. A. 235
Coldwell, Harriet 206
Cole, Emaline 220
Geo. W. 150
James H. 141
John H. 129
Margaret 132
Mary 154
Missouri V. 234
Nelson 167
Thomas 235
William T. 112
Coleman, Abram M. 84
Adelphia 248
Amanda M. 105
Ann 157
Bartlett 167
Betty 164
Blackman 59
Carolina 86

Coleman, (cont.)
Catherine 155
Charity 164
Charles 226
Chastain 66
Chastain A. 15
Claiborne 167
Daniel 147
Edwin 112
Elizabeth 15, 52, 72,
103
Elizabeth A. 29
Emeline 243
Fayett 167
Francis 72
Green 167
Grief 15
Guy 248
Hannah 186
Harriet 229
Houston 167
James 248
James A. 122
James E. 108, 112
Jesse 15
Jesse A. 126
John 15, 119, 132, 135,
167, 226
John H. 150
Jordan 15
Joseph 15, 90
Joshua 119
L. J. 238
Lavinia F. 128
Lilly Ann 167
Lively Ann 103
Margaret 167
Martha 163
Martha A. 148
Martha E. 147
Mary 46, 51, 59
Mary Ann 179
Mary L. 167, 195
Mat 167
Milley 15
Mordecai 15
Nancy 43, 119
Patrick H. 150
Rebecca 15, 167
Rebecca H. 108
Robert B. 167, 195
S. E. 233
Samuel C. 119
Sarah A. E. 89
Sarah Ann 118
Sarah Anne Rebecca 8
Sarah J. 197
Sarah W. 54
Spencer 167
Susan 149, 240
Susannah 54
Sutton 119
Tennessee 161
Miss U. E. 249
William 15, 86
Wm. A. 15
William C. 108
Wm. D. 129
Wm. F. T. 135
Coles, Harrison 241
Collier, David 241
Eliz. 224
Elizabeth 72
Emily H. 88
Henry 167
Ingram B. 15
James M. 105

Collier, (cont.)
John A. 126
Lindsay 167
Martha G. 35
Martha J. 100
Matilda 193
Nancy 56
P. P. 15
Susan 172
Collingsworth, Benjamine
F. 15
Collins, Aberilla 105
Adeline 167
Charlotte 94
David R. 226
Ellen 213
Hill 167
James 135
Jane 78
Jas. S. 15
John 167
Joseph 167
Louisa 176
Lucinda 97
Lucretia 127
Margaret 35
Simeon 217
Tennessee 188, 253
Thomas 108, 119
Colman, Edmund 207
Eliz. 197
Geo. 217
Isaac M. 167
Isham 217
James 207
James K. 167
Jane 157
Jane E. 143
John C. 207
Julia A. 219
Lucy 222
Miss Lucy M. 210
Martha 212
Matilda F. 216
N. A. 167
Rachel 205
Sarah Ann 142
Tennessee 216
Toney 167
Walter E. 126
Walter P. 167
Colwell, Mahala 239
William 15
Comer, Adam 34
Alexander 167
C. R. 235
Charles 159
Eliz. 156
Geo. M. D. 226
George 66
Jerry 167
Jim 195
Martha Jane 209
Mary J. 157
Michael 25, 35, 156
Sarah 88
Susan 212
Commer, Jane 58
Compton, Maj. Banister
217
Elisha 116
Emma H. Vaught 195
Lou M. 232
Richard H. 195
Susan A. 236
Tabitha 124
Con, James N. 15

Conatser, Nicholas 15
Cone, George W. 112
J. J. 153
Conley, Elizabeth M. 114
Hardy S. 102
J. A. 153
Louisa 122
Mary Ann 86
Mary S. 109
Nancy 86
Orpha L. 103
Conly, Alfred W. 96
Louisa Jane 83
Mary A. 86
Conn, George A. 15
Josephus H. 15
Connelly, George W. 15
Hardy S. 15
James B. 15, 122
John W. 15
Thomas J. 15
Conner, Polly 36
Thomas W. 132
Connie, Willobe A. 96
Cook, Abraham 35
Agness 88
Austin 68
D. L. W. 153
David, Jr. 147
Edmund G. 88
Elbert 147
Eliz. D. 230
Elizabeth 6, 67, 68,
105, 123
Elizabeth E. 117
Ellis E. 102
F. E. 151
Fanny 111
Geo. C. 150
George S. 99
George W. 15
J. G. 226
J. P. 207
James 15, 156
James H. 143
James P. 147
Jane 198, 217
John 15
John S. 153
Joseph 15
Joseph H. 153
Kitturia Ann 200
Lucinda 173
Manerva 164
Mariah 23
Marinda B. 90
Mary Ann 16
Mary E. 156
Mary J. 123
Mary L. 154
Nancy 94, 97
R. A. 207
Rebecca 74, 185
Robert 93
Samuel W. 143
Sarah 24
Sarah J. 128
Stephen 156
Thomas 15
Thos. 24
Wiett W. 15
Wm. C. 157
Wm. D. 126
William G. 22
Cooke, Elizabeth G. 34
Green 15
James 25

Cooke, (cont.)
James R. 150
John D. 15
John H. 129
John J. 61
Mary 12
Nancy 48
Priscilla 128
Rebecca 57
Richard D. 112
Sallie N. 152
Sally 45
Thomas M. 147
Wm. L. 129
Cooksey, W. H. 129
Coon, Shadrack 36
Coonce, Nancy C. 158
Cooper, Alvin 167
Anderson 235
Archibald 53
Bedford C. 16
Betty 235
Caleb 153
Charles D. 16
Edward 16
Eliza 85
Elvira 195
Geo. 167
Henry 207
Isaac 28
James 167, 195
John 5, 16, 195
John A. 150
John B. 16
John L. 16
Lucinda 210
M. T. 167, 195
Margaret 28
Mary Jane 202
Micajah T. 16
Nancy 31, 67
Nelson 16
Noah 16
Rebecca 10
Richard 16
Robert 207
Miss Sallie E. 223
Sarah 166, 240
Tabitha 47
Thomas 207
Coosa, Rebecca 84
Copeland, Frances 83
George 217
J. M. 241
Lewis 207
Minerva Jane 235
Tom 241
Coplin, James 16
Coppage, Harriet 183
Louiza 201
William 122
Corben, John 147
Corbett, Henry 207
Richard 153
Corbin, Christopher C.
132
H. B. 167, 195
Corbitt, Peter 167
Corble, Peter 167
Cordell, Thomas M. 102
Corder, Emnline 89
Jackson 119
John 126
Mary 16
Mary E. 154
Mary Jane 150
Raner 206

Corder, (cont.)
  Sarah 23
Corlile, Jane 240
Cornatzor, Thomas R. 119
Corner, Adam 93
Corns, Eliza 194
Cornwell, Eli 217
Corsthwait, Geo. D. 67
Corwell, ' See also Cro-
  well)
  Ann 167
Cosbey, Alfred G. 16
  W. M. 159
  Williamson 16
Cosby, Alfred G. 53
  Catherine 87
  Rebecca 53
  W. M. 143
  Wallace 16
Cosey, Martha A. 95
Cothran, A. H. 196
  Isabella 158
  Sarah E. 157
Cothrin, Frances C. 106
Cotten, Abner 16
  James 122
  Jemima 176
  Martha 190
Cotter, James L. 150
Cotton, Jana 105
  John H. 126
  Lacey Ann 231
  Levenia 103
  Manaus C. 132
  Martha 105
  Mary 104
  Rebecca 129
  Sallie 161
  Sarah Ann 147
Couch, Dolly 245
  H. W. 235
  Henry 241
  Isaac M. 129
  Jane 226
  Malinda 3
  Martha 157
  R. W. 153
  Thomas J. 196, 207
  William 16
Coughanour, David 126
Coulter, Aaron 167
  Amanda 167
  Asa 8, 16, 90
  Bartlett 83
  Eliza 100
  Fanning 84
  Manning 129
  S. 143
  Sherley 112
Council, J. L. 159
Counsel, Jacob W. 153
Countryman, Catherine 22
  Elizabeth 29
Counts, Geo. 16
  George 16
  George S. 16
  Jesse 16
  Phillips 39
  William 16
Coursey, John B. 116
  Joseph 141
  Tyree 116
  W. J. 218
  William 16
Courtney, Julia 117
Courts, George W. 122
Cove, Matilda 251

Covington, Armenia 126
  David 16
  Dianna 231
  Edmund 16
  Edwin J. 96
  Eliz. J. 152
  Miss Eliza 41
  Elizabeth 48
  Elmira 124
  Emely E. 135
  Frances J. 119
  Jackson 16
  James N. 153
  Jemima Jane 100
  Jesse 6, 16
  John 16
  Joseph 122
  Julia A. 32
  Julia Ann 233
  L. A. 196
  Larkin 16
  Larkin A. 135
  Larkin M. 126
  Lucinda 128, 137
  Lucinda E. 111
  Martha 15
  Martha J. 120
  Mary 56
  Mary J. 138
  Naoimia 117
  Narcissa 167
  Pink 157
  Robert 248
  Miss Sue A. 249
  T. H. P. 147
  Tabitha Jane 4
  Thomas 157, 196
  Tom 167
  Wm. 147
Cowan, Calip 167
  Dellie Z. 229
  Isabella 181
  Joseph 196, 207
  Joseph D. 147
  Margaret H. 146
  Martin 167
  Nancy 17
  Nelson 167, 241
  Patsy 172, 243
  Sallie J. 154
  Slartin 167
  V. D. 2
  Varner D. 16, 17, 20
  William 17
  William B. 17
  William M. 17
Cowans, Julia 233
Cowen, Anna L. 213
  Annie 157
  Catharine E. 136
Cowger, Harriet 133
Cox, Bell 244
  Caroline E. 102
  E. C. 156
  Elisah 147
  Elisha 1, 17
  Eliz. 219
  Ephraim 17
  Eveline 85
  Ezekial 17
  George 207
  Hiram 17
  Isham 35
  J. G. 56
  James I. 17
  James L. 17
  Jane R. 111

Cox, (cont.)
  Jas. R. 19
  John F. 88
  Joshua T. 99
  Margaret 80, 131
  Martha 154
  Martha A. 94
  Mary 80
  Michael 196, 207
  Rachel G. 79
  Samuel 102
  Sarah N. 87
  Susan 112
  T. W. 235
  Thomas W. 17
  William 79, 105
Coyne, John 167
Cozart, J. W. 248
  John 207
  W. J. 248
Crabtree, Nancy M. 233
Craddick, Necy 183
Craddock, Elicum 17
  G. G. 150
  John N. 17
  Nathaniel 218
  William 83
Cradick, Ann 242
Cradock, M. A. E. 146
Craford, Sara 14
Craft, Hester 25
  Rebecca 9
Craig, F. D. 137
  John 17
  William B. 105
Crainor, Thomas B. 96
Cram, John 167
Cranahan, (See also
  Carhahan, Carnahan)
  Hugh 13
Craner, Moses 196
Crary, Mary A. 124
Crass, Wm. 16
Cravens, Thomas 96
Crawfoed, Preston 159
Crawford, Agatha 229
  Amelia 227
  Miss Anna E. 224
  Bedford 16, 226
  Charles B. 17
  David 17
  Delia M. 39
  Diana 164
  Ellen P. 138
  Elvira 167
  Essex 248
  Frances 230
  Gid 226
  James 99
  John 17
  Joseph G. 105
  Joshua 218
  Lockey E. 151
  Martha 164
  Mattie E. L. 202
  Meriky 238
  Temperance B. 71
  William 17, 102
  William C. 17
Crawley, M. D. 147
  Martha J. 133
Creason, Lewis 87
Creasy, Mary M. 142
Creech, John W. 144
  Mary 104
  Mary Ann 36
Creek , John 17

273

Creek, (cont.)
Mary 109
Permelia J. 209
Crenshaw, John W. 132
Creson, Mary A. 160
Pricilla P. 160
Crews, John W. 159
Squire 17
Crichlow, Hellin M. 140
James 78, 96, 105
Martha 220
Sarah C. 132
Thomas H. 105
W. D. 144
Crick, Eliz. 130
Eliz. E. 149
F. G. 153
James 112
Jesse A. 235
John 36
Miss Martha T. 252
Mary 122, 128, 236
Mary Ann 235
Merriman 135
Nancy 102, 104, 158
Perry 112
Richard 126
Sarah 115, 127
Wm. H. 159
William M. 122
Criswell, R. T. 167
Critchlow, Joseph E. 167
Nancy 88
Thomas N. 226
Critts, Sebastian 196
Crocker, Alenbert 78
Amanda E. 112
Elizabeth M. 116
Isaac 105
John C. 96
John T. 17
Lambert 17
Manirva 132
Martin 78
Martin L. 89
Mary 90
Mary E. 130
Matilda 34
Thomas B. 122, 129
Crockett, A. S. 129
Alice B. 218
Allen B. 126
America S. 5
Ann M. 34
Bettie 229
C. 155
Calvin 196
Charles A. 218
Cordelia 156
Dandridge M. 99
F. P. 10, 54, 59
Dr. F. P. 207
Fountain O. 17
Frank 241
G. H. 226
Granville S. 17
Harry 167
Henry 226
John A. 87
Louisa 99
Mary J. F. 94
Mary Jane 5
Milly 172
Nathan 167, 196
O. W. 3, 218
Overton W. 5, 112
Patience 167

Crockett, (cont.)
Robert P. 150
Sallie 207
Sally 235
Samuel O. 116
Sarah 119
Sarah C. 121
Sarah G. 129
W. C. 207
W. G. 56
William G. 99
Wm. M. 137
Cromer, Joseph H. 129
S. F. 241
Cronister, Adam 26
Crook, Malinda 47
Mary 110
Cross, George W. 105
John 17
John C. 141
M. 248
Martha 33
Mary Ann (?) 214
S. J. 159
Susan 248
Susan A. 106
Crosslin, A. M. 153
J. S. 248
Mollie J. 226
Polly 16
Crossthwait, George D. 17
Crosthwait, Geo. D. 8, 45
George D. 60, 77
Mary 73
Mary C. 60
Rebecca 60
Crosthwaite, Emeline 127
Croswaite, Jennie 222
Crouch, Miss M. J. 247
Crouse, Alfred 226
Miss Amanda B. 161
America E. 156
Elizabeth 122
Elizabeth F. 197
George J. 248
H. A. 144
Harriet 168, 199
Henry 70
J. A. 205
Jane 143
John 167
Joseph L. 196
Lucinda C. 145
Martha H. 130
Martha I. 197
Mary 131
Matthias 17
Spencer 17
Thomas 153
Crow, John 10
Crowder, Ailsy A. 108
Emiley Ann 97
George G. 119
Jane 61
Jesse 17
John R. 102
Marg. 213
Nancy 103
Nathaniel 18
Rebecca L. 86
Sally 61
Samuel 60
Stephen 102
Crowe, Daniel 207
Crowell, (See also Cor-
well)
Moses 167

Crowford, Peggy 178
Crownover, Polly 52
Crowse, B. S. 207
Henry 86
Henry C. 116
Mary 108
Nancy A. 146
Cruchway, Wm. 241
Crump, M. R. R. M. 196
W. B. 167
Cruse, Beverly A. 102
Martha 77
Crutcher, Brown 167
Emma H. 143
J. A. 241
Jane E. 132
Laura 206
Martha 164
Nannie H. 241
Neal 207
Richard 167
Tennessee 167
Tennessee A. 138
Crutchfield, B. J. 226
Dilly 6
Elizabeth 88, 117
Gideon 18
John 105
John H. 112
Mary 84
Oliver M. 17
Oliver W. 69
Rebecca 196
Sarah 197, 202
Thomas N. 119
Crutchfielf, Susan C. 115
Cuff, John W. 18
Culan, Thomas 18
Culbertson, Mary 61
Culf, Easter 244
Cullum, Casarinda 112
Culp, Charles 167
Margaret 41
Culver, Edith 3
Frances 12
Cummings, Alfred M. 126
Emma 246
Jacob 167
Uriah S. 55
Cummins, Andrew 79
Benjamine 18
Elizabeth 46
Nelton 12
Robert 18
Robert G. 18
Sarah 22
U. S. 45
Uriah 18
Cunigan, Susan 242
Cunningham, C. P. 150
Cary A. 209
Dicey 96
Ellin 98
George 126
James 18
Jane 68
Jesse 167
John 147
Joseph 18
Leviny 96
Martin 61
Mary 61
Mary M. 100
Moses 150
Phebe 132
R. W. 73
Richard 65

274

Davis, (cont.)
Isaac 19, 207
Jacob 16, 168
James 19, 168
James A. 116
James B. 19
James N. 153
James S. 81
Jane 8, 11, 19, 75,
168, 173
Jennie 253
Joe 248
John 30
John A. 196
John M. 7
John P. 19
John W. 153
Joseph 168
Judith 7
Julia 168
Kenira 170
L. 3
Lewis 72, 168
Lizzie 244
Miss Lizzie C. 246
Louvinia 236
Lucinda 157
Lucy A. 146
M. E. 143
Miss M. E. 235
Maggie T. 173
Malinda 192
Manie 224
Margaret 79, 214
Mariah 164, 168
Martha J. 135
Martha L. 87
Mary 7, 55, 64, 83,
102, 165, 243
Mary A. S. 104
Mary C. 135
Miss Mary C. 212
Mary E. 235
Mary J. 105
Mary Louisa 97
Mattie 253
Media G. 211
Miles 168
Mira 192
Mosbey 207
Nancy 36, 87, 104,
107, 166, 179, 237,
253
Nancy E. 84
Narcissa 64
Parthena 225
Peggy 70
Perry 168
Persila 111
Phillip 105
Phillis 189
Puss 222, 230
Mrs. Q. E. 221
Rachel 225
Rebecca L. 20
Richard 93, 226
Robert I. 207
Robert J. 196
S. B. 159
Sallie 250
Sally 30, 168, 193
Samuel 93
Sarah 150
Sarah C. 178
Sarah L. 179
Simon 168
Susan 240

Davis, (cont.)
Susannah 40
Syrenia 168
Thomas 19, 235
Thomas D. 19
Thomas P. 19
Timothy 19
Tom 168
Turner 218, 226, 235
Vilet 169
W. L. 144
W. T. 235
William 16, 105, 207
William E. 119
William H. 3, 64
Wm. K. 135
Wm. L. 39
Willy Ann 72
Young, 132
Dawson, Ann 168
Washington 168
Day, J. I. 226
Manerva 69
Daysey, Mary Ann 168
Wm. 168
Deahne, Jenny 166
Dean, Candas 22
E. H. 93
John W. 106
Josephine 209
Mary ? 242
Mary C. 47
Wm. 248
Deason, D. G. 150
Isabel 168
John 19
Milly 118
Tabitha 130
Wm. 168
Deasont, Margaret E. 122
Deaton, Mary 228
Debs, Samuel C. 19
Deckard, Henry 168
Deckerd, Henry 226
Deer, Mary 26
DeJarnatt, Annis 168
Bill 168
Daniel M. 102
Jane 163
Tobe 168
DeJarnett, Jack 168
James G. 116
John 235
Julia 116
Martha 168
Martha W. 121
Moses 168
Nancy 80
Miss Nannie 235
Phillis 251
Reuben 168
Vicey 168
DeJarnette, Edmund 168
DeJarrett, Gabe 248
DeJernett, Edna 78
Delbridge, Amanda 241
E. W. 218
Edward H. H. 132
Elizabeth 106
Fred 168
James T. 144
Jerry 168
Mary Eliza 162
Mary P. 67
Susan H. 97
Dell, Martha A. J. 152
Deloath, Boykin 19

Delyell, Nathan 159
Dement, Abner 235
Abraham 19
Agnes 97
Allen 19
America 165
Ann E. 122
Cader 19
Charles 19
Charles L. 168
Charlotte 70
David 112
Elizabeth 26, 51
James 19, 29
John 19, 241
John B. 108
Joseph A. 112
Mary 99
Mary B. 94
Mary J. 155
Sarah 30
Sereany 51
Susan 208
Susan C. 97
Wilson 168
Wilson Y. 138
Demumber, William 19
Denen, Hiram A. 19
Denham, A. E. 241
Esquire W. 241
Dennes, Giney 83
Denney, Matilda 90
Sarah 88
Dennis, Josephine 224
Josephine C. 215
Priscilla 123
William 218
Dennison, Amanda M. F.
131
Eliza R. 119
Denny, Anamda 182
B. R. 226
John 35
Margarett 95
Robert 19
Robert A. 19
Samuel 19
Denoho, Mary B. 9
Denson, Martha 125
Denton, Charles 19
Hannah 99
James 102, 241
William 93
Depriest, Charles C. 19
Nancy 32
Derbin, Jane 184
Derly, Wm. 168
Dervin, Meriah 186
Dethel, Palmyra A. 132
Devaden, Delon 8
Devault, Nancy E. 127
Peter 18
Dial, John C. 19
Dicas, Lear 80
Dickens, John 168
Dickerson, Eliz. 153
Marg. 178
Matilda 203
Tinzey 132
Dickey, Frances 4
James 19, 44
John L. 4, 19
Matthew 19
R. A. 159
W. P. 196
William E. 106
Dickie, Chelnisa D. 106

276

Dickie, (cont.)
Francis E. 113
James H. 141
Martha J. 141
Mary L. 119
William L. 119, 122
Dickins, Baxter 20
Ja. H. 119
William 20
Dickinson, Alfred 20
Ann 14
Fanny Pricilla 100
Gallant D. 20
Isham S. 20
Jennie 229
M. A. 218
Margaret L. 130
Martha Ella 109
Sally 6
Samuel 20
Sarah 168
William 7, 20, 168
Zilly 62
Dickson, Adalade 244
Alexr. S. 17
Alfred 20
Amos 20
Cynthia H. 6
David 20
Edwin R. 64
Eliza A. 116
Emeline 60
Enoch N. 87
Enos H. 20
Ezekiel 20
Geo. 196
Hannah H. 77
Henry 248
John 168
John D. 106
Joseph 20
Lizzie 231
Lucinda 88
Maduci E. 68
Malinda 98
Margaret H. 72
Mary G. 41
Rosana 246
Sarah M. 6
William 19, 20
William R. 20
Dicus, Margaret 64
W. D. 218
Digins, Adline 246
Dill, Amanda 242
Amanda T. 87
Catharine L. 137
E. E. 150
Eliz. J. 125
Eliza 83, 150
Elizabeth 109
H. C. 207
J. M. 144
James 196, 235
John 158
Joseph 20, 74, 218
Lavenia 198
Martha J. 142
Marvell M. 20
Mary 71
Mary G. 153
Marye E. 158
Narcissa 137
Newton C. 20
Noah W. 20, 63
Sarah T. 145
Thomas 150

Dill, (cont.)
W. C. 150
Wm. 150
Dillard, John 218, 248
John L. 9
Joseph 41
Martha A. 15
Rose J. 121
Sarah 94
Dillin, Albert 218
Rebecca 199
Sarah Ann 204
Dillion, Allen 20
James A. 138
Dillon, Bell 216
Clemmontine F. 188
Fanny 175
Jane 181
John 106
Mary 167
Nancy 86
R. A. 144
R. J. 196
W. E. 248
Wm. H. 141
Dillow, Jacob 168
Dirikson, Davis S. 20
Dismukes, Thomas U. 20
Z. T. 248
Ditto, Jane 169
Dixon, May 23
Doak, Eliza A. 99
J. M. 147, 248
Joseph 20
Mary A. 100
Nancy E. 99
Nelson 65
Robert 20
Sam 168
Dobbins, D. P. 144
Fanny 168
Margaret A. 125
Thomas 83
Wm. 153
Dobrowsky, P. M. 144
Dobson, Benjamine 20
Jane 95
Joseph C. 20, 78
Nancy 216
Rebecca 75
Sarah E. 199
Dobyns, Dennis R. D. 20
Dodd, Elmira L. 37
Griffin 60
Jane C. 60
Nancy H. 60, 61
Dodson, Paul W. 122
Doke, T. J. 196
Dokes, Jordan 207
Dollan, Diner 221
Dolly, Elizabeth 34
Nancy 180
Dolton, Wm. 159
Donaho, Margarett J. 144
Donald, Mary M. 71
Sarah 28
Donaldson, Archibald Y. 102
J. W. 207
Donel, Mary C. 243
Donels, William A. 87
Donelson, Andrew J. 20
Calvin 20
Donnell, Arabellah K. 100
Calvin 207
Charles 168

Donnell, (cont.)
Daniel 168
Dinah 187
Eliza. M. 132
Elmira 180
Fanny 205
Jack 207
James 153
John 207
John W. 129
Levi 20
Lockey J. 130
Martenia 168
Martha Ann 207
Nancy 201
Nannie 231
Robert S. 43
S. C. 144
S. J. M. 213
Samuel 20
Sarah E. J. 124
Miss Susan 219
Wesley 168
William 20
Donnelly, Catharine 106
Homora T. 130
Lucy 77
Donnelson, John L. 88
Donoho, Jane 98
Lucy 206
Parthenia E. 101
R. D. 20
Robert D. 56
William 20
Doodman, Eliza J. 33
Dooley, Martha 101
Doran, Alexander 20
James G. 21
Neoma S. 46
Rebecca L. 86
Doring, Eliz. 131
Dorrell, Evergreen 158
Dorsey, Alexander 108
Charles 21
Dorson, Warren 168
Dosher, Daniel 21
John 21
Dosheta, Nancy 28
Doss, Elizabeth 1
Doty, W. E. 218
Doughlass, Asa 147
Doughtry, William 106
Douglas, Fanny 34
James H. 108
Mary 242
Nathan L. 10
Nathaniel 10
Rodham 21
Thomas 138
William 41, 196
Douglass, Abram 112
Amanda 133
B. H. 248
Dianna 193
Edy E. 194
Fred 207, 218
George W. 102
James 112
John W. 218
M. J. 241
Mary 134
Mary A. 139
P. 235
Polita Ann 130
Rachel A. 113
Sallie 221
W. T. 196

Eades, (cont.)
Hannah 126
Isaac 21
Samuel A. 147
William 21, 147
Eads, A. J. 169
Martha 240
Mathew W. 150
Milly 149
Rhodie E. 217
Sally 71
Solomon 147
Eagleton, Alex 218
Eliza 127
Elvira 102
Fanny 169, 214
John A. 141
Margaret 104
William 1
Wm. C. 132
Young 169
Eakes, Daniel 106
Eakin, Abraham 169
Miss Jane C. 224
Mindo 169
Nelson 208
W. G. 208
Eaks, Leathy 123
Lucy Ann 135
Ealon, Samuel 196
Ealy, Mary Eliz. 141
Earley, Miss Eliza 174
Martha 158
Earls, Nancy J. 212
Early, Henry 21
Jessee 196
Sarah A. 143
Earp, E. J. 169
Jefferson 23
Mariah 2
Earps, Martha R. 210
Earthman, Mary 83
Sarah 110
William W. 112
Earwood, William 21
Easley, Miss Tennie 250
East, A. 39
Anderson 21, 63
Easters, Susan 5
Eastice, John 157
Eastland, Thomas B. 21
Eastus, Henderson 21
Eastwood, Eliz. 219
John 248
Martha Jane 231
Mary 105
Miss S. J. 246
Susan 112
William 112
Eatherly, Martin A. 241
Patrick A. 227
Eathman, Margaret J. 88
Eaton, Elizabeth 60
Jenny 175
Martha Jane 223
N. J. 164
Nancy J. 160
Newton J. 150
Rebecca 149
Rebecca E. 239
Tabitha 131
Edding, William 36
Edens, Ezekiel 21
Edes, William 112
Edkridge, Margaret K. 107
Edmonds, Eliz. E. 145
Frances A. 113

Edmonds, (cont.)
Henry L. 108
Martha 30
Miss Martha 234
Thomas C. 102
Edmondson, Anne 17
Baldey 169
Baldy 169
Charles 208
Ed. 169
Eliza 106
Harriett 201
Henry 169
John 21
John James 196
Louisa E. 161
Martha 187
Peyton 169
Solomon 169
Susan 62
T. P. 241
Edmonson, Jane 44
Edmonton, John James 169
Edmunds, Louisa C. 156
Edualy, David 23
Edward, Daniel 169
Thomas 147
Edwards, A. S. 2, 3
Alice K. 225
Amanda G. 110
Andrew S. 3
Arthur M. 21
Augusta 25
Augustus 21
Charles A. 22, 80
Daniel 169
Dennis 227
Edward 22
Eliz. 137
Elizabeth 50, 64
Elizabeth T. 113
Fannie J. 230
Frances 91
George W. 119
Granville 235
Harrison 169
Henry 169, 208
Hiram G. 208
Hughs 116
Isaac S. 138
J. W. 218, 241, 248
Jack 169
James 43
Jane 233
Miss Jane 242
Jarman B. 144
Jeff 227
John 22
John A. 93
John J. 22
John W. 169
Joseph 55, 65
Mrs Judith 52
Judith C. 127
Judith W. 42
L. H. 218
Levi 22
Louisa W. 51
M. J. 223
Margaret J. 200
Mariah 164
Marillis 29
Martha 206, 208
Martha Ann 14
Martha L. 131
Martha S. 125
Martin 69, 90

Edwards, (cont.)
Mary Ann 40
Mary L. 219
Minerva 71
Moses 169
N. A. 147
Narcissa H. 98
Nat 169
Nathan 169
Penelope 54
Phebe 50
Polly T. 19, 67
Presley 3
Richard A. 22
Roderick 22, 89
Miss S.A. 253
Sallie K. 174
Sam 169
Sarah A. 141
Sarah M. 41
Sterling C. 116
Susan 169
Sylva 169
Thomas 16, 22, 93, 169
Thomas G. 218
Thomas J. 22
Thomas M. 108
Welden 22
Wm. 135, 169
William C. 8, 22
Eggleston, John W. 22
Ehart, Christian 22
Ehrenseller, Martha 139
Eillon, Eliz. H. 142
Elam, America R. 123
Daniel F. 138
Dora 241
Edward 22, 37
Frances C. 104
George F. 99
Henrietta 37
Jane E. 215
Joel 22
K. E. 144
Mary O. 103
Mattie E. 218
Nancy 49
Rebecca O. 123
Thomas J. 156
Tom 169
William 22
Elder, Anne 156
Benj. A. 196
Benjamine 22
Betsy 56
Betty 154
Elias A. 141
Emily J. 132
George W. 169
James 22, 37, 49
James G. 135
John S. 156
Joshua 22, 51, 68
Levi W. 150
Lucy E. 118
Mary 14
Matilda 152
Matilda E. 115
Nancy 83
Miss Serena B. 228
William 22, 227
Wm. K. 129
Elgin, F. G. 157
Samuel 22
Elkin, Shedrich W. 169
Elkins, Laura 231

Elkins, (cont.)
  Ruth 46
Elliatt, Thomas J. 99
Ellington, Wm. 156, 218
Elliot, Catharine 149
  Louisa F. M. 147
  Mary L. 125
  Wm. G. 147
  Miss Willie A. 234
Elliote, Joseph 108
Elliott, Alfred 45, 70
  Amanda 206
  Amanda C. 132
  Archibald 144
  Barney 22
  Delila 243
  Eleanor 111, 115
  Elizabeth 38, 83, 90
  Glasgow 169
  Harriett C. 137
  James 218
  John 43
  Knacy H. 22
  Laura 228
  Louisa 79
  Lucretia 151
  Margarett 102
  Martha 127, 145
  Martha A. E. 90
  Martha W. 104
  Mary 66, 131
  Mary J. 105
  Matilda 98
  Milton M. 144
  Nancy 13
  Nelson 169
  P. M. C. 90
  Peter N. 22
  Richard B. 119
  Richard S. 22
  Robert 22
  S. R. 212
  Sallie 159
  Sarah 11, 12
  Sarah B. 103
  Sarah W. 111
  Simon 22, 38, 79
  Stacy 48
  Susan 134
  Tennie P. 227
  Thomas 22, 37
  Wm. 169
Ellis, Albert 169
  Caroline 208
  Edward N. 132
  Greensberry 89
  Hick 22
  Hicks 126
  Hicks E. 52
  Josiah 22
  Louisa 135
  Lucinda 113
  Mary P. 137
  Melissa A. 99
  Neal 248
  Pamela A. 119
  Radford G. 99
  Rody 83
  Susan 4, 181
  Susan F. 84
  Thomas B. 22
  William W. 22
  Wyat H. 70
  Wyatt H. 23
  Wyley 23
  Zachariah W. A. 144
Ellison, Charlotte 90

Ellison, (cont.)
  Hugh H. 23
  Mary A. 100
  William 27
Elliston, Hugh H. 40
Elmore, Miss E. J. 247
  Lucian C. 196
  Sarah Catherine 226
Elrod, Adam 141
  Adam A. 23
  George 23
  Harmon 28
  Harmond 23
  James M. 153
  John 23, 48
  Montgomery 23
  Phebe 69
  Sarah 45
  Thomas S. 93
Elseback, Wilson 169
Embry, Charles 218
  Edmund 138
Emory, James K. 218
  Lizzie 249
Endsley, Abram D. 85
England, Mary J. 172
Engleman, Geo. F. 144
English, Eliza 66
  Susan 158
Ensley, Allen 241
Eperson, Carson 218
Epps, Anne 78
  Bridgett 21
  Ely 23
  F. R. 241
  Lafayette 2, 23
  Lawrence 241
  Wm. 235
Erp, Claiburn 248
Ervin, Miss Lizzie 253
Erwin, Charles 23
  Elizabeth 28
  Isaac 27
  James A. 241
  Jincy 69
  Malinda 77
Esatrop, Nancy 61
Esby, Hannah 187
Esco, George 248
Escue, Hardin 112
Eselton, Margaret 22
Eshredge, Nancy C. 150
  Wm. D. 150
Eskredge, Amanda 168
  Sarah A. 148
Eskridge, Bettie 208
  William R. 99
Esler, Sarah 96
Espey, Alexander 23
  Catherine 171
  Charles 23
  Dolly 208
  George 23, 112
  Jo 248
  John 23, 77
  John W. A. 108
  Lou A. 233
  Margaret 31
  Rachel 28
  Robert 23, 122
  Sally 9
  Usley M. 112
Espy, Evaline 180
  Hannah 189
  Moses 169
  Samuel E. 144
  Sarah 162

Essinger, Rachel 231
Estes, Andrew 169
  Coleman 93
  David M. 77
  Dicey 169
  Frances 84
  J. K. 169
  Martha 56
  Penelope D. 77
  Sarah 29
Esther, Prudence 48
Estus, John 208
  Malinda 208
Etheridge, Jerry 227
  Matthew 235
Ethredge, Sarah A. 147
Etta, Arabella 169
  Ben 169
  Jane 169
  Milly 169
  Nathan 169
  Tom 169
Etter, Chancy 141
  Dorothy 56
  Elizabeth 65
  Emeline 209
  Jack 218
  Lydia 22
  Nancy 9
Eudaley, Margaret 65
Eustice, Charles 227
Evans, Amanda 140
  Angline 138
  Anna 198
  Daniel 87
  Eliza 84
  Frances 101
  Isaham 196
  Isham 218
  Jacob 235
  James 208, 227
  Jim 169
  John 23, 78, 93
  Joseph 23
  Julia H. 111
  Lavinea 78
  Marg. 241
  Margaret 39
  Martha 122
  Mary Ann 102
  Mary E. 148
  Peter 126
  Riley 108
  Sarah 87
  Wm. 138
  William B. 23
Everett, Barbara 16
  Swinfield 43
  Taylor 235
Evett, Wm. 208
Evins, Caroline 143
  Daniel 23
  Mary J. 132
  Sarah Jane 232
Ewell, Dabney 23
  Jesse 23
  Jessee 108
Ewes, Elizabeth 55
  Thomas 97
Ewing, Florence 196
  Henry 1
  John A. 132
  Josiah W. 138
Eyson, Richard 23
Ezell, Amanda 209
  C. C. 90
  Julia 203

Ezell, (cont.)
Margaret 199, 205
Uberto D. 23
Ezzell, Susan E. 120
Fagan, H. W. 44
Henry W. 23
M. D. 142
Robert 23, 78
Robert A. 89
Sarah E. 126
Fagett, Maria 177
Fain, John 97
Miss Martha E. 209
Nancy J. 134
R. W. 218
Falkenberry, Thomas J. 23
Fan., Winifred 69
Fane, E. L. 159
Fannell, Rody 174
Fanning, A. J. 129, 208
Farbus, Robert 23
Faris, Rosetta 170
Roxana 175
Farlar, Ed. 241
Farless, Martin 108
Obediah 126
Washington 235
Farliss, Elisha 106
Farmer, Miss A. L. C. 136
Bailey W. 23, 33
Benj. F. 153
E. J. 135
Fronia E. 160
George J. 135
James A. 138, 144, 158
James C. 144
Lucy 19, 93, 211
Mrs. M. A. 224
Mary E. 151
Nancy 104
Sarah 110
Susan 87
Thomas 24, 150
Washington 170
Wm. 126
Willis H. 156
Farnbrough, Lucinda 5
Farr, Ann 100
Anna E. 228
E. L. 16, 24
Miss E. M. 204
Eliza M. 16
Johannah 46
John S. 84
Joseph C. 97
Margaret 57
Marnada A. 210
Sarah J. 188
William L. 24
Farris, Eliz. 192
Ellen 230
John 24
Lamora 84
Martha 198
Nancy 167
Sophia E. 222
Miss Sue A. 199
Wm. 170
William D. 24
Farriss, Charlotte 9
Frances E. 93
Joel 85
Fathara, Mary E. 69
Fathera, Artelia 222
James C. 4
Martha 252
N. R. 170

Faucett, Archibald 97
Catharine C. 151
Faulkenbury, Jacob 24
Thomas 70
William 11
Faulkner, Lucy 177
Favour, James 24
Fearguson, Pathenia 213
Fears, Eben E. 24
Mary 40
Mary Ann 67
O. B. 67
Oben 67
Prier 126
Featherson, Wm. L. 27
Featherston, Alizira 29
Berintha M. 30
Catherine 80
Mary E. 204
Prestley 129
W. G. 227
Featherstone, Burwell 68
Calvin 153
Edward 39
Levina 95
Nancy 6
Oliver P. 153
Presley 24
Press 248
Featheton, Catherine 24
Felker, John A. 79, 93
Nancy 72
Felps, William C. 122
Feltcher, (See also
Fletcher)
John B. 87
Susan J. 91
Felts, Corinda A. 136
Lucy A. 142
Rebecca 98
Richard 135
Sarah 90
Fentress, David 24
Fergason, Gran. 170
Levi W. 153
Lucy 170
Sam 170
Sarah 30
Susan 207
Fergus, James L. D. E.
147
Ferguson, Dougald 51
Dugald G. 21
Frances E. 51
Jim 170
Mary 15
Mary I. 217
Rebecca A. 48
Susan 68
Toliver 24
Feris, Lewis 170
R. W. 170
Ferrell, James 24
Stephen 119
Ferrill, Charles 159
Fanny 214
James R. 196
Ferris, Caroline 186
Charles B. 87
Elizabeth 64
Martha J. 136
Mary J. 120
Sarah 186
Ferriss, Elizabeth G. 61
Frances 74
Frances E. 96
John C. 24

Ferriss, (cont.)
Louisa 106
Louisia 97
Wm. D. 24
Fields, Alibella 200
Bennett G. 99
Harriet 128
Ira W. 93
Joseph H. 141
Martha 109, 170
Richard 66, 157, 170
Riley 24
Filker, John A. 91
Finch, Adam 126
Elizabeth T. 80
George 24
James A. 132
Jarrott 24
John 24
Mary 18
Mary L. 132
Nancy 40
Sarah 74
Sarah E. 128
Sarah J. 242
Findly, Nathan 25
Finey, Eliz. 198
Finger, Miss Eliz. M. 211
Elizabeth 4
Margaret 80
Fink, A. C. 159
Finley, Isaac 24
Nancy 49
Finney, Andrew 11, 24,
44
Ann 94
Caroline 166
Catherine 38, 87
Evelina 42
Jane 44
Martha 120
Milton 196
Percilla A. 36
Susan 110
William 24
Finny, Ann 94
G. P. 144
Fips, Edmond 196
Fisher, Benjamine 23
Edward 24, 27, 79
Elizabeth 28
Frances 194
Isaac 170, 196
John 24, 170
Malenda 202
Malinda 214
Violet 205
Fite, Amanda 190
Arthur 235
Fitzgerald, Ann 215
Fitzjarrald, Wesley 144
Flaming, Jane M. 24
Fleming, Austin 170
Ditcy 170
Doshia H. 165
Eleanor 24
Eliz. M. 135
Elizabeth C. 54
Esther 10
G. D. 170
Jackson 89
Jacob M. 122
James 235
Jane 120
John 24
Joseph 196
Lucinda 128

Fleming , (cont.)
Miss M. E. 177
Martha 170
Martha J. 136
Miss Martha J. 249
Mary B. 153
Mary J. 135
Mary M. 125
Miss Millie J. 167
Nancy A. 219
P. E. 144
Peter E. 119
Rebecca 42
Rhuah A. 127
Richard L. 24
Samuel 129
Thomas 218
Wm. 132, 170
Flemister, Mack 196
Flemming, George W. 106
John 30
Martha M. 110
Mary E. 85, 105
Nancy 36
Rebecca M. 120
Ruan 9
Thomas F. 24
William 106
Flenaman, Celly 167
Fletcer, Jennie 235
Fletcher, Andrew J. 196
Angeline 217
Beckey 170
Betty 205
Boney 170
Caroline 217
Charlott 207
D. D. 150
Dock 170
Mrs. E. A. 236
Eliza 169
Eliza Jane 219
Elizabeth 207
Elvira A. 86
Frances 87, 101
Granderson 24
Henry 227
Isabella W. 120
Jack 170
James B. 227
James F. 24, 138
James F., Jr. 235
James M. 135
Jane M. 126
Jas. F. 13
Jeremiah W. 37
Jinny 201
John 24, 26, 241
John D. 2, 24, 25, 31, 35
John W. 24, 106
Keshiah 167
Lou 235
Louisa 180
Lucinda 218
Lucy 224
M. H. 24
M. J. 151
Malinda 42
Margaret 170
Mariah 176, 246
Martha 80, 135
Martha H. 90
Mary 166, 195
Mary D. 139
Mary M. 37
Mat 170

Fletcher, (cont.)
Millie 227
Minos L. 94
Mira 179
Montford H. 25
Montfort H. 24, 47
Moses 170
Miss Naw 234
Nelson 170
Reuben 218
Richmond S. 30, 83
Roxannah S. 137
Samuel 241
Sarlin 208
Sterling 170
Sue F. 229
Susan 194
Susan C. 88, 125
Tabitha 35
Thomas 227
Thomas H. 144
Washington 227
Wm. 227
William C. 25, 141
Flowers, A. J. 153
Ann C. 222
Cornelius J. 99
J. A. 153
John H. 20
Joseph 13
Josiah 25
Larry 25
Lusinda 98
Mary 102
Sarah D. 142
Tabitha 90
Transiquilla 67
William 25, 67
Floyd, A. H. 156
Amanda 180
Amelia 66
America E. 250
Ann 204
Benjamin W. 119
Chaney 225
Charles 241
D. D. 147
Edward 170
Eliza 208
Ellen 211
Fannie 250
George W. 97
Harriet 193
J. H. 159
Jacob 170
Jake 248
James H. 103
James P. 132, 158
Jason 170
John 170
Joshua A. 135
Josiah W. 99
L. H. 227
Leanna M. 227
Lizzie T. 159
Luke 235
Martha S. 128
Mary 211, 250
Mary Agnes 179
Mary J. 216
Moses 170
Nancy 196
Nannie 237
Narcissa J. 125
Ned 227
Nelson 170, 242
Sarah C. 129

Floyd, (cont.)
Thomas 116, 227
Thomas A. 112
Tom 170
W. H. 208
W. J. 218
Wiley 235
William S. 109
Flutral, Reubin 196
Fly, Miss Tenny 224
William D. 25
Foltheringham, Alex 170
Foot, Louisa 196
Peter 196
Foote, Willis 170
Forbes, Frances 85
Forbish, Albert A. 170
Forbous, George W. 103
Forbs, Benjamine 62
John 36
Mary E. 194
Sarah 54
William 15, 25, 112
Ford, Abram 122
Andrew M. 99
Delila 28
Edward 25, 90
Eliza 155
Harrison 227
Henry 144
John 25, 63
Judith 26
Lee Ann 118
Lewallen 108
Louisa E. 117
Malinda 218
Margaret 214
Mary J. 118
Mary S. 242
Pleasant 108
Simeon 25
Solomon 25
Wm. 159, 218
Forehand, Sarah 111
Forgus, John F. 242
Forgy, Melinda 69
Forrest, Elisha 25
Forrester, J. E. 218
Forsythe, E. M. 159
Fortenberry, Elizabeth 48
James 25
Nancy 26
Fortenbury, William 67
Fortner, Celia 196
Joshua 196
Fossett, James 106
Foster, Anny 47
Chestine 106
Cyntha Ann 124
Eliz. 155, 73
Eliza 217
Elliott R. 122
Frances M. 126
Geo. 196
George 25
Guinn 25
Isaac 208
James 50
James A. 103
James E. 144
James J. 25
John 25, 106, 235
John H. 116
Lewis 235
Lucinda C. 241
Martha 120
Martha A. 98

Foster, (cont.)
  Mary 1
  Mary E. 225
  Miss Mary F. 251
  Mary Jane 214
  Nancy 86
  Phebe 47
  Richard H. 122
  Rose 208
  Rufus H. 94
  Sarah 123
  Sarah E. 105
  Sarah J. 130
  Susan 153
  William 25, 103, 144
  William F. 103
Fouch, Mary 44
Fourmawalt, Ann C. 95
Foutch, Thomas 25
Fover, James H. 218
Fowler, Absolom 52
  Elinder 24
  Elizabeth 67
  James B. 126
  Jemima 67
  John G. 112, 135
  Mary S. 122
  Rezin 25
  Sarah Ann 126
  Thomas B. 218
  Thomas C. A. 25
  Wm. R. 197
  Zineby 70
Fox, Bettie 228
  Cattie 243
  Eliza 57
  Elizabeth A. 114
  Emily 171
  Isaac W. 135
  James F. 208
  Jane 108
  John 25, 248
  John E. 197
  John M. 197
  John W. 116
  Joseph 10, 25
  M. A. 211
  Manerva 148
  Mar. Jane 170
  Mary 10
  Mary E. 145
  Mary F. 151
  Mary J. 188
  Matthias 25
  Polly 1
  Rebecca 86
  Sam 242
  Samuel 153
  Sarah 57
  Sarah Eliz. 223
  Tennessee 236
  Wm. 138, 150
Francis, Eliz. 170
  Henry 170
  John 197
Franklin, Doctor 218
  Isham 35
  Jane 12
  Knox 84
  Nathan 197
  Polly 35
  Thomas 197
Fransley, Charles A. 32
Frasier, Wm. 126
Frazer, Mary 184
Frazier, ---- 247
  Adam 170

Frazier, (cont.)
  Chany 246
  Eliza 245
  Ephraim 242
  Harrison 170
  Henry 248
  Isaac 119
  Jane 243
  John 70
  Lucy 221
  Marshall 208
  Ross 170
  Sandy 235
  Simon 248
  Susan 235
  Wm. E. 248
Freas, Jacob W. 119
  Dr. S. H. 242
Frederick, Hezekiah 25
Free, Joseph 235
Freeling, Abraham 170
Freeman, Areanah 131
  Asberry 25
  Cader 25
  Condice 18
  Daniel 25
  Daniel M. 106
  Elizabeth N. 100
  Green 25
  James H. 109
  Joab B. 49
  John 25
  John M. 208
  Joshua 126
  Levander 153
  Lucinda 95
  Margaret P. 90
  Mariah 45
  Marshall 123, 132
  Mary 96
  Mathew 25
  Mayfield 197, 208
  Nancy Ann 60
  Nancy B. 116
  Patsey 53
  Petty 11
  R. C. 242
  Rebecca 22, 70
  Robert 170
  Robert W. 109
  Sara 16
  Squire 26
  Susan M. 189
  Thomas R. 129
  Vinie 234
  W. F. 153
  W. M. 159
  William 26, 106
Frensley, Charles A. 15,
  26
  James M. R. 26
  Matthew P. 26
Fresley, James McR. 23
Fretwell, Joshiah 106
Frier, Susan 241
Frierson, Ballam 218
  Epheba 170
  Napoleon 170
  Porter 227, 235
  R. M. 248
Griffin, Alice A. 227
Frilus, Charlie 218
Frizell, H. H. 197
Frizzell, Allen 26
  Edith 178
  Hugh 26
  John 135

Frizzell, (cont.)
  Margaret Jane 227
  William J. 26
Frizzelle, Brice 26
  Isaac 26
Frost, Elvira E. 111
  Holly A. 114
  John W. 138
  Mary E. 84
  Natha A. 132
  Mrs. S. M.226
  Sarah H. 89
Fry, John 129
  Malinda 245
  Mary 157
Frye, Jane 169
Fryor, Garrett 26
  Isaac 26
Fudge, John B. 26
Fugatt, Albert 170
Fugett, Barkley M. 91,
  94
  Benj. 132, 197
  Mathew S. 126
Fugitt, Albert 235
  David 242
  Sarah 47
Fulks, Caroline 37
  Jane A. 100
  Joel 26
  John D. 26
  John W. 170
  Mary 107
  Mary A. 151
  Mary Ann 29
  Nancy E. 106
  Samuel 84
  Sarah 99, 193
Fuller, Benjamine 26
  Eliza 98, 215
  Elizabeth 33
  Emily 122
  James 26
  John N. 227
  Joseph 89
  Lucinda 35
  M. J. 148
  May 54
  Minty 201
  Nancy J. 32
  Patsy 25
  Thomas 112
Fulton, Elizabeth 41
  Jerry 170
  Martha 180
  Mary M. 143
  Permelia 173
  Sarah 171, 203
Fuquay, Harrison H. 170
  Joel 153
  Miss L. D. 193
  Samuel 208
  William B. 26, 89
Furgason, Andrew 248
  Beriman 141
  Joel J. 26
  Malinda 197
  Mary A. 196
  Obadiah 26
  Samuel D. 129
Furgerson, Elizabeth P.
  90
  George W. 112
  Jordan 119
  Louisa 75
  Martha 96
Furgeson, Alfred 170

Gibson, (cont.)
Joseph 227
Mamie R. 153
Manerva 144
Moses 27
Patsey 23
Permelia R. 153
Phillis 246
Rachel 101
Rebecca 31
Rhody 73
Robert D. 150
Ruth 56
Ruthanna 159
Sarah 59, 158
W. F. 144
Washington 27
Wm. 171, 242
Gifford, Joseph G. 197
Gilbert, Charles 126
James 27, 144
John F. 144
Margaret 218
Gilchrist, Abram 235
Carter 227
Daniel 27
Philip P. 126
Gilden, Peyton 171
Sally 171
Giles, Wilson B. 27
Gill, Caroline 147
Gillem, Martha Ann 99
Gillerease, Ann 219
Gillespie, Daniel J. 129
Elizabeth 21
Jane 80
John 27
Mary 23
Sarah 69
W. C. 144
Gilley, Caleb 27
Elizabeth 47
Jesse H. 27
John 87
Peterson 27
Simeon 27
Gilliam, Abbey 171
Anderson 123
C. H. 144
Emily 176
James 25, 27
James W. 116
Jesse 40, 99
John 27
Julous 171
Louisa 195
M. G. 248
Mary J. 123
Nancy 1
Richard 99, 129
Sarah 216
Thomas 27, 132
William 27, 35, 46
Gilliland, Jane 62
John 62
Joseph 27
Mary 2, 3
Milly 3
Samuel E. 103
Gilliman, Mary Jane 76
Gillis, John F. 171, 208
Gillispie, Nancy 98
Gillmore, John 27
Robert 208
Gilly, J. A. 197
J. R. 171
Lucinda 12

Gilly, (cont.)
Mary 77
Gilmon, Herbert 197
Gilmore, Arthur M. 27
Catherine 215
Elenor 152
Emeline 116
J. D. 219
John D. 76
Peter 123
Sarah C. 117
Wm. M. 138
Gingary, Mary A. E. 122
Gingery, Jacob 28
Ginkins, A. 167
Ginnings, Catharine 173
Given, Sarah 113
Glascock, Baswell C. 34
Glass, James W. 3
Lillian E. C. 136
Martha 200
Glasscocke, Polly 9
Glaze, William 28, 36
Gleaves, Mary D. 24
Glenn, Daniel 208
Judy 170
Lemiza S. 145
Luke 171
Lutha Ann 127
M. M. 154
Martha A. F. 153
Stephen M. 141
Susan C. 121
Wm. 171
Wm. T. 141
Glimp, John H. 144
Louisa 141
Martha A. 122
Sarah E. 209
Glinn, James D. 12
Glouchland, Joseph W. 28
Glover, Joe 197
Glymp, Emily 212
George W. 138
Milley F. 132
W. T. 157
Winaford 97
Gober, Samuel 208
Gobson, William 90
Godsey, Lacy 28
Godwin, Samuel 28
William P. 28
Goforth, John M. 28
Polly 27
Golden, Josias 219
Mariah 191, 204
Thomas M. 87
Goldin, Mary Ann 81
Goley, Mary Ann 24
Golfin, Hezdkiah 235
Gollerher, John 86
Golliger, Michael 103
Golston, Serry 228
Goober, Mary 149
Gooch, Aaron 171
Add 219
Alexander 235
Allen T. 28, 208
Anderson 235
Arey 171
Batsy 191
Betsy 217
Charity 208
D. R. 63
Dick 171
Edith 197
Edmund 235

Gooch, (cont.)
Egbert 235
Elis 197
Elizabeth A. 117
Frances 205
George 219
Hattie 243
Henrietta 246
I. S. 159
J. C. 126
James 242
James H. 141
Jerry 208
Jesse 227
Jim 171
Joe 242
John C. 28
Joseph 208, 219
Josephine 220
Josette 222
Laura 225, 239
Levina 199
Lucas 171
Lucinda T. 40
Martha T. 152
Mary 219
Mary E. 96
Mary L. 119
Meseah 196
Monroe 171, 219
Narcissa 236
Nathaniel 235
Phillis 177
Sina 229
Thomas Romind 171
Thomas T. 28
Wm. 219
Good, Eliz. W. 141
Hugh 28
J. N. 242
James A. 72
James O. 87
Mary 87
Mary Ann 69
Mary E. 131
Robert 87
Sarah W. 63
Goode, Edward 28
Elizabeth 108
Gooden, Cornelius 28
John D. 106
Queen 169
Goodin, Levicy 16
Malindy 224
Gooding, Nicholas 28
Susanna 46
Goodloe, Aquilla 28
Artillia P. 96
Caleb 171
Cinthy 53
Elizabeth 1, 112
George 28
Henry, Jr. 28
J. Camp 248
John, Jr. 28
Julia 39
N. C. 16
Nancy 83
Priscilla 29
R. M. 227
Rebecca 37
Reuben 171
Theodocia B. 103
Tilmesia M. 86
William H. 106
Goodlow, John W. 144
Goodman, Amanda M. 111

Goodman, (cont.)
  Bettie 242
  Cynthia 227
  David 208
  Edmund 28, 100
  Eliza 203
  Emily G. 207
  H. L. 156
  Jack 197
  Jethro 87
  John 97
  Kitty 219
  L. A. 148
  Liddie 148
  M. J. 221
  Margaret 153
  Melinda 228
  Miss S. J. 235
  Samuel H. 144
  Sarah A. 119
  Thomas H. 94
  William 28, 68
  Wm. A. 242
  William B. 28
Goodner, Matilda 154
  Nancy 26
Goodrich, Edmund 91
  Elizabeth 91
  John 28
  Mary 212
  Thomas E. 37
  Washington 28
Goodson, Jane 48
Goodwin, Alred 171
  Caroline 191
  Catharine 217
  Cresia 171
  Eliza 192
  G. M. 242
  Harriet 171
  Isaac T. 171
  J. D. 153
  James 28
  Jim 171
  Maggie 226
  Margaret C. 186
  Mariah 189, 196
  Martha 211
  Mary 190
  Rose Ann 163
  Sallie 208
  Sam 171
  Tabitha 169
  Miss Tennie L. 245
Gordan, J. B. 159
  Samuel 197
  Wm. 208
Gorden, A. W. 153
  John B. 141
  W. A. 171
Gordon, David 3
  Isaac 28
  J. B. 157
  John 28
  M. J. 221
  Martha Ann 50
  Nancy 50
  Nannie 227
  Parmentine A. 180
  Reuben M. 50
  Wiley B. 85
  Wm. 138
Gosney, Richard C. 129
Gosos, Mary Ann 214
Goss, Charles B. 112
  Elijah 83
  Hannah 182

Goss, (cont.)
  John W. 197
  Margaret 182
  Sarah A. 106
  Sylvia 177
  Thomas C. 116
  Willis H. 97, 100
Gosset, Lavander 197
Gotcher, Henry P. 138
Gott, Joseph 28
Gotto, Clarinda 214
Goulding, Sarah 81
Gowan, A. P. 28
  Alfred P. 48
  Cynthia M. 13
  James 159
  Mary J. 110
Gowen, Alfred P. 31
  Allen 7, 18, 35
  Eliza 57
  Kendrew 109
  Martha 52
  Susan 52
Grady, William H. 83
Graham, Annie 184
  Daniel 28
  Dudley J. 112
  H. 5
  Isabella J. 120
  John 129
  John A. 156
  John L. 197
  John P. 6
  L. A. 213
  Lucy B. 4
  M. V. 150
  Robert 219
  Wm. 197
Gramps, John 129
Grant, Edmond P. 87
  Henry 248
  James M. 158
  James T. 138
  Mary B. 222
Grason, Isham 171
Graves, America E. 142
  Ann M. 133
  Eliza 171
  Joseph L. 141
  Lewis 91
  Lucy 238
  Margaret D. 66
  Mary Ann 143
  Richard R. 150
  Susan H. 116
Gray, Abraham C. 112
  Charlie 219
  Christian 33
  Elizabeth 38, 67
  Freemon 208
  Henry L. 28
  Miss Margarett 234
  Mary 235
  Matthew 72
  Parmely 18
  Samuel 77
Grays, Jane 219
Greaves, Mary E. 86
Green, A. H. 151
  Amanda E. 235
  Ann 124
  Miss Bersheba 1
  Clarissa 184
  Deborah 115
  Elizabeth 111
  Miss Ella 250
  G. J. 242

Green, (cont.)
  Geo. 171
  Henry W. 171
  Hilliard 171
  Irvin 159
  Isaac 171
  Isham S. 30
  J. 242
  Jane 128
  Jefferson 171
  Jessie 242
  Jo 248
  John 28
  Joseph 227, 235
  Joseph A. 106
  Joseph J. 126
  Josephine M. 21
  Julia 251
  Julia Ann 171
  Miss Kate 251
  King 171, 235
  Levenia 111
  Lucinda 205, 225
  M. F. 235
  Margaret 171
  Martha 78, 171
  Mary 89
  Mary A. 104, 132
  Miss Mary A. 208
  Mazana 25
  Miss Mollie 249
  Molly 203
  Nancy 102
  Richard 219
  Sallie 171
  Santee 171
  Susan 242
  Thomas J. 106
  Virginia 151
  Virginia C. 149
  W. W. 171
  Wm. 242
  William T. 123
  Winney A. 213
  Wray 171
Greenlee, Amy B. 163
Greenlief, Julius 208
Greer, Andrew 129
  Charles 208
  Elijah V. 141
  Eliza 132
  Henry 106, 235
  John 94
  Mary 88
  Mary E. 155
  Nancy 106
  Nancy M. 150
  Nathaniel 88
  Nelson 248
  Rebecca 149
  S. E. 157
  Sarah 148
  Samuel 236
  Stephen 112
  Thomas 129
Gregory, Abraham 116
  Alexander 29, 106
  America 93
  Andrew 116
  Ann 84
  Betty 181
  Catherine 16, 171
  Edwin 29
  Elender 173
  Emily 248
  Green 208
  Miss Hattie 250

Hall, (cont.)
   Franklin 90
   Ferdinand P. 100
   Gideon B. 119
   Gordan 172
   Hansford R. 103
   Harriett 180, 207
   Henderson 219
   Henry 119
   Hilry 242
   Irvin 29
   Isaac 88
   Isabella 144
   J. C. 242
   Miss J. E. 199
   J. T. 236
   Jacob 208
   Jacob G. 106
   James 29
   James C. 119
   Jane 1, 4, 44
   Jane K. 131
   Jo 172
   Joannah 28
   John 14, 29, 132, 172,
    197, 219, 236
   John A. 29, 172
   John C. 30
   John Chisen ? 219
   John N. 227
   John W. 30, 62, 89,
    150
   Joseph 197, 219
   Judy Ann 129
   Julia 187
   Julia D. 144
   Julien 172
   L. C. 248
   Lion D. 156
   Lizzie 229
   Louisa 101, 126
   Luanna 144
   Lucy 171
   Malinda F. 159
   Manerva 214
   Martha 100, 168, 208
   Martha A. 96
   Martha J. 115
   Mary 121, 215
   Mary E. 136
   Mary Etta 221
   Mary Jane 222
   Mary M. 233
   Melissa 102
   Miss Mintie 249
   N. N. 220
   Nancy 6
   Nat 227
   Nathan A. 94
   Prudence 110, 114
   Ralph R. 172
   Randolph B. 30
   Rebecca 252
   Richard 172
   Sally 3
   Sam 208
   Samuel 219
   Sarah 31
   Sarah P. 106
   Seth J. 112
   Spencer 172
   T. F. 236
   Thomas 30, 129
   Tom 172
   W. C. 109
   William 30, 40, 45,
    150, 208

Hall, Wm. A. 172
   Wm. J. 138
   William M. 30
   Wm. T. 172
   Zacharaih 30
   Zachariah 249
Halleburton, John E. 97
Halliburton, Jim 172
   Susan 130
   Syrena 173
   Wm. 172
Hallum, Mary 99
Hallyburton, America 200
   D. F. 197
   Eliz. P. 201
   Hampton 172
   J. O. 150
   James O. 135
   John E. 30
   M. P. 144
   Mary P. 137
   Milton 197
   Solomon 172
   Sue P. 237
   Miss Tennie V. 253
   Wm. H. 68
Halsen, Zusilla E. 140
Halstead, Benj. 219
   Calvin 158
   Evergreen 219
   Miles 91, 94
   Susan M. 215
   Susie C. 226
Halston, Benjamin 112
Ham, James 30
   Robert 172
Hamblin, Mary E. O. 45
Hamby, J. G. 157
Hames, Jenny 194
Hamilton, A. M. 20, 74
   Andrew 219
   Andrew M. 30, 94
   Berry 172
   Dovery 9
   Eleazer 30
   Eliz. 224
   Elizabeth 107
   Francis T. 30
   George 30
   Hance 30
   Henry 197, 209
   Iby 44
   Isaac 197, 209
   J. W. 219
   James 144
   James D. 30
   James W. 40
   Jane 10, 172
   Jas. W. 38, 55
   Jesse 172
   John 30, 219
   Louisa J.4
   Lucian 158
   Mary D. 134
   N. B. 76
   Nancy 10, 29
   Nannetta S. 136
   R. J. 219
   Rebecca A. 158
   Sarah W. 143
   Thomas 112
   Thomas N. 197
   William 30, 91
Hamm, Eliza 35
Hammon, Hiram 30
Hammond, H. C. 197
   J. N.249

Hamon, John 30
Hampton, Benjamine 30
   James 30, 77
   John 30
   Polly 77
   Thomas 30
   Wade 209
Han, Elizabeth 81
Hancock, Abedia 196
   Benj. C. 30, 129
   Benjamine 30
   Caroline 154
   Caroline M. 63
   E. D. 150
   Edm. 172
   Eliza 88
   Elmira 119
   Francis 30, 57
   Hariet N. 68
   James 30
   Mary Ann 77
   Robt. 28
   Roxanna 125
   Samuel 30
   Sarah A. 96
   Tom 172
   Venus 172
Hand, Samuel 30
Handerson, Isabella S. 45
Hanesay, Jesse 172
Haney, Elizabeth 49
   Isaac 30
   William 30
   William A. 51
Hankins, Berryman G. 12
   Didema 29
   Ellis W. 16
   John 30
   Sarah G. 107
Hanna, Andrew 30
Hannah, Citty 167
   Edy 211
   Elizabeth 62
   Emaline 196
   Jennie T. 139
   Mary A. 125
   Mary H. 112
Hanner, Lavinia 220
Hannis, Brinthey M. 46
   David P. 30, 53
Harbern, Rebecca 11
Harbin, Alfred S. 31, 46
Harbour, Elisha 31
Hardcastle, Kesiah 75
Hardeman, Agatha 61
   Constant 52
   Mary 101
   Mary E. 13
   Matilda 109
   Sarah E. 36
   Susannah P. 67
   Thomas 52
   Thos. 40
Hardin, Jim 172
   Nancy 10
Harding, Alfred 197
   Ellen Amy 242
   George 197
   Giles S. 90
   Gus 249
   James H. 209
   Lizzie 201
   Miss Mary A. 234
   Nellie 252
   Sally 197
   Samuel 197
Hardy, John S. 59

Hawkins, (cont.)
Henry 197
I. D. 160
James S. 32
Nancy 238
Nora 200
Hawley, Joseph 109
Hayes, David 4
Henry 49
James 84
Jane 32, 69
John 32, 135
Lucy 89
Martha E. 147
Mary 103
Newett 109
Rhebe 104
Thomas C. 86
Thomas H. 132
Thomas P. 116
Hayley, Margaret 25
Haynes, A. C. 240
Abram 148
Amanda 188
Ann 172, 173
Barbary 56
Betty 232
Caroline 210
Catey 173
Catherine 151, 215
Christopher 227
Colan 243
Elvira J. 134
Everett 32
Evritt B. 88
Fannie 186
G. C. 236
Geo. 172, 197, 227
Harriet 227
Harriet V. 139
Harry H. 94
Harvy J. 141
Henry 172, 197
I. J. C. 153
Isaac 123
Ivy J. C. 86
J. W. A. 209
James J. 209, 242
Jane 199, 227, 249
Jane S. 113
Jefferson 172
Jesse 172
Joanna 225
John 227
John A. 227
John M. 32
John S. 88
John W. 132, 144
Lewis 172
Louisa A. 141
Louise J. 195
Malinda 197, 211
Manerva 152
Margarett 115
Margarett D. 87
Martha A. 87
Mary Ann 134
Mary E. 161
Mary J. 199
Matilda 56
Melinda 208
Minerva 184
Minirva 182
Nancy L. 139
Nathaniel 30, 50, 85
Ned 172
Nelly 205

Haynes, (cont.)
Nicholas 109
Nicholas S. 119
Phillis 207
Rebecca S. 211
Reuben 172
Ritta 172
Robert 236
Rose Ann 172
Sandy 173
Sarah A. 150
Sarah Ann 120
Silas 197
Simon 173
Thomas K. 32, 156
W. A. 157
W. H. 160
Wiley 173
Wm. 173, 219, 236
William A. 32, 56, 97
Willis 173
Zachary 197
Hays, Amos 87
Archibald 83
Caroline 219
Geo. W. 227
H. J. 160
Harmon 209
James 32, 242
John P. 197
John R. 209
Lawrence G. 86
Louis 227
Martha 100
Martha E. 130
Mary J. 150
Nancy A. 16
Ned 219
Rebecca 120, 137
Sarah 53
Susan Ann 232
Thomas H. 156, 141
Wm. 130
William J. 32, 141
Hayse, Elizabeth 62
Haywood, Lizzie 248
Wm. 209
Hazelett, Melzer W. 32
Menervia 83
Hazelwood, Benjamin F.
123
Sarah Ann E. 124
W. R. 227
Hazlett, Catherine 47
Catherine W. 44
Spencer 73
Head, Eliza 100
John F. 32
John R. 32
Patsey 10
Sarah 4
Headley, John W. 197
Heal, J. W. 151
Health, Rebecca 40
Heard, Elizabeth 50
Martha 44
Hearden, Martha 175
Hearn, Elizabeth 69
William 70
Heart, Ann 79
Heartless, Louisa 74
Heasbitt, Margaret 142
Heath, Anderson 89
David 219
Eliz. 206
Elizabeth 98
James 32

Heath, (cont.)
James H. 54
Levi 32
Levy 32
Martha 116
Martha Ann 39
Mary 89
Mary A. 95
Rebecca J. 216
Robert 197
Solomon 32
Tempy 111
Thomas J. 119
Wm. H. 236
Wilson 116
Heaton, Lucinda E. 145
Heaventon, Caroline 203
Hedge, Cloa 186
Hedgepath, A. W. 227
Mossouria A. 141
Hedgepeth, Edny M. 109
Mossouria A. 142
Hedgeth, Nancy 46
Hedgpath, Elizabeth 47
Hedgpeth, Elisha 197
Houston 242
Lucinda 110
Heffling, Joseph 173
Heflin, James 32
Jonathan 32
Pamelia 76
Hegdon, M. E. A. 160
Mary 196
Height, James W. 109
Heist, C. W. 32
Helfin, Jesse 32
Helton, A. P. 173, 198
Abram H. 90
Anderson P. 135
Arena 102
Barbary 111
E. L. 231
Elizabeth 121
J. B. 219
James 32
James N. 144
John 32
John B. 227
Joshua 100
Miss Lemmie 248
Margaret J. 206
Mary 36
Mary E. 214
Pompey 173
Sarah 121
Sarah E. 153
Susan A. 161
Susannah 105
W. N. 173
William 32
Henderson, A. G. 94
Abby 235
Albert G. 32, 113
Alec 236
Alexander 173
Alice 234
Becca 239
Caroline 194
Charlott 189
Cornelia 192
David M. 9
Demerris 192
Edward 173
Eli 219
Eliz. 128
Eliza Ann 226
Eliza E. 64

Henderson, (cont.)
Elizabeth A. 4
Elizabeth G. 72
Francis 252
Frankie 223
Greenville 32
Harmon L. 109
Isaac 209
James 4
Joe 173
John 32
John L. 62
John P. 209
L. F. R. 51
Laura 238
Lizzie 164
Louisa 72
Louisia C. 109
Lurinda 212
Malvina 180
Margaret B. 46
Margarett I. 94
Marshall 209
Martha L. 6
Martha T. 2
Mary 74, 212
Mary R. 10
Matilda B. 46
Matilda W. 8
Miss Medora 235
Meriah 173
Milly 199
Nelson 198
Miss Octie 224
Patrick 236
R. 2
R. K. 198
Richard 219
Robert 3, 173
Sarah 239
Susan A. 185
Susan E. 97
Syrus 209
Violet L. 4
Wm. P. 148
Hendon, J. R. 226
Hendrick, Daniel 32
R. F. C. 147
Hendricks, Charlotte 178
David B. 119
Mary 126
Wm. 227
Hendrix, Elisha W. 236
Hester A. G. 195
Isaac 242
J. G. 227
Jack 198
Malisa A. 147
Mantania 214
Mary N. 148
Nancy 123
Nathan W. 123
Rebecca Ann 149
S. G. 218
Miss S. N. R. 244
Susana 189
Symantha A. 142
Thomas 100
Tom 236
W. P. 116
William W. 119
Henisy, Jessee 173
Henkle, Amelia E. 145
Henley, Amanda 95
Rebecca L. 103
Richard L. 138
Turner B. 32

Henly, James 173
Martha 173
Wm. 173
Hennicy, Jane 217
Henning, James G. 94
Henry, Miss ---- 224
Ann 188
B. T. 173
B. W. 198
Benj. F. 148
Beverly W. 103
Bill 173
Eliz. C. 131
Fantleroy, 103
Flora 180
Fontain J. 150
James B. 32
James P. 32
Joel G. 106
John 33, 228
John L. 153
Lucretia 138
M. C. 147
Margaret 31
Martha 173
Mathews 120
Overton 173
Reuben 236
Sarah L. 64
Susan 108
Thomas 173, 249
Virginia 133
W. C. 236
Washington C. 132
William B. 109
Hensley, Alfred 173
Hannah 173
Leah 48
Peter 209
Rachel I. 159
Henson, John 33
Herald, J. S. F. 209
Heraldston, Joseph S. 141
Herbert, Eliza Jane 139
Herd, Armstrong 44
Heriford, Miss Ella 247
John 25
Herncon, Eliza J. 142
Herndon, Elizabeth 14
Joe 53
Joseph 6
Matilda Jane 147
Reuben 33
Samuel 106
Herod, Emily C. 172
Emily Jane 236
Louisa Jane 11
Herof, Hannah 228
Herral, J. T. 242
Herrald, Miles 23
Herrall, Calvin C. 138
Herrell, Elizabeth 94
Miss Emmeline J. 124
John T. 138
Mary 103
Miles 153
Noah 100
Ruben 144
William 100
William F. 103
Herrild, Wright 85
Herrill, William 84
Herrin, Elizabeth 103
Susan 100
Washington 209
William D. 33
Herring, Charles 33

Herrington, James 109
Herrod, David 209
Edward 116
Elizabeth 77
J. T. 249
Lucinda M. 158
M. N. 160, 242
Mary F. 198
Rebecca C. 108
Right 126
Rubin 130, 138
Simme 105
Susan 46
Herrold, Lemuel B. 58
Herron, B. F. 150
Frederick 148
John S. 156
Michael 160
Hert, John 228
Hesbroner, Jacob A. 144
Hess, Joseph D. 33
William R. 33
Hester, Alexander 94
Charity 95
Jane 101
Miss M. A. 129
Mary E. 108, 120
Mary J. 143
Rebecca 86
Heuett, Leander 173
Heugley, John 113
Hevel, Mary A. 151
Hewett, John 33
Hewitt, Cyntha 142
John 73
Stacy 15
Hibbett, George 219
James R. 138
Joseph C. 228
Joseph F. 33
Thomas C. 219
Hibbetts, Fayett 173
Hibbits, Ella 241
Hibbitts, Mollie 248
Hibits, Ira 198
Hickenbottom, Alemede 223
Hickerson, Isaac 173
Lexie 230
Hickinbottom, Louise 75
Hickins. Eveline 135
Hickman, Geo. W. 160
John 33
John H. 132
Miss Julia 246
Mary A. 151
Mary E. 127, 155
Nathaniel 33
Thomas G. 249
Hickmon, Susan 148
Hicks, Albert 173
Allen 173
Ann E. 117
Ben 173
Ellen 162
Emma 215
Evelina 137
Feeby 236
Frances 173
Frankie 202
Henry 173, 249
Henry H. 135
Henry N. 242
Isaac M. 33
J. H. 209
John 19, 33, 173
John M. 144
Judith E. 144

Holden, (cont.)
Effie 164
Eliza J. 129
Ellen 229
F. C. 209
Frances A. 108
Geo. W. 141
George 34, 83
Goodman 130
Granville C. 132
Harriet M. 160
Isabella 219
J. M. 160
James 109
James M. 120
James P. 135
Miss Jane 245
Jerdan 116
John 236
John B. 236
Jonathan 100
Jordan 34, 85, 97,
  153, 160
Joseph 34, 113
Levi 174
Miss M. C. 199
Malinda 127
Malitie A. 87
Margaret A. 152
Martha 104, 236
Martha F. 194
Martha J. 174
Mary 100
Mary A. 149
Mary H. 161
Mary J. 118
Matilda A. 197
Menervi 88
Minerva 173
Nancy 98
Nigara A. 117
Nigary 160
Permelia 153
Philip 174
Rachel 120
Rolly 34
Roxanna 205, 208
Sallie 155
Sallie R. 146
Sally 47
Samantha A. 114
Sarah J. 137
Susan C. 115
Syote E. 88
T. 50
T. W. 160
Thomas 209
Thomas C. 249
Thomas J. 132
Vesty 78
William 47, 72, 83,
  100, 209
Wm. M. 219
Wm. S. 156
Winston 249
Holder, Margaret A. 210
  Oelvia 147
Holdin, Mary 189
Holland, Green 25
  Michael 174
Holleck, Lucretia 69
Holley, Crawford 34
Hollingsworth, William
  89
Hollins, Sam 249
Hollis, David 34
  James 34

Hollis, (cont.)
James B. 34
John 34
Joseph 6, 16, 34
Margaret 221
Sarah 240
Simeon 34
Holloway, John B. 34
John G. 21
Julia 141
Margaret 16
Mary 250
Mildred 88
William B. 14
Hollowell, Miss Bettie
  212
Carrie 156
Cynthia A. 128
Ed 198
Edwin C. 34
Henry 174
J. W. 228
James J. 113
James P. 198
Jennie 173
Joseph 34
L. R. 209
Mary C. 143
R. T. 153
Sallie C. 137
Sarah 179
Solomon S. 174
William B. 34
Holly, Eliza A. 112
Ledy 63
Sally 99
Holman, William S. 89
Holmes, Arthur 174
Charles R. 141
Critty 174
Eliza 83, 185
Harry 209
J. T. 132
James 34
Joseph 198
Lucinda B. 123
Wm. F. 249
Holoway, Ellen 223
Holowell, Sarah E. 196
Holsted, Judeth S. 160
Holt, Betsy 68
Caty 70
Daniel 174
Druzilla 87
Harold 34
James 34
John H. 135
Joseph P. 22
Lavina 223
Martha E. 223
Mary M. 106
Richard 12, 35
Sarah 101
Throneberry 73
W. G. 209
William 5
Wm. T. 174
Holton, Miss Anna E. J.
  247
John R. 100
Nancy 20
Sarah A. 101
William B. 35
Honeycutt, James 198
Louiza 169
Rufus M. 242
Hooberry, Finus 132

Hooberry, (cont.)
Jacob S. 174
Jesse J. 103
Salina A. 174
Hoobury, Jacob 86
Hood, Chesley 35
Eliz. C. 142
John 174
John F. 236
L. C. 156
Martha 131
Mary 236
Mary J. 152
Nancy E. 125
Sue 163, 216
Susan 45
Hooker, Abram 249
Betsey 9
Celia Ann 186
Elizabeth 76
James 35, 198, 228
John 97
John P. 242
Joshua 35
Mary 252
Nancy 223
Sally 127
William 70
Hooper, Elizabeth A. 79
Frances A. A. 135
George 35
Sarah 125
W. J. 144
Wm. J. 150
Hoosby, John H. 35
Hoover, A. H. 123
A. J. 19, 32, 71
Abraham 35
Alice 166
America A. 211
Andrew J. 48, 76
Ann E. 29
Anny 94
B. A. 236
B. S. 198
Barbery 85
Benj. F. 126
Benjamin S. 94
Byron 138
C. 182
Catherine 73
Christopher 7
Daniel 35
Daniel D. 138
Delitha 163
Eliz. J. 160
Elizabeth 84, 123
Ephraim 35
Filmore 198
Frederick 35
Geo. 198, 228
Henry 228
Henry J. 123
Isaac 94, 174
J. A. 236
J. C. 160
Jacob 90, 94, 97
James 94
James M. 141
Jane 201, 235
Jasper 236
Jasper N. 133
Jemima 67, 108
Joab 138
John H. 100
John L. 35, 57
John P. 106

Hoover, (cont.)
John W. 85
Joseph P. 156
Julias 100
Julius 144
Leah 198
Levi 219
Louisa 97
Louisa J. 157
Lucy 206
Margaret 167, 209
Mariah J. 47
Martha 107
Miss Martha A. 235
Martha J. 120
Martin 64, 123, 249
Martin V. 97
Mary 7, 195
Mary A. 110, 118
Mary Jane 209
Mary L. 154
Mathias 150
Mathias W. 97, 113
Milly 174
Nancy 64, 93
Miss P. A. 244
Paralee 186, 212
Polly T. J. 98
R. L. 209
Rachel 87
Rebecca 119
Sally 58
Sam 242
Sarah 124, 147
Simeon 83
Susannah 32
Tabitha 149
Van 242
W. H. 228
W. M. 148
Wm. 228
Wm. F. 141
Hope, Alexander 160
David B. 35
James W. 126
Rachel A. 160
Rebecca 160
Wm. 219
William P. 35
Hopkins, Amanda 175
Elisha 35
Eliz. 125
Hampton 35
Henry 242
James C. 109
John L. 249
Margaret 201
Margaret T. L. 127
Martha 195
Polly 174
Sam 174
Samuel 120, 198
Sarah E. 158
W. H. 198
William 123
Willie 35
Hops, Sip 219
Hord, Ada Byron 138
Miss Allis G. 215
Ann 244
Brice 174
Briden 209
Julia Ann 174
Levina 174
Pary 236
Patsey 183
Sarah Ann 140

Hord, (cont.)
Thomas 35, 174
Horn, Clement W. 50
Horton, Amanda 181
Catharine 125
Elijah 35
G. B. 160
Henry 242
Isaac W. 219
James H. 130
James H. 228
Jefferson 35, 249
John 198
John N. 126
Louisia 97
Martha Ann 138
Morenda 155
William 97
Wm. J. 126
Hoshone, Rebecca 18
Hoskins, Adam 174
Dorothy 80
Eliz. M. 125
Eliza 45
Elmena 139
George 219
Jane 174
Jenny 154
John 35
Margaret 185
Mary W. 116
Milly 174
Nancy 47
Samuel 174
Simon 174
Spill C. 45
Hotchfield, Jacob 174
House, Ailsey 163
Bettie 194
Chaney 191
Charity 164
Claiborn 174
Claiborne 35
Edmond 174
Eliz. G. 149
Eliza 5
Elvina 206
Frotia 176
Frusanna 196
George 242
George W. 5
H. T. 146
Henry 198
Hezekiah 22, 35
Isaac L. 6
Isabel 169
J. W. 150
James 141
Jane 252
Jesse A. 63
John 174
Josephine 250
Judy 174
Kisey 181
Lit 249
Liza 174
Louisa 187
Miss M. E. 243
Martha 198
Martha L. 186
Mary 165
Mary A. 61
Nicks 209
Peter 174
Robert 174
Roberta 169
Sally 174

House, (cont.)
Sarah 52
Sophia 249
Susan 47
Thomas 209
Wesley 198
Wm. 249
Woodley 174
Woodly 174
Houston, Margaret 40
R. W. 174
Samuel 174
Wm. 126
Howard, Anna W. 204
Annie 228
Giles 198
Jinnia A. 220
John 249
Mary E. P. 133
Howberry, Jacob S. 86
Howell, A. W. 198
Abner 7
Alfred 94, 103
Alfred T. 88
Amanda M. 224
Andrew 174
Benjamine 56
Benjamine W. 35
Bettie 225
Caroline E. 15, 107
Catherine 43
Cynthia 20
David 35
Eliz. J. 144
Elizabeth 4, 93
Elizabeth C. 104
Emaline 103
James D. 35
Joel 43
John 29, 35
Martha 151
Nancy A. 200
Sarah 4
Susannah 69
William 24, 45, 150
William G. 97, 103
Howerton, Martha Ann 66
Howland, Amanda 133
Burrel 174
Cassay N. 123
Celia 140
Clinton 228
David 209
Dock 174
Elizabeth 117
Ephraim 150
Fannie 238
Gloster 174
Harriet 163
Hettie 180
J. W. 160
James 47
James L. 116
John 21, 109, 249
John F. 2, 11, 242
Leroy D. 130
Lewis 35
Lewis H. 142
Lottie 251
Marg. 180
Margaret 112, 248
Martha 155
Mary 212
Mary A. 222
Mary Ann 2, 118
Nancy 106
R. L. 150, 174

Howland, (cont.)
 Rebecca 194
 Rebecca E. 99
 Miss Rosie E. 246
 Sarah Ann 41
 William 94, 174
 Wilson 219
Howse, Adaline W. 78
 Charles A. 106
 Charlotte P. 109
 Clem 236
 Eliza 198
 Francis K. 143
 G. A. 150
 George W. 106
 Henry 174
 Isaac 36
 Isaac L. 5, 23
 Jack 174
 John C. 120
 John R. 228
 Keziah 240
 Miss Laura 218
 Leander J. 123
 Louisa Y. 152
 Margarett C. 146
 Martha 207
 Martha A. 120
 Martha L. 64
 Mary A. 118
 Mary E. 118
 Nancy J. 94
 Nelson 174
 Nicholas 174
 Philip M. 40
 Robert 228
 Robert C. 35
 Susan E. 223
 Tom 174
 Washington 174
Hoyle, Jane 73
Hubanks, Sandy 174
Hubbard, Caldonis 240
 Miss Calfernia 244
 Geo. 174
 John 35
 Louisa 203
 Martha Della 166
 Mary A. 145
 Sue 193
 Susan 141
 W. H. 228
 William 35, 66
Huchens, John W. 148
Huddleston, Bos 219
 Coleman 174
 Eliza Jane 185
 Emily 187
 Frank 249
 George M. 133
 Henry 174
 Indy 174
 Lutetia 230
 Mary 166
 Mary E. 203
 Mary Jane 176
 Mat 174
 Nelson 174
Hudson, Alex 219
 Alfred 94
 Enoch M. 35
 Frances M. 83
 J. C. 242
 James 174
 Jesse 11
 John 12, 35
 Lodden 48

Hudson, (cont.)
 Lodewick 36
 Mary 41
 Susan A. 161
 William 87, 198
 William S. 94
Hueston, Hartwell 209
Huff, Alexander 198
 Eliz. 174
 John 174
 Josie 230
 Julie S. 149
 Polly 12
Huggins, A. D. 209
 Camillus D. 138
 Cornelia A. 104
 Ducenia A. 95
 Harrison 249
 Isabella S. 136
 James 174
 Jonathan 30
 Judeth 215
 Kate 228
 Louisa R. 132
 Luke 174
 Martha 174, 227
 Mary A. 85
 Mary E. 125
 Netty 243
 Sarah H. 141
 Tempey 174
 Weakley 228
Hugh, Nathan 209
Hughes, America W. 138
 Elizabeth 122
 Francis W. 148
 Hardin 236
 Jacob 228
 James 133
 Rev. John F. 236
 Louisa 228
 Margaret 48
 Martha 12
 Nancy M. 204
 Thomas F. 130, 151
 Virginia 129
Hughs, David H. 36
 Orange 219
 Richardson 36
Huist, Christian 36
Huitt, Wm. N. 142
Humbel, Sarah 199
Hume, Evalina B. 159
 Jesse W. 106
 Mary J. 153
Hunnicut, John 174
Hunt, Aaron 242
 Adline 241
 Andrew J. 120
 Aupha 198
 Barbary 209
 Bennett S. 113
 Catherine 146
 Charity 133, 174
 Derindia 17
 E. D. 148
 Edmund 249
 Eliz. 231
 Eliza 181
 Elizabeth 7
 Francis A. 36
 Frank 209, 249
 Henry 36, 86, 174
 Hickman 36
 Howard 228
 Hustus 133
 J. W. 2

Hunt, (cont.)
 Jane 86
 Jeremaih 36
 Joe 209
 John 151
 John P. 144
 John W. 51, 97
 Julia A. 201
 Lucinda 96
 Miss Lucy R. 246
 M. J. A. 234
 Mahala E. 115
 Malinda 162
 Martha 114
 Martha A. 116
 Mary 17, 89, 147
 Mary A. 103
 Nancy 113
 Rosannah A. 146
 S. W. 155
 Samuel 36
 Samuel G. 242
 Simon 219
 Thomas 113
 William 36, 153
Hunter, Ann O. 86
 Bettie 159
 David 113
 Dennie 242
 Edatha 33
 Eliz. A. 154
 Fanny 202
 H. T. 249
 Isabella 165
 James H. 109
 Joab 36
 Margaret J. 126
 Mary C. 143
 R. L. 242
 Robert 94
 Miss Tabitha 244
 William 48
Huring, Cuzi 69
Hurse, Rebecca 108
Hust, Sally 57
Huston, Wm. 220
Hutchens, Mary 159
Hutcherson, A. P. 148
 Amanda D. 121
 Isaac 209
 Jennie 242
 John 144
 John L. 106
 Jos. 138
 Joseph 148
 Mary E. 116
 Olevar A. 109
 Rachel 233
 Sarah 71
 Thomas 138
 William 113
 Wm. M. 174
 William S. 109
Hutchfield, James 175
Hutchins, Henry N. 228
Hutchinson, G. W. 249
 James M. 123
Hutchison, Amanda 210
 Anna 201
 David C. 36
 Emily 12
 Harriett 200
 Sallie 160, 161
 William 36
 Zack 175
Hutson, Alex 249

Hutson, (cont.)
Eliz. 130
Miss Emiline 242
Henry M. 6
Johanna 134
Hutton, John W. 36
Mary 155
Ruth 180
Sallie 221
Susan 35
Hyde, Hartwell B. 135
John 236
Mariah E. H. 126
Hynds, Benjamine D. 36
Ingleburger, Wm. 198
Ingles, George W. 36
Inglis, Garland E. 91
Inglish, Elihu 123
Thomas N. 153
Ingram, Miss Jane 158
Inhoff, Fannie E. 203
Inhoof, Michael 91
Nancy 118
Inhoos, Michael 94
Inman, P. H. 154
Insell, George 148, 243
Isabel 242
Jane 223
Minerva 130
Susan 223
Thomas S. 123
Irby, Clacy 194
Harriet 175
Mary 169
Sam 175
Willis 36
Iron, Augustus 32, 36
Irvin, Amanda 227
Angeline 219
Elisa 204
Eliz. 223
Nancy 157
Robert S. 220
Irwin, George T. 142
Jack 175
Isbell, George 175
Isham, Absalom 138
Ellen 153
Isom, Absalum 130
Ivery, Charles 36
Ivey, Abram S. 100
Anthoney 175
Benjamine 36
Benjamine W. 36
Burrel 36
Burrell 144
Elizabeth 46
Margey J. 54
Martha 140, 181
Martha M. 42
Ivie, Andrew J. 86
Caroline 226
Eliza J. 152
John G. 154
Lizzie A. 151
Margaret J. 93
Mary Ann 30
Mary J. 169
Nancy D. 154
Patrick 220
Tabitha V. 22
Thomas 236
Wm. H. 5, 54, 58
Ivins, Albert P. 133
Eliza 63
John 36
Ivy, Malinda 63

Ivy, (cont.)
Martha 27
Mary 58
Sarah H. 96
Sarah M. 66
Tabitha 42
Jackson, Aaron 36
American 232
Anna 145
Barnett 90
Charles 175
Eleanor H. 197
Eliz. 170
Eliz. J. 153
Eliza Jane 164
Emily 241
Evergreen A. 111
Florida 94
Frances 111
Francis M. 249
Frankie 252
George 198
Giles 100
Hardy 175
Henry 175
Hosea 36
Indiana 140
Isaac 198
J. N. 160
James 58, 113, 249
James H. 154, 198
James L. 106
James W. 100
Jasina 28
Jessee 175
Jessie 209
Jim 198
John C. 138
John F. 126
John Stonewall 249
John W. 145
Josephine N. 170
Julia A. 145
Laura 166
Lizzie 164
Lucretia 155
Miss M. S. 253
Martha 63, 242
Mary 136, 243
Mary E. 107
Mary V. 124
Matilda J. 113
Matthew 36
Mead H. 142
Milinda 167
Mollie 250
Moses 175, 243
Myra 201
Nancy 175
Nathan 36
Newton C. 113
Puss 240
Rachel 180, 192, 226
Rebecca L. 110
Richard 36, 100, 175
Robert 249
Samuel 36
Sarah 126
Sarah C. 159
Sylva 198
T. M. 175, 249
Thomas 228
Thomas J. 198
Thomas M. 126
Wm. 198
Wm. H. 113
Wm. J. 123

Jackson, (cont.)
William P. 97
Wm. R. 209
Willis 36
Jacobs, Alfred 36, 123,
142, 228
Alfred M. 97
Alvin 123
Arminda 153
Asenath 113
Bassel 90
Cinthia 65
Clinton 103
D. P. 209
Eliza 16
Elizabeth 35
Houston 116
Jackson 103
James 198
James H. 249
Jeremiah 123
Jerry 36
John 36
John G. 106
John W. 133
Josephine 225
Lawyer 243, 249
Mahaley 105
Margarett N. 115
Mary A. 130
Mary J. 122
Mary P. 177
Matilda 173
Matthias 37
Melvina 29
Nannie E. 243
Pinkney 198
Pleasant 37
Polly 166
Rachel 151
Rebecca 86
Sally 69
Sarah 57
Sarah E. 224
Stokley 138
T. B. 160
Tabitha 102
Tabitha B. 199
Talitha 65
Thomas H. 138
Viney 196
W. P. 198
William 94, 116, 123
Jakes, Ben 249
Edith 170
Geo. 145
John 41
Malissa 213
Milly 207
Wimon 209
Jamerson, Robert 154
James, Allen W. 116
Ann 246
Benjamine C. 8, 26,
37, 66
Braxton 175
Cary 2, 3
Charles 175, 236
Dorotha 53
Edm. 175
Elizabeth 93
Elizabeth L. 78
Emma C. 131
Fanny 200
Miss Francis 249
G. T. 249
Geo. 175

James, (cont.)
Gilbert 220
Harriet 184
Isaac 209
J. F. D. 142
John 175, 209
John A. 126
John P. 37
John W. 138
Joseph 53
Jsper N. 209
Lizza 199
Maggie 199
Martha 34
Martha E. 146
Mary 28, 131
Mary J. 114
Mary L. 86
Mary T. 90
Nancy D. 76
Nannie R. 192
Rebecca S. 75
Robert 236
Robert L. 37
Sallie 244
Sarah A. 118
Sarah H. 23
Sary 4
T. Carrie 228
Thomas 37
Virginia 200
W. F. 198
Wm. 175
William N. 37
William R. 76
Jameson, Allen 220
Gus 175
John 175
Kitty 219
Samuel 37
Thomas 106
Jamison, A. 209
Aggy 207
Allen 37
B. H. 154
Caroline 181
Cook 175
Cornelia 153
E. D. 249
Edm. 175
Elizabeth 83, 89
Entram 175, 243
Harriett 175
Henry 113
Henry D. 3, 26, 37
Hugh B. 37
Isaac 175
James 91, 94
Jane B. 96
John W. 142
Joseph 228
Julia A. 84
King 175
Louiza 180
Mac 198
Maggie 221
Mahaly 169
Mariah 249
Martha E. 136
Mary 175
Mary J. 95
Nancy L. 173, 198
Nelson 175
Oliver 243
Phillis 175
Polly 10
Sallie G. 153

Jamison, (cont.)
Sarah 110, 175
Wm. R. 145, 156
January, Joseph A. 133
Lizzie 215
Robert W. 106
Sarah J. 112
Wm. 175
Janusary, L. M. 147
Jarman, Miss Ada E. 236
George W. 120
J. H. 249
Mary 134
Richard 175
Robert H. 120
Will 175
Jarmon, L. B. 236
Lorenia 192
Wm. R. 145
Jarnagan, Jerusha 33
Jarnagen, Kinchen 97
Jaratt, Lucinda 193
Jarratt, A. P. 143
A. T. 202
Adelaide 225
Alexander W. 135
Allzaera 198
Amanda 173, 208
Amanda V. 122
America 146
Andrew 175
Aribella 117
Benj. A. 228
Benjamine 37
Benjamine F. 120
Casha R. 126
Daniel 228
David M. 37, 94
Dilcy 203
Elizabeth 32
Elizabeth J. 99
Elmira F. 118
Emma 167
George 175
Harriett 175
Hattie A. 237
Higdon R. 37
Jacob 175
James A. 130
John J. 37
Judy A. 108
Judy M. 118
Julia R. 112
Levi 175
Levi D. 135
Levina S. 103
Levinia 88
Lucretia 100
Manuel 175
Mariah 193
Martha 141, 238
Martin 198
Mary C. 104
Mary E. 95
Mary F. 80
Mollie 219
Nancy 84
Miss Nancy 230
Nelson 175, 198, 210
Patrick 228
Peter 175
Phillis 175
Prudy 167
Purlina E. 99
Richard 210
Robert 142
Sallie 230

Jarratt, (cont.)
Sally 212
Sandy 175
Sandy B. 103
Sarah 215
Snow S. 220
Sophia 97, 163
Susan 175, 198, 231
Theodica 91
Thomas L. 123
Wade 37
Wm. R. 228
Jarratte, L. J. 151
Jarrell, James W. 151
Lewis 86
Jarret, Levina 47
Mary A. 62
Jarrett, D. M. 154
David M. 47
Dennis 249
Elizabeth R. 21
Ellen 242
Jim 243
Jonichan 37
Judith M. 37
Lilly 219
Miss M. 174
Martha 248
Olivia A. 190
Purliner D. 53
Rhoda Ann 130
Robert 24, 40
Sallie P. 241
Sally 58
Sylva 166
Thompson 37, 58
Wade 4
Jasper, David 175
Patsey 175
Jaunary, William H. 109
Jeans, Susannah 135
Jeffers, J. Hooberry 86
Jefferson, Fanny 232
Thomas 175
Jency, Fleming 243
Jenkins, Albert 236
Alice 199
David 156
E. M. 148
Ellen 175
Emeline 226
Fanny 212
Henry 198
Hiram 37
J. W. 153
James 88, 198
Jane 202
Jones 210
Julia 175
Lavina 179
Liddy 175
Louisa 175
Mary 211
Melinda 230
Nancy 91, 224
Nimrod 135
Peter 228
Randal 175
Sam 175, 243
W. R. 220
Wesley 175
Wm. C. 210
Jennings, Ameliza 148
C. A. 154
Eliza A. 150
Gordon 37
James H. 156

Jennings, (cont.)
Jerry 228
Lafayett 198
Lockey 169
Mary 179
Mollie 253
Robert 175
Jeregin, Annis 85
Jerland, Delilah 116
Mary Ann 121
Jernigan, Eliz. 154
J. S. 236
J. W. 151
Mary Ann 240
Reuben 220
William 94, 243
Willie 35
Jerrell, Edmond T. 103
Jett, Andrew 175
Hannah 175
Thomas D. 236
Jetton, A. J. 49
Albert 175, 210
Amanda 182
America 193
Andrew Jackson 88
Anne 205
Asenath 14
Auston 210
Betsey 187
Bob 175
Buck 228
Cicely H. 93
Eliza A. 147
Elizabeth 37, 105
Harriett 185
Isaac 37
J. F. 236
J. W. 45
Jane 5, 41
Jane O. 95
Jas. S. 2
John 37, 228
John D. 135
John H. 138
John L. 37, 49, 79
John W. 17, 37
Jno. W. 49
Lafayett 198
Lewis 37
Lewis D. 89
M. L. 222
Margaret 17
Margarett W. 83
Maria 237
Martha A. 107
Mary E. 203
Nancy A. 10
P. D. 106
Peggy Louisa 80
Polly 2
R. B. 220
Robert 37
Robert B. 88, 123,
    145
Rufus B. 37
Sarah B. 89
Sarah W. 84
Susan 181
Tabitha 102
Taylor 236
Walkup 243
William 100, 220
Jewel, I. C. 249
Miss Lucy H. 244
Jewell, Sallie 214
William C. 113

Jinkins, Anderson 175
Calvin 198
Eliza 191
Jane 201
John 198
Tabitha 24
William 37
Job, Elihu C. 37
Jobe, Berry P. 37
Charlotte 247
Minerva 189
Miss Nannie P. 209
John, Eliz. 147
Lucinda 175
Johns, Adeline 232
Amanda 210
Ann 169
B. H. 198, 243
C. R. 4
Catharine E. 94
Daniel 210
Ed. 175
Edmund G. 220
Eliz. 143
Elizabeth 3
Frances 86
Frank 249
Frederick 38
George 220
Henry 175
Isaac 38
James 175
Jefferson 175, 243
John D. 154
Joseph 198, 243
Joseph B. 113, 243
Joseph G. 38
L. W. 249
Laura 235
Lucinda 175
Lucy 198
Lucy M. 133
Martha 72, 168
Martha Ann 175
Martha E. 151
Mary 51, 54, 175
Miss Mary 207
Mary E. 17
Mary G. 56
Mildred 54
Narcissa 162
Nelson 228
Nicholas H. 91
Oney 192
Paralee 209
Paul V. 38, 103, 151
Rachel 244
Randolph V. 38, 51
Richard 175
Robert 176
Rody F. 20
Sarah 21
Sarah L. 55
Stephen B. 38
Miss Sue Tommie 219
Susan B. 16
Susan F. 107
Thomas 38
Vicy 186
William 48, 94, 145
Wm. R. 210
Johnson, Miss A. M. 253
Albert A. 148
Alimedia 176
Allice 217
Alzira 63
Amanda 163, 202

Johnson, (cont.)
America 128
Andrew 28, 176
Andrew W. 84
Ann 175
Anna 249
Archibald 38
Arey 19
B. P. 228
B. T. 236
Benjamin 103
Bettie 234, 235
C. M. 135
Caroline V. 130
Charles 109, 210
Clementine 89
Columbus M. 38
D. H. 176
Dallas 236
Eakin 109
Edward 4, 135
Eliz. 138
Eliz. A. 132
Eliza 160
Elizabeth 21, 96,
    102, 105, 108
Emiline 176
Ephraim 249
Eugene M. 220
Exeline 226
F. R. 234
Fannie 234
Fanny 90
Frances E. 153
Frank 176
Gabriel 176
Geo. 176
George E. 120
Gideon 176
Grandison 176
Granville 126
Harriett 121
Miss Harriett T. 247
Harry 176
Henry 27
Hiram 198
I. H. 154
Isaac 23
Isaiah 249
J. B. 250
J. N. 151
James 90, 176, 199
James H. 38
James M. 38, 100, 113
James N. 106
James P. 133
James W. 145
James Wm. 236
Jane 2, 28, 68
Miss Jane 165
Jemimah 176
Joel 109, 158
John 35, 38, 85, 176,
    220, 250
John B. 116
John F. 116
John S. 145
Joseph 210, 228
Joshua 38, 109
Miss Judith C. 250
Kesiah 63
L. M. 150
Lafayette 243
Larkin 38, 176
Larkin J. 84
Lea 176
Miss Lou 208

Johnson, (cont.)
Louisa 236
Lucinda 176
Luvery 219
M. 157
Miss M. E. 246
Malinda 221
Margaret 137
Margaret S. 130
Mariah 44
Martha 77
Martha L. 7
Mary 19, 105, 115, 1
161, 193
Mary E. 159
Mary J. 122, 233
Mary Jane 230
Matilda 197
Mike 228
Mildred 25
Mollie 237
Moses 176
Nancy 11, 84, 176,
218
Nancy A. 85, 112, 118,
128, 154
Nancy J. 138
Narcissa 91
Nelson 250
Oliver C. 38
Patrick 176
Patsey 181
Peter 176
Polly 54
R. L. 236
Rachel 195, 207
Rebecca 125, 209, 229
Rheny 46
Robert 145, 176
S. H. 126
Sallie E. 252
Samuel 199
Sarah 61, 156, 176
Sarah E. 140
Sarah Jane 210
Sherrod 199
Snep 199
Squire 176
Steven 176
Sue C. 210
Susan 169
Susan Ann E. 144
Susan E. 147
Sylva 252
T. B. 158
Taylor 210
Tennessee 199
Thomas 38, 42, 51,
176
Tillman, 176
Virginia 107, 133
W. T. 228
W. W. 160
Wash 176
William 22, 25, 38,
126, 145, 160, 250
William A. 120, 148,
250
William E. 103
William H. 106
Wm. W. 145
Winney 167
Zilpha C. 139
Johnston, Benjamine 38
Edward 38
Elizabeth 48
Henry J. 58

Johnston, (cont.)
Isaac 23, 38
John 11, 38
Rebecca 49, 77
Robert 38
Thomas 38
William 22, 38
Wm. A. 142
Zachariah 38
Joiner, Charlott 176
Tucker 220
Victoria 210
Wiley 176
Jolly, John J. 148
Rebecca H. 119
Thomas J. 113
Jonakin, Sarah 10
Jones, A. P. 176
Abigail 203
Abner 88, 157
Ada Lee 243
Allen 38
America 245
Amzi 38
Anderson 38
Andrew 199
Ann 48
Ann Eliaz 126
Anna C. 98
Anthony 176
Arnet 9
Arnett 38
Arthur 176
B. A. 199
Barber 176
Beckey 181
Bedford C. 106
Betsy 163, 197
Betty 164, 176, 202
Bob 176
Caroline 93
Celia 158
Cena 199
Charles 97, 176
Christina J. 120
Cora E. 236
Daniel 39
Darling 100
David 39
David, Jr. 39
E. H., Jr. 228
E. R. 231
Edm'nd. 4
Edward 176
Elihu 220
Elijah 39
Eliz.230
Eliza 72, 179, 249
Eliza J. M. 19
Mrs. Eliza S. 237
Elizabeth 14, 37, 39,
85
Elizabeth A. 101
Elizabeth E. 96
Emaline 203
Enoch 39
Enoch H. 154
Esther 236
F. M. 220
Fannie 175
Fanny 159
Miss Fanny 212
Felix 39
Frances 197
Frank 176, 228
G. M. C. 145
G. W. 243

Jones, (cont.)
Gaston 106
Geo. L. 138
George 15, 109
Giles 39
Granderson 199
H. H. 39
H. M. A. 157
Harrison 176
Henrietta 178
Henry 176
Henry M. 28
Hetty (?) 180
Hollow N. 87
Miss Ida Lee 243
Idell 231
Isabel 43
Isabella 176
Iverson 176
J. B. 14
J. M. 250
J. W. 157
James 60, 176
James E. 120
James H. 130, 250
Jane 90
Janus 220
Jo 176, 250
Joanna 176
Johanna 214
John 39, 48, 65, 97,
126, 135, 176
John B. 39
John C. 199
John L. 156
Joseph B. 39
Julia Ann 123, 146,
190
July 197
Miss Laura 216
Leticher H. 113
Levi 20
Lewis 176, 199, 250
Line 238
Littleberry 39
Mrs Lou 243
Louisa 51
Louisa A. 140
Louisa Fall 106
Lucinda 22
Lucy 73, 212
Luzinda B. 99
M. H. 220
Mrs. M. J. 219
Malinda 176
Marg. 211
Margaret 42, 84
Margaret A. 85, 239
Margaret C. 97
Mariah 250
Martha 69, 95, 101,
110, 190
Miss Martha 244
Martha D. 145
Martha E. 102
Mary 29, 34, 157, 170,
176, 210, 245
Mary A. 152
Miss Mary E. 244
Mary J. 135
Matilda 194
Matilda J. 154
Matt 220
Matthew 39
Mattie A. 194
Miss Millie 245
Mira 176

299

Jones, (cont.)
  Monen 55
  Nancy 136, 212, 228
  Nancy A. 133, 136
  Nathan 39
  Ned 176
  Pamela 142
  Parthenia E. 138
  Patsy 164
  Peter B. 39
  Pinkey 39
  Pinkney 94
  R. C. 243
  Rebecca 40
  Richard C. 91, 120,
    130
  Richard H. 135
  Robert 199
  Robert S. 65, 116
  Miss S. E. 219
  Sally 192
  Sam 220
  Sam'l. 1
  Samuel 14, 39, 51,
    116, 154
  Samuel P. 176
  Sarah 39, 43, 65, 85
  Sarah A. 149
  Sarah E. 149
  Sarah M. 117
  Sarah R. 113
  Spottwood 39
  Spotwood 39
  Sterling B. 123
  T. A. 157
  Tennessee 206
  Thomas 39, 176
  Turner 176
  W. A. 148
  Wilburn 176
  William 39, 154, 228,
    243
  William A. 109
  Wm. E. 138
  William L. 39, 59
  Wm. R. 210
  Willie 39
  Willis N. 210
  Wilson Y. 116
  Zilpha A. 114
  Zina 24
Jonican, Polly 10
Jordan, Addie 237
  Alexander 39
  Amanda 163
  Amy 177
  Anderson 176
  Ann E. 221
  Betsey 13
  Betsy 14
  Bettie 234
  Bill 250
  Blanch 103
  Blount 103
  Caroline 244
  Charlott 215
  Constantine 113
  David 39
  Miss E. A. 247
  E. B. 236
  E. L. 151
  Easter 175
  Ed. 176
  Edward L. 90, 199
  Edy 253
  Eliz. M. 192
  Eliza Ann 184

Jordan, (cont.)
  Eliza E. 112
  Elizabeth 116
  Elmira 250
  Emily 210
  Fanny 223
  Dr. Garner M. 199
  Georgiana 229, 237
  Harriet 221
  Harrison 228
  Harvey 176
  Holden 160
  Isaiah 113
  Isam 250
  J. M. 250
  J. R. 148
  Jacob 199
  James 220
  James B. 113
  James F. 138
  James M. 127
  Jeff 176
  Jennet 240
  Jennie 225
  Jennyling 234
  Jim 176
  John 177, 228
  John A. 199
  John W. 156
  Joshua 133
  Kincheon 177
  Laura C. 144
  Leland 250
  Lewis 177
  Lina 202
  Lizzie 234, 236
  Louiza 177
  Lucinda 177
  M. D. 130
  Miss M. E. 247
  Mahala Jane 185
  Manerva 208
  Marg. 211
  Margaret Ann 223
  Mariah 206
  Mark 39
  Miss Martha A. 244
  Martha Ann 116
  Martha J. 98
  Mary 178, 244
  Mary Ann 200
  Mary E. 230
  Mary W. 159
  Maryland 177
  Mason 176
  Miss Mattie J. 181
  Michael B. 113
  Millie 241
  Mira 251
  Mollie E. 238
  Nelly 182
  Polly 237, 239
  Richard 177, 199,
    210
  Rosa 177
  Rufus 177
  Ruthey 177
  Miss S. A. 221
  Sallie 176, 210
  Sarah 176
  Stephen 113
  Sue 238
  Susan 243
  Miss Susan 223
  Tempy 195
  Tennessee 235
  Tom 177, 243

Jordan, (cont.)
  Wm. A. 130
  William D. 9
  Wm. N. 160
  Wilson 250
Jorton, Melissa F. 229
Joslin, Lewis 39
Jourdan, Arena 96
  Marah 19
Jourden, Eliza A. 146
Joy, Elizabeth 106
  Mary D. 17
  Robert C. 120
Joyner, Mar. 198
Jude, Ellis 220
Juell, Sarah A. 196
Julian, Charles 39
Jurnigan, Martha 159
Justice, James C. 148
Kade, Mariah 178
Karney, Charles 142
Keeble, Miss A. S. 58
  Armstead 220
  Baldy 177
  Billy 177
  Betsy 177
  Catherine B. 95
  Celia 191
  Celia A. 236
  Clem 220, 250
  Dicy 169
  E. A. 250
  Edward A. 78
  Edwin A. 39, 51
  Forbs 210
  Frissa 177
  Green 236
  Harriet 198
  Harrietta 9
  Henry 228
  Horace P. 113
  Humphrey W. 39
  John G. 17
  Jordan 177
  Joseph 236
  Julia 228
  Kitty 210
  Louiza 178
  Mack 177, 210
  Maria 184
  Mariah M. 61
  Marshall 250
  Martha 111
  Mary B. 241
  Robert R. 39
  Rose 168
  Sarah 77
  T. M. 243
  Tena 237
  Thomas 177
  Walter 7, 39, 106,
    120
  Wm. G. 220
Keel, Francis E. 144
  G. C. (or Maston)
    87
  Hannah 36
  Jemima 55
  Peyton 86
  Susan 161
Keele, Frances 55
  G. W. 236
  James W. 250
  Mary 53
  Nancy 27
  Richmond 97
  William 1

300

Keels, Thomas 7
Keesee, Charles 40
Keith, Charles L. 177
  Lee 39
  Washington 39
  William 29
Kelby, Manerva J. 131
Keller, James M. 142
Kelley, Bell 192
  Samuel 40
  Stephen 40
Kellis, Haywood 177
Kellough, Lizzie 157
  Mary A. 111
  Samuel 130
  Sarah T. 75
  William A. 109
Kellow, Eliz. 152
  James M. 148
  N. J. 243
  Nancy C. 132
Kelly, A. G. 109
  Albert 40
  Amanda 174
  America 246
  Edm. 177
  Elizabeth 243
  Emaline 198
  Felix G. 36
  Isabella 216
  Jane 198
  John 228
  Josiah S. 37
  Lucinda 222
  Tennessee 197
Kelso, Caroline 210
Kelson, Jane 231
Kelton, Adolphus A. 228
  Alice J. 229
  Ann 152
  Caroline 164
  E. A. 197
  Miss E. R. 150
  Eliz. 131
  Eliza 87
  Eliza R. 83
  Elizabeth 79, 113
  Elizabeth M. 120
  Emily 14
  Emily M. 119
  G. E. 183
  George 40
  Isabella 136
  J. P. 144
  James H. 94
  James L. 103
  Jane 112
  Jane M. 104
  John 40
  John T. 158
  Margaret 95
  Margaret A. 98
  Margaret L. 55
  Martha S. 135
  Miss Mary 247
  Mary A. 153
  Mary Ann 53
  Mary L. 109
  Matilda C. 113
  Nancy S. 107
  Poline M. S. 115
  Polley 10
  Rachel 229
  Robert E. 145
  Robert J. 145
  S. T. 243
  Samuel 40, 86

Kelton, (cont.)
  Sarah A. 122
  Susan F. 206
  Tempy 220
  Thomas C. 113
  Thomas N. 236
  William 40
  Wm. A. 177
  William H. 94
Kenady, John C. 210
Kenashaw, Nathan 59
Kendal, Ephraim 40
Kendell, Amanda 183
Kennedy, Edmond 40
  Emaline 216
  Geo. E. 87
  John 40, 123
  Julia 175
  Lucinda 112
  Mary 74
  Sam'l. 40
  Washington 220
Kerby, America E. 121
  Christopher A. 138
  James H. 116
  Jane E. 120
  Laura A. 137
  Lavina 134
  Louisa M. 136
  Martha A. 98, 108
  Mary 111
  Mary M. 120
  Parmelia 98
Kerr, G. W. 40
  Jane 11
  M. M. 199
  Mary I. 189
  Narcissa 20
  Peachie Ann 238
  Phillip 220
  Rachel 56
  Saml 177
  Miss Sarah Ann 249
  Stephen 156
  Thomas 210
  V. W. 144
  Wilson 40, 237
  Wilson H. 20, 39
  Wilson Hugh 40
Kester, Alexander 94
Key, Alexander W. 237
  Ben 250
  Jane 251
  Nancy 47
  Walter T. 90
Keys, A. M. 143
  Eliza C. 79
  Erasmus S. 106
  Harriet 71
  John 243
  Nancy T. 88
  Polly Z. 46
  Samuel 40
Keyser, Catherine U. 83
  Ezra 83
  Martha 95
  Matilda 32
Kidd, G. W. 127
  Thomas 228
Kilian, Kessian 44
Killen, Henry T. 38
Killiam, Mary Anne 17
Killingsworth, J. C. 210
  William B. G. 40
Killingworth, Elizabeth 24
Killough, Easter 177

Killough, (cont.)
  Harry 177
  Isaac 40
  James 39
  John 40, 41
  Sallie 233
Kilpatrick, Jane 19
Kimbro, Adeline 171
  Alice 229
  Amanda 88, 119
  Andrew 177
  Angeline 171
  Ann 198
  Anthony 210
  Clarah A. 208
  Fannie 175
  Frances 52
  George 228
  Hal 177
  Harriet 184
  Harvey 250
  Isaac N. 148
  Jane 168, 187
  John 40, 157
  Joseph 40, 177
  Lorenda 166
  Lucinda 74
  Martha 98
  Martha L. 96
  Mary L. 177
  Matilda 177
  N. G. 156
  Sarah 241
  Sarah A. 219
  Sarah W. C. 104
  Stephen 177
  Toney 177
  W. L. 145
Kimbrough, Mary 36
  Mary E. 118
Kimmons, Isaac 199
  Jack 243
Kincannon, Landon A. 40
Kindrick, Joseph 29
  Judith 16
  William R. 40
King, Aaron 243
  Adam C. 40
  Alfred 220
  Andy 210
  Anne 25
  Anthony 177
  Benj. S. 133
  Bettie 156
  Boling 32
  C. M. 199
  Calvin 177
  Charles 177
  Charlotte 174
  Daniel 40
  David 210
  Edwin J. 40
  Elias 97
  Eliza 222
  Elizabeth 41
  Elizabeth E. 102
  Ellen 177
  Elzira 202
  Enes 40
  Fed 177
  G. S. 160
  G. W. 250
  Hardy 177
  Henry 228
  Isaiah 228
  Isiah 177
  Jack 220

Lane, (cont.)
Julia 179
Malcijah 41
Martha 137
Martha A. 83
Melissa 182
Micajah 41
Moses 210
P. 220
Purnal 220
Sarah E. 152
Sophia W. 160
Susan 75, 123
William T. 100, 109
Langley, Charlott 167
Langlin, Tom 199
Langstaff, Hannah 121
Langston, Polly 60
Sally 30
Lanier, Geo. W. 148
Nicholas S. 100
Lannis, Wm. N. 220
Lannom, A. R. 250
A. T. 151
Cinthia 25
Elvina M. C. 144
Fanny 224
Frances 250
H. C. 250
John M. 109
Joseph 109
Joseph N. 97
Joseph W. 220
Levi 97
Lucinda 95
Mary B. 109
Mary E. U. 125
Mary M. 99
Milton 83
Nancy A. 115, 150
Rechel 162
Robert T. 199
Selina H. 89
Thomas E. 199
Tilman W. 3, 97
Lannon, Miss Bettie B.
245
Green 41
J. T. 237
John 41
Mary S. 3
Sarah 88
Thomas 86
Thomas E. 237
Wm. A. 135
Wm. D. 123
Lannum, Alfred T. 133
Elizabeth J. 105
Levina 7
Nancy 20
Polly 63
William 41
Lannun, Green B. 44
Lanom, Zabieth F. 58
Lantern, Henry 127
Thomas 94
Lark, Evelina 162
Larkin, C. A. 240
Larkins, Lewis 210
Lasater, Basil B. 229
Lasiter, E. E. 195
Eliz. H. 130
James 100
Julia 156
Mary J. 130
Wm. 130
Wm. M. 148

Lassater, Catherine 67
Susan 130
Lassiter, Alexander 41
Armedia 51
Delana 59
Emilin 174
John 133
Kitty 31
Lester 59
William 41
William M. 106
Zane 38
Lasswell, Martha J. 89
Latimore, Geo. 220
Lattemore, B. F. 154
Lattimore, Margaret 117
Laudmilk, James 160
Laughlin, James 56
Jane 56
John R. 32, 38, 41,
62, 76
Joseph Y. 130
Laura E. 73
Nancy 2
S. H. 22
Samuel H. 7, 42
Stith M. 45
William 18
Young 42
Laurence, Margaret C. 84
Lavender, Samuel 210
Law, Tom 177
Lawhorn, Exum 106
Thomas M. 106
Lawing, Frances H. 128
I. A. 202
John J. 48, 88
Mary M. 116
Nancy W. 182
Robert 42, 106
Miss Sallie 236
Susan 104
William 103
Lawrence, Angeline 224
Carney 203
Celia 226
David 229
Edmund 42
Edward 94, 97
Eliz. 220
Elizabeth 4
Elizabeth J. 102
Elizabeth M. 96
Felix 177
Geo. 220
George 177
George W. 120
Harriett 222
Harrison 220
J. S. 154
James 89
Jeremiah 42
Jesse 42
John B. 138
John D. 94
John L. 94
John W. 177
Joseph 117
Judith M. 120
Julia 193
Lemon 177
Lidia 210
Louisa 184
Lucy F. 149
Miss M. A. 212
Malinda L. 183
Margaret 220

Lawrence, (cont.)
Maria 177
Martha 67
Martha E. 239
Martha Louisa 103
Mary A. 143
Miss Mary A. R. 244
Mary E. 102
Mollie 218
Munroe 138
Nancy T. 148
Narcissa 222
Nathaniel 177
Sallie 207
Samuel 42, 177
Samuel W. 42
Sarah 160
Sarah C. 126
Sarah J. 241
Sarah L. 119
Sarah P. 53
Thomas H. 97
Walker 229, 237, 243
William 89, 97, 177
William H. 42, 199
Lawson, Nathan 177
Lawten, Eliza Ann 172
Lay, Margaret 223
Layhew, Joseph B. 237
Layne, A. J. 210
Alfred J. 130
Geo. M. 158
Mary A. 210
Robert 135
Leach, Jane 198
Nancy D. 133
Leakray, Eliza 203
Martha 203
Milly 201
Leath, Amanda 145
Anna 250
Eliza B. 120
John A. 103
John W. 151
Lewis 237
Lizzie 247
Louisa F. 124
Mary J. 125
Peterson G. 89
W. J. 229
Winney 64
Leatherman, Charles 42,
59
D. M. 229
Fannie M. 158
Jefferson 42
Leathers, Allen W. 103
Elizabeth C. 120
J. T. H. 199
Jennie 245
Jonathan 177
Julia Ann 209
Martha H. 34
Mary F. 155
N. R. 155
Theophilus H. 87, 133
Leatherwood, Ennen 242
Leathwood, Winny 246
Ledbetter, Ann 133
Catharine 142
Eliz. 190
Elizabeth M. 69
Miss Emma 252
Isaac 17
Isaac H. 84
Jordan 199
Julia 40

Ledbetter, (cont.)
  Maggie 240
  Malisa 57
  N. C. 220
  Patsy 239
  Raford 210
  Rebecca 32
  Richard 16, 17, 24,
    28, 32, 43, 52, 67,
  Sarah 210
  William 8, 11, 37,
    52, 56, 61, 199
  Wm., Jr. 145
Lee, Ann 207
  Caswell A. 88
  E. E. B. 154
  Eliz. 199
  Elizabeth 17, 72
  Emma 247
  George W. 11, 12, 42
  James M. 127, 177
  Jerry 177
  Joel T. 85
  John S. 97
  Miss L. C. 250
  M. 144
  Martha A. E. 152
  Nancy 81
  R. H. 177
  Rebecca 231
  Rebecca J. 121
  Robert A. 135
  Miss Sallie E. 234
  Sarah A. 128
  Thomas 29
  Thomas J. 177
  W. D. 229
  Washington 42
  William 42, 237
  William H. 100
Leech, James S. 59
Leehu, James 90
Leek, Eliz. 132
  John 154
  Nancy M. 117
  Paralee 108
Leeper, Marion 202
Leftrich, John 177
Legg, Allen 237
  Harrison 199
  Jemima 199
Legrand, Lucy N. 31
  Peter 6
  William T. 42
Lehue, Fanny 200
  Sarah A. 86
Leigh, Allen 177
  Daniel 103
  William 12
Leinan, Levinia A. 34
Leiper, (See also Pei-
  per)
  James E. 229
  James W. 17
  John 42
  Lucy E. 168
  Maria 213
  William F. 34, 67
  William P. 42
Leith, Spencer 177
Lemay, Kate 232
Lenear, James R. 117
  Jane 116
Lennex, Sarah 12
Lennox, Richard 16
Lenoir, Miss Callie 252

Lenoir, (cont.)
  Isaac P. 109
  John P. H. 42
  S. J. 241
  William P. 97
Lenore, John W. 210
  Licurgus 210
Leonard, Anacy 182
  Fannie 216
  Frederick 42
  Miss Georgeanna 247
Lesetter, James 158
Lester, Brinkley 41
  C. S. 220
  Eliza 198
  Emily Jane 157
  Esther Jane 71
  J. H. 220
  Martha L. 151
  Mary A. 161
  Rebecca 159
  Zelphy 78
Letherman, Martha 189
Level, John 42
Levy, Henry 210
Lewis, A. A. 178
  Abraham 220
  Abram 113
  Allen 229
  Andrew 42
  Ann E. 98
  Archibald 42
  Benj. 135
  Benjamin 120
  Clara 178
  Crecy 59
  Eliz. P. 134
  Elizabeth 39
  Elizabeth J. 114
  Frances E. 149
  Frank 220
  Franklin 210
  G. B. 250
  Gabriel 42
  Henry 178, 243
  J. M. 151
  J. W. 220
  James 42
  James A. 123
  John 178
  John W. 117
  Joseph 113
  Leven 117
  Lucy 240
  M. 151
  Margarett Jane 141
  Miss Martha 244
  Martha Ann 139
  Martha E. 112, 241
  Mary 78, 168, 175
  Miss Mary A. 244
  Mary A. E. 237
  Mary E. 123
  Melinda 180
  N. M. 229
  Nancy 146
  Nancy A. 117
  Nancy W. 113
  Richard H. 106
  Samuel 53, 178
  Sarah A. 117
  Susan 15
  Wm. 199, 210
  William A. 117
  William C. 86
  Wm. J. 127

Lickens, James 178
Liddon, William A. 66
Ligon, Ann E. 102
  Mathew 90
Lillard, Alex. 178
  Alexander 42
  Amanda 186
  Benjamine 7, 34
  Catherine 172
  Charlie 250
  David 178
  David W. 94
  Dilsey 202
  Ellen 153
  Miss Flora 244
  Frances L. 102
  Francis J. 89
  Geo. 199
  Geo. W. 75
  George W. 107
  Henry 237
  Jack 210, 220, 250
  James M. 148
  Jemima 184
  Jim 220
  John 199
  Jones 250
  Julia 236
  Margarett 91
  Marilda J. 210
  Martha 117
  Martha E. 115
  Mary 107, 228
  Mary Ann 139
  Matilda 178
  Minerva 180
  Mordecia 237
  Nancy R. 68
  Pierce 250
  Rhody Ann 191
  Robert 210, 220
  Sam 178
  Shepherd 210
  Sophia 102
  Spencer 220
  T. O. 237
  Miss Tempie B. 252
  Thomas W. 133
  Virginia E. 227
  W. G. 229
  Wesley 229
  William B. 42, 97
Linch, Aden 42
  Erasmus C. 42
  Hugh 42
  Susan 42
Lincoln, W. H. 210
Lindsay, Candis 252
  Charlotte 178
  Elizabeth V. 16
  Joseph 158
Lindsey, Bob 178
  Catherine 204
  Dudley H. 42, 80
  Elijah 199
  Frances C. 16
  Garriel 178
  Hannah 200
  Martha 166
  Nancy 201
  Salley 191
  Solomon 178
Lindsley, Eliz. 190
Linebaugh, B. F. 148
Lingo, Hettie 245
Link, Polly 55
Linster, Ann E. 101

Linster, (cont.)
Margaret 131
Margaret H. 128
Tom 178
Lion, Elijah 42
Lipscomb, Addie 233
Caroline 189
James 229
Lipsey, Morgan 42
Peggy 41
Lisenby, Decca 62
Elizabeth 51
Mary 7
Lisendy, Mary A. 98
Lish, D. A. 160
David 160
Little, Louisa J. 115
Mary 224
Richard 250
Sanpherd H. 88
Lively, David E. 100
Sarah A. 107
Livings, Allen G. 127
Lloyd, Joel M. 43
Sarah 76
Lochard, Preston 85
Lock, Agness 197
Charles 22
Margaret M. 108
Lockard, Caroline 197
Elijah 133
Jenny 210
Louisa 130
Lucy 223
Miss Mary C. 234
Newton 178
Preston 97, 237
Wm. 220
Locke, Anne 13
Charles 62
Hugh S. 8
Joseph 42
Martha J. 45
Mary 13
Nancy 45
Robert 34
Susan 12
Lockhard, Harriett 3
Lucretia 78
Lockhart, Elias 43
Shady 78
Loften, Phebe 168
Washington 210
Loftin, Elizabeth M. 120
Lewis 178
Lucy 20, 53
Robert M. 36
Thomas 43
William 25
William L. 120
Lofton, Lewis 229
Logan, Eliza 109
Samuel F. 135
Violett B. 103
William C. 109
Logon, P. A. E. 151
Logue, Lucinda 171
Lokely, John W. 210
Lomx, Wm. C. 133
Long, Clinton 178
Hannah 38
James 151, 220
Jessee 199
John 43, 178
Luther 250
M. E. 214
Margaret 28

Long, (cont.)
Solomon 43
Squire 43, 78
Vaney 43
Lorance, Adaline 84
Easter 93
Ephraim M. 43
George W. 43, 113
Isaac 199
J. E. 160
Jane 36
Manervia 112
Mary 60
Nelly 189
Sallie 215
Sally 224
Sarah 91, 94
William 43
Wright 229
Lord, William 43
Loughry, Charlott 167
J. N. 127
W. D. 237
Louis, Margarett Jane 141
Love, Allen R. 43
Bunyan 220
Charles 43
Charles T. 117
Dock 243
Elizabeth M. 113
Eveline M. 94
F. P. 237
Harriet 178
Henderosn 221
Hugh 94
James H. 97
Jeffery 199
John 199
John R. 178
Martha Ann 128
Mary J. 139
Peggy 31
Peter 221
Reuben 178, 229
Ruben 210
Rubin 210
Sumner 229
Thomas B. 113
Wesley 178
Lovel, Eliza 143
Lucy 51
Mary 46
Wm. A. 178
Lovell, Markham 43
Susan A. 120
Loven, Edmond 120
James A. 130
Mrs. M. A. 239
Lovericke, Frederick 154
Lovern, Edmund C. 2
Lovin, Elizabeth 125
Hugh F. 138
Nancy 4
Loving, Francis 143
Lovorn, H. F. 154
Lovvorn, John W. 156
Low, Alfred P. 90
Henrietta 85
John 84
Lowderwilk, Miss S. A. 247
Lowe, Amanda M. N. 114
Areminta 228
Bettie D. 198
Calvin C. 120
Cassandra 208

Lowe, (cont.)
Catherine 194
Cecelia W. 19
Charles F. 67
Charlotte 224
Claborne 210
E. E. 155
Elizabeth 118
Elizabeth S. 28
F. P. 237
G. N. 237
Gabriel 43
Harriett 174
Henrietta 31
Hugh K. 151
James 43, 103
James G. 229
John S. 43
John W. 243
Lizzie 230
M. F. 243
Malinda 77
Mary E. 100, 160
Mary J. 160
Miss Mattie S. 244
Melissa 194
Milton M. 138
Nathan 250
Miss R. I. 236
R. L. 237
Robert W. 109
Sarah Isabella 252
Sievy 250
Stephen 210
Susan 89
Susan C. 93
Sylva 216
Thomas F. 154
W. E. 160
W. S. 229
Walter 14, 135
Walter, Jr. 43
Walter S. 91
William 43
William S. 97
Willis 229
Lowell, William 43
Lowery, Alvin 120
Florinda 198
James P. 45
William 43
Lowrance, George W. 43
Katherine 6
Lowrence, Margaret C. 27
Lowrie, John W. 43
Lowry, Albian 72
Albin 43
Charles 178
Cynthia 86
Elizabeth 55
Florida 2
Henry D. 243
John 49
Louisa 178
Mariah 10
Nancy 16
Patsy 49
Loyd, Ann 22
Jenry F. 199
Rebecca B. 135
Rebecca J. 114
Sarah J. 98
Luck, Lurenia T. 108
Luman, James J. 107
Lumly, Green 43
Polly 59
Lusk, Burton 43

Malone, (cont.)
William N. 47
Maloy, Milley 179
Manahan, Fanny R. 77
James 34
Mancy , Leana 202
Manear, Jane 201
Tilla 250
Maneever, Solomon 178
Manely, Jesse 47
Maner, Elizabeth 43
Maney, Anthoney 178
David 229
David D. 120
Fanny 224
Ferby 250
Frank 211
Geo 178
Giles 199
Harriet 178
Henry 178, 221
Joseph 250
Levanna 191
Lizzie 180
Lucy 231
Mariah 211
Mary 252
Mary W. 39
Nancy 178
Nathan 178
Nathan J. 229, 237
Riel 199
Riley 178
Spencer 221
Thomas H. 94
Tom 178
William 47
Mangrum, Jesse 136
Jesse W. 120
Joseph 136
Joshua 127
Lucinda J. 131
Martha 126
Rebecca 112
Manier, Jack 243
John H. 250
Lemuel 148
Manire, A. C. 231
Amasa 148
David C. 133
Edmund H. 113
Philip H. 130
Mankin, A. J. 211
Bettie 237
Miss Bettie 223
Charles 47, 100
Eliz. J. 139
Elizabeth 53
Ella J. 243
Ellen H. 208
Frony 227
G. R. 237
Harriett 171
James 47, 53
James A. 139
James H. 160
Jesse 18, 47
Jesse W. 97
John 47, 75
M. A. 146
Martha 18
Mary E. 117
Stephen B. 47
Susan 209
W. C. 243
Welcome 142, 200
Welcome H. 117, 130

Mankin, (cont.)
William 47, 117
Mankins, Miss Margaret
234
Martha 148
Mary 50, 236
Nancy 52
Newton F. 229
Sophronia W. 177
Susan 10
Susan E. 227
Thankful 158
W. P. 229
Wm. 229
Manley, Isaac 178
Mrs. Martha E. 245
Mary 10
Turner B. 47
W. R. 243
Wm. R. 130
Manly, Elizabeth 40
Harriet 215
Malinda R. 195
Mann, Aaron 154
Mary I. 147
Miss Nancy C. 248
Manning, Charlotte 62
Francis S. 47
Jane 144
Joseph S. 160
Willie D. 47, 72
Mannon, John 47
Manor, David 250
David M. 120
James 47
James W. 133
Judeth A. 160
Levi 47
Levina 49
Lizzie B. 226
Martha 37
Milley 57
Priscilla 58
Rebecca 61
Rhody 86
Smithie 86
V. R. 159
Manson, Adam 178
Betty 172
Darcus 252
Emeline 186
Mat 229
Sue 216
Manus, Eleanor C. 71
Marable, Albert 178
Allen 179
Angleine 241
Anthony 179
Benj. 76
Benjamine 6
Catherine C. 220
Clem 179
Daniel 179
Eliz. L. 158
Eliza 39
Elizabeth 63
Ellen 179
Fountain 151
George W. 33
Isaac L. 142
Isaac M. 47
J. R. 221, 229
Jerry 179
John 47
Lucinda 174
Martha L. 52
Martha M. 39

Marable, (cont.)
Mary Ann 51
Mary Anne 6, 8
Mary E. 140
Narcissa 174
Philip 179
Robert 211
Silas B. 123
Susan 248
Taswell 179
Wm. H. 59
William M. 33, 47
March, Moses 221
Marchant, Wilie 107
Marchbanks, James 47
Miss Kate 224
Marlen, Susan J. 126
Marley, Robert 37
Marlin, Abner 85
B. M. 229
B. W. 250
Cath. 213
Edward 221
Elenor 123
Ellen 230
Evelina 220
Isaac 145
James 47
Jane 16, 83
Jane W. 93
John 47
John P. 145
Joseph 200
Lemuel L. 47
Mary 88
Matthew 250
Samuel 200
Sarah 160
T. C. 179
Thomas 47, 61
W. B. 243
William 47, 86
Marr, James A. 90
Marritt, Albert 250
Marrs, Alfred 47
Marsh, Sion 47
Marshal, Jasper 154
Marshall, A. D. 16
Alexander 243
Dilcey 193
Edmond 200
Eliza 30
Geo. 151
Isabella 23
James 179
Julia 31
Julia G. 12
M. W. 241
Margaret 161
Mrs. Martha 253
Martha Ann 21
Matilda 188
May 83
Milly 18
Penny 173
Robert 47
Susan D. 153
Thomas 83
Thos. W. 48
William 47
Wm. A. 142
Martin, America 168
Amy 206
Andrew B. 221
Caleb 48
Caroline 229
Catharine 107, 127

Martin, (cont.)
Charles 179
Charlotte 75
Cordelia 250
Eliz. A. 144
Eliza 94
Eliza E. 103
Elizabeth 110, 123
Ellen 251
Essick 237
Ester 115
Ezekiel 200
Fannie 179
G. W. 229
H. C. 221
Hannah 79
Henry 179
Ive 211
J. Ella 236
James B. 123
Jane 21, 120, 221
Jemima J. 100
Jesse 179
Jessee 211
Jim 179
Joe 211
John 48, 113, 221
John D. 28, 103
Joseph G. 123
Joseph L. 200
Lamanda M. E. 105
Levi 237
Lewana 87
Lewis G. 48
Lewis H. 120
Lidy 167
Louisa 121
Lucy 87
Lucy W. 126
Margaret J, 124
Maria 125, 252
Marilla 4
Marina 247
Mary 18, 179
Mary C. G. 117
Mary F. 242
Mary R. 197
Matt 145
Milly 174
Nancy 235
Nannie 208
Nicholas 237
Noah 109
Olivia D. 81
Onie 237
Parthenia 188
Rebecca J. 103
Richard 179, 221
Robert W. 86
Sam 179
Sarah 226
Spencer 200
Syntha 199
Tennessee 167
Thomas 48, 221
W. D. 200
Wm. 154, 179
Wm. C. 130
Maryweathers, Eliza 77
Mason, Adeline 179
Clarissa 179
Eady 242
Eliz. 167
Eliza 224
Eliza H. 45
Elizabeth 13, 15
Ellis 179

Mason, (cont.)
Henry 48, 113
Isaac H. 48
Isabella 138
J. H. 211
John 179
John B. 211
John F. 48
Josephine 154
Julia E. 29
Julia Emma 231
L. H. 211
Lafayett 211
Luke 179, 200
Luke T. 148
M. L. 154
Manerva 173
Margaret 179, 200
Martha 48, 177
Martin S. 136
Mary 41
Miss Mary 249
Mary E. 150
Mary G. 109
Miss Mattie S. 250
Melly 164
Milly 196
Mourning 41
Parthena A. 70
Parthenia N. 110
Philip 179
Reynsor H. 48
Richard 179
Roberta S. 138
Sallie J. 237
Sisan 73
Susan 236
Susan A. 145
William N. 120, 160
Winnie 179
Massey, Drury 48
Eliza 223
Elizabeth 39
Fanny 226
Frances C. 228
Mary 60
Nancy 11
Osburn 48
T. J. 156
William G. 48
Masten, Peter 179
Masterson, Sally G. 80
Thomas 48
W. W. 41, 71
Maston, G. C. (?) 87
Mathenia, Mary 15
Matheny, Job 48
Mathes, Ann A. 153
Mathews, Adaline 195, 207
Amanda 117
Charles 179
E. D. 86
Eliz. 154
Elizabeth A. 49
Ellen 220
Emily 183
Emma 230
Fanny 205
Frank 211
James T. 200
John 120, 179
John K. 151
Joseph 211
Josephine 211
L. H. 179
Louisa 205

Mathews, (cont.)
Margaret A. 106
Martha E. V. T. 136
Mary 105, 157
Mary A. E. 146
Mary Ann 124, 198
Mary I. 112
Mima 179
Molly 206
Nancy A. 222
S. H. 211
Samuel 200
Tennessee 51
Wm. G. 211
Wm. H. 133
Mathis, David C. 127
Frances A. 22
Hannah H. 125
Harriet F. 212
Kellar 1, 25
Martha E. 134
Mary 127
Permelea M. 125
Wm. T. 136
Matlock, Julian J. 200
Matthew, Chappel 48
Matthews, Chappel 48
Drury 48
Elizabeth 69
Elizabeth C. 108
Epps L. 89
Isham 237
Jacob 48
James H. 48
James R. T. 48
John 47
Kellar 27
Kelley 48
Mary 52
Mary Anne 73
N. J. 151
Nathan 221
Rebecca 32
Robt. 48
Tennessee 48
Wm. 57
William R. 48
Mattox, Albert 151
Mauberry, Delitha 149
Maupin, W. C. 243
Maury, Sarah 178
Maxey, Joel 48
Mary 49
Philip 49
Maxwell, A. T. 243
Abner T. 109
Edw. L. 211
Elizabeth 51
Gerusia 223
Green B. 237
J. L. 151
James H. 117
James T. 109
Jane C. 129
Jeffry 211
Jno. 48
John 237
John A. 109, 221
Martha 98
Mary Ann E. 120
Mary E. 114, 232
Nancy 112
R. D. 200
William 100
William A. 113
William F. 113
William P. 109

Maxwell, (cont.)
Wm. T. 211
May, Abram 179
Alamenta 85
Charloote J. 128
Domina 179
Edmund 48
Evelina D. 129
Frances 106
Franky 76
G. W. 200
Hester A. R. 130
J. H. 221
John C. 200
Judah M. 87
Lucinda 42
Marilla 8
Mary 54, 83, 100
Matty 210
Rebecca S. 107
Sarah 14, 59
Susan T. 65
Thomas 48, 211
William W. 113
Zeina 179
Mayberry, Charlotte 158
Margaret 77
Peggy 77
Mayfield, Christopher 48
Daniel 179
Diana 78
Eliz. 148
Eliz. E. 133
Elizabeth 49
Fountain S. 97
Freeman 211
Geo. M. 200
Hance W. 48
Isaac 84, 103
Israel P. 91
J. S. 200
J. W. 179
Jane E. 107
Jesse W. 103
Johanna F. 8
John C. 107
Margaret E. 86
Mary C. 36
Minerva 233
Octavia P. 91, 94
Rebecca J. 90
Sarah 86
Sarah J. 151
Susan F. 148
Tolbert 48
William 48
Mayhew, David 48
Mayho, Benjamin 49
Mayne, John J. 229
Mayo, Susan 79
Mays, Greenberry 237
J. E. 237
Mrs. Kate 216
Maze, Sherrod 49
Mazy, Joseph 200
McAdo, Mary J. 86
McAdoo, Addrana 245
Albert 200
Alfred P. 97
Miss Alice M. 238
Alsey 206
Anderson 251
Anna 185
Brantley H. 43
Calvin 180
Darthula A. 142
Dick 180

McAdoo, (cont.)
Ed. 221
Frances A. 157
Gabriel 180
George 180
Green 221
Harriet 181, 188
Henry 230
Isham 221
J. P. 237
Jackson 181
James 181
Jenetta 185
Jerry 230
Joseph 181
Locky 65
Louisa 211
Liss Lucy 188
Miss M. L. 241
Maggie A. 214
Major 237
Mary E. 121, 141
Mrs. Nannie E. 224
Nicy Ann 181
Noah 211
Puss 207
Randel 181
Robert 211
Russell 251
Miss S. E. 237
S. F. 144
Solon H. 181
Sophia 242
Tom 244
Vera 172
Virginia C. 203
Wm. 211, 212
McAfee, James T. 181
McAlister, Ben 221
McAllister, Louisia A.
100
McBowen, William 117
McBride, Charles 44
James 56
Willis H. 127
McBroom, Abel 139
Alexander 160
Henry D. 69
J. D. 44
Maria J. 157
McCabe, Alexander L. 60
Joseph B. 113
Julia A. 85
Nancy G. 60
William H. 85
McCain, James 44
John 21, 44
McCalister, Sarah 142
McCall, Cinthia 11
Susan C. 56
McCallister, Mary J. J.
C. 123
McCan, William M. 60
McCandless, James T. C.
120
McCanlis, John 151
McCann, John J. 139
McCarden, James 181
McCarrill, Margaret 32
McCaslin, Emeline 130
Hugh R. 130
Matthew 44
William 124
McCathey, Edm. 181
McCaul, James J. 113
McCauley, Mrs Sallie 248
McCauly, Henderson 181

McCauly, (cont.)
Mary 181
McCay, Martha 18
McClahahan, Matthew 22
McClain, J. H. 151
John 12, 44
Mary 74
McClanahan, Casandra 75
E. W. 145
Ezekiel W. 124
Harriet N. 93
James R. 89
Jane 88
John B. 103
John D. 145
Mary 75
McClannahan, Sarah 133
McClaran, Daniel 133
John D. 100
McClareb, Tishey 168
McClaren, Alexander P.
244
James P. 251
Kiner 174
Martha 174
Mary A. E. 129
Milly 193
Rolly 181
Miss Susan J. 199
William L. 44
McClarin, Lewis 181
McClaron, Deniel C. 97
McClarrin, T. J. 221
McClary, Garland 44
Jonathan W. 80
Susan 235
McClean, Temperance C.
148
McClendon, Green 44
Hettie A. E. 127
McCloud, Nancy J. 136
McClroy, Elizabeth E. 36
McClure, Dicy 200
Eliza 83
Elizabeth 38
Isabella 207
James R. 113
William M. 52
McCollock, Miss M. A.
214
McCollom, Alexander 103
McCollum, John 181
McCombs, John R. 133
Robert 44
Rosanna 120
William 44, 59
Wm. A. 23
McConnell, Jane 207
McCord, John 244
Rich'd. E. 44
W. H. 221
Wm. 181
McCorkle, Geo. W. 160
Jehiel M. 44
John 44
McCormack, Joseph 44
Mary 9
McCormick, Eli 44
McCowan, M. T. 204
McCoy, Andrew A. 120
Catherine 53
Edy E. 147
Elizabeth A. 52
Frances 139
Hardy 44
Henry 53
James P. 136

309

McCoy, (cont.)
John T. H. 130
Miss Judeth J. 169
Mary 54
Mary R. 220
Nancy 30
Ruthy C. 134
Sarah Jane 117
William 44
McCracken, Cynthia C. 109
Elam 48
Eliz. 125
Elizabeth 90
Joseph T. 120
Mary E. 114
Sarah 54
McCrackin, George 3, 44
McCrae, Wm. A. 145
McCrary, Alex E. 139
Arthur 10, 44
Arthur A. 148
Elizabeth 102
Elizabeth A. 110
G. N. 230
George 3
George M. 44
Isabella 20
James F. 124
Jane 98
Joseph N. 237
Lucy 3
Miss M. M. 171
Margaret E. 154
Mary Ann 115
Mary E. 158
Mary J. 139
N. J. 197
Robert 120
Sarah 67
Sarah B. 105
Susanah J. 138
McCray, Ann Elizabeth 114
Elizabeth 114
Elmira S. 119
Louisia 102
McCrcken, Joseph 84
McCrea, C. T. 161
Harriett V. 158
Mary 167
Mary A. 127
McCree, Ruthy 46
McCrie, Edward 44
McCroken, Margaret M. 90
McCroy, Mary A. 95
Reden M. 94
McCulley, Henry 44
Joseph 44
Robert 44
William 44
McCulloch, G. J. 145
Mary C. 113
Miss Mattie P. 176
Sam D. 97
Sarah 66
McCullouch, David 44
J. W. 12
Martha 12
McCullough, Alexander 78
Catharine 181
Celia 171
D. S. 181
Daniel 181
Ellen B. 121
Henry 7, 110
Henry C. 117

McCullough, (cont.)
Isaac 91, 94
Isabella C. 144
J. F. 221
J. W. 221
Jamas M. 100
James 83
James D. 120
Jane 88
Joseph 160
Martha 108
Mary 127, 198
Mary E. 35
Mas. R. 212
Nancy 232
Pheby 243
Philip 181
Phillip D. 110
R. C. 142
R. T. 221
Richard P. 44
Robert L. 44
Sarah Ann 121
Sarah E. 139
Sarah J. 127
Susan C. 121
Tennessee 211
Vinie 237
Wesley 181
McCutchen, David C. 44
Elizabeth 33
Fines 103
John F. 44
Thomas 44
McCutcheon, John F. 62
McDaman, James 44
McDaniel, A. J. 212
America 150
Easter 206
Eliza A. 106
Elizabeth 118
G. W. 212
George 44
James W. 85
Jane 200
John 113
Louisa 194
Lucinda 239
Luvenia 196
Mrs. Margaret 244
Martha 45, 145
Mary 134, 211
Nancy C. 111
Nelson 200
Sarah E. 159
Serena 156
Staunton M. 44
Susan H. 116
Thomas 85
Wm. 151
William A. 117
Wilson 44
McDeanman, Richard 45
McDeannan, Joseph 45
McDermott, Fann 203
Fanny 214
John 89, 230
Miss Lizzie 248
Mary 209
Sarey 237
McDonald, James A. 107
Margaret 184
Martha S. 233
McDonnell, Geo. 200
James R. 100
McDonough, J. P. 148
McDowel, J. P. 160

McDowel, (cont.)
Jesse 65
McDowell, David 145
Dokey 23
Elizabeth 13
Elizabeth A. 89
Frances 130
Gideon 45
Harrison 45
James 19, 97
Jennet 223
Jesse 45
Joseph F. 133
Judith 25
Lizzie 225
Martha 75
Mary 89
Mary A. 222
Mary J. 123
Matthew 79
Nancy 13
Rhoda Ann 126
Rhonda Ann 112
Richard 200, 237
Samuel 31
Wallace 97
McElrath, Mary T. 154
McElroy, A. M. 142, 181
Adam 45, 88
Andrew M. 45
Ann 47
Elizabeth 113
George 1
J. W. 37
John C. 117
John W. 64
Miss M. J. 248
Malenda 192
Margaret A. 87
Margaret S. 62
Martha J. 85
Martha N. 197
Matilda 104
Matthew L. 45
Melissa 226
Miss Nanne E. 234
Newton A. 114
Wm. E. 127
McElwrath, William C. 100
McEntire, William 110, 114
McEwen, James 32
Mary A. 97
Nancy A. 134
Sarah 32
Sarah L. 32
McEwin, Sarah 103
McEwing, Lucinda F. 156
Martha A. 111
McFadden, Allis 184
Anna 206
Candor 127
Caroline 14
Eliza L. 105
Hollie A. 184
Jack 212
James 181
James S. 103
Malinda 213
Manerva 181
Mary J. 117
Nancy 91, 94
Parlee 228
Ralph 17
Sarah J. 146
Susan H. 154

McFadden, (cont.)
 Wm. 181, 212
 Wm. H. 212
 William R. 14, 97
McFaddin, Miss Lou C.
 209
McFarland, Benjamine 45
 Ellen 38
 Eliza Y. 110
 Esther 31
 John 83
 Sarah A. 85
 Thomas 45
McFarlin, Benjamine 45
 Eliza G. 147
 Elizabeth A. 18
 Henry 94
 John 212
 John A. 136
 M. P. 130
 R. B. 154
 Sarah 30
McFerrin, A. E. 67
 Alexander F. 43, 45
 B. L. 3, 34
 Henry 212
 Jane C. 15
 Mary 212
 Mary P. 68
 Wm. 181
McGahey, Polly M. 45
McGaughey, Geo. B. 212
 W. G. 251
McGee, Patsey 234
McGehe, Joseph 200
 Samuel 200
McGhee, Nelson 221
McGill, A. M. 200
 Alfred 181
 Caroline 181
 Mrs. Casandra 205
 David 120
 Delphia 181
 Elizabeth 89
 Fannie 241
 Fanny L. 206
 Frances 224
 Francis 199
 George 181
 Harvy 181
 Henry 181
 Isaac 110
 James 84, 114
 Joanna 181
 John 84, 237, 251
 Lewis 181
 Lizza 146
 Maggie C. 231
 Mariah 198
 Mary 194, 241
 Mary J. 142
 Minervy 251
 Nancy 56, 192, 224,
 251
 Nancy J. 111
 Ned 200
 Pleasant R. 221
 Robert 244
 Robin 181
 Sallie 234
 Wm. 221
McGinnis, Andrew 120
 Joseph 136
 Mary 121
McGlothan, Charlotte
 216
McGlothlin, Margaret 164

McGonagil, Barbara 39
McGoigal, Lear 12
McGough, Matthew 45
McGoughey, J. L. 160
McGowan, Ceazer 181
 Harpeth H. 45
 Isaac W. 136
 John 45
 Mary E. T. 150
 Samuel W. 156
 Susan 149
 Thomas M. 158
 W. F. 181
McGowen, C. E. 154
 Josie 225
 Judy 181
 Lucy B. 98
 Martha A. 36
 William B. 45
McGraw, Caleb 45
McGrefor, Jane 226
McGregor, Albert 45
 Alford 244
 John 1
 Mary A. 102
 Milbry J. 123
 Ransford 45
 Rensford 38
 Sarah 195
 William J. 84
McGregory, Eliz. 125
McGrew, Mary Anne 57
 Sarah 40
McGrier, Curry 21
McGrigor, Clinton 136
 Milbra J. 130
 Ransford 5 , 64
McGucken, George 221
McGuffin, Jane 16
McGuire, John W. 145
 Thomas J. 136
McHenry, Amanda 243
 Bettie 209
 Eliz. 161
 Elizabeth 88
 Fanny 200
 Geo. 181
 Ginny 187
 Henry 145
 Jane 79
 John 45, 120
 Lindy 239
 Martha A. 143
 Mary J. 130
 Miranda 181
 N. M. 143
 Phil. 181
McHugh, James 200
McInlise, James 89
McIntire, James 107
McIntyre, Geo. 230
McIver, Evander 45
 Maria 28
 Matilda C. 24
McKafee, Patsey 39
McKain, John 38
McKay, C. W. 181
 Caroline T. 114
 Haly 175
 Jane 95
 John 84
 Louisa 64
 Lucretta 53
 Martin 230
 Rena 60
 Robert 89
 Sarah 115

McKay, (cont.)
 Silas 117
 Slias H. 148
 William 45, 64, 76
McKean, Arenia C. 91,
 94
 Eli 45
McKee, Ambrose 23, 85,
 90, 100, 110, 230
 Andrew 107
 Andrew M. 45
 Caroline 28
 Daniel 71
 Eliza 114, 127
 James 97, 136, 151,
 238
 James H. 110
 Jas. 58
 Jincy 23
 John 45
 John B. 45
 Margaret E. 89
 Margarett J. 145
 Martha A. 134
 Mary 35, 127, 169
 Mary C. 123, 132
 Matilda 5
 Nancy 59, 109
 Nancy A. 27
 Nannie A. 230
 Rebecca 229
 Robert 244
 Rufus R. 230
 Sallie B. 182
 Sarah 71
 Sarah M. 140
 Miss Sophia 171
 Sophronia 206
 Susan A. 106
 William 45, 120
 Wm. A. 145
 Wm. P. 114
McKeen, Mary D. 40
McKelvey, Hugh 45
 James 46
 John 45
 Mary 8
 Willis W. 45, 46
McKerley, John 46
McKever, Robert 181, 200
McKey, James 81
McKinley, Emila 130
 John 46, 64, 71, 72,
 79
 John T. 151
 Mary A. 94
 Sarah 16
McKinney, Joe 251
 Lucy M. 132
 Mary 147
 Rebecca 28
 Susannah 144
 William 1
McKissick, Daniel 146
 Hugh L. W. 130
 Margaret 106
McKite, Rachel 94
McKnight, Alex. 13
 Amanda 193
 Andrew M. 100
 Calvin H. 46
 D. M. 142
 David 53
 David M. 94
 Emeline 216, 229
 Emma 189, 249
 Enos 120

311

McKnight, (cont.)
F. A. 200
Isabela 18
Isabella 64
Isabella M. 9
Iverson W. 142
James 21, 46
James D. 110
James G. 133
James N. 139
Jane 51, 53
John 50, 238
John A. 221
John N. 230
John P. 139
John R. 181
Joshua 181
K. P. E. 145
Margaret 41
Margaret M. 119
Martha 222
Martha P. 136
Mary 189
Mary E. 1, 134
Mary S. 135
N. V. 218
R. M. 221
Robert 46
Robert J. 142
Samuel 79
Samuel F. 46
Samuel H. 91
Sarah M. 98
Thomas 46, 63, 201
Virginia 239
Will T. 244
William 46
William W. 110, 124
Wm. J. 120
Wm. T. 133, 142, 212
McLain, Florence 231
J. H. 221
McLane, John 212
McLaren, Hannah 237
Martha Ann 232
Micha 108
McLaughlin, A. E. 230
Frank 181
George W. 139
Henry 201
Isaac 46
Laura 247
Levi 46
William H. 107
McLean, Alney H. 107
Anderson 244
Ann 184
Bob 181, 212
Charles G. 46
Cynthia A. 113
D. V. 57
Fannie 236
Fanny 181
Geo. 238
Harriet 191, 247
Henry 181
James 46
John 46
John C. 221
Joseph M. 148
Julia 216
Julia Ann 139
Lucy 236
Lyrena 180
Mallinda 181
Martha 172, 228
Priscilla P. 44

McLean, (cont.)
Sara Jane 4
Solomon 181, 201
Susan D. 134
Unis 245
Wesley 238
McLeek, Mary M. 101
McLemore, Charles 238
McLendon, Geo. T. 46
Martha 103
Thomas J. 46
McLilland, Wm. N. 201
McLin, Anne 13
Eunice 39
James S. 110
Jean 53
John A. 55
Miss Lizzie 250
Mary E. 119
McLine, Sallie 237
McMahan, A. D. 212
Geo. W. 88
James A. 46
McManton, Henry 212
McMason, Wm. 244
McMeekin, Wm. 221
McMenamy, James 46
McMennemy , James 62
McMillan. Jackson 46
Malcolm 46
McMillion, Franklin P. 133
McMilon, John 201
McMinamy, James 31
Mary Anne 31
McMinaway, S. E. 238
McMinn, Lucy 208
Paralee F. 142
McMurray, Elizabeth 15
Geo. W. 127
Lizzie 203
Mittie 174
N. J. 207
Nelson 181
Samuel 52
Sarah N. 180
McMurry, Arabella 152
George W. 98
Jane 38
John 46
Nancy J. 126
Samuel 47
William 46, 50
William H. 46, 63
McNabb, C. A. 148
Eliz. 129
James M. 148
McNairy, Francis E. (?) 51
John 238
McNamara, Edward W. 201
McNary, Henry 212
John N. 46
McNeal, Eliz. J. 145
McNeely, Jemima 74
Sophia 32
McNees, Samuel C. 46
McNeil, Adie C. 234
McNichol, Barney 181
McNiel, Mary E. 145
McNight, James 46
Sarah 46
McPeak, Elizabeth 93, 96
Henry 46
John 46
Mary E. 197
Patton 84

McPeak, (cont.)
Rachel 43
Richard 244
Washington 84
Wm. 251
McPeake, Lucinda 58
McQuirter, Lorena 162
McQuisheon, John F. 11
McRae, Flora 135
Francis E. 239
Harriett N. 130
William A. 46
McRay, Curtis 46
McRea, Thomas R. 136
William 46
Wm. D. 127
McRoy, Martha 100, 107
McRunnels, Charles 181
Eliza 181
McSpadden, Robert D. 46
McTaggart, Daniel 201
McWhorter, Mollie W. 206
McWilliams, J. H. 212
Mead, Sarah 154
Meadors, Ephraim 15
Mary 14
Meadows, Geo. W. 154
John A. 142
Means, Izabella C. 113
Mearhead, Matilda 106
Meban, Anna 24
Meddling, Mary 94
Mederith, William 57
Medford, Aberilla 7
Medfrey, Nancy A. 241
Medley, Bashiba 117
Medlin, John M. 142
Medling, Wm. A. 130
Meeky, Edmond 221
Melchor, Miss F. H. 251
Meller, Lewis 49
Melton, Martha J. 118
Mary 201
Sarah 119, 121
Mences, James 49
Mercer, Alexander 237
Wm. 200
Meredeth, Joseph 127
Meridith, John 85
John D. 100
Miss S. V. 251
Tabitha 133
Meridy, Sarah A. 101
William 49
Meritt, Clemmy 205
Martha 145
Merrett, Charles 200
Merritt, Charles 179
Elizabeth A. 121
Franklin 243
George R. 136
James 85
James P. 49
Louisiana C. 101
Lucinda 175
Martha 113
Nancy 49
Samuel 100, 179
Susan F. 99
Merton, Martha 192
Mesbitt, Martha A. 242
Meshaw, Henry 211
Messick, Richard 179
Metheny, Job 57
Metter, Susan J. 161
Miceall, Margaret 99
Michael, Lemuel C. 49

Michael, (cont.)
  Lucy Ann 57
  Thomas 49, 70
Mickey, Rosanna 209
Mierhead, Sarah J. 129
Miers, Luzanna 151
  Samuel 142
Miles, Amanda 229
  Ann 171
  Bell 250
  Ben 211
  C. M. 151
  Caswell M. 127
  Charlie 237
  Cordelia 224
  Dock 179, 243
  Ellen 220
  Frances 132
  Franklin 211
  Geo. 200
  Green 179
  Harden 250
  Isabella 141, 230
  Jack 179
  Jane 165
  John Z. 133
  Josephine 251, 252
  Lou 230
  Louisa P. 74
  Lucy 179
  Mahaly 179
  Marshal 229
  Martha 183
  Mary 242
  Mary Jane 248
  Nancy C. 98
  P. P. 156
  Philip 179
  Polemna T. 136
  Sallie 237
  Sarah 167
  Syntha 162
  Teller 179
  Thomas B. 94
  Thomas W. 74
Milican, John 211
Miliner, Mike 200
Miller, Adline 240
  Alfred 42, 87
  Amanda 231
  Anne 60
  Annie 247
  Arena 199
  Bate 179
  Benj. 229
  Betsy 60
  Bettie 241
  Miss Bettie 248
  Bill 211
  Caroline 208
  Catharine 152
  Charles 49
  Charlotte 11, 170
  Cole 211
  Daniel R. 133
  Dick 179
  Dorinda 211
  Durrel G. 133
  E. L. 243
  E. S. 221
  Edward S. 127
  Eliza 190
  Elizabeth 16, 74, 77, 108, 117
  Ellen 229
  Emma 229
  Ester C. 112

Miller, (cont.)
  F. G. 179
  F. H. 243
  Miss Fanny 211
  Felix G. 49, 113
  Fountain H. 179
  Geo. 179
  H. H. 250
  H. N. 179
  Hannah 212
  Hannah E. 133
  Hannah P. 63
  Hannibal 200
  Hardy 86
  Harriet 180, 199
  Henrietta 167
  Henry 139, 229, 237
  I. J. 154
  Isaac 2, 29, 123, 179
  Isaac L. 40, 107
  J. E. 204
  J. F. 157
  J. R. 211
  Jack 211
  Jackson 179
  James 107, 250
  James C. 113
  James R. 49, 123, 151
  Jane 4, 98
  Johanna 52
  John 52, 98, 179, 221, 229
  John A. 88
  John R. 117
  Jos. 179
  Joseph 113
  Josephine 223
  Judith A. 135
  Kitty 194
  Laura 225
  Lavicy 199
  Lawson 179
  Leann 107
  Levi 211
  Lizzie 215
  Lucinda 47, 238
  Lucy 238
  M. C. 139
  Madison 180, 211
  Margaret 22, 57, 152, 216
  Margaret E. 100
  Margarett 145
  Maria 184
  Mariah 172
  Martha 153
  Martha V. 148
  Mary 9, 29, 61, 127, 212, 248
  Mary A. 213
  Mary E. 151, 226
  Mary F. 150
  Mary Jane 155, 162
  Mary N. 116
  Mathew C. 139
  Matt 229
  Mattie 247
  Mildred 52
  Minerva 173, 179
  Nathaniel 49, 51
  Octavia 129
  P. A. 212
  P. C. F. 221
  Pamela 40
  Peter 249
  Rebecca 7, 23, 60
  Miss Rebecca A. 243

Miller, (cont.)
  Richard 211
  Riley 117
  Robert 120, 180
  Robert C. 117
  Rolly H. 221
  Ruthy 242
  Sallie 245
  Sallie E. 221
  Samuel G. 117
  Sarah 176, 227, 232
  Sarah A. 186
  Scott 180
  Solomon 180
  Susan 192
  Susan J. 193
  Sylvanius S. 156
  Sylvanus 154
  Taylor 229
  Temperance 136
  Thomas 180, 200
  Thomas J. 180, 237
  Viney 185
  W. I. 180
  William 49, 90, 243, 250
  William W. 49
  Wilson B. 229
  Miss Z. C. 250
Milley, Gaither 73
Millhouse, Millman 200
Milligan, Melvina 232
Milliken, George H. 113
Millins, Martha J. 151
  Mary 1
Mills, Benj. 180
  James 221
Milton, James 109
  Louisia 109
  Newton 109
Mindrow, Ann M. 51
Minifee, Ann 16
Minor, Mrs Fannie 214
  William 49
Minter, Eliz. 239
  Harry 180
  Jeptha 49
  John M. 142
  Judy 237
  Lavinia 167
  Mary 237
  Samuel 237
  Viny 229
  Wm. 229
Minters, Catherine 24
Mintor, Jim 243
Mitchell, ---- 241
  A. 38
  Ada 139
  Bettie 245
  C. G. 23
  Calvin G. 113, 139
  Caroline 77
  Charity 172
  Charles C. 49
  David 49
  Dicey 162
  Ebenezer 49
  Eli C. 107
  Eliz. A. 137
  Eliza 31
  Ella A. 237
  Ester 87
  Fanny 144, 215
  Green 251
  Henry 200
  James 49, 84, 117,

Morris, (cont.)
Adaline 53, 218
Caroline 125
Clary 119
Eliza V. 51
Evalina S. 32
G. W. 211
George 32
Henry 103
Jackson 120
James 50
James H. 200
Jas. S. 44
John B. 67
Joseph 136, 211
M. J. 157
Martha W. 52
Mary 26
Mary A. 146
Overton B. 5
P. A. 244
Prudence 95
Robert 109, 244
Robert S. 10, 11, 16,
72, 73, 76, 80, 83
Sally 13
Sarah A. 64
Sarah B. 70
Stansheary 149
Susanna 208
Thomas W. 117
Wm. 180
Morrison, Ezekiel 14
William G. 100
Morrow, Jerry 229
John H. 113
Nancy J. 108
Sarah 109
William T. 110
Morse, Charles D. 1
Delila 54
Henry 200
Martha 150
Morton, A. H. 143
Anderson 230
Ann 146
Annie T. 230
Arbam W. 113
Miss C. H. 37
Caroline E. 60
Catherine W. 8
Charles P. 88
Cicily M. 66
Elizabeth V. 28
Evaline A. 5
Fanny 11
George 200
Harriette C. 140
Henry 180, 244
Hiram 145
J. D. 151
Jacob J. 110
James 50
James W. 19, 117
John 180
John B. 136
John W. 136
John Z. 50
Joseph 50, 94
Joshua 180
Levi 180
Lucy 217
Malissa A. 135
Margaret A. 180
Margaret J. 126
Mariah 180
Martha M. 65

Morton, (cont.)
Mary 220
Mary A. 136, 161
Mary Ann 144, 210
Mary F. 18
Matt 180
Nancy 181, 192
Nancy C. 2
Nancy N. 113
Priscilla W. 48
Robert H. 123, 139
Roxana 203
Sallie 181
Samuel T. 151
Susan C. 157
Tennessee L. 139
W. Henry 211
Wm. 156
Wm. H. 221
Mosbey, Miss Ellennora
245
Miss M. W. 248
Mary 158
Mosby, Elizabeth 75
Fountain C. 87
John 50
Kitturah 95
Moseley, Albert 120
Dorcas 236
Mary 118
Mary Ann 196
Peter B. 94
William W. 84
Mosely, Henry 139
Jane G. 76
Nancy 242
Mosley, Chesley 123
Gilliam 98
Guilliam 50
Hartwell 117
J. C. 180
James 103
John W. 221
Mary C. 114
Nancy 6, 113
Rebecca 121
Sally 61
Sarah Ann 106
Thomas G. 110
William 98, 157
Mosly, Washington 211
Moss, Caroline 116
George H. 50
Gilbert 50
Louisa 160
Margarett 147
Mary Jane 154
Neaty C. 129
Sarah J. 228
Susan 86
Willy Ann 90
Motheral, Joseph 50
Mount, John B. 230
John T. W. 123
Mary Jane 157
R. L. 244
Simon 180
Moxby, James C. 221
Moxley, J. W. 244
Mozer, Chesterfield 180
Muckelbatten, Emily 220
Muerhead, William D. 117
Muirhead, John 117
Mulky, Dr. Wm. L. 200
Mullen, Lucinda 189
Mullenax, L. S. 237

Mullins, America Ann E.
150
Andrew 230
Andrew J. 136
Ann 29
Ann E. 111
Catherine 29
Christian 15
Cornelia A. 132
David 50
Edm. 180
Edna 201
Edward 51
Eliz. 210, 218
Francis 196
Franklin 124
H. A. 154
Hannah 180
J. V. 200
Jacob 230
James P. 145
Jane 73
Jesse 51
Joel 117
John 51, 73, 88, 100,
127, 145, 151
John R. 51
Jonas 160
Julia 118
Louisa A. 145
Lucinda 74
Margaret J. 136
Martha 51, 234
Martha J. 152
Martin H. 237
Mary 70, 84, 245
Mary E. 108, 112
Mary Jane 212
Melvina 133
Milly 199
Nelson 50, 51, 103
Nelson W. 230
R. F. 158
Radford L. 133
Rebecca 147
Robert 211
Sallie 240
Sarah E. 117
Thomas J. 142
W. L. 151
William 21, 51, 180
Mulloy, Arthur 124
Munday, Margaret 88
Wm. S. 200
Mundy, Manervia 100
Murfree, Adaline 180
Caroline 166
Dread 180
Ephraim 180
Esther L. 145
Fannie D. 150
Felix 200
Henny 180
Henry 230
Isabella 228
James 200
James B. 157
Jenny 222
John 180, 211
Kitty 197
Lavinia V. 155
Leanna 180
Marcus 230
Mariah L. 152
Martha A. 47
Mary M. 99
Miles P. 51

315

Murfree, (cont.)
Nat 237
Robert 180
S. H. 211
Sally 211
Sarah 180
Sarah Ann 144
Sophia 177
Stephen 200
Sylva 178
Thadeous 180
Toney 180
Viney 180
Washington 180, 244
William L. 100
Murhead, John 230
Murphey, Anne 37
Clay T. 200
Eliz. 136
H. G. 230
James K. 160
James P. 139
John 88
John D. 55
John G. 86
Josephine 137
Louisa 123, 145
Mary E. 166
N. G. 79
Nancy G. 106
Murphrey, Mary E. 183
Murphry, Nat 221
Murphy, Ezekiel 51
Harrison 221
James K. P. 230
John 51
Julie Ann 149
Mary 228
Mary J. 55
Miles P. 230
Nathaniel G. 51
Vinnie 234
Wayne W. 51
Murray, Asa 180
Gabriel 180
Harriet 219
Hiram W. 100
Joseph 180
Leonard 180, 230
Martha 180
Mary 197
Reubin 221
Robert 51
Stephen 180
Thomas 230
Wm. H. 4
Murrell, Pleasant 237
Murry, Anthoney 180
Caroline 180
Charley 211
Easter 204
Elizabeth 96
Frank 211
James 51
Jane 200
Lemuel G. 120
Mary J. 131
Nancy W. 149
Nathan 200
Samuel 51
Susan 159
Tobe 244
Turner 230
Muse, Betty 191
Howard 200
J. W. 221
Lucy A. 149

Muse, (cont.)
Ned 251
Sam'l. C. 52
Mustain, Alfred J. 90
Devrix 94
Harriet 21
Mustean, Martha D. 97
Myers, Benjamine 51
David 22
G. W. 251
I. C. 152
Nancy 65
Mynight, Marthy 18
Myrick, Alvis 136
Francis A. 133
Walter 51
Nabers, James W. 212
Nailor, Woodfin 2
Nairy, Francis E. 51
Nance, Agness 88
Allen 26
Amanda L. 136
Ann 188
Anna 56
Burrel 222
Clement W. 51
Clementine L. 37
D. F. 151
Elizabeth 34, 64, 75,
76, 99
Frederick W. 85
Henry 51
Isaac 63
Isaac N. 181
J. N. 230
James A. 133
Jane 26
John 51
John W. 145
Joseph 212
M. E. 218
Mariah 167
Martin 51
Mary 19
Mary A. E. 108
Mary T. 135
Nancy 73
Nancy J. S. 128
Richard 51
S. R. 242
Sarah 9, 32
Sarah A. 142
Tabitha 22, 31
William 51
William S. 94
William W. 88, 103
Napper, James W. 230
Narkley, Eliz. 171
Naron, Eliz. 137
Sarah E. 139
Nash, Amanda E. 155
Amanda M. 108
C. M. 158
Eliza 99
Eliza Jane 177
Elizabeth P. 109
Francis 65
Franklin 90
Geo. N. 145
Geo. R. 39
George 51, 75
George R. 51, 94
Hannah E. 141
Hannah V. 132
Mary 123
Miss N. E. 168
Nancy 77

Nash, (cont.)
Patsy 65
Sarah 34
Sarah F. 145
Seluda 32
Travis C. 52
Virginia 145
William 16
William W. 52, 74, 77
Nashv, Miss Eldora 232
Nations, Christopher 136
Naylor, Amanda L. 140
Calvin H. 117
Eliz. C. 138
Louisa J. 148
Neal, Amanda 100, 181
Miss Amanda 235
Ann 209
B. L. 154
Burchett 31
Caladonia 122
Charley 181, 212
Claiborne 181
Cyntha 88
Cyntha A. 99
Elizabeth 28
Flora 192
Grant 230
Harriet 232
Isabella 217
J. E. 201
Jane 48
Jemima 228
Joel 15
John 31, 83
John E. 148
Josie 239
Lewis 181
Loudicy K. 109
Louisa 201
Lucinda 214
M. C. 203
Margaret J. 109
Martha E. 140
Mary M. 133
Nancy 53, 54
Napoleon 201
Narcissa 195
Narcissa J. 104
Phillip 124
R. J. 212
Richard 53
Salem 181
Sam 181
Samella 233
Sarah A. 134
Seth 52
Susan 95
Susan C. 133
Susan E. 134
Thomas 133
W. P. 157
William 52, 84
Neale, William 42
Nealy, Wm. W. 145
Neel, Alexander 52
Armstead 29
Eliza 97
Mary 68
Mima 181
Philip 181
Rebecca A. 34
Neeley, Isabella 91
Joshua R. 139
Mary 139
Nancy A. 117
Neelly, Joshua 52

Nichols, (cont.)
Susan A. 107
Nickens, Mary A. 152
Nickson, Margarett 96
Night, Isaac 182
Nancy 151
Sarah 182
Niles, Charles 45, 70
Niper, Ambrose B. 77
Nipper, Lizzie 215
Patsey 40
Nisbet, Joseph 52
Nisbett, Alexander 76
Betsy 193
Ephraim 130
Jinny 162
Nisbitt, Mary 94
Nivins, Eliz. C. 152
Lucinda 66
Mary 119, 122
Nixon, Francis B. 29
John 52
Lavenia 104
Lurainy 15
Mary 55
Pulaski 62
Uriah 74
William 107
Noakes, Amy 54
Noe, Aquilla 201
Benj. 212
Geo. W. 154
James 52
John 52
Lucinda 129
M. F. 221
Martha 212
Mary 148
Nancy 157
Purlina N. 125
Sarah 119
Susan I. 207
W. R. 157
Nokes, Mary J. 160
Nolan, Martin 139
Noland, David 244
John 70
John L. 201
Lewis 79
Nancy M. 157
P. G. 17
Robert C. 182
Nolen, Daniel 230
James 222
Lewis 182
Martha A. 98
Mary F. 146
Nolin, Moses T. 182
Nord, Mahaly 171
Norfleet, Nelson 182
Thomas M. 52
Norman, Allen 212
Amanda 91, 170, 219
Benjamin P. 110
Berryman 27, 52
Bradley 182
C. W. 244
Calvin 212
Carney 100
Caroline 182
Catharine 225
E. A. 151
E. A. C. 8
E. P. 228
Eliza 217
Elizabeth 14
Ephraim 48

Norman, (cont.)
Ephraim A. C. 83
Furney G. 2, 53
Granville L. 136
H. H. 201
Henry 124, 251
Isabella 162
Jane 202
Joe 182
John 53, 68
Joseph 182
Logan H. 114
Louisa 52
Margaret 49
Martha E. 220
Nancy 2
Narcissa 171
Pettis W. 91
Rose Jane 183
Rosanna 218
Rosannah 14
Rozetta 127
Sophia 179
Susan 156, 191
Thomas 182, 244
Thomas H. 53
Wm. 222
William J. G. 53
William M. 53
Norris, Elizabeth 45, 53
Frances 25
James D. 53
Joseph 53
Lou 251
Norsworthy, Anne 41
North, Ann 220
Anna 203
Anthony 53, 201
David 182, 230
Davy 182
Eliz. 160
Frances 61
J. A. 222
M. J. 153
Martha S. 140
Mary 61, 182
Nancy 35
Nathan 182
Richard 251
Miss Sallie M. 249,
250
Sarah F. 227
Thordorick 117
W. J. 244
William E. 37, 47, 53
Northcott, Amanda 102
Andrew J. 114
Benj. F. 133
Caroline 112
D. P. 151
Delong 159
Eliz. C. 137
G. N. 158, 238
James M. 114
John 127
John W. 124
Margaret Angeline 219
Mary M. V. 201
Nancy 133
Ruby E. 213
V. H. H. H. 201
William J. 124
Northcutt, Eliz 148
G. N. 244
Geo. N. 145
Hosey 53
Joel B. 84

Northcutt, (cont.)
Love 25
Mahala 63
Mary 79
Nancy R. 157
Polexany 43
Robert S. 100
S. K. 244
Sarah C. 156
William 53
Northern, Thomas Y. 98
Norton, Ann 165
Eliza 219
Jefferson 251
Norman 78
William 53
Norvell, Abram 121
Charles W. 139
Elizabeth 35
Matilda 104
Norvill, Nathaniel 53
Norwell, James 89
Norwood, Wm. 201
Nuckles, Elizabeth R. 18
Joshua 18
Nuckolls, Dr. Garret S.
230
Nugent, Melindah 29
Null, Nicholas 8
Nurney, Nelson 103
Oaff, James 201
Oakley, Harriet 89
James W. 101
Lucretia 101
Martha J. 200
Stanford P. 98
Oaks, Cynthia 47
Isaac 53
Isable 53
Isble 53
Sarah 68
O'Briant, Wm. 142
O'Brien, John 148
O'Bryant, David 121
O'Callaghan, W. A. 130
Odel, Margaret 128
O'Dell, Hiram F. 158
Odell, J. A. 238
James 85
Jeremiah 53
R. S. 230
Siothia 102
Odem, B. F. 212
Oden, Amanda 83
Edm. 182
Fannie J. 238
John 238
John A. 103
Lucinda 163
Nelly 245
Tempy 52
Thomas M. 133
Odeneal, T. J. 127
Odle, Mary (?) 102
Odom, Sherman 244
Walter 238
Wm. F. 201
Odum, Mary 206
Oglevie, Jasper 244
Old, Elizabeth 62
John H. 148
Oldridge, Levina 66
Olds, Daniel S. 53
Eliz. 159
Mary (?) 102
Oliphant, Amelia E. 65
Isaac N. 42, 83

Neely, Dr. D. M. 244
  David M. 117
  Dorothy J. 100
  Elizabeth 99
  Ezabella 44
  J. H. 181
  Jackson 181
  James Q. E. 181
  Jane 115
  John 69
  John C. 124
  John D. 114
  John J. 148
  M. H. 145
  Margarett A. 127
  Martha K. 149
  Mary A. 99
  Mary L. 100, 127
  Nancy 75
  Nancy E. 109
  Sallie A. 186
  Sarah W. H. 111
  Susan 114
  Susan A. F. 147
  Tabitha 152
  W. W. 182
  Wm. 212
Neil, C. D. 42
  J. F. 222
  John T. 86
Neill, James F. 145
  Richard 16
Neilly, Benjamine F. 52
  John 52
  Susan F. 12
  William 52
Neilson, Hugh D. 80
  Oswell 29
  Sallie 167
Neisbet, Alexander 46
  Nancy 18
Neisbett, Isabellah 120
Nelson, Adam 238
  Allen 201
  Amanda J. 153
  Beverly 52
  Catherine 20
  Charity 253
  Daniel 52
  Drury D. 103
  Ed 222
  Eliz. E. 167
  Eliza 204, 218
  Eliza A. 22
  Elizabeth C. 103
  Evin 100
  F. 212, 222
  Geo. 182, 201, 230
  George F. 117
  Hal 182
  Henrietta S. 61
  I. L. 154
  Isaac R. 139
  J. A. 251
  J. S. 244
  James C. 52
  Jas. W. 74
  Jerry 222
  John R. 80
  Jos W. 81
  Joseph 52
  Joseph W. 57, 86
  Kate 165
  L. 154
  Lavica E. 207
  Lizzie 228
  Logan 201

Nelson, (cont.)
  Malcomb R. 19
  Marshal 182
  Martha 189, 211
  Martha A. 108
  Mary 76, 162, 182,
    185, 210, 229
  Mary L. 152
  Matilda 240
  Mildred F. 77
  Minter 182
  P. M. 154
  Pleasant H. 52
  Ralph 182
  Rosabella 201
  Samuel 20, 52, 71
  Sella 211
  Simon 182
  Sophonia E. 38
  Susan 169
  Susan H. 151
  Susan M. 57
  Thomas 52
  Thomas C. 4, 64
  Tom 182
  Wm. 39
  William D. 52
Nesbett, Alexander 13
  Alexander A. 13
  Miss Bettie 181
  Ephraim 39
  N. C. 212
Nesbit, Alexander 88
  Ephram 151
Nesbitt, Ephraim 72
  Ephriam 201
  Julius 244
  Lucy S. 231
  Rosannah 143
  Susan 193
Nettle, George 244
Nevels, Hamton 182
  Susan 251
Nevil, William 56
Nevill, Emeline E. 103
Nevils, Elizabeth 12
  Lucy 234
  Sarah Ann 84
Nevina, Ann 56
Nevins, Elizabeth 38, 50
  Henley 29
  Jane G. 8
  Martha J. 192
  Mary 79
  Mary J. 192
  Miss Tennessee 200
  William 8, 222
Newgent, David D. 100
  Elizabeth 110
  John D. 59
  Lucinda 96
  Mary E. 95
  Nathaniel 85
  Sarah Ann 54
  William H. 84, 100
Newget, Catharine 141
Newman, Albert 222
  Allen 100 , 124
  Amanda 243
  Anderson 130
  Andrew 222
  Ann 141
  Caroline 198
  Cassie 244
  Mrs Cassie 220
  Charles 182
  Dick 222

Newman, (cont.)
  Drucilla A. 148
  E. A. 163
  Eliz. 150
  Elizabeth 56, 98
  G. J. 182
  Gabrial 145
  George 182
  J. T. 222
  J. W. 160
  James 52
  James K. 230
  James M. 85
  Jane 103, 193
  John 52, 251
  John A. 98, 120
  John D. 127
  John E. 103
  Joseph 52
  Kate; W. 193
  Lucy 207
  Martha 109
  Mary 107, 229
  Mary Jane 225
  Melinda 182
  Mihaley 89
  Minerva M. 37
  Nancy 76
  Narcissa 184
  Rosanna 52
  Thomas 212
  William 124, 222
  William M. 120
Newsom, Miss A. 192
  Ann 240
  Balam 114
  Caroline E. 153
  Elizabeth 83
  Francis C. 52
  James R. 148
  John B. 52
  Lucy 63, 112
  Mary J. 126
  Missora Ann 104
  Samuel 94
  Sarah 85
  Sugar 251
  Thomas 52, 230
Newson, Henry 244
  Thomas 43
Newton, Eppy 49
Nice, John W. 148
Nichol, J. Y. 157
  James 222
  Tempy 170
  William 52
Nicholas, Eli 15
Nichols, Daniel 4
  Daniel B. 52
  Eli 38
  Esther 38
  Euphraima 73
  Isaac D. 212
  James A. 120
  James L. 52
  Jennie 215
  Joshua 52
  Margaret 81
  Margaret Ann 116
  Margarett 113
  Martha 4
  Martha E. 116
  Mary A. 140
  Mary E. 145
  Nancy E. 136
  Sally 15, 78
  Sarah A. 120

Pace, (cont.)
 Peggy 14
 Riney 39
 Ruth 4
 William 81
 William C. 114
Pafford, Wilie 95
Page, Elizabeth 10
 Jesse T. 133
 John B. 54
 John E. 151
 Jordan 201
 Lucinda 40
 Mary Ann 57
 Sallie 243
 Susan 93
 William 54
 William D. 10, 36
Pain, Rachel 21
Painter, America T. 179
 Miss Eliz. 248
 Elizabeth 40
 John 74
 John F. 182
 Juliann 121
 Margarett 143
Pallet, Agnes 20
Pallett, Thomas A. 54
Palmer, Andrew 88
 Greenville 95
 Jacob 230
 Joseph 136
 Julia 222
 Miss M. E. 203
 Mary E. 148, 182
 Milley 167
 William 54
 William H. 54
Palmore, E. L. 196
 Wm. 160
Paneely, John F. 222
Parham. Joshua N. 54
 Peter 54
Pariker, Dinah 209
Paris, Sarah Ann 229
Parish, Elizabeth R. 88
 Jack 244
 Roxana 180
 Samuel A. 142
 Susan 182
 William G. 54
Parker, A. B. 222
 A. Y. 182
 Albert Y. 156
 Alfred K. 130
 Amanda E. 114
 Ann 70
 Ben 222
 Benj. 201
 Catharine 63
 Deborah 42
 Dollison 35 , 54
 Donelson 38
 Dorton 95
 E. A. 206
 Eliz. 144
 Elizabeth H. 101
 Frances L. 231
 Francis 54
 Garrison 54
 Hardy 42, 54
 Isaac 26, 54
 Isaac P. 136
 Jane 201
 Joel 49
 John 98, 130
 John A. 121

Parker, (cont.)
 John W. 151
 Joseph 151
 Joseph A. 238
 Lucy 226
 Malery 87
 Margaret L. 142
 Margaret S. 138
 Martha 131, 148, 240
 Mary 52, 78, 203
 Mary Ann S. 118
 Nancy 120
 Nehemiah 154
 Patsey 25
 Phineas 2
 Richard 91
 Sarah 159
 Spicy G. 154
 Susan 108
 Thomas 160
 William 91, 182
 Zedda 221
Parkes, Martha 89
Parkman, Martha 95
 Mary A. 87
Parks, Charles 88
 Cinthy 72
 Lewis 230
 Rachel 221
Parkson, Emeline 86
Parmer, Emaline 217
 Emma 238
Parnack, Geo. 87
Parnck, Geo. 87
Parnell, John S. 160
Parrent, Louis 145
Parris, Eliz 147
 W. B. 201
Parrish, America 24
 Catherine 121
 Charlotte 24
 Elizabeth C. 121
 Eliza J. 18
 Miss Jemima 213
 Mary 91'
 Mary F. 127
 Mary R. 39
 Roxana 247
 Sarah Jane 158
 Thomas L. 117
 W. G. 18
 William 54
 William C. 110
 William G. 20, 72
Parsley, Miss Alice 247
 J. A. 222
 James J. 136
 Jesse S. 54
 John L. 54
 John Q. 88
 Miss Josephine 247
 M. C. 212
 M. J. 251
 Mary Anne 19
 Moses M. 50
 Rosanna 50
 Stephen 13
 William N. 104
Partee, Ann 201
 Charles M. 54
 Rodolphus G. 136
 Sarah F. 201
Partlow, James W. 114
Paskel, Wm. 251
Pasley, Isabella M. 133
Pass, D. M. 244
Pate, Catherine E. 140

Pate, (cont.)
 Delaney 32
 Fanny 207
 George 222
 Henry H. 145
 Houston 182
 Martha 182, 220
 William 3, 54
Patey, B. F. 244
Patillo, Harrison 6
 Minerva 192
 Samuel 54
 Sarah A. 99
 Sarah Ann 33
Patillow, Netty 217
Paton, Lewis 201
Patrick, Levi 54
 Matilda C. 104
 William 33, 104, 244
Patten, James 157
Patterson, Alexander 30
 Alpha 95
 Amaziah C. 101
 American A. 227
 Bailey 54
 Balsonia 129
 Beverly D. 151
 Bob 201
 C. A. 244
 California A. 105
 Miss Camelia 154
 Caroline 118
 Caudis F. 129
 Charley 230
 Rev. D. R. 212
 E. E. 244
 Edward 54
 Elenor 93
 Ellen 194
 Emaline 113
 Everard 222
 Fanny 166
 Felix H. 86
 Fenton M. 54
 Frank 230
 Frelingheison 182
 George 238
 Gideon 54
 Green 83
 Hillery 107
 Isaac 121
 J. A. 212
 J. L. 238
 James 85
 Jane 60, 61, 110
 Jemima 31
 John 54, 127
 John W. 238
 L. B. 121
 Lewis 182
 Malinda 242
 Martha J. 135
 Mary 222
 Mary A. 153
 Miss Mary E. 183
 Mattie 153
 Maxmilly 151, 152
 Moses 212
 Nannie B. 214
 Naomi 33
 Queen E. 132
 R. H. 130
 Robert W. 182
 S. A. 212
 S. A. R. 217
 Salle 158
 Mrs. Sallie 243

Pool, Alexander 6
  Benj. 251
  Polly Ann 41
Pope, A. J. 251
  B. F. 212
  Benjamine 56
  Charles 56
  Christopher 127
  Ezekiel 11
  Francis K. 201
  Hardy 56
  J. J. 183
  J. K. 201
  Miss J. L. 240
  John 56
  John W. A. 146
  Julia 161
  Louisa A. 196
  Martha 35
  Mary 35, 131
  Moses 183
  Nancy 26, 121
  Penelope 11
  Rebecca E. 148
  Sarah J. 135
  Solomon 56
  Sophia 145
  Tabitha 124
  Tempeance 123
  William 56, 104, 202
  William J. 88
  Winifred 3
Poplin, Green L. 51
Popp, Nancy 19
Porter, Agga 202
  Anne 81
  Burton 202
  James L. 68
  James M. 139
  Jane L. 44
  John N. 56, 89
  Margaret 46
  Samuel 44, 56
  Thomas B. 56
  William 124
Porterfield, D. H. 157
  Leonidus F. 124
  Peggy B. 68
  Samuel S. 56
  Susan 17
  William S. 56
Portis, Elizabeth 103
  Joseph H. 139
Poser, Catherine 220
Posey, Dennis 56
  Elizabeth 67, 79
  Elizabeth A. 120
  Green 183, 251
  John 56
  Julia Ann 206
  Julia Ann L. 141
  Martha 90
  Martin 213
  Mary 104
  Mary A. 209
  Mollie 236
  Nancy 44
  Nancy E. E. 93
  Nancy J. 126
  Nicey 76
  P. F. 146
  Rethenia 186
  Richard 183
  Rosannah 19
  S. A. 241
  William H. 32, 83
  William S. 56, 136

Posey, (cont.)
  William Y. 110
Post, Ann 70
Poterfield, C. M. 222
Potter, Benjamine H. 56
Potts, E. L. 240
  Elizabeth 59, 96
  George B. 56
  Henry 68
  Lucinda 133
  William 19, 56, 238
Potty, Phebe 53
Powel, Nancy M. 144
  Salley A. 191
Powell, Amanda 161
  B. C. 54
  Dallis 161
  Eddy 37
  Miss Eliza J. 246
  Jane 154
  Joseph 148, 154
  Martha 93
  Mary Ann 58
  Mary L. 141
  Nancy 1, 20
  Osburn 56
  Rebecca 46
  Robert J. 130
  Sarah J. 150
  Susan Ann 137
  Tabitha 72
  Tenison 56
  Thomas 20, 38, 56
  Thomas, Jr. 55
  Virginia 152
  W. M. 158
  W. O. 222
  William 56
  William E. 56
Powers, Augustus 213
  George 57
  William B. 107
  William D. 104
Powling, Miss P. E. 249
Prater, Aaron 57, 107
  Amanda 253
  Amanda E. 158
  Austin 121, 142
  Celia 194
  David 146
  Elijah 57
  Eliz. 167, 204
  Elizabeth 109
  Ellen 253
  Harriett R. 213
  Henry 151
  Jennier 57
  Jerry 213
  John 101, 142, 146
  Lucinda 173
  Malinda 48
  Mary E. 230
  Mary J. 238
  Mattie E. 160
  Monroe 114, 213
  Philip J. 136
  Phillip G. 151
  Rebecca M. 225
  Sarah N. 157
  Susan 197
  Susan J. 177
  Thomas 57
  Vinie 229
  W. I. 183
  W. P. 244
  Wm. H. 130
Pratt, Baldwin 154

Prawley, Cinthia 25
Presley, Miss Mattie 246
Presly, Betsy 170
Preston, Alfred 183
  Mariah 212
Prewett, David L. 148
  Eliz. 158
  Henry 57
  John 61
  Locky 123
  Mary 91, 130
  Rebecca 158
Prewitt, Clard 183
  Eliz. 138
  Jane E. 138
  Larry E. 121
  M. H. 57
  Mary 103
  Phillis 193
  Piety 17
  Susan 183
Price, America 146
  Benj. 222
  Cynthia 13
  Harriet 212
  Miss Hattie E. 234
  Henry 222
  James 154
  Jane 148
  Jesse P. 231
  Jessie 238
  John 57
  John M. 57
  John W. 57, 101
  Martha 88
  Preston G. 213
  R. C. 156
  R. L. 154
  Sarah 169
  Susan 113
  T. J. 154
  Thomas 19
  Wesley 231
  Wilson B. 146
Prichett, Caladonia C.
  132
Pride, John S. M. 139
Priestly, Elinor J. 94
  James 57, 84
  John T. 110
Prim, James 183
  William 68
Primm, Frank 183
  John G. 107
  Judith Ann 123
  Judy A. 213
  Margaret S. 205
  Martha L. 212
  Mary 183
  Sarah 141
Prince, ---- 121
  Alfred 107
  Emily 172, 182
  Louisa 120
  Susan 111
Prior, John 57
Pritchett, Aeriadne T.
  121
  Charity 165
  Mary H. 115
  Sarah A. J. 24
  Sarah L. 148
Proby, Burrow 213
  Wilmoth 246
Proctor, Eliza 183
  Joe 183
Profitt, Isiah 202, 213

324

Randolph, (cont.)
Vina 220
Wm. 251
Wm. W. 136
Randsom, John 61
Raney, Hannah 26
Isham 244
John E. 121
Rankin, A. 73
A. W. 251
Addie 196
Alexander 39
Anne 27
E. E. 184
Edmond 184
Eleanor 21, 24, 59
Elizabeth V. 124
Fannie 235
Franklin W. 136
Henry 251
James 39
James H. 161
Jane 122
Je. E. 201
Jerry 245
John A. 245
Joseph 58
Lewis 251
Martha 198
Mary 61
Mary E. 203
Mary M. 49
Miss Mintie M. 249
Robert D. 35
Samuel 58
Sarah 16
Sarah L. 140
Thomas C. 58
William C. 58
Rankins, Martha E. 143
Rannaway, Caroline 212
Rannols, Charlie 251
Ransom, Alexander 184
Alfred 56, 58
Amanda 184
Athelston 58
Benjamine 58
Bettie 224
C. 222
Caroline 112, 184
Cinthia 184
Daniel 184
Easter 188
Ed. 245
Einey 184
Elizabeth 71
Elizabeth K. 114
Miss Fannie 232
Frances 219
Geo. 184
Green 184
Harry 231
Henry 184
Henry D. 13, 58
James 184, 251
Jane 192
Jerry 251
John 58, 61, 104
Katy 182
L. A. R. 195
Lemuel 58, 154
Levina 192
Lizzie 240
Lucinda 210
Miss M. P. 237
Margaret 111, 225
Margaret K. 87

Ransom, (cont.)
Martha 252
Mary 183, 184, 252
Mary E. 140
Mary J. 87
Medicus 154
O. W. 238
Peter 184
Reuben 238
Richard 67, 71
Richard P. 127
Robert 202
Robert N. 136
S. H. 156
Sam 245
Samuel 184
Sarah 184, 242
Sciota Jane 175
Simon 184
Sophronia 170
Tom 184
William A. 98, 107,
117
William K. 34, 70, 90
Rasson, Geo. 161
Rather, Celia 241
Creasy 231
Daniel 148
Mattie F. 218
Peter 213
Polly 246
Susan M. 138
Wm. 130
Rawlings, Elizabeth L. 94
Miss Ellen 253
German D. 117
John 58
John Marshall 101
John W. 58
Lewis 84
Lucy A. 123
Martin H. 98
Mary 26
Mary J. 153
Mathias 58
Matthias 58
Nancy N. 109
R. L. 202
Sarah 103
William 107
Rawlins, John 58
Nancy 37, 45
Wm. 17
Rawls, John 58
Ray, J. H. 202
John 58
John C. 121
John G. 58
Thomas 58
Wm. R. 152
Wm. Y. 222
Rayborn, Charles 251
Samuel 251
Sarah 227
Rayburn, French 184
Read, Almira 104
Ann 87
Catharine 136
Clement T. 110
Dorothy 51
Eliza 107
Elizabeth 55
Elizabeth B. 15
Francis 29
Jemsha T. 228
Joel 90
John 58

Read, (cont.)
John A. 59
John H. 59
John N. 59
Julia 2
Margaret 89
Martha 80, 133, 232
Martha Ann E. 49
Martha E. 137
Mary 63, 122
Mary E. 99
Mary H. 124
Mary J. 135
Matilda 114
Nancy G. 125
Polly 75
R. W. 238
Racheal 99
Rachel 19
Radford W. 86
Richard G. 114
Robert A. 91
Sally C. 100
Sara Ann 44
Sarah 2, 51, 56
Silas 51
Silast L. 59
Silvy 51
Sion L. 59
Solomon 59
Susan 56
Susan A. 103
Susan C. 128, 140
Thomas H. 5
William 83, 98
William A. 110
Wm. R. 213
Ready, Albert 202, 213
Miss C. Alice 221
Caroline 30
Catharine O. 131
Charles, Jr. 81
Ella 245
Miss Ella L. 250
Ellen 235
Harlow 215
Isabella 248
James 26, 59
Jane 247
Jane C. 20
John 238
Mary 34, 248
Mary A. 108
Miss Mattie 157
Peline 213
Susannah M. 96
Thomas 184
Tony 245
Reames, James 59
Reaves, Moses G. 32, 37
Red, Lizzie 212
Redby, Claiborn 202
Redding, Margaret J. 109
Redman, Betty 222
Redmon, Jane 229
Reece, Eggleston 184
Elizabeth E. 100
George E. 245
Isham 59
Mary V. 136
Reed, Anna 195
Barbery 162
Berry 83
Betsy 184
Betty 199
Caroline 25
Caswell 184

Richardson, (cont.)
Pat 184
Reuben 184
Robert B. 107
Mrs. Sallie 218
Sandy 184
Susan W. 148
Thomas 60
William M. 60
Wm. T. 139
Richie, John 60
Richmon, John D. 146
Richmond, Anderson 60
Mary 213
Rick, Sarah C. 123
Ricketts, M. J. 153
R. S. 58
Ricks, Amy 184
Exum 60
Margaret 85
Mary A. 98
Riddle, Mary L. 231
Rideout, Martha 187
Martha L. 56
Susan 206
Thomas 222
Ridgeway, Elizabeth 17, 62
Jane 55
John 17
Mary 27
Wm. 27, 62
Riding, Thomas 60
Ridley, Amanda 171
Angeline 210
Betsey 184
Boyd 222
Bromfield L. 60
Burrell 184
Catherine 249
Claiborne 184
Clara 252
Clarisa 213
Clayborn 202
Dick 222
Edward 184
Eliz. 250
Emmanuel 184
Fannie 228
G. C. 202
George V. 60
George W. 184
Hance A. 60
Hannibal 184
Harriett 170
Henry 1, 3, 184
Hense 202
Hershal 213
Jackson 184
James 60, 213
James A. 107
James B. 139
Jim 184
Joanna 223
John C. 60, 95
Joseph 184
Laura 184
Lizzie 184
Louisa 184
Louisa A. 26
Lucy 184
Miss Maggie 235
Malinda 184
Mary 174
Mary E. 137
Mary J. 139
Mary Jane 184

Ridley, (cont.)
Mat 184
Melinda 184
Mima 66
Moses 251
N. A. 152
Nancy 95
Nancy A. 134
Narcissus F. 97
Patty 184
Penny 177
Polk 213
Sallie E. 138
Samuel J. 121
Sarah B. 52
Selestia Ridley (?) 184
Serena 184
Stewart 231
Susan 52
Virgil 184
Washington 184
William A. 80, 139
York 184
Ridman, Wm. 222
Ridout, Ann B. 140
Ann C. 83
Braxton 231
Eliz. H. 139
John 184
Miss M. G. 173
Mariah 187
Pleas Ann 168
Susan J. 6
Rieves, Ira O. 152
Riley, Eliz. 233
Rine, Ellen 167
Ring, Joseph F. 136
Lucretia E. 134
M. L. 142
Thomas 60
Rinkard, Sarah 250
Rino, Clem C. 159
Rion, C. J. 251
Francis P. 245
Martha W. 132
Reuben 52
Thomas D. 136
Rippetoe, Burrus W. 60
Ritner, John 95
Ritter, Preston H. 60
Rivers, Ellen 179
Roach, Neal 104
Roads, Armon 222
Robert 202
Roan, Charles H. 213
Roane, J. H. 146
Roans, Ann 221
Robason, James M. 133
Robb, Ann 151
Eliza H. 144
Mary Y. 6
Nancy C. 14
Sophia A. 89
W. W. 146
Robbins, Harmon 95
James H. 95
Lemuel 98
Mary 88
Thomas 61
Roberson, A. J. 202
Alexander 213
Harriet 247
Isiah 157
Miss Jennie 250
Lee 245
Mandy 222

Roberson, (cont.)
Mary 160
Mary Ann 117
Narcissa 252
Polly 75
Pompy 238
Robert 202
Robert, James 184
John I. V. 95
Roberts, Abram 222
Allen 202
Ann 226
C. A. 142
C. J. 213
Caroline 98, 166
Catharine 94
Christiana 68
Clarisa 215
D. M. 161
George W. 124
Henry 21
Jack 156
James M. 63, 83
Jane 97
Jesse 15
Josephine 174
Louisa M. 145
Mary 74
Mary A. 140
Matilda A. 96
Melvina 190
Nancy 52, 65
Susan 112
Thomas 60
Warren 245
Wm. 184
Wm., Jr. 231
William J. 121
William T. 15
Winney 5
Robertson, A. B. 64
A. M. 202
Adam 185
Amanda 141, 185
Ann 69
Barney 251
Burgus 222
Catherine 19
Charles 185
Charlott 199
Chester 185
Christopher 60
Cynthia H. 23
Cyrena 40
D. M. 231
Daniel 87
Drury 48
Edward 60
Edward H. 60
Elisha 60
Eliz. 201
Eliz. E. 141
Eliza 84, 183
Elizabeth 52
Geo. 202
Greef 185
Green B. 127
Higdon J. 130
Hiram 202
Holly 139
James M. 185
Jane 76, 176
Johannah 37
John 72
Joseph 21
Kinchen 60
Lovy O. J. 151

327

Robertson, (cont.)
  Lucinda 175
  Luke S. 60
  Mary 21, 55
  Mary C. 149
  Nancy 46, 76
  Peter 185
  Pleasant 60, 61
  Polly 61
  Pompy 185
  Rachel 144, 178
  Rhoda 212
  Richard 60
  Sarah 46, 47
  Sarah F. 161
  Sarah P. 240
  Solomon 222
  Thomas 60
  Tom 185
  Victoria 163
  Vina 221
  William 60, 61
  William B. 38
Robins, Joseph 185
  Lemuel 61
Robinson, Alexander 89,
  133
  Bell 245
  Miss Bettie 244
  Calvin 151
  Christopher 61
  Cinthia 185
  David 61
  Edward H. 61
  Eleanor 3
  Elizabeth C. 96
  Elizabeth F. 97
  Ellen V. 140
  Ellis 185
  Ensey 185
  Fulton 61
  G. W. 149
  George W. 117
  H. 2
  Hannah 44
  Miss I. M. 246
  Isaac 23
  Isaiah 61
  J. R. 76
  Jacob 154
  Jane 13, 55, 133
  Joe 185
  John 61, 185
  John H. 61
  Joseph 86
  Lee 245
  Louisia 87
  Lucinda 250
  Luke S. 61
  Martin 238
  Mary 21, 27
  Miss Mary 179
  Mary A. 102, 125
  Mary Ann 116
  Micajah 61
  Micha 28
  Milly 185
  Nancy 61
  Phillip O. 154
  Samuel 121
  Samuel B. 61
  Susan M. 22
  Susanna 49
  Thomas 90
  Thomas J. 156
  Uriah 124
  William 61

Robinson, (cont.)
  Wm. A. 158
  Wm. H. 64
  Willie G. 98
Robison, Alice 219
  Calvin 222
  Harriet 239
  James R. 231
  Jemima 233
  Col. W. D. 231
  Wm. 231
Rock, Stephen 231
Roden, Rachel 43
Rodgers, Andrew 61
  Elizabeth W. 85
  Flora 171
  George B. 107
  James 95, 124
  Joseph W. 85
  Margarett 90
  Martha 114
  Martha Ann 118
  Mary 86
  Mary A. 102
  Peggy 37
  Ranzel H. 127
  Robert 127
  Susan M. 130
Rogers, Anna 202
  Benj. F. 130
  Miss Elender J. 170
  Eliza 231
  Ervin 61
  Fannie 226
  Harriet 231
  J. C. 98
  Jerry 238
  John 61, 130
  John D. 61
  John R. 23
  L. A. 231
  Louisa 165, 195
  Mary E. 132
  Nancy L. W. 97
  Nelly 221
  Nicholas 98
  Oliver 89
  S. M. 231
  Temperance 15
  Thomas 89
  W. M. 213
  W. W. 158
  Zalpha 105
Roges, Felix 213
Roland, John 61
  T. M. 213
Roling, America 142
Rolins, Mary 123
Rollin, Mariah 38
Rollins, Cherry 174
  Harriett 165
  James 213
  Joseph 161
  Margarit 150
  Mariah 208
  Mary J. 208
  P. T. 160
  Sallie A. 144
Rooker, David 185
  Jennings 61
  Patience 189
  Rose Ann 178
  William 104
Rooney, Michael C. 61
Rorister, Geo. 213
Roromines, George 88
Rory, Luviny 184

Rosborough, Mary E. 146
Rose, B. 213
  Clementine 104
  Elmira 153
  Miss F. E. 250
  Jacob B. 238
  Julia 93
  Miss Laura A. 250
  Margaret J. 84
  Robert 146
  Sarah 149, 211
  William 90
Rosenfield, Hellen 155
Rosewell, Buford A. 61
Ross, Abram 238
  Alfred 83
  Amanda C. 150
  Amos 185
  Bettie 237
  Booker 251
  Caswell 202
  Elizabeth L. 89
  Fanny 226
  Felix G. 133
  Frances 19
  Francis 195
  Frank E. 231
  Geo. W. 154
  Harriett 185
  Henry 238, 245
  John 61, 86, 238
  Judith 211
  Miss Kate 215
  Lucy 214
  Margarett W. 96
  Martha 208
  Martha A. 197
  Mary 238
  Miss Mary 176
  Mattie L. 169
  Melie Ann 251
  Minty 171
  Oscar 238
  Peter 185
  Richard 185
  Sam 185
  Sarah Jane 181
  Sterlin 185
  Thomas 231
  Wm. 43
  Wm. W. 62
Rostetter, Thomas 213
Roulet, Wm. 185
Roulett, Major 161
Roulhac, George 61
  Jas. P. 33
  Margaret P. 33
  William G. 61
Rouse, Berry 50
  Edmond 185
  Edmund 61, 86
  Hiram 91
  Isaac 127
  James 202
  Jinsey 68
  John 61, 68
  Joseph 133
  Louisa 230
  Margaret 50
  Martha 138
  Polly 202
  Richard 127
  Sally 104, 238
  Sarah 198
  Thomas 202
  William 61, 213
Routon, James M. 90

Rowan, Filey A. 236
  James 252
  Martha 174
  Robert 238
  Stokely D. 107
  William B. 110
Rowden, Roxy 80
  Thomas 222
  Tinnie 150
Rowe, Susan 81
Rowen, Mary 41
  Valentine 213
Rowett, Miss R. A. 183
Rowland, Benj. V. 90
  Benjamine 61
  F. M. 245
  James C. 213
  Jane 73
  John 117
  L. B. 185
  Louisa 160
  Lucy A. 10
  M. P. 245
  Martha Ann 73
  Mary J. 207
  Samuel 231
  Sarah Jane 236
  Thomas T. 101
  William 110
Rowlett, Adaline 124
  Benj. 185
  Benj. F. 161
  Caroline 193
  City M. 141
  Edward A. 110
  Frances 97
  John 124
  Joseph W. 185
  Leonard 61
  Lucy R. 161
  Lydia 234
  Martha A. 208
  Martha E. 133
  Mary S. 124
  Peter M. 110
  Rebecca 113
  Rebecca R. 151
  Sarah A. 112
  Sarah E. 116
  T. N. 161
Rowse, Edward 68
Rowton, Edwin 18
  Eliza 211
  Francis E. 29
  Nancy 36
  Peyton 38
  Richmond 61
  Rulant 98
  Ryland 114
  V. P. 153
  William D. 44, 65, 83
Roy, Caroline 228
  Sarah 185
Royster, Fannie 251
  Fanny 249
Rozell, Blackman L. 88
  Martha D. 88
Rozella, Ashley B. 61
Rucker, Adaline 185
  Albert 213
  Alice 228
  Amelia 185
  America 243, 253
  Anderson 185
  Ann 220
  Ann Eliza 225
  Belinda 48

Rucker, (cont.)
  Benjamine 61
  Bennett 127
  Bettie 221
  Butler 252
  Catesby 185
  Catey 185
  Charity 185
  Charley 202
  Clarissa 176
  Clinton 185
  Cloa 185
  D. L. 149
  David 185
  Deanna 209
  Delany 194
  Dick 185
  Donia 224
  Easter 185
  Edmond 202
  Edmund M. 61
  Elijah 252
  Eliza 185, 202
  Eliza R. 37
  Elizah 185
  Elizabeth 96, 116
  Elizabeth A. 42
  Ellen 210
  Emiline 182
  Emily 13, 174
  Ezabella E. 108
  Felix 252
  Frances M. 120
  Frank 185
  Gideon 30
  Gideon L. 61
  Glasgow 185
  Hancie 185
  Handy 231, 245
  Harriet 215
  Harriett 185
  Harry 185
  Henry 185
  Isaac 185, 252
  Isabella 226
  Isham 252
  Ishmael 185
  J. N. 158
  James 213, 238, 245, 252
  James H. 61
  Jane 185
  Jean 185
  Jennie 230
  Jesse 185
  Jim 185
  Joanna L. 123
  Johanna 57
  Johanna S. 162
  John W. 61
  Joice R. 62
  Joseph A. 213
  Joseph B. 62
  Josephine A. 145
  Josephine B. 102
  Julia 234
  Katey 185
  Katherine 56
  Kittie 238
  Kebber 185
  Lidia 185
  Lucinda E. 5
  Lucretia 208
  Lucy A. 222
  Lucy F. 110
  M. 154
  Miss M. L. 249

Rucker, (cont.)
  Madison 202
  Maggie A. 212
  Marg. 188, 229
  Mariah 185
  Martin 62
  Mary 185
  Mary Anne 58
  Mary R. 133
  Melinda 202
  Mildred R. 179
  Milly A. 213
  Minda 185
  Mundora 137
  Nannie C. 154
  Nathan 185
  Ned 185
  Nelson 185
  Osborn 185
  Pauline 48
  Peggy 207
  Peter 185
  Phelis 185
  Philip 185
  R. M. 213
  Ransom 62
  Richard 185
  Robert B. 107
  Rose 182
  Ruthey Ann 181
  S. R. 58
  Samuel 127, 213, 231
  Samuel C. 52, 57, 62
  Samuel J. 110, 139
  Sarah 18, 124, 194, 205
  Sarah A. 67
  Sidney 185
  Sophia B. 149
  Stephen 238
  Susan 215
  Miss T. M. 217
  Tenacy 3
  Terry 62
  Thelia 185
  Thomas O. G. 62
  Thomas S. 62
  Tildy 185
  Viney 180
  Vinnie E. 235
  Washington 185
  William 77, 117, 185, 186, 231
  William H. 98
  William R. 62
  Winney 185
  Zacheriah 186
Rucks, Benjamine 70
Rudder, Caroline 233
Ruff, Louisa 97
Ruffner, John F. 127
Ruker, Mary J. 211
Runnells, James D. 139
  Nancy C. 138
Runnels, Aaron 238
  Calvin 155
  Caroline 229
  Miss Catherine 245
  Charles 252
  Clara 186
  H. A. 186
  Jack 213
  Jenny 186
  John 186
  P. R. 245
  Phebe Jane 229
  Pollard 114

Runnels, (cont.)
  Sam 186
  Vicey 104
  Wm. 186, 202
Rushing, Abel 62. 88
  Bartley M. 110
  Eliz. 133
  J. C. 155
  Jane 22
  Joel 95
  John C. 110, 130
  Nelson E. 62
  Patrick 62
  Rachel 69
  Sarah 109
  Sarah E. 129
  W. P. 231
  William 62
Russ, Caroling 100
Russel, Chesley P. 155
Russell, Albert F. 252
  Alexander 62
  Clayborn 213
  Eliz. Ann 131
  Fanny 201
  Henry 252
  Indiana 250, 253
  James A. 88
  Jasper H. 186
  Jefferson 186
  John 252
  L. 186
  Margaret W. 8
  Martha 199
  Mary 72
  Miss Mary E. 245
  Nancy 87
  Newton 130
  Robert 186
  Virginia 236
  William 62, 231
Russworm, Eliza 191
  Julia 243
  Laura J. 221
  Lockie A. 223
  Lucy 237
  Minerva 224
  Samuel C. 149
  Sarah 151
  Virginia 85
Russworn, Mary L. 232
Russwurm, Elinor 95
  Elmire 107
  Julia 179
Rust, Isaac 62
Rutherford, Miss Martha
  E. 252
  Nancy 27
  Thomas 27
Rutledge, Alexander C. 85
  Albert 152
  Benj. 139
  David 62
  Eliz. 151, 158
  John 33
  Joseph M. 62
  Judah T. 79
  Martha Anne 7
  Mary A. 158
  Monroe 86
  N. D. F. 232
  Pleasant 62
  R. P. 223
  Richard 152
  Rosemond 14
  Susan L. 94
  William A. 101

Ryan, Berry 47
  C. F. 152
  C. J. 252
  Charles 186
  Eliz. 139, 205
  Emily 235
  George 62
  James M. 139, 156
  John R. 152
  John W. 146
  Lizzie 218
  Mary 193
  Mary A. 248
  Michael T. 62, 104
  Milly 186
  Newton 130
  Paterick 104
  Polly 238
  Susan 87
Rylee, J. E. 231
Ryon, Catharine 125
  Lucinda 138
  Sarah A. 127
Sackett, Jane 119
Sadler, F. E. 161
  John 213
  Sarah E. 155
  Wm. 223
Saffill, Andrew J. 146
Saffle, Martha 34
Sage, Jesse 62
  John W. 186
  Lucinda 41
  Lucinda E. 159
  Mary A. 105
  Nancy C. 126
  Wm. F. 136
Sagely, Eliza 30
  Joseph 62
Sailors, Daniel 27
  Mary Ann 67
Salmons, Abner 62
  Watson 62
Salone, Mary 252
Salscorter, Meyer 231
Sampler, L. P. 160
Sampley, Mrs. L. P. 230
Sander, Demaris 55
  Menerva C. 21
Sanders, A. B. 146
  Abram 223
  Amanda 186
  Miss Amanda 238
  Amanda M. 117
  Anderson 186
  Andrew T. 139
  Angeline 188
  Bedy 28
  Miss Callie 212
  Caroline 175
  Catharine 98
  Catherine 244
  Charlotte 94
  Cherry 63
  Cornelius 55, 62
  D. J. 156
  David 186
  Dorothy 37
  Dovie E. 224
  Edward F. 84
  Ellen 235
  Elisha 21, 62
  Eliz. 140, 158, 159
  Eliz. America 153
  Eliza 102, 186
  Eliza A. 28
  Elizabeth 8

Sanders, (cont.)
  Ellis 46
  Fannie E. 227
  Frances J. 160
  Frances R. 118
  Frederick 62
  Garrett 62
  Geo. 231
  George 62, 104, 186,
    238
  Harriett 186
  Harriett E. 118
  Hiram 62, 133
  Houston 252
  Isaac 62, 63, 245
  Isabella 235
  J. C. 157
  J. E. 238
  J. P. 146
  James 63
  James J. 104
  James M. 63, 252
  Jane 186
  Jean 182
  Jennie 173
  John 4, 245
  John C. 136
  John C. 63
  Josephine 241
  Julia A. 164
  Laney 213
  Leonard W. 158
  Levy Ann 107
  Lindy 219
  Lou 226
  Louisa 234
  Lucinda W. 111
  M. J. 146
  Miss M. N. 223
  Mahulda 12, 147
  Malissa 188
  Mankin S. 124
  Marandy D. 106
  Marandy E. 146
  Margaret 25
  Mariah 186
  Mark 202
  Marshall H. 110
  Martha 185
  Martha A. 146
  Martha E. 161
  Martha M. 85
  Mary 97, 99, 100, 187
  Mary A. 139, 154
  Mary A. E. 131
  Mary Ann 20, 101
  Mary C. 151
  Mary E. 104, 127
  Mary F. 153
  Mary J. 185
  Mary M. 186, 214
  Mason 252
  Mima 169
  Minerva 55
  Missouri 171
  Nancy 158, 202
  Nancy C. 114
  Nelly 61
  Noel 44
  Nonan 165
  Permelia 122
  Permilia F. 105
  Phebe 89
  Phillip 186
  Phillip S. 186
  Pinkney G. 63
  Ransom 186

Sanders, (cont.)
Rich. 213
Richard 63
Richard B. 110
Robert 9
Robert A. 202, 238
Rose 218
Miss Sallie L. 245
Sallie T. 220
Sam 186
Samuel R. 110, 136, 155
Sarah 5
Sarah A. 141
Sarah L. 152
Solomon 214
Squire 202
Stephen C. 121
Susan 213
Susannah 13
Miss Symantha 223
T. M. 238
Thomas 8, 60, 63, 223
Thomas L. 114
Thomas W. 124
Unity V. 239
Victoria 224
W. A. 225
W. D. 146
W. L. 245
Whitfield 114
Wiley 63
William 46, 63, 186, 202
William A. 95
Sanderson, Eliza Jane 196
Sandford, James 3
John 63
S. J. 240
Sandwich, Westey 214
Sanflor, Candor 127
Sanford, Betsy 186
Caroline M. 124
Chaney 253
Eliz. 186
Eliz. R. 137
Eliza 106
Elizabeth G. 96
Fanny 224
George W. 63
J. W. 202
James 63
James H. 161
John 72
John A. 98, 133
Lucinda A. 96
Martha J. 201
Martha M. 91
Mary 87, 211
Mary A. 6
Nancy 172
Peck 186
Peyton 161
Rial 186
Sarah J. 142
Susan 145
Thomas 252
Willis 121, 186, 202
Sartan, Elizabeth 116
Sartin, Eveline 116
James R. 223
Sartor, William 107
Sarver, Jacob A. 107
Saterwhite, Frances 35
Satten, Mallie 246
Satterwhite, S. T. 239

Sauls, Henry 161
John 18
Ruth M. 18
Saulter, John 63
Saunders, Benjamine 42
Donaldson 32
Elizabeth 124
Elmira 107
Jarratt 110
Jesse B. 107
M. R. 218
Mary L. 116
Mary S. 98
Robert W. 63
Sally 75
Samuel 86
Thomas 63
Thomas S. 110
Usler 186
Savage, G. M. 245
James 63
Richard 117
Saver, America 234
Sawyer, Edward 186
Sawyers, Andrew C. 239
Daphney 223
David 223
Hiram 186
James 63, 72
James C. 223
Kate 220
Mahala 186
Martha 186
Melissa 227
Nelly 72
Peter 186
Miss R. D. 196
White 223
Saylors, Catherine 65
John 67
Scales, Daniel R. 127
David 186
Harriet 194
Isaac 223
Jessee 214
Joseph R. 127
Lucy Jane 188
Mary J. 156
Mary Jane 253
Minerva 239
Peter P. 63
William T. 101
Scarberry, Mary J. 169
Schiff, A. 155
Schofflin, Archer 186
Julia 186
Schorn, Wm. 214
Scisom, Ann 252
Scoggins, John 63
Scott, Caroline 252
Crockett 202
Jane 162
John A. 202
John W. 63
Judith 6
Julia 72
Mary 249
Miss Mary Jane 244
Moses 63
Rachel 68
Sallie J. 176
Sarah 195
Scovel, Arthur 231
Screws, Littleton 63
Scroggins, Squire Henry 186
Scrugg, Henry 252

Scruggs, Ann 229
B. C. 214
Christina 202
Edmond 239
Eliza 176
Ellen 203, 215
Fanny 220
Gross 98
Joshua 231
Lizzie 218
Lucinda 240
Martha 193
Mary 196
Narcissa 230
Peter 214
Polly 186
Spencer 214
W. M. 202
W. T. 214
William 63, 104, 186
Scules, Miss Cora 251
Seagrove, Mary A. 214
Searcy, Alsy 194
Anderson 63, 139
Catherine W. 80
Charles 239
Ellen 207, 218
Hannah 204
Isaac 63
Isham G. 41
John W. 63
Julia E. M. 103
Lucie W. 141
Lucinda 186
Lucy 77
Lucy W. 58
Mary J. 210
Robert W. 8
S. A. 144
Sarah M. 5
Tabitha 88
Tabitha J. 149
Tarlton 186
W. W. 152
Seargint, Edward H. 107
Sears, Cinthia Ann 186
Dennis 186
Seat, James G. 186
Seawell, Benjamine P. 41
Mary 24
Seay, A. 158
Frank 245
Franklin 186
Hager 186
John W. 223
Malissa A. 206
Mark 186
Martha Jane 130
Mary A. 147
Mary Ann 134
Riley 186
Sarah Jane 173
Seek, Jacob 87
Seekers, Mary 227
Seem, Abraham B. 63
Segraves, William 114
Self, Nathan 63
Sellars, Alfred 63
Cumley 186
Emma A. 216
Sellers, Wesley M. 121
Semmons, Martha J. 139
Sergeant, John W. 157
Serrell, Nancy E. 127
Sessom, Jesse 63
Settle, Flem 223
Louisa 182

Smith, (cont.)
Candes 234
Caroline 9, 59, 108,
146, 194, 198
Caroline M. 38
Caroline R. 117
Catharine 198
Catherine 67, 187,
230
Caty 210
Charles 65, 187
Charles G. O. 65
Charles P. 146
Chatarine 248
Christina 188, 232
Cinthia A. 41
Clemons M. 131
Cornelia 165
Crene 231
Cueley 121
Cunningham 65
Miss D. F. 217
Daniel 45, 65, 203
Daniel G. 134
Daniel J. 133
David 187
David M. 214
Delilah 22
Della 240
Dennis B. 95
Dora 239
E. 187
E. B. 228
E. R. 209
Edm. 187
Edmund 203
Eli 9, 65
Elias 239
Elijay 239
Eliz. 203, 217
Miss Eliz. 161
Mrs. Eliz. C. 212
Eliz. J. 135
Eliz. W. 135
Eliza 56, 165, 251
Eliza Anne 61
Eliza R. 128
Elizabeth 4, 30, 36,
44, 73, 96
Elizabeth C. 118
Elizabeth D. 120
Ellen 179, 187
Elvira 210
Emma 219
Ephraim F. 98
Esther 69
Eveline 96, 101
Fannie 176
Fanny 178, 208
Frank 187
Gabe 223
Geneveeve 200
Geo. 187, 203, 239
Geo. W. 128
Goerge S. 107
George W. 65
Golden L. 187
Gran. 231
Granderson 187, 223
Green 187, 214, 252
Greenberry 74
Griffith 65
Hardy 121
Harriet 190, 234
Harriet B. 38
Harrison 187
Harvey 231

Smith, (cont.)
Hattie 250
Henderson 239
Henry 187, 223
Henry B. 128
Henry P. 131
Hiram 149
Iley 187
Isabella 153, 191
Isadora 149
Isham 65, 68
Iverson G. 86
J. B. 143
J. E. 187, 214
J. F. 223
J. L. 152
Jack 187
Jack Woods 245
Jackson 114, 203
Jacob 223
James 65, 98, 107,
114, 128
James A. 136
James D. P. 152
James E. 101
James H. 65, 223
James M. 117, 128,
155
James R. 11
James S. 65, 78
Jane 12, 70, 80, 193,
216, 243, 252
Jane C. 39
Jane E. 142
Jennie 177
Jesse 91, 95
Jesse B. 128
Jessee 187
Jim Polk 187
Joanna 115
Johannah 131, 215
John 5, 65, 66, 110,
187, 203, 214
John, Jr. 66
John B. 161
John D. 136
John E. 104
John G. 143
John H. 45, 49, 101,
121
John J. 121
John P. 40, 66, 75
John T. 128
John W. 104
Jonas 252
Jonathan J. 107
Joseph 47, 66
Joseph B. 149
Joseph H. 152
Joseph P. 187
Josephine 195, 197,
208
Miss Josephine A. 244
Josephine Zachry 140
Joshua 187, 223
Josiah 66
Josiah L. 136
Julia 196, 207
Julia G. 17
Julius 187
Julous 187
Karon 15
L. 84
Lamb 187
Larkin 66
Laura 160
Laura Ann 187

Smith, (cont.)
Lee 164
Lenius 223
Levi 187
Lewis 88
Lidia A. 159
Lishy 252
Lizzie 216
Louisa 179, 187, 207,
226
Lov. 194
Lucinda 178, 187
Lucy 15, 163, 165,
198
Lucy J. 197
Lucy Jane 94
Luvenia 187
M. E. 241
Miss M. E. 224
Maggie 159
Malcomb 110
Malina A. 194
Margaret 6, 18, 35,
74, 217
Margaret A. 224
Margaret J. 112
Margarett Jane 149
Maria 191
Mariah 187, 216
Marinda J. 115
Marshall 187
Martena 251
Martha 9, 57, 171,
183, 228
Martha A. M. 122
Martha E. 140
Martin 187, 231
Martina 188
Mary 3, 15, 37, 42,
44, 68, 80, 91, 106,
120, 130, 180, 188,
204, 215, 237, 239
Mary A. 86, 129, 176
Mary C. 77
Mary D. 214
Mary E. 109
Mary F. 13
Mary J. 43
Mary N. 38
Mary S. H. 129
Mary W. 126
Matilda 6, 163
Matthew 66
Mattie 218
Meredith 66
Mickey W. 129
Midy 204
Millie A. 157
Millington, 66
Milly 85, 242
Minerva 186, 187
Morgan 107
Moses 203
N. J. 203
Nancy 12, 50, 57, 88,
127, 167, 176, 187,
233
Nancy C. 137, 199
Nancy N. M. B. 195
Narcissa 243, 250
Narcissa L. A. 54
Nat 187
Nathan 252
Ned 187
Nepoleon B. 139
Newton 203
Nicy 205

Smith, (cont.)
Nimrod 66
Noah 66
Obediah 86
Oliver F. D. 126
Oliver H. 221
Olivia 229
Oney 65
Ozella   187
Pallona 98
Parlee 141 (See
  also Garrison, Par-
  lee Smith 141)
Partheny 60
Patience 187
Penelope A. 114
Peter 187, 223
Peyton 2, 3, 4, 31
Philonica Ann 208
Polly 31
Priscilla 187, 189
Queen E. 220, 221
Rebecca 105
Rebecca C. 67
Rebecca M. 141
Rebecca P. 65
Retha 200
Richard W. F. 66
Robert 40, 110, 121
Robert A. 231, 245
Robert D. 66
Robert G. 95
Robert H. 95
Robert M. 95
Robert P. 146
Rosa 204
Rufus 239
S. B. 214
S. Hardy 231
S. W. 146, 157
Sallie 213, 223
Sallie Bet 232
Sam 187
Sam Houston 187
Samuel 66, 77
Sanders 252
Sarah 13, 34, 88, 187
Sarah Ann 139
Sarah Jane 5
Sarah O. 114
Sherwood W. 131
Simeon 117
Simon 187, 252
Solomon 203
Sophia 3, 8, 83
Sophronia 196
Steben 188
Stephen 203
Sue 197
Susa E. 132
Susan 13, 71, 158,
  227
Susan C. 25
Susan T. 104
Susanna 13
Swinfield 57
Synthia 172
Tarlton 203
Taswell S. 121
Tely 235
Temperance Ann 116
Temperance J. 66
Temperance W. 61
Tenney 216
Tenny 163
Thaddeus 245
Theo 214

Smith, (cont.)
Thomas 18, 58, 66,
  188, 214, 223
Thomas B. 66
Thomas J. 161
Thos. Washington 66
Tudor N. 86
United America 66
Unity 165
Unity C. 38
Viola 233
Virginia A. 105
Virginia F. 110
Virginia W. 104
W. A. J. 214
W. J. 231
W. W. 139
Warren 188
Washington 203, 223
Watson 188
Wealthy 67
William 31, 66, 78,
  91, 95, 110, 188,
  203, 214, 231, 239,
  252
William A. 110
Wm. E. 214
William H. 66
Wm. M. 252
William R. 107
Williamson 88
Wislon R. 66
Zack 223
Zady 10
Zelia 167
Smithey, Joseph 223
  Timothy 101
Smithia, William 95
Smithy, Jim 252
  Wm. 239
Smoot, Jemima 104
Smotherman, Abraham 66
  Alfred 114
  Amanda 143, 219
  Amy L. 110
  Azariah 245
  Balinda 124
  Bartholemew 139
  Bartholomew 101
  Barton 104, 232
  C. C. 239
  C. T. 152
  Deanna 196
  Dennis W. 134
  Miss Dorinda 245
  Dorinda S. 130
  E. 227
  Elbert 107, 245
  Eldridge 104, 252
  Eliz. 209, 223, 232
  Elizabeth 91, 101,
    114
  Elmore 128
  Emily 106, 188
  F. A. 218
  Fanny 212
  Francis 95
  Frank 188
  Greenberry 98
  Harriet J. 117
  Henry 143
  Isham 95
  James 161
  James A. 134, 139
  James F. 107
  James M. 188
  Jane 109
  John 117, 124, 143

Smotherman, (cont.)
  John R. 117
  John W. 203
  Jonathan P. 107
  Joseph 124, 136
  Joshua 155
  Julia A. 140
  Lewis 66
  Lorinda E. 206
  Louisa 109
  Lucinda T. 91
  M. A. 203
  M. J. 226, 243
  M. P. 156
  Malissa E. 220
  Marcus 21, 66
  Margaret A. 124
  Margaret C. 109
  Mariah 164
  Martha 216
  Martha A. 126
  Martha J. 143
  Martha R. 116
  Mary 50, 87, 88, 95,
    111, 128
  Mary A. 136, 242
  Nancy 109
  Nancy A. 243
  Nancy M. E. 203
  Parton 239
  Phebe F. 126
  Polina J. 213
  R. H. 161
  Rebecca 87
  Rebecca S. 135
  Robert 223
  Robert M. 203
  Samuel 66, 188
  Sarah 101, 188
  Solomon 188
  Sophia 100, 106
  Sophronia 188
  Susan 100, 201
  Miss Tennessee 248
  Thomas 101
  Turman 214
  Uriah 146
  W. L. 245
  William 66, 73, 121,
    139, 143
Smothers, Delitha 137
  Eliz. 142
  Harriet 51
  James 66
  John 15, 66
  Mary 4
  Milkey 79
  Rebecca 10
  Thomas F. 66
  William 101
Smott, Thomas9, 66
Snadridge, Sarah 129
Sneed, Alexander 143
  Ann 63, 88
  Miss Anna E. 246
  Beckey 188
  Charles 131
  Charlott 204
  Constantine P. 67
  D. H. 146
  Dabney 124
  David 188
  Eliz. 168
  Elizabeth 110
  H. H. 214
  Henry 188
  James B. 124

Stafford, (cont.)
John A. 143, 146
Mary J. 214
Staggs, Sally 8, 25
Stainback, J. M. 245
Staky, Drucilla 88
Stallin, Elizabeth 64
Stam, Jackson 91
Stamford, George W. 98
Stamper, Lucy 223
  Wm. 203
Stanburg, Lewis 155
Standley, James C. 55
Standord, Bettie 251
Stanfield, Miss M. R.
  199
  Wm. 2
Stanford, Lafayette 239
Stanley, Catherine 53
  Elizabeth 13
  James 53
  Jeptha 29
  John 67
  Mary 174, 175
  William C. 60
Stansil, Harvey 67
Stansler, Harvey 188
Stanton, Joseph 232
  Mrs. M. E. 234
  Pickney 146
Stapleton, John 40
  Mary 40
Starkey, Emeline 110
  Lucinda 13
Starnes, James 98
Starns, ---- 60
Starvens, Geo. 203
State, James A. 67
Staten, Elijah 114
Statham, John G. 67
  Malinda 107
  Mary 70
  William H. 67
  William P. 67
Statland, Walter H. 158
Statler, Samuel 71, 139
Staton, Charles W. 245
  E. W. 24
  Elijah 8
  Frances 137
Stattens, Joseph 188
Stattler, Samuel 68
Statum, Jane 91
Stearns, D. 232
Steel, Jane 55
  Robert 214
Steele, Calvin 188
Stegall, Elijah 68
  Lewis 188
  Obediah G. 68
  Sarah A. 108
Stegar, Elizabeth 124
  Francis 68
  Mary 106
  Sarah 125
Steger, Charles C. 68
  William 68
Steinhagen, R. T. 214
Stell, L. A. 206
Stem, Angeline 157
  Asa L. 131
  Huriah 223
  James 95
  Mary Jane 178
  Sarah E. 156
  Susannah 223
Stephens, Aminadah 68

Stephens, (cont.)
Delilah 5
Eliz. 134
Elizabeth 27
Geo. M. 140
George 27
George Washington 232
Joseph D. 68
R. E. 143
Sarah 166
Sarah W. 84
Ticey J. 124
Stephenson, John L. 239
  Mary 130
  Robert 40
  William M. 95, 98
Sterchie, F. P. 214
Stevans, Alexander 188
Stevens, Anny 44
  Caroline 204
  Elijah 71
  Hannah 180
  J. B. 157
  L. J. 144
  Sampson 68
  William 68
Stevenson, Ephraim 203
  Jane 65, 129
  Jerry 214
  John 31, 65, 68
  Simon 203
Steward, Cintha A. 68
  Wesley B. 68
Stewart, Alfred 223
  Amanda L. 208
  Anderson 95
  Andrew 232
  Cezar 203
  Daniel M. 68
  Elias 223
  Harrison 252
  Jack 188
  James B. 68
  James W. 40, 75, 114,
    124
  John E. 68
  Joseph H. 124
  Julia 103
  M. L. 86
  Martha 146
  Martha Ann 202
  Mary 10
  Nancy 188
  Permela 32
  Peyton 68
  Presley 68
  Presly 24
  Richard 146
  Samuel T. 29
  Sane 133
  Susannah 29
  William 68, 107, 188
  William B. 56
Still, John 2
  Miss L. H. 219
  Lavinia 43
  Littleberry 68
  Nancy 57
Stinson, Archibald 4, 10
  Green 68
Stitt, Louise J. 152
Stoball, Samuel 214
Stockard, Arie 216
  Caroline 213
  Fannie J. 156
  Helly 199
  James E. 98, 232

Stockard, (cont.)
John D. 89
Miss S. A. 248
Susan 204
Wm. S. 223
Stockel, Charles 214
Stockird, Absolom 68
  James 68
  William 60
Stoe, Peggy 76
Stokes, Anna 240
  Betty 188
  John 232
  Miss Martha J. 251
  Robert 188, 203
  Sterling 29, 68
  T. H. 50
  Thomas H. 68
  William 5, 68
Stone, Ada 160
  H. B. 203
  Harriet 179
  James G. 161
  James P. 252
  Malissa 132
  Mary 28
  Nancy 75, 156
  Sarah 134
  Sarah A. 75
  Miss Sarah A. 168
Stoner, John M. 203
Stout, Absolom 17
Stovall, Agatha Ann 167
  Amanda J. 114
  Bill 203
  Elvira 112
  Jane 30
  Jephtha 128
  Jesse C. 68
  John A. 68
  John D. 33
  Joptha D. 101
  Joseph 214
  L. S. 236
  Maria T. 20
  Martha J. 102
  Mary Jane 67
  Nancy D. 31
  Patten A. 68
  Perlina 77
  Ruth 26
  Sally D. 33
  Samuel 68
  Susan J. 121
  Vanda E. 159
  William P. 68
Stover, Geo. W. 188
Stovers, George W. 239
Stoves, Eliza 228
Strain, Matilda 6
Strange, Jemima 22
Straughter, Spence S.
  155
Strickland, Alfred 214
  Lizzie 214
  Mathew 188
  Wiley 214
Strong, Francis 69
  Nelson 69
  William S. 69
Stroop, Beckey 170
  Catharine 101
  Elizabeth 100
  John 69
  Miss M. A. 213
  Sarah L. 127
  Tennie 245

Strother, John 69
  Matilda 59
  Robert 69
Stroud, Ann 237
  Jane 238
  John 25
  John W. 69
  Thomas 69
Struder, Adam 1
Stuart, Samuel T. 69
Sturdephant, Stephen 188
Sturdivant, John 69
Sublet, Washington 232
Sublett, Addie 141
  Albert 188
  Campbell 232
  Charlotte 224
  Ellen 249
  Geo. A. 2, 32, 34,
    56, 60
  George 245
  George A. 40, 57, 69
  Houston 214
  Jasper 188
  Jim 188
  John 188, 214
  Joseph 203, 239
  Josephine 226
  Mary 6
  Mary Ann 42
  Mary M. 114
  Nancy 17
  Norance A. 203
  S. J. 156
  Sam 188
  Sarah A. 124
  Susan A. 141
  V. M. 78
  William 69
Sudberry, John 84
  John H. 152
  Mariah C. 101
  Mary E. 90
  Pattrick H. 101
  Susan E. 101
  Wm. 203
  William T. 90
Sugg, Aquilla 69
  Jane A. 143
  John H. 69
  Thomas 69
  Wm. 137
Suggs, Eliz. 214
  Eliza 148
  G. L. R. 223
  Harvey 223
  Isham 188
  Lizzie 203, 250
  Lockey C. 152
Sugs, Isham 232
Sullens, Jane 181
Sullings, Sally 3
Sullivan, Ann 19
  Ann M. 88
  Anny 19
  C. T. A. 223
  Calvin 188
  Eliz. 215
  H. R. 161
  James 19, 69
  Jane 200
  Jesse 69
  John 5
  John E. 117
  Miss Josephine 245
  Josephine C. 155
  Miss Mary 245

Sullivan, (cont.)
  Mary F. 145
  Melissa J. 242
  Nancy 81
  Nancy Ann 188
  Peter 188
  Richard 252
  Robert 45, 69
  Robert J. 140
  Rufus D. 223
  Wm. B. 203
  William G. 114
Sullivant, John 69
  Mary 6
Sumler, Bell 221
Summar, Smanda 241
Summars, Milly 107
Summer, Carolone 183
  Jackson 114
  Joanah 103
  John 101
  Julia A. 156
  Leanah 101
  Luninda 107
  Mathew 131
  Moses 101
  Patsey 65
  William 85
Summerall, Henry 69
Summerhill, A. H. 121
  Catharine 141
  Eliza 133
  Elvira 213
  Norvel R. 134
  T. A. 203
Summers, Abner 104, 245
  Alfred 69
  Alvin F. 104
  America 155
  Benjamin 107
  Betsy 50
  Biney 90
  Catharine 131
  Charlotte 194
  David 69, 90, 104
  Davidson 118
  Derinda 9
  Elizabeth 95, 116
  Elizabeth H. 98
  Elvira 72
  George 69
  James Ira 69
  John 69, 245
  John D. 89
  John W. 137, 161, 214
  Lafayette 128
  Lewis 69, 203
  Louisa 161
  Lucinda 69
  Malinda 43, 104
  Mallissa 162
  Martha 238
  Mary 31, 36, 65
  Mary Ann 121
  Mary Ann D. 131
  Milus 124
  Miss Nancy M. 246
  Polly 200
  Rachell 89
  Rebecca 120
  Sally 109
  Miss Sarah 248
  Sarah N. 139
  Tabitha 43
  U. T. 118
  Uriah T. 117
  V. T. 128

Summers, (cont.)
  William 57, 85, 89,
    101, 110, 143
  Wm. A. 232
  Winifred 53
  Zachariah 98
  Zachariah T. 89
  Zachariah W. 89
Sumner, Lewis 189
  Osborn 252
  Susan E. 128
Sursa, Joseph 14
Sutherds, Monroe 203
Sutherland, Anne 17
  Elizabeth 38
  James 69
  Jesse 69
Suttle, Ben 203
  Elbert 189
  Ellis 69
  Margaret 215
Sutton, Miss Alice J. 243
  Ed. 252
  Elisha 69
  Frances A. G. 100
  J. P. 203
  John 189, 252
  Joseph 203
  Lemuel 69
  Nancy 36
  Roxannah P. 79
  Sarah 71
Swafford, John 214
Swain, D. F. 252
  Miss Lulia 216
  Miss Mahala 235
  Miss Mary J. 223
Swan, Albert 245
  Amanda 166
  George D. 69
  Lavinia 98
  Lunsford Y. 137
  Martha L. 233
  Mary Ann 177
  May 45
  Moses 42, 152
  Naoma 130
  Rebecca E. 137
  Sarah 42
  Wm. R. 214
Swancey, Cataline 155
Swane. T. E. 199
Swanger, David 152
Swann, Amanda 144
Swater, Henry 215
Sweet, David 69
  John 21
Swense, Adeline 189
Swett, Henry 152
Swift, John 189
Swiney, Calvin 121
Swink, Clementine 122
  Docy M. 90
  Frances 157
  Geo. W. 223
  James H. A. 101
  John 203
  L. J. 243
  Martha P. 124
  Mary E. 90
  Michael 69, 89
  Sarah C. A. 130
  Thomas 189
  William L. 118
Swope, Roscow 70
  Roseow 70
Swynk, Catharine 102

338

Sykes, Joseph 189
Syllivan, Queen Victoria
    A. 232
Taber, John 10
Tabern, Cornelius 215
Tabour, John 90
Tailor, John 70
Talant, Nancy C. 231
Talbert, Josephine 231
    Wm. T. 137
Talent, Miss Mahana 245
Taliferro, Abigil 119
Tallant, Wm. 232
Tallent, Wm. 252
Talley, Ada J. 157
    D. H. 223
    James S. 246
    John 189
    Miss M. A. 245
    Martin 252
    Melissa H. 219
    Reuben 239
    Rufus 189
    Will 189
Tallon, John L. 223
Tally, Ann 189
    Emma 210
    Jake 239
    Newman 70
    Peter C. 98
    Pleasant 70
    Pylin 235
    Robert 215
    Thomas 215
Tankert, Harbet 189
Tanner, Robert 134
Tapley, Mary 231
Tappan, James C. 137
Tarlton, Julia 149
Tarpley, Burton 215
    Cader D. 114
    Edward 70
    Geo. W. 203
    Henry L. 152
    James A. 70, 114
    Jane 80
    John A. 140
    Lockey 161
    Miss Lockey 189
    Mary A. 89
    Sally 51
    Sarah H. 19
    Thomas 79
Tarver, Lewis 215, 252
    Nelson 70
Tassey, Alexander 121
    David F. 104
    John W. 140
Tassy, Isabel N. 125
Tatum, Absolom 70
    Absolum 95
    David 70
    Eliz. 139
    J. H. 246
    Jesse B. 114
    Jesse M. 70
    John B. 70
    Joseph 31
    Luke 70
    Marcus 70
    Mary 70
    Sarah 67
    Sarah S. 107
    William 70
    William M. 98, 137
Taylor, ---- 85
    Aaron 70

Taylor, (cont.)
    Adam 85
    Adin 70
    Amanda A. 134
    Andrew J. 107
    Caroline 90
    Charles T. 114
    Creed 146, 239
    Daniel W. 121
    David 70
    Delila 87
    E. E. 189
    Eliza 89
    Elizabeth A. 105
    Mrs. Emeline 226
    Eny 107
    Evan 19
    George N. 88
    Harriet 198
    Harriett E. 125, 158
    Henry 155
    Henryetta 189
    I. L. 68
    J. W. 189
    Jacob T. 70
    James 51, 70, 110, 121
    James C. 7
    James H. 89
    James J. 70
    James M. 203
    James P. 111
    James R. 70
    Jane 125
    Jennetta 119
    Jesse 70
    John 36, 70, 111
    John D. 70
    John H. 137
    John M. 232
    John N. 83
    Joseph M. 108, 134
    Joseph R. 35
    Josiah 61, 70
    Josiah R. 70
    Leonard 75
    Lewis 70
    Lorena 189
    Louisa 75
    Lurenia 189
    Malinda J. 116
    Malinda L. 153
    Margaret A. 91
    Margarett A. 93
    Martha B. 19
    Martha C. 202
    Martha E. 227
    Mary 76, 86, 130, 204
    Mary F. 141
    Mary Jane 226
    Melissa 126
    Michael 70
    Milley 49
    Nancy 47, 50, 61, 86
    Ned 215
    Nehemiah 70
    Miss Nora 234
    Obedience 122
    Miss Ony W. 244
    Phoebe 34
    Powell 70, 108
    R. W. 232
    Rebecca 51, 173
    Rebecca J. 136
    Robert 70
    Robert H. 95
    Ruthey Ann 165
    S. H. 246

Taylor, (cont.)
    Sallie 207
    Miss Sallie 247
    Sam 189
    Sarah 36
    Sarah C. 197
    Sarah J. 119
    Simeon 75
    Stacker J. 252
    Susan 27
    Susan H. 140
    Thomas E. 77
    Thomas G. 91
    Thomas L. 118
    Thomas S. 114
    Tom 189
    Uriah 215
    Vincent 4, 70, 124
    W. C. 161
    William 13, 70, 155
    William C. 95
    Winston 53
Teague, John 71
Teal, Barbary 143, 146
    James 71
    Susannah 78
Tear, Richard V. 71
Teasley, Alexander 239
Teate, Wm. 203
Tedder, William 71
Tedo, James 88
Teel, Anna 15
    Martha 243, 249
    Rebecca 249
Teer, Richard V. 83
Teete, David J. 239
Teeter, Stout 71
Telman, Rose 173
Temple, Hiram James 253
    Miss Mary E. 253
Temples, Lourany 217
Templeton, Burgess 114
    Nancy 240
Tenison, Archibald 13
    Rutherford 71
Tenning, William A. 71
Tennison, A. J. 155
    Abraham 71
    Archiblad 20, 71
    Edmund 46
    H. 2
    Hiram 24
    Joseph 9
    Levivey 75
    Martin 71
    Sarah A. 139
Tennon, Emma 239
    Mary A. 85
Tennyson, Martha Jane
    233
Terry, Ann 232
    D. P. 215
    John 232, 252
    Walter 203
    Willis 232
Tey, Zachariah 223
Thacker, Charles M. 101
    M. A. 183
    Rebecca 48
Tharp, David 246
    James 71
Thewer, Reese 137
Thom, James 239
Thomas, Anna 8
    Anne W. 69
    Benj. 152
    C. E. 189

Thomas, (cont.)
Caroline 237
Catharine 108
Catherine 58, 85
Charles A. 189
Christian 11
Edward 71
Elementine 197
Eliz. J. 131
Elizabeth 41
Elizabeth A. 11
Ellen 110
Emily 204
Gideon W. 134
Harchas 189
Harriet 193
Henry 71, 189
J. M. 246
Jacob 71
James 89, 152, 161,
232
James H. 215
Jane 74, 83
Jinnie 189
Joe 189
John 189
John A. 85, 131
John F. 71
John W. 131
Johnathan 215
Lavinia 189
Louisiana 155
Lucinda 112, 116
Martha J. 119
Mary 7, 175, 238
Mary E. 156
Mary H. 65
Mrs Mary Jane 246
Miss Molly E. 217
Nancy 68, 83
Narrissa 123
ParIee 153
Peter 71
Peter J. 42
Rachel 31
Rebecca 72
Robert 140
Robert G. 128
Sampson 101, 128
Sandy 239
Sarah 111, 213
Sawney 155
Stephen 137
Susan 216
Susan R. 43
Thomas 71
Wiley Jefferson 223
William 71, 98, 155,
239
Wilson 71
Wilson B. 71
Thomason, Spencer 75
Thompkins, Charlotte 175
Geo. I. 158
Thompson, A. M. 196
Abraham 13
Abram 203, 215
Albert C. 118, 137
Amanuel 189
Angline 241
Anna 38
Annie 156, 230
Arehy 189
Azariah 124
Beatins 119
Bill 189
Burton 189

Thompson, (cont.)
Cal 189
Caroline 207
Catharine 115
Catherine 161
Catherine E. 159
Christian 42
Miss Christina 250
David 143
David S. 114
Dela F. 140
Dicy Ann 239
Mrs. E. A. 242
Eddy 76
Edy 83
Eldridge 246
Eli N. 104, 134, 203,
252
Eliz. 206
Eliza 32
Elizabeth 13, 40, 86,
115
Elizabeth M. 122
Elleanor 233
Ellen 172
F. C. 146
Franklin 161
G. R. H. 232
Geo. W. 204
George 57
George W. 137
Granklin 189
Hannah 213
Harkles P. 15
Harriet R. 139
Henrietta S. 136
Henry D. 71
Isabella 153
Isham 215
Jacob 71
James 12, 71, 95
James A. 71, 89
James P. 8
Jean 46
Jesse 33, 69, 71
Jessee 189
Jim 189
John 32, 37, 71, 76,
189
John A. 159
John H. 88
John S. 189
Joseph 63, 71, 101
Joseph M. 121
Kate 235
Ladosha 106
Lawrence C. 66, 71
Lucinda 34, 246
M. P. 204
Malinda Jane 204
Mansfield 72
Margaret 38
Margaret J. 144
Margaret T. 129
Maria 159
Mariah 220
Martha 41, 170
Mary 13, 71, 225
Mary Ann 176
Mary E. 160, 163, 214
Mary J. 84
Mary Jane 138
Miss Mary L. 251
Mary M. W. 36
Mattie C. 233
Micajah 18
Milly 189

Thompson, (cont.)
Minerva 204
Mizakiah 204
Nancy A. 118
Nancy Ann 231
Nelly 187
Nimrod 118
Orville 72
P. P. 224
Peggy 189
Philip 40
Phillip 98
Pleas 246
Ples 189
Rachel 189
Rebecca 54, 71
Mrs. Rebecca 5
Richard 204
Robert 72, 89
Robert C. 72
Rose 171
S. 73
S. J. 151
Sallie 227
Sam 189
Samantha A. 143
Sam'l. C. 72
Sam'l. G. 7
Samuel 215, 239
Sarah 106, 238
Sarah A. 110
Sarah E. 31
Sarah G. 111
Sarah M. 177
Sarah R. 87
Simon 232
Sindy 218
Sissy 226
Sophia 184
Stephen 232
Susan 9, 79
Tenia 214
Thomas B. 121
United America 124
Vilet 189
Wilie B. 72
William 72, 252
.William L. 72
William M. 95
Wm. W. 232
Young 111
Thorn, Ann 22
Betty 215
Isabella 226
James (?) 239
M. J. 144
Missouri 221
Rachel 18
Rachel W. 135
Sarah 75
Sarah Ann 114
Thomas 85
Thomas D. 143
W. T. 252
William 72, 80
Thorne, Jane 73
Thornhill, W. L. 157
Thornton, Elizabeth 62
John 72
Louisa L. 127
Louise 44
Mary Ann E. 128
Nancy 46
Patsey 39
Sally 47
Thraer, Reece 124
Thrailkill, Henry H. 161

Thrasher, William 79
Threat, Henry 80
  Rhoda A. 137
Threatt, Frances E. 127
Threet, Harman 95
  Henry 72
  Joseph M. 143
Thresher, George 72
Throer, Harry 189
Thurman, Benjamine 72
  Berry 39, 72
  Eliz. 126
  Elizabeth 116
  Elizabeth S. 123
  Hollis 72
  N. F. 149
  Nathan 45
  Peachy 56
  Sally 39, 47
  Susan 33
  Wiley 72
  William 33
Thweate, Elizabeth 66
Thweatt, Joseph O. 137
Tidball, John 252
Tider, Mary 108
Tilar, John 68
Tilford, Henry W. 152
  James M. 72
  Jane 9
  Malisa 149
  Mary 154
  Monroe 239
Tilghman, Dasey 189
  Emlfry 164
  Lilly 163
  Mary 164
Tilker, John A. 95
Tiller, George A. 224
  Henry 104
Tillman, Angeline 189
  Henry 189
  James 239
  Jim 189
Tilly, Joseph 215
Tilman, Benjamine 72
  Cely 189
  James 189
  Mary P. 9
  Sally P. 35
Tilmon, Marg. 194
Timms, C. W. 155
Tindel, Furnery F. 101
Tines, Charles M. 124
  Matilda A. 133
Tinsley, Sam'l. B. 12
Tippet, John 72
  Susan 63
Tippett, Richard 72
Tite, Elizabeth James 86
Todd, A. E. 152
  Aaron 149, 204
  Addie 156
  Anderson 98
  Ann 21, 117
  Ardenia F. 106
  Asa 72
  Benjamine 69, 72
  Betsy 172
  Betsy Jane 225
  C. W. 232
  Caleb 104
  Eda A. 72
  Eliza. J. 128
  Elizabeth 13
  Ellen 222
  Fielding 95

Todd, (cont.)
  Frederick E. B. 101
  Harrison 143
  Henry 189
  Hiram 72
  J. T. 232
  Jackson 131
  Jacob M. 140
  James 72
  James C. 252
  Jane 83
  Jefferson 72
  Jemima 9, 72
  Jeremiah 104
  Jesse F. 87
  John 43, 140
  Julia Ann 203
  Lavicy 128
  Louisa 7
  Lucinda 104
  Malinda 118, 130,
    150
  Mamie 204
  Martha Jane 211
  Martha L. 191
  Mary 20
  Mary A. 132
  Mary M. 135, 151
  Melvina 87
  Miner 237
  Mirna 23
  Mollie J. 236
  Nancy 101, 201
  Nancy D. 106
  Nancy M. 146
  Nancy P. 202
  Peggy 7
  Phebe 105
  Phoebe 25
  Pinkney 72
  Polly 43
  Polly H. 139
  Reuben 72, 118
  Reubin 69
  Robert 64
  S. A. 160
  Samuel 232
  Sarah 69, 85
  Miss Sarah 252
  Sarah E. 203
  Serenia 117
  Synthia 72
  Thomas A. 189
  Tobe 246
  W. N. 252
  Walker 121
  William 72, 98, 204
  William J. 56
Tolbert, John 232
Tolds, Liddy 191
Toliver, Henry 146, 232
  William 121, 140
Tolliver, Wm. 224
Tombs, Eliz. 144
  Lucy 107
  Manuel 41
  Nancy 103
  Sarah O. 141
  Susan 91, 95
  William 104
  Willie 111
Tomlinson, Hugh 3
Tompkins, A. G. 215
  D. C. 140
  Henry 189
  James E. 157
  James M. 43, 61

Tompkins, (cont.)
  Lavinia 189
  R. T. 232
  Robert 189
  Sarah M. 143
  Silas 72
Toney, Hetty 180
  Sarah 197
Toom, Nancy 44
Toombs, Elizabeth 18
  Hardin 72
  Harriet 189
  James W. 98, 149
  Joel 124
  John 189
Tooms, Dicy 73
  Harden 73
  Manuel 72
  William 73
Totty, Catherine 28
  M. H. 156
Towle, Patsey 41
Towns, Eliz. 239
  Mary Ann 214
  Tempie Ann 227
  Wm. C. 128
Townsend, Abram 189
  D. C. 155
  Liza 189
  Thomas 98
Townson, Stafford 232
Towsend, Martin 215
Trail, Caroline 74
  Elizabeth 108
  Felix G. 95
  Martha 112
  Rebecca M. 88
  Valentine 131
  Wiley 121
  Young 73
Trailor, Isham 124
Trale, Isabella 146
Travers, Daniel, Junr. 73
  Daniel, Senr. 73
Travis, Amanda 156
  Amos 73
  Ann 227
  Arthur 73
  B. F. 239
  Barton S. 73
  Benj. 143
  David 71, 83
  E. A. 160
  Eliz. 223
  Miss Eliz. 253
  Elizabeth 27
  Euphemia L. 140
  Hardy 7
  J. Z. 239
  Jane 30
  John 27
  Julia A. 180
  Miss Julia F. 250
  Louisa 146
  Marable 26
  Mary C. 63
  Milus 7
  Robert 204
  Solomon 73
  William 98, 101
  William A. 101, 161
Traylor, Miss Alexander
    250
  Berry 189
  Charlotte 169
  E. P. 118
  Edmund P. 111

Via, Lucy 8, 19
Viar, William 99
Vicary, Wm. G. 253
Vickers, Wm. 204
Vickery, Eliz. 201
  John M. 74
  Mary 201
  Mary C. 207
  Patsey 65
  Winright 74
Vickey, Daniel G. 232
Vickory, Catharine 208
Victory, Nancy A. 148
Vincent, A. M. 159
  Alexander A. 62, 114
  John N. 74
  John W. 101
  M. A. 161
  Mary 210
  Sally 25
Vincents, A. A. 51
Vinson, Ann C. 65
  Eliza L. 70
  George 74
  Henry, Sr. 74
  Jackson 114
  Mary A. 103
  Nancy 84
  Sarah A. 16
  Wm. 1, 2, 134
Vis, Frances W. 17
Vivrett, John B. 74
Voris, Thomas 232
W----, Francis 155
Waddey, Geo. W. 74
Wade, Abigail Ann 74
  Adaline 207
  Adam 246
  Addie 248
  Adeline 196
  Alexander 190
  Ann 71
  Archie 190
  Aron 246
  Ben 239
  Betsy 190
  Bettie C. 183
  Caliborn 190
  Caroline 76, 200
  Caroline M. 122
  Catherine 91
  Charles 190
  Dabner 114
  Dick 190
  Dora L. 231
  Drew 190
  Eliz. 138, 190, 204
  Eliza 67, 204, 224
  Eliza A. 22
  Eliza J. 89
  Elizabeth 14
  Elizabeth L. 117
  Ella 221
  Miss Ella 233
  Ellen 226
  Evelin 190
  Fanny 179
  Francis 177
  George 190
  Green 190
  Hal 190
  Henry 190
  Miss Ida L. 244
  Isaac 204
  Israel 232
  Miss Izora 250
  Jacob 253

Wade, (cont.)
  James 74, 204
  Jane 10, 165
  Jennie 242
  Jerry 190
  Joe 239
  John 190, 232, 246
  John C. 74, 95
  John M. 74
  John W. 232
  Joshua 190
  Judy 188
  Julia Ann 60
  Julius C. 146
  L. D. 253
  Levi 54, 74, 88, 159, 161
  Levina 211
  Lewis 74
  Littleton 190
  Louisiana 80
  Lucinda 38
  Lucretia 84, 172
  Lucy 151
  M. B. 232
  Mahala 74
  Malissa 195
  Marg. 190
  Margaret 147
  Margarett J. 113
  Mariah 190
  Martha 11, 126, 190
  Mary 190
  Mary Ann 99
  Mary C. 122
  Milly 190, 225
  Minerva 225
  Mordecai B. 74
  Moses 190, 204
  Nancy 6, 190
  Nathan 233
  Nelson 204
  Nettie G. 251
  Nicy 179
  Noah 75
  O. H. 91
  Patsy 58
  Phil. 190
  Philip 190
  Polly 183
  Quill 246
  Rachael 75
  Rebecca 22, 50
  Richard W. 104
  Robert 121, 224, 233
  Rose Ann 190
  Sallie 190, 191
  Sally 190
  Sally S. 141
  Sam 190
  Sarah 34, 122, 190, 217
  Sarah C. 67
  Spencer 190
  Susan 50, 185
  Susan G. C. 123
  Susanah 136
  T. C. 157
  Miss Texie 220
  Theny 232
  Thomas J. 190
  Titus 190
  Victoria 186
  Washington 190, 246
  Wat. 190
  Watson 224
Wadley, Amanda 217

Wadley, (cont.)
  C. M. 149
  Ceily 99
  Daniel 99
  Isaac 190
  James 34
  John W. 118, 128
  Julia 190
  Kate E. 179
  Lizzie 235
  Martha J. 209
  Matilda 20
  Moses B. 17
  Rachel 35
  Sa. 241
Wafer, Dick 246
Wagner, G. W. 233
  Wm. 233
Wagoner, Nelson 215
Wail, J. L. D. 215
Waits, Ann 122
Walace, Richard W. 204
Walden, Amy 214
  Caroline 165
  Cena 173
  Daniel 233
  David 233, 253
  Eliz. 223
  Erastus S. 108
  Gran 190
  Harriet 184
  Henry 190
  Isora H. 134
  James A. 149
  John 29, 140
  John W. 101
  Lucy A. T. 143
  Malissa 249
  Martha 40
  Nancy D. 134
  Richard E. 101
  Sam 190
  Susanah M. 131
  Weldon 253
Waldran, James W. 146
Waldron, Charles H. 131
  John W. 104
Wale, George W. F. 131
Walker, Allen 204
  Amanda 191
  Ann 219
  Benj. 30
  Bird B. 75
  Cathrine 155
  Cezar 204
  Charles B. 95
  Delina 34
  Elizabeth 70
  Elizabeth H. 30
  Ephraim 75
  Fannie E. 241
  Fanny 204, 205
  George 75, 95, 190
  Iley 99
  J. T. 215
  J. W. 233
  James 121, 253
  James A. 111
  Joseph 85
  Lattie 250
  Lewis 149, 204
  Marcia 18
  Martha 2, 59
  Martha A. 138
  Miss Martha E. 168
  Mary 7, 55, 143
  Mary Ann 242

Walker, (cont.)
  Matt 224
  Mattie I. 158
  Minerva 168
  Moses 190
  Nancy 50
  Pleasant H. 75
  Miss R. J. 212
  Rebecca 86
  Robert 53, 65
  Sam 246
  Samuel 204
  Violet 220
  W. D. 224
  William 84, 86, 157,
    190
Walkup, Eliza 59
  James 75
  Jane 77
  John D. 233
  Mary C. 90
  Nancy 118
  R. O. 215
  Rebecca 9
  Robert 75
  Wiggy 78
  William J. 36
Wall, Alexander A. 125
  Henry M. 75
  Sallina A. 132
Wallace, A. M. 128
  C. M. 89
  Eliza 30
  Elizabeth 85
  Geo. W. 191
  Hugh 60
  Jackson 54, 75, 79
  James 83
  Jane 84
  John 42, 62, 75, 87
  Jonathan 75
  Jonathan M. 68, 75
  Joseph 75
  Louisa 29
  Mary 42, 54, 75, 83
  Samuel 75
  Sarah 238
  W. H. 146
  Wm. 233
Wallden, Pertandy 64
Waller, Ben 239
  Benj. 191
  Benjamin P. 108
  Miss Bettie 210
  Catharine 111
  Edward 75
  Eliz. C. 130
  Elizabeth A. 120
  Ephriam 215
  Geo. R. 204
  Hannah 162
  James R. 240
  Jane 109
  John B. 152
  Manervia 127
  Martha 53, 116
  Martha A. 130, 131
  Susan C. 127
Wallin, J. E. 215
Wallis, Amos S. 24, 75
  Anne 4
  Hannah P. 81
  Robert 204
  Violet 222
  William 158
  William P. 75
Walls, G. W. 246

Walls, (cont.)
  Mary Ann 225
  Robert 146
  Simeon D. 75
  Thomas 121
Walpole, Ailey F. 137
  Catherine J. 128
  Chas. H. 128
  Eliza 75
  Neely Ann 228
  Thomas D. 90
Walpool, Benjamin H. 102
  Miss Caroline 173
  Elizabeth C. 102
  William E. 75
Walpoole, Rebecca H. 26
Walsh, Thomas 118
Walter, Lewis 204
Walters, Geo. 215
  William 75
Walton, Charles H. 75
  Willis R. 137
Wammuck, James 191
Ward, Albert 191
  Amanda 200, 205
  Andrew 233
  Austin 75
  Avey 71
  Azekiel 54
  Benj. 134
  Benj. F. 137
  Benjamine 27
  Best 75, 84
  Betsy 191
  Burwell 75
  Caley 191
  Caroline 137
  Charlotte C. 73
  Cilla 191
  Clarkey 98
  Daniel 191
  Delaney 74
  Dilcey 248
  Elenor 106
  Miss Ella 233
  Eliz. 142
  Eliza A. 87
  Elizabeth 54, 89
  Eveline 107
  Ezekiel 54. 75
  F. C. 191
  Miss F. C. 246
  George 191
  Harrison 121
  Henry 75
  Isabella 200
  James 215
  James B. 191
  James H. 204
  James I. 125
  James J. 99
  James N. 215
  James R. 137
  Jerry 204
  Jesse 75
  John 75, 191
  John P. 137
  Josephine Alice 229
  Judy 178
  Julia 198
  Julius 191
  Katey 191
  Kinchen 131
  L. A. 224
  L. J. 158
  Mrs. L. M. 205
  Levi 224

Ward, (cont.)
  Lewis 191
  Louis 191
  Louisa 99
  Margarett 112
  Marshall 246
  Martha 118, 124, 247
  Martha A. 147
  Martha E. 147
  Mary 24
  Mary E. 151
  Mary J. 129
  Mary W. 135
  Melinda 105
  Milton Y. 137
  Nancy 22, 24, 68, 84,
    110, 114
  Narcissa 120
  Nicholas G. 99
  Patience 11
  Polly 59
  Raford C. 137
  Robert N. 204
  Sallie 207
  Sam 215
  Sarah A. 118
  Solomon 204
  Sophia A. M. 120
  Spious 161
  Thomas 215
  Thomas C. 75
  Thomas S. 75
  Victoria 225
  W. W. 253
  William 75, 95
Wardlaw, James C. 118
Warmoth, Oney 200
Warmuth, H. J. 204
  Lucinda 209
Warner, Bob 253
  Joseph H. 215
Warnick, John 75
  Martin 215
  Nancy B. 8
Warpole, Miss Catherine
  249
Warpool, Lucy J. 104
  Wm. P. 240
Warren, Abram 191
  Benjamine 35, 75
  Bettie 231
  Burrell 75
  Cara 3
  Celia 196
  Edwin 104, 131
  Elizabeth 90
  Emily L. 145
  Enoch 75
  Gabriel 233
  George E. 76
  Henry 233
  J. P. 233
  James 128
  Jane 69
  Jeremiah 76
  John 26, 76, 111
  John A. 215
  John J. 46
  John T. 95
  Joseph N. 146
  Miss Julia S. 236
  July A. 153
  Louisa 58
  M. S. 153
  Margaret J. 135
  Margarett 80
  Martha S. 117

Warren, (cont.)
  Mary J. 161
  Matilda 186
  Nancy 57, 91, 154
  Nannie A. 239
  Nathaniel 76
  Peterson G. 76
  Peyton S. 118
  Robert 76, 137
  Robert B. 3, 22, 49,
    87
  Sarah 20, 26
  Thomas 49, 76
  William 17, 76, 89,
    121, 128
  William M. 76
Warrin, Mary A. 164
Warrne, Elizabeth 108
Warson, Delly 197
  Taylor 204
Washington, Albert 215
  Cinthia 178
  David 191
  Frances 227
  Francis W. 121
  George 191, 246
  Hannah 191
  Henry 224
  James 233
  John 246
  Lizzie 174
  Mahala 220
  Martha 191
  Mary 187
  Randolph 191
  Sally 48
  Sam 191
  Thos. 14
Wasson, Helen M. 105
  John 76
  Lasson M. 115
  Logan A. 102
  Matilda J. 104
  Ophelia 228
  Richard 102
  Richard P. 76
  Sophia W. 136
Waterhouse, Alex 191
  Sarah 191
Waters, Arpha 191
  Elisha E. 134
  James 155
  Prince 191
Waterson, Nelson 233
Watkins, A. G. 246
  Absalom 125
  Amy 191
  Arey 178
  Charles 191
  Daniel 224
  Delila 86
  Eliza 223
  Eveline 169
  Henry 191
  Hezekiah 17
  Isabella 169
  Isaiah 76
  James 152, 204
  Joseph 76, 128, 131
  Joseph M. 76
  Miss L. J. 214
  Mrs. L. J. 208
  Lizzie 168
  Locky A. 93
  Lucy Quarles (?) 192
  Martha 206
  Mary 62, 211, 231

Watkins, (cont.)
  Mary E. 150
  Matilda 133
  Milly 172
  Mollie A. 201
  Rebecca E. 161
  Richard 191
  Richard (?) 192
  S. D. 58, 60
  S. S. 253
  Samuel B. 99
  Stephen D. 25, 76
  Susan 110
  Thomas G. 5, 11, 76
  Thos. S. 36
  W. D. 215
  W. S. 128
  William L. 32
  Wilson L. 76
Watson, Cap. 224
  David C. 240
  David H. 76
  Davis 191
  Elizabeth 100
  Esther 60
  Fissonia 89
  George 191
  J. M. 161
  Jane 22
  Jerry 233
  John 191
  John M. 134
  Martha A. E. 135
  Mary J. 188
  Mary L. 17
  Merida 76
  Pleasant A. 125
  Rebecca 66
  Susan E. 240
  Susannah 119
  T. W. 253
  Wilkins W. 76
  Wm. 204
  Zusilla E. 140
Watt, Jesse 80
  Margaret 7
Watterson, Nelson 191
Watts, Charles 91
  Ellen 151
  J. H. 146
  L. C. 253
  Martha A. 106
  Mary F. 207
  Syotha 85
  Thenia 159
  Travis 13
  William E. 99, 122
Weakley, Albert 191
  Anderson 191, 246
  Caroline 169
  Celia 169
  Cinda 248
  Daniel 191
  David 204
  Eliza 171
  Eveline 240
  Evie B. 154
  Harriet N. 132
  Harvey 191
  Horace 191, 204
  J. P. H. 149
  John 240
  Louisa 252
  Lucinda 169
  Margaret 194
  Martha 171
  Mary J. 106

Weakley, (cont.)
  Messech 191
  Narcissa 248
  Robert L. 39
  Sandy 233
  Susan N. 114
  William 76
Weakly, Betsy 191
  Billy 191
  Bob 191
  Dorcas 191
  Edm. 191
  Garland 191
  Harriet 191
  Henry 191
  Joe 191
  Lewis 191
  Louisa 191
  Nancy 191
  Sam 191
  Wm. 191
Weatherford, Allen S. 99
  Ann 115
  Charles M. 118
  Eliza 90
  Elizabeth 84
  Martha 54
  Mary A. 203
  Ramsey 85
  Richard 215
  Stephen D. 125
Weatherly, Bob 246
  James M. 20, 76
  John B. 134
  Lockie 187
  Martha J. 141
  Mary 84
  Nancy E. 12
  P. W. 128
  Rebecca 163
  W. P. 128
Weatherspoon, Fanny 9
  Martha 20
Weaver, Adam 76, 89
  Daniel 3
  David 76
  Frank 253
  Hannah 191
  Rev. J. P. 158
  L. J. 253
  Mary 142
  Mary J. 250
  Mat 191
  Mollie 240
  Sallie 181
  Miss Sue 252
  Temperance 3
  William 76
Webb, Aaron 76
  Aden 76, 149
  Aggy 162
  Alex 253
  American 226
  Angeline 171
  Annie 241
  Arsey Harriet 179
  Benjamin 115
  Bettie 194
  Caroline 238
  Cassandra 45
  Clarissa 191
  Crockett 233
  Cynthia Ann 79
  David 155
  E. J. 131
  Edy V. 102
  Emaline 107

Williams, (cont.)
James L. 216
James R. 104, 111
Jane 96
Jason 78
Jesse 78
Jesse W. 155
John 45, 76, 78, 192, 224
John A. 224
John Bell 233
John H. 78
John N. 155, 192
John Watson 192
Joseph 71
Katherine R. 214
Lavinia C. 125
Levicy 12
Lewellen 78
Lewelling 15
Miss Lizzie 245
Loderick 78
Lotta 233
Louisa 198
Lucinda P. 99
Lucy 17
Lyda 109
Lydia 70
M. N. 150
Manirva 157
Margaret 8, 130
Mariah 55
Martha 12, 23, 32, 90, 95
Martha J. 213
Martha M. 96
Mary 66, 95, 131, 163
Mary J. 240
Mary Virginia 233
Melberry 51
Melissa N. 158
Mildred 151
Moses 216
Nancy 100, 196
Narcissa 244
Nelly Jane 149
Nelson 192
Nicholas H. 125
Nick 240
P. J. 225
Philip 192
Rachel 233
Miss Rachel 188
Rebecca 58, 112
Rebecca L. 90
Rhoda Ann 68
Richard 78, 155, 192
Robert 78
Robert B. 111
Roena 251
S. J. 192
S. Macon 221
Samuel H. 146
Samuel M. 78
Sara T. 45
Sarah 4, 80
Miss Sophia 237
Stephen 240
Suraney 128
Susan 5, 218
Susan E. 137
Tennessee 234
Thomas 12, 23, 78
Thomas G. 192
Thomas J. 152
Tressy 2
Victoria 220

Williams, (cont.)
Virginia 161
W. B. 246
W. N. 157, 253
Wiley 253
William 78, 111
William B. 96
William D. 152
William J. 115
William L. 78
William M. 137
Williamson, Albert 192
Angelina 62
Betsy 192
Bowling 78
Edward 84
Elizabeth L. 125
Geo. W. 78
George W. 57
H. G. 115
Harriet 187
Henry C. 78
James 192
John A. 192
Judy 189
Judy Ann 243
Lizzie 219
Martha J. 208
Martha Matilda 236
Nancy 45
Nannie E. 222
Nannie V. 195
Richard 79
Robert 79, 253
Robert J. 233
Sarah 114
Thomas S. 96
Williford, Cynthia 102
Elizabeth 103
James 159
Jesse W. 118
Jordan 3
R. P. 155
Samuel 78, 79
Sarah 138
Willis, C. J. 155
Henderson 192
James B. 79
Rhoda 192
Willis 79
Willoughby, J. M. 224
Miss Painlee 233
Wills, Adaline 106
Benj. 192
Elizabeth 10
George 79
John 102, 205
Judith 33, 44
Polly 11
William 56
Willson, John 157
Wilman, Sarah 182
Sarah Ann 27
Westly 192
Wilson, ---- 37
Alex 240
Amanda 237
Amanda J. 242
American 192
Ann E. 96
Aron 79
Ben 192
Benjamine F. 79
Cath. 211
Cherokee 192
D. W. 246
David S. 79

Wilson, (cont.)
Eleanor 113
Eliz. C. 141
Eliza 168
Elizabeth 32
Geo. 216
George B. 115
Harriet 233
Henry 79
J. B. 224
J. H. 253
James 18, 40, 79, 134
James E. 122
James H. 50, 68
James T. 137
Jane 20, 39, 211
Jim 246
John 86
John B. 118, 155
John D. 89
John M. 96
John R. 73, 79
John W. 149, 155
Joseph 131, 216
Josephine 236
Josiah L. 79
K. 118
Louisa 127
M. P. 147
Malinda 164
Manervia 127
Mariah 120
Martha 211
Martha I. 94
Martha O. 227
Mary 63, 64, 205
Mary C. 95
Mary F. 187
Mary T. 96
May L. 20
Melvina 114
Nancy 31, 205
Nancy G. 141
Nancy J. 128
Nancy K. 20
Miss Narcissa C. 218
Parthenea 115
Rachel 33, 40, 229
Rebecca 115
Robert 224
Sam 240
Samuel 64, 79
Samuel S. 79
Sarah S. 24
Sarah A. 90
Sylva 181
Thomas 192, 233
W. L. 152
Washington 131
Wesley 240
William 22, 79, 104, 140
Wm. J. 134
William K. 16, 118
William M. 122
William N. 125
Wimberly, Henry O. 131
Julian 63
Windman, Sylvia 175
Windrow, Byars 79
Indiana 36
John W. 240
Lucy 164
Miss M. L. 253
M. T. 152
Maria 233
Martha 189

Windrow, (cont.)
  Matilda A. 161
  Nelson 193
  Queen 182, 201, 223
  Sarah C. 156
  Travis 10, 41, 57,
    140
Winford, Matilda 135
Winfre, Miss Sarah 244
Winfree, Eliza 190
Winfrey, Alfred 155, 158
  Allen 111
  George 79
  Henry 79
  James 79
  James A. 224
  Martha 138
  Martha J. 197
  Melvina 187
  Susan 123, 126
Wingo, T. R. 128
Winn, Cader 216
  E. P. 137
  George 240
  Henderson 216
  Jordan A. 157
  July E. 155
  Mary 216
  Narcissa 222
  Rachel 216
Winrow, Ellen 161
  Geo. 193
  Wyatt 193
Winsett, Abraham G. 111
  Amos 79
  Billy 193
  Cary Ann 132
  David G. 125
  E. K. 200
  Elvey 139
  Elvy 228
  Harley 79
  J. F. 149
  J. J. 158
  Jack 193
  James J. 161
  John T. 111
  Jonas J. 111
  Josiah F. 111
  Lititha 198
  Malinda 237
  Manerva V. 156
  Martha 199
  Martha E. 198
  Mary A. 119
  Nancy 193
  Peney 135
  Rachel 37
  Robert W. 128
  Sarah A. 185
  Virginia C. 135
  W. W. 161
Winston, Andy 193
  Anthony 79
  Miss Barbary 162
  Celia 162
  Eliz. 133
  Eliza 17
  Eve 53
  Fannie 162
  Fanny 162
  Francis 87
  Harriet M. 87
  Harriett W. 104
  Isaac 115, 193
  Miss Isabel E. 234
  Julia Ann 218

Winston, (cont.)
  Mahulda W. 110
  Mary E. 127
  Mary Jane 157
  Nancy 50
  Nancy Ann 128
  Samuel 20, 22, 108
  Susan E. 121
  Thompson 193
  Walter 99
Winters, Mary 27
Wise, Charles 240
Wisen, Sarah E. 147
Wisner, Mary W. 197
Witherspoon, Alexander
    B. 115
  Benjamin F. 115
  David 8
  Eliz. 148
  Hannah 8
  Isabella E. 86
  J. M. 224
  Jane J. M. 138
  Jane M. 45
  Miss M. M. 247
  Margaret T. 9
  Pernissa S. 3
  Rachael 70
  Susan E. 181
  Thos. A. 79
  William 79
  Wimphrey 79
  Winphrey 79
Witt, A. T. 240
  Lucius 224
Woldridge, Nelson 193
  Rachel 193
Womack, John K. 253
  Michael 79
Wood, A. J. 131
  A. T. 216
  Andrew J. 137
  Ann 199
  David S. 79
  Davis T. 205
  Drury 79
  Elizabeth 87, 89,
    114
  George W. 104
  Hiram H. 85
  James 79, 115
  Jesse 59
  Joel 96
  John 66, 79, 108
  John H. 111
  John H. (of Warren)
    79
  John J. 80
  Johnson 108, 128
  Joseph 137
  Judith 36
  Judith C. 139
  July Ann 36
  Lafayette 128
  Layfayette 115
  Liza 161
  Lou 194
  Lucisaiana 59
  Martha 242
  Martha Jane 39
  Mary E. T. 139
  Mary F. 97, 100
  Mary Jane 216
  Nancy 18
  Nancy J. 131
  Obediah 137
  Owen 48, 52

Wood, (cont.)
  Polly 22
  R. H. 216
  Richmond 22
  Robert H. 108
  S. H. E. 195
  Sam 193, 224
  Sarah 84, 105
  Selinia A. 94
  Susan 24
  Susan C. 137, 151
  Thomas 104, 161
  Virginia 111
  W. C. 224
  William 80
  William T. J. 99
  Willie 249
Woodard, Cornelius 224
Woodfin, H. W. 216
  Harriett R. 135
  James G. 205
  Jasper N. 125
  John J. 96
  Martha F. 121
  S. C. 216
  Samuel 80
  Thomas E. 84
  William G. 84
  William L. 108
Woodroff, Richard 158
Woodrough, John 193
Woodruff, Allen N. 80
  Hall 193
  Isham 253
  James 80
  James T. 134
  John 161
  John M. 128
  Lucy 193
  Richard 99
Woodrum, Stephen 80
Woods, Aaron 205
  Aggie 193
  Alfred 205
  Anne 161
  Benton 61
  Bettie 197
  Caroline 193, 217
  Catherine 238
  Charlotte 232
  Dock 233
  Edm. 193
  Eliz. 188
  Elizabeth 111
  Gabriel 193
  Henry 205, 253
  J. N. 161
  James B. 42, 80
  Jane 67, 193, 201
  Jasper N. 193
  John 80
  John, Jr. 122
  John W. 233
  Joseph 193
  Lucy 193
  Ludia 218
  M. A. E. 195
  Mandy 221
  Mar. 195
  Marg. 193
  Margarett 195
  Maria 228
  Mary 174, 204, 233
  Mary E. 95
  Mary J. 84, 205
  Milly 191
  Nancy 12

Yeargan, (cont.)
  Gilbert 240
  Hilary H. L. 118
  James 246
  Jim 193
  Nannie 220
Yearger, Edmon 146
Yearwood, Aaron 36, 80
  Anne 73
  Cyntha 105
  Eliza J. 233
  Elizabeth 103
  Hannah 166
  Harriet 170
  Jacob S. 137
  James 37, 73, 115
  James J. 80
  John 81, 83, 240
  M. E. 220
  Mahala 182
  Martha J. 137
  Mary 153
  Paralee 243
  Rachel 182
  Miss Sallie E. 247
  Sarah 84, 177
  Sarah L. 146
  W. A. 253
  Wm. 205
  William M. 71, 81
  William P. 118
Yell, John C. 224
Yews, Sarah J. 136
Yoakum, H. 77
York, Geo. 193
  Louisa 241
  Mahala P. 199
  Mary Ann 225
  Milly 223
  Mitchell 224
  Moses 216
  Ralph 193
  Tom 193
  Uriah 128
Youes, George 84
Youlett, James 216
Youman, Elixa 236
Young, Abram 81
  Alphia 81

Young, (cont.)
  Any 33
  B. C. 233
  Cardy 193
  D. C. 253
  Davis 233
  Emanuel 233, 246
  George 246
  Harry 233
  Henrietta 201
  Henry 233
  Hiram 81
  Isaac 87
  Isaac B. 118
  James 81
  James L. 71
  Jane 55
  Jesse 81
  John 81
  John L. 224
  Lorence D. 81
  Lorenzo D. 78
  Lucinda 87
  Maria 208
  Martha 227
  Martha A. 201
  Mary 59, 181, 247
  Mary Ann 146
  Mary E. 230
  Mollie 198
  Nancy T. 124
  Peter 240
  R. H. 253
  Rebecca 15
  Sam'l. 81
  Samuel 81, 233
  Wm. 131
  Wm. C. 157
Youngblood, Easter 223
  Sarah 62
  Syrus 193
  William 81
Yount, Abram 81
Youree, Andrew H. 81
  David 44
  Dorothy 139
  Eliz. 200
  Elizabeth 46, 100
  Francis A. 68, 80

Youree, (cont.)
  Francis H. 118
  Francis O. 104
  Isabella 85, 102, 124
  James F. 131
  John 152
  Joseph 30
  Margaret J. J. 88
  Martha J. 97
  Mary A. 52
  Mary D. 148
  Mary H. 137
  Nancy P. 114
  Rachel E. 79
  Rebecca Ann 130
  Sarah 229
  William 52
  Wm. F. 128
Ytth, Ransel 246
Zachary, Caleb 81
  Elizabeth 81
  Godlpho 81
  Godolpho 81
  J. S. 81
  Joshua 81
  Josiah W. 81
  Josie 81
  Mary 81
  Nathan 216
  Spencer 81
Zachery, Nancy C. 100
Zachry, Cynthia 91, 95
  Hartwell S. 81
  Sophia 70
Zachy, Sophia 70
Zackray, Adaline 102
Zumbro, Adam J. 233
  Allen J. 118
  George W. 111
  Hannah N. 103
  Miss Jennie 248
  John A. 253
  Martha 101
  Mary A. E. 134
  Mary J. 220
  Mattie 242
  W. F. 193
  William 105

ADDENDA

Arbuckle, Julia 221
Arnold, Mary Dean ? 242
Batey, John W. 240
Bowling, J. S. 234
Bryan, William A. 99
Cola, Ellen 37

Colman, Daniel 156
Crews, Martha V. 218
Davis, Luncinda 229
Fearn, Julia 243
Halton, Martha A. 141
Jacobs, Richard Ann 225
Johnson, Samuel C. 38

Merefee, John 179
Miller, Sabrien 166
Smith, High 10
Turner, Josie 228
Willeford, Clabron H.
  104
Williams, Locrick 102

www.ingramcontent.com/pod-product-compliance
Lightning Source LLC
Chambersburg PA
CBHW060139280326
41932CB00012B/1568